WHO KILLED THE KING?
VOLUME ONE: WHO WERE THE REGICIDES?

ROBERT TEMPLE

Who Killed The King?

The Story behind the Execution
of King Charles I

In Three Volumes

VOLUME ONE: Who Were the Regicides?

eglantyne books

Published by Eglantyne Books ltd,
The Club Room, Conway Hall, 25 Red Lion Square, London WC1R 4RL.
www.eglantynebooks.com
All rights reserved
©2021 Robert Temple.
ISBN 978-1-913378-05-9
Printed in the UK by Imprint Digital ltd.
A CIP record for this title is available from the British Library.

DEDICATION

This book is dedicated to my wife, Olivia.
No one will ever know how much effort
she put into the compilation of this
book over many years.
But I know.

ABBREVIATIONS USED

Add. MSS.	Additional Manuscripts in the British Library
Bart	Baronet
CJ	Journals of the House of Commons
DL	Deputy Lieutenant (of a county)
DNB	Dictionary of National Biography
Oxford DNB	Oxford Dictionary of National Biography
HMC	Royal Commission on Historical Manuscripts
JP	Justice of the Peace
Keeler	Mary Frear Keeler, The Long Parliament 1640-1641, Philadelphia, 1965.
LJ	Journals of the House of Lords
MP or M.P	Member of Parliament
Noble	Mark Noble, Lives of the English Regicides, 2 vols., London, 1798.
r.	recto
v.	verso
VCH	Victoria County History (for a particular county)

MANUSCRIPT COLLECTIONS CONSULTED

A. National Depositories:

1. Public Record Office

C.3. Chancery Proceedings
C.78. Chancery Decree Rolls
C.142. Chancery, Inquisitions Post Mortem
E.121, E.316, and E.358. Exchequer Papers
REQ.2. Cases in the Court of Requests
HCA.13. High Court of Admiralty Papers
STAC.8. Cases in the Court of Star Chamber
PROB-6. Prerogative Court of Canterbury, Administrations.
PROB-11. Prerogative Court of Canterbury, Wills.
S.P.12. State Papers Domestic, Elizabeth I.
S.P.14. State Papers Domestic, James I.
S.P.16. State Papers Domestic, Charles I.
S.P.18. State Papers Domestic, Interregnum.
S.P.29. State Papers Domestic, Charles II.
S.P.46. State Papers Domestic, Supplementary.
S.P.19. Papers of the Parliamentary Committee for Advance of Money.
S.P.20. Papers of the Parliamentary Committee for Sequestrations.
S.P.21. Papers of the Parliamentary Committee for Both Kingdoms.
S.P.23. Papers of the Parliamentary Committee for Compounding.
S.P.24. Papers of the Parliamentary Committee for Indemnity.
S.P.25. Order Books of the Councils of State, Interregnum.
S.P.28. 'Commonwealth Exchequer Papers' (traditional name)
S.P.63. State Papers, Ireland.
S.P.77. State Papers, Flanders.
S.P.78. State Papers, France.
PRO 30/ 53. Papers of Edward, Lord Herbert of Cherbury.
T.51. Treasury Books.

2. The British Library

Additional MSS.
Egerton MSS.
Harleian MSS.
Lansdowne MSS.
Sloane MSS.
Stowe MSS.

3. The House of Lords Record Office

Main Papers Collection
Braye MSS.

4. The Bodleian Library

Ashmole MSS.
Aubrey MSS.
Clarendon MSS.
Nalson MSS. (deposit of part of the Portland MSS.)
Rawlinson MSS.
Tanner MSS.
MS. ENG. HIST. C.487: Edmund Ludlow's Memoirs

B. **County, regional, local, or foreign depositories consulted:**

5. Ashmolean museum, Oxford (Sutherland Collection)
6. Archives of St. Bartholomew's Hospital, London
    (HA1/5 Journal of Governors)
7. Berkshire County Record Office, Reading
8. Birmingham Public Reference Library, MSS. Department
    (Letter Books of Sir William Brereton)
9. Borthwick Institue for Historical Research, York
10. Brotherton Library, University of Leeds
    (Loder-Symonds-Marten MSS.)
11. Buckinghamshire Record Office, Aylesbury
12. Canterbury Cathedral Archives
13. Chetham's Library, Manchester
    (MS. A.3.90-91. Letter Books of Assheton Family)
14. Christ's Church College, Oxford
15. City of Coventry Record Office
16. College of Arms, London
17. Cornwall Record Office, Truro
18. Dr. Williams's Library, London
    (MS. 24.50: Diary of Thomas Juxon)
19. Duke of Devonshire's Collection at
    Chatsworth House, Derbyshire
20. Duchy of Cornwall Archives, London
21. East Sussex Record Office, Lewes
22. Essex Record Office, Colchester
23. Gloucestershire Record Office, Gloucester
24. Guildhall Library, London
25. Henry Huntington Library, San Marino, California, USA
26. Herefordshire Record Office, Hereford
27. Huntingdonshire Record Office, Huntingdon
28. Hull Record Office, Kingston-upon-Hull, Yorkshire
29. Isle of Wight Record Office, Newport, Isle of Wight
30. Inner Temple Library, London
31. John Rylands Library, Manchester
    (Rylands English MSS.:
    45. Genealogical Miscellany (inc. Ludlow)
    136. Lilburne Pedigree
    296-333. MSS. Of W. D. Pink
    451. transcript of portion of Parliamentary Diary of the
      regicide John Moore, MP
32. Kent County Record Office, Maidstone
33. Lichfield Joint Record Office, Lichfield
34. Liverpool Record Office (Moore MSS.)
35. Longleat House, Wiltshire (Whitelocke MSS.)
36. National Library of Wales, Aberystwyth
    (MSS. MSC 11440D and 11441-3: Letter Book and Papers of
    John Jones the regicide
    MS. Powis Castle 314A: Herbert Correspondence)

37. National Portrait Gallery Archives, London
38. Norfolk Record Office, Norwich
39. Northamptonshire Record Office, Northampton
40. Northumberland County Record Office, Newcastle-upon-Tyne
41. Nottinghamshire County Record Office, Nottingham
42. Norwich Central Library Archives Department
43. Oxfordshire County Record Office, Oxford
44. Pembrokeshire Record Office, Pembroke
45. Somerset County Record Office, Taunton
46. Surrey County Record Office, Kingston-upon-Thames
47. Warwickshire County Record Office, Warwick
48. West Sussex Record Office, Chichester
49. Wiltshire County Record Office, Trowbridge
50. Windsor Castle Library (HM The Queen's Extra-Illustrated Clarendon)
51. Worcester College Library, Oxford (Clarke MSS.)
52. York Minster Library, York
53. MSS. Collection of Robert Temple

CONTENTS OF VOLUME ONE

Annotated replica of the Death Warrant of King Charles I.

Chapter One:	Identifying the Regicides
Chapter Two:	Family Backgrounds of the Regicides
Chapter Two, Appendix One:	Further Details of the Family Backgrounds
Chapter Two, Appendix Two:	Transcribed Manuscripts and Full Texts Prior to Editorial Abridgement of the Biographical Dictionary Entries
Chapter Three, Part One:	Two Courtier Regicides
Chapter Three, Part One, Appendix:	Transcribed Manuscripts
Chapter Three, Part Two:	The Early Careers of the Regicides
Chapter Three, Part Two, Appendix:	Transcribed Manuscripts

FAC-SIMILE OF THE
DEATH-WARRANT FOR THE EXECUTION OF CHARLES THE FIRST, KING OF ENGLAND.
WHO WAS BEHEADED ON THE 30TH JANUARY, 1649. IN THE 49TH YEAR OF HIS AGE AND THE 24TH YEAR OF HIS REIGN.

At the high Cot of Justice for the tryinge and iudginge of Charles Stuart Kinge of England January xxixth Anno Dm 1648:/

Whereas Charles Steuart Kinge of England is and standeth convicted attaynted and condemned of High Treason and other high Cr[y]mes And sentence vppon Saturday last was pronounced against him by this Cot to be putt to death by the seuerings of his head from his body Of wch sentence execution yet remayneth to be done These are therefore to will and require you to see the said sentence executed In the open Streete before Whitehall vppon the morrowe being the Thirtieth day of this instante moneth of January betweene the houres of Tenn in the morninge and Five in the afternoone of the same day wth full effect And for soe doing this shall be yor sufficient warrant And these are to require All Officers and Souldiers and other the good people of this Nation of England to be assistinge vnto you in this service Given vnder our hands and Seales

Jo. Bradshawe	Ha: Waller	Tho. Wogan
Tho. Grey	John Blakiston	Symon Mayne
O. Cromwell	J. Hutchinson	Tho. Horton	John Venn
Ed. Whalley	Tho. Pride	Per. Pelham	Gregory Clement
M. Livesey		Ri. Deane	Jo. Downe
John Okey	Robert Tichborne	Ed. Whalley	Tho. Wayte
J. Danvers	H. Edwardes	Henry Marten	Tho. Scot
Jo. Bourchier	Daniel Blagrave	Vinct. Potter	Jo. Carey
H. Ireton	Owen Rowe	Wm. Constable	Miles Corbet
Tho. Mauleverer	Wm. Goffe	Rich. Ingoldsby	
	Ro. Tichbourn	Will. Cawley	Jones
	Pe. Temple	J. Barkstead	John Bourne
Tho. Harrison	P. Scroope	Isa. Ewer	Gilbt. Millington
J. Hewson	James Temple	John Dixwell	G. Fleetwood
		Valentine Wauton	J. Alured
			Rob. Lilburne
			Will Say
			Anth Stapley
			Gre Norton
			Tho. Challoner

A replica of the Death Warrant of Charles I. There are three regicide signatures which are difficult even for historians of the period to decipher, due to the peculiar handwriting. They are: THOMAS PRIDE, which is the fifth down in the third column from the left, HUMPHREY EDWARDES, which is the fifth down in the fourth column from the left, and JOHN MOORE, which is the fourth down in the sixth column from the left.

The signatories are, in descending order down the vertical columns, starting at the left:

John Bradshawe,	Sir Michael Livesey, Bart.,	Sir Hardress Waller,	Henry Smyth,	Augustine Garland,	Symon Mayne,	Thomas Wogan,
Thomas Grey [Lord Grey of Groby],	John Okey,	John Blakiston,	Peregrine Pelham,	Edmund Ludlow,	Thomas Horton,	John Venn,
Oliver Cromwell,	Sir John Danvers,	John Hutchinson,	Richard Deane,	Henry Marten,	John Jones,	Gregory Clement,
Edward Whalley,	Sir John Bourchier,	Wiliam Goff,	Robert Tichborne,	Vincent Potter,	John Moore,	John Downes,
	Henry Ireton,	Thomas Pride,	Humphrey Edwardes,	Sir William Constable, Bart.,	Gilbert Millington,	Thomas Wayte,
	Sir Thomas Mauleverer, Bart.,	Peter Temple,	Daniel Blagrave,	Richard Ingoldsby,	George Fleetwood,	Thomas Scot,
		Thomas Harrison,	Owen Rowe,	Willikam Cawley,	John Alured,	John Carew,
		John Hewson,	William Purefoy,	John Barkstead,	Robert Lilburne,	and Miles Corbet.
			Adrian Scrope,	Isaac Ewer,	William Say,	
			James Temple,	John Dixwell,	Anthony Stapley,	
				Valentine Wauton,	Sir Gregory Norton, Bart.,	
					Thomas Chaloner,	

(The regicide John Cook was not permitted to sign the Death Warrant because he acted as Prosecutor. John Lisle, one of the two Vice Presidents of the Court (the other being William Say), presumably forgot to sign or left too soon.) John Bradshaw (who here signs his name Bradshawe) signed first because he was the President of the Court. Thomas, Lord Grey of Groby, was invited to sign second, as he was of the highest social standing, being the only lord. Above left of the signatures, the text of the Warrant says to its military addressees, who were in charge of carrying it out: 'To Collonell Francis Hacker Colonell [Hercules] Huncks and Lieutenant Colonell [Robert] Phayre and to every of them.' The seals are impressed in red wax. The original document is preserved in the House of Lords.

CHAPTER ONE

Identifying The Regicides

Who were the regicides? – This is a question which has not been sufficiently addressed in the three and a three-quarters centuries which have elapsed since the execution of King Charles I. It is true that in 1798 a book by Mark Noble appeared bearing the promising title *The Lives of the English Regicides*.[1] But it is a book so full of scurrilous and groundless rumour, so lacking in accuracy, and so vindictive in tone that it is essentially worthless for historical enquiry. The author had so much misinformation to purvey that he extended his performance to two volumes. It appears that he wished to curry favour with the Establishment of his day by heaping odium upon the regicides under the pretext of making a historical investigation of them.

Strange as it may seem, no other book has ever appeared dealing with this interesting subject.

In attempting then to answer the question 'Who were the regicides?' one is left rather at a loss as to where to turn. Much of the most basic and elementary information about them has been lacking until very recent times. Their very identities have wavered uncertainly in the half-light. Were they shadows or were they men?

Five of the regicides had no entries at all in the old *Dictionary of National Biography* (hereinafter referred to as the DNB), until I myself wrote them for the supplementary *Missing Persons* DNB volume.[2] The entries of many of the others in the old DNB are scanty, and all are riddled with factual errors to such a degree that probably not one DNB entry for a regicide could be considered really reliable before the 2004 Oxford edition was published, in which some errors have now been corrected. (Unfortunately, I was not approached regarding this project, as I could have corrected all the errors for all of the regicides.)

Information about the regicides found in other standard books tends to repeat the errors of other authorities. These errors have been endlessly perpetuated in long chains, some acknowledged and some not. Scholars inevitably borrow from one another. But when they borrow one another's factual errors, the results tend to be disastrous.

In pursuing my study I sadly realized that I should have to start essentially from scratch.

At the end of this chapter may be found an alphabetical summary of the identification information concerning the regicides. From time to time confusion has arisen over who did and who did not sign the Death Warrant of King Charles I. The situation has not been helped by the fact that three of the signatures (those of Humphrey Edwardes, John Moore and Thomas Pride) are practically indecipherable. The book of 1798 referred to a moment ago does not get it right. The author maintained that Francis Allen and Thomas Hammond both signed the Death Warrant, whereas neither did. It is no great credit to the author of the only previous book which ostensibly dealt with the regicides that he didn't even know who signed the Death Warrant (he also claimed that John Moore did not sign it, whereas he did).

The English Regicides is probably a misnomer, since some of the regicides were Welsh. But since their act of regicide took place in England, and the usage has become accepted, we shall retain it.

The 'English' regicides, therefore, were essentially the men who signed the Death Warrant of Charles I.

However, for the purposes of this study, I have made two slight extensions and one diminution in the term of regicide. I include in the term the Prosecutor, John Cook. He was not allowed to sign the Death Warrant because of his role as prosecutor, but not to consider him a regicide would clearly be unacceptable. Additionally, I have included John Lisle in the study and consider him very much a regicide even though he didn't sign the Death Warrant. The reason for this is primarily that I have been able to establish that he acted as Vice-President of the High Court of Justice and was a constant attender at its sessions. The lack of his signature on the Death Warrant must either have been an oversight or an act of caution on his part. (This question is discussed later on, in the section on 'Circumstances of the King's Trial', in Volume Two of this work.) But Lisle certainly took part in the judgement and condemnation of the King. Others of ambiguous standing whose signatures are missing from the Death Warrant but for whom some claims could be made that they had essentially been regicides have been omitted from this study. There were, after all, more than enough people to get on with, considering that I was faced with 61 different men to study and practically nothing existed to guide me when I started.

The diminution in the concept of regicide to which I referred a moment ago is of a rather different nature. I decided that because so much had been written about him already by others, I would eliminate Oliver Cromwell from my study except insofar as his inclusion was necessary for tables, percentages, descriptions of events, and comparisons – and of course in contexts of analysis and discussions. There is, for instance, an entire section on 'The Regicides under the Protectorate' which obviously has its entire theme based upon Cromwell's regime and the attitudes of the various regicides towards him personally and towards the Protectorate which he established. It was thus clearly impossible to eliminate Cromwell entirely from a study of the regicides. One might view this study as being in one sense a complement to all those studies by others which have concentrated on Cromwell largely to the exclusion of the other regicides.

There is another reason why Cromwell should not be allowed to monopolize the attention of a study of the regicides as a group, although this only came up in the course of my research and was a most unexpected finding. To my surprise I found that a careful study of the detailed evidence concerning the trial and execution of the King could not be said to bear out the ubiquitous assumption by all historians until now that Oliver Cromwell had been the prime mover behind these events. The facts, I discovered, are quite otherwise. Cromwell really had a surprisingly minor role in the whole affair and was essentially on the sidelines. My own analysis, presented in the section dealing with 'Circumstances of the King's Trial', revealed that the trial and execution of Charles I was organised by a group of five men, - Thomas Chaloner, Augustine Garland, John Lisle, Henry Marten, and Thomas Scot. They were the individuals who really originated and carried out all the key business, and they operated as a very tight and intimate group, with the indefatigable lawyer Augustine Garland doing most of the 'donkey work' of drafting, which must have kept him up most nights, as the amount of work which he produced in short time periods bordered on the superhuman. It might be possible to claim for Augustine Garland the title of 'most motivated' of all the regicides, at least to judge from the levels to which he drove himself in overwork, like a man obsessed.

One curious result of this necessity has been my extraordinary reliance upon primary source material to a degree greater than is usual in so recent a period as the 17th century. But the simple fact is that much of the secondary source material time after time revealed itself to be treacherous, unreliable, and positively wrong. Regardless of the theories being expounded by whichever author it was, almost without exception his or her basic factual data concerning the regicides was incorrect. This was so uniform a feature of the secondary source material that less blame may be heaped at the feet of particular individuals because it is something they all share, both the good ones and the bad ones. My duty of correcting all of these factual errors became so tedious that I eventually ceased making lists of them all, as they were positively overwhelming in number, more like an avalanche of false data by which all the authors had, wittingly or unwittingly, been smothered. I had only one option, to build up my own edifice of fact from the solid foundations of the primary source material, which alone could be considered reliable.

It is no exaggeration to say that in the pursuit of the facts about the regicides, I have unearthed approximately 2000 new documents which had never been known to historians before. I have worked in 52 record offices and archives (as recorded in the list of them and their manuscript collections in the Bibliography). The fact that no other substantial account of the regicides existed meant that I did not engage in discussions of my predecessors: there were none.

This does not at all mean that I have paid no attention to other authors dealing with this period; far from it. We all 'stand on the shoulders of giants', as Newton said. Without the mighty labours of Sir Charles Firth and Samuel Gardiner, what would we know about the history of the Interregnum at all? Subsequent studies were only made possible by their pioneering work, and have built upon and considerably refined their gigantic joint edifice, which gave the superstructure and the guidance to all studies since their time. But for all the great work that has taken place over the past century and a half that these subjects have been taken at all seriously, the regicides have tended to slip through the cracks. An intensive enquiry into who they were and what they did simply never took place. Those authors who look upon Charles I as 'the martyr king' have shrunk away from the regicides in horror, and have made no serious attempt to find out about them, presumably because they were the horrid fellows who murdered their hero. There are some extreme examples of this attitude, where vituperation took the place of discussion and slander was substituted for facts. The authors who indulged in that kind of thing may have 'felt better for it', but it did not advance scholarship, it held it back. I have personally known one such author, and it was not an acquaintance which was delightful.

Thus it was that I undertook my enquiry by falling back, with some desperation and exasperation, upon the most basic of all questions for a person writing about the regicides: 'Who *were* the regicides?' And at first it seemed like a question shouted into the void, for no echo came back.

When dealing with a large number of men who may or may not have had many things in common, it is inevitable that a study will have to rely from time to time on the preparation of lists and tables. This may be inelegant, but it simplifies presentation and makes it possible to compress much discussion into arrangements of data which may be taken in at a glance. If, therefore, many lists and tables appear in this study, it was because it was the only way to deal with intractable data about a very large number of people simultaneously. It is not easy to talk about sixty people at once. It is even less so to discuss sixty families at once, as was necessary in the section 'The Family Backgrounds of the Regicides' and its lengthy appendix. Of necessity, alphabetical listings are often the only possible solution.

I hope that this study satisfactorily answers the question: 'Who were the regicides?' It was no easy task. I extended the enquiry to uncover not only the identities, families, and places of origin of the regicides, but to sketch their careers leading up to the act of regicide, with particular attention to those regicides who had had connections with the Court or who had legal backgrounds. We shall discover that the High Court consisted essentially of a mixture of important MPs and the colonels of most of the New Model Army regiments. We shall examine the possibility that these colonels were thought of at that time as somehow 'representing' their regiments rather in the way that MPs represented their constituents, with the regiments being thought of as large (albeit mobile rather than geographically anchored) bodies of 'the people', and we shall see that as a regiment often contained far more people than a borough constituency seat had voters, some of the soldiers might have considered a regiment far more democratically representative than a parliamentary borough seat. What is more, most of the men in the regiments would not have been enfranchised in the constituencies where they lived, so that treating their regiments as quasi-'constituencies' effectively gave them the vote and thereby extended the franchise. In this sense, it could be argued that the High Court of Justice represented the people in a new and enlarged way, however novel and strange. I do not put this forward as a theory, but rather I point out that something of this kind seems to have been in the minds of the regicides.

In attempting to elucidate the identities and positions of the regicides in the political spectrum, we shall uncover many surprising insights into the history of the period which had not previously been known. We shall find that the moderates and the radicals in Parliament were in a desperate factional struggle with one another earlier than had been thought. We shall look with new eyes upon the phenomenon of 'recruiting', or filling up the vacant parliamentary seats by means of byelections. It shall become evident that without such 'recruiting', the High Court would hardly have been possible.

We shall also uncover strange conspiracies against the republican regicides by a previously unknown combination of forces. We shall see that those men later known as the 'Cromwellians' acted in league long before the establishment of the Protectorate to destroy the power of the republican regicides in Parliament and in the counties. We shall uncover extraordinary corruption, deceit, and 'dirty politics'. We shall find factional struggles going on amongst the Parliamentarians with unbelievable intensity in the counties as well as at the national level. It is not a pretty picture, and it reveals a kind of inner civil war going on within the parliamentarian camp extending far beyond what had ever previously been realized. It was only possible to discover these things because of my finding the primary sources which revealed them, as they are not to be found mentioned in any secondary sources, and no historian has ever heard of them.

During the preparation of this study of the regicides, the need to know more about the New Model Army officers became so acute that I made extra efforts to try to achieve clarity in that area. I was able to discover in the House of Lords Archives the original officer list of the New Model Army in the hand of Lord Fairfax himself, indicating a numbering system for the regiments (which I have extended and adopted), and with the Lords' amendments added. Rather than holding that document back to form part of this study, I prepared it for publication at the earliest possible date, so that it could be shared by all. Car thieves stole the only copies of the original notes and first draft of that, and I had to recreate all of the research from scratch, which had just reached the state of being ready to publish. (That was in the days before personal computers, and of modern 'backups' of data. Then we had only typewriters.) That resulted in a delay of three years, which is how long it took to find out for a second time who all of the New Model officers were in order to do the annotations and footnotes for a full publication of the list. (I was not interested in publishing only a list, the only point of it was for the list to be as fully annotated as possible.) Up until then, the New Model officers had been only a little less obscure than the regicides themselves, despite the Herculean efforts of Sir Charles Firth in his books on military matters, which I read and re-read so many times I nearly memorized them. It seemed clear to me that Firth had nearly drowned in his data, being frankly overwhelmed by it, because of having no organising system for numbering the regiments properly. On the other hand, I hesitated to introduce an innovation of my own for numbering the regiments, because it would only mean that some other scholars would dispute it and condemn it as arbitrary and presumptuous, because I had thought of it and they had not. I was fortunate, therefore, that Fairfax himself provided the lead for the numbering system, so that the system which I introduced could be traced back to the general who actually commanded that Army, which gave the system the unassailable pedigree which was needed to prevent pointless academic disputes by wounded egos. (If Firth were alive, I am certain he would personally have welcomed the system with alacrity, as he was a great scholar and not a petty person, interested more in the subject and in historical truth than in his personal status and career.)

When this material was finally ready for the second time, it was published in the journal now called *Historical Research*, but which at that time was still called the *Bulletin of the Institute for Historical Research*.[3] The identifications of the officers made possible for the first time an informed discussion of the political background to the formation of the New Model. Previously, the necessary information was lacking to render possible any reliable conclusions about this important subject. Such discussion is to be found in the section, 'The Honourable Members from the Army', which account should be supplemented by the account which I published in the journal.

Subsequent to publishing my article and completing my account of 'The Honourable Members from the Army', I gave copies of both to the Canadian historian Ian Gentles, as an assistance to him in the writing of his book *The New Model Army*, which was published in 1992.[4] Over a period of many months, I assisted Gentles with long discussions, sharing of information, and clarifications of points of detail, in order to help him. We often found ourselves working at the same time in the Public Record Office and the Institute of Historical Research, where we met frequently. Although my article was freely available to all, the chapter of this work which I gave him in confidence was not. I gave him permission to refer to it in moderation on the condition that he cite the source properly. Despite my generosity towards him, Gentles pointedly excluded mention of my name from the long list of scholars who had 'generously shared with me their detailed knowledge of army affairs from 1647 to 1660', in his Acknowledgements. My name is only mentioned in the text of his book once, in a single sentence where he quotes from my published article, and my name appears twice in his footnotes.[5] It does not cost an author anything to acknowledge assistance, especially as merely one name in a long list, but he chose not to do it. Hence, the lack of courtesy of Gentles did not provide occasion for me to retain any personal good feelings. Years later, when he unexpectedly wrote to me and offered me some money to give him more information about the regicide Thomas Pride, I found no difficulty in ignoring his letter.

As an extension of my attempt to identify the parliamentarian military officers, I also published an article entitled 'The Massey Brigade in the West', which was also based upon my discovery of its manuscript officer list.[6] This article was meant to be the first of a series of three articles containing valuable findings about this obscure military entity, and describing some events which involved certain of the regicides (though there were no regicides serving in the Massey Brigade, which was looked upon by most of the regicides with horror as an out-of-control rampaging force of cavalry despoiling the countryside and under the control of unscrupulous and corrupt individuals). Unfortunate circumstances prevented the drafting of the two successor articles for which the material had been gathered, and that material has remained unpublished, which is especially unfortunate in that it contained some uniquely interesting material relating to the New Model Army and also concerning the regicide Vincent Potter.

My third military publication (but the first to appear, in 1981) was 'Discovery of a Manuscript Eyewitness Account of the Battle of Maidstone', drawn from a manuscript letter of the regicide Peregrine Pelham, MP, which I found at Hull, and reporting the actions of the regicide Colonel John Hewson.[7]

Other published accounts of regicides by myself include ten entries in *A Biographical Dictionary of British Radicals in the Seventeenth Century*.[8] (In addition, I collaborated on several more entries which appeared under the names of other scholars, to the extent that the editors said I had acted 'almost as a third editor'.) In those volumes I wrote the entries for two sympathisers of the act of regicide who were not themselves regicides, and who are therefore not studied here, namely Alexander Rigby, MP, and Lord Monson [aka Mounson].

It is only to be expected that, having compiled the first extended study of the regicides ever seriously attempted, many new facts have come to light which suggest revised interpretations of the history of the period concerned. The regicides were, after all, the prime actors on the national stage at that crucial moment when a monarch was executed allegedly for crimes against his people and for betraying his contract with his people.

What follows in this chapter is an Alphabetical List of the regicides and a brief guide to the identities of the individual regicides, distinguishing them from others of the same name, and listing all the variant spellings of their surnames which I have come across over the years in both printed and manuscript sources. Sometimes a variant spelling can lead to a regicide being overlooked entirely. For instance, the parliamentary diary of the regicide John Moore went unnoticed for many decades because it was catalogued in the British Library (when it was the British Museum Library and all manuscripts were listed on index cards in old Victorian wooden drawers) under the name of More rather than Moore, since the alphabetical listing threw it out of sequence by it being filed under M-O-R instead of M-O-O. I was the person who first discovered this. Many who read Burton's *Parliamentary Diary* could be excused for not realizing that 'Colonel Hewitson' was the regicide John Hewson. And so on. A list of variant spellings of the surnames, then, is the least that one requires in sorting out the confusions which can arise regarding such a large number of people, who lived in an age when spelling was not precise in any case. Although I cannot remember the exact reference, since I made no note of it at the time, I do recall seeing a single page document once written by a man of the period (the regicide Valentine Wauton) in which he spelled his own name five different ways on the same page. In some cases, it seems to have been a fashionable affectation to see how many different ways one could spell one's own name by way of showing off one's stylishness and flair. Fortunately, this was not a universal practice. But spelling was done by ear in the seventeenth century, and we shall see that the variations ranged enormously. It is hoped, therefore, that this guide will be helpful to anyone wishing to pursue research into the regicides further.

The following pages contains for reference purposes an alphabetical list of all the regicides.

I shall now proceed to give brief comments concerning these individuals, in alphabetical order, which specify any factors which in any way might concern or render difficult their correct identifications. These include known variant spellings of their names (and some of them spelled their own names in different ways at different times, as whim took them, since as I have already pointed out, Valentine Wauton even wrote his own surname in five different forms apparently as an intentional exercise in versatility), or contemporaries of the same name with whom they might be or already have been confused. I also call attention to other possibilities of confusion, for instance the difficulty of knowing whether John Carew, MP, or John Crew/Crewe, MP, is being referred to in the *Commons Journals* at any particular time. These two MPs were not related to one another but were contemporaries, and since the clerks of the House of Commons sometimes confused them (or at least did not differentiate them) on occasions, it is no wonder that we sometimes find it difficult to avoid doing so also. Other confusions can arise when two different men are confused by contemporaries who did not know them personally because they have the same surname, as happened from time to time with Sir Hardress Waller and Sir William Waller, for instance. The pitfalls of potential error are many, and so I conceived of my first task as being the construction of a guide to true identification. Since until now few people have been clear as to who all the regicides were, and some of their signatures on the Death Warrant were not even correctly read (as for instance that of Thomas Pride, for centuries rarely if ever correctly deciphered), an absolute guide to who they were, with these notes on the possible dangers of mis-identifications, must be the starting point for any enquiry.

General readers can conveniently skip the rest of this chapter, for these technical identification details are intended primarily for historians, in order to try to prevent confusion of identities of the regicides by scholars in the future.

ALPHABETICAL LIST OF THE REGICIDES
Note: The two men listed in parentheses did not actually sign the Death Warrant.

John Alured
John Barkstead
Daniel Blagrave
John Blakiston
Sir John Bourchier
John Bradshaw
John Carew
William Cawley
Thomas Chaloner
Gregory Clement
Sir William Constable, Bart.
(John Cook)
Miles Corbet
Oliver Cromwell
Sir John Danvers
Richard Deane
John Dixwell
John Downes
Humphrey Edwardes
Isaac Ewer
George Fleetwood
Augustine Garland
William Goffe
Lord Grey of Groby
Thomas Harrison
John Hewson
Thomas Horton
John Hutchinson
Richard Ingoldsby
Henry Ireton

John Jones
Robert Lilburne
(John Lisle)
Sir Michael Livesey, Bart.
Edmund Ludlow
Henry Marten
Sir Thomas Mauleverer, Bart.
Simon Mayne
Gilbert Millington
John Moore
Sir Gregory Norton, Bart.
John Okey
Peregrine Pelham
Vincent Potter
Thomas Pride
William Purefoy
Owen Rowe
William Say
Thomas Scot
Adrian Scrope
Henry Smith
Anthony Stapley
James Temple
Peter Temple
Robert Tichborne
John Venn
Thomas Waite
Sir Hardress Waller
Valentine Wauton
Edward Whalley
Thomas Wogan

JOHN ALURED. He had no entry in the DNB until I wrote it for the *Missing Persons* volume which appeared in 1993, when I wrote entries for all five 'missing' regicides, and brought them into the DNB for the first time.[9] Noble's supposed account of him is really not an account of John Alured at all, but of his brother Matthew Alured, Noble having confused the two men.[10] Keeler discussed him, but confused him with his son and also had him die eight years too late.[11] John Alured was a Colonel, but so was his son, also named John Alured. And Colonel Matthew Alured, the regicide's younger brother, is far better known. In many sources, when one finds 'Colonel Alured' mentioned, it takes a great deal of thought to decide which one might be meant. The regicide died in 1651, so all references after that to a living Colonel John Alured are to his son. Variant spellings: Aldred, Alred, Allured, Owlered, Eldred. (There was at least one contemporary named John Eldred, who was not politically prominent. The regicide Miles Corbet was married to a Molly Eldred, probably related to John Eldred. These Eldreds were of a different family, unrelated to the Alureds. But that did not prevent contemporaries sometimes referring to John Alured as 'John Eldred', possibly because they themselves confused the Alureds with the Eldreds, especially if they did not know them very well.)

JOHN BARKSTEAD. Variant spellings: Berkstead, Berksted, Barksted.

DANIEL BLAGRAVE. Variant spellings: Blackgrave, Brograve. But there was apparently a family genuinely named Brograve, who seem to have been of no relation. However, today in the Reading area I have been in touch with some people named Brograve who actually claim to be descended from the Blagraves and related to the regicide, and who insist that Brograve is a true variant form of Blagrave. I am sceptical about this, however, as I look upon the few occasions when Daniel Blagrave was referred to as Brograve as being mistakes. It seems to me more likely that the two separate families have common origins in the Middle Ages, than that Brograve is an acceptable form of Blagrave from a time as recent as the seventeenth century. An interesting and well-informed biographical account of this regicide is found as an extended addendum under the heading of Joseph Blagrave (the regicide's uncle) in *Athenae Oxonienses* by Wood.[12]

JOHN BLAKISTON. Noble became extraordinarily confused about this regicide. He insisted that he was called Joseph rather than John, and that John was his brother.[13] This was of course nonsense. There was no Joseph Blakiston at all, with the exception of the son of the regicide born in 1635, who died an infant. It is clear that Noble never saw the Death Warrant, where the signature 'John Blakiston' is one of the clearest. Variant spellings: Blackiston, Blackstone, Blaxton, Blackston. There is some reason to believe that the regicide pronounced his own surname 'Blaxton', which would account for some of these spellings on phonetic grounds, although a present day collateral descendant assured me most earnestly that the pronunciation of the family name must be 'Blake-his-ton'.

SIR JOHN BOURCHIER. He had an uncle Sir John Bourchier, knighted ten years before, of Hanging Grimston, Yorkshire. Variant spellings: Bourcer, Bowcher, Boucher, Bourcher, Bowser, Bowcer, Bouchier, Bourghchier, Burgchier, etc. In his chapter on the origins of surnames in his book *Remains concerning Britain*, published in its revised edition in 1637, William Camden discusses surnames which were later borne by many of the regicides. He mentions the surname of Bourchier, one of the 'names of ancient good families, as they are written in old Latin Records and histories, with them now in use', giving its correct spelling as Bourchier and claims that it derives from the Latin *de Burgo charo*. He also notes with dismay the decay of its pronunciation, which by his day had already declined to Bouchier and was becoming alarmingly corrupted to Bowcer by the lazy processes, which horrified Camden, of 'contracting, syncopating, curtolling, and mollifying'.[14]

JOHN BRADSHAW. The regicide always seems to have signed his own name with a final 'e', so that the correct spelling as far as he himself was concerned was Bradshawe. However, as he is such a prominent figure and the convention has existed in historical and scholarly literature for three and a half centuries now of calling him John Bradshaw without an 'e', it would be destabilising to sensible discourse to attempt to change the conventional usage at this late date. I shall therefore knowingly continue the fiction of calling him Bradshaw rather than Bradshawe for the sake of clarity and comprehension. The surname comes from a Saxon name, Bradshaigh, and this spelling seems to have been used on very rare occasions, perhaps out of affectation (though not to my knowledge by the regicide himself, only by other family members). There appears to have been another contemporary John Bradshaw who was involved in Parliamentary politics at the local level in Cheshire, but who was never active nationally. Probably they were related, but there is very little occasion for confusing them.

JOHN CAREW. A common variant spelling is Carey. Since it is still fashionable to pronounce the name of the Carews 'Carey' to this day, and the family is the same, one may presume that in the seventeenth century the same was the case. It is very hazardous to draw firm conclusions in attempting to differentiate this regicide from his contemporary, the MP John Crew or Crewe, who was no relation, in the *Commons Journals* after the regicide's entry into Parliament as a recruiter in 1647. Both were prominent. One must therefore always bear in mind that Crew and Crewe may occasionally be mistakes for Carew.

WILLIAM CAWLEY. It is possible to confuse him occasionally with his son, also called William Cawley, as both were Justices of the Peace in Sussex during the 1650s. Although the spelling Calley might be used on rare occasions by mistake, there were genuine Calleys who seem to have been an entirely separate family, and an obscure contemporary named William Calley did exist.

THOMAS CHALONER. He himself spelled his surname Chaloner, although historians have often preferred the spelling of Challoner. Another common variant spelling is Challenor. William Camden pointed out in *Remains* that the correct spelling was Chaloner, and that it originated as a name for someone who had come from Chalons in France.[15] The regicide's father and grandfather were also called Thomas Chaloner, but both were knights and the father died as early as 1615. There was a contemporary Thomas Challoner from Sussex, who was a Justice of the Peace from 1644; these Challoners of Lindfield were apparently no relation whatever to the Yorkshire family of the regicide. The Sussex Thomas Challoner never entered onto the national stage, but some historians have assumed that the regicide was a Sussex JP and have been puzzled by that. It is however a case of mistaken identity. There is a life of the regicide in Wood's *Athenae Oxoniensis*.[16]

GREGORY CLEMENT. He had a son also called Gregory Clement, who was admitted to Lincoln's Inn in 1657. The name was often spelled Clements, and occasionally Clemens. The author Samuel Clemens ('Mark Twain') claimed direct descent from the regicide.

SIR WILLIAM CONSTABLE, BART. This name was sometimes spelled Cunstable, which is how it is pronounced even today by people bearing the name, as I know very well, since I have some close friends who are Constables.

JOHN COOK. Variant spelling: Cooke.

MILES CORBET. Variant spelling: Corbett. William Camden in *Remains* pointed out that Corbet originated from the Norman French word for 'raven'.[17]

OLIVER CROMWELL. Occasionally his name was spelled Crumwell, which is how many older people still pronounce it, and which was presumably the pronunciation of his time as well.

SIR JOHN DANVERS. He himself signed his name Davers with a bar across the 'a' to denote the 'n', in the style of the time. William Camden in *Remains* noted with dismay the decline of Danvers to Davers, a process of decay of which he disapproved.[18] The origin of the surname in Norman times was obviously d'Anvers, or man from Anvers in France.

RICHARD DEANE. Also Dean, rarely Deene. Sometimes he is confused with his younger cousin, Captain Richard Deane, who is mentioned in the regicide's will and with whom he was on friendly terms, treating him as a protégé. In addition, the regicide had an obscure uncle called Richard Deane, who seems to have taken no part in public affairs of any kind, as well as a great-uncle, Sir Richard Deane, Alderman and Lord Mayor of London in 1628-9, who did not die until the middle of 1635. At one time or another the following variant spellings have found use: Deene, Deine, Dean, A'Deane, Adeane. aDayne, Adeyne, Adeine, Michael Edward Adeane, later Lord Adeane (1910-1984), who was Private Secretary to Queen Elizabeth II, told me that he was a direct descendant of this regicide, and was thrilled when I provided him with information about him.

JOHN DIXWELL. Variant spellings: Dixewell, Dickswell, Dickeswell, Dixwel, Dickswel. After the Restoration, as a refugee who fled abroad to avoid execution, he assumed the name of James Davids, which preserved his same initials.

JOHN DOWNES. Often called Downe.

HUMPHREY EDWARDES. In the old DNB and elsewhere he is called Edwards, as he was also in his lifetime. But he always signed himself Edwardes with the 'e', and his brother and descendants of the brother always meticulously kept the 'e', no doubt to assert their identity and to differentiate themselves from all the other countless Edwards's in the world. Since Humphrey Edwardes is an obscure regicide, there is no need to keep to an existing scholarly convention to avoid confusion, and so I shall spell his surname the way he and his family did. It should be remarked that this regicide's signature was so florid that it is often not recognised by those unfamiliar with it, and has rarely been deciphered on the Death Warrant. (In fact, it bears a truly bizarre resemblance to the signature 'Pembroke and Montgomery' of the contemporary Earl of Pembroke, both being tall and thin with letters squeezed together like box springs. One almost wonders if they had the same tutor when young, who taught them to write that way.)

ISAAC EWER. The variant spellings are numerous: Ewers, Ewre, Ewres, Hewer, Hewers, Eure. The regicide had a nephew, Captain Isaac Ewer, who by 1655 was an under-clerk to John Milton and who later had a distinguished legal career.

GEORGE FLEETWOOD. Variant spellings: Fleetwoode, Fleetewoode, Fletewood.

AUGUSTINE GARLAND. His father was Augustine Garland the Elder, and died in 1637/8. In an assessment record, the regicide was called 'Austin Garland', and in his admission entry to Lincoln's Inn he was called 'Augustus Garland'. There was another contemporary Augustine Garland, probably related, alive and a minor in 1636 in Kent, who was mistakenly thought by Brunton and Pennington to be the regicide.[19]

WILLIAM GOFFE. Variant spellings: Goff, Gough, Goughe. There was a Lieutenant-Colonel William Goffe serving under Monck in 1659 who was probably a relation of the regicide; he had a prominent quarrel with the regicide's father-in-law Edward Whalley the regicide. (It is very important not to confuse the two William Goffes in analysing this incident, for obvious reasons.)

THOMAS, LORD GREY OF GROBY. He always signed his name 'Tho. Grey', which has on occasion led to his not being recognised as Lord Grey of Groby. Grey is sometimes spelled Gray, and Groby is frequently spelled Grooby. There were many contemporary Greys, several of high military rank, and some were related to the regicide. Many of these Greys were associated with the same part of the country, which on rare occasions can lead to confusion with him. There was another Thomas, Lord Grey, namely the 15th Lord Grey of Wilton, but he died in 1614, without issue, and confusion need not arise.

THOMAS HARRISON. There were several contemporary Thomas Harrisons. Apart from the regicide, the most prominent was a naval captain of that name, who seems to have been considerably older than the regicide. So for a brief time, while the regicide held the rank of army captain, there were two Captain Thomas Harrisons. The regicide had a brief contact with Reading, where there was a locally prominent Thomas Harrison, so that some confusion is possible there. Later, when the regicide was a colonel, there is the possibility of confusion between him and his father-in-law, Colonel Ralph Harrison, if a Colonel Harrison is spoken of and his first name is not given, and the context does not make the reference unambiguous. It is ironical that a Colonel Harrison was married to the daughter of another Colonel Harrison. Thomas Harrison was the only regicide whose wife had the same surname as himself.

JOHN HEWSON. The name is frequently spelled Huson, Hughson, Hewetson, Hewitson, etc. For instance, in Burton's *Parliamentary Diary*, the regicide is invariably called Colonel Hewitson. Hewson's family is obscure, but the evidence suggests that he is probably the son of another John Hewson. It is possible that the old DNB's note of John Hewson, Cobbler, selling shoes to Massachusetts in 1628 is really a reference to his father. I have found a portrait of Hewson in armour which certainly makes him too young to have been the 1628 cobbler. (There is also a false portrait of Hewson which is really a portrait of Sir William Waller, also in armour, but that is a different image altogether. And finally, there is a contemporary cartoon image of Hewson. I have all three in my collection. Hewson only had one eye, which helps with identification.)

THOMAS HORTON. He had a son Thomas Horton who was under 21 when his father died in 1649.

JOHN HUTCHINSON. The name is very rarely spelled in the variant form of Hutchingson. His third son was called John Hutchinson, but there is no possibility of confusing them.

RICHARD INGOLDSBY. His father was Sir Richard Ingoldsby. The regicide himself was knighted after the Restoration. He had a son Richard Ingoldsby, born 1654. There are countless opportunities for confusing the regicide with other people: he had several brothers who were also officers on the side of the Parliament, all listed in the appendix to the section on The Family Backgrounds of the Regicides. Variant spellings: Inglesby, Ingleby. There was a Yorkshire family called Ingleby (today seated at Ripon Castle), and some of them seem to have been officers in the Yorkshire militia, making confusion a possibility though not a likelihood.

HENRY IRETON. He had a son named Henry Ireton who was a small child when the regicide died. In the mid-1640s both the regicide and his brother Thomas were Captains of Horse in the New Model Army at the same time, but the regicide was very soon promoted to Colonel. Variant spellings: Eierton, Irton, Eyrton. (These spellings are chiefly encountered in earlier generations of the family and had died out by the regicide's time.)

JOHN JONES. There were so many colonels named Jones during the Civil War and in its aftermath, that sorting them out is enough to drive anyone to despair. It is probable that no one could ever identify all references to 'Colonel Jones', even with many years' dedicated research. There was Colonel Michael Jones, there was Colonel Philip Jones, there was Colonel John Jones, and others, mostly just called 'Colonel Jones' in reports. The regicide had one surviving son also named John Jones, who died about 1717. It should be noted that the regicide's father, Thomas Jones, had two versions of his surname: Jones and 'ab John', which in Welsh of course means 'son of John', indicating that the regicide's grandfather was also a John Jones. There is no evidence that I have encountered to show that the regicide himself continued the Welsh tradition by ever calling himself John ab Thomas, or John ap Thomas (in the more modern spelling) officially, although he may well have done this as a child and when mingling with Welsh friends and family members.

ROBERT LILBURNE. The regicide, a colonel, can sometimes be confused with his brother Colonel Henry Lilburne or even his other brother, Lieutenant-Colonel John Lilburne (the Leveller). There was also a first cousin, Captain Thomas Lilburne. Confusions between these men would generally only arise early in the Civil War. Variant spellings: Lylburne, Lilborne, Lilburn, Lilborn.

JOHN LISLE. The Lisles were an extremely ancient family who took their name from their home on the Isle of Wight, where they had lived since 'time immemorial', as the saying goes. The original form of the surname was the Latin 'de Insula', meaning 'of the Isle'. William Camden called attention to the Latin origin of this surname in his *Remains*.[20] Lisle's close colleague Bulstrode Whitelocke always wrote the regicide's name as John l'Isle. The regicide was also known as John de Lisle, John de l'Isle, and even sometimes during his own lifetime was called John de Insula by contemporaries of an antiquarian disposition. The regicide also had a son called John Lisle, who died in 1709.

SIR MICHAEL LIVESEY, BART. He is frequently called Sir Miles rather than Sir Michael, especially in pamphlets and newsletters. His surname appears in a variety of spellings on many occasions, including these forms: Livesley, Levesey, Lewesey, Livesay, Livesaye, Lvesy, Luesy, Levesy, and even rarely and mistakenly, Lucy or Lucey. Of all the regicide surnames, Livesey appears to be the most multifarious in terms of spellings.

EDWARD LUDLOW. Often Ludlowe. He had a grandfather Sir Edmund Ludlow (died 1624) and in his earlier life he can be confused with his uncle, who was also named Edmund Ludlow (died 1666). The regicide also had a first cousin named Edmund Ludlow who died 1645/6. The Ludlow who was captured by the royalists at the beginning of the Civil War was not the regicide but his brother Robert Ludlow, who died a prisoner of war in 1643 at Oxford. There were many Ludlow relations who were active at the local level, held militia commissions in Wiltshire, etc. It is difficult to sort them out, and early in his career, the regicide may occasionally be confused with some of them.

HENRY MARTEN. His father was Sir Henry Marten, MP, and a remarkable fact is that their signatures are practically indistinguishable from one another. The regicide had a son Henry Marten by his second wife, who was admitted to the Inner Temple in 1657. The regicide evidently hated to be called Henry and would only let people call him Harry, and he is sometimes referred to in print as Harry Marten. He was particular about the spelling of Marten with an 'e', but very commonly his name was mis-spelled Martin or Martyn. Since he was a colonel, there is some danger of confusion between him and Colonel Francis Martin (or Martyn), who served in the Earl of Essex's Army, and whose name appears from time to time in unexpected contexts.

SIR THOMAS MAULEVERER, BART. This man's surname appears to have driven his contemporaries to distraction. No one seemed able to spell it properly. The four syllables are a real tongue-twister at the best of times. The name was spelled in a variety of ways, including these: Maleverer, Mallevery, Mauliverer, Mallever, occasionally even degenerating as far as the obviously incorrect Mallory. It was the brilliant William Camden, in his *Remains*, who revealed the mystery of this bizarre surname: 'Many names also given in merriment for Bynames or Nick-names have continued to Posterity; as Malduit, for ill scholarship or ill taught; Mallieure, commonly Mallyvery, *i.e. Malus Leporarius,* for ill hunting the Hare …'[21] The regicide's Mauleverer family of Allerton Mauleverer, West Riding, Yorkshire, can sometimes be confused with the Mauleverer family of Arncliffe, in Yorkshire, whose descendants are living today. The two families were related distantly, but quite distinct from one another. It is possible sometimes to confuse the regicide, who was a colonel, with a distant relation, Colonel John Mauleverer, who died in 1650.

SIMON MAYNE. He signed his first name Symon. The regicide's father was also called Simon Mayne, but died at the age of only 40 in 1617. The regicide also had a son called Simon Mayne, born about 1644, who later became a Judge and in turn had his own son called Simon Mayne. Variant spellings: Meyn, Meyne, Meine.

GILBERT MILLINGTON. Occasionally Myllington. He also had a son called Gilbert Millington, born circa 1648.

JOHN MOORE. He is another regicide who had no DNB entry until I wrote one for him in the *Missing Persons* volume, although my entry was cut substantially by the editor for reasons of space.[22] (I give the original test of the entry in full in the Appendix to the section on The Family Backgrounds of the Regicides.) I had previously done a lengthy entry for Moore in the *Biographical Dictionary of British Radicals in the Seventeenth Century*.[23] Keeler has discussed him.[24] Noble believed that 'his name is not in the death warrant'.[25] However, John Moore had probably the worst handwriting I have ever seen from the entire seventeenth century, and in his signature, although 'John' is clear enough, 'Moore' is so obscure that it practically requires a cryptographer to decipher it. Hence it is that many have been unable to read it and thought he had not signed the Death Warrant of Charles I, which he did in fact do, immediately after John Jones. (The three signatures on the Death Warrant which are very difficult to read are those of Humphrey Edwardes, John Moore, and Thomas Pride.) One reason why Moore has received so much less attention than he deserves is probably due to this fact that his signature is illegible and no one ever recognises it on documents. The name Moore is also spelled More, Moor, and rarely de la More (which was the original form of the surname for this family). Descendants of this regicide spelled their name More to distinguish themselves from the many Moores of this world. Because More and Moore are separated by some distance in alphabetical listings, the regicide John Moore's Parliamentary Diary manuscript went unrecognised in the British Library (then the British Museum Library), since it was indexed not under Moore but under More. And since the man did not have a DNB entry at that time anyway, whether under Moore or More, few really knew who he was in any case. I was the first person to find this Diary in the British Library and appreciate what it was, sometime about 1973. I remember looking through the listings which in those days were written on paper index cards in a large wooden case just outside the old Manuscripts Room. Finding nothing under Moore, I kept going for a very long time until, by sheer bloody-mindedness, I had gone as far as More, and there it suddenly appeared. I must have had a hunch. I made a fuss about it, the word got round, and suddenly people were queuing up to go and consult John Moore's Parliamentary Diary! This was a very rewarding experience, to get the lost diary into circulation again. The fact that the Diary is in such atrocious handwriting that it can barely be read has not deterred people, apparently.

SIR GREGORY NORTON, BART. This was another man missing from the old DNB until I wrote his entry for the *Missing Persons* volume.[26] Norton was not discussed by Keeler, since he only entered Parliament as a recruiter MP. I also wrote Norton's entry in the *Biographical Dictionary of British Radicals in the Seventeenth Century*.[27] This was the first biographical sketch of him ever written, with the exception of a silly fantasy sketch by Noble, which is full of errors from beginning to end.[28] There was also a Sir Richard Norton, Bart., of a different family (although they may have had common origins), whose daughter married the regicide's son Henry. The regicide also had a son called Gregory Norton, who unfortunately died before his father in the same year, 1652. The regicide might on occasion be confused with Colonel Richard Norton.

JOHN OKEY. He had a son John Okey, born 1642, who entered Gonville and Gaius College, Cambridge, in 1657.

PEREGRINE PELHAM. He had no entry in the DNB until I wrote it for the *Missing Persons* volume.[29] Noble said of him: 'It is singular how little can be learnt of this man.'[30] However, we do know a great deal about him now, and I have discussed him in an article in a journal as well, having found a considerable amount of his correspondence.[31] Keeler also has an entry for him.[32] His father was also called Peregrine Pelham. It is sometimes difficult or impossible to distinguish between the regicide and his first cousin Henry Pelham when a 'Mr. Pelham' is mentioned in the *Commons Journals*, for they were contemporaries and both were prominent MPs.

VINCENT POTTER. He also had no entry in the old DNB until I wrote it for the *Missing Persons* volume.[33] Keeler does not mention him, as he was not an MP. Between 1643 and 1645 the regicide can easily be confused with his brother John, since they were both called Captain Potter (Captain John Potter died at the Battle of Naseby in June, 1645). In some documentation concerning the Parliamentary Commissioners to the Army (an office in which the regicide succeeded his brother) it is still possible to confuse the two men, and great care has to be taken, due to the fact that two Captain Potters carried out the same job in succession.

THOMAS PRIDE. Often spelled Pryde. He had a son, Captain Thomas Pride. A special caution needs to be given: this regicide's signature is most peculiar, and not always recognised. Furthermore, it seems to have changed somewhat over the course of the years, as if the regicide had not been fully literate as a youth, struggled to learn to write his name as a businessman, and later developed an easy command of writing skills. But like John Moore (who was fully, copiously literate and had no such excuse), Pride's surname is written in a way which is only barely legible, even by one familiar with it.

WILLIAM PUREFOY. The name is variously spelled: Perfrey, Purfey, Purefey, Purifoy, Purefay, etc. There were many Purefoys alive at the time of the regicide, but of them all, only he seems to have been a colonel.

OWEN ROWE. Frequently spelled Roe. Care has to be used to avoid confusing him with the Irish Catholic leader, Owen Roe O'Neill, who is very often referred to at that time simply as 'Owen Roe'. The context, however, generally makes a confusion impossible. The regicide was a colonel, but so was his brother, Francis Rowe, who became Scoutmaster-General but died about December, 1649, in Ireland. Up until that date, the two men can easily be confused. A third Colonel Rowe, named William, also became Scoutmaster-General, which does not make the situation any clearer. As with the two Captain Potters who held the same job in succession, we have also the two Colonel Rowes who held the same job in succession. The name was also spelled Row. So many Rowes existed at that time, that when a 'Mr. Rowe' is mentioned, one needs to be extremely careful; the regicide was a prominent merchant in the City and also a merchant adventurer, and his name as 'Mr. Rowe' occurs in many unexpected places.

WILLIAM SAY. Also spelled Saye. Sometimes it is not clear, when 'Say' or 'Saye' is mentioned, whether the regicide or Lord Saye and Sele is meant. This might appear unlikely at first thought, but I have encountered such instances where the ambiguity is impenetrable. The regicide's father was also called William Say, but he died in 1613, so cannot be confused with his son. It should be remarked that although the regicide was a prominent barrister, he had a brother Edward who was called to the bar on the very same day as himself. So in legal references, confusion is possible between the two men. Another 'Mr. Say' who should also be mentioned is Leonard Say, Dean of St. Paul's Cathedral, who was a distant cousin of the regicide.

THOMAS SCOT. He always signed his name Scot, although most historians have referred to him as Thomas Scott. I choose to use his own spelling of his name. He had a son, Colonel Thomas Scot. The regicide (who was MP for Aylesbury) has often been confused by historians with another MP named Thomas Scott, who was a Major rather than a Colonel, but who nevertheless was often *called* Colonel. This latter MP was MP for Aldborough, and was a passionate Leveller, who died 8 January 1647/8. It was this other MP, not the regicide, who married Grace Mauleverer, the daughter of Sir Thomas Mauleverer, the regicide. Most historians have made the mistake of believing Grace Mauleverer to be the second wife (of an imagined three) of the regicide. In fact, the regicide only had two wives, not three, and Grace Mauleverer was not one of them.

ADRIAN SCROPE. Also spelled Scroope and Scroop, which is how it has always been pronounced, and still is. Five years before he was born, a relation of his, Adrian Scrope, son of Adrian Scrope, was born, but he does not seem to have lived to adulthood. The regicide is often confused with the much younger Sir Adrian Scrope of Lincolnshire, who was a royalist and a distant relation. The royalist was involved in a riot at an Inn of Court when young, and has been wrongly identified as the regicide, who actually attended a different Inn of Court fifteen years earlier (see extended discussion of this point in the section on 'The Regicides and the Law', where it is pointed out that part of the convenient theory of the regicides being rebellious youngsters, who rebelled against authority when young as a foretaste to executing the king, is based upon this misidentification, and thus loses much of its basis).

HENRY SMITH. Also Smyth. His father was also called Henry Smith, and died in 1623. The true surname of this family had been Heriz (from the Norman French word for 'hedgehog'), and they changed it to Smith to inherit a legacy in the 15th century. All of their pedigrees describe them as 'Smith alias Heriz', and descendants living today call themselves Heriz-Smith.

ANTHONY STAPLEY. Also Stapeley. His father was named Anthony Stapley, and died in 1606. His youngest son, Captain Anthony Stapley, was born circa 1630, was admitted to Gray's Inn in 1647 and, by switching Inns of Court for some reason, to the Inner Temple in 1648. The regicide's father had been of Framfield, Sussex, and the regicide was of Patcham, East Sussex, which is on the edge of modern Brighton. It is necessary to stress these place names to avoid confusion with the other Stapley family of Hickstead Place, East Sussex, whose papers are preserved in the East Sussex Records Office at Lewes, and who are another branch of the family, *not* the regicide's branch. This other branch of Stapleys also had two other Anthony Stapleys.

JAMES TEMPLE. Rarely Tempull. He had a son James Temple, born 1630. He and the regicide Peter Temple are often confused, especially as both were colonels. In the *Commons Journals* they are called 'Col. Temple' or 'Mr. Temple' at random and interchangeably, though perhaps James was more frequently called Colonel than Peter, and Peter more frequently called 'Mr.' (James was the more martial of the two men.) It is often possible to tell them apart, but not always. But once outside the House of Commons, the complications multiply enormously, because of the existence of Colonel Edmund Temple, Colonel Purbeck Temple, and Colonel Thomas Temple, and all of these Temples, regicides and otherwise, were related to each other.

PETER TEMPLE. Rarely Tempull. He had a son Peter Temple, born 1635, who later became the Rev. Peter Temple, obtained an MA from Cambridge, 1659, went to Virginia at the Restoration and returned to England to be Vicar of Sible Hedingham, Essex, 1672-1690. There were two other contemporary Peter Temples, both distant relations: Sir Peter Temple, Knight, of Stantonbarry and Little Linford, Bucks., who was politically inactive and published one book of a religious nature in 1658 (containing engravings of himself and his wife, of which I have originals); Sir Peter Temple, Bart., was also an MP and was named to the High Court of Justice but never attended. (His oil portrait hangs at Radley, the public school, near that of his mother Lady Hester Temple, née Sandys). The regicide James Temple also had a son Peter Temple born in 1633.

ROBERT TICHBORNE. His father, Robert Tichborne the Elder, was Warden of the Skinners Company. The regicide himself was later to be Master of the Skinners Company. The regicide had children, but it is unknown whether he had a son Robert. Confusion between the regicide and his father is easy when considering their activities in the City of London. The regicide had long-standing associations with the parish of St. Michael le Querne, of which his father had also been churchwarden. The father was on the Common Council and in 1639 was called 'Mr. Deputy Tichborne' by the new churchwardens of his parish. Variant spellings: Tichburn, Tichburne, Tychborne, Titchborne, Titchburn.

JOHN VENN. Also Venne. He had a son John Venn born in 1629; although the son was alive in 1634, he seems to have died young. The name Venn was sometimes spelled Fenn or Fen; in a Visitation for 1634, the regicide's family was actually described by the heralds as 'Ven alias Fen'.

THOMAS WAITE. Frequently spelled Wayte. There were several contemporary Thomas Waites. It has been thought by some that the regicide was the son of Thomas Waite of Keythorpe in Leicestershire, but this man seems to have been his grandfather, and who in 1612 was issued arms and was the King's Receiver for Warwickshire and Leicestershire, dying in 1642. The regicide was definitely the son of Henry Waite of Wymondham in Leicestershre. The regicide attended Gray's Inn and is a different person from the Thomas Waite who was admitted the very same year to Lincoln's Inn, son of yet another Thomas Waite of Haxby in Yorkshire. There was a Captain Francis Waite of Leicestershire, son of Thomas of Keythorpe, who was apparently the regicide's uncle, and he can be confused with the regicide during the time when the regicide was himself a captain, before he became a colonel.

SIR HARDRESS WALLER. When referred to only as 'Waller' he might be confused with his first cousin, Sir William Waller. It should be noted that this is rendered slightly more likely by the fact that they were both generals. Sir Hardress was a Major General of Foot, which is not widely appreciated, and this is a fact not mentioned in the old DNB.

VALENTINE WAUTON. Although he is listed in the old DNB as Walton, the regicide signed his name Wauton. He was probably called Walton far more often than Wauton, but Wauton is the correct surname, and as he is not prominent enough for the false convention to be maintained for purposes of clarity, I shall use the correct spelling of Wauton in discussing him. Variant spellings include Watton, Wanton (a mis-spelling which occurs in a Visitation of Norfolk), and Wawton. The mis-reading Manton often occurs in the CSPD and sources of that kind, where transcribers have been at work, and the 'W' has been mistaken for an 'M'. The regicide had a son, Captain Valentine Wauton/Walton, who served in Oliver Cromwell's regiment of horse and was killed at the Battle of Marston Moor in 1644. Since the regicide was a captain himself at the beginning of the Civil War, there was for long a question as to whether it was he or his son who was a prisoner of war in Oxford Castle as late as July, 1643. But I have been able to establish with certainty that this was the regicide himself. The regicide is, of course, more familiar as Colonel Wauton, which he became later. Here too there is some slight possibility of confusion, since there was a royalist Lieutenant-Colonel Wauton or Walton mentioned by Thomas Mytton in a letter of January, 1646/7,[34] whose identity I have not been able to establish. He may have been a relation. The regicide's eldest surviving son in 1650, George Wauton, was a captain in his father's regiment, but there is no possibility of confusion, since his father was by then a colonel.

EDWARD WHALLEY. He had a son Edward Whalley born in 1656. There is much evidence to indicate that the name was pronounced as in 'whale', including the discovery I made in Nottinghamshire of the use of the whale as a heraldic motif and crest by the family. I have seen carved whales in wooden panels saved from their old houses. The name is frequently spelled Whaley, or Whaly, but rare as Walley or Waley. Many descendants of this family today pronounce the surname as in 'whale', though others pronounce it to rhyme with 'Ollie'. William Camden in his *Remains* points out that the surname Walley originally signified a man of Wales: 'Many strangers coming hither, and residing here, were named of their Countries, as ... Welsh, Walsh, Walleys ...'[35] and this supports the belief that, as Wales was referred to by the name originally, Wales should dominate the traditional pronunciation.

THOMAS WOGAN. Another Welshman, a variant spelling of his surname sometimes encountered is Woogam, and a rare variant spelling, mostly of the sixteenth century, is Wegan or Wegyne. Although the regicide eventually became a colonel, he was Captain Wogan during the same time as the renegade Captain Edward Wogan, and a very great deal of confusion has resulted between the two men. All references to 'Captain Wogan' have to be treated very carefully for this reason.

1. Mark Noble, *The Lives of the English Regicides and Other Commissioners of the Pretended High Court of Justice Appointed to Sit in Judgement upon Their Sovereign, King Charles the First*, John Stockdale, London, 1798, 2 vols.
2. C. S. Nicholls, ed., *The Dictionary of National Biography: Missing Persons*, Oxford University Press, 1993. The entries which I contributed were for John Alured, John Moore, Sir Gregory Norton, Bart., Peregrine Pelham, and Vincent Potter.
3. Robert K. G. Temple, 'The Original Officer List of the New Model Army', *Bulletin of the Institute of Historical Research*, Vol. LIX, No. 139, May, 1986, pp. 50-77.
4. Ian Gentles, *The New Model Army in England, Ireland and Scotland, 1645-1653*, Blackwell, Oxford, 1992.
5. *Ibid.*, p. 19, and footnotes 105 and 109 on pp. 451-2.
6. Robert K. G. Temple, 'The Massey Brigade in the West', *Somerset and Dorset Notes and Queries*, Vol. XXXI, Part 322, September, 1985, pp. 437-45.
7. Robert K. G. Temple, 'Discovery of a Manuscript Eye-Witness Account of the Battle of Maidstone', *Archaeologia Cantiana*, Maidstone, Kent, Vol. XCVII, 1981, pp. 209-220.
8. Richard L. Greaves and Robert Zaller, eds., *Biographical Dictionary of British Radicals of the Seventeenth Century*, Harvester Press, Brighton, 1982-4, 3 vols.
9. Robert Temple, 'John Alured', in *Dictionary of National Biography: Missing Persons*, xxxx
10. Noble, Vol. I., pp. 75-80.
11. Mary Frear Keeler, *The Long Parliament 1640-1641, A Biographical Study of Its Members*, American Philosophical Society, Philadelphia, 1954, p. 85.
12. Anthony a Wood, *Athenae Oxoniensis*, second edition, 1721, I, 370-1. (The pages of this work are double-paginated in vertical columns.) This is the edition I have, and as it contains more than 500 lives which were absent in the first edition, I cannot say whether Daniel Blagrave is in the first edition. When using Wood, it is always essential to use this second edition, because in addition to a vast expansion of material, it contains countless corrections as well.
13. Noble, *op. cit.*, p. 91.
14. William Camden, *Remains concerning Britain*, John Russell Smith, London, 1870, pp. 160-1.
15. *Ibid.*, p. 119.
16. Wood, *op. cit.*, II, 264-5.
17. *Ibid.*, p. 138. Other bird-origins for surnames include Arundel from the French word for 'swallow', and of course, Dove, Nightingale, Peacock, Sparrow, Alcock, Hancock, Howlet, Wren, Parratt, Finch.
18. *Ibid.*, p. 160.
19. D. Brunton and Donald H. Pennington, *Members of the Long Parliament*, Archon Books, USA, 1968, p. 51. See *Archaeologia Cantiana*, Vol. XX, p. 25.
20. Camden, *op. cit.*, p. 162.
21. *Ibid.*, p. 144.
22. DNB, *op. cit.*, xx.
23. Richard Greaves and Robert Zaller, eds., *Biographical Dictionary of British Radicals in the Seventeenth Century*, Harvester Press, Brighton, UK, 1984. The entries are alphabetical. I did many entries for this work, and edited several others which appeared under other people's names.
24. Keeler, *op. cit.*, p. 277.
25. Noble, *op. cit.*, Vol. II, p. 85.
26. DNB, *op. cit.*, xx.
27. Greaves and Zaller, *op. cit.*
28. Noble, *op. cit.*, Vol. II, p. 102.
29. DNB, *op. cit.*, xx.
30. Noble, *op. cit.*, Volume II, p. 118.
31. Robert K. G. Temple, 'Discovery of a Manuscript Eye-Witness Report of the Battle of Maidstone', *Archaeologia Cantiana*, Vol. XCVII, 1981, pp. 209-220.
32. Keeler, *op. cit.*, pp. 300-1.
33. DNB, *op. cit.*, xx.
34. Bodleian Library, Oxford: Tanner MS. 59/2, 677-8.
35. Camden, *op. cit.*, p. 130.

CHAPTER TWO

Family Backgrounds Of The Regicides

Hitherto, our ignorance of the regicides has been so great that no one knew who the parents of many of the regicides were, or where they came from. And in many cases, the parents claimed for the regicides by such sources as the old DNB were wrong. In tackling the problem of the regicides, therefore, I had to commence with the question: who were they? This was not an easy question to answer in most cases. For instance, in trying to find the parentage of Sir Gregory Norton, Bart., when my work began, I was reduced to going through just about every Norton pedigree for the whole of England. It is no exaggeration to say that it took me several years to find out who Gregory Norton was and where he came from. Fortunately I was able to discover this before I wrote his entry for the *Missing Persons* volume of the DNB, so that the correct information has been made publicly available for years. This information was incorporated into the entry for Norton written by J. T. Peacey for the Oxford DNB. However, there is a problem with both his entry and mine. I gave the place name of origin for Norton's mother as Chaldeworth, Berkshire, and did not trouble to double-check that (I merely copied it from my source). Peacey changed this to Challeworth, upon what authority I do not know. However, according to Bartholomew's *Survey Gazetteer of the British Isles*, neither a Chaldeworth nor a Challeworth has ever existed in the British Isles, whether in Berkshire or elsewhere. I am inclined therefore to believe that Norton's mother must have come from Chaddleworth in Berkshire, which is seven miles from Lambourn, and which has the advantage of really existing. These kind of details may seem exasperating and insignificant to non-historians, but alas, those of us engaged in this work have to strive like Hercules to achieve the endless series of Labours. Having written two biographical dictionary entries for Norton (Peacey only cites one of them, and before my efforts began, Norton had none at all anywhere and no one really knew who he was), I now find myself correcting yet another detail. They say, and it is true, that a historian's work is never done, until he himself or she herself joins the ancestors and enters into the dark mists of history in person.

Identifying the families and parents of the regicides is so basic and essential that it takes precedence over most discussion. If you don't know who a man was and where he came from, what can you really say about his origins? – Nothing. (I say 'he' in this work because there were no female regicides.)

My search for the parents of the regicides was therefore one of the most intensive areas of my research. And I am glad to say that of the 61 regicides, I found the parents for all but two of them. And of those two, John Hewson and Vincent Potter, I have found highly probable parents for Hewson and enough leads and possible relatives of Potter – apart from clarifying his county of early adulthood, where he joined the county militia at the beginning of the Civil War – to make the eventual discovery of his parents' names highly likely, if not by myself, then by some other researcher in the future.

I have compiled massive family histories for the regicides (apart from Cromwell, whose family is already documented to the most extensive degree imaginable[1]), and these are to be found in the Appendix to this chapter. A further Appendix section then follows these family histories, consisting of transcribed documents and other primary source material. The family histories themselves are substantiated by well over five hundred references, which follow the family histories found in the Appendix. This material may be consulted for literally thousands of new facts which had never before been discovered, as well as for countless corrections to existing accounts of the regicides found in such sources as the old DNB, where erroneous parents have frequently been given for regicides, and which are riddled with misinformation. In the newer Oxford DNB many of the factual errors have been corrected, but not all. Many of the corrections appearing in the Oxford DNB stem from my own research, which was circulated fairly widely by my friend the late Ruth Spalding, and also by John Adamson of Peterhouse in Cambridge University, who left it sitting on the open shelves of the History of Parliament Trust for a very long time, so that when I went to retrieve it without warning one day, I found it bristling with notes of other researchers, which I have retained in case anyone doubts this story.

Very little of the material in the Appendix will be repeated here, so it must be understood that for detailed information about the family histories of the regicides, one must refer to the Appendix, where the regicide families are listed alphabetically under the name of each regicide. All known siblings of regicides are also listed, together with dates and career information for them where available. This is of particular importance for the military regicides, since in so many cases the brothers and sons of regicides were also officers, and confusion is often possible, a point which was dealt with in a preliminary fashion in the preceding chapter.

A rigorous and deep study of the regicide families has yielded more than just a mass of information. Several key points have emerged from the study which are of considerable consequence. These will become clear as the discussion proceeds.

Precedents exist amongst modern historians of the seventeenth century for elaborate studies of family histories. Perhaps most notable are those of Alan Everitt in his book *The Community of Kent and the Great Rebellion 1640-60*.[2] Everitt in a sense based his entire book upon this foundation. On the first page of his Introduction he says: 'Perhaps we have tended too much to look at the period through the eyes of the government, and especially of parliament. The social and political life of the vast majority of Englishmen, even among the gentry, was lived almost wholly within the confines of their county – their "country" as they significantly called it.'[3] Thus does he launch upon his account of what he aptly calls the *community* of Kent, with his concentration upon its gentry. It was its gentry who led its community. His studies of the family histories and interrelations of these gentry were fundamental to his purpose.

Everitt says early in his book: 'Socially and politically, most English counties were dominated either by a single great family, like the Derbys in Lancashire, or by two or three rivals as in Leicestershire and Somerset, or by a knot of closely related families of comparable standing. Kent was among these last. ... The real leaders of Kentish society were composed, besides (the Earl of) Thanet, of twenty or thirty related "county" families such as the Derings, Haleses, Twysdens, Scots, Diggeses, and Oxindens of Deane as a *group*. Most of these families comprised several separately established branches and they were not usually in origin distinct from the lesser or "parochial" gentry, who were often drawn from their junior scions.'[4]

He adds: 'The existence of such "clans", with many separately established branches, is not a phenomenon peculiar to Kent ... Their connexions spread far and wide and united the whole body of the gentry. ... Such a corporate sense was of course shared by many counties. ... The origins of the gentry help to explain it. Despite the proximity to London, only one-eighth of the gentry were complete newcomers to the county, arriving since Queen Elizabeth's reign ... Virtually all the leading families – Culpepers, Derings, Oxindens, Sondeses, Scots, and Twysdens, for example – and nearly three-quarters of the knights and four-fifths of the peers were drawn from these indigenous gentry. Moreover, though many parochial gentry stemmed from Tudor yeomen, between 80 and 90 percent of the gentry as a whole, including virtually all the "county" families, were reckoned gentle well before the Tudor period. Families like the Culpepers, Sondeses, Haleses, and Walsinghams had been appointed to the commission of the peace since before the Reformation.'[5]

We can see here to what extent Everitt tackled the family histories. Establishing how old a family was and what offices it had held at what early dates he viewed as fundamental information to enable a sensible discussion of the Great Rebellion to take place. We shall see just how correct such a course of research is, when applied to the country as a whole. Indeed, we shall discover through the researches into the family histories of the regicides that many of the regicides formed "clans" spreading throughout the country, and not only within single counties, which were every bit as important and powerful nationally as those discovered by Everitt at work within Kent and determining its political history.

Although Everitt adopted a valuable – indeed, crucial – methodology, which we shall emulate, his research is not always faultless. In an article I published about Kent in 1981 in *Archaeologia Cantiana*, it was necessary for me to call attention to his lack of grasp of certain military matters.[6]

And as far as the Kentish regicides are concerned, Everitt lets us down entirely. He fails to notice a number of key facts about the regicides' families, and this undermines his theory that "new" families were more politically radical. His slips also show the vital importance of the most thorough possible biographical/genealogical research. He mentions three Kentish regicides in his book: John Dixwell, Augustine Garland, and Sir Michael Livesey, Bart. Everitt was not aware that the regicide James Temple was someone who spanned three counties, Sussex, Kent, and Essex, that his parents were buried in Rochester Cathedral, and that one of his two childhood homes was at St. Mary Hoo in Kent.

Everitt wholly mispresents the origins and social standing of Dixwell, Garland, and Livesey. He is correct when he refers to Augustine Garland as a newcomer to Kent, to the extent that Garland was a Kentishman at all, for he was not actually a 'Kentish regicide' in fact. Everitt was unaware that Garland became a recruiter MP for Queenborough in Kent only because he inherited some property there from his father (who otherwise had largely cut him out of his will). The Garlands were never really a Kentish family, and the regicide himself had no pretensions about being a Kentishman. The regicide's great-grandfather Richard Garland had lived at Hayes, but after that the Garlands migrated to London, where they were a family of lawyers and merchants. Garland's grandmother was from Calais and may have been French. (For the details of this, see the Appendix.) Garland was thus a Kentish MP by accident, as a means of getting a seat. He was forced to affiliate himself with Kentish politics due to the circumstance that his father had essentially disinherited him, so that he was driven back upon a minor family property which happened to be in Kent.

Everitt, being unaware of all this, is therefore somewhat misleading when he speaks of Garland as a newcomer to Kent and as not being representative of Kentish opinion.[7] But he is positively led astray when he uses Garland mistakenly as one of the supposed 'newer families' to illustrate his thesis that 'the newer families tended to take extreme political positions: Garland, Parker, Lancaster, Plumer, Butcher, and Aldersey were all relative newcomers, and Monson, Rich and Temple had no roots in the county.'[8] Indeed, we have already seen that it is not true that James Temple had no roots in the county, a fact also unknown to Everitt, which goes somewhat further to weaken his thesis. The Temples not only had a home in Kent, but they were the hereditary captains of Tilbury Fort directly across the Thames from Kent and were in constant communication with the captains of Kent's Gravesend Fort opposite, in order to coordinate the matter of the defence of the Thames, so that their business with Kent was continual and urgent. Furthermore, James Temple's parents were both buried in Rochester Cathedral, and his mother was daughter and co-heiress of John Somer of Rochester; his step-mother and his first wife were both from Haremare Hall on the Kent/Sussex border. In addition, Temple's brother-in-law was a Kentish baronet, and he was also closely related to the leading Kentish family of Sandys, since his aunt was a Sandys. Everitt's lack of all this information therefore led him to make an unwise assertion.

But it is when he comes to discuss the Kentish regicide Sir Michael Livesey that Everitt goes most seriously astray. Everitt says of him: 'Since these extremists were men of great determination, thinking in terms not of local politics but of national principles, it was not difficult for them to grasp the reins in an emergency. But most of them, like the regicides Sir Michael Livesey and John Dixwell, were drawn from new or comparatively unimportant families in the county, unrelated to the natural leaders of the shire, and unable to render their control permanent.'[9] He adds: 'Dixwells, Riverses, Liveseys, Garlands, Springates, Sandyses, and Blounts were all comparative newcomers to Kent ... Such a group was not likely to control the county for long without some degree of support from the older landed families of the shire, who outnumbered them by at least six to one.'[10]

We have already seen that the Garlands were not a Kentish family at all and do not really belong in Everitt's context. Furthermore, since the regicide's wife died two months after he was elected to Parliament, and he had no surviving children, there was no Garland family in any case. There was only a single man without a family.

Further remarks about Livesey by Everitt continue the same theme: 'Who now completed the core? ... among them were Sir Michael Livesey, Thomas Blount, and Sir William Springate – men of an altogether different stamp and the only members of the core who were newcomers to Kent.'[11] Also: '... most of the rest were newcomers to the county: Thomas Plumer and Sir Michael Livesey came of a Tudor lawyer and a London merchant ...'[12] A little later on he calls Dixwell, Garland, and Livesey 'gentlemen-lawyers'.[13] And although it is true that Dixwell and Garland were both barristers, there is no record of Livesey ever having studied the law or having had anything whatever to do with it. One wonders how Everitt could have called Livesey a lawyer when there is no evidence for it of any kind.

Again, Everitt continues his theme that the new families of Kent were the radicals by saying: 'Control of the County Committee had passed from these county gentry to other men. It had passed to the small group of extremists, mainly of new and unpopular families like Sir Michael Livesey the regicide ...'[14] Later Everitt even describes Livesey as being of the *nouveaux-riches* and of legal and mercantile origin.[15]

Everitt's view of Livesey's social standing and family background simply do not hold up. First of all, Livesey's pedigree goes back to at least the eleventh century, and the description of him as a *nouveau riche* of mercantile or legal origin is absurd. His father was Sheriff of Kent in 1618. Although the Liveseys only came south from Lancashire and the Midlands in the regicide's grandfather's time, the grandfather, Robert Livesey, was twice Sheriff of Sussex and Surrey (in 1592 and 1602) and of considerable local distinction. The Liveseys seem to have shifted their abode to Kent in connection with the regicide's father's marriage. For he married Anne Sondes, daughter of Sir Michael Sondes of Kent.

Everitt is at great pains to portray the Sondes family as one of the leading old gentry families of Kent.[16] And yet, despite the fact that Livesey's mother was a Sondes (which is stated clearly even in the old DNB, normally so full of errors for the regicides), Everitt strangely persists in trying to portray Livesey as a man with no local Kentish connections of any importance. This is a most peculiar contradiction, and suggests a stubborn adherence to his theory by Everitt in the face of facts, and a wilful overlooking of readily available facts, such as Livesey's being a son of a Sondes as so clearly stated in that readiest of all sources at the time Everitt was writing, the old DNB. This does not encourage us to rely upon any theories put forward by Everitt, who at times seems more intent upon theories than upon evidence.

Furthermore, Livesey's father was descended from the distinguished Berkeley family, who traced their descent back to at least 1086, as well as the Barons Welles who go back to at least 1311 in their pedigree, and included a Lord-Lieutenant of Ireland in 1438. Yet another ancestor of Livesey's was Sir Thomas Lawne (or de la Launde), who was knighted by Henry VII 'at the bridge foot on the King's entering London after the Battle of Blackheath'. The regicide himself obtained a baronetcy in 1627.

Livesey was thus of an ancient and distinguished ancestry, far from being a *nouveau riche*, certainly not remotely of mercantile origin, certainly not a lawyer, and intimately related to one of the leading old Kentish families. So much for Everitt as a source of information about Livesey!

We have seen that Everitt went astray in his views of Livesey, Garland, and James Temple. What of John Dixwell, the remaining Kentish regicide? Here he is on firmer ground, but still his treatment of him is rather misleading. He was correct in viewing him as a lawyer, since he did indeed qualify as a barrister (see the later section of this book on 'The Regicides and the Law'). But he was mistaken about the regicide's parentage. He thought the regicide was the brother of Sir Basil Dixwell, Bart., whereas he was actually his nephew.[17] John Dixwell is one of the many regicides whose true parentage I have been able to establish for the first time. As with all the regicides discussed in this chapter, the Appendix must be consulted for references and further details. This was made necessary by the vast bulk of material which I uncovered, a mass of information far too great to include in the main body of this work.

Everitt is correct in stating that the Dixwell family were 'comparative newcomers to Kent'.[18] The Dixwells' relationship with the Oxinden family, one of the leading Kentish gentry families, only commenced when the regicide's sister-in-law lost his protection after the Restoration and on February 6, 1661/2, married Sir Henry Oxinden.[19] I have found evidence that the regicide had a wife alive in 1644,[20] but there is no knowledge of her identity. We must thus hold open the option that the regicide might have been related by marriage to a leading Kentish gentry family. This would certainly go some way towards explaining Dixwell's extraordinary prominence in Kent. (Dixwell re-married as an exile in New England after the Restoration, and left children there,[21] but that is not relevant to this discussion, since it took place too late to be of concern to us here.)

But lest the Dixwell family be thought of as *nouveaux riches* and of obscure yeoman stock, we must make the situation clearer and explain their connection with Kent. The Dixwells traced their lineage back to at least the mid-1400s. Originally they were the lords of the manor of Dixwell in Hertfordshire. They then became seated by 1551 at Coton Manor, Churchover, Warwickshire. The family association with Kent commenced with the regicide's great-uncle, John Herdson, son of Henry Herdson of Stourton, Lincolnshire, and Alderman of London. This John Herdson 'had a considerable estate … at Folkestone and other parts in the County of Kent', which he left to his nephew Basil Dixwell (later Bart., uncle of the regicide).[22] This estate included the splendid manor house of Folkestone Priory. Basil Dixwell was created a baronet on February 18, 1627/8.[23] (He must not be confused with the two later Sir Basil Dixwell, Barts., of a separate post-Restoration creation, the first of whom was the regicide's nephew.) In 1622, Basil acquired the manor of Brome Park at Barham in Kent.[24]

The parents of the regicide died young, and he and his younger brother Mark Dixwell were raised by their uncle Sir Basil at Folkestone. (Doubtless the Court of Wards pillaged the family fortunes in the process.) Sir Basil had been a fourth son, and had been seated at Folkestone as a result of his uncle's generous legacy by at least 1619.[25] Sir Basil became elected MP for Hythe in 1626 and Sheriff of Kent in 1626-7.[26] He was therefore a man of some stature in Kent, although the first of his name to live there. As mentioned already, we do not know whom the regicide married, but his younger brother Mark married in 1635 to Elizabeth, daughter of Matthew and Alice Read and heiress of William Reid (her brother) of Folkestone. As for Uncle Basil, he was a bachelor. When he died in 1642, the regicide seems to have been in possession of Folkestone Priory already and Sir Basil's residence of Brome Park was left to the younger nephew, Mark. Early in the Civil War, Mark sold Brome Park to his brother for £13,000, and then died prematurely. In order to spend so large a sum on an extra property which he did not need, the regicide must have been extraordinarily wealthy.

John Dixwell was extremely generous to his brother's widow and children. He spent £250 a year just on the education of the children. He expended thousands of pounds on their support. For 17 years he maintained the estate of Brome Park, which he owned, for their benefit, and apparently lived either at Folkestone Priory or Brome Park as the whim took him. His wife evidently died young, as he was a widower by the time of the Restoration and he had two wives in succession in New England during his lengthy exile (he died there in his 80s). When Firth stated in Dixwell's DNB entry of the regicide 'as temporary holder of these estates [Brome Park] John enjoyed great local influence' he was speaking in ignorance of the true facts, and several historians have gone astray as a consequence. The fact is that John Dixwell was one of the wealthiest and most propertied men in Kent entirely in his own right.

The regicide's nephew, young Basil Dixwell, of whom he had taken such good care, married Dorothy, daughter of Sir Thomas Peyton, Bart., of Knowlton in Kent. Through this alliance the regicide became connected with a leading Kentish gentry family, though probably not until the Civil War had ended.

We see therefore that although Everitt was correct in saying that the Dixwells were a new family in Kent, they were not entirely without local connections by marriage, and the regicide was certainly of considerable standing by virtue of his extensive property and great wealth. Nor was his family a 'new' family in the social sense. They had been gentry for at least two centuries. John Dixwell was raised in Kent and can be presumed to have had wide acquaintance in the county. Although 'new' to Kent, Everitt was certainly unjustified in claiming of Dixwell that he was 'unimportant' there.[27]

This examination of the treatment of the regicides of one particular county by the main historian of that county during the relevant period has been instructive. We see that despite his careful and largely meticulous research, Everitt was entirely unable to get to grips with the true facts about the regicides in Kent. The obscurity of the subject and the difficulty of discussing the regicides and their families may now begin to become more apparent. But lest Everitt be seen to be alone in his difficulties with the regicides, let us turn our attention to another major study of a county, this time to J. T. Cliffe's *The Yorkshire Gentry: from the*

Reformation to the Civil War.[28] This fine work is again meticulous and detailed. As its title indicates, it takes as its basis the study of family histories, and thus adopts the methodology so successfully pursued in the main by Everitt. But what do we find in this work about the Yorkshire regicides? One of them, Peregrine Pelham, is not even mentioned, nor is his family. Two regicides, Sir Thomas Mauleverer, Bart., and Thomas Chaloner, are mentioned only twice each in passing. The surname of Mauleverer is misspelled Maleverer. The only thing the expert on the Yorkshire gentry has to tell us about the regicide's family is that it had a Norman surname.[29] That is certainly true, and in the previous chapter we saw the meaning of the name, 'bad hare-chaser', as recorded by William Camden. Indeed, the Mauleverers traced their ancestry to the Conquest. Cliffe occasionally mentions the Mauleverers of Ingleby Arncliffe, but they were only distantly related to the regicide. Cliffe nowhere discusses the different branches of the Mauleverer family, nor did he go into the family's origins at all other than to note the Norman nature of the name.

Three other Yorkshire regicides fare better. John Alured is mentioned four times and Sir John Bourchier and Sir William Constable, Bart., are mentioned several times each. There is no discussion of the Alured family as such. Cliffe does mention that the regicide, and his father and uncle, were well off, were friends of the Boyntons, Puritans, and opposed to the Court before the Civil War, but that is about all. Bourchier and Constable are the only Yorkshire regicides who are treated fairly fully. But this still means that only two out of five of the Yorkshire regicides receive proper attention in Cliffe's book, and the existence of the fifth (Pelham) is not even mentioned.

However, the scanty attention given to regicides in countless books about the period is a widespread phenomenon, and Cliffe and Everitt are cited in particular because they are two of the more careful historians of the period who have concentrated specifically on family histories. If even they have not said much that is useful about the regicides and their families, then the general situation may well be imagined.

There is a distinct difference between the observations of Everitt and those of Cliffe with regard to the political allegiances of families during the Interregnum. We have already seen that Everitt maintained that 'new' families tended to be more radical. We have also seen that Everitt's grasp of information about the regicides was so tenuous that he misrepresented them in the context of his assertions concerning his theory about the 'new' families being radical. In fact, Everitt's contention will not hold up in general for the country at large either. We shall be examining the families of the various regicides and seeing whether they were 'new' or not. We shall see that mostly they were not. Perhaps it is true that 'new' families tended to be radical, but if so, the reverse certainly is not true, namely that radicals tended to be 'new' families. The massive data we have accumulated on the regicide families disposes of this theory of Everitt's decisively and completely.

But first let us consider the general observations on families made by Cliffe, as they are so much more interesting than those made by Everitt. First of all, it should be noted that Cliffe agrees with Everitt on the crucial importance of studies of the histories of families and groups of families. With those sentiments I most heartily agree. Cliffe's entire book is devoted to this principle. Cliffe gives a resounding account of the crucial importance of social status in the seventeenth century, a subject discussed in the later section 'The Regicides and the Law' when I explain the social significance of achieving the rank of barrister. He then remarks: 'In view of the importance of status and degree in the eyes of the gentry it was natural that they should take a close interest in their personal ancestry and kinship. Men with social pretensions who had purchased coats of arms tended to be regarded with amusement or derision: ancient lineage, on the other hand, was a source of pride and respect. ... Kinship was not simply a matter of genealogical interest. Contemporary opinion held that ties of blood, however tenuous, involved special obligations and loyalties and this concept of clan solidarity was an important factor not only in normal social intercourse but also in public life.'[30] We shall see just how important it was in public life when I present the findings of the 'clans' operative amongst the regicides.

Cliffe makes these interesting observations: 'Even in the reign of Charles I there were many country squires who could trace their ancestry back to the mediaeval knightly class from which the gentry had evolved. Of the 679 families of 1642 at least 270 had been represented in the ranks of the Yorkshire gentry as early as 1500.'[31] The 679 families he mentions are the families which in 1642 constituted, according to Cliffe, the Yorkshire gentry.[32] I compute this to be 39% of the Yorkshire gentry who could in 1642 trace their ancestry back to 1500. We shall see that this figure was greatly surpassed nationally by the number of regicides who could do so, which suggests a view which is the very opposite of Everitt's theory.

Cliffe makes interesting comments about the nature of the families which adopted radical political stances during the Civil War. He refers to the 'rise of the gentry' controversy which many years ago burdened scholarly brows: '... "the rise of the gentry" is a concept which requires qualification. ... no real link can be found between economic decay and political dissent in the period leading up to the Civil War. Sir William Constable, who was imprisoned in 1627 for refusing to contribute to the forced loan, had previously sold extensive property and was still heavily in debt but he was hardly typical of the Yorkshire squires who stood out in opposition to the Crown. In the main these were men of considerable substance who owned more than they had inherited. ... In terms of landed income there were no fundamental differences between the royalist gentry and the parliamentarian gentry ... In fact the rising gentry and the declining gentry were both well represented in the royalist party. ... In the final analysis ... the economic position of the parliamentarian gentry as a group was basically sound. Between one-third and one-half of the families represented had increased their estates by one means or another since the accession of James I, while on the eve of Civil War scarcely more than one family in ten was experiencing financial difficulties. ... On the whole, the parliamentarian gentry were in better financial circumstances than the royalist gentry ...'[33]

This is an extraordinarily interesting finding, and goes far towards dispelling any notion that the side of the Parliament was supported in the Civil War only by disgruntled 'declining gentry'. As regards the position of Sir William Constable, however, his position was thoroughly exceptional in ways which were unknown to Cliffe. Cliffe was unaware of the fact that Constable's financial troubles were not innate but were actually the creation of the Court; Sir William was owed £8,000 by Charles I, who refused to repay the money. This forced Constable artificially into an impossible level of debt. Alas, it was not an uncommon situation for someone who had made the mistake of being a courtier acceptable to Queen Anne, thereby incurring the contempt of King James's party, and naively trusting to the honour of either James or Charles in matters of money. But Cliffe knew nothing of all this, and marked Constable out as a figure of the group of the failing county gentry (due perhaps to bad estate management? riotous living?), which goes to show the perils of over-generalizing. Constable has never really had a 'good press'. William Hepworth Dixon even called him a Roman Catholic,[34] when in fact he was the very opposite, a Puritan. There has often been the presumption amongst historians that people who are going down in the world have a sense of grievance which leads them to want to overthrow the system, which they blame for their own failings, and that they are like this because of wounded vanity and a desire for vengeance. Such simplistic psychological theories are an insufficient basis for interpreting the past, especially when examples are found and then forced to fit the mould, because a historian needs examples to demonstrate his theory. The early career of Sir William Constable will be recounted at length in the later section 'The Early Careers of the Regicides', and we shall then see the real story of his life, rather than an imagined one.

A theory put forward by R. H. Tawney in 1941 that the rise of a new group of 'agricultural capitalists' overthrew the monarchy in the 1640s will not hold up.[35] Cliffe has demonstrated this conclusively for Yorkshire, as we have just seen. Perez Zagorin has also produced a summary of good reasons why the thesis is untenable.[36] But as we shall see, the strongest evidence to my mind is the evidence to follow later in this chapter. For my studies of the regicide families – who, after all, were the leading radicals of the period and constitute a large sample indeed – conclusively dispense with Tawney's immature and rash theory. Tawney exemplifies the unfortunate and all too common tendency of some historians to rush into theories on insufficient evidence, or for other motives such as adherence to a predetermined general theory of history. There are several reasons why historians behave like this: intellectual vanity and the naïve belief that they can explain everything with a theory (a fault very common with physicists, who are always trying to prove how clever they are by formulating 'grand unified theories', or what they immodestly call 'theories of everything', which always fail), laziness and the refusal to work hard enough locating and studying primary source materials (which involves not only work but travel and considerable expense), unhealthy peer pressure not to excel too much, not to rock the boat, not to challenge other historians about their mistakes, and the need to keep one's head down and not make waves if there is to be any chance of a scholarly promotion and a better salary. Also, there are the consensus blindnesses of any scholarly community: the things everyone agrees not to see, or to pretend not to see, as the recognition and articulation of those awkward things would make life too difficult for the community. Renegades do not last long in the closed world and closed ranks of a scholarly community which is focused on a narrow field of specialisation. And finally, there are the powerful undercurrents of bias which effect different sections of such a scholarly community. There are some historians who are wedded to various dogmas, some political, some religious, and they see everything through the lenses of their dogmas, and seek to make events fit into theories. That is unprofessional.

It is only long and careful, and often tedious, research such as that carried out by Cliffe, which can yield sufficient data for decisions on theories to be possible. Tawney simply did not do enough work. Nor did Hugh Trevor-Roper, who stands at the opposite end of the controversy. He maintained in the early 1950s that the King was overthrown by 'declining gentry'.[37] Although Trevor-Roper was closer to the truth in some respects than Tawney, if only because he started from a less doctrinaire stance, we have seen that Cliffe has also disproved Trevor-Roper's thesis in Yorkshire. The material which I shall present here also contradicts Trevor-Roper's thesis. Indeed, those regicides who were 'declining' were often doing so because they had been robbed! What are we to make of the fact explained in the section on 'The Early Careers of the Regicides' that the Chaloner family had been robbed of £100,000 by the King? Does that genuinely make them 'declining gentry'? Of course not. It makes them *robbed gentry*. And that is a very different thing.

There has been far too much premature and useless theorizing in seventeenth century studies. Some historians have shown that they are much more interested in their own theories than in the evidence or in the truth about the period. This does not advance scholarship. And the rush – the indecent haste, I would call it – to put historical personages into categories where they can more readily be manipulated for purposes of supporting theories is central to the faults shown by the passionate theorizers. Personally, I am perfectly happy to go without theories altogether. Facts suit me just fine. The reductionist passion to turn history into theory is an evil contagion, a kind of mental virus, which is the curse of our age.

To cite a regicide example, it would be easy to describe Sir William Constable as 'declining gentry' (as even Cliffe did, despite his better sense in most things), because of the obvious decline in his fortunes. This puts Constable in a box which can be shuffled around in the theorizing game. But it is not accurate, for it takes no account of *the causes of his condition*. My much closer examination of Constable's condition than that attempted by any previous researcher enabled me, after much time and effort, to discover that Constable was owed £8,000 by the Crown. This was central to his dilemma. He was *artificially declining*, not *naturally declining*. The same was true of poor Sir John Danvers, whose sad tale of woe is recounted in the later section as well. People like the Chaloners, Constables, and Danverses cannot be called 'declining gentry', because the fact is that their financial conditions were entirely artificial. They were victims of systematic Court theft, of the sort which would today be something fit to be investigated by what used to be called the Serious Fraud Office. We cannot use their financial condition to draw up sweeping theories about sociology. Cliffe has very wisely said of Constable that in any case 'he was hardly typical of the Yorkshire squires who stood out in opposition to the Crown.'[38] Cliffe is very much to be praised for his exemplary approach and for his preference to facts over hasty theories.

Let us turn our attention to the regicides as a whole and begin by adopting Everitt's technique of establishing how old their families were and what offices they had held at what early dates. The first thing which will become obvious is that Everitt's idea that 'the newer families tended to take extremely political positions' does not apply at all to the regicides.

In considering the antiquity of the regicide families and how far back they could trace their lineages we often are reduced to saying how far back *we* can trace their lineages today. It is thus to be understood that the information about to be presented is conservative, and that the ages of the families known to the regicides themselves may in many cases have been far greater. After all, at the Restoration many regicides such as Thomas Scot burned all their papers to protect themselves and their friends, others fled into exile, and the Estates of the regicides were confiscated, with such flimsy things as pedigrees of the hated King-killers doubtless being thrown onto bonfires in disgust. We have to make do with what evidence survives, and remain aware that much has perished. What follows, therefore, is only what I have been able to accomplish with what evidence I could glean from that which remains, which is inevitably incomplete.

Of the 61 regicides, ten could trace their ancestry back before the Norman Conquest. A further eight could trace their ancestry back to the Conquest itself. A further three could trace their ancestry back to the 11th century, within one of two generations of the Conquest. That means that 21 out of 61 regicides could boast of lineage antedating the year 1200. Clearly these men were not of 'new families'.

But a considerable number of other regicides could boast of origins which were at least mediaeval. One could trace his ancestors back to the twelfth century, four could trace their ancestors back to the 13th century, seven could trace their ancestors back to the 14th century, and a further seven could trace their ancestors back to the 15th century. That means that 19 of the 61 regicides could boast of lineages extending back to the period between 1200 and 1500, in addition to the 21 regicides whose lineages went back even further than that.

Thus, 40 of the 61 regicides were of families which went back at least to the year 1500, according to evidence which still survives today. With two thirds of the regicides therefore being of such old families, the theory that the radicals of the period were 'new families' must be abandoned.

As for the remaining regicides, four could trace their families back to the early 16th century and five to the mid- or late 16th century. All of these men's antecedents extending back at least as far as a great-grandfather are therefore still known. (It must be remembered that one regicide's family has still not been identified and one is only probable, so we cannot be certain of much regarding them.) Of the 61 regicides, only 12 cannot with certainty be traced today back to someone earlier than a grandfather. However, even amongst these twelve, there is one important exception: Henry Marten. I have established for certain that a pedigree of the Martens going back several generations before Henry does exist in the College of Arms,[39] but I have been refused photocopies, and have been unable to consult it because of the difficulties put in the way of researchers by the Heralds, who are a commercial group who try to limit the access to their amazing collections by independent scholars in case it might effect their financial interests. Although I have worked in the archives of the College of Arms, it has been under severe restrictions and limitations, which were far from being satisfactory, and I was not allowed to see the Marten pedigree. I therefore count Marten as being a regicide who has not been traced back further than his grandfather only because I have personally not done this, and I cannot verify or vouch with certainty for the more extensive pedigree despite the fact that I know it exists because I had the card reference to it in my hand.

Another remarkable fact about the descents of the regicides is that no less than six of them could boast of royal descent of some kind, whether English, Irish, or Welsh. These six were Oliver Cromwell, Humphrey Edwardes, George Fleetwood, John Jones, Henry Smith, and Thomas Wogan. In the case of Jones, his pedigree tracing his royal descent was actually drawn up *on the day of the execution of Charles I*. That is not just making a point, it is making a 'statement'!

The following chart has been compiled from the data found in the Appendix, regarding the antiquity of the regicide families.

FAMILY BACKGROUNDS OF THE REGICIDES

DESCENT TRACED FROM BEFORE THE CONQUEST

SAXON:
John Bradshaw
James Temple
(Saxon earls)
Peter Temple
(Saxon earls)

PRE-CONQUEST NORMAN:
Sir William Constable, Bart.

PRE-CONQUEST WELSH OR IRISH:
Thomas Chaloner

Oliver Cromwell
(Princes of Powys)
Humphrey Edwardes
(Welsh kings of Powys; family residing in England by early 1100s)
George Fleetwood
(Welsh princes)
John Jones
(Welsh kings; also royal descent from English kings)
Thomas Wogan
(Welsh kings and Irish kings)

DESCENT TRACED FROM THE CONQUEST

Miles Corbet
Sir John Danvers
(who wore on his signet ring the motto DANVERS 1066 AD)
Henry Ireton
Sir Thomas Mauleverer, Bart.

John Moore
(multiple descent from the Conquest)
William Say
Henry Smith
(also royal descent from Henry I)
Edward Whalley

DESCENT TRACED FROM THE ELEVENTH CENTURY

Lord Grey of Groby
Sir Michael Livesey, Bart.
Sir Hardress Waller

DESCENT TRACED FROM THE TWELTH CENTURY

Robert Tichborne

DESCENT TRACED FROM THE THIRTEENTH CENTURY

Richard Deane
Thomas Horton

Richard Ingoldsby
William Purefoy

DESCENT TRACED FROM THE FOURTEENTH CENTURY

John Blakiston
Sir John Bourchier
John Lisle
Peregrine Pelham

Adrian Scrope
John Venn
Valentine Wauton

DESCENT TRACED FROM THE FIFTEENTH CENTURY

John Carew
John Dixwell
John Hutchinson
Robert Lilburne

Edmund Ludlow
Sir Gregory Norton, Bart.
Thomas Scot

DESCENT TRACED FROM THE EARLY SIXTEENTH CENTURY

John Alured
Daniel Blagrave

John Cook

DESCENT TRACED FROM THE MID OR LATE SIXTEENTH CENTURY

Augustine Garland
Thomas Harrison
Thomas Pride

Anthony Stapley
Thomas Waite

GRANDFATHER TRACED

John Barkstead

FATHER TRACED

William Cawley
Gregory Clement
John Downes
Isaac Ewer
William Goffe

Henry Marten
(However, as already mentioned, a pedigree exists in the College of Arms tracing his ancestry back several generations, and it is probable that it is accurate; access to this pedigree has not been allowed by the College of Arms for proprietorial reasons.)
Gilbert Millington
John Okey
Owen Rowe

FATHER PROBABLE

John Hewson

UNKNOWN

Vincent Potter

We saw earlier that Cliffe discovered that in 1642 as many as 39% of the Yorkshire gentry could trace their ancestry back before 1500. He implies that this is remarkable. If it be remarkable, then the regicides were far more remarkable, for we have seen that *we* have been able to trace their ancestries back to such an extent (and it is certain that *they* could have done even better) that we have discovered that 65.5% of the regicides' families go back before 1500. This means that the regicide families were of far greater antiquity than those of the Yorkshire gentry, and doubtless of equally far greater antiquity than those of any single county in England. (I do not know of any studies comparable in depth and breadth to that of Cliffe having been done either for any other county or for the country as a whole.) I shall be discussing later in this chapter what significance this strange 'family antiquity' issue may have, for I have come to conclude that the extreme antiquity of the regicide families is central to our understanding of the act of regicide in a most unexpected way.

Lest it be thought that the antiquity of the regicide families was unmatched by county status, let us take a lead from Everitt's book and examine the office-holding of the regicide families. This was a central feature of Everitt's estimations of the importance of the gentry families in Kent. It should be mentioned straightaway that two regicide families were evidently largely of yeoman stock for several centuries, namely those of Thomas Horton and John Venn, although John Venn seems to have been related to Sir Richard Venn (or Fenn), who was a Lord Mayor of London and with whom he shared the same coat of arms. Therefore, the antiquity of the Horton and Venn families is not to be taken as an indication of gentry status for centuries, but of 'sturdy yeoman' stock, as I explain in the Appendix.

With the exception of Horton and Venn, however, all the regicides who could trace their antecedents to the early sixteenth century may be considered as having been unquestionably gentry for some generations. Including Horton and Venn, we thus have 19 of the 61 regicides who were *not* certainly gentry for generations. Or, to put the matter the other way round, 42 of the 61 regicides were certainly gentry for generations. That is a percentage of 69%.

Here, then, is the list of office-holding in some of these old regicide families:

DANIEL BLAGRAVE. His uncle was MP for Reading in 1601 and Sheriff of Berkshire in 1605. First cousin was Sheriff of Berkshire in 1624; another first cousin was Sheriff of Berkshire in 1646, having been passed over for the office in 1638. Three great-uncles plus his aunt's father were MPs of the Long Parliament.

JOHN BLAKISTON. Related to various bishops (see Appendix for list).

SIR JOHN BOURCHIER. Descended from a Lord Chancellor of England of 1342, and also from a Duke of Gloucester. His great-great-grandfather was Lord Berners, the famous translator of Froissart. Grandfather was MP for Yorkshire from 1588 to 1592 and had been Sheriff of Yorkshire in 1581. Great-uncle Sir Thomas Barrington was a Long Parliament MP.

JOHN CAREW. Great-great-great-grandfather John Carew was Sheriff of Cornwall. Great-great-grandfather was Treasurer to Queen Catherine in the time of Henry VIII. Great-grandfather was MP for Saltash.

THOMAS CHALONER. Grandfather was an MP and Ambassador. Father was manager of Queen Anne's estates and Governor of Prince Henry from 1603.

SIR WILLIAM CONSTABLE. Descended from Ivo Viscount Constantine of Normandy and Ivo Lord Vescy, as well as Barons Halton or Haillton (one of whom died in 1189 at Tyre on Crusade). Countless ancestors had been Sheriffs of Yorkshire and MPs. Several generations were knighted in the field for valourous conduct in warfare.

MILES CORBET. Summoned as barons by Edward I.

SIR JOHN DANVERS. Grandfather Lord Latimer had been the second husband of Catherine Parr, who was later sixth wife of Henry VIII. This Latimer's father had been Lieutenant-General and Commissioner of the North. A forebear was Justice of the Common Pleas. Father was Sheriff of Wiltshire in 1588. Step-father was a first cousin of Queen Elizabeth I.

RICHARD DEANE. Descended from Burgesses of Wallingford of the 13th and 14th centuries. Great-grandfather and grandfather were both Collectors of the Subsidy in 1524. Maternal great-great-great-great-grandfather was made Knight of the Bath in 1306 by Edward I. Descended from William of Wykeham, founder of New College, Oxford, and Bishop. Great-uncle was a Lord Mayor of London.

JOHN DIXWELL. Great-grandfather was an Alderman of London. Uncle was Sheriff of Kent and MP for Hythe.

GEORGE FLEETWOOD. Great-grandfather was Master of the Mint. Grandfather was an MP. Great-uncle was Receiver of the Court of Wards. Uncle was Bishop of Worcester. Great-uncle was Earl of Norwich, several times MP.

LORD GREY OF GROBY. Descended from a Norman Lord of Groby of 1086, an Earl of Leicester who died 1190, an Earl of Winton who died 1219, Lords Ferrars and Derby, Suffolk, Poynings, Clifford, a Duke of Norfolk, Marquess of Dorset, an ancestress who as her second husband married King Edward IV, etc. Lady Jane Grey was his great-grandfather's first cousin. His great-grandfather was Lord Burghley, Secretary of State.

THOMAS HARRISON. His father was four times Mayor of Newcastle-under-Lyme.

JOHN HUTCHINSON. Father was Sheriff of Nottinghamshire 1620-1 and MP for the shire in 1626, prevented by the Court from being reelected in 1628, but reelected in 1640.

HENRY IRETON. Great-grandfather was George, Tenth Baron Zouch, summoned to Parliament, 1553-1566 and died 1569.

JOHN JONES. Directly descended from Jevan ap Jevan, Constable of Harlech Castle in the reign of Henry VI.

ROBERT LILBURNE. Directly descended from Sir William Lilburne, Lord Warden of the Middle Marches in mediaeval times. Grandfather was Yeoman of the Wardrobe to Queen Elizabeth I. Uncle was MP for Sunderland.

JOHN LISLE. Directly descended from John de Insula, summoned to House of Lords by Edward II.

SIR MICHAEL LIVESEY, BART. Grandfather was twice Sheriff of Sussex and Surrey, in 1592 and 1602. Father was Sheriff of Kent in 1618. Directly descended from a Lord Lieutenant of Ireland in 1438, and many others of distinction (see Appendix).

EDMUND LUDLOW. Directly descended from William Ludlow, Butler to Kings Henry IV, V, and VI, and MP, who died in 1478. Great-grandfather was Marshal of the Household to Queen Elizabeth I. [Note that this ancestor of Ludlow would have been a friend and colleague of Lilburne's ancestor, above.] Father was MP for Hindon in 1603, and Sheriff of Wiltshire. Grandfather had been Sheriff of Wiltshire also.

HENRY MARTEN. Father was MP, Judge, and Member of the Court of High Commission.

SIR THOMAS MAULEVERER, BART. Countless illustrious forebears (see Appendix). Great-grandfather was Sheriff of Yorkshire in 1552. Father was Sheriff of Yorkshire in 1588.

SIMON MAYNE. Father was Sheriff of Buckinghamshire and died in 1617.

JOHN MOORE. His ancestors were MPs for Liverpool continuously from 1307 to his own time! Father was Sheriff of Lancashire in 1620, MP for Liverpool in 1625. Uncle was MP of the Long Parliament.

SIR GREGORY NORTON, BART. Great-great-grandfather was Sir Anthony St. Leger, Knight of the Garter, agent of Thomas Cromwell, member of the jury which condemned Anne Boleyn, Gentleman of Henry VIII's Privy Chamber, Lord Deputy of Ireland. Directly descended from a High Sheriff of Kent in 1428. Uncle was Secretary for Ireland.

PEREGRINE PELHAM. Grandfather was Field Marshal and Lord Justice Sir William Pelham (see his DNB entry written by myself). Great uncle was Chief Baron of the Exchequer in Ireland. Another great-uncle was MP. Great-great-great-great-grandfather was Treasurer of England under Henry IV. Great-great-great-grandfather was Chamberlain to Queen Katherine and died 1471. Great-great-grandfather was Lord Chamberlain of England.

WILLIAM PUREFOY. Great-grandfather was Escheator of Warwickshire under Mary Tudor.

WILLIAM SAY. Ancestors included various mediaeval Knights of the Bath, etc. (See Appendix).

THOMAS SCOT. Either his father or his grandfather (impossible to know which, as both had the same name) was MP for Aylesbury in 1585.

ADRIAN SCROPE. Directly descended from Henry Scrope, Third Baron Scrope of Masham, Knight of the Garter, who attempted to assassinate King Henry V. Also directly descended from a Lord Treasurer of England in 1367, a Steward of the Royal Household to Richard II and Chancellor of England 1378-80, a Governor of the Fleet who died in 1498, a Marshal of the Army under Queen Elizabeth I, a Chief Justice and Secretary of Edward III, and so forth.

HENRY SMITH. Descended from King Henry I, and countless high nobility. Great-uncle was Lord Burghley, Secretary of State. One uncle was an MP, Ambassador, and Clerk of the Privy Council. Another was an Alderman of London. Another was a Privy Councillor.

JAMES TEMPLE. Grandfather was Clerk to the Privy Signet. Father was MP in the 1620s and Captain of Tilbury Fort. Uncle was Viscount Say and Sele.

PETER TEMPLE. Grandfather was Sheriff of Warwickshire in 1597. Great-grandfather was an Auditor of the Exchequer under Henry VIII.

ROBERT TICHBORNE. Directly descended from two Sheriffs of Hampshire under Edward III, one under Henry IV, one under Henry VII, one under Queen Mary Tudor, one Sheriff of Wiltshire under Edward II, one under Edward III, and so on. Uncle was Attorney-General of the Duchy of Cornwall.

SIR HARDRESS WALLER. Great-grandfather was Sheriff of Kent in reign of Henry VIII, dying 1555. Grandfather was also Sheriff of Kent under Elizabeth I. Uncle was Lieutenant of Dover Castle.

EDWARD WHALLEY. Father was Sheriff of Nottinghamshire 1595-6 and MP for Boroughbridge in 1602. Directly descended from a Sheriff of Derbyshire between 1351 and 1361. Great-grandfather was MP many times, Steward to Duke of Somerset under Edward VI, agent of Thomas Cromwell, etc.

THOMAS WOGAN. Father was MP for Pembrokeshire in the Long Parliament, having been a member of every parliament since 1614 except for that of 1624; he was a Deputy Lieutenant of his county and its Sheriff in 1636.[40] Uncle was MP of the Long Parliament.[41]

Although the preceding list of offices may seem long, it is by no means exhaustive. I have omitted all but a few legal offices and have not bothered to mention the lowlier position of Justice of the Peace (JP), which was enjoyed by so many members of most of the regicide families that it may in most cases be presumed, without even having to be mentioned. The preceding list is only a mere sampling, as for instance, I did not bother to trace the number of MPs in the Alured family who preceded John the regicide in Parliament. Everitt had expressed himself as being impressed that leading families in Kent 'had been appointed to the commission of the peace [as JPs] since before the Reformation'.[42] He certainly had a low threshold of what would impress him! From even a cursory examination of the office holdings or high dignities achieved in the regicide families, we see that they were largely families which had produced Sheriffs and MPs for their counties. A significant minority of the families had held major national positions such as Lord Chancellor in the more distant past. The majority of regicide families were clearly not just of great antiquity, but were also of long service in offices higher than the lowly commission of the peace, when seen in comparison to any other group of families below the peerage which I have ever seen discussed.

The evidence therefore shows the regicide families to have been exceptional in ways never before recognised. They tended to be of greater antiquity than other families and to have held significant offices for longer. However, only a minority had held great offices at Court, and those which had had mostly done so before the arrival of the Stuarts.

The regicide families therefore seem to have represented a peculiar kind of traditional family which has not been much discussed in the literature. One reason for this is obviously the fact that they could not be recognised or discussed unless one had done massive genealogical research in dozens of archives all over the country, and not many people have ever done that. But before we consider just what these peculiarities may be, we shall first consider some additional extraordinary facts about two of the regicide families which may offer some clues to help us gain some further insight.

We remarked briefly that Adrian Scrope had an ancestor who had attempted to assassinate King Henry V ('Lord Scroop' in Shakespeare's *Henry V*). This family precedent for attempting the act of regicide had itself had a kind of precedent within the family. An earlier ancestor, the first Baron Scrope of Bolton, was Lord Chancellor under Richard II and as such refused to put the Great Seal to many of the grants the King made to his favourites. Although the King was enraged, Scrope managed to face him down. Another member of the family, Treasurer under Henry IV, was executed on the King's orders in 1399. As for the aspiring regicide, Henry, Third Baron Scrope of Masham, speaks of him and his two collaborators in *Henry V*: 'And by their hands this grace of kings must die.' Adrian Scrope can hardly have been ignorant of these dramatic episodes from his family's history. Nor did rebellion against monarchs die with the regicide. His grandson took part in the Monmouth rebellion.

If we turn now to Sir Hardress Waller's family, we find the most extraordinary tale of this family's relation with the institution of monarchy. We read the following 17th century account, of the regicide's direct ancestor:

'Richard Waller of Gromebridge in Sussex [*sic, should be Kent*] Esqr serving in ye warres in France in ye time of Kinge Henry ye 5th did take Charles Duke of Orleance fath^r to Lewis ye 12th & kept him Prisoner in England 25 yeares during wch time hee built that goodly house wch yet remaineth at Gromebridge & afterwards paid for his ransome foure hundred thousand crownes hee was Grandchild to Charles ye 5th & died 1464.' (See Appendix.)

Such a dramatic tale can hardly have been unknown to Sir Hardress Waller. His family's fortunes were based upon the kidnapping of the father of a French king (whom Richard Waller seems to have seized at Agincourt), who was kept prisoner in the family house (acquired by the Wallers circa 1400) where Sir Hardress himself grew up in Kent, doubtless amidst tales of the daring of his ancestor of two centuries before, and with a wing of his own house probably still referred to as the apartments where the Duke of Orleans had lived for a quarter of a century in 'the old days'. But despite the fact that the family seat of Sir Hardress Waller was for more than two centuries the grand fortified mansion of Groombridge Park (replaced in 1662 by the present edifice, Groombridge Place, but the old gardens still partially remain), three and a half miles south of Tunbridge Wells in Kent, he is not mentioned by Everitt as having any association with the county. Everitt merely says, in discussing his first cousin, Sir William Waller, that he and Sir Hardress 'both came of the same minor Wealden family'.[43] However, 'minor Wealden families' do not normally live in gigantic early 13th century moated fortress style houses large enough to hold the father of a foreign king a secure prisoner for 25 years.

All of these family traditions seem to me to have something psychologically in common with the fact that John Jones chose to have his pedigree tracing his royal descent drawn up and dated on the same day as King Charles's execution, and the fact that Sir John Danvers signed the Death Warrant with a seal that said 'DANVERS 1066 AD' on it (*note:* this seal is perfectly preserved on other documents; see Appendix). What all this says to me is that many of the regicides may have felt themselves *equal or even superior to Charles I* in terms of their lineage and family histories.

Of course, Sir John Danvers was a step-cousin of Charles I. But apart from that, the regicides had no connection with the Stuart lineage more recent than a common descent from Henry I. No regicide could therefore have imagined himself to be equivalent to Charles I. What I believe many of them did imagine, however, was that Charles I was their inferior.

One aspect of the psychology of this situation which I cannot discuss except in a passing mention is the contempt with which the Stuarts were regarded by many distinguished Englishmen as uncouth Scots who had come south with a scandalous king, who leered after 'fresh-cheeked boys' and hated the company of women and children (including his own), who pillaged the country to give fortunes to his boyfriends, sold the life of Sir Walter Raleigh for Spanish gold, allowed all offices of state to be sold by his favourites, perverted the state, robbed the people, and laid waste the proud traditions of England and perverted the monarchy. It is as well to recall that there was a widespread contempt for the Stuarts amongst traditional Englishmen ever since the death of Elizabeth I. Everyone knew that King James's mother had murdered her husband by blowing him up in bed with gunpowder. There were also rumours flying round about the true paternity of Prince Henry and Prince Charles: was the former the son of a Mr. Stuart (the Queen's first Scottish lover) who was burnt to death in his own house by King James in Scotland, was the latter the son of the Earl of Gowrie (the Queen's lover at the appropriate time), who was also murdered by King James as part of a so-called 'Gowrie Conspiracy' which many said was wholly invented to cover the deed? Indeed, had King James ever consummated his marriage to Queen Anne at all? Was Prince Henry really poisoned by the connivance of his 'father' because his 'father' was not his father at all and hated him as much as he was himself hated by Prince Henry (who did not hesitate to say so openly)? Was the little stuttering pipsqueak Prince Charles, only four feet eleven inches tall, whose favourite book was the Catechism, really only a pathetic whingeing bastard? Was his mother a whore? Was his domineering wife a harridan? Were they all closet Catholics? We should also not underestimate the virulent hatred of King James for his homosexuality (what today is called 'homophobia'). And we should not forget that King James was physically disgusting, with a tongue too large for his mouth, drool always oozing down his chin, a weirdly rolling eye, a refusal ever to wash his hands under any circumstances, and other personal peculiarities which were less than endearing. Since this work does not deal with the reign of King James I, these subjects cannot be discussed, but only alluded to as stories which were going round, perhaps true, perhaps not, but certainly believed in by many, or known to be true by some. I would suggest that the regicides included many who believed them. Several of the regicides had been linked to Queen Anne or Prince Henry, the anti-James factions of the court circles, and 'knew a thing or two' and 'had many a tale to tell'. We should never allow ourselves to overlook this psychological background to the eventual act of regicide. However, having called attention to these matters, I pass on without evaluating the evidence for these stories, as that is not our business, but is rather something to be dealt with by those who make the Reign of James I their special concern.

We have already seen how astonishing the antiquity of the regicide families was. The Wogans claimed to trace their descent from the certainly mythical date of 250 AD, but what is important is not whether it was true but whether they believed it. And it seems they did. Several of the regicides were unquestionably of a distant royal descent and boasted of it. The two Temples believed themselves to be the custodians of the Saxon tradition of resisting the Norman yoke, believing themselves (and it may even be true) to be descended from the Saxon Earls Leofric, Algar, Edwin, and Morcar, who were the last Saxon leaders to resist the Norman Conquest after the Battle of Hastings. Certainly Sir Peter Temple, Bart., their relative and political sympathiser in the Long Parliament who was named to the High Court of Justice but chose not to attend, was obsessed by these very genealogical issues. Sir Peter spent most of his life and vast sums of his money chasing all over the country for genealogical information, much of it concerning his descent from the Saxon Earls of Mercia, a pedigree going back at least to 850 AD. (Hundreds of pages of genealogical manuscripts collected by him still survive, some in the Huntingdon Library, some with the family of the late Baroness Kinloss, and there is no doubt of his conviction, which he would have passed on to both James Temple and Peter Temple the regicides, who sat beside him in the House, and whose political views he shared, that they were all descended from the last resisters of the Norman Invasion, with the implication probably being that they were not only superior to any upstart post-Conquest kings, but certainly to the mangy, scurvy Scots who had come down with James to pillage England like a second Norman Plague.)

Many of the regicides could precisely identify the Norman warriors and magnates from whom they were directly descended. The Moores had been MPs for Liverpool since 1307 without a break, which meant continuously for 342 years by the time of Charles's execution. Compared to that, the Stuarts had only been Kings of England for 46 years. A family which had held the same seat in Parliament for 342 years could look upon the upstart Scottish dynasty only 46 years old as inferior in antiquity and therefore inferior in intrinsic worth. The Wallers had kidnapped and held to ransom a French king's father. The Scropes and the Says had looked kings in the eye and said 'No'. Men with such family traditions alive in their minds, and displayed in their emblazoned pedigrees, - or even displayed on shields hung round a great hall, as with John Moore, - felt inferior to no one. The idea of challenging or facing up to a king was not unthinkable to them. It had been done before, why not again?

One of the concepts which appears to have been at work was that intrinsic worth was more reliably indicated by long continuance than by transitory or momentary status. In the section on 'The Regicides and the Law', I demonstrate that more than half of the peers sitting in the House of Lords were creations of the Stuarts and thus parvenu peers whose families had not traditionally held that dignity. ('Court toadies to an upstart dynasty' would be a less kind way to refer to them.) What recourse had families such as those of the regicides for sustaining of their sense of dignity and self-esteem in the face of all these new creations which placed people higher than them in status whom they may have viewed as intrinsically their inferiors? The prime example of inflated mock-status to their eyes was certainly the case of the Duke of Buckingham, a younger son of a minor Leicestershire gentry family who because he was sleeping with James I was given a dukedom, a peerage generally reserved at that time for members of the royal family or for very ancient families who had held it for generations. Such an outrage to established views of nobility as the elevation of Villiers to a dukedom (not to mention his effective control of the Government and sale of most offices of state, for which he stuffed money in his pocket) was merely the most prominent case in what must have been seen by many as an onslaught by the Stuarts against the established patterns of social status in England. The sale of peerages (the Earldom of Warwick was purchased for £10,000, as an example) and of baronetcies – a new dignity created to raise money for the Crown – has been discussed by historians on many occasions, and little more can be added here. However, it is worth noting lest objections be raised that the regicide Sir William Constable purchased his baronetcy for £2,000 and thus could hardly be outraged at the sale of dignities, that his was a special case. (The details are given in the section on 'The Early Careers of the Regicides'.) To put it briefly, he had been knighted but apparently stripped of his knighthood, so that the purchase of a baronetcy was the only means open to him to redeem his social status by recovering the appellation of 'Sir'. It is of interest, certainly, that seven years after purchasing his baronetcy, he had still not yet received his patent for it.

In general, the regicide families were of remarkable antiquity and in many cases had long records of office-holding. But few had much experience of favour from the Stuarts, many doubtless either because they would not sleep with them or refused to pay. An apparent exception to this lack of favour from the Stuarts might at first sight appear to lie with the Danvers family, for the regicide Sir John Danvers's brother experienced such favour and was created Earl of Danby; but as is shown later on, Sir John Danvers himself was the object of a sustained and relentless vendetta by James I. So it may safely be said that none of the regicides was ever in favour to any degree with James I or Charles I. Several of the regicides and their families were deeply in favour with Queen Anne and Prince Henry, but these court associations gained them only persecution and hatred from James and Charles. Detailed accounts are to be found in the section 'The Early Careers of the Regicides'. There we see that those regicides and their families who made attempts to come to terms with the Stuart Dynasty met with vicious rebuffs, of breathtaking severity.

We have already seen, from the remarks of Everitt and Cliffe, - and it is evident at every turn in surveying the period – that social status was of paramount importance to the men of the seventeenth century. Let us accept therefore that this premise cannot be seriously questioned. Granted that seventeenth century men were deeply preoccupied with social standing, what was to be done about the fact that the regicide families were meeting with rebuffs and affronts? It may well be that *because* the regicide families were of such remarkable antiquity they were the more sensitive to these rebuffs and affronts than newer families would have been. A family which had only recently moved up to gentry status after centuries of yeoman status might feel it had done rather well, and would be less sensitive to affronts from the Court. But we have seen that the regicide families were largely old gentry families. They had been around for centuries. They had often been *important* for centuries. And now they were being passed over and forced to endure the indignity of watching newer and 'inferior' people being elevated to favour and status above them. This must have stung. No one who has any degree of self-confidence in his own worth likes to see someone he regards as inferior to him promoted above his head, especially if seniority is outraged in the process. What university don who is the most senior in his department and – he thinks – of the greatest repute and standing in his field in that department can feel happy at some new and younger man, of less brilliant attainments, being brought in and appointed Chairman of the Department over him? Any academic can understand the position of the regicides.

One way a seventeenth-century man could regain his self-respect when he was being affronted by parvenus was to say to himself that his family was older, his family traditions more distinguished, his coat of arms bore more quarterings, and his connections were more rarified, than those of the newer men who were being shown favour. Furthermore, he could claim that his principles were nobler, and as by definition he was probably not a court creature, this would almost inevitably have been the case. After all, it is a standard comfort for those who are not favourites of those in power to boast of their independence. They do not compromise their principles to curry favour, since they are denied the opportunities to do so. This general observation is not intended as a slur upon the regicides, since only a few of them (such as Richard Ingoldsby and Gilbert Millington) showed much evidence of weak character, and most of them appear to have been of inordinately and genuinely strong principles. It is difficult to know to what extent the regicides actually held republican principles from early dates. In the section on early careers I suggest that perhaps the first to do so was Thomas Chaloner, closely followed by his intimate friend, Henry Marten.

The four most intellectual regicides were probably Thomas Chaloner, Augustine Garland, Henry Marten, and Thomas Scot. Scot even held a degree of Master of Arts, which was highly unusual at that time, and showed that he was a serious scholar. In the section on 'Circumstances of the King's Trial' we shall see that these four men constituted four of the five main republican organisers of the King's trial and execution. They may be considered genuine ideologues and, being intellectuals, were probably the first regicides to formulate republican principles overtly. The principles of the regicides generally would in the early 1640s probably have been less in the manner of ideological positions than instincts deriving from a sense of what was right, proper, and just. And a crucial point is that in arriving at estimations of what was right, proper, and just, they would almost certainly have used as a touchstone their sense of *tradition*. And it was tradition which was to their minds being outraged by the excesses of the Stuarts, every bit as much as the people's liberties. For, after all, such liberties of the people as they could have expected to see were sanctioned by tradition and long usage. And was not the main legal system of England one of common law, which derives entirely from precedents? Many of the regicides were lawyers, and trained to think in terms of precedents. The antiquity of a family was itself a precedent: a family which had long continued, and even more so, a family which had long continued in distinction, was the very utterance of a rule of what we might call 'the common law of society'. The Stuarts were shattering this subtle structure.

How can we explain the curious fact that the regicides came from unnaturally ancient families, out of all proportion to the average? We can explain this by acknowledging that by virtue of their families they were more acutely sensitive of the threat the Stuarts posed to tradition in England. Being more sensitive, they were more outraged, and being more outraged, they were more active. All the more so in that their own families and persons were being affronted by the upheaval wrought by the Stuarts in the traditional social structure. Their dignity and self-esteem were being undermined. Add to this that many of them were the objects of illegal acts of prerogative, were robbed by the Crown, humiliated by the clerical authorities (John Blakiston being one of the prime examples of this), and had members of their families killed, or were themselves outlawed, abused, and imprisoned for what were not genuine offences under the common law, and you have a very angry group of outraged gentry. And that is precisely what the regicides were, by and large, - *a very angry group of outraged gentry.*

It is central to an understanding of the question that the Stuart Dynasty was parvenu, and foreign to boot. It did not adhere by its very nature to English tradition. It was, in fact, not even English. This made it easier to justify opposition to it. Some of the regicides' families had resisted the Tudors on the battlefield (as, for instance, the Temples, who had sided with Richard III at Bosworth Field); resisting encroachments of the Stuarts was a continuation of the pattern and was by comparison small beer. I believe that in order to understand what was in the minds of the men who signed the Death Warrant of Charles I, we must be fully aware that those men were convinced, in many cases, that they were not only his equals, but actually his *betters*.

Nor should we underestimate the self-confidence afforded even to those regicides whose families were of yeoman stock, with no social pretensions, if their families were known to be firmly rooted and of long duration. In order to have an inordinate love of tradition and even a ferocious resentment against its being undermined, one need not be at the highest levels of society. Yeomen of ancient families probably felt more acutely the outrages against tradition than did many peers. Yeoman are no less proud than gentry, as anyone who has been friends with ordinary farmers can testify, and I am one of those, as I have spent most of my life living in the countryside. Even Thomas Horton and John Venn (in whose house in Somerset, which still stands, I have been a guest), though from a sociological viewpoint one would have to say of them that they were on the lowest fringes of the gentry as prosperous yeoman/gentry (if there is such a category), could trace their families back hundreds of years. One does not need a coat of arms emblazoned by a herald to be proud of centuries of forebears who have tilled the same soil as oneself. I know many a farmer who strikes his chest and boasts that his farm was his father's farm, and one generation will do to give him that sense of pride. If there was a grandfather at the same farm, so much the better. But what matters is not the numbers of generations so much as that there has been some continuance, some tangible tradition. That is what makes people take pride in themselves, as members of a family. Add centuries to the weight of this tradition, and the pressure of their combined quotas of family members add, with each generation, another layer of gold to the golden-plating process of the family's reputation, its standing, and its sense of itself.

Just as the political arguments for opposing the King were so often based on real or imagined traditions such as the 'Norman yoke' theory, similarly, individual men had to have their own theories about themselves to justify what they were doing. The family backgrounds of the regicides gave them in most cases good, solid reasons to think well of themselves. They might not have been grandees at Court, but they viewed themselves as illustrious none the less – and with the added bonus of having remained uncorrupted. If a man knew very well that he had the blood of many kings running in his veins, - kings of olden times, of 'the good old days' when kings were proper fellows and were neither leering, predatory homosexuals like James I, nor stuffy priggish 'midgets' like Charles I, - he felt he had an inherent right in nature and blood to judge the misdeeds of a contemporary monarch. John Jones's dating of his family's pedigree on the date of Charles I's execution is but one overt manifestation of the connection many of the regicides must have had in their minds between the act of judging a king, and their own worth. Charles I had forfeited his right to kingship; the regicides were asserting their own rights to greater family honour by bringing him to justice. It was simply one more noble act for one's country, in a long series boasted of in most of their families.

In many cases the regicides probably conceived of themselves, often subconsciously, as redeeming their distinguished families from shameful and undeserved public obscurity or neglect which had been caused over long periods by the wicked and corrupt practices of a decadent Court. The Stuarts had raised many lesser and unworthy favourites to peerages, creating a sycophant aristocracy epitomised by Buckingham, and had as a result packed the House of Lords with a majority of supporters of the King. Several peerages had been sold for large sums, reducing nobility to a commodity traded in the marketplace. But the regicides, so many of whose families had been shut out of the Court, or had refused to become Court creatures, were righting all these wrongs. The real, the true nobility would now purge the country of a degenerate monarch and all his decadent malignants. The good old families would rally to the Good Old Cause.

Thus do I believe that many of these men saw the situation. And when we consider this, we begin to realize that classification of men by estimations of their economic status loses much of its point, and is an artificial criterion of analysis which has only achieved such excessive and unbalanced prominence in historical studies because of the influence of Marxism, with its insistence upon the predominance of economics over all other factors in history. Indeed, Marxism so insists upon the effacement of individuals in favour of 'forces of history' that such factors as self-esteem and psychological motivations do not really exist for many Marxists, who see all human beings as being motivated solely by economic imperatives: as economic automata, in fact. The Marxist Religion has exuded a poison deep into the heart of historical studies, which distorts much otherwise good historical work and has ruined many a fine scholarly mind by enslaving it to a rigid dogma as extreme as that of any other religious fanaticism.

The classification of men by economic status as a means of interpreting history, without taking other factors into consideration, takes no account of what a psychologist would call 'self-image'. Even granted that one can reliably estimate the true economic status of an individual of the seventeenth century (which I have rarely seen done with any degree of accuracy; and we have seen that the glib phrase 'declining fortunes' can be no such thing, as we saw with Sir William Constable, where we had merely a victim of Court theft), I am convinced that it is absurd to believe that the amount of money in a man's pocket could outweigh his own view of himself and of his family. This is especially true of men like the regicides. For in considering them we are considering men who put themselves at the ultimate peril, who took the greatest risk possible in their day, - killing their king, - and this reveals them as men of exceptionally intense motivation. They did not do it in a desultory fashion. They did not do it for money. It was not a casual act. They committed themselves so emphatically and unambiguously that there are few occasions in history when one can so plainly say of a group of men: *They knew what they were doing.*

And the corollary of this is: 'They knew who they were.' They had vivid 'self-images' of themselves and of their families. Thus do the stories of their families provide a crucial element in our evaluation of them. They represented traditions, ancestors, families, hoary with antiquity. When they signed the Death Warrant of Charles I, countless hands guided theirs from beyond the grave. Ancestors who had been executed or who suffered under monarchs stood ghostly round the regicides as they signed and sealed the historic document. The family traditions were alive in the minds of the regicides, they felt and knew them as they acted. In some cases, such as that of Miles Corbet, a near relative (in his case a brother) had died as a result of a Stuart monarch. That required little imagination, as it was an immediate and direct memory, and a continuing sense of personal loss on the part of the regicide. But the more obscure and distant family sufferings and grievances, of which they had heard as boys from their grandfathers and from old maiden-aunts, clustered round their thoughts, rose up from the mouldering family tombs and whispered in their ears. Such a momentous and dangerous act, - the men performing it could not but experience a real sense of these things. Echoes of what they were doing resounded down their family trees. And from this, they could not but derive much comfort and a sense of satisfaction. This would have been a salutary strengthener of resolution. It is the invisible ingredient in a recipe for revolution.

A more ambitious programme than I have found it possible to undertake could build upon these researches into the family histories of the regicides and trace the political and philosophical antecedents of the regicides, by examining more minutely the actions of their own ancestors (which would have been known to each regicide through his family history). Several of the regicides' families had associations with reforming factions in previous reigns; there were associations with Thomas Cromwell and Queen Katherine Parr, and there were histories of opposition to the authoritarian reign of Henry VIII as well as sufferings under him. There were also connections with early humanist or puritan thinkers or leaders (Peter Temple's family had connections with Lutterworth, of which John Wycliffe had been Rector, Temple's immediate ancestors were protégés of the puritan Earl of Huntingdon and had long been sponsored by the Hastings family). But these early ideological roots have only been sketched. It is a task of too great magnitude to go that far back in time for full consideration of the individual ancestors of the regicides, what they thought and what they did. Although these things must certainly have been influences on the regicides, we would also have the problem of trying to find some specific evidence to prove rather than merely to suggest such influences. It is enough to suggest here that in many cases, such influences cannot have been absent. In the section on early histories, we shall commence our consideration of the ideological roots of the regicides in connection with our survey of their early careers by starting no earlier than the Essex Rebellion of 1601.

We take our leave now of the family backgrounds per se. We must turn our attention to the remaining major task which is required of us in connection with the families. That is to discover the relationships between the regicides and the extent to which 'clans' such as those spoken of by Everitt might be seen to exist in relation to them. Much has been written about the extraordinary web of family relationships which was used by Oliver Cromwell in the exercise of his aims and power.[44] We shall not recapitulate this valuable work, done at such length by others. But at least 21 regicides had relationship either by blood or by marriage with Oliver Cromwell, and through him, of course, with each other. This is in itself quite a web! But it is only part of the story. My detailed investigations of the families of the regicides makes possible a much fuller understanding of regicide interrelationships and reveals countless ones which not only were not previously known, but which could not have been known in any other way than by the extensive genealogical researches which I pursued for their sixty families all over the country for many years, in many cases visiting their former homes, meeting their descendants, and exchanging information with many of these families which still exist.

Here it is necessary to refer to the voluminous appendices in which the family histories are given at length, alphabetically arranged. Each regicide's relationships with other regicides are given in each case under the heading of 'Prominent Relations'. But it should be noted that not all such interrelationships between regicides are thus given in every instance. Every relationship is noted under one or the other parties, but not all are noted under *both* parties. This situation is remedied in the tables which follow.

A methodical survey of the interrelationships of the regicides is absolutely essential. Table One deals with which regicides were related to other regicides and which were not. Forty regicides were related to other regicides, whereas 21 were not. We thus see that two thirds of the regicides were related to other regicides.

Table One.
REGICIDES RELATED TO OTHER REGICIDES

BY MARRIAGE ONLY:	BY BLOOD ONLY:	BY MARRIAGE AND BLOOD:
John Alured	John Cook	Sir John Bourchier
John Blakiston	Sir John Danvers	Daniel Blagrave
John Carew	Thomas Harrison	Thomas Chaloner
Miles Corbet	Sir Gregory Norton	Oliver Cromwell
William Goffe	**TOTAL: 4**	Humphrey Edwardes
Lord Grey of Groby		George Fleetwood
John Jones		John Hutchinson
Robert Lilburne		Richard Ingoldsby
Sir Michael Livesey		Henry Ireton
Henry Marten		John Lisle
Simon Mayne		Sir Thomas Mauleverer
Thomas Pride		Peregrine Pelham
William Say		William Purefoy
Henry Smith		Adrian Scrope
Robert Tichborne		Edmund Ludlow
Valentine Wauton		Anthony Stapley
TOTAL: 16		James Temple
		Peter Temple
		Sir Hardress Waller
		Edward Whalley
		TOTAL: 20

GRAND TOTAL OF THOSE RELATED: 40.

Table Two.
REGICIDES NOT RELATED TO OTHER REGICIDES

John Barkstead	Thomas Horton
John Bradshaw	Gilbert Millington
William Cawley	John Moore
Gregory Clement	John Okey
Sir William Constable	Vincent Potter
Richard Deane	Owen Rowe
John Dixwell	Thomas Scot
John Downes	John Venn
Isaac Ewer	Thomas Waite
Augustine Garland	Thomas Wogan
John Hewson	**TOTAL: 21**

The above list is not infallible. It is *possible* that Owen Rowe and Thomas Scot were related by marriage, but I have not been able to prove it. I have classified John Dixwell and Richard Deane as being unrelated to other regicides, although they were both extremely distantly related to some, because the relationships were so distant that it would perhaps not be sensible to claim any significance for them. I have therefore erred on the conservative side. Similarly, Thomas Wogan's connection by marriage to Thomas Pride was also too distant to be counted. These relationships were simply too tenuous for us to treat them as important. Also, of course, we do not have complete knowledge, and there may have been relationships of which we are in ignorance, through the loss of documents and the passage of time. One further qualification should be made as well: some of the above were related to men who could have been regicides if they had been able or willing to take up their seats on the High Court of Justice. For instance, Constable was the uncle of Lord Fairfax, and John Moore was related by marriage to Alexander Rigby (whose DNB life I have written in the 'Missing Persons' volume).

We now come to the essential survey of which regicides were related to which. The easiest way to give this information is to run through the alphabet quickly and give the relationships as briefly as possible.

Table Three.
INTERRELATIONSHIPS OF REGICIDES
(OTHER THAN OLIVER CROMWELL'S)

John Alured	Pelham by marriage
John Barkstead	None
Daniel Blagrave	Danvers and Lisle by blood; Tichborne by marriage
John Blakiston	Bourchier by marriage three times over; Mauleverer twice by marriage distantly, and once through Bourchier; Cromwell through Bourchier
Sir John Bourchier	Mauleverer a first cousin; Cromwell a third cousin; Blakiston by marriage three times over
John Bradshaw	None
John Carew	Pelham by marriage
William Cawley	None
Thomas Chaloner	Fleetwood a third cousin; Cromwell through Fleetwood; Ingoldsby by marriage
Gregory Clement	None
John Cook	Harrison a cousin
Sir William Constable	None
Miles Corbet	Tichborne by marriage
Sir John Danvers	None closely, but many distantly, particularly Blagrave and James Temple
Richard Deane	None closely enough to be noted
John Dixwell	None closely enough to be noted
John Downes	None
Humphrey Edwardes	Jones by marriage, and through him, Cromwell (after 1656); probably Norton and probably step-cousin of Purefoy
Isaac Ewer	None
George Fleetwood	Chaloner a third cousin; Cromwell by marriage
Augustine Garland	None
William Goffe	Whalley by marriage (father-in-law), and through him, Cromwell
Lord Grey Of Groby	Smith by marriage
Thomas Harrison	Cook a cousin
John Hewson	None
Thomas Horton	None
John Hutchinson	Ireton a second cousin; through him, Cromwell
Richard Ingoldsby	Cromwell a cousin; Chaloner and Waller by marriage
Henry Ireton	Hutchinson a second cousin; Cromwell by marriage (father-in-law)
John Jones	Cromwell (after 1656), Edwardes, and Mayne by marriage
Robert Lilburne	Marten, Mayne, and Cromwell by marriage
John Lisle	Blagrave a second cousin; Livesey and Say by marriage

FAMILY BACKGROUNDS OF THE REGICIDES

Table Three (continued).

Sir Michael Livesey	Stapley by marriage; probably Lisle by marriage
Edmund Ludlow	Scrope a distant cousin and also related by marriage
Henry Marten	Mayne by marriage; Lilburne by marriage, and through him, Cromwell
Sir Thomas Mauleverer	Bourchier a first cousin; Blakiston by marriage twice distantly and also through Bourchier; Cromwell through Bourchier
Simon Mayne	Cromwell, Jones, Lilburne, Marten, James Temple and Peter Temple (separately), all by marriage
Gilbert Millington	None
John Moore	None
Sir Gregory Norton	Edwardes probably a close relation
John Okey	None
Peregrine Pelham	Stapley doubly by blood and singly by marriage, Alured and Carew by marriage
Vincent Potter	None
Thomas Pride	Wauton by marriage very late (i.e., their children married each other); Cromwell through this connection to Wauton
William Purefoy	Distant cousin of Peter Temple; probably step-cousin of Edwardes
Owen Rowe	None
William Say	Lisle, Scrope, and Stapley by marriage
Thomas Scot	None. (He was not the son-in-law of Mauleverer as many historians have claimed; that was the other Thomas Scott, MP for Aldborough.)
Adrian Scrope	Ludlow a distant cousin and also by marriage; Cromwell, Say, Tichborne, and Waller by marriage
Henry Smith	Grey of Groby, James Temple and Peter Temple (separately) by marriage
Anthony Stapley	Pelham doubly by blood and singly by marriage; Livesey, Say, and James Temple by marriage
James Temple	Distant cousin of Peter Temple; distant cousin of Danvers; Mayne, Smith, Stapley, Tichborne, Whalley (doubly), and Waller by marriage, and Cromwell through Whalley
Peter Temple	Distant cousin of James Temple; distant cousin of Purefoy; second cousin of Waller; Smith and Mayne by marriage; Cromwell through Mayne
Robert Tichborne	Blagrave, Corbet, Scrope, James Temple, and Waller by marriage
John Venn	None
Thomas Waite	None
Sir Hardress Waller	Second cousin of Peter Temple; Scrope, James Temple, and Tichborne by marriage; Ingoldsby by marriage and through him to Cromwell
Valentine Wauton	Cromwell by marriage (brother-in-law); Pride very late by marriage (their children married)
Edward Whalley	Cromwell a first cousin; Goffe by marriage (son-in-law); doubly by marriage to James Temple
Thomas Wogan	None

The above Table does not carry the relationships through to the 'second generation' of relationship, other than to point out the links with Cromwell. (Cromwell's own many relationships, looking outwards from his position, are not listed here, because they have been published for a very long time, as mentioned earlier.) If carried further, the relationships proliferate enormously. For instance, there were 21 regicides who were related to Cromwell. If one were to carry the relationships through to the 'second generation', one would have to add in each case the other twenty to each one of the 21. And indeed, apart from the Cromwell connections, this would have to be done with each related regicide in turn. For instance, William Say who was related by marriage to John Lisle would then in the 'second generation' of relationship be related to Lisle's second cousin Daniel Blagrave. Thus, as soon as we extend the interrelationships beyond the simple first and direct stage of connection, we are enmeshed in a gigantic and highly complex web. To prepare such a vastly inflated chart would be tedious and unnecessary and would no longer fit on any normal paper or screen, but anyone can plot the further stages of relationships for himself or herself from Table Three, if a large enough sheet of paper is at hand and one has all day! All one has to do is as follows: if you want to know all the regicides Henry Marten was related to *through other regicides*, you simply go to the names in the Table of all those regicide relations listed under his own name, go to their names in the Table, and write down all the regicide relations listed under *their names*. To carry it through to the 'third generation' of relationship, you simply then go in turn to their names, and so on indefinitely until you have exhausted the generations of relationship at last. At that point, the total number of regicide relationships will have been reached.

Of course, in order to prepare the very simple and basic list which constitutes Table Three, and make all the information easily accessible in tabular form, I have had to suppress artificially the total number of regicide relationships of each regicide (except for those who had none). But the advantage of presenting the information in this way, apart from simplicity and directness, is that we can see the routes by which the relationships occurred. This 'generational relationship' mode allows us to trace the tortuous connections of the regicides to each other by blood and by marriage with an unusual ease.

The second generation of relationships were often highly important to the regicides themselves, and we must not assume that because they were so multifarious, and because I have omitted them from Table Three for the sake of simplicity, we are entitled to overlook them. I have no doubt whatsoever that Daniel Blagrave was very glad indeed to find himself related to William Say through John Lisle, and hastened to claim kin with yet another distinguished lawyer for the sake of his legal career before he ever entered politics. Turning to the military scene, we may readily imagine that Waller and Whalley were very keen, as New Model Army colonels, to get all that bit closer through their second generation relationship via James Temple. Smith was related by marriage to Grey of Groby, and we may safely presume that Peter Temple, as a close crony of Grey of Groby's, was delighted to have a 'second generation' connection to Grey of Groby through Smith (they were all from the same county). And so on. (It is unfortunate that Smith's relationship to Grey of Groby, and even Smith's proper identity, were not discovered by Jeff Richards, who in 2000 published a lengthy and interesting biography of Grey of Groby.[45]) Certainly these further tentacles made for closer and stronger bonds between the men, and would often have had considerable significance. The vast multiplicity of criss-crossing interrelationships makes the word 'web' almost inadequate when considering a very large number of these regicides. 'Multiple web' might be better!

The 'most related' regicide, apart from Oliver Cromwell, was James Temple. The 'second most related' was John Blakiston. I have compiled Table Four (below) to show the 'scores' which indicate how interrelated each regicide was with other regicides. In the case of someone like Simon Mayne, who had a high score, we may conceive of him as buoyed up and supported by all of these family connections, for he had a reputation of being a weak character on his own, and was mocked by some of his colleagues. But if we look for such a pattern of buoying-up operating universally, we will be disappointed. James Temple's high score doesn't seem to have done him much good; he never made it onto the Council of State or became a committee magnate. (It is probably true, however, that his wide set of family relationships saved his life at the Restoration, so that he could die in prison in Jersey rather than be hung, drawn and quartered. But that is not for discussion here.) James Temple, despite his high 'score', was always on the sidelines in the political arena. On the other hand, Thomas Scot, with a score of zero, and Miles Corbet, with a score of only one, were dominating figures in Parliament. But of course, this reminds us of the perilous nature of our survey: the relationships between regicides are of only a very restricted importance insofar as they pertain to any one individual. The importance of the relationships is their vast collective and cumulative nature, and their importance in terms of *groups*. For they bound together disparate men with ties of mutual respect and claims of familial obligations which cannot have been negligible factors in the formation and operation of the High Court. As Everitt said, in speaking of 'the existence of such "clans"', 'Their connexions spread far and wide and united the whole body of the gentry ...'[46]

We must not make the mistake of thinking that regicide relationships to other regicides are the be-all and end-all. We must retain perspective and realize that Constable, though not related to other regicides, was the uncle of Fairfax, which was certainly more important. And Grey of Groby, though related to only one regicide by marriage in the 'first generation of relationship' and two others in the 'second generation of relationship', had more than enough important relations of other kinds! Our consideration of the regicide interrelationships is therefore not intended to take precedence over other factors which may have been more important; however, its importance is sufficient to warrant our giving it our concentrated attention. And to that end, the following table will be of considerable interest.

Regicides not related to other regicides are obviously omitted from the following table.

Table Four.

NUMBERS OF RELATIONSHIPS WITH EACH OTHER OF THE FORTY INTERRELATED REGICIDES MINUS CROMWELL, BY BOTH BLOOD AND MARRIAGE (WHICH ARE NOT HERE DIFFERENTIATED), MINUS THE 'SECOND-GENERATION' RELATIONSHIPS EXCEPT CROMWELL'S OWN

(Those related by either first or second generation relationships to Cromwell are also all related to each other, as indicated by the phrase 'plus Cromwellian'.)

John Alured	1
Daniel Blagrave	3
John Blakiston	7 plus Cromwellian
Sir John Bourchier	5 plus Cromwellian
John Carew	1
Thomas Chaloner	3 plus Cromwellian
John Cook	1
Miles Corbet	1
Sir John Danvers	2
Humphrey Edwardes	4 plus Cromwellian (from 1656)
George Fleetwood	2 plus Cromwellian
William Goffe	2 plus Cromwellian
Lord Grey Of Groby	1
Thomas Harrison	1
John Hutchinson	2 plus Cromwellian
Richard Ingoldsby	3 plus Cromwellian
Henry Ireton	2 plus Cromwellian
John Jones	2 plus Cromwellian (from 1656)
Robert Lilburne	3 plus Cromwellian
John Lisle	3
Sir Michael Livesey	2
Edmund Ludlow	2
Henry Marten	3 plus Cromwellian
Sir Thomas Mauleverer	5 plus Cromwellian
Simon Mayne	6 plus Cromwellian
Sir Gregory Norton	1
Peregrine Pelham	5
Thomas Pride	2 plus Cromwellian (from (1650s)
Willia Purefoy	2
William Say	3
Adrian Scrope	6 plus Cromwellian
Henry Smith	3
Anthony Stapley	6
James Temple	10 plus Cromwellian
Peter Temple	6 plus Cromwellian
Robert Tichborne	5
Sir Hardress Waller	6 plus Cromwellian
Valentine Wauton	2 plus Cromwellian
Edward Whalley	4 plus Cromwellian

Relationship to Cromwell himself is counted as 'one' in the numbers given above, but always followed by 'plus Cromwellian' to indicate the other twenty regicides thus connected (note that this does not form part of the 'score'). The relationship to Cromwell himself is either first-generation or second-generation, and these are not differentiated here, but may be determined either from the main text of from the Appendix in each case. No other second-generation relationships are counted as part of the 'score'. When one regicide is doubly or triply related to another regicide, each separate relationship is counted as 'one' for purposes of the scores.

Twenty-one regicides were related to Cromwell, and Cromwell's own 'score' has not been computed. We have only considered those regicides who were related to him in first and second-generation relationships, and not how many relationships he enjoyed, looking outwards from his position.

But the Cromwell family, strange as it may seem, was not the dominant *family* amongst the regicides. The single family which far and away dominated the regicides was the Temple family. And this is not because James Temple had the highest 'score', closely followed by Peter Temple's separate 'score', or because the Temple family was the only one which actually produced two regicides.

I have computed the number of regicide relationships of James Temple in the combined first and second-generation of relationships, as also those of Peter Temple. If we eliminate, first of all, the second-generation relationships of each from the tally of the other, we get a 'score' for James Temple of 67, and for Peter Temple of 52. But, since they were related to each other, if we add their second-generation increments to one another, they each then have scores of 84. This means that their total number of regicide relationships individually far exceeded the actual number of regicides, as their joint total was 168 (representing 275% as many 'regicide relationships' as there were actual regicides to be related to, or 420% as many 'regicide relationships' as there were *related regicides*). These astonishing facts mean that between them, the two Temple regicides manifested what we could, for want of any better way of expressing it, describe as a truly extreme *relationship-density* to other regicides.

This extraordinary finding calls for us to pause for a moment, and to consider some possible 'theoretical biological' aspects. This is the second bizarre *biological density phenomenon* associated with the Temple family at this particular time in history. In one sense, the two phenomena are certainly related, and the second is partially caused by the first. The first such phenomenon was reported by Thomas Fuller, in his famous book, *History of the Worthies of England*, which was published posthumously in 1662 (he died in 1661).[47] Fuller was certainly in a position to know what he was talking about as far as the Temple family was concerned, as his second wife (who married him in 1652 and bore him several children), Mary Roper, was the grand-daughter of Sir Peter Temple, Bart., of the Long Parliament (named to the High Court of Justice but declined to sit), who was first cousin of James Temple the regicide. In his *Worthies*, Fuller records that Lady Hester Temple (who was his own wife's great-grandmother and who was the grandmother of James Temple the regicide) lived to see 700 of the descendants of her own body. I once brought this fact to the attention of the late Norris McWhirter, editor of the *Guinness Book of Records*, with whom I had an acquaintance. He agreed that this appeared to be a world record for human fecundity, but whether he ever entered it into his *Book of Records* I do not know, because I have never actually opened a copy, as it is not my sort of reading, being too sensationalist and superficial by nature to appeal to me. Books of that kind appeal to the people who do crossword puzzles and who like facts in isolation, whereas I only like facts when they can be placed in context and have some kind of meaning. The second phenomenon is the one we have already discussed, namely the extraordinarily high 'relationship-density' of the Temple regicides to other regicides. It is immediately obvious that, to some extent, the large number of regicide relationships of James Temple, who was a grandson of Lady Hester Temple, was a direct result of having such a huge number of relations of all kinds. However, Peter Temple the regicide was not descended from Lady Hester Temple, being only a distant cousin of her husband, and yet he had an extraordinarily high 'relationship-density' with other regicides also. Therefore, we are somewhat at a loss here to figure out what is cause and what is effect. Was there something strange about the Temple family in the 16th and 17th centuries which caused these unusual biological phenomena? This may seem an abstruse point to be mentioning in a book which deals with history, as it is a point which is possibly of a scientific nature. However, I should point out that I have been a part-time Professor of the History and Philosophy of Science (i.e., a Visiting Professor, and previously at a different university was an Adjunct Professor of Humanities, History and Philosophy of Science, 'Adjunct' being the word the Americans love to use, though I find it ugly and inelegant and received special permission from that university not to have to use it when speaking of my position outside the United States, when I was authorised to say 'Visiting' for that appointment as well), and I have spent a great deal of time studying the subject known as 'theoretical biology'. I knew Professor Conrad Waddington of the University of Edinburgh, who founded this discipline in the 1950s and 1960s. In a book of popular science which I published in 1983, I also discussed biological density issues, and it is clear that species of animals have concealed mathematical patterns regulating these.[48] (These mathematical phenomena appear to be related to the concealed order-in-chaos nowadays clarified and expounded by modern chaos theory, which was unknown to Waddington and his early collaborators, as it had not yet been developed, though it received some of its impetus from them.) It is by no means improbable that something of this kind operates amongst humans, though not at the species level, rather at the 'clan' level. I mention this only in passing, because I feel that I would be negligent if I did not call attention to it at all, even if this be no occasion to go into any detail. I suspect that such phenomena do from time to time effect historical events, and that this may have been the case with the regicides. I regret that I dare not go any further into scientific and mathematical matters here, however, as it would be inappropriate to do so in a specifically historical treatise.

Certainly if we wish to suggest a 'mega-family' incorporating most of the regicides, the Temple family would be the candidate name for it. The Temple family-at-large had the greatest sprawl and subsumed the greatest number of regicides the greatest number of times. In terms of numbers, the Cromwell connections were of secondary importance, except that we must not forget that at the individual level, Oliver Cromwell personally would have had a greater 'relationship-density' than either of the two Temples on their own (though not greater than the two combined).

Perhaps we could say that the regicides as a group – to whatever extent one can actually speak of them as a group – largely consisted of two giant 'mega-families': the extended Temple family and the extended Cromwell family. These two also overlapped. If one considered these two 'mega-families' as webs, then one had a spider at the centre and one didn't. The closest the extended Temple family had to a family manipulator was Lord Saye and Sele (uncle of James Temple). But he was no regicide nor had he any ambitions to run the country. On the other hand, a spider at the centre of the Cromwell family web gave us the Protectorate. Cromwell was a man of insatiable ambition. But without his web of relations, it is inconceivable to think of him successfully establishing the government of the Protectorate. (This is not to say that all of his relations supported his personal ambitions, and several of them such as Valentine

Wauton vehemently and strenuously opposed him, as we shall see especially in the section 'The Regicides under the Protectorate'.) However, the trial and execution of the King were by no means primarily the work of Oliver Cromwell, as is made clear in the chapter on 'The Circumstances of the King's Trial', so that Cromwell's work as spider was not fully operative as early as 1649. The true importance of Cromwell's 'mega-family' was to come later.

Earlier we noted Cliffe's remarks about kinship, and it would be as well to repeat them again here:

'Kinship was not simply a matter of genealogical interest. Contemporary opinion held that ties of blood, however tenuous, involved special obligations and loyalties and this concept of clan solidarity was an important factor not only in normal social intercourse but also in public life.'[49]

The bias against the subject of historic families, social tradition, and blood ties can sometimes be passionate. This was the case with the historian Donald Pennington of Balliol College, Oxford, who was doctrinaire in the extreme. He once screamed at me like a mad man on that subject. When he was in a rage he turned purple to a most alarming degree. His dogmatic bent doubtless arose from his association with his mentor, Christopher Hill, also of Oxford. As soon as Hill died in 2003, he was exposed in the newspapers as having been a notorious Soviet spy. Pennington shared his views, and was, like Hill, a mental prisoner of dogma. Pennington was also a very sloppy scholar, often criticised in later sections of this work for his countless errors of fact and for his professional laziness. I early became aware of his working methods, and their insufficiency. When I first began my study, before I realized at all what Pennington's background was, and when I thought of him only as co-author of the book *Members of the Long Parliament*[50], I went to see him at his rooms in Oxford. This was one of my earliest attempts to gather information about the regicides, many of whom were obviously members of the Long Parliament. I asked Pennington about his co-author Brunton, and he said he had been killed in a car crash years before. I asked Pennington whether he had any further notes about the MPs which had formed the subject of his study, hoping that if he did, he might be willing to let me see them and they might contain leads and information which I could then pursue, with his blessing, of course. He said no, that the notes he and Brunton had made had all been on index cards, and they had been thrown away because everything on them had been used. I was rather shocked to discover that Pennington had no notes or files relating to the MPs of the Long Parliament, and never had had any proper ones. The idea of compiling a book such as his solely from index cards with jottings on them appalled me. My own files on the regicides, including vast amounts of information which could not be incorporated in this study, are now so voluminous that it is a major problem of where to store them. The basic notes alone fill two large filing cabinets. I have never understood how anyone could write a book surveying a large number of people and have no meaningful notes or papers. I also have an enormous specialist library on the subject of the regicides and their period, including many rare contemporary editions, not to mention a voluminous collection of 17th century manuscripts, and a huge collection of portrait engravings and photos which I have taken of oil paintings and houses. And yet, Pennington admitted that he had nothing. Dare I say that I could readily understand later on how it was that Pennington and Brunton's book was so unreliable and full of errors? They simply didn't do their work properly. It was a sloppy job, unworthy of any true scholars.

But Pennington's association with Christopher Hill was an even worse matter. As the London *Times* commented in 2003: 'One of the most influential historians of the 20th century, who went on to be Master of Balliol, Oxford, stands accused today of taking a dark secret to his grave: he was a Soviet mole. ... Hill used his position as head of the Russian desk at the Foreign Office to push pro-Soviet policy ... [including] that all White Russian émigrés teaching Russian at British universities and schools should be sacked and replaced with Soviet-approved staff.'[51]

After Hill's death, the revelations about him poured out thick and fast in the press. In the London *Evening Standard* a report said: 'The unmasking this morning of Oxford historian Christopher Hill as a secret Communist Party member and Soviet spy does not surprise fellow historian Professor Norman Stone ...'[52]

The London *Observer* wrote: 'In 1940 [George] Orwell's fury was provoked by [Hill's] juvenilia, *The English Revolution: 1640*, a book with a fair claim to be the most simplistic Marxist version of history published in Britain in the twentieth century.

'Orwell identified a persistent fault of the far Left. Like those who give a knowing wink and insist that the war against Iraq is "all about oil", Hill and his comrades were too "cocksure". They wrote off "religion, morality, patriotism [as] a sort of hypocritical cover-up for the pursuit of economic interest" when they insisted that the Parliamentarians' war against Charles I could be reduced to a battle between the rising class of capitalists and the dead weight of the feudal monarchy. ... [Hill] formed a friendship with Peter Smollett, head of the Russian Desk at the Ministry of Information and an acquaintance of Kim Philby. Before fleeing to the Soviet Union, Smollett performed many small services for Stalin, including persuading several publishers to turn down Orwell's *Animal Farm*.

'When I talked to [Anthony] Glees [of Brunel University], he said Hill had been "sinister and disgraceful". His research proved that Hill was a Soviet agent in the Foreign Office, and a demoralised Hill had come to his home in 1983 and admitted that he was guilty as charged. Glees went on to wonder whether Balliol should go through its records and discover what Hill had been up to when he was Master. The apparently fair and kind scholar may well have promoted left-wing students in the 1960s and 1970s while obstructing the careers of Conservative undergraduates.'[53]

It is best if historians pursue their work without being constrained by their personal dogmatic views. Historical enquiry should be the pursuit of truth, wherever that truth may lead. The historical figures one is researching were often partisan enough in their lifetimes, without the historian piling his or her own partisan passions on top of the findings, which is like putting a rotten fish rather than a cherry on top of a cake.

1. Mark Noble, *Memoirs of the Protectoral-House of Cromwell*, 2 vols., London, 1787. Also: James Waylen, *The House of Cromwell*, London, 1897.
2. Alan Everitt, *The Community of Kent and the Great Rebellion 1640-60*, Leicester University Press, 1966.
3. *Ibid.*, p. 13.
4. *Ibid.*, p. 35.
5. *Ibid.*, pp. 35-6.
6. Robert K. G. Temple, 'Discovery of a Manuscript Eye-Witness Account of the Battle of Maidstone', *Archaeologia Cantiana*, Vol. XCVII (1981), pp. 209-20. (This article may be downloaded from my entry in www.researchgate.net and also from my website, www.robert-temple.com).
7. Everitt, *op. cit.*, pp. 151, 271, and 311n.
8. *Ibid.*, p. 311n.
9. *Ibid.*, p. 55.
10. *Ibid.*, p. 118.
11. *Ibid.*, p. 147.
12. *Ibid.*, p. 151.
13. *Ibid.*, p. 152.
14. *Ibid.*, p. 185.
15. *Ibid.*, p. 234.
16. *Ibid.*, pp. 36, 47, 50-2, 64, and 70-3.
17. *Ibid.*, p. 33.
18. *Ibid.*, p. 118.
19. Listing in *Marriage Licenses Issued at Canterbury*, an index found in the Library of the Institute of Historical Research, London.
20. British Library ADD. MS. 42,586, f. 22.
21. Accounts of the life of John Dixwell in exile after 1660 (when he lived under the pseudonym of James Davids, thus preserving his original initials), his marriage there, and his children, may be found in Lemuel Aiken Welles, *The History of the Regicides in New England*, Grafton Press, New York, 1927, and Lemuel Aiken Welles, *The Regicides in Connecticut*, Tercentenary Commission of the State of Connecticut, Yale University Press, New Haven, Connecticut, 1935. (The other regicides who survived in exile in New England after the Restoration were William Goffe and Edward Whalley, who are also described.)
22. British Library ADD. MS. 24,120, ff. 250-1.
23. *Ibid.*
24. *Ibid.*
25. *Visitation of Warwickshire 1619*, Harleian Society, Vol. XII (1877), p. 297.
26. Rylands Library, Manchester: Ryl. Eng. MS. 3001769.
27. Everitt, *op. cit.*, p. 55.
28. J. T. Cliffe, *The Yorkshire Gentry: from the Reformation to the Civil War*, University of London, The Athlone Press, 1969.
29. *Ibid.*, p. 13.
30. *Ibid.*, pp. 10-11.
31. *Ibid.*, p. 13.
32. *Ibid.*, p. 5.
33. *Ibid.*, pp. 351-4.
34. William Hepworth Dixon, *Personal History of Lord Bacon from Unpublished Papers*, Tauchnitz, Leipzig, 1861, p. 96.
35. R. H. Tawney, 'The Rise of the Gentry: 1558-1640', *Economic History Review*, Vol. XI, 1 (1941).
36. Perez Zagorin, *The Court and the Country*, Routledge, London, 1969, pp. 19-21.
37. Hugh Trevor-Roper, 'The Elizabethan Aristocracy: an Anatomy Anatomized', *Economic History Review* 2nd Series, Vol. III, 3 (1951); *The Gentry 1540-1640*, Cambridge, 1953.
38. Cliffe, *op. cit.*, p. 351.
39. College of Arms references which I was able to discover, for possible use by those more fortunate of access in the future:

    C12/95.2^d Ind.; Vts. Berks. 141-2-3, p. 81; I 8. f.433. See also I.C.B.84 (an entire volume of 'Regicides').
40. Mary Frear Keeler, *The Long Parliament 1640-1*, American Philosophical Society, Philadelphia, USA, 1954, p. 399.
41. *Ibid.*
42. Everitt, *op. cit.*, pp. 35-6.
43. *Ibid.*, p. 208.
44. See for instance Waylen, *op. cit.*, and Noble, *op. cit.*
45. Jeff Richards, *The Life and Times of Thomas, Lord Grey of Groby*, New Millennium, London, 2000.
46. Everitt, *op. cit.*, p. 35.
47. Thomas Fuller, *Worthies of England*, Allen and Unwin, London, 1952, pp. 42-3 (in the section dealing with Buckinghamshire).
48. Robert Temple, *Strange Things: A Collection of Modern Scientific Curiosities*, Sphere Books, London, 1983. See in particular 'The Bigger They Are, the Fewer'.
49. Cliffe, *op. cit.*, pp. 10-11.
50. D. Brunton and Donald H. Pennington, *Members of the Long Parliament*, reprint edition of the original 1954 edition, Archon Books, 1968.
51. Ian Cobain, 'Was Oxford's Most Famous Marxist a Soviet Mole?', *The Times*, London, 5 March 2003, p. 3.
52. London's Diary, London *Evening Standard*, 5 March 2003, p 10.
53. Nick Cohen, 'Left in Stalin's Shadow', article about Christopher Hill, the London *Observer*, 9 March 2003.

CHAPTER TWO APPENDIX ONE

Further Details of the Family Backgrounds

JOHN ALURED. Born March, 1607, and baptized April 4, 1607, at Preston, son and heir of Henry Alured (1581-1628) of the Charterhouse, Sculcoates, on edge of Hull, and Frances, daughter of Francis Vaughan of Sutton upon Derwent. Parents married at Sculcoates, February 12, 1603/4. Mother buried June 22, 1626. Father buried at Holy Trinity, Hull, April 14, 1628. Regicide's father, uncle, grandfather, and great-grandfather were all M.P.s.[1] Siblings: Colonel Matthew, born circa 1613 (not circa 1620-4 as presumed by Pink)[2]. Thomas, born September 1, 1608. Christopher, baptized January 27, 1609/10. George, born 1612. William, born 1621, Kitt, birth date unknown, died 1623. Ellen, baptized April, 1611, died 1624. Elizabeth and Frances, dates unknown. See Appendix to this Chapter for previously unknown will of the regicide's father, transcribed in full.

The Marvell family lived next door to the Alureds, and Mrs. Marvell acted as a substitute mother for the Alured children after their own mother's death. Andrew Marvell, the son and later poet, evidently got his introductions to the Fairfax family and high-powered London contacts through John Alured later in life. Marvell's original patrons had previously always been a mystery to biographers.[3]

Prominent Relations: Henry Darley, M.P., was a cousin and later brother-in-law, being brother of Alured's first wife. Peregrine Pelham, M.P. and regicide, was a cousin of Alured's wife.

Pedigrees: MS. pedigree in MS. in York Minster Library, *Collection of ... Descents* by John Hopkinson, corrected by Thomas Wilson. Most comprehensive source with annotated pedigree is W.D. Pink, "Alured of the Charterhouse, Co. York". *Yorkshire Genealogist*, ed. by J. Horsfall Turner, Vol. I (Yorks., 1888).

JOHN BARKSTEAD. Probably born around 1610. Son of Michael Barkstead of London, whose second wife was Rose, daughter of Anthony Herring, Goldsmith, of London; they were married August 27, 1621, at St. Olave, Old Jewry, London. Ian Gentles has discovered that Michael Barkstead was son of Harman Barkstead and was bound apprentice to his later father-in-law (or perhaps *his* father), Anthony Herring, Goldsmith, in 1587, and was made free of the Goldsmith's Company on August 29,1595. The regicide himself was bound apprentice to Thomas Campe, Goldsmith, in 1627, and made free January 8, 1635/6, becoming Prime Warden of the Goldsmiths in 1653. (Apprenticeship and Freedom Index, unpaginated, at Goldsmith's Hall.) Hence we can be sure Rose Herring was his step-mother, not his mother, since he could not have become an apprentice at the age of six. We thus do not know who Barkstead's mother was, and there is no London marriage recorded, which makes it likely that the marriage took place in her home parish somewhere outside London. He was related to a Robert Glover (see Grosart, below), and that is just about all we know of his relations. There are three Robert Glovers listed in Chester's *London Marriage Licences* of the period, one from faraway Norfolk, but two in London. One was married in 1591 and the other in 1615. I have not undertaken further research into this, which is not to say that more could not be discovered by someone determined enough. There is a large oil portrait of John Barkstead preserved in Dr. Williams's Library in London.

Prominent Relations: Probably Sir Christopher Pack, an Alderman of London in 1647 and prominent in the Parliament of 1656, who married widow of Michael Herring, an Alderman of 1651, who was probably a very close relation of the regicide's step-mother. Michael Herring himself was prominent as the Treasurer at Goldsmith's Hall during the 1640s, a kind of civil servant. The regicide may well have been closely related to the poet, actor and playwright,

William Barkstead/Barksted, who flourished 1607-1610. In 1610, this man wrote a tragi-comedy called *The Insatiate Countess* which still survives.[5] It was once wrongly attributed to John Marston but is now known to have been Barksted's work. William Barksted definitely spelled his name 'Barksted'. In 1876, the Rev. Alexander Grosart published a limited edition of only fifty copies of *The Poems of William Barksted*, which fortunately is available in a modern reprint from Scholar Select (no date or place given). In his Introduction and in his Postscript at the end of the volume, Grosart says how disappointed he is at the sparsity of biographical information about Barksted. But he reveals that two documents signed by Barksted are known (dated 1611 and 1615/6), and that Barksted, who described himself as an actor and as 'one of the servants of his Majety's revels', 'was of the most renowned Company of "Actors" in England in 1615/16'.

Pedigrees: None known. Family history obscure; however, they may have had arms. Although Barkstead was granted arms in 1654, this was probably a confirmatory grant of real or claimed family arms, since they are the same arms used by him on a document eight years earlier.[4]

DANIEL BLAGRAVE. Born 1606. The old DNB says he was nephew of John Blagrave of Reading the mathematician (which is true) but gives no parents. Very great confusion has arisen over the multifarious Blagrave family, and the identities of the regicide's parents. Brunton and Pennington,[6] C.H. Josten,[7] and T.L. Underwood in *Biographical Dictionary of British Radicals in the Seventeenth Century* (1982)[8] erred in believing the regicide to have been son of Anthony Blagrave and Jane Burlace or Borlase. He was actually the fifth son of Alexander Blagrave (brother of the Anthony just mentioned) of Southcote, and Margaret …..[9] The only historian to get this right has been Christopher Durston, in his Ph.D. thesis, who, however, did not know the mother's name.[10] The regicide had a brother John, born circa 1588, married to Frances Gregory of Bentley, Hampshire, and alive in 1665.[11] The regicide's grandmother, Anne Hungerford, came of a Gloucestershire family which had been M.P.s since the fourteenth century.[12] The regicide's uncle, Anthony Blagrave, was M.P. for Reading in 1601, and Sheriff of Berkshire in 1605.[13] His son, Sir John Blagrave, the regicide's first cousin, was Sheriff of Berkshire in 1624, and this man's younger brother, Anthony Blagrave, was considered for Sheriff in 1638 but passed over, but later became Sheriff in 1646.[14] The Blagrave family came from Staffordshire to London in the early 1500s and business and fortunate marriage resulted in their acquiring eventually former Reading monastery lands, which brought them to Berkshire in 1551.[15] There were so very many Blagraves that it was difficult for their prosperity to be spread satisfactorily over the entire clan; their fortunes were uneven and there were bickerings over money.[16] The regicide was related to the astrologer Elias Ashmole[17] and may have had a brother, who at least was a close relation, named Joseph Blagrave who wrote almanacs and astrological/medical works, between 1658 and 1685.[18] The regicide's mathematician uncle, John Blagrave, published as his main work in 1585 a book called *A Mathematical Jewel*, and he was esteemed "the flower of Mathematicians of his age".[19]

Prominent Relations: Sir Ralph Verney, Bart., married Mary Blacknall, who was daughter of the regicide's first cousin Jane. Sir John Borlase, Bart., M.P., was the father of the regicide's Aunt Jane. Anthony, Sir Edward, and Henry Hungerford, - all M.P.s of the Long Parliament, were apparently the regicide's great-uncles, being sons of Sir Anthony Hungerford, whereas the regicide's mother was daughter of Sir Anthony Hungerford, apparently the same man (but certainly the same family in any case). Related to the regicide John Lisle (see under Lisle).

Pedigrees: Blagrave of Southcott (the regicide being pointedly omitted, since this was after the Restoration), p. 238, Vol. V, *The Genealogist*. Blagrave of Bulmarsh (family of regicide's uncle Anthony), p. 23 7, Vol. V, *The Genealogist*. Blagrave of Southcote and Sonning (including accurate parentage of the regicide), p. 21, Vol. II, *Berkshire and Its County Gentry 1625-49*, a Ph.D. thesis by Christopher Durston deposited in the Berkshire County Record Office.

JOHN BLAKISTON. Born in the Rectory at Sedgefield, Durham, and baptized at Sedgefield, August 21, 1603. Second son of the Rev. Marmaduke Blakiston, Prebend of Durham, etc. (a high-churchman), and Margaret James, thought to be a niece of Bishop James. The regicide's older brother, Toby, married Frances Briggs and died 1646; he resided until then at his father's seat of Newton Hall, Durham.

The regicide had no less than three younger brothers who were high-church vicars: Rev. Robert Blakiston, baptized January 7, 1606/7, who succeeded his father as both Rector of Sedgefield and Prebend of Durham (1631), and was married to Elizabeth, daughter of John Howson, Bishop of Durham; Rev. Thomas Blakiston (date of birth unknown, but older than Robert), Vicar of North Allerton, 1628, Prebendary of Wistow, ejected 1640s, married (wife unknown); Rev. Ralph Blakiston, M.A., baptized June 24, 1608, Rector of Ryton, County Durham, died unmarried, buried at Ryton, January 30, 1676/7. There were three other brothers: Henry, Peter, and George. The first two both married Mauleverer girls, but not of the regicide Mauleverer's particular branch of that family. The regicide also had three sisters: the eldest, Frances, married John Cosin, Bishop of Durham, on August 13, 1626 (she was baptized February 2, 1605/6); Mary Blakiston, baptized June 30, 1613, married a Durham merchant, Ralph Allenson, September 9, 1629; Margaret Blakiston (date of birth unknown), married November 28, 1631, Thomas Shadforth of Eppleton, Durham, and their daughter Elizabeth married Robert Hutton of Houghton-le-Spring (died 1681), who was a Captain of Horse under Robert Lilburne the regicide, and later under Sir Arthur Heselrige. This last-mentioned nephew was pretty well the only other supporter of Parliament in the entire Blakiston clan apart from the regicide, his wife, his brother George, and assorted cousins. But all of the regicide's large immediate family were to his view "prophane", idolators, and royalists, with the exception of his brother George, who was also a Puritan.

Prominent Relations: Apart from the clerical celebrities mentioned above, the regicide's first cousin, George Blakiston, was son-in-law to Sir John Bourchier, the regicide. Bourchier was doubly related by marriage, however, as he was also the father-in-law of a John Blakiston who seems to have been John Blakiston the regicide's own son of that name, who was born 1633, attended Cambridge and Gray's Inn, and died 1702. The latter identification is not certain but extremely probable, for lack of another contemporary of the name, and the fact that this Martha Bourchier married John of Newton. Two nephews amongst the Mauleverer Family although distantly related to the regicide, Sir Thomas Mauleverer, may have meant a feeling of kinship between the two regicides.

Pedigrees: A conflation of pedigrees of 1575, 1615, and 1666, is printed at p. 19 of J. Foster, *Durham Visitation Pedigrees*, followed by another such conflation of another branch of the family at p. 21. A brief collateral pedigree is at pp. 107-8 of Vol. I, *Complete Baronetage*. However, the origins of the family going back to 1341 are given in an elaborate pedigree in Surtees's *History of Durham*, III, 162ff., 402. And a mammoth pedigree commencing with the regicide's father is printed on pp. 54-64, and 172-179 of Vol. II of the *Maryland Historical Magazine*, in the article "Blakistone Family" by Christopher Johnston (1907), which carried the descent down to the time of publication, through the regicide's son, Nehemiah, who emigrated to America.

SIR JOHN BOURCHIER. Born circa 1592, son of William Bourchier (born 1559?) and Katharine, daughter of Sir Thomas Barrington, Bart., of Hatfield Broad Oak, Essex.

The Bourchiers were an extremely ancient and distinguished family. The regicide's direct ancestor Robert Lord Bourchier was Lord Chancellor in 1342.[20] A later ancestor was Thomas, Duke of Gloucester (died 1438). The famous translator of Froissart, John, Lord Berners, was the regicide's great-great-grandfather through an illegitimate son, James Bourchier (not a son of Catherine Howard); the regicide's grandfather, Sir Ralph Bourchier, was M.P. for Yorkshire from 1588 to 1592, and had been Sheriff of Yorkshire in 1581. Study of the law at Gray's Inn was a family tradition: the regicide's uncles Sir John, Ralph, William, and Verney, his father, and his brothers Robert and Thomas, as well as himself, all attended Gray's Inn. The regicide had brothers Robert (died unmarried, born circa 1590); Thomas, a supporter of Parliament born circa 1601, died November 11, 1658, married to Elizabeth Pickering of York; and sisters, Winifride, married the physician Dr. Lister of York (probably identical with Sir Matthew Lister, physician to Queen Anne and Charles I); Elizabeth, married to William Scudamore of Overton, Yorkshire; Anne, married to the above-mentioned William's brother, John Scudamore, at Belfreys, June 17, 1620.

Prominent Relations: Sir Thomas Mauleverer, Bart., the regicide, was Bourchier's first cousin. John Blakiston, the regicide, was Bourchier's son-in-law's first cousin and almost certainly his daughter's father-in-law as well. Oliver Cromwell and John Hampden were both third cousins of Bourchier. Sir Thomas Barrington, Bart., M.P., was Bourchier's great uncle, and his son, Sir John Barrington, Bart., Bourchier's uncle. Martin Lister, M..P., was probably the nephew of Bourchier's sister Winifred. Through the Barringtons, Bourchier was related also to the Wallops, Gerards, Lyttons, and Oliver St. John.

Special Note: Bourchier was one of three John Bourchlers who were knighted within ten years of one another. Firth, in the old DNB, possibly intimidated by such confusing possibilities, sidestepped the issue and mentioned nothing at all about his knighthood. A place of origin of only one of them is given, - the first of the three is described as being "of Co. York", and was knighted on either May 23 or June 2, 1609, at either Whitehall or Greenwich.[21] This man was the regicide's uncle, who was of Hanging Grunston or Grimston in Yorkshire; it can hardly have been the regicide himself, for he had only been admitted to Gray's Inn the same March. This uncle was still "Mr. John Boursher of Grimston" on May 15, 1609, at the marriage of his daughter; Norcliffe erred in believing him to have been knighted only in 1619,[22] whereas we have documentary evidence that he was already knighted by the time of the recording of a fine in 1617.[23] The second John Bourchier to be knighted was knighted at Dublin Castle by Sir Arthur Chichester, Lord Deputy of Ireland, on March 24, 1610/11.[24] The third was knighted at Theobalds on November 11, 1619.[25] The regicide was one or the other, and was most likely the third, since it would have been more appropriate for a knighthood to follow his being called to the bar the year before, on August 1, 1618, and he would still have been only 27 years old in 1619. It is difficult to imagine his being knighted at the age of only 19, if he were the second knight. The identity of the second knight remains a puzzle, and he must have been from quite a different family of Bourchiers altogether.

Pedigrees: The best, "Bourchier of Benningbrough", is found on pp. 305-8 of *Dugdale's Visitation of Yorkshire*. One which goes back to the 1300s is "Bourchier Earls of Eu" faving p. 401 in Vol. IX of the *Yorkshire Archaeological and Topographical Journal*, 1886. MS. pedigree with variations for the earlier generations is preserved in the MS. in York Minster Library, *Collection of ... Descents of ... Families* by John Hopkinson and Thomas Wilson.

JOHN BRADSHAW. Baptized December 10, 1602, at Stockport, Cheshire, third but oldest surviving son of Henry Bradshaw of Marple, Cheshire, and Catherine Winnington, daughter of Ralph Winnington of Offerton; they were married February 4, 1592/3, at Stockport. Bradshaw's elder brothers were dead, and he was the heir, at least by the age of 17, when he was admitted to Gray's Inn, May 26, 1620. The DNB errs in describing the regicide as second son; the first son, William, baptized January 2, 1596, died in infancy and was buried November 19, 1597. The second son, Henry, was baptized June 23, 1600. There is then confusion about his identity; he cannot have been the Colonel Henry Bradshaw mentioned in a prominent pedigree who died March 15, 1661.[26] Further research is necessary locally in Cheshire, but we may perhaps assume that this Henry died an infant and that a younger brother of the regicide was then born who was named Henry once again, as happened in several families at this period. However, this matter remains an open question, and remains to be settled in the future. "W.L.", writing for the Chetham Society in 1855, correctly noted that the regicide was a third rather than a second son.[27] Unknown to the old DNB, to the *Biographical Dictionary of English Radicals of the Seventeenth Century*, and apparently to all authorities, is the existence of a collection of personal papers concerning Bradshaw, going back to a letter from a cousin in 1639.[28] The Bradshaws traced their descent back to a Saxon family seated at Bradshaw-juxta-Bolton-le-Moors, several generations before the Norman Conquest, "and continued there in uninterrupted male succession for twenty-five generations, being connected in marriage with most of the families of distinction in the county".[29] The regicide had a younger brother Francis, called Frank, baptized January 13, 1603, and sisters Dorothy, baptized August 11, 1598, married George Newton, still alive in 1659 with several children and Anne, baptized November 9, 1599, who died March 22, 1669/70.

Prominent Relations: The regicide's first cousin was John Milton, whose mother was Sarah Bradshaw, the regicide's aunt. Major-General John Lambert was apparently a cousin of Bradshaw, according to a casual remark made in a 1659 pamphlet.[30] This must have been a distant relationship which only took on some importance when Lambert and Bradshaw found themselves rising to national importance and coming into political contact; attempts to trace the relationship have not so far met with success, but a deep study of Lambert's family has not been attempted in this connection.

Pedigrees: "Pedigree of Bradshaw-Isherwood, of Marple Hall", unpaginated, in Vol. I, *Lancashire*, of Joseph Foster's *Pedigrees of the County Families of England* (1873). See also in the Rylands Library at Manchester, Rylands English MS. 745, "Memoirs of the Family of Bradshaw of Marple in Cheshire", by Holland Watson.

JOHN CAREW. Born July 3, 1622, at Antony, Cornwall. Baptized July 7. Was son of Sir Richard Carew, Bart., of Antony House, East Antony, Cornwall, and his second wife, Grace, daughter of Robert Rolle of Heanton; they were married at Pentrockstowe, August 18, 1617. The regicide's father has his own entry in the old DNB; he was created baronet August 9, 1641, and died about 1643. Sir Richard was first married to Bridget, daughter of John Chudleigh, of Ashton, Devonshire, by whom he had four daughters, Elizabeth, Martha, Mary, and Gertrude, and his eldest son, Sir Alexander Carew, 2nd Bart., and M.P. for Cornwall from 1640 until he was disabled to sit September 4, 1643, "for adhering to the king and betraying his trust".[31] Keeler unaccountably says that Alexander was the "only surviving son" of Sir Richard, whereas there were two others including the regicide; Keeler also seems to have been unaware that Alexander inherited his baronetcy from his father and says he was himself created baronet in 1641, which was actually his father.[32] Alexander married Jane

Antony House in Cornwall, built in the early 18th century on the site of the original childhood home of John Carew the regicide.

Richard Carew, grandfather of the regicide John Carew.

Rolle, daughter of Robert Rolle of Heanton, who was either his step-mother's sister or her niece. Alexander was executed on Tower Hill December 23, 1644; his widow died April 25, 1679, aged 74. The regicide had a full brother who was younger, born 1624, Thomas Carew, later knighted July 21, 1671, of Barley, Devon, married Elizabeth, daughter of John Cooper of Bowell, Devon; he was later an M.P. for Exeter under Charles II.[33] The regicide was not popular with the descendants of his family and was omitted from some pedigrees, and was looked upon as a disgraceful person. His excellent surviving miniature portrait by Samuel Cooper, in the possession of Sir John Carew Pole, Bart., of Antony House, which I saw when I visited him, is mistakenly labelled "Sir John Carew", the spurious knighthood possibly having been intended at one time by some member of the family to lend an air of respectability to him, or even to disguise his identity as a regicide. I am indebted to P.L.Hull, the County Archivist for Cornwall, for obtaining details of the regicide's birth, by a special visit to Antony House, where the only surviving source giving the facts is a manuscript kept pedigree there, for which see below. (The parish records prior to 1678 had been lost or destroyed.) The Carews were a distinguished and ancient family. The regicide's great-great-great grandfather John Carew had been a Sheriff of Cornwall; his great-great grandfather had been Treasurer to Queen Catherine in the time of Henry VIII and was knighted at the accession of Edward VI; his great-grandfather was M.P. for Saltash; and his grandfather, Richard Carew, was a famous antiquary who was also Sheriff of Cornwall, Surveyor of Cornwall, and M.P. for Saltash, being an "ingenious man, learned, eloquent, liberal, stout, honest, and well skilled in several languages".[34]

Prominent Relations: The regicide was first cousin once removed to Richard Erisey, M.P. (1590-1668), who had been raised as a ward at Antony House. John Rolle, M.P. (1598-1657) and Sir Samuel Rolle, M.P. (1588-1647) were both uncles of the regicide through his mother as well as brothers-in-law of the regicide's half-brother Alexander. Sir Thomas Hele or Heale, Bart., M.P., was first cousin of the Rolle brothers, according to Keeler.[35]

Pedigrees: MS. pedigree preserved at Antony House in Cornwall, property of Sir John Carew Pole, Bart., in a manuscript book entitled "Carew and Other Records Collected by the Revd. Gerald Pole Carew" (19th century). "Carew, of Anthony", pp. 99-101 in John Bernard Burke, *Extinct and Dormant Baronetcies of England*, 2nd edition (1844).

WILLIAM CAWLEY. Baptized November 3, 1602, at St. Andrew's Oxmarket, Chichester, West Sussex. Only son of John Cawley of Rumbleswick, Chichester, and his second wife Mary Michell (married June 1, 1599, at Chichester), of Bridgwick. The regicide apparently had seven half-sisters: Marie, Alice, Anne, Elizabeth, who died a child, Susane, Jane, and Elizabeth (born 1591) the youngest, given the name of her dead sister. At least four of them married, etc. These sisters were by the first wife, who was apparently called Marie and died at Easter, 1599. The father apparently married a third time to a Catherine …….. John Cawley was a wealthy brewer who was Mayor of Chichester three times, in 1590, 1601, and 1613, owner of much property in his area of Sussex, and was buried at St. Andrew's Oxmarket in Chichester May 3, 1621, a memorial with a fine portrait bust still surviving (having been rescued from demolition, and myself having tracked down the missing surmounting coat of arms in the possession of a local architect, etc.) An excellent oil portrait of Cawley as a young man survives at Chichester, in the alms house which he endowed.

Prominent Relations: No nationally prominent or even regionally prominent relations that we know of. The regicide's younger son, Rev. John Cawley became Archdeacon of Lincoln, March 2, 1666/7. The regicide's older son, William Cawley of the Inner Temple, became a prominent legal author twenty years after the Restoration, when he published *The Laws of Q. Elizabeth, K. James, and K. Charles the First concerning Jesuites, Seminary Preists, Recusants, &c. and concerning the Oaths of Supremacy and Allegiance Explained*, London, 1680; it is a small folio of 267 pages plus extensive Table, of which I own a copy.

Pedigrees: A pedigree appears in Berry's *Pedigrees of Sussex*, but a copy of this printed pedigree heavily annotated has much further information, and was made available along with a sketched MS. pedigree of her own by Mrs. Valerie Cawley, the leading Cawley family historian, of St. Andrews, Scotland. Much of the information given above comes from this source, some of it with references to definite sources and some of it not. I am extremely grateful to Mrs. Cawley for her help.

THOMAS CHALONER. Born 1595 at Steeple Claydon, Buckinghamshire, third son of Sir Thomas Chaloner the younger of Steeple Claydon and Guisborough, Yorkshire, and his first wife Elizabeth, daughter of William Fleetwood of Great Missenden, Buckinghamshire, Serjeant-at-Law and Recorder of London. The father died November 17,1615, is buried in Chiswick Church with effigy tomb; the mother died November 22, 1603. The regicide's eldest brother William was created a baronet July 20, 1620, and died unmarried at Scandaroon [modern Iskenderun, a major port in southernmost modern Turkey near the Syrian border and Aleppo; it was the main port under the Ottomans for trade with Baghdad and India] in Turkey in 1641. The second brother was the Rev. Edward Chaloner, D.D., Chaplain to Charles I while Prince of Wales, and Principal of St. Alban's Hall, who died of the plague at Oxford, aged only 34, in 1625; I have a book of his published sermons. After 1641, the regicide was thus the eldest male of the large family. His younger full brother was James Chaloner, also an M.P. in the Long Parliament and named to the High Court of Justice, where he sat but did not sign the Death Warrant. James was a scholar who wrote a history of the Isle of Man, etc. James married Ursula, daughter of Sir Philip Fairfax and sister of Sir William Fairfax. There were three full sisters: Mary, Elizabeth, and Dorothy, all married, etc. The regicide's father married a second wife at St. Peter-le-Poer, London, on July 10, 1604. She was Judith, daughter of Sir William Blount of London and widow of John Gregory of Hull. By this marriage there were four sons: Henry, Charles, Frederick, and Arthur, and three daughters: Anne, Katherine, and Frances, who married Sir William Fairfax of Steeton. She had been baptized February 12, 1610/11 at St. James's, Clerkenwell, London, and was buried at Bolton Percy, January 6, 1692. The wife of the regicide was a Sotheby, almost certainly Anne Sotheby, born 1626 or 1627, daughter of Robert Sotheby (b.c. 1580) of Pocklington, Yorkshire, and Jane Constable (b. April 29, 1589, daughter of Sir Philip Constable, of Everingham, Yorkshire, 1547-1619). One of her brothers died of a drinking bout in York in 1646, as related in a letter to the regicide of May 24. (Henry Cary, *Memorials of the Great Civil War in England*, 2 vols., London, 1842; Vol. I, pp. 64-66: 'Robin Gardner ... did give your wife's brother, Mr. Sothabie, so great a quantity of sack at Mrs. Corney's, that he did instantly die in the room, and we buried him the next day.') The regicide's much younger wife was from a side branch of the ancient Constable family from that of Sir William Constable the regicide; the Constables of Everingham in the East Riding of Yorkshire were royalists and Roman Catholics, which must have made for a great deal of tension and hostility between the regicide and his in-laws. No information is known about these aspects of Chaloner's private life, there is no record of any children of his marriage, and pedigrees show him as without issue.

The Chaloners were an ancient Welsh family from Denbighshire. The regicide's grandfather, Sir Thomas Chaloner the elder (1521-1565), was an M.P., ambassador, author, translator of Erasmus and friend of leading scholars such as Sir John Cheke, etc. and his only son, the regicide's father, Sir Thomas Chaloner the younger, was also an author and a naturalist and mineralologist, a favourite of James I, manager of Queen Anne's estates, governor of Prince Henry from 1603, etc. It should be noted that the regicide usually signed his name Chaloner, rather than Challoner, and the family is generally known by the more common spelling, but he is treated as Chaloner for the purposes of our discussion.

Prominent Relations: Richard Ingoldsby the regicide was Chaloner's nephew's brother-in-law. Sir William Fairfax was married to his half-sister Frances. Both General Charles Fleetwood and Colonel George Fleetwood the regicide were Chaloner's third cousins.

Pedigrees: The best is from "Dugdale's Visitation of Yorkshire", pp. 118-124, *The Genealogist*, New Series, Vol. XIX (1903). MS. pedigree in York Minster Library in MS. book Collections of ... Descents of ... Families by John Hopkinson and Thomas Wilson. Pedigree of "Chaloner, of Guisborough" in Burke's *Extinct and Dormant Baronetcies*, 2nd edition (1844), p. 105. Pedigree of "Chaloner of Claydon" p. 80 of George Lipscomb, *History and Antiquities of the County of Buckingham*, Vol. III (1847). Pedigree of "the Chaloners of Gisborough", p. 221 of John Walker Ord's *History and Antiquities of Cleveland* (1846).

GREGORY CLEMENT. Baptized Nov. 21,1594 at St. Andrew's, Plymouth, son of John Clement and Judith, daughter of John Sparke of Upper Plymouth.[36] His great-grandfather may have been Sir Richard Clement, of the Mote, Ightham, Kent, whose two wives (one being Lady Anne Grey, widow of Lord John Grey, brother of the Marquess of Dorset) seem to have borne him no issue; he did, however, have illegitimate issue (one daughter married Thomas Lovelace of Hever[37]). This Sir Richard was Sheriff of Kent in 15312. Otherwise, the regicide may be descended from Sir Richard's brother John Clement.[38] Continuing friendships at Ightham may have led to the regicide's son James (it has also been suggested it was the youngest son Gregory) marrying Frances Sedley of that village, daughter of Sir John Sedley, Bart., who was High Sheriff of Kent in 1621.[39] The regicide probably had uncles and brothers who included the following men: Nicholas Clement, of Plymouth, married to Jane, died 1657; Robert Clement, married November 25, 1616, to Elizabeth Driver, widow, at St. Dunstan's. Stepney, Middlesex, ship owner and merchant of Wapping Wall, manufacturer of ship equipment, church-warden of St. Dunstan's and buried there, September 25, 1645;[40] Edward Clement, ship's captain alive 1637/8.[41] Also, definitely related to the regicide and probably a brother was George Clement,[42] alive 1641 and possibly the George Clement, married to Mary, who died 1657, of Tiverton, Devon.[43] One brother of the regicide's who is firmly established as such was the high-churchman, the Rev. Robert Clement, B.A., instituted by Lord Pawlett as Rector of Seavington St. Michael with the Chapel of Dinington, Somerset, on May 17, 1632, but ejected by Parliament in 1652 (the same year the regicide was expelled from Parliament, thereby doubtless losing the power to protect his brother).[44] The Rev. Robert was a Laudian to such an extent that he introduced fringed altar and pulpit cloths.[45]

Prominent Relations: The Rashleighs of Cornwall, by marriage through a cousin named John Sparke (see regicide's letters to Jonathan Rashleigh about a seat in Parliament, transcribed by me and included in the Appendix to the Chapter on 'The Regicides as Recruiters'). Another close relation was the noted clockmaker William Clement (1638-1704).

Pedigrees: Truncated pedigree of one generation in *Visitation of Kent, 1530-1*, p. 6, Harleian Society, Vol. 74. MS. pedigree at f. 65a of MS. Rawlins on B. 74 in the Bodleian Library, giving several generations of Clements who may or may not be related to the regicide.

JOHN COOK/COOKE. Born 1608. at Husbands Bosworth, Leicestershire. Eldest son and heir of Isaac Cook alias Brodfield or Bromfield, of Husbands Bosworth, Burbage, and Lutterworth, Leicestershire, and Elizabeth, daughter of John Twigden of Husbands Bosworth. The double surname of Cook alias Brodfield goes back at least three generations before the regicide (who as far as is known never used the double name, only using 'Cook'); an aunt of the regicide's married an Anthony Bromfield of Eaton, Warks., but this is presumably not connected to the surname Brodfield. The regicide was apparently the great-great-grandson of a Sir Thomas Hardwick,[46] although a knight of that name is not listed in William A. Shaw's *The Knights of England* (1906), so that this information is apparently faulty or taken from an incorrectly deciphered or corrupted text. The regicide had brothers: James Cooke (born 1610, admitted to Gray's Inn, August 3,, 1629, the same day as Sir Gregory Norton, the regicide; William Cook (born 1613; and sisters: Elizabeth Cook (born 1614) and Susanna Cook (born 1618).

Prominent Relations: Apparently Cook was "a near relative" of Thomas Harrison the regicide, though the precise relationship has not yet been ascertained.[47] It may not be correct.

Pedigrees: A pedigree showing five generations of the regicide's family appears in the *Visitation of the County of Leicester, 1619*, p. 108.

SIR WILLIAM CONSTABLE, BART. (Knighted by the Earl of Essex in Ireland, July 12, 1599; Created a baronet June 29, 1611.) Born circa 1575. Eldest son of Sir Robert Constable of Flamborough on the Yorkshire Coast and of Holme Manor, Spalding Moor, Yorkshire, and of Anne, daughter and heiress of John Hussey of Driffield. The old DNB does not give the mother's name; Noble[48] and Rynder in the *Biographical Dictionary of English Radicals of the Seventeenth Century*[49] err in believing the regicide's grandmother Dorothy Widdrington to have been his mother, whereas she was really his grandmother. *The Complete Baronetage* makes clear that the regicide's father and grandfather had the same name (Robert) and were thus confused.[49] Burke's *Extinct and Dormant Baronetcies* thus omits an entire generation.[49A] The Constables were an extremely ancient and distinguished family. The surname of Constable was assumed from the family's then position of Constable of Chester, held since about the time of the Norman Conquest; apparently for a long time a family sinecure. The family's descent in fact is said to come directly from Ivo Viscount Constantine of Normandy and his wife, Emma, sister to Adam, Earl of Britain. Another ancestress was Beatrix, only daughter and heiress of Ivo Lord Vescy. While still based at Chester, the title of Baron Halton or Haillton was conferred on the family, one ancestor of the title dying on a crusade at Tyre in 1189 under Richard I. The family estate at Flamborough seems to have been acquired circa 1200, and many Constables were knights, sheriffs of Yorkshire, and M.P.s in succeeding generations. The junior branch, represented by the baronetcy of Constable of Everingham, became extinct in the male line in July, 1746.[50] The senior branch of the family was represented by the regicide. Many of the regicide's forbears had gone in for military adventuring, so this seems to have been very much a family tradition, continued over several centuries. Sir Robert Constable of Flamborough, the regicide's great-great grandfather was knighted in the field by Henry VII for valorous conduct; his son, the regicide's great-grandfather Sir Marmaduke Constable, was knighted in the field by Henry VIII for valorous conduct and made a knight banneret by Edward VI; Sir Robert Constable the regicide's grandfather was knighted in the field by the Earl of Sussex for valorous conduct on May 11, 1570.[51] It would appear that the regicide's father Robert Constable was knighted by the Earl of Essex in Ireland ten days after the regicide himself, unless this was a brother of whom nothing else is known, in which case we are at a loss to find a recording of the knighthood of the regicide's father.[52] But it should be obvious that a Constable was not considered a Constable until he displayed his valour on the battlefield, which goes far to explain the regicide's constant involvement throughout most of his life in whatever military adventures were available, and his being wounded at the siege of Rouen in 1591 when he was only about sixteen.[53] After his involvement in the Essex Rebellion (discussed in a later place), Constable was lucky to have his life spared; his knighthood conferred by the Earl of Essex seems to have been declared void (though no record of this is known), since he was "Esq." when he received his baronetcy in 1611.[54] Or he may just have declined to use a title conferred on him by a disgraced person, and pretended it had never happened. But it goes some way to explain why he was keen to get a baronetcy in the first year of their creation, so that he could be "Sir" again; he must have looked upon it as a rehabilitation of his status in society, and an outward sign that he had finally recovered from his disgrace. It is not difficult to imagine the fury he must have felt in June, 1630, when by one of the financial exactions of Charles I, he was actually forced to compound and pay a fine for knighthood along with Thomas Mauleverer the regicide and others even though he was already a baronet, and in Constable's case he had been a knight already for thirty-one years![55] In Yorkshire property fines of 1616, and 1621/2, he was described as "Knight and Baronet".[56] The fact that he was officially recorded as a knight as well as a baronet in 1616 is extremely important for resolving a controversy which has arisen since the publication of the *Oxford Dictionary of National Biography*, in which David Scott, author of Constable's entry, expressed his belief that the regicide was not the same man as the William Constable knighted by the Earl of Essex in 1599. According to Scott's theory, the regicide could not have been a knight as well as a baronet, as there is no record of any other Sir William Constable having been made a Knight at that period. Scott believes that there was an older William Constable, and that the two men were different. Scott thought Constable was born and baptized in 1590. Numerous authorities have long claimed he was born circa 1580 (see below for an example). However, having been wounded at Rouen, as mentioned above, I do not believe he could have been born later than 1575. We have no knowledge of any brothers or sisters of this regicide. A William Constable was baptised 25 August 1574 at St. Peter's Church, Limpsfield, Surrey, which is a few miles south of Croydon. No parents were listed in the baptismal entry. If the Constables had been staying there at the time of the birth, they would have been at the old manor house of Limpsfield called Fenchleys (now called Tinsley Park) with a gentry family named Holmeden. The date and the name match but without the parents' names being given, this is only a possibility. Too little is known of the Holmedens, except that they were socially prominent, and Robert Constable's friendships from his military service under the Earl of Sussex and others could have included anybody. Other researchers, more familiar with the Holmeden family history, might be able to throw more light on this matter. But why would a William Constable be born in the tiny village of Limpsfield, which had no known association with any Constables?

Prominent Relations: Thomas, First Lord Fairfax was his father-in-law, and had, like Constable himself, been knighted by the Earl of Essex. Ferdinando, Second Lord Fairfax was thus the regicide's brother-in-law, and Sir Thomas, later the Third Lord Fairfax, was the regicide's nephew. The regicide was doubly related to Sir Thomas Widdrington (1600-1664), M.P. Widdrington was son-in-law to the regicide's brother-in-law Ferdinando, Lord Fairfax, but also related to the regicide by blood through his grandmother Dorothy Widdrington. The royalist M.P., Sir William Widdrington (1610-1651) was a distant relation of the former Widdrington according to Keeler; I do not know which branch of Widdringtons was more closely related to Constable.[57] Sir William Carnaby, M.P. (1593-1645) was related to both Widdringtons.[58]

Pedigrees: *Complete Baronetage*, Vol. I, p. 44, is the entry for the regicide himself with what is probably the most accurate information, describing him as having been born 'about 1580'. Burke's *Extinct and Dormant Baronetcies*, pp. 126-7, is probably less accurate. An MS. pedigree in the Bodleian is MS. Rawlinson B. 74, ff. 94b and 95a.

MILES CORBET. Born 1595.[59] Second son of Sir Thomas Corbet of Sprowston, Norfolk, High Sheriff of Norfolk in 1622; and Anne, daughter of Edward Barrett, of Belhus Hall (a spectacular painting of which dated 1710 survives at Thurrock), of Aveley, Essex. Anna was heiress of her mother Elizabeth daughter and coheir of Sir Robert Lytton, of Hertfordshire, who had been knighted by King Edward VI on the day of his coronation (February 20, 1546/7).[60] The regicide's childhood home of Sprowston Hall near Norwich was built in 1559 and has long been demolished; I have located what appears to be the only existing photo of the house (taken in the 1880s), showing an enormous mansion, and this photo was intended to be reproduced for the first time, together with a portrait of Corbet, in *Norfolk Archaeology*, 1989, along with my article "The Last Days of Miles Corbet", however this article was never completed and was set aside unfinished owing to circumstances. The regicide's grandfather, Sir Miles Corbet, was among those knighted by the Lord Admiral at Cadiz in Spain, June 22, 1596.[61] This Corbet was married to the daughter of Sir Christopher Heydon of Norfolk; it should be noted that a Christopher Heydon was knighted at Cadiz on the same day as Corbet,[62] and the two men were evidently comrades-in-arms. It is not known whether this could have been Corbet's father-in-law, or was perhaps his brother-in-law (since another Christopher Heydon was knighted circa 1549, which could have been the father-in-law). The regicide's family was extremely ancient. His great-great-great grandfather is described in a mid-17th century pedigree as follows: "John Corbet, of Brockdish in the County of Norfk Esquire was

Sprowston Hall near Norwich, Miles Corbet's childhood home.
It was demolished long ago, and this photo is thought to be from the late 19th century.

a third Brother of the House of Morton Corbet Castell in the County of Salop and came from thence in the Reigne of ...... and bare with a Mallet in the first as a note of difference these Coates (shown). He maried ...... He lieth buried at Brockdish & hath a marble Monument."[63] The family of which the regicide's Norfolk branch were thus an offshoot were prominent followers of William the Conqueror, mentioned as "famous at the time of the Conquest" by Camden, the founder of the English family being apparently named Corbeau ("a noble Norman"), whose grand-daughter Sybil Corbet was wife of Henry Herbert, the Chamberlain to King Henry I. Later Corbets were summoned as barons by King Edward I and lived at Caus Castle. The direct ancestors of the regicide became seated at Moreton Corbet in Shropshire at the beginning of the thirteenth century.[64] The regicide's elder brother, Sir John Corbet, Bart., died in 1628, leaving the regicide as eldest male of his generation. This Sir John was son-in-law of Sir Arthur Capell, later Lord Capell, the royalist leader. It must be stressed that Sir John Corbet was strenuously opposed to the arbitrary exactions of Charles I's reign and died as a result of his opposition in the following way, recorded in the 17th century pedigree mentioned earlier, but with gaps, due to holes in the MS.: "He was committed to prison & lay in the Gatehowse in Westminster almost for the space of a yeare for refusing th .... Subsidies demanded in the Reigne of King CHARLES .... with others, with others (after they were remanded to prison by the Judges of the Kings Bench having brought their Habeas Corpus were gratiously sett at liberty .... Sir John Died about ..... dayes after at Westminster being .... & lieth buried in ye Chancell of St Margarets Chu: in Westm on y^e ...." From this note of Sir John's death, although the details are partially missing due to deterioration of the document, it is obvious that his health must have been so drastically impaired by the harsh imprisonment, that he died as a result of it.[65] The regicide thus had a very strong basis for personal hatred of Charles I, whom he would rightly have considered responsible for his brother's death. The regicide would have been a personal witness of the episode, since he himself records that he became an M.P. for the first time in 1626 (his brother was also an M.P.), and was thus from that time an observer of events at London.[66] The regicide had an elder sister Elizabeth, who died s.p., and his many other siblings were: Rev. Edward, married three times to 1. Thorneton, 2. Colthorp, and 3. Russell; Thomas, died a child; William, married Doughty; Rev. Thomas who on April 4, 1643, married only daughter of Colonel Laurence Bromfield of Tower Street, London (a prominent City militia figure some documents relating to this brother of the regicide, including his little book of births, marriages, and deaths, are to be found as part of MC 46 at the Norfolk Record Office in Norwich); Katherine, married Sir John Mead (presumably the one of Lofts, Essex, knighted March 2, 1622/3[67]); Amy, married Robert Brewster; Anne, married Foxon; Jane, unmarried; Ellen, married Herrick; ...ely, married Thomas Sotherton; Mary, died young; Dorothy, married Slany; Bridget, died s.p. Two of the regicide's brothers were thus churchmen.

Prominent Relations: Lord Capell, the royalist, was his brother's father-in-law. The grandson of this brother, Sir Thomas Corbet, Bart. (succeeded 1649) was a zealous royalist who was sequestered and sold the family mansion at Sprowston.[68] Sir John Corbet, Bart., M.P. of the Long Parliament (1594-1662) was a distant cousin (it is remarkable that their dates coincide exactly except that Sir John was born one year earlier). This distant Corbet M.P. cousin was an opponent of ship money and Laudianism, and later became a Presbyterian elder.[69] Sir John Corbet's first cousin was Sir Richard Lee, Bart., M.P., a royalist who was disabled in September, 1642.[70] A somewhat less distant cousin of the regicide was Sir William Lytton, M.P. for Hertfordshire in the Long Parliament, whose mother was a St. John, and who was related to the Lukes, Fleetwoods, Wallops, and whose second wife was sister of Sir Thomas Barrington, Bart., M.P. Through this cousin, therefore, the regicide was connected with a large network of M.P.s and prominent leading families. Although no evidence has yet been discovered indicating the extent of the ties between Lytton and Corbet in Parliament, an important clue indicating possible close relations may be found in the fact that Lytton's first wife was a Slaney,[71] and Corbet's sister Dorothy was married to a Slaney. Close connections between Corbet and Lytton early in the Long Parliament may perhaps safely be presumed. Lytton worked closely with Hampden, and was only secluded in 1648. Lytton's joint mission with Capell in 1640 also indicates another connection with the Corbets, as Capell was connected as abovementioned.[72] Capell was also related to Sir Thomas Barrington, Lytton's brother-in-law.[73] The regicide had business relations with Colonel Laurence Bromfield through his brother the Rev.Thomas Corbet in regard to lands in Ireland in 1646,[74] and within months, in 1647, Bromfield and Corbet were on opposite sides, with Bromfield being a leader of the Presbyterian counter revolution in the City and arrested.[75] Corbet accused him of high treason and acted personally to assure that he was secured, which cannot have improved family relations![76]

Pedigrees: Mid-seventeenth century MS. pedigree is MS 15577/43b in the Norfolk Record Office at Norwich. See also *Complete Baronetage*, Vol. I, pp. 219-20. Also, Burke's *Extinct and Dormant Baronetcies* (1844), pp. 132-4.

SIR JOHN DANVERS. (Knighted March 3 or 5, 1608/9, at Whitehall.[77]) Born 1585 (which we know because he was 16 in July, 1601, when he was admitted at Oxford), which is a correction to the old DNB. He was third and youngest son of Sir John Danvers of Dauntsey, Wiltshire, a Sheriff of Wiltshire in 1588 who had been knighted in 1574,[78] and Elizabeth Neville, fourth daughter and coheiress of John Neville, the last Lord Latimer. The regicide's descent from his mother was particularly illustrious. His grandfather the third Lord Latimer had been the second husband of Catherine Parr, later sixth wife of King Henry VIII. He had been implicated in the Pilgrimage of Grace in 1536. (See old DNB.) The father of this Latimer, the second Baron, was Lieutenant-General and Commissioner of the North (see old DNB.) We shall here neglect a further tracing back of the Neville pedigree, for reasons of space. As for the Danvers family, its extensive history is traced at great length in the book *Memorials of the Danvers Family of Dauntsey and Culworth* by F.N. Macnamara (London, 1895), which takes the family down from the time of the Conquest, and it would be repetitive to do so again here. No less than three of the Danvers clan were knighted on the same day, November 14, 1501, at the marriage of Prince Arthur (Henry VIII 's older brother): John of Dauntsey, Thomas, and William, who was Justice of the Common Pleas.[79] The regicide's two older brothers have their own separate notices in the old DNB, which see. The elder was Sir Charles Danvers, who was one of the leaders of the Essex Rebellion; he was entrusted with seizing the presence-chamber and the halberds of the guard at Whitehall, and. was beheaded on Tower Hill for his role in the Rebellion. He would have been a friend and colleague of the younger man, Sir William Constable, the regicide who was a minor actor in the Rebellion, who would later join Sir Charles's younger brother (ten years younger than Constable himself) in signing a later monarch's Death Warrant. Sir John Danvers the regicide may thus be viewed as continuing a tradition established by his older brother in opposing the monarch of the day. The other brother of the regicide, Henry Danvers, was also close to Essex and Southampton, but was in Ireland at the time of the Rebellion and escaped involvement; James I created him Baron Danvers of Daunstey in 1603, and Charles I created him Earl of Danby in 1626, becoming a member of the Privy Council in 1628, with many further honours and positions of trust. He seems to have been a royalist, but was of ill health and died early in the Civil War unmarried (see DNB). Both the regicide's brothers thus left no issue. The regicide had several sisters, and the quarrels between him and his sister Katherine, who married Sir Richard Gargrave of

Nostel, were so notorious (she being a fanatical royalist) that they clogged up the machinery of Parliament and its committees probably, more than any other single personal issue of the entire era. This situation can only be described as utterly outrageous by any standards. An attempt made by the author to trace the history of the dispute has led to the discovery of such a vast quantity of documentary material that it would make a book by itself. The ostensible basis of the quarrels were money and property, but the passions were personal and highly political, sucking in countless M.P.s and notable persons as participants. The subject simply defies summary and is thus reluctantly set to one side. The author may one day try to write an account of the scandal, for that is what it was - a national scandal, the most extreme instance of its kind, proving that public machinery could be paralyzed by intractable personal matters, for dealing with which no adequate means existed. The point is that the primacy of public business was without sufficient safeguards, due to major flaws in the governmental structure and the lack of a civil service. The temptation must be resisted to conclude that Danvers was obstructing public business for his personal gain. In my opinion, after surveying so much of the primary material of the case, Worden is not justified in his severe criticisms of Danvers over the dispute with Lady Gargrave, where he says of Danvers that his "behaviour does leave a decidedly unpleasant taste in the mouth" and whom he accuses of "ruthless pursuit of his private interests in the House".[80] What Worden describes as "insatiable requests"[81] are seen, upon closer inspection, to be largely the result of the total inadequacy of the governmental system of the time to be able to cope with the case and its ramifications. This may tie up with Danvers's extraordinarily keen preoccupation with law reform, discussed in the chapter on "Regicides and the Law". It simply remains here to say that Lady Gargrave was, if anything, more "insatiable" in her requests than her brother was in his, - a point not to be overlooked by anyone attempting to draw any conclusions about character. Sir John's other sisters were: Anne (died 1632, an oil portrait of her survives), married Sir Arthur Porter of Llantony; Lucy, married Sir Henry Boynton of Bromham; Eleanor, married Sir Thomas Walmesley (died 1642) of Dunkenhalgh; Elizabeth, married Sir Edward Hoby of Bisham; Mary, died an infant; and Dorothy, married Sir Peter Osborn of Chicksands Priory in Bedfordshire, being the parents of the noted Dorothy Osborn (often spelled Osborne) who wrote the famous Letters to her future husband, Sir William Temple, Bart., the author and diplomat.

Prominent Relations: An anomalous situation existed regarding the M.P. of the Long Parliament, Peregrine Hoby of Bisham. This M.P. was the illegitimate son of Danvers's brother-in-law.[82] Whether Danvers nevertheless treated him as his nephew is not known. Hoby was a moderate Parliament supporter, secluded at Pride's Purge. Danvers was distantly related to a wide range of M.P.s, including the Hungerfords, the Fiennes (and of course Lord Saye and Sele), probably John Fettiplace, a supporter of Pym who later became an active royalist,[83] with whom the relationship may have been double, and by extension to the network of relations of these men. Sir Edward Boynton or Bayntun, M.P. for Chippenham in the Long Parliament, named to the High Court of Justice but who did not sit, was the nephew of Danvers. This man's son, Edward, M.P. for Devizes in the Long Parliament, was thus Danvers's great-nephew. Through his brother-in-law Sir Arthur Porter, Danvers was closely related to Endymion Porter, the royalist M.P. Danvers's mother married as a second husband, Sir Edmund Carey, a first cousin of Queen Elizabeth I. This resulted in further relations, but only through a step-father, and not by blood. It is a considerable irony that Sir John Danvers was a step-cousin of King Charles I, who felt his wrath, only through a marriage contracted by his mother for the express purpose of protecting the regicide's brothers from the wrath of a previous monarch.[84] This information is preserved by the regicide's cousin and close friend, the royalist scholar John Aubrey, author of *Brief Lives*. Lady Carlisle, the great friend of Pym, was Danvers's first cousin. Through his second wife, Danvers was brother-in-law of Sir Hugh Stukeley, Bart., a close relation of the Luttrells of Dunster Castle in Somerset. Danvers's first marriage, to a woman "old enough to be his mother" as Aubrey bluntly puts it[85] resulted in Danvers becoming the step-father of a man older than himself: This was Lord Edward Herbert of Cherbury, of Montgomery Castle. A younger step-son of Danvers was George Herbert, the poet and divine, who, however, was only seven or eight years younger than Danvers himself, and died in 1633. Although Lord Herbert of Cherbury was a royalist early in the Civil War, it may safely be presumed that it was largely Danvers who talked him round to making his peace with the Parliament in 1644. Another of Danvers's step-sons was the M.P. of the Long Parliament for Bewdley, Worcestershire, Sir Henry Herbert, who was disabled to sit for royalism in 1642.[86] The son of Lord Herbert of Cherbury, and Danvers's stepgrandson, was another M.P. disabled for royalism in 1642, Richard Herbert, M.P. for Montgomery borough.[87] Another M.P. of the Long Parliament, Edward Herbert, M.P. for Old Sarum, was first cousin of Danvers's step-sons, a royalist and friend of Laud.[88] Finally, three other M.P.s: William Herbert, another William Herbert, and Philip Lord Herbert, were all somehow related to Danver's step-children, not to mention assorted other Herberts including several noteable peers like the Pembrokes; but an examination of the Herbert family tree has not been undertaken for want of space. Danvers's first wife was sister of the royalist M.P. Francis Newport and daughter of the royalist Sir Richard Newport who was a member of the Council of Wales.[89] The regicide's daughter Anne married first Sir Henry Lee, 3rd Bart., of Ditchley, Oxon., and Quarendon, Berks., and secondly, Henry Wilmot, first Earl of Rochester, the royalist general, conspirator, and companion in exile of Charles II. The regicide's daughter Elizabeth married the truly extraordinary Robert Wright, alias Danvers, alias Villiers, alias Viscount Purbeck (see DNB entry for him under Danvers), whose amazing and tragic life would make a book of itself.

Pedigrees: The pedigree of the branch of Danvers of Culworth may be consulted in Burke's *Extinct and Dormant Baronetcies*, where it is pointed out that the family are descended from Roland d'Anvers, one of the companions in arms of William the Conqueror. Assorted and related pedigrees are to be found in the book by Macnamara on the Danvers family mentioned earlier, together with lengthy textual comments.

RICHARD DEANE. Baptized July 8, 1610, at Guiting Power Church, Lower Guiting, Gloucestershire. Son of Edward Deane of Pinnock (within walking distance of Guiting Power), near Winchcombe, Gloucestershire (a farm within walking distance of Sudeley Castle), and his second wife (married 1609) Anne Wass or Wase (died 1670) thought to have been the daughter of Christopher Wase, goldsmith of London, of the family of Wase of Wycombe, Bucks. The regicide was the eldest child by the second wife. His half siblings by the first wife, Joan Colet (died 1608, were: George; Robert (born 1606); Margaret (born and died 1596); Elizabeth; Anne (born 1599); Margaret (the second one, born 1604). The regicide's full siblings, all younger, were: Naomi (born 1612); Hannah (born 162-); Samuel (died an infant; Nathaniel (born 1617); Joseph (born 1624); and Jane, married first to Dru Sparrow, Secretary to the Generals at Sea, who was killed in action, February 18, 1652/3, and secondly to ………..Monteage. The Deanes have been traced tentatively back to 1298, and John de Dene, Manucaptor of John Margot, Burgess for Wallingford in that year. His son William was Manucaptor to Richard Gratard and Nicolas de la Barre, Burgesses for Wallingford, 131921. Eight generations later, William à Dene was Collector of Subsidy for Wallingford in 1524. It was his son, William à Dene, Junior, joint Collector of Subsidy with him, who moved to Gloucestershire and was grandfather of the regicide. He made a good match with Margaret Wickham (died 1602), of the family of Wickham of Swalcliffe, Bucks., whose ancestors are traceable at least to 1275, and whose great-great-great-great grandfather Sir

Robert de Wykeham, was made a Knight of the Bath on May 22, 1306, by King Edward I, at the same time as the then Prince of Wales, later Edward II.[90] These Wickhams were related to the famous William of Wickham, the Bishop (1324–1404), listed in DNB under spelling of Wykeham, who founded New College, Oxford, being descended from his brother. (The present Lord Saye and Sele is descended from the sister of the bishop, and believes himself to be the heir general of that family, as he told me himself; in fact, he is unaware that the descendants of this Wickham family are the correct heirs-general.) The Wase family of the regicide's mother were relations of the Hampden family, their neighbours in Buckinghamshire, and the regicide shared common Hampden ancestors with John Hampden, M.P.

Prominent Relations: John Hampden, M.P., was a fairly distant cousin, as just mentioned. Sir William Armine, Bart., M.P. and member of the Council of State in 1649, 1650, and 1651 (see DNB), seems to have been Deane's step-uncle and his mother's step-brother, as her step-father was Sir William Armine (presumably the Senior, of Osgodby, also an M.P. and High Sheriff, who died 1621). Deane's Aunt Judith Wase was daughter of Sir John Gow, a Lord Mayor of London. Sir Richard Deane, great-uncle of the regicide, was a Lord Mayor of London, and his three daughters married prominent figures, all of whom were cousins by marriage of the regicide: John Goodwin, the important M.P. of the Long Parliament (whose brother Robert Goodwin was also an M.P.); William Methold, the important City merchant and East India trader; and Robert Mildmay and William Rolfe (first husband of the daughter married to Methold), members of important Parliamentary families. Through all these connections, Deane would have been linked also to wider networks of relationship and patronage.

Pedigrees: Several linked pedigrees are to be found in the biography of Deane written by a descendant: John Bathurst Deane, *The Life of Richard Deane*, London, 1870.

JOHN DIXWELL. Born 1606 or 1607 (since he was aged 82 when he died March 18, 1688/9).[91] All previous authorities have erred in claiming that this regicide was son of William Dixwell and Elizabeth, daughter of Roger Brent. They were in fact his uncle and aunt. The regicide was the older son of Edward Dixwell of Coton Manor, Churchover, Warwickshire, and Mary Hawksworth. This can be established by a pedigree signed by the regicide's nephew Sir Basil Dixwell, Bart., preserved in the British Library (Add. MS. 5507, 286b). The Dixwells had been seated at Coton since 1551.[92] A seventeenth century MS. in the British Library says of the family's origins: "This family were Antiently of Dixwell Hall and Lords of the Mannor of Dixwell in the County of Hartford, Which they Possessed till the Beginning of the Reign of King Richard, When they Exchanged the said Mannor with John of Durham for that of Great Munden in the same County; some Considerable Length of Time after which, William Dixwell, (the Lineall Offspring of this Family) did, by Marriage, Remove from thence to Tingreth [now known as Tingrith] in Bedfordshire ...", etc.[93] Although the regicide's grandmother, Abigail Dixwell, had bwen the daughter of an Alderman of London named Henry Herdson (of Stourton, Lincs.), none of the regicide's other immediate family were of any discernible political importance whatsoever. The regicide seems to have been entirely unrelated to other M.P.s, very much a lone wolf in a Parliament filled with enormous all-encompassing cousinhoods. This cannot have strengthened his political position. However, he was not narrowly provincial, since he was deeply concerned with a county different from his family's home county, and most of his associations throughout his lifetime were with Kent as opposed to Warwickshire. The regicide had a younger brother, Mark Dixwell, who was born 1609 and married November 28, 1635, Elizabeth Read, aged 19, daughter of Alice Read of Folkestone, Kent. This brother became a Kentish militia Colonel and member of the Kent County Committee early in the Civil War, but died in 1643. (Nineteen years later, his widow

Broome Park near Barham in Kent, the home of John Dixwell the regicide.

John Dixwell's house Broome Park advertised for sale in 1978.

remarried to Sir Henry Oxenden.) John and Mark's parents must have died young, for they appear to have been raised by their uncle, Sir Basil Dixwell, at Folkestone, since the regicide was described as "of Folkestone" when he was admitted to Lincoln's Inn in 1630/1. This uncle of the regicide's was left very extensive lands and manors in Kent by his maternal uncle, John Herdson, enabling him to set himself up as something of a Kentish magnate. This Basil was knighted February 18, 1627/8,[94] on which day he was apparently also simultaneously created a baronet.[95] But he died unmarried in 1641 and his title became extinct; it must not be confused with the 1660 baronetcy of Dixwell which was held successively by two other Sir Basil Dixwells, Barts.[96] Upon his death, this uncle Sir Basil seems to have left his property to his two nephews: the regicide evidently received an enormous amount of money and Folkestone Priory, together with much other property too extensive to discuss here. Mark Dixwell received Brome Park (also known as Broome Park), at Barham, in Kent. He appears to have been short of cash, and so he sold this property to his brother, the regicide, for £13,000, possibly as part of an arrangement on his deathbed for support of his wife and children.[97] The regicide then became the guardian of his brother's children, paying his widow £300 a year, paying £250 a year for the education of the children, and eventually laying out a further £2500 of his own money for these relations, plus maintaining the estates for 17 years at his own expense, and then these relations ended up getting the estates in the end and refusing help to the regicide's own son in the 1680s.[98] The reason for mentioning all of this is because all previous commentators have (with the exception of Dexter) made the mistake of believing that John Dixwell built his importance and position in Kent upon his dead brother's estate, that his political career and financial standing were derived only in that way. The insinuation has been that the regicide would have been a nobody if his brother (thought by other writers to be older) had not died prematurely, with John stepping into his shoes, taking over hi's estate, and exploiting the widow and children with a heartless and ruthless determination to advance himself. Brunton and Pennington fortunately avoid any such imputation.[99] But Firth in the old DNB said that "as temporary holder of these estates John enjoyed great local influence", being in total ignorance of the true situation. Happily, Everitt does not purvey this misinformation, and does not mention anything about Dixwell's property situation at all.[100] The erroneous view is unfortunately perpetuated by E.A. Andriette in the *Biographical Dictionary of British Radicals in the Seventeenth Century*, where we read: "Upon the death of his older brother Mark, John became guardian for his nephew, Basil, and temporary holder of lands in Kent which had belonged to an uncle, Sir Basil Dixwell."[101] See Addendum, below.

Prominent Relations: None, except for his uncle, Sir Basil Dixwell, Bart., who died 1642, and had been M.P. for Hythe in 1626.

Pedigrees: *Visitation of Kent in 1663-8*, Harleian Society, Vol. 54, p. 49. *Visitation of Warwickshire, 1619*, Harleian Society, Volume 12 (1877), pp. 40-1 and 296-7. Two Dixwell pedigrees are on pp. 161-2 of Burke's *Extinct and Dormant Baronetcies* (1844), not wholly reliable. The Dixwell family in the 17th century was extraordinarily large and complex, and no pedigree exists which gives a full or accurate picture of it. I have made some progress towards sketching a fuller version than exists elsewhere, but this is work for the future, in connection with the transcription and editing of a number of Dixwell family letters of a personal nature, some extraordinarily interesting, which I have discovered from the period.

ADDENDUM

I have discovered in the Kent Archives Office the will of the regicide's uncle, Sir Basil Dixwell, Bart. This provides conclusive proof that the regicide and his brother Mark Dixwell were, as I said earlier, the sons of Edward and Mary Dixwell, since the uncle in appointing Mark Dixwell his sole executor, describes him as "my nephew Marke Dixwell sonne of my Late deceased brother Edward Dixwell".[533] However, all my speculations and attempts to sort out John Dixwell the regicide's position with relation to this uncle's estate are thrown into complete perplexity by the contents of the will and its very lengthy annexed schedule of bequests. One interesting revelation is that the regicide had another brother, Charles, who was left £200 by Sir Basil; Charles's existence had not hitherto been known. But apart from the many individual bequests, in which the regicide does not figure, everything is left to Mark Dixwell, and the regicide is not mentioned anywhere in the will at all - *except* that he was a witness to it: The will was drawn up in 1635, by which time the regicide was already a lawyer; did he draw it up for his uncle? Being a witness hardly indicates an estrangement: therefore, did his uncle settle on the regicide by indentures the properties suggested by me earlier, prior to his will? In the will he seems to leave only leases, money, and possessions to Mark; probably the regicide was already in possession of Folkestone Priory by gift as early as 1635.

JOHN DOWNES. Born 1610. He was elder son of Richard Downes of Manby, Lincolnshire, who died 1618/9, and Elizabeth ....The regicide had an uncle, the Rev. John Downes, of Lusby, Lincolnshire, who had a daughter Martha who in 1624 married a Ralph Towneraw of Ashby (born 1594). Beyond this, nothing of Downes's family background is certain, until his own generation. It is possible that he may have been related to the Downes family of Melton Hall, Great Melton, Norfolk, who seem to have been financially devastated in 1604 by a combination of indebtedness and penal action because of their Papism, and to have dispersed away from Melton.[102] But this is sheer speculation. The regicide had a younger brother, Richard Downes, born circa 1617, who married Sybil ....; the christenings of their children are recorded in the parish register of St. Margaret's, Westminster. This Richard became an Alderman of London, September 16, 1652, at which time he was of the Fishmonger's guild.[103] By 1660, Richard was a Draper. He served as a Commissioner for the Excise in 1650 and Customs Commissioner in 1659. He sat on the High Court of Justice to try Goring, Capell, Holland, etc., and signed their Death Warrant on March 6, 1648/9, along with the regicides Vincent Potter and Owen Rowe. He submitted a lengthy deposition in his brother's defence at the Restoration which included his account of what he saw at the last day of the King's trial.[104] The Downes brothers had three sisters, the eldest of which married Samuel Vynter of Redburne.

Prominent Relations: The step-mother of the regicide's second wife was Abigail, daughter of Sir Arthur Heveningham, so that the regicide was connected by marriage with William Heveningham, M.P., who sat on the High Court of Justice though he did not sign the Death Warrant. The second wife of the regicide had an eldest brother who was brother-in-law to Sir William Playters, Bart., M.P., a crony of the regicide Henry Marten but secluded at Pride's Purge.[105] And a sister of hers was married to Sir Richard Lechford of Selwood, Surrey.

Pedigrees: None known of the regicide's immediate family, but the regicide is mentioned in one for Moseley, *Visitation of London 1633-5*, II, 114.

HUMPHREY EDWARDES. Probably born circa 1615. Younger son of Thomas Edwardes of Shrewsbury, Shropshire, High Sheriff of Salop.1622 and J.P. by 1623, died aged 79 and buried March 19, 1634, in St. Chad's, Shrewsbury beside his parents (Hugh and Alice Edwardes), and not his first wife, Anna, daughter of Humphrey Baskerville of London and widow of Stephen

Ducket (who was buried November 12, 1607, at St. Chad's), as stated by all previous writers. His mother appears to have been instead the second wife, Mary Norton, who died July 18, 1641, and is buried at St., Chad's.[106] The Edwardes family were descended from the ancient Welsh kings of Powysland, and were seated at Kilhendre, Salop., in the reign of King Henry I. The earliest ancestor to assume the name of Edwardes was John ap David ap Madoc, of Kilhendre, in the reign of Henry VII: he was the great-grandfather of the regicide.[107] The regicide's eldest brother Henry died without issue, as did another brother, Jonathan, who is buried at St. Chad's. The only brother of whom much is known (all of these beings sons of the first wife) is Sir Thomas Edwardes, Bart., created a baronet by Charles I in 1644 (the title being renewed with the original precedence in 1678 by Charles II for this man's son, and only becoming extinct in 1900). Due to his royalism, this brother's lands in Salop. were granted by Parliamentary Order to the regicide, September 23, 1645, the original order being preserved in the House of Lords Record Office.[108] Perhaps this financial pressure induced his royalism to abate, as this brother seems to have become a Salop. committeeman eventually.[109] There were two sisters: Alice, married Michael Lewis of Salop., and Lucy who first married Thomas Pope of Salop. (no doubt related to the regicide's wife Hester, daughter of Roger Pope of Shrewsbury), and second married Sir ……..Ottley, almost certainly Sir Francis Ottley or Oatley of Pitchford, Salop.[110] This Lady Lucy Ottley was granted administration of her brother's estate (his wife being dead and no children having been born) October 26, 1658.[111]

Prominent Relations: This regicide was on such intimate terms with the regicide Sir Gregory Norton, Bart., that they were like twin brothers. It seems likely that they were somehow, probably distantly related, through this regicide's mother, Mary Norton. This remains speculation until such time as it can be determined from which Norton family she came. Edwardes was a close cousin of the first wife of the regicide John Jones. He was probably also related to William Purefoy (whom see). See also *Visitation of Shropshire, 1623*, Harleian Society, Vol. XXVIII (1889), pp. 172-4, and Vol. XXIX (1889), p. 405.

Pedigrees: Until the Edwardes baronetcy became extinct in 1900, pedigrees continued to appear in Debrett's. Ashmole copied a pedigree drawn up in 1663, and this appears to be preserved in MS. Ashmole 858, pp. 132-3, in the Bodleian.[112].

ISAAC EWER. (Special note: for this regicide see Appendix to Chapter Two, where may be consulted photocopies of my original entries submitted for several regicides to the *Biographical Dictionary of British Radicals in the Seventeenth Century*, which are fuller, especially in their references, than the entries as they appeared in that work.) Born circa 1612. Close relation and probably son of Richard Ewer of Hatfield Broad Oak, Essex, Surveyor of the Highway in 1634 in his parish.[113] Mother unknown. This Ewer family seem to have been of prosperous yeoman status, perhaps hovering on the border of parochial gentry. They seem to have been related in some way to the Ewer families of Pinner, Middlesex, and Cheshunt, Herts., who were far more distinguished. The head of the latter, William Ewer, was Serjeant at Arms to Charles I. Joan Ewer, of South Myms, Middlesex, loaned £14 to the Parliament and was assessed for £100 in 1644.[114] The basis for assuming a relationship with these other Ewers is that when the regicide was granted arms by the heralds, February 22, 1647/8,[115] the chief heraldic feature (allowing for various martial elements referring to the Colonel's military exploits) was a tyger passant, sable. The tyger passant was the central feature of the arms of the Ewers of Herts. and Middlesex, the tyger being sable for the ones in Middlesex, perhaps indicating a closer relationship with them than the Ewers of Herts., who had a tyger or.[116] There were also Ewers as far away as Herefordshire with arms identical to those of Middlesex.[117] It is interesting to speculate that the Ewers of Strood, Kent, may also have been some relation, for Thomas Ewer, born there March 10, 1592/3, who emigrated to New England, is reported by Governor John Winthrop of Massachusetts to have been charged in 1637 with having said of Charles I "that, if the King did send any authority hither against our patent, he would be the first should resist him".[118] But much more research would be necessary to establish a relationship, and this is pure speculation. Mark Noble, never one to allow a regicide a respectable pedigree if he could avoid it, and who was in possession of much genealogical information of the eighteenth century which is now lost to us, states quite categorically that 'the regicide "was of the ennobled family of the Barons Ewer, in Yorkshire".[119] I interpret this to mean that Noble had come across some evidence indicating that Ewer had family associations of somewhat higher status than his immediate Essex parish, for Noble seems to have had the run of the College of Heralds (a privilege denied to modern historians). I consider a relationship with the Yorkshire Barons Eure extremely unlikely, if only because their arms were entirely different, though there may have been shared ancestors at some very distant date. The regicide had two brothers, John and William. The former had a son John, and the latter had sons William and Captain Isaac Ewer. This latter nephew of the regicide had a distinguished career as a young diplomat, then barrister, and important figure at Lincoln's Inn, becoming Keeper of the Black Book by 1692. He was one of John Milton's underclerks in 1654/5.[120] I have sketched his career briefly in the Entry for his uncle found in the Appendix to this Chapter.

Prominent Relations: John Thurloe, Secretary of State to Cromwell, was this regicide's brother-in-law, and was named sole executor of the regicide's will and made guardian of his children in 1650. Thurloe made his nephew the young Captain Isaac Ewer his protegé (see document in Appendix).

Pedigrees: The Ewers of Hertfordshire have a pedigree, "Ewer of the Lea and Cheshunt", in the *Visitation of Hertfordshire* for 1634, pp. 51-2. This takes their descent back to the time of Henry VIII. This pedigree may be supplemented by notes taken by Elias Ashmole from the church at Watford, Herts., of the same family, printed in C.H. Josten, ed., *Elias Ashmole*, Vol. IV, *Texts: 1673-1701*, pp. 1436-7.

GEORGE FLEETWOOD. Baptized February 15, 1621/2, at Chalfont St. Giles, Bucks. Eldest son of Charles Fleetwood of the Vache (a grand house which still stands), Chalfont St. Giles, Bucks. (died May 28, 1628) and Anne, daughter of Nicholas and Margery Watkins, of Aldgate Ward in London.[121] The regicide's father died aged 36, only eight years after his own father, Sir George Fleetwood of the Vache (knighted May 11, 1603, died 1620), so the regicide was left as heir at the age of six; wardship papers have not yet been discovered, but probably exist. The Fleetwoods were an ancient family who originated in Lancashire; a John Fleetwood was lord of the manor of Plumpton Parva, Lancashire in 1339, and his son Henry was alive in the reign or Henry VI. This Henry Fleetwood had a great-grandson Thomas Fleetwood, of the Vache, who was Master of the Mint and whose son Everard Fleetwood was an M.P. By a second marriage, this Thomas Fleetwood was the great-grandfather of the regicide.[122] The regicide's great-uncle Sir William Fleetwood of Cranford, Middlesex, was Receiver of the Court of Wards (and grandfather of the Lieutenant-General Charles Fleetwood of the Cromwellian party). The regicide's uncle was the Rev. James Fleetwood, D. D., Bishop of Worcester, for whom see his own entry in the DNB. This uncle was the chaplain of the future Charles II, a heavy irony for the uncle of a regicide. He had been sequestered during the Interregnum[123] and as a staunch royalist was named Provost of King's College, Cambridge, at the Restoration despite a remarkable and poignant protest by many Fellows of the College,[124] later becoming Vice-Chancellor of Cambridge University, and finally in 1675 Bishop of Worcester. The Fleetwoods were themselves actually descended from the ancient Princes of Wales of the twelfth century (Owen Gwynedd) through a Welsh ancestress who married the first recorded Fleetwood in the fourteenth century.[125] The regicide had a brother David and a sister, Catherine, who married George Clerke, a merchant of London, and died 1678.[126] The brother David is obscure; he may be the David Fleetwood alive and living in Stratford-upon-Avon in 1642 and 1643.[127]

Prominent Relations: Lieutenant General Charles Fleetwood, the New Model Army colonel and later mainstay of the Protectorate, was the regicide's second cousin. The regicide was thus related to Oliver Cromwell by marriage, since this cousin Charles married Cromwell's oldest daughter Bridget, widow of the regicide Henry Ireton. Charles had a brother, Colonel William Fleetwood, who was a royalist, and a very remarkable brother, Baron General Sir George Fleetwood (knighted by Charles I on June 3, 1632, when he was a Colonel under Gustavus Adolphus of Sweden, and created a Swedish Baron by Queen Christina on June 1, 1654, becoming a Swedish Lieutenant General in 1656), for whom see his own entry in the DNB; the latter's descendants, the Swedish Barons Fleetwood, and their large family, survive in modern Sweden, where they even have a family society. The regicide was related (as a third cousin) to the regicide Thomas Chaloner, whose mother was Elizabeth Fleetwood, daughter of William Fleetwood, Recorder of London.[128] The regicide was a cousin of Lord Grey of Wilton, since his own great-great-grandfather had been an earlier Lord Grey of Wilton. The regicide's great-uncle was Edward Denny, Earl of Norwich, several times an M.P., who died 1630; see his own entry in DNB. (He was no relation to the later Earl of Norwich, George Goring!) The regicide was third cousin of Sir William Spring, Bart., whose father-in-law was the theologian Sir Hamon l'Estrange (died 1654, see DNB) who was the anonymous author of an interesting posthumously published book of which I have a copy, *The Reign of King Charles* (1655), and whose brothers-in-law were the author Sir Roger l'Estrange (see DNB) and Sir Nicholas l'Estrange, Bart. It would be possible to list many more such relationships for this regicide, who was obviously enmeshed in a vast web of important family connections, but to prolong the list would be tedious.

Pedigrees: MS. pedigree and notes by Browne-Willis in MS. Rawlinson B. 263, pp. 2412, in the Bodleian. (Browne-Willis gives the regicide's date of baptism as February 28 rather than February 15, supposedly from the register as it appeared in the eighteenth century. Perhaps, therefore, February 15 was really, the date of birth. Pedigree of the Friherrliga Utten Fleetwood take the family back to 1320 in the male line, in Vol. II of *Den Introducerade Svenska Adelns Attartavlor* (*The Introduced-to-Court Swedish Nobility Family Trees*) *med Tillagg och Rättelser* (with additions and corrections) by Gustaf Elgenstierna, Norstedt, Stockholm, 1926. "Fleetwood of Caldwick" in Burke's *Extinct and Dormant Baronetcies* (1844, pp. 199-201). A vast amount of genealogical discussion and information is to be found in assorted contributions to *Notes and Queries* such as the following: 9th Series, Vol. IX, pp. 48-9, 175 234-5, 261-2, and Tenth Series, Vol. I, pp. 422-4. It would be an understatement to say that the Fleetwood family genealogy is complex, and has confused many people over the years.

AUGUSTINE GARLAND. Baptized January 13, 1602, at St. Antholin's Budge Row, London. Only son of Augustine Garland, Senior, Attorney of London and resident of Coleman Street, and his first wife, Ellen Whitteridge, daughter of Jasper Whitteridge of London. The regicide's grandfather, also Augustine Garland, was a member of the Fishmongers'

Guild, and his father Richard Garland was from Hayes in Kent. Apart from this, little is known about the Garland family's origins, and they seem to have been obscure. The regicide's grandmother, Jane, daughter of Cornelius Carden, came from Calais, and seems not to have been English. She was quite possibly of the same family as Sir Thomas Carden, knighted by King Henry VIII, apparently at Boulogne, after the conquest of the town, September 30, 1544.[129] Perhaps this family were prominent merchants of the Calais-Boulogne area involved in trade with England and supporting the English interests (in which case almost certainly Protestants). A Ferdinand Carden wrote to Secretary Cecil January 17, 1603/4.[130] Research into the Carden family might prove interesting, but has not been practical here. The regicide had a full sister, Elizabeth, who married William Newbold of London, "one of the Clerks of the Poultry Counter". He had two half-sisters by his father's second wife, a widow named Alice Johnson, daughter of a London draper named Cliffe (married Garland January 16, 1603/4, at St. Dunstan's. Stepney, Middlesex; she died December 11, 1633; the regicide's father died January 22, 1637/8): Rebecca Garland, married to Henry Cole of Carshalton, Surrey (who died January 14, 1637/8), and Mary Garland, who married Thomas Chester of London sometime prior to 1634. The regicide's coat of arms is identical to the arms of the family of Garland of York, but whether there is any significance to that fact is unknown.[131]

Prominent Relations: Apparently none, which might explain why Garland never made it into the highest positions despite his being indispensable at the secondary level.

Pedigrees: "Garland" in the *Visitation of London 1633-5*, Vol. I, p. 301. The regicide's sister is mentioned in the pedigree of "Newbold" in *Ibid.*, Vol. II, p. 123.

Special Notes: Pink errs in saying that Garland was from Tulsham Hall, Kent. He confused Augustine Garland with Augustine Skinner, who was from Tulsham Hall.[132] See the Appendix to this chapter for my entry for Garland as prepared for the *Biographical Dictionary of British Radicals in the Seventeenth Century*.

WILLIAM GOFFE. Born at Haverfordwest, Pembrokeshire, Wales, probably circa 1615, during the time his itinerant father was preacher at St. Mary's, Haverfordwest.[133] Third son of the Rev. Stephen Goffe, D. D., and Deborah (surname unknown, born circa 1587 and died November 8, 1626, a brass plaque to whose memory may be seen in Stanmer Church in Sussex). The Goffes seem definitely to be of Welsh descent, and the regicide's father probably retreated to Haverfordwest to preach after encountering opposition in England (described in a moment because he had relations there). I have found a Phillip Gough of Haverfordwest who in 1656 signed with other locals a testimonial to London on behalf of a petitioning prisoner named Daniel Wise.[134] In his researches at the end of the last century, James Phillips discovered a "Balthazar Goffe, tailor" resident in Haverfordwest about the same time.[135] I have analyzed the seal of the regicide which is perfectly preserved on the envelope of a letter he wrote to Henry Cromwell in 1658,[136] and the arms are: Two boars' heads armed couped, in a canton a lion rampant holding dexter a baton. The Gochs, Goghes, Goughs, of Wales and Bristol, Gloucestershire, Somerset, and similar areas, have arms the central feature of which is the use of the boar's head couped, which also has served as their crest.[137] Of the Goughs in Bristol, a contemporary of the regicide, Henry Gough, merchant, was obviously well to do and supported the Parliament, since on March 16, 1653/4, he was described in London as "well affected" and reimbursed £1,604/ 06/ 02 for goods used by the State;[138] and "one Goff" together with the Mayor of Bristol in the 1640s was reported as corresponding with the Parliamentary forces in a plot to betray the Royalist-held Bristol to the Parliament, as we learn from an intercepted royalist informants' note.[139] These two men may well have been the same, and it is not unlikely that the plotter and Parliament-supporter Henry Gough was related to the regicide, who was one of the officers of foot who took part in the successful siege of Bristol under Fairfax. Perhaps the Gough of Bristol's correspondence with the Parliament forces was with William Gough himself, if they were indeed related. What appears to have been an extended family of at least distantly related Goffes produced at least one law student at the Middle Temple: a George Goffe, son and heir of William Goffe of Hewelsfield, Gloucestershire (a few miles from Chepstow), deceased, was admitted there November 4, 1615. There is evidence of a James Goffe of London directly associated with the regicide in 1656 in connection with Protectorate business.[140] He was probably his younger brother. We know the regicide had many relatives, because in 1659 he was publicly accused of making several of them Army officers: "his Relations, who never fought with us in the late Wars".[141] One of these protégés must have been the Lieutenant-Colonel William Goffe who in the spring of 1658/9 was based at Lambeth and in Westminster Hall had an notorious quarrel, siding with Colonel Richard Ashfield against the regicide William Goffe's own father-in-law, Lieutenant-General Edward Whalley, about politics.[142] We thus have a superfluity of known and suspected relations of William Goffe the regicide, without any family tree of that period to place them in their relation to one another. None of the Goffes appears to have been important gentry, but they seem by their industry and application to have achieved a certain amount of mercantile prosperity or educational attainments, which can nowhere be seen better illustrated than by the curious career of the regicide's father, which I have thought best to sketch briefly as follows:

Stephen Goffe went to Oxford in 1592, obtaining his B.A. on November 3, 1595, and becoming a Fellow of his college, Magdalen, in 1598, obtaining his M. A. December 11, 1599. From 1595 he acted as a tutor to "several that proved afterwards very noted scholars", one of whom was Dr. Robert Harris, later President of Trinity College, Oxford, whom Goffe "instructed very profitably in godly exercises". Anthony à Wood says of Goffe at this time that he was "a good logician and disputant, but a very severe Puritan, eminent for his training up, while a tutor, several that proved afterwards very noted scholars".[143] Magdalen College appointed Goffe Rector of Bramber-cum-Botolphs in Sussex, in 1603. But by 1607, Goffe was deprived of his living by Bishop Lancelot Andrewes, apparently for refusing to wear the surplice or use the sign of the cross in baptism.[144] By 1614 at the latest, Goffe was preacher at St. Mary's, Haverfordwest, though he may have held the position of a Puritan lecturer rather than being the vicar or rector. In both 1614 and 1615, Goffe is recorded as having been away from his duties in Haverfordwest, the second occasion specifically having been at London.[145] In the 1620s, Goffe returned to Sussex, living at Stanmer, where his wife was interred in 1626, and where he was resident in 1628 when his son John became Rector of nearby Ripe.[146] By the summer of 1632 at the latest, a Goffe was Preacher to the regiment of Lord Vere in the Netherlands, where he became the centre of a complex religious controversy, but this was a different man.[147] By the summer of 1634, Goffe was still living at Thakeham. It was there that the regicide lived when, July 15, 1634, he was admitted apprentice to William Vaughan, grocer, in London.[148] I am indebted to Ian Gentles for this information, a correction to the old DNB where Vaughan is called a salter (drawing on an erroneous report published in a pamphlet of 1658.[149]).

The regicide had four brothers: Stephen, John, James, and Timothy. Timothy, the youngest, was baptized November 5, 1626, at Stanmer, Sussex, but may have died young, as nothing more is known of him. Three notices have been found in 1656 mentioning James Goffe of Canning Street in London, including a mention of him as his brother by the regicide.[150] Little else is known of him except he was obviously willing to let his elder brother the regicide put him forward in some minor government business under the Protectorate. But the two older brothers of the regicide were as different from the regicide in their beliefs as they could possibly be. The younger of these two older brothers was at least on speaking terms with William despite it all. He was the Rev. John Goffe, D.D. (born circa 1610), an author and high churchman who was expelled by the Parliament as Vicar of St. Stephens, Hackington, Kent, and even thrown into prison in Canterbury. But by 1652, "by the endeavours of his brother William", Rev. John was inducted into the rectory of Norton near Sittingbourne, having been persuaded by the regicide to behave himself and keep a low profile.[151] At the Restoration, Rev. John petitioned successfully to the House of Lords and was reinstituted as Vicar of Hackington.[152] For more about him, see his entry in DNB; he died November 20, 1661. The regicide's eldest brother, born circa 1605, also has his own entry in the DNB. He was the notorious Rev. Stephen Goffe, D.D., who was chaplain first to Charles I, and then to Queen Henrietta Maria, assisted Charles I in his flight from Hampton Court, was imprisoned, escaped, was employed as envoy in Europe and acted as confidential royalist agent, became tutor to the young Duke of Monmouth, and converted to Roman Catholicism. Any two less likely brothers at this period it would be difficult to imagine. So extraordinary were their differences of every kind, both religious and political, that many historians naturally found it too incredible to believe that they really were brothers at all. But any doubts of this kind were laid finally to rest, as I pointed out in an article in 1980, by the discovery of the manuscript of part of Ludlow's Memoirs, where Ludlow explicitly speaks of them as being brothers.[153] Rev. Stephen died 1681 at Paris.

Prominent Relations: Lieutenant-General Edward Whalley was Goffe's father-in-law and close companion and friend. Through Whalley, who was first cousin of Oliver Cromwell, Goffe was related by marriage to the Cromwell clan.

Pedigrees: An elaborate history of the Goffe family, incorporating many successive pedigrees, was complied by G. L. Goff in 1895, entitled *Memoirs of the Goff Family*; this is an elaborately bound typed manuscript which was many years ago in the possession of the regicide's descendant, Colonel Robert Goff, O.B.E., M.C., whom I knew fairly well. It does not trace the pedigree back earlier than the regicide's father, however. Another pedigree which also goes back no further than that is "Goff, formerly of Standerwick Court and Hale Park" in Burke's *Landed Gentry*, 18th edition, 1968, Vol. 2, pp. 250-1.

THOMAS GREY, LORD GREY OF GROBY. Born 1623, eldest son of Henry Grey, First Earl of Stamford (died August 21, 1673) and Anne, daughter of William Cecil, Earl of Exeter. The regicide's parents married at St. Bennet Sherehog in London in July, 1620. The descent or this regicide, who was of the highest social stratum, was almost bewilderingly illustrious. He was descended from Hugo de Grentesmainell, a Norman who was Lord of Groby as early as 1086; from an Earl of Leicester who died 1190; an Earl of Winton who died 1219; an Earl of Ferrars and Derby; an Earl of Suffolk; a Lord Poynings; a Lord Clifford; a Duke of Norfolk; an ancestress who as her second husband married King Edward IV; a Lord Harrington; a Marquess of Dorset; etc.

The famous Lady Jane Grey, who was Queen of England for a few days, was the first cousin of the regicide's great-grandfather. Lord Burleigh, Queen Elizabeth's Secretary of State, was the regicide's great-grandfather, through his mother. The family connections are legion, and cannot be traced in full here. The regicide had two sisters, one of whom seems to have died young, or is unknown at least to this author. The other, Lady Diana Grey ("second daughter") married Robert, Second Earl of Elgin and First Earl of Ailesbury and had at least six children. The regicide also had a brother, Lieutenant John Grey, a royalist who was taken prisoner in March, 1643/4, by a Parliamentary officer named Henry Grey who apparently was a cousin of the regicide.[154] The regicide also seems to have had another younger brother who in the spring or 1643/4 was acting as a Cornet of Horse for the Parliament, but this may just be a misunderstanding due to confusing wording of a contemporary pamphlet.[155] There may have been other siblings, but it has proved extremely difficult to disentangle the Greys.

Prominent Relations: Through his marriage to Lady Dorothy Bourchier, second daughter and coheiress of Edward Bourchier, Fourth Earl of Bath, the regicide was related to her family: the Fifth Earl of Bath, who died 1654, was his brother-in-law; the Earl of Denbigh and Sir Chichester Wrey, 3rd Bart., were married to the regicide's wife's sisters; Thomas Howard, Lord Howard of Charlton, Viscount Andover, and eventually First Earl of Berkshire, was related by blood and by marriage. The regicide's younger brother John Grey, mentioned above, married Katherine, daughter of Lord Dudley and Ward. The regicide was also related to the regicide Henry Smith by marriage though the Cecils.

Pedigrees: Under "Earl of Stamford" in successive editions of Debrett's *Peerage*, though as this title became extinct in August, 1976, any future editions (if they are ever published again) will drop this pedigree. Also see Pedigree on p. 633 of Vol. IV of John Nichols, *History and Antiquities of Leicestershire*.

THOMAS HARRISON. Baptized July 2, 1616, at Newcastle-under-Lyme, Staffordshire. Only son of Richard Harrison of Newcastle-under-Lyme, and Mary ……..(surname unknown). The descent of the regicide is only known as far back as his great grandfather. T. Pope describes the family as "a sturdy commercial stock well respected in the old borough. His father, grandfather and great-grandfather had been butchers and graziers, all of them had taken their share in serving as borough officers, and the first two had between them occupied the position of mayor on six occasions.… In the middle of the sixteenth century we find that Richard Harrison, butcher, grandfather of the major-general, during the years 1552 to 1565 was a councillor who served as church-warden three times, receiver three times, bailiff twice, sergeant once and constable once.[156] This grandfather was Mayor in 1594 and 1608. I have discovered his will, which I have transcribed and included in the Appendix to this chapter, due to the importance of Harrison and the lack of knowledge about his antecedents. The regicide's father, also Richard Harrison, was Mayor of Newcastle-under-Lyme four times, in 1626, 1633, 1643, and 1648. He was buried March 25, 1653, at Newcastle; the regicide's mother was buried there May 18, 1658. The regicide's uncle was Colonel Ralph Harrison of Highgate, Colonel of the City's Yellow Regiment in 1647, a Draper and Citizen of London. This uncle was a radical, and signed the Death Warrant of Goring, Capell, Holland, and Hamilton on March 6, 1648/9.[157] He died 1656. The regicide married his daughter Katherine, the regicide's own first cousin. The regicide had three sisters: Jane, baptized June 2, 1612; Dorothy, baptized March 29, 1618; and Anne, baptized August 3, 1619, who married Randle Lovatt, who was Mayor of Newcastle-under-Lyme in 1656.[158]

Prominent Relations: Colonel Ralph Harrison mentioned above, his uncle and father-in-law. He was also related to John Cook (see *ante*).

Pedigrees: Harrison Pedigree constructed by T. Pope and published on p. 175 of his book *Newcastle-under-Lyme in Tudor and Early Stuart Times*, No. LXXV of Historical Series of Publications of University of Manchester (1938).

JOHN HEWSON. Date of birth unknown. Parentage unknown, but thought to be son of John Hewson, Shoemaker, who supplied the Massachusetts Company with a consignment of shoes February 26, 1628 (mentioned in the old DNB as if it were the regicide himself), and Margery …… (surname unknown), both subjects of satire in a 1650s pamphlet, *A Choice and Diverting Dialogue*

FURTHER DETAILS OF THE FAMILY BACKGROUNDS

The caricature of John Hewson showing the upright sword, which is the main feature of his coat of arms. (Collection of the author)

between Hughson the Cobler and Margery His Wife. The regicide's wife, alive at this time, was named Anne, so this would seem to be his parents who are here intended. John Hewetson, a family historian, maintained that the regicide was no relation to the family of which he wrote, but that he was "of the family of 'Huson' already seated at Tenterden in the county of Kent in the year 1600".[159] His reason for this assertion is "from the fact of his bearing the same arms", which Hewetson (quoting a seventeenth century source) gives as: Quarterly, Gules and ermine, an eagle displayed or, in the dexter chief quarter a lion passant argent."[160] Unfortunately for Hewetson's theory, the regicide did not use these arms. His arms as preserved on the Death Warrant of Charles I and on a document in the British Library[161] dating from 1647 have none of these features whatsoever. The arms have as their central feature a chevron on which are four crescents. Above the chevron stand two extraordinary animals which look very like donkeys, regarding each other. And beneath the chevron is an upright sword. This latter feature is caricatured in a contemporary cartoon caricature which I have in my collection of old engravings (source for this unknown, alas), which bears as its caption the following: "Like will to Like, else why should HEWSON be Still among Knaves. Knaves love his Company." The figure is shown with one eye, which was Hewson's main trademark. The sword he holds upright in his hand is not a sword of the time, but is a replica of the sword on his coat of arms. This little cartoon may have been published perhaps in 1653 by some who knew Hewson and had hoped he would not support the Protectorate, or it may be after the incident of the City apprentices; it is certainly pre-Restoration. I have tried without success to discover whether the regicide was the John Hewson, brother of Penelope Hewson of "Burro Court" in Gloucestershire, who was granted her Administration on January 3, 1649/50.[162] The Gloucestershire Record Office have been unable to trace either the house or Penelope Hewson. A relation of this regicide's, and probably his eldest son (he had three) was Geoffrey Hughson who was commissioned Captain in the Middlesex militia under Colonel Edmund Harvey, November 20, 1650.[163] Two Hewsons are listed as living in London in 1638 in one survey: John Huson in Whor's Yard, All Hallows, Barking; and Mr. Hughson in Pancras Lane, St. Pancras, Soper Lane.[164] Further progress on reconstructing the Hewson family has not been made.

Prominent Relations: Apparently none.

Pedigrees: Apparently none relating to the regicide's immediate family, but refer to John Hewetson, *Memoirs of the House of Hewetson or Hewson of Ireland*, London, 1901, pp. 204-6.

THOMAS HORTON. Born 1602 at Gumley in Leicestershire. Second son of William Horton of Gumley (who died 1638 and described himself in his will as "yeoman") and Isabell Freeman. The father's will is transcribed and included in the Appendix to this chapter; the regicide is made co-executor with his mother, and his brothers (especially his older brother) are pointedly excluded from that role. The Hortons were an ancient yeoman family descended from Henry de Horton, who came from Horton, Northamptonshire, and settled at Knaptoft, Leicestershire, sometime between 1268 and 1277. Thus was founded the Family of Horton of Mowsley, an offshoot of which became the Hortons of Saddington, Leicestershire after 1450, and an offshoot of which in turn became the Hortons of Gumley, the regicide's immediate family.[165] For four centuries, the Hortons remained precisely what they were: sturdy, generally prosperous, unimportant yeoman farmers. The regicide was the first Horton to become important in the political world, if being a New Model Colonel can be said to be political (for which subject see the later chapter "The Honourable Members from the Army"). The regicide's older brother, John Horton, married Margery Caslin, and was named a Parliamentary Sequestrator for Leicestershire, February 11, 1649/50.[166] The regicide had a younger brother Andrew (married, had a daughter Liddia, but his wife's name is unknown), who was recommended by the Leicestershire County Commissioners as Agent to the Commissioners of Sequestrations for Leicestershire, September 29, 1659.[167] There were also younger brothers James, Robert, and William, and sisters Elizabeth, Mary, Ellen, Margaret, and Frances. Gumley, the seat of the Hortons was six or seven miles from Noseley, the home of Sir Arthur Heselrige (Hazlerigg), the radical M.P. Horton was a close friend of the Heselriges and in his will in 1649 left Sir Arthur and Lady Heselrige £10 apiece to buy rings to remember him by.[168] His horse was even named Haselrigg![169] The old DNB erred absurdly by suggesting that Horton had been Heselrige's servant, a point wisely corrected by H. R. Engstrom in the *Biographical Dictionary of British Radicals in the Seventeenth Century* (1982). Horton was a Captain in Heselrige's regiment of horse at least as early as October, 1642,[170] and was evidently Heselrige's protégé, which is the tiny grain of truth in the drastically misconstrued notion that he was Heselrige's servant.

Prominent Relations: Although the regicide was not related by blood to anyone prominent, his brother-in-law John St.-Loe was well-connected. I have recently been able to establish which of several contemporary John St.-Loes this brother-in-law was, and it transpires that his mother was the niece of Bishop Lancelot Andrewes.[171] He himself was born 1630 and appears as a three year-old child in the *Visitation of London 1633-5*, ed. by J.J. Howard and J.L. Chester, London, 1880, Vol. I, p. 222 (Saintloe of Tower Street Ward).[172] He was a royalist, and in 1660 Charles II appointed him Receiver-General of the Crown Revenues or the Seven Western Counties and Farmer of the Excise in Dorset "in respect of his services and sufferings in his Ma[ties] Cause".[173] He died 1680, when Administration was granted to his widow, Margaret.[174] The regicide's son Thomas Horton lived with him after the regicide's death, being admitted to the Middle Temple on February 12, 1666/7.

Pedigrees: Incredibly elaborate and annotated pedigrees of the Horton family have been compiled by L.G.H. Norton-Smith, in two articles on "The Hortons of Leicestershire" in *Transactions of the Leicestershire Archaeological Society*, Vol. XXII (1944-5) and Vol. XXIII (1947). The author appears to have been unaware that one of the Thomas Hortons in his mammoth genealogy was the regicide. I find it extremely difficult to believe that the author was genuinely ignorant of the fact, which is so easily established, and am tempted to conclude that he concealed it on purpose. When challenged publicly about it by a man named Carter, Horton-Smith in 1943 boasted in *Notes and Queries*: "I am profoundly thankful to be able to assure Mr. Carter that this man was most certainly not 'one of the family, ... Thank Heav'n we have nothing in blood With a Traitor ..." (the latter part of the quotation is from a peculiar bit of doggerel verse written by Horton-Smith insisting he is not related to a man who "betrayed his own King"). It has been necessary to go into this because anyone consulting Horton-Smith's compilations of material on the Horton family would, without guidance, find it impossible to locate the regicide. The pedigree of his immediate family is the elaborate fold-out pedigree of "The Hortons of Gumley" (he is on the third line down between his brothers John and James). He is referred to in a single-line description on page 19 (at the top) of the Vol. XXIII mentioned above. On the previous page there is half a page about his older brother John Horton. An article by Dorothy Horton also called "The Hortons or Leicestershire" in *The Genealogists' Magazine*, Vol. 14 (1964), pp. 295-300, is of interest. She says: "There is a tradition in the family that one of its members signed the death warrant of Charles I ... but Mr. Horton-Smith ... denies all kinship with this regicide." Any doubts about the matter are totally dispelled by a reading of the regicide's last will and testament.[172]

JOHN HUTCHINSON. Baptized at St. Mary's, Nottingham, September 18, 1615. Eldest son of Sir Thomas Hutchinson of Owthorpe, Nottinghamshire, and Margaret, daughter or Sir John Byron (married at Bulwell, Nottinghamshire, April 11, 1612). Sir Thomas was knighted at Hinchinbroke March 20, 1616/7,[175] was a J. P. by 1618 and Sheriff of Nottinghamshire,1620-1. He was M.P. for his county in 1626, imprisoned for refusing to act as loan commissioner so that he could not be reelected in 1628, but was again M.P. in 1640 until his death August 18, 1643.[176] He remarried at St. Mary's, Nottingham, December 17, 1631, to Katherine, daughter of John Stanhope. Captain Lawson Lowe has written of the regicide's family: "The Hutchinsons of Owthorpe, who were a younger branch of an ancient Yorkshire family, sprang from Thomas Hutchinson, second son of Anthony Hutchinson *of* Cowlam, near Driffield in Yorkshire, who purchased lands at Owthorpe and elsewhere in Nottinghamshire, about the commencement of the sixteenth century."[177] The Hutchinsons were included in the Visitation of Nottinghamshire for 1569 and inter-married with the Zouch and Sacheverell families.[178] The regicide had a younger full brother, George Hutchinson, who married Barbara Apsley, sister of the regicide's own wife Lucy Apsley, and who served as the regicide's Lieutenant-Colonel and close and constant political and military ally and associate. They were somewhat estranged from their half-sister Isabella, who married Charles Cotton of Berrisford, Derbyshire, on June 30, 1656, at St. Mary's, Nottingham, and their half-brother Charles (born circa 1637, married at St. Paul's. Covent Garden, London, in 1663 to Isabella Boteler, daughter of Francis Boteler, and died 1695).

Prominent Relations: According to Lucy Hutchinson, Henry Ireton the regicide and John Hutchinson were closely related. She says: "Collonell Hutchinson was, after his brother, one of the neerest kinsmen he had ..."[179] Until now, no one has ever been able to figure out how they were related. I have been able to establish that they were second cousins twice removed.

The full explanation of the matter will be found in my article "The Relationship between Henry Ireton and John Hutchinson", in the *Nottinghamshire Historian*, though publication is postponed until I am able to incorporate further material at a later date. [I never pubished this.] The regicide's step-mother was half-sister to the Earl of Chesterfield and sister of William Stanhope, M.P. for Nottingham in the Long Parliament, but disabled for royalism in 1644.[180] This Stanhope was a cousin of Denzil Holles, M.P., and half-uncle of Ferdinando Stanhope, M.P. (died 1643).[181] The regicide was also related to William Ellis, M.P. for Boston in the Long Parliament, and to Thomas Grantham, M.P. for Lincoln in the Long Parliament.[182] Sir Richard Byron the royalist was the regicide's first cousin, John and Richard, Lords Byron, were his uncles, and through his wife, Sir Allen Apsley the royalist was his brother in-law.

Pedigrees: *Visitation of Nottinghamshire, 1569/1614*, Harleian Society, Vol. 4, 1871, pp. 115-6. *Visitation of Nottinghamshire, 1662-4*, Thoroton Society, Vol. XIII, 1950, p. 11 (certified by the regicide himself in the MS.)

RICHARD INGOLDSBY (later SIR; created a Knight of the Bath by Charles II at his coronation, April 20, 1661). Baptized August 10, 1617, at Buckingham. Second son of Sir Richard Ingoldsby of Lethenborough, Buckinghamshire, and Elizabeth, daughter of Sir Oliver Cromwell, Knight of the Bath, of Hinchinbroke, Huntingdonshire. The regicide's father had been knighted by James I upon his visit to Sir Oliver Cromwell's house at Hinchinbroke, October 22, 1617.[183] The Ingoldsby family were of extremely ancient descent, traceable at least to Sir Roger Ingoldsby, Lord of Ingoldsby (Ingleby), in Lincolnshire, in the year 1230.[184] The fact that this family origin had a strong influence on the regicide's sentiments is proved by the fact that he actually purchased the Manor of Ingleby in Lincolnshire despite the fact that he had to accept three "sitting tenants" and the benefits of his purchase would effectively be realized only by his descendants. I have transcribed and include in the Appendix to this chapter, a document from the Public Record Office, "Richard Ingoldsby's Restoration Petition for Ancestral Home (1663)", with a letter of recommendation from Lord Southampton, who seems to have been a strong supporter of Ingoldsby, to the King about the matter, who tactfully mentions the regicide's interest in the Manor being "for the names sake". I also include in the Appendix to this chapter a transcription of the will of the regicide's father (died 1656), although the document was in an advanced stage of disintegration. The regicide had one older brother, Francis (baptized August 14, 1614, at Lethenborough), married Lettice, daughter of Crowley Norton of Offleys, Herts. He was M.P. for Bucks. in the Protectorate Parliaments of 1654, 1656, and 1658. He gained the royal favour at the Restoration and was to have been knighted, but being a fantastic wastrel, he dissipated his fortunes, sold the family home, and died in debt, October 1, 1681. The regicide's other siblings, in descending order by sex, were: Oliver, born 1619, admitted Inner Temple 1639, is thought to have married a Cromwell of Hinchinbroke (possibly a confusion with his mother), became Major in Parliamentary forces and was reduced in May, 1645 (see document in the Appendix to this chapter "Letter from Colonel Charles Fleetwood and his Major, Thomas Harrison, to Robert Scawen ... 1645" in which this is presented, and clears up confusion which had previously arisen about the identity of this Ingoldsby), was as Lieutenant-Colonel in the New Model Army in 1647 killed at Pendennis Castle in Cornwall; John, born 1621, a Parliamentary officer who died at sea, easily confused with a cousin, Major John Ingoldsby[185] so that it is not clear which John was Colonel at the siege of Drogheda in Ireland;[186] Henry, born 1622, served as a royalist officer early in Civil War but switched to Parliament side and was a Captain in his brother, the regicide's, regiment of foot at the creation of the New Model Army (see chapter on "The Honourable Members from the Army" and its Appendix, where I give the newly-found original list of New Model officers, and where I distinguish Ingoldsby's regiment as the Sixth of Foot), was a Colonel in Ireland by August, 1652, where he was closely associated with his father-in-law, the regicide, Sir Hardress Waller, and brother-in-law, Walter Waller,[187] became M. P. for Limerick, Clare and Kerry in the Protectorate Parliaments of 1654, 1656, and 1658, along with his father-in-law and brother-in-law,[188] was Governor of Limerick in 1659 and vowed "he would withstand (the reinstated Commonwealth) to the wearing out of his old shoes",[189] was created a baronet by Oliver Cromwell, March 31, 1657/8, besieged and took Windsor Castle for the King at the Restoration, was recreated a baronet by Charles II, August 30, 1660, married Anne, daughter of Sir Hardress Waller the regicide, leaving issue, and died in Ireland in 1701; George, married ..... Gold, became a Major in Parliamentary Army in Ireland and was of Ballybricken;[190] was knighted in 1671, and died in the Dutch wars;[191] Thomas, married widow of Alderman Langhorne, became Captain in the regicide's New Model regiment, apparently promoted Captain at the siege of Bristol, where he was wounded, in succession to two Captains successively killed at the same siege - Captains Andrew Ward and (Robert?) Williams, was accepted as Captain in regiment of Colonel Matthew Alured in 1659 only by special vote of Parliament,[192] but continued as Captain January 12, 1660;[193] William, born 1627; Elizabeth, born 1618, died unmarried; Sarah, died unmarried; Anne, born 1626, married Sir Edward Chaloner, nephew of the regicide Thomas Chaloner; Mary, born 1629, married Major Thomas Reade of the New Model Army's Eleventh Regiment of Foot, who was wounded at the siege of Taunton when his Colonel was killed, and later was highly praised by the regicide Thomas Horton for his fighting at the Battle of St. Fagan's in 1648, became a Colonel, and died 1662, by which time his widow was another woman, named Priscilla.[194]

Prominent Relations: Oliver Cromwell was the regicide's mother's first cousin, so that Ingoldsby was through that connection related to the vast Cromwellian family-complex. Thomas Chaloner the regicide and his brother James Chaloner, M.P. were both uncles of Ingoldsby's sister's husband. Sir Hardress Waller the regicide was father-in-law to Ingoldsby's brother, Henry, but by 1658 at the latest these two regicides were at odds over a debt, and Ingoldsby was very hard on Waller about it (see document "Petition of Richard Ingoldsby (1660)", in which Ingoldsby says that he "did seize upon and mark ... for his own use" the goods and chattels of Waller , - this document is in the Appendix to this Chapter). Ingoldsby's wife was daughter of Sir George Croke, a judge of the King's Bench, who had been an M.P., and who spoke up against ship money and in defense of John Hampden (see DNB); through this connection, the regicide was related by marriage to Robert Croke, M.P. for Wendover in the Long Parliament (disabled for royalism, November 13,1645)[195] and other Crokes who were mostly royalists, and Bulstrode Whitelocke, a relation of the Crokes whose son nearly became the regicide's son-in-law in 1671 but didn't because the Ingoldsbys were asking for too great a jointure settlement.[196] It should perhaps be noted that the regicide's first cousin Major Philip Cromwell (second son of Sir Philip) served as the regicide's Major in the Sixth Regiment of Foot in the New Model Army, and died of wounds received at the storming of Bristol.

Pedigrees: *Visitation of Buckinghamshire, 1634,* Harleian Society, London, Vol. 58, pp. 75-6. Burke's *Extinct and Dormant Baronetage,* 1844, pp. 277-8. And there is an annotated pedigree of some length in Mark Noble, *Memoirs of the Protectoral House of Cromwell,* 1787, pp. 181-91.

HENRY IRETON. Baptized November 3, 1611, at Attenborough, near Nottingham. Eldest son of German (or Germain) Ireton, of Attenborough, Nottinghamshire, and Jane ....(surname unknown). The regicide's father was buried at Attenborough on May 18,1624, leaving the young Henry head of the family at the age of only 12, which may go some way towards explaining his reported seriousness of manner. I have done an enormous amount of work on the Ireton family, and have discovered that they can be traced back to the time of William the Conqueror, and a man called Sewallus. It was his great-grandson, Fulcherus, who first took the designation "de Ireton" in the reign of Richard I. He had a son Henry de Ireton who had a son Henry de Ireton who married Ellena, daughter of the Baron Langton (reign of Edward I), of Newton. One of his grandsons, William Ireton, married Philippa, daughter of Henry Chandos, presumably related to the Lords Chandos; but they were not direct ancestors of the regicide. I have accumulated a number of wills and inventories of goods of early Iretons, and these commence with John Ireton of Ireton (died 1534), whose wife was Anna Curzon, apparently of the family of which the present Earl Howe and Baroness Zouch are descended; the father of this Anna was John Curzon of Kedleston. It is a curious fact that at an earlier date the Ireton and Curzon families were party to a legal dispute: Richard de Curzon, valet of Philip Lovel the High Treasurer, sued Henry Ireton of Ireton (son of Fulcherus de Ireton) for taking and detaining his cattle in the 39th of Henry III. The same Curzons of Kedleston from whom this ancestress of Henry Ireton the regicide came were represented in the Long Parliament by Sir John Curzon, Bart. (1598-1686), M.P. for Derbyshire, secluded in December, 1648, at Pride's Purge. Keeler remarks on his "old county family, famed for their riches and hospitality".[197] This M.P. and Henry Ireton were probably something like fourth cousins three times removed, but I have not worked it out precisely yet; one wonders whether they were aware of it. Probably Ireton realized Curzon was a distant cousin of some kind. The Iretons for centuries were a Derbyshire family, seated at Ireton, from which they took the surname. The regicide's great-great-great grandfather, John Ireton (mentioned above, married Anna Curzon) was seated at Ireton at his death, and it is interesting that in his will he left, amongst many other charitable dispensations, five shillings to the church. at Kedleston, the Curzon family's church; a transcription of this will is given in the Appendix to this chapter, and it will be seen there that it mentions both his son. and his grandson, the first German Ireton, by name. By the time of the regicide's grand father's generation, the Iretons were spreading down into Nottinghamshire; the second German Ireton, the regicide's greatuncle, resided at Hurst Grange, Cuckney, Notts., and Administration was granted to his widow Frances on February 11, 1595/6.[198] This German Ireton's brother, William Ireton, married Maria, daughter of George, Tenth Baron Zouch, who was thus the regicide's great grandfather. Lord Zouch was summoned to Parliament, 1553-66, and died, 1569. He was succeeded by his son, Edward, Eleventh Baron Zouch, who died 1625, and was the regicide's second cousin (or the regicide was his first cousin twice removed, however one prefers to view it). About 1605, the regicide's father purchased a lease of the rectory of Attenborough, a small hamlet near Nottingham, and settled there.[199] The regicide's siblings, in descending order by sex, were: Clement, born between 1611 and 1615, who became a well-known Fifth Monarchy Man,[200] and was appointed one of the City of London Commissioners for the Militia by the Committee of Safety in November, 1659;[201] John, baptized October 17, 1615, became Lord Mayor of London in 1658, was knighted by Cromwell, and had a career too complicated to survey here (see DNB); Matthew, baptized between 1615 and 1619 (entry illegible in parish register) but is not heard of after 1639; Thomas, baptized May 4, 1619, at formation of the New Model Army, was Captain of Horse in the Seventh Regiment of Horse intended for Colonel Algernon Sidney, but eventually commanded by Colonel Nathaniel Rich, was a radical officer who signed June 18, 1647, letter drafted by Lewis Audley at St. Alban's,[202] became Major, and died 1652, leaving a fascinating and lengthy will which revealed many curious facts about his family and circumstances, - he owned the Manor of Ireton Wood, Derbyshire, and left £100 to his "cousin" Thomas Cockeram, to whom he was only related through his seven-times great grandmother in the year 1340!! (John Ireton in 1534 left John Cockeram a young ram, in the will in the Appendix, so the Iretons and the Cockerams seem to have been keeping in touch for three centuries); Mary, married William Bainbridge of

Lockington, Leicestershire, on November 12, 1638;[203] Sarah, married the royalist Edward Ford, eldest son of Sir William Ford of Harting, Sussex. This royalist brother-in-law and Henry Ireton the regicide were on very friendly terms despite the fact that Ford was made a Colonel and High Sheriff of Sussex by Charles I, who knighted Ford during the Civil War, on October 4, 1643, at Oxford.[204] Thomas Ireton left Ford £5 for a ring, and his wife £40 for a jewel.[205]

Prominent Relations: Apart from those mentioned already, Ireton was second cousin twice removed of the regicide John Hutchinson; this has already been mentioned under Hutchinson, and is discussed at length in my forthcoming article in the *Nottinghamshire Historian*, "The Relationship between Henry Ireton and John Hutchinson". [This article was not completed or published owing to circumstances.] Ralph, Lord Grey of Warke, married Ireton's niece, Catherine Ford. The royalist Lord Culpepper was father-in-law of one of the Ford daughters. Oliver St. John described himself as Ireton's "cousin", but the nature of their relationship has not yet been determined. Ireton was related to the Sacheverell family, since his great-aunt Jane married Henry Sacheverell. Last, but by no means least, Oliver Cromwell was Ireton's father-in-law, and the story of their association is too well known to need description.

Pedigrees: MS. pedigree in the British Library: ADD. MS. 6,669, pp. 211-2. Also, there are six pages in Latin by Thomas Shirley about the Ireton family as far as Henry VI's time, on pp. 25-30 of MS. Harleian 4028 (also called ADD. MS. 6671 for some reason!). An Ireton pedigree is found in MS. Vincent 146 for Derbyshire, in the College of Arms in London, f. 23 9.

JOHN JONES. Said to have been born in the parish of Tregaron, Anglesey, in 1579, though I am certain the regicide was much younger than this;[206] if this information were true, he would have been 81 at his execution in 1660! *The Dictionary of Welsh Biography* altered the suggested birth date to "1597?", which suggests that the earlier "1579" may have been discovered to have been a mere typographical error.[207] But in my opinion, even 1597 is too early. Jones was born in the newer of the two family houses at Maes-y-Garnedd, at Llanbedr, Gwynedd (using the modern name), near the celebrated Pass of Drws Ardudwry, in what was previously called Merionethshire, Wales.[208] This substantial stone house, in a dramatically wild and lonely setting, is still standing and is a Grade II officially Listed building described as 'probably early 17th century'. Jones's second wife, Catherine Cromwell, was born in 1597; so we must presume he was not too much younger than that himself. He was the second son of Thomas ab John or Jones, of Maes-y-Garnedd and of Kilcychwyn (or Cilchochwyn), Merionethshire,[209] and Elin (or Ellen), daughter of Robert Wynn, of Taltreuddyn, Llanenddwyn, Merionethshire. The regicide's father more fully styled himself in a document of 1622 (the marriage settlement of the regicide's older brother Edward) "Thomas ap John ap Ievan ap Hugh, of Llanbeder, Co. of Merion., gent."[210] (Maes-y-Garnedd's "new mansion house", the one still standing, was retained by the father for life, but its "old mansion house" was reserved as jointure for life on the regicide's mother; many family properties are mentioned.)[211]

John Jones was descended from both the English and Welsh kings. It is truly remarkable that the very day of King Charles I's execution is the date given on an elaborate pedigree compiled for John Jones which commences with the following introductory paragraph: "This is the Pedigree and Achievement of the honourable and truly noble Colonell John Jones, Esquire, a Member of Parliament, and one of the honourable counsell of the state of England, declaring his descent, together with the descent of his vertuous consort, as well from the

Royall blood of the Norman and Plantagenetts, Kings of England, as from all the Royall races and nobilitie of Wales, and selected out of the Exchequer rolles, and other records remayning at Caernarvon, and also out of antient charters, Euidence, and works of the best approved Antiquaries and Bards of Wales, vidlit. Caradoc of Llangarnon, Cwnddelw Brydydd Mawr, Iolo Goch, Lewis Glyn Cothi, Guthyn Owen, Gwilim Tew, &c., by the industrie and trauail of Robett Vaughan of Hebgwrt in the county of Merioneth, Esquire, and finished the 30th day of Januarie, Anno Dom. 1649⁰."[212] Although the document was prepared after Jones became a member of the Council of State, the author obviously wished to underscore an incredible historical coincidence, that he had finished the pedigree on the day of the execution of the King, showing that Jones was descended from kings himself. This Robert Vaughan "was a very celebrated antiquary and genealogist, and a country gentleman of high position".[213] The regicide's immediate antecedents were not as illustrious as his distant ones: "Though of no great wealth, his family was of ancient descent, being derived from the great House of Nanney, through Howel ab Ynyr Vychan an Ynyr an Meurig, Lord of Nannau, ab Madog ab Cadwgan ab Bleddyn ab Cynfyn, Prince of Powys."[214] In the father's line, the regicide was directly descended from Jevan ap Jevan, Constable of Harlech Castle in the time of Henry VI, and from Osborne Fitzgerald, Lord of Ynsymaengwyn.[215] As another scholar put it in 1872: "Colonel Jones was a younger son of an ancient descent, but, in his own branch of it, of small property and of little weight, in the county of Merioneth. He was, however, lineally descended from the great house of Nanney, in that county, ... (through) Howel ap Ynyr Vychan, who was coroner for the county of Merioneth from 11 to 17 Edw. III, an office then of more importance than at present."[216] It should be perhaps noted that Ludlow said of Jones that he "was a gentleman of North Wales; of a competent estate and good interest in his country".[217] Jones had an older brother, Edward, who married in 1622 Elizabeth, daughter of Ievan ap Humphrey of Llanenthoyn, Merionethshire, and died 1623 leaving an only daughter. The regicide's younger brothers were: Humphrey, mercer, of Paternoster Row, London, who was the regicide's banker, business agent, and finally executor, dying 1690; Henry, who became Deputy Governor of Dublin under his relation Sir Theophilus Jones, was still in Ireland in 1659 but died before 1664, he and Humphrey were joint purchasers in 1648 during the sale of Bishops' lands of the manor and lordship of Istervin in Flintshire and Denbighshire for £1254[218] - and a youngest brother, Richard Jones.

Prominent Relations: The regicide's second wife was Catherine Cromwell, third sister of Oliver Cromwell. But this marriage in 1656 was only a very late association with the Cromwell family, not relevant to his earlier career. The regicide Humphrey Edwardes was a cousin of the regicide's first wife, Margaret Edwardes. Through his mother, the regicide was a cousin of Sir Hugh Middleton, Sir William Middleton, and Sit Thomas Middleton. The latter, who was M.P. for Denbighshire in the Long Parliament, actually brought Jones to London as his agent and clerk in the early 1640s. Middleton's brother-in-law was Sir Robert Napier, Bart., M.P. for Peterborough in the Long Parliament.[219] More closely related to the regicide through his mother, née Wynn, than the Middletons, was Sir Richard Wynn, Bart., M.P. for Liverpool in the Long Parliament, who had two nephews in the Long Parliament, John Bodvel (or Bodville or Bodevile), M.P. for Anglesey (who became a royalist) and John Mostyn, M.P. for Flintshire (also became a royalist).[220] The naval Captain Henry Whitstone was the regicide's step-son, as his second wife Catherine Cromwell's first husband had been Roger Whitstone; another step-son, Sir Thomas Whitestone, petitioned unsuccessfully for the regicide's estates at the Restoration.[221] The regicide was related to Lewis Jones, Bishop of Killaloe, and his four sons, Henry Jones, Scoutmaster General, General Michael Jones, Sir Theophilus Jones, and Bishop Ambrose Jones (for them see DNB).[222] (The regicide was not related to Colonel Philip Jones.)

Pedigrees: The extensive and elaborate pedigree prepared for the regicide, mentioned above, apparently still exists, along with one or two copies of it. Two brief excerpts from it have been printed.[223] At the turn of the century it was still in the possession of a descendant of the regicide, the Rev. Cyrus Moirall, of Plas Yolyn, Chirk.[224] Preliminary efforts to find it have failed, but I shall continue the search.

The coat of arms of Robert Liluburne the regicide (and of his brother John, the Leveller.)

ROBERT LILBURNE. Born 1613/4. Eldest son of Richard Lilburne of Thickley Puncherdon, Durham (1583-1667), and Margaret, daughter of Thomas Hickson or Hixon, Yeoman of the Wardrobe to Queen Elizabeth. The Lilburnes traced their descent from Sir William Lilburne, Lord Warden of the Middle Marches, in mediaeval times.[225] The brother of the regicide's five-times-great grandfather was Constable of Alnwick in the reign of Henry VI, and the regicide's great grandfather, Bartholomew Lilburne, "was at Bullon with Henry VIII".[226] He died in 1562.[227] The regicide's uncle George Lilburne was M.P. for Sunderland and died 1667. His son Thomas became an officer in Monck's Army.[228] Gregg says George Lilburne died 1676; but these figures must have been accidentally reversed![229] The regicide's father and uncle, George, were both on the Committee of Durham during the Civil War.[230] They were known locally as "the two Lilborns" and worked closely together.[231] The regicide had one sister, Elizabeth, who married first Robert Chambers and second Thomas Gower. The regicide had two brothers: John (1615-1657), who was the famous Lieutenant-Colonel John Lilburne the Leveller (see DNB and countless other sources) about whom so much has been written that it would be pointless for me to recapitulate his career here; and Henry (1618-1648, Governor of Tynemouth who on August 9, 1648, declared for the King but was killed the next day in a successful assault by Parliamentary forces.[232] Since the regicide's relations with his notorious brother, John, are still the subject of much dispute and speculation (J.S. Morrill recently saying of the regicide: "He stood alongside his brother John at the latter's trial in 1649, but otherwise dissociated himself from him ..."[233]) I include in the Appendix to this chapter the transcription of a document I have found amongst the Clarke MSS. at Worcester College, Oxford, headed "Robert Lilburne Tries to Save His Embarrassing Brother by Offering His Emigration to America (1649)".

Prominent Relations: Apart from his own family, Lilburne was related through his wife, Margaret Beke, to Colonel Richard Beke of Haddenham, Buckinghamshire, descended from Queen Elizabeth's chief equerry, important during the Protectorate, and the last man knighted by Richard Cromwell before the Restoration, came to terms with the Restoration, later becoming M.P. for Aylesbury and then Wendover.[234] This man was the brotherin law of the regicide; the old DNB erred in making him his father-in-law. Lilburne's wife was also the niece of Simon Mayne, the regicide. She was also related to the Lovelaces and, by marriage, to Henry Marten the regicide. Oliver Cromwell was uncle by marriage to Lilburne's brother-in-law Beke. Through these connections by marriage, one could extend the network with which Lilburne became associated.

Pedigrees: An MS. pedigree exists in the John Rylands Library in Manchester: ENG. MS. 136. A pedigree of "Lilburne of Thickley" going back 13 generations and signed by the regicide's father is found in Foster, ed., *Durham Visitation Pedigrees Recorded 1575, 1615, and 1666*, pp. 214-5. Pauline Gregg has printed a pedigree constructed by herself and going back to 1526, on p. 360 of *Free-Born John, A Biography of John Lilburne*, Harrap, London, 1961.

JOHN LISLE. Born 1606. Eldest son of Sir William Lisle (knighted May 20, 1606 at Whitehall,[235] died October 21,1648[236]) of Wootton on the Isle of Wight, Hants., and Bridget, daughter of Sir John Hungerford of Down Ampney, Gloucestershire. The Lisles were an extremely ancient family, originally called de Insula. In the 1650s, their neighbour Sir John Oglander wrote of them: "There have been many families of the Lisles or de Insulas, as so many conduits from the springhead, Wootton. Our family hath matched divers times with theirs, our 2 families being the most ancient of any in the Island by many hundreds of years, and they always lived well, which I hope will continue."[237] The regicide's ancestor John de Insula was summoned to the House of Lords by King Edward II.[238] Robert de Insula, Bishop of Durham from 1274 to 1283, and excommunicated in 1280, appears to have been of this family (see his entry in DNB for account of his life). Thomas Lisle, Bishop of Ely who died 1361, may have been of the family (see his entry in DNB). I have not found a satisfactory account of the Lisle family by this date of writing. Keeler claims that the regicide was a "younger son", but he was actually the eldest son.[239] The second son was William Lisle, admitted to Middle Temple 21 April, 1634, called to the bar 4 June 1641, Bencher 30 October, 1663, Master in Chancery, June 1665, became a royalist, and was knighted by Charles II on the same day as his neighbour William Oglander, July 4, 1665.[240] The regicide had two sisters, Lettice and Bridget. Bridget, on September 24, 1632, being "a rude girl and ill brought up, her parents letting her have her way in all things, ran away with one Mr. Jennings, an ironmonger's second son. She was a handsome gentlewoman, aged 20 years."[241] The third son, and the regicide's youngest brother, was Daniel, admitted to Middle Temple, November 16, 1646, called to bar, February 7, 1650/1. There is a possibility that a Thomas Lisle was another son, for he signed a petition with the regicide's father to the Parliament, October 24, 1644, in favour of Lord Pembroke as Governor of the Isle of Wight; or this man may have been a cousin of some sort.[242] It should perhaps be remarked that a very large number of the regicide's ancestors are to be found in William A. Shaw's 2 vols. *The Knights of England*;

that Johannes de Insula, Lord Lisle of the Isle of Wight, and his son, Walter, were both made Knights of the Bath by King Edward I, May 22, 1306; that a later John Lisle was made Knight of the Bath by King Henry IV at his coronation, March 17, 1400; that Nicholas Lisle was summoned to be created Knight of the Bath at the coronation of King Edward V, but as the ceremony did not take place, he eventually received this honour at the coronation of Elizabeth, Queen of Henry VII, four years later, in 1487; and so on.[243]

Prominent Relations: Dennis Bond, M.P. of the Long Parliament, was second cousin of the regicide's second wife. Sir Thomas Bond, Bart., Comptroller of the Household to Queen Henrietta Maria, was the same wife's third cousin twice removed. It is possible, but not established, that the regicide's second wife was a relation of the M.P. of the Long Parliament Richard Long (died 1648), through her mother Ann Long. Chief Justice Sir Henry Hobart was the regicide's father-in-law through his first wife, Mary, who died 1633. The regicide's brother-in-law married to another Hobart girl was the M.P. of the Long Parliament, Sir Robert Crane, Bart., who died February 17, 1643.[244] Through his mother, a Hungerford, the regicide was related to all the Hungetfords, which included three M.P.s of the Long Parliament: Anthony, Sir Edward, and Henry Hungerford, -who were brothers. The regicide was also closely related to the regicide Daniel Blagrave, whose grandmother, Anne Hungerford, was of the same family as Lisle's mother, - probably her aunt - so that these two regicides were probably second cousins. The regicide William Say was, according to Ludlow, "a kinsman of Mr. Lisle's wife",[245] meaning Lisle's second wife of course. The relationship was through Say's grandmother Patience White, daughter of Robert White of Christchurch, Hants., who was related to the second Mrs. Lisle's father.

Pedigrees: A manuscript pedigree is in the Bodleian Library at Oxford: MS. Rawlinson B. 77, f. 65a-b. The regicide is mentioned in the three following printed pedigrees: "Bond, of Grange", in John Burke, *A Genealogical and Heraldic History of the Commoners of Great Britain and Ireland*, Vol. I, London, 1836, p. 241. "Descendants of Alice Lisle", *The Genealogist*, Vol. V, p. 186. "The Descendants of Alice Lisle". *The Genealogist*, Vol. VI, p. 13.

SIR MICHAEL LIVESEY, BART. (Created a Baronet, July 11, 1627.) Born 'either 1611 or 1614', though obviously the former, because otherwise he would have been made a baronet aged only 13.[246] Only surviving son of Gabriel Livesey of Lynstead, of Hollingbourne, and of the Parsonage, East Church, Kent, and his second wife, Anne, daughter of Sir Michael Sondes (knighted at Greenwich June 18, 1598, by Queen Elizabeth[247]), of Throwley, Kent. Gabriel's first wife had been Anne, daughter of Sir Thomas Crompton, but there was no-issue. The regicide had a brother, Robert, who died in infancy, and no other siblings. Gabriel's first marriage had been at Hounslow in June, 1598. His second was July 7, 1608, by license, at Throwley, Kent. He was Sheriff of Kent in 1618, and died March 18, 1622. The regicide had many illustrious and distinguished ancestors. The Liveseys themselves originated at Livesey, Lancashire, and by way of Nottinghamshire and Derbyshire they came south in the person of the regicide's grandfather, Robert Livesey of Streatham and Tooting-Bec, Surrey. He was twice Sheriff of Sussex and Surrey, in 1592 and 1602. He died August 21, 1608, aged 81, and John Aubrey has recorded the tomb inscription, in which he is further described as "an Auntient Justice of Peace of approved Wisdome, Integritie, Courage, and Industrie".[248] Through this Robert's second wife, the regicide's grandmother, Elizabeth Berkeley, the regicide's descent was of considerable antiquity and distinction. His ancestors included: Sir Thomas Lawne (or de la Launde), knighted by Henry VII "at the bridge foot on the King's entering London after the Battle of Blackheath", in 1497;[249] Lionel de Welles, Sixth Baron Welles, who accompanied Henry VI to France and was later a Lord Lieutenant of Ireland 1438-40 (see his entry in the old DNB), was the regicide's great-great-great-

great grandfather (these Welles's go back at least to Adam, Baron Welles who died 1311, who has an entry in DNB); the family of d'Engayne (d'Angain, and other variant spellings) who were prominent warrior knights under King Edward III and the Black Prince;[250] the northern warrior knights, the Watertons; and the very distinguished Berkeley family who can be traced back to at least 1086 (see "Family of Berkeley" entered in DNB) and to list whose prominent personages, amongst the regicide's ancestors, would take too much space here.[251]

Prominent Relations: Sir Edward Peyton, Bart., M.P., of Isleham Cambridgeshire, was the regicide's uncle; he died in April, 1657.[252] His son, Sir John Peyton, Bart., was thus the regicide's first cousin, who in turn was first cousin of Sir Thomas Peyton, Bart., of Knowlton, who was M.P. for Sandwich in the Long Parliament (disabled February 5, 1644).[253] The regicide's cousin Sir John Peyton married, first, a Bellingham girl who was related to Sir Henry Bellingham, Bart., M.P. for Westmorland in the Long Parliament (disabled October 11, 1645);[254] this Sir John's second wife being a Hobart, it is by no means improbable that the regicide was related by marriage to Sir John Hobart, Bart., recruiter M.P. from Norfolk, who was in turn related to the regicide John Lisle, whose first wife had been a Hobart.

Pedigrees: "Livesey, of East Church", in Burke's *Extinct and Dormant Baronetcies*, 1844, pp. 317-8. "Livesey Pedigree" in *Archaeologia Cantiana*, Vol. XXVI, 1904, pp. 326-7. Four lines, hardly a pedigree, starting and ending with the regicide, are in the Bodleian Library: MS. Rawlinson B. 77, f. 74a.

EDMUND LUDLOW. Born 1619. Eldest son of Sir Henry Ludlow (1592-1643), M.P. for Wiltshire in the Long Parliament until his death, and who has an entry in Keeler,[255] and Elizabeth, daughter of Richard Phelipps, of Whitchurch, Dorset (she was buried at St. Andrew's, Holborn, London, November 6, 1660). The regicide's parents were married January 6, 1611/2, at the Chapel of the Rolls in Chancery Lane, London. The regicide's grandfather, Sir Edmund Ludlow (knighted by Queen Elizabeth, September 14, 1601[256]), had been M.P. for Hindon in 1603. He died 1625, and his Inquisition Post Mortem is printed.[257] He had been Sheriff of Wiltshire in the 28th year of Elizabeth, and his father before him had been Sheriff for the county in 1567. The regicide's father was Sheriff in 1633, and the regicide himself was Sheriff in 1645. The regicide's father was one of the most fiery and determined opponents of prerogative government and of Charles I.[258] The Ludlows traced their descent from William Ludlow of Hill Deverill, Wiltshire, who was Butler to Kings Henry IV, V, and VI, and became M.P. for Ludgershall, Wilts., dying in 1478. The regicide's great-grandmother was Edith, third daughter of Lord Windsor, of Stanwell, Middlesex, and two generations earlier he had an ancestress who was one of the Bulstrodes. The regicide's grandmother was Margaret, daughter of Henry Manning, who was Marshal of the Household to Queen Elizabeth, and whose previous husband had been Thomas Howard, Viscount Bindon, the third son of Thomas, Duke of Norfolk. The regicide's next brother was Robert Ludlow, who was himself a firebrand against Charles I, along with Dr. John Bostwick and "two other famous firebrands of this State"; Robert Ludlow was seized by the royalists, imprisoned in York Castle, July, 1642, and died a prisoner the following year, aged only 22.[259] The regicide describes in his Memoirs how Charles I had wanted to execute Robert Ludlow and was only prevented from doing so by Parliament threatening retaliatory executions of royalists if the King did it.[260] This brother was, during his brief active time, a Captain of foot.[261] The regicide's next brother was Thomas, who was on friendly terms with Oliver Cromwell,[262] was alive in 1660, but of whom not much is known. The next brother was Nathaniel, baptized at Maiden Bradley, Wilts., April 13, 1624, and died 1701. Since he was executor of various family wills, including his father's, he may well have been a lawyer. Next in age was a sister, Frances, baptized at Maiden Bradley, October 6, 1626, and buried there April, 1632, aged 5.

The next sibling was Philip, baptized at Maiden Bradley, April 15, 1628, became Lieutenant of the ship under Admiral Edward Popham, and was entrusted by Popham with command of an entire sea convoy of eighteen captured Portuguese ships and English ships to guard them, which sailed back to England, and as "commander-in-chief of the Brazeele merchant ships" convoy, he died on board the *Sephier*, August 13, 1650, either of wounds or sickness. He was buried with honour in Westminster Abbey.[263] The next sibling was Henry, baptized at Maiden Bradley, February 19, 1629/30. He was the ancestor of the Earls Ludlow (title extinct, 1842), but little is known of him otherwise. There were three further sisters: Elizabeth, married Colonel Nicholas Kempston (see below); Margaret, married (in 1623) Giles Strangeways (1602-1677) of Charlton Adam, East Charlton, Somerset; Mary, married 1656 to John Brent of Cossington, Somerset.

Special note: The regicide must not be confused with a notoriously unpleasant and obnoxious first cousin named Edmund Ludlow (will proved in London, February 23, 1645/6), who married Elizabeth, daughter of Giles Penny, of Coker, Somerset. This Edmund's own father (also a Henry, as with the regicide) described him in a letter to Sir Robert Phelipps in the summer of 1632 as "my foolish son now in Yeovil Prison".[264] An undated document (which must be between 1639 and 1646) preserved for no obvious reason amongst the State Papers in the Public Record Office describes this Edmund's "sinister Waies and delayes ... to distresse ... and keepe ... from maintenance and Livelyhoods" his seven brothers and sisters, whose money he stole, and whom he treated abominably. A very severe judicial order was issued against him, giving him only twelve days to become a reformed character. He seems to have exasperated everyone he met.[265]

Prominent Relations: Edward Phelipps, M.P. for Ilchester in the Long Parliament, and secluded for royalism February 5, 1644, was the regicide's second cousin. Sir Thomas Phelipps. Master of the Rolls, had been the regicide's mother's uncle and guardian. Sir Henry Vane the Elder's wife was daughter of Sir Edward Phelipps, Master of the Rolls and Speaker of the House who died 1614, so that there was thus a relationship by marriage between the regicide and the two Sir Henry Vanes. Robert Wallop, the M.P. for Andover in the Long Parliament, who sat on the High Court of Justice but did not sign the Death Warrant, was described in the Memoirs by Ludlow as "my cousin".[266] This Wallop's father, Sir Henry Wallop, was also an M.P. (for Hampshire) in the Long Parliament, but died, November, 1642, before Ludlow entered the House. The Wallops were related to many M.P.s in the Long Parliament: William Heveningham, who sat on the High Court of Justice but did not sign the Death Warrant, was Sir Henry Wallop's son-in-law, who was in turn related by marriage to the regicide John Downes (see *ante*); Lyttons, Barringtons, Worsleys, Palmes, Holles, Harleys, Jervoises, and others, were relations.[267] Sir John and Giles Strangeways (father and son, M.P.s of the Long Parliament, were only distant cousins of the regicide's brother-in-law, another Giles Strangeways, but they were doubly related to the regicide, since the M.P. Giles Strangeways's son, Thomas, married the grand-daughter of the notorious, obnoxious, Edmund Ludlow, the regicide's first cousin. The regicide was distantly related to the Bulstrodes and to Bulstrode Whitelocke, M.P., with whom he was on amicable though not intimate terms. The regicide's grandfather (through his mother) was Sir John Stradling, and Ludlow was thus a cousin of numerous Stradlings, most of whom were prominent as royalists. A letter to Ludlow which shows a fair degree of intimacy, from Colonel Thomas Stradling, whom Ludlow calls his "uncle"[268] "who had been constantly of the King's party", as had his brother Sir Edward Stradling, survives. I have transcribed it and it will be found in the Appendix to the chapter "The Regicides under the Protectorate". Ludlow had much to do with his brother-in-law, Nicholas Kempston, an officer in the Army who was Lieutenant-Colonel to the regicide

Colonel Robert Lilburne for some time, and later served in Ireland. There are frequent references to him in Ludlow's *Memoirs* (see Index). An account of Kempston's career and an explanation of certain curious aspects of his political position (especially in 1647) would be too lengthy for the space available here, though I have found a very great quantity of documentary material about this man.

Pedigrees: A manuscript pedigree dated 1646 and culminating in the regicide himself, is in the Bodleian Library: MS. Rawlinson B. 77, f. 108b. An enormous fold-out printed pedigree is in *Wiltshire Archaeological and Natural History Magazine*, Vol. XXVI, 1892, at page 173.

HENRY MARTEN. Born 1602 at Oxford. Elder son by his first wife of Sir Henry Marten (knighted at Theobalds by James I, December 21, 1616[269]), M.P. and Judge and Member of the Court of High Commission, who died 1641. The regicide's father has his own entry in DNB, and the regicide and his father are each separately noticed at length by Anthony à Wood in *Athenae Oxoniensis*.[270] (It is Wood who records the regicide's birth in a house opposite Merton College Church.) Wood, who was no admirer of the regicide, praised his father's legal and judicial abilities, calling him "the best, for ought that I know, that ever appeared in our Horizon, and therefore venerated by all good and learned Men."[271] The regicide's mother was named Elizabeth, and her maiden name is thought to have been Reynolds, though not with any degree of certainty. There is widespread disagreement and confusion over the regicide's antecedents. Williams has maintained that the regicide's father was "the son of an obscure yeoman worth no more than £60 a year".[272] Mrs. Cole has said: "The origins of the Marten family are obscure." She puts above the regicide's father in a pedigree drawn by herself "Parents doubtful".[273] Durston says: "The origins of the Marten family of Longworth and Shrivenham Berkshire are somewhat obscure . ... The only agreed facts about Sir Henry's parents are that they were of low social status, and owned a small estate worth between £400 and £600 a year."[274] Several writers have maintained that the regicide's father was son of Anthony Marten of London, who was the son of William Marten of Oakingham, Berkshire.[275] Wood himself maintained this, and he must have acquired his information so early that his testimony is of great weight.[276] After much searching, I have located a seventeenth century manuscript pedigree showing the descent of the Marten family which seems to resolve these doubts. This pedigree, deposited in the College of Arms, confirms the regicide's descent from Anthony Marten as maintained by Wood.[277] The pedigree goes back a surprising number of generations, and in light of further study of it and the leads it offers for confirmation from other quarters, a complete reevaluation of the regicide's family antecedents will be required. Due to the extreme difficulty of making use of material in the College of Arms, a study of this kind has had to be deferred and cannot be incorporated here, and awaits a future occasion. In the meantime, it must be stressed, that all matters concerning the regicide's antecedents earlier than his father must be considered an "open case", and the jury is still out. This means an inevitably incomplete consideration of the regicide's relations. The regicide had several younger siblings and halfsiblings: a sister, Jane, was living 1618 but is presumed to have died fairly young. There was a brother, George, admitted to the Inner Temple, November 1631 (same year as the regicide John Downes and the year after Marten's kinsman Simon Mayne, the regicide), married Frances Weld (who died 1677), and died 1666. Several letters to the regicide from this brother are preserved at Leeds, in one of which the intimacy and friendship between the two brothers is well expressed by George, who says to Henry from Barbadoes in 1655: "Pray be pleased sometimes to let me hear from you, for I hope you doe not thinke there is any person can wish you more happiness or more reioyce at the newes of it then, Good Brother, Your most faitfull & affectionat Brother & servant George Marten".[278] There was a sister, Elizabeth, called Eliza, born 1603 and died 1694, who married Charles, son of

Sir Clement Edmonds (see DNB, an M.P. named Secretary of State in the year he died, 1622); a letter from her and one from her son, Charles, to the regicide in 1652, survive.[279] There was also a sister, Mary, who married firstly Sir Richard Rogers (knighted at Royston, July 19, 1621,[280] died 1635), and resided at Bray, but married secondly in or about 1661 to John Fenwick. One letter from her to the regicide in 1648 and two of his to her survive.[281]

Prominent Relations: I have not yet been able to establish whether the M.P.s of the Long Parliament, Hugh Rogers and Richard Rogers, were related to Marten through his brother-in-law mentioned above. Sir George Stonehouse, Bart., M.P. for Abingdon in the Long Parliament and disabled for royalism, January 22, 1644, was the regicide's first wife's brother-in-law. Through the same first wife, the first Lord Lovelace was Marten's father-in-law and the prominent royalist, the second Lord Lovelace, was Marten's brother-in-law. Simon Mayne the regicide was the nephew of Marten's first wife. Major John Wildman, the Leveller, was related to Marten by marriage and was his intimate friend; an account of their friendship and publication of their letters remains for a future occasion; this may be planned by Dr. C. M. Williams as part of his forthcoming book. [The updated account of Henry Marten by Professor Williams, based upon his earlier 1954 thesis, was never published, and it is unknown whether he ever finished it.]

Pedigrees: There is a manuscript pedigree in the Bodleian Library: MS. Rawlinson B. 77, ff. 160b161a. The pedigree in the College of Arms is: MS. Vincent, Berkshire 143, f. 81. Mrs. Cole has published a sketch pedigree: J.C. Cole, "Some Notes on Henry Marten, the Regicide, and His Family", *Berkshire Archaeological Journal*, Vol. 49, 1946, p. 41. Durston has sketched a pedigree: Christopher Durston, *Berkshire and Its County Gentry 1625-49*, a Ph.D. thesis in typescript deposited at the Berkshire County Record Office, Reading, p. 101 of Vol. II. See also C. M. Williams, *The Political Career of Henry Marten*, a 1954 Ph.D. thesis deposited in the Bodleian Library.

SIR THOMAS MAULEVERER, BART. (Created a baronet, August 2, 1641.) Baptized April 9, 1599. Elder son of Sir Richard Mauleverer (knighted by Queen Elizabeth February 16, 1583/4[282]), of Allerton Mauleverer, West Riding, Yorkshire, and his second wife Katherine, daughter of Sir Ralph Bourchier of Yorkshire (who may have been knighted on the same occasion as the regicide's father in 1583/4[283]). The regicide's father was Sheriff of Yorkshire in 1588, and died 1603. His first marriage (no issue) was November 19, 1562, to Johanna or Jane Mauleverer who was his own aunt by blood (i.e., his grandfather's daughter) and who had been married twice before, first to Henry Wharton and secondly to Robert, Lord Ogle; she died 1594. (This marriage raises interesting questions about what is and is not considered incest.) The Mauleverers were of extraordinary antiquity. Mark Noble says of them that they were "a most ancient and knightly family, seated at Allerton-Mauleverer, in Yorkshire, ever since the reign of William the Conqueror."[284] One 18th century pedigree MS. which I have found (the one which reveals the incest) traces the regicide's ancestors back a dizzying twenty generations before the regicide himself![285] The son of the first Mauleverer on the pedigree "built the Church at Allerton-Mauliverer", so he must have been a wealthy Norman magnate. There are other examples of Mauleverers marrying each other; the regicide's nine-times-great grandfather John married a relation, Mary Mauleverer. This pair's grandson, Sir John Maulverer, was knighted by Henry, Duke of Somerset at the Battle of Wakefield, December 30, 1460.[286] His son, Sir Alnathe (or Halneth) Mauleverer, was created a Knight of the Bath at the marriage of Arthur, Prince of Wales, November 14, 1501, by the proud father, Henry VII.[287] His great-grandson, the regicide's great-great-great grandfather, Sir Thomas Mauleverer, was knighted by the Earl of Hertford, the King's Lieutenant, at the burning of

Edinburgh, May 11, 1544.[288] His son, Sir Richard Mauleverer, was among those knighted to celebrate the coronation of Queen Mary Tudor, October 2, 1553.[289] His son Thomas was Sheriff of Yorkshire in 1552, and married Eleanor, daughter of either Sir Richard or Sir Henry Oughtred, and they were the great-grandparents of the regicide. The regicide had a younger brother, William, baptized at Allerton Mauleverer, 1602, matriculated pensioner St. John's College, Cambridge, Michaelmas, 1619, B.A. 1623, admitted (curiously) to Gray's Inn, November 1, 1619 (indicating that he studied at two places simultaneously?) There were two sisters: Elizabeth, baptized May 3, 1597, died within days and was buried, May 15, 1597; and Olivia, baptized April 9, 1598.

Prominent Relations: Sir John Bourchier the regicide was his first cousin, through his mother. Sir Philip Musgrave, Bart., M.P. for Westmorland in the Long Parliament, was the regicide's brother-in-law through his first wife, according to Keeler.[290] John Blakiston the regicide had a brother, Henry Blakiston, who married Mary Mauleverer, a distant relation, of the family of Arncliffe (a very tenuous connection). Thomas Scott, M.P. for Aldborough, was the regicide's son-in-law and married his daughter, Grace. Contrary to what other authorities have maintained, Mauleverer's son-in-law was not Thomas Scot the regicide: The son-in-law was the Leveller, Major or Colonel Thomas Scott, who has often been confused with the regicide, as they were M.P.s at the same time. The regicide had a well-known son, Sir Richard Mauleverer, Bart. (1623-1675), who was a well-known royalist and was declared an outlaw in 1654. Judge Sir Richard Hutton, one of the leading jurists of the seventeenth century, who died February 25, 1638/9, was the regicide's father-in-law in his first marriage. Through his second wife, the regicide was related to the Wilbrahams, and it appears that his father-in-law was the royalist,. Sir Thomas Wilbraham, Bart., of Woodhey, Cheshire, who "distinguished himself in the royal cause during the great rebellion."[291]

Pedigrees: MS. pedigree, "Mauliverer of Allerton-Mauliverer", pp. 2202, John Hopkinson and Thomas Wilson, *Collection of ... Descents of ... Families*, in York Minster Library. Burke's *Extinct and Dormant Baronetcies*, 1844, pp. 315-5. Brief section in MS. Rawlinson B. 77, f . 172a, in the Bodleian Library.

Special Note: I own a book in Latin which once belonged to this regicide, and bears his signature. The book is so intensely intellectual, that it suggests the regicide must have been so also.

SIMON MAYNE. Baptized February 17, 1611/12, at Dinton, Buckinghamshire. Only son of Simon Mayne, of Dinton Hall, Dinton, near Aylesbury, Buckinghamshire (this house is still standing and my wife and I have been to tea there), and Coluberry, daughter of Richard, the First Lord Lovelace (rather than his sister as maintained in the old DNB, who was widow of Richard Beke, who died 1606). The regicide's father was Sheriff of Buckinghamshire, dying aged 40, July 13, 1617, and is buried in Dinton Church. The regicide's mother died January 10, 1628/9, and is buried in Dinton Church. The will of the regicide's father was proved at London, September 11, 1617, by his relict, in which he kindly left £20 apiece to each of his wife's seven children by her first husband.[292] According to Browne Willis, the regicide's family were "a younger branch of the family of Co. Herts."[293] They were apparently not of an illustrious descent, though by the regicide's time they were very substantial in their county, which was only adopted by the regicide's father, who was a son of Henry Mayne of Bovenden or Bovington, Herts. The latter's grandfather was from Ascott.[294] None of the Maynes was ever knighted. The regicide had one sister, Coluberry, who married Thomas, son and heir to Henry Bulstrode, of Hedgly, Buckinghamshire.

Prominent Relations: Henry Marten the regicide was brother-in-law of Mayne's mother. Oliver Cromwell was the uncle by marriage of Mayne's nephew Richard Beke. Mayne was more closely related to both the Temple regicides than they were to each other: James Temple the regicide was the first cousin once removed (through the Andrews family of Lathbury, Bucks.) of Mayne's aunt, Maria Mayne; Peter

Dinton Hall in Buckinghamshire, the home of the regicide Simon Mayne. (Photo by Robert Temple)

Temple the regicide was the second cousin of Mayne's wife, Jane Burgoyne. Colonel Richard Beke, M.P. after the Restoration, was Mayne's nephew. Robert Lilburne the regicide was the husband of Mayne's niece, Margaret Beke. Through his sister, as mentioned above, Mayne was related by marriage to the Bulstrode family, and thus to Bulstrode Whitelocke, M.P. The first Lord Lovelace was the regicide's grandfather, and the second Lord Lovelace was his maternal uncle. But Mayne was doubly related to the Lords Lovelace, since his aunt was also a Lovelace. Sir John Burgoyne, Bart., M.P. of the Long Parliament, was the regicide's father-in-law. The regicide's nephew Richard Beke was married to Levina Whitstone, step-daughter of the regicide John Jones, and niece of Oliver Cromwell (as above mentioned). One piece of evidence survives of Mayne's having dealings with his relation, Henry Marten, in 1643, when Marten seems to have been of assistance to Mayne with regard to financial and property dealings.[295]

Pedigrees: MS. pedigree in the Bodleian Library: MS. Rawlinson. B. 77, ff. 127a-128b; the regicide is at the bottom of 128a, and his son Simon at the top of 128b. *Visitation of Warwickshire, 1619*, William Camden, Harleian Society, Vol. XII, 1877, pp. 330-1. *Visitation of Buckinghamshire in 1634*, Harleian Society, Vol. 58, p. 90.

Special Note: Included in the Appendix to this chapter, see my entry for Mayne prepared for the *Biographical Dictionary of British Radicals in the Seventeenth Century*.

GILBERT MILLINGTON. Born in or shortly before 1598. Elder son of Anthony Millington of Felley Abbey, Nottinghamshire (the house still stands), and Prudence, daughter of William Gilbert of Colchester, Proctor of the Arches. Although the regicide referred to his house as Felley Abbey, both before that time and since (and at the present), the house has more properly been known as Felley Priory, being on the site of the Priory of St. Mary, founded in 1156 for the Augustinians. The origins of the Millington family are thoroughly obscure, and they had not been at Felley before 1603, when Felley was granted to the regicide's father by James I.[296] The regicide's father died in 1620 and was buried at Greasley, Nottinghamshire, not before September (the parish register entry is illegibile for the date). His will was proved at London, November 4, 1620, by the regicide.[297] At the time the will was drawn up, in 1618, the regicide's father described himself as "of the parish of St Clement Danes Without Temple barr, in the county of Middlesex gentleman". Felley seems merely to have been his country seat. He had another country property at Nasinge, Essex, which was left to his younger son. Felley went to the regicide. And the house in London, which was held on lease from the Countess of Arundel, was left to the two sons jointly. The regicide's father left so much property, land, gold, and jewels, that one cannot but wonder where it all came from. Further research remains to be done on this family, and also on the Gilbert family. The regicide seems to have had three uncles: John Millington of Kimberley, Notts. (alive 1618); Nicholas Millington, buried at Greasley, Notts., December 18, 1612; and Percival Millington, who married Ellen Sugar or Singar, August 19, 1576, at St. Mary's Church, Nottingham, in 1583) lived at Long Rowe, Nottingham, and in 1597/8 was a leader of an attempt by the burgesses of Nottingham (of which he was one) to challenge corruption in the town's Common Council and overthrow the grip of an oligarchy there.[298] The regicide had one brother, John, who lived at Stanton, Nottinghamshire (and possibly also at Nasinge, Essex, unless he sold that property). He was, like the regicide, a lawyer. He was admitted to Lincoln's Inn, March 2, 1620/1, and called to the bar June 24, 1628. Before his legal training, he had attended Peterhouse, Cambridge (admitted pensioner, Michaelmas, 1613). He obtained a place as Purveyor of the Cellar to the King in 1626, and died before May 10, 1655, at which time his son and heir, John, was admitted to Lincoln's Inn. (Much of the above information was made available by myself, at his request, to Professor Bernerd C. Weber, who incorporated it in his entry for Millington in the *Biographical Dictionary of British Radicals in the Seventeenth Century* (1982-1984), but no acknowledgement was made, and so I am forced to mention the fact lest it be thought that I took the information from him which in fact I gave to him. Professor Weber appears to have died aged only 60 in 1987.)

Prominent Relations: None known.

Pedigrees: None known.

JOHN MOORE. Born 1599. Eldest son of Edward Moore of Bank Hall (not Banks Hall as in Keeler[299]), Walton, Liverpool, Lancashire, and the adjoining Old Hall, and Katherine, daughter of John Hockenhull or Hocknell, of Prenton, Cheshire, and his wife Margaret, who was apparently née Hockenhull or Hocknell also, who then remarried Edward Ravenscroft and died 1613.(This last refers to the regicide's grandmother.) The regicide's father was a J.P. by 1611, Sheriff of Lancashire on November 20, 1620, M.P. for Liverpool in the Parliament of 1625, and died 1633. What was by the time of the regicide the family's dower house, called the Old Hall, and formerly called Moore Hall, had been inhabited by the regicide's direct ancestor, Sir John de la More, as early as 1235.[300] A pedigree which had been in the possession of the regicide himself drew his descent from the time of William the Conqueror, commencing with this ancestor: "Steven de More, lord of Morehall in ye Com. of Lanc. in ye time of Will. Le Bastard, Duke of Normandy & Conqr of England: tooke part wt Butler Barron of Warranton & had ye grant for his lands all yt he was then in possession of belonging to his family, ther being this seall engraven at it, as may more fully appere in ye Deed to Butler in Domesday Booke in ye Tower of London."[301] It has been remarked by one antiquary on this score that a Butler is mentioned as Richard Pincerna in the Doomsday Book, as holding Pontone (Poulton) near Chester.[302] The early Moores did hold land in Chester, and many deeds and charters of considerable antiquity survive.[303] The regicide's great-grandfather (through his grandmother) was Sir Richard Molyneux, of Sefton, Lancashire (knighted June 24, 1586),[304] through whom the regicide was also descended from a family described by Burke as "Amongst the Norman nobles who entered England with the Conqueror, in 1066." The first of whom, "William de Molines, appears to have been one of the most distinguished (of the Normans), as well from the Battle Abbey roll, wherein his name standeth the eighteenth in order as from the old chronicles ..."[305] By the regicide's time, the Moore family had 27 quarterings to their arms, which the regicide had carved on shields which were hung in his ancient hall above his dining table. Moore's ancestors had been Members of Parliament for Liverpool more or less continuously since the year 1307.[306] The first M.P. in the family was named Richard, and his father Randle had been Reeve of Liverpool; this M.P.'s nephew John also sat in the Parliament of 1307, and married the daughter of Amauricus Butler, Baron of Warrington; his son in turn was Mayor of Liverpool in 1351. The "new" house of the regicide was built by his ancestor Thomas in 1388; his son William married Margaret Mauleverer, of the family of the regicide Sir Thomas Mauleverer, but as this took place in the fourteenth century, it was hardly a close relationship between the two![307] One could go on and on, but the point seems sufficiently established, that this regicide's family were of extreme antiquity, traceable in many lines from the leading Norman barons and knights, and had since the Conquest held a prominent social position, involved in politics at the national level over many centuries, though always as representatives of their region, and never as court creatures. The regicide had three brothers and four sisters: Robert, of Water Street, Liverpool, married Eleanor (surname unknown, died February, 1677/8); Thomas, died without issue, January 15, 1635/6; Rev. William, attended Magdalen College, Oxford, was ordained by Bishop of Bath and Wells in 1634; Eleanor, baptized at Walton, April 13, 1604, married William Ireland who was Mayor of Liverpool in 1640; Elizabeth, married a Scotsman named James Bailey; Dorothy, apparently married Edward Chesnall; Victoria, baptized at Walton, May 17, 1617, married a John Brimashaw or Brimsgrave or Brimadge, who seems to have been a lieutenant of horse who died in Ireland of wounds, - she was buried February 3, 1688/9.[307A]

Prominent Relations: The regicide's wife was niece of the Earl of Meath, and Roger Kirkby, M.P. for Lancashire in the Long Parliament, who became a royalist and died in August,1643, was her cousin. The regicide's uncle was Major-General Ralph Assheton of Middleton, M.P. for Lancashire in the Long Parliament, who died February 17, 1650/1.[308] They were close political allies. The other Ralph Assheton, M.P. for Clitheroe in the Long Parliament, was related, as were the royalist M.P. Peter Venables and Peter Legh, M.P. for Newton, in the Long Parliament.[309] As mentioned earlier, the regicide, Sir Thomas Mauleverer, and Moore had shared ancestors from the fourteenth century; this may not have meant anything to Mauleverer, but it would certainly have been known to Moore, who was something of a genealogical fanatic. In all probability, the two men admitted to an extremely distant kinship, and as they were exactly the same age and held identical political views, they may well have had a friendship which drew some extra strength from the relationship. Moore's wife was daughter of the royalist, Alexander Rigby of Burgh and Leighton. She was cousin of Moore's close political ally and crony, Alexander Rigby, M.P., Colonel, and Judge (for whom I have done the entry in the *Biographical Dictionary of British Radicals in the Seventeenth Century* (1982), and which, see). The regicide was a fairly distant cousin of Sir Francis Molyneux, Bart., whose eldest son and heir married Lucy Rigby, daughter of the Judge just mentioned. Through these Molyneux's who were contemporaries of his, the regicide was connected with the families of Sir James Harrington, Lord Monson, the Foljambes, and so on. The regicide was a close cousin of the Viscounts Moore of Drogheda (later Earls of Drogheda), who represented an offshoot of the regicide's family and were on familiar and friendly terms with him; some correspondence between them survives.[310]

Pedigrees: "More, of More Hall", in Burke's *Extinct and Dormant Baronetcies*, 1844, pp. 367-8, where is mentioned the regicide's ancestor who was knighted by the Black Prince at the Battle of Poictiers, etc.; Burke does not identify the regicide as a regicide, but simply and coyly says he "defended Liverpool against Charles I." An elaborate and much-annotated pedigree by Ronald Stewart-Brown may be found in *Transactions of the Historic Society of Lancashire and Cheshire*, New Series, Vol. XXVII (Vol. 63), 1912, pp. 92-119 (it should be noted that it extends over 27 pages). Three extremely elaborate and complex, privately printed, Moore family pedigrees, have most kindly been sent to me by the present Earl of Drogheda. The regicide does not appear on them, nor do any of the Moores of Liverpool; the descent is traced from Moores of Kent in the reign of Henry II. This may mean that the regicide and the Viscounts Moore of Drogheda merely imagined a relationship, that the Moores of Kent and the Moores of Liverpool had somehow intermarried, or that the descent of the Moores of Drogheda from the Moores of Kent is an error. I have not yet managed to solve this puzzle. Since the son of the regicide was created a baronet by Charles II, there are pedigrees in the *Complete Baronetage* and some 19th century *Debrett's*, under the spelling of "More".

Special Note: The full original text of my entry for John Moore for the *Biographical Dictionary of British Radicals in the Seventeenth Century* (1982-1984) is included in the Appendix to this chapter. (That entry was extensively cut down by the editors prior to publication.)

SIR GREGORY NORTON, BART. (Created baronet April 27, 1624.) Born circa 1603. Son of Henry Norton of Charlton, Wantage, Berkshire, and Elizabeth, fourth daughter of William Nelston (spelled with the "t"), of Chaldeworth, Berkshire. [Correction made in 2021: this should be Chaddleworth, Berkshire, not Chaldeworth, Berkshire, or Challeworth, Berkshire, as suggested by J. T. Peacey as a possible correction.] The Nortons can be traced back at least ten generations before the regicide.[311] His uncle was Sir Dudley Norton, knighted by James I at Newmarket, January 19,1614/5, "at his going over into Ireland" where he was Secretary for Ireland.[312] The regicide's great-great-grandfather was Sir Anthony St. Leger, made a Knight of the Garter on the same day as the 24th Earl of Arundel, by Henry VIII, April 24, 1544,[313] agent of Thomas Cromwell, member of the jury which condemned Anne Boleyn, Gentleman of Henry VIII's Privy Chamber, escorted Anne of Cleves to England, became Lord Deputy of Ireland, 1540 (confirmed by Edward VI, 1547), died March 16, 1558/9 (see his entry in DNB). The regicide's ancestors included a Thomas Ellis, who had been High Sheriff of Kent under Henry VI in 1428. The regicide had an only brother, Horden, who died young, prior to 1623.

Prominent Relations: As mentioned under Edwardes, *ante*, it is suspected that Norton was related to the regicide Humphrey Edwarde through his mother, Mary Norton, but not closely (otherwise Norton in his will would have called Edwardes his cousin, which he did not[314]) . Apart from the uncle mentioned above, who had been Secretary for Ireland, the regicide's third cousin was Sir William St. Leger, M.P., Privy Councillor, President of Munster, who died 1642 (see his entry in DNB). The regicide's son married the daughter of Sir Richard Norton, Bart., of Rotherfield, Hampshire; it is not known whether these two Norton families were related.

Pedigrees: "Norton, of Charlton in Wantage", *Visitation of Berkshire, 1623*, Harleian Society, Vol. LVI, 1907, pp. 115-6. "Norton" in *Middlesex Pedigrees*, Harleian Society, Vol. 65, pp. 114-6. *Complete Baronetage*, Vol. I, pp. 257-8, and see p. 195 for Sir Richard, mentioned above.

Special Note: My entry for the regicide for the *Biographical Dictionary of British Radicals in the Seventeenth Century*, in its whole text, is included in the Appendix to this chapter.

JOHN OKEY. Baptized August 24, 1606, at St. Giles in the Fields, London. Third son of

William Okey and Margaret Wetherley, who were married September 7, 1595, at St. Giles-in-the-Fields, London. The regicide's father may have come from the vicinity of Brogborough, Bedfordshire. The regicide's mother's name may have been more properly spelled Witherley, and related to Hammond Wetherley or Witherley, who was born circa 1654, became a Gentleman of the Chapel Royal after the Restoration, and was buried October 4, 1717, at Westminster Abbey.[315] Both the Okeys and the Wetherleys or Witherleys were sufficiently obscure to have defied attempts to trace them to date. Dr. Ian Gentles has found a John Okey who was apprenticed to the Haberdashers' Company, January, 1625/6, and who was then described as being of Ross-on-Wye, Herefordshire.[316] Since this John Okey was a suitable age to be the regicide, it may mean that the Okey family were a Herefordshire family, but the Herefordshire Record Office have been unable to find anything on them. Gentles may well have found a crucial clue, but further research is required, and this regicide's family background remains very much a mystery, except that we may, I believe, safely assume that he was not of any substantial gentry status.

Prominent Relations: Apparently none.

Pedigrees: A pedigree starting with the regicide's parents may be found at p. 172 of H. G. Tibbutt, *Colonel John Okey, 1606-1662*, Vol. XXXV of the *Publications of the Bedfordshire Historical Record Society*, 1955.

PEREGRINE PELHAM. Baptized September 27, 1602, at Bosham, Sussex. Elder son of Peregrine Pelham, who appears to have left Sussex to take up residence at Hull, and Anne …….. (surname unknown). The regicide's father also had a brother, Robert, who was a merchant at Hull. They were the sons by a second marriage of the celebrated Field Marshal and Lord Justice Sir William Pelham, who has an entry in DNB. Not only is the regicide's grandfather listed in the DNB, but the grandfather's full brother, Sir Edmund Pelham, Chief Baron of the Exchequer in Ireland, and his half-brother, Sir Nicholas Pelham, soldier and M.P., are also both noticed in DNB. This makes the regicide's own absence from the old DNB somewhat more ironical, but I was able to remedy this by contributing an entry for him and four other 'missing' regicides in the *Missing Persons* volume of the DNB (1993). The Pelhams can be traced back to at least 1300, but the first to rise to national prominence appears to have been the regicide's great-great great-great grandfather, Sir John Pelham, who has an entry also in DNB, where he is described as son of a Sussex knight; he was a close supporter of Henry IV, who brought him to power with him and eventually made him Treasurer of England. He died 1429 and his son Sir John Pelham was Chamberlain to Queen Katherine and died 1471. Through the mother of Sir John, the regicide was apparently descended from the Grey family, whose illustrious Norman magnate descent has already been surveyed to some extent under Lord Grey of Groby (*ante*). The regicide's great-great grandfather was William, Lord Sandys of the Vyne, who also has his own entry in DNB. He was Lord Chamberlain of England. Peregrine Pelham may thus be viewed as head of a side branch of a greater gentry family, and, as will now be seen, he was related to many of the greater gentry in his own day.

Prominent Relations: Henry Pelham, M.P. for Grantham and briefly Speaker of the House of Commons during Lenthall's absence with the Army in 1647, was the regicide's first cousin. So was the royalist officer, Sir William Pelham of Brocklesby, Lincolnshire, who died 1644.[317] The regicide was second cousin of Sir Thomas Pelham, Bart., M.P. for Sussex in the Long Parliament, who was expelled at Pride's Purge and died in 1654.[318] The regicide's grandfather had had as his first wife a daughter of the fifth Earl of Westmorland, resulting in relation by marriage with the Nevilles. The regicide's half-uncle married a daughter of Charles, Lord

Willoughby of Parham, so that the regicide was thus a cousin of the Parliamentary officer and leader of the "Presbyterian" faction, Francis, fifth Lord Willoughby of Parham. Through his cousin Sir Thomas Pelham, the regicide was connected with the elder and junior Sir Henry Vanes, Sir Thomas Walsingham, M.P., James Rivers, M.P., Henry Shelley, M.P., and the regicide Anthony Stapley, M.P.[319] But he was also related to Anthony Stapley the regicide by blood, through Stapley's mother; the two regicides were third cousins, both being descended from Thomas Pelham of Laughton, Sussex, who died circa 1517. The relationship with Stapley through Sir Thomas Pelham's branch was also by blood, it should be noted; the two regicides were in fact double-third cousins. The regicide was doubly related by marriage to Colonel Herbert Morley, of Glynde, Sussex, M.P. for Lewes, but not closely. The regicide was also a cousin of the wife of John Alured the regicide. The regicide wasalso somehow related to the Constables of Everingham, very distant relations of Sir William Constable, Bart., the regicide, since he speaks in an unpublished letter of "Sr Phillip Constable although he be my kinsman".[320] The regicide was a distant cousin of Oliver St.John, M.P. He was also fairly distantly related by marriage to the Lords de la Warr, the Carews (including the regicide John Carew), the Sackville Earls of Dorset, the Earls of Essex, the Capells, and so on.

Pedigrees: Mrs. Arthur Pelham and David McLean, *Some Early Pelhams*, Hove, Sussex, 1931, large fold-out pedigree and *passim*, especially pp. 236-41.

Addendum: It was neglected to notice that the regicide had a brother and a sister who were baptized in Sussex in 1611 and 1613; the sister, Eleanor, married the Rector of Brocklesby, Lincolnshire, in 1629. The brother's name has not yet been discovered, and it is to be doubted that he lived to manhood.

VINCENT POTTER. Born 1614 (since he was aged 21 when on May 6, 1635, he was transported to New England).[321] Potter's parents are unknown. He may have been of a Warwickshire family, and served as a Captain in the Warwickshire Militia early in the Civil War, as is discussed in a later chapter. Mark Noble said that he was related to Hugh Potter, M.P. of the Long Parliament, who came from Iddesleigh, Devon, and died 1662.[322] However, their arms were different, although sharing the central feature of a fesse ermine. The arms of Potter of Iddersleigh, Devon, were Sable, a fesse ermine between three cinquefoils argent.[323] The arms of the regicide are perfectly preserved on the Death Warrant of Goring, Capell, Holland, and Hamilton, in the House of Lords Record Office, and are: A fesse ermine between three owls (or what appear to be owls:) The regicide may have been a close relation of the Rev. Nathaniel Potter, Vicar of Stockton near Southam, Warwickshire in 1654. There were Potter families at Honington, Sudbury, and other places in Warwickshire, and a search of various parish registers might yield the information which could enable Potter's family history to be sketched, which is so far impossible. It is probable that the regicide had a relation in Boston in America, whom he joined there as a young man; this may have been Robert Potter, mentioned by John Winthrop, who was an extreme religious radical who in 1643 was set to forced labour in leg irons for heresy.[324] Eventually he was banished, and his estate confiscated by the Masschusetts officials; he went to England and during the 1640s he was restored to his estate by official order and returned to New England fully vindicated and under protection, dying in 1655.[325] The regicide had a brother, Captain John Potter, who was one of the four original Parliamentary Commissioners to the Army, but died of wounds at Naseby; the regicide then succeeded him and obtained his place. In 1647 there was a young John Potter associated with the regicide in his business who was undoubtedly a relation, being the regicide's son or nephew, or perhaps cousin.[326]

There are numerous genealogical problems and uncertainties, however. According to records of those who went to America, Vincent Potter was first taken to America in 1620 aged six, and then went again to America in 1635, aged 19. On the earlier journey, in 1620, he was accompanied by Antony Potter and Robert Potter. This Robert Potter is in all probability the Robert Potter mentioned by John Winthrop. Vincent himself was profoundly Puritan, as we know because I have discovered his private journal containing his religious sentiments, extracts from which are to be found in the Appendix to the chapter on 'The Regicides and Religion' in a later volume. It thus makes some sense that Vincent the regicide and the Robert Potter mentioned by Winthrop would be associated. It is further possible that Robert was either his father or his uncle. Antony Potter may be the Antony Potter who was married in 1574 at St. Peter Mancroft in Norwich, suggesting that he was Vincent's grandfather. In 1621 they were joined in America by Samuel Potter, born 1595 at Besthorpe, Norfolk. It is clear that these people were all related, though Vincent's brother John Potter is nowhere to be seen. All of these Potters appear to have been from Norfolk, either from hamlets and tiny villages, or from Norwich. The implication is that they were yeomen. The absence of John Potter, however, is suspicious, and it is possible that the Vincent Potter who went to America may not be Vincent Potter the regicide at all. We know that the Samuel Potter mentioned above had a mother named Prudence (and father Samuel). On 28 August 1648 a Prudence Potter was buried at Crediton in Devon, which as already mentioned was the county of Hugh Potter's family. Could it be that the uncommon name Prudence was carried over to a younger Potter, and that the Norfolk Potters and the Devon Potters were related? But why then was Vincent in the Warwickshire militia as a young man? In other words, were there two contemporary Vincent Potters, one from Norfolk and one from Warwickshire? The key to the solution of this enigma is to find early evidence of the association of a Vincent Potter with a John Potter, as we know for certain that they were brothers. Or perhaps other evidence may come to light one day which can resolve these dilemmas. As there were so many Potters in England at this time, all I can say to some possible future researcher is: 'Good luck!'

Prominent Relations: Apart from Hugh Potter, M.P., who may have been a relation as mentioned above, none are known. There was a Potter of the same period, probably a near relation, who was an Alderman of Coventry, and this avenue of research might perhaps be pursued further by a local historian. I am confident that a Warwickshire historian could resolve the mystery of Vincent Potter's parentage.

Pedigrees: None known which are certain to be relevant to the regicide's family. Hugh Potter's immediate family are represented in *Visitation of the County of Devon, 1620*, Harleian Society, Vol. VI, 1872, p. 218.

THOMAS PRIDE. Probably born latter half of 1608, younger son of Robert Pride of Cossington and Pedwell (which is in the parish of Ashcott), Somerset. If so, the regicide had an older brother, Roger, baptized November 22, 1607, at Cossington, of whom nothing else is known.[327] The name of their mother is unknown; their grandfather was John Pride of Cossington (buried 1634), who married Joan ……….. (buried February 19, 1606). Association of these Cossington Prides with Ashcott parish goes back at least to 1582, since the above-mentioned John Pride was assessed for £3 for goods under Ashcott in that year.[328] Therefore, the Cossington Prides are probably earlier from Ashcott parish, and John Pride is probably son of Richard Pride of that parish, whose will was proved in 1546 but does not survive in the original.[329] The above parentage and descent of the regicide is strengthened by these demonstrated associations of the Cossington Prides with Ashcott Parish (a few miles from Cossington), and the known absence of Prides in the Ashcott parish register. A contemporary source, a newspaper of 1649,

It is not known whether this portrait is of Colonel Thomas Pride the regicide, or of
Lieutenant-Colonel William Pryde (died 1632), whose tomb is at Canterbury Cathedral.
They were apparently related, as they had similar coats of arms featuring three Somerset otters' heads.

claims that the regicide came from Ashcott in Somerset.[330] I am indebted to Ian Gentles for the information that on January 30, 1622, a Thomas Pride of Pedwell, Somerset, was admitted a haberdasher's apprentice at London.[331] Pedwell is a tiny hamlet in Ashcott Parish, an easy walk from Ashcott village. It would appear that the Prides were prosperous yeoman farmers of Pedwell in the sixteenth century (when there would have been essentially the one main farm there, with surrounding cottages of farm-workers), who then expanded to Cossington, running two properties simultaneously. I have found proof that the regicide was actually a haberdasher, and seems to have valued his description as such above the description as "brewer" (his actual trade). This information appears in the *Journal of the Governors* of St. Bartholomew's Hospital in London, when "Col. Pride, haberdasher," was admitted a Governor in July, 1652; the description "haberdasher" was sufficiently surprising to the historian Nellie Kerling to merit an expostulatory "sic!" from her, since she obviously thought Pride should have been styled "brewer".[332] This evidence that the regicide was a haberdasher proves that he is the Thomas Pride from Pedwell discovered by Gentles, and confirms the 1649 account that the regicide came from Ashcott parish; the only possible parents then appear to be the ones given above, and we may be fairly confident of them. The Prides may have risen above yeoman status to be in the realms of the lesser, or parochial, gentry, at Cossington. This may partially be presumed from the marriage of the regicide's aunt Agnes on August 24, 1606, to Edward Popham, husbandman, of Cossington, a grandson of Alexander Popham of Huntworth (1555-1602), who was himself nephew of Sir John Popham, Lord Chief Justice. Marriage into the magnate Popham family must imply a certain minimum social standing for the Prides; according to the Popham family historians, there were no children of this marriage[333] and the regicide's Aunt Agnes was buried as early as 1634.[334] I have discovered the regicide's seal perfectly preserved on a document in the Public Record Office from 1650/1.[335] There it may be seen that the arms he used were: A chevron inter three otters' heads erased. [Otters were common then on the Somerset Levels, at the edge of which Pedwell sits, at the foot of the Polden Hills.] On the chevron are two outstretched serpents looking at each other with their tongues sticking out. This use of the otter's head as the chief motif of the regicide's coat of arms poses some other interesting questions. The otter's head (with a fish in its mouth) was the crest and three otters were the arms, of an intriguing character known as "Colonel Pride" from the generation preceding the regicide's. Perhaps they were somehow related. The earlier Colonel Pride's highly elaborate effigy tomb can hardly have escaped the notice of anyone sufficiently motivated by antiquarian curiosity who has visited Canterbury Cathedral (it is true that one must insist on passing the barrier to St. Michael's Chapel, which may not suit a timid person). There we see in all his glory Lieutenant-Colonel William Pryde, who fought "in the Belgick Warres, Slayne at ye Siege of Maxtritch [Maastrich] the 12 of July 1632". It is interesting, from the inscribed poem, to learn that "He bore as much of Pietje as Armes" and that he had been "A Souldier, till neere Sixty from Sixteene". He sounds like a personality-clone of the regicide, having died "In his religious thoughts". I have not yet managed to carry a photograph of the portrait of "Colonel Pride" thought to be the regicide to hold side by side the effigy of this earlier man, but I fear the portrait is really of the earlier one, and not of the regicide at all. The family of this earlier Colonel Pride were well-connected, as mentioned in a moment. The regicide may have exploited such relations, for he seems to have become extraordinarily well-connected early on in London. As we shall be considering in a later chapter, he was on close terms with the Earl of Pembroke and made a very good marriage early in life; and he enjoyed the clear patronage of the House of Lords in 1645.

Prominent Relations: The regicide's aunt was married to an Edward Popham who was second cousin three times removed of the well-known Colonels Edward and Alexander Popham of the Civil War, the former becoming an Admiral and recruiter M.P., and the latter being an M.P. in the Long Parliament; their father was Sir Francis Popham, also an M.P. in the Long Parliament (died 1644), who may possibly have helped the young Pride get on in the world, as his uncle was the elder Popham's first cousin three times removed, and must have been known to him personally. It should be noted that John Pyne, the Somerset "boss", was a grand-nephew of the elder Popham.[336] If the regicide were actually related to the earlier Colonel Pride mentioned above, he would have had an extraordinary circle of relations, though this group of Prides later adopted the spelling of Prowde and thus are easily missed in lists of names. The earlier Colonel had married Mary, daughter of Sir Adam Spracklin, Spratling, or Sprakeling; this family and the Proudes are described in Everitt.[337] Everitt says the Sprakelings and the Proudes "were infamous for their violence and their feuds" and the Sprakelings in particular seem to have committed an extraordinary number of murders, leading Everitt to speak of "the blood of the Sprakelings" in ominous tones as something tainted, as in a horror story.[338] But tainted or not, the blood managed to become compounded with the finest tinctures, for the earlier Colonel Pride's daughter Katherine became Lady Zouch,[339] his son Searles married the daughter of the Kentish gentry figure, John Denne,[340] and his daughter Mary was the daughter-in-law of the immensely wealthy and prominent Sussex magnate, Henry Lord Dacre, of Herstmonceux Castle, marrying his second son Fiennes Lennard.[341] There are various reasons to suspect that Pride may have been related somehow to the regicide William Goffe, but this is too speculative until further evidence is found, so I do not give the details. Pride married a daughter of Thomas Monck, of Portlinch (or Potheridge), Devon, who was a royalist.[342] This father-in-law's younger brother was the well known Colonel George Monck, later Duke of Albemarle. Pride's daughter Elizabeth married, as her second husband, Robert Wauton, son of the regicide Valentine Wauton (Walton). One of Pride's sons married the daughter of William Brydges, Seventh Lord Chandos.

Pedigrees: Two generations of Prides appear in a pedigree of Ketleby, in a Visitation of Shropshire of 1623, in the College of Arms (MS. Vincent 13 4, f. 533), but they have no evident relationship with the regicide.

WILLIAM PUREFOY. Born circa 1582-1584. Unlikely to have been born circa 1580 as stated in both DNB and *Biographical Dictionary of British Radicals in the Seventeenth Century* because his father was only 16 years old in 1580![343] The regicide was eldest son of Francis Purefoy of Caldecote Manor (site of present Caldecote Hall), Warwickshire (died 1613, aged 49), and Eleanor, daughter of John Baskerville of Curdworth, Warwickshire. The Baskervilles were an ancient and distinguished family with many knighthoods. The Purefoys were seated at Misterton, Leicestershire, as early as 1277, and purchased the Manor of Drayton, Leicestershire, in 1397, where the regicide's great-grandfather was born.[344] This great-grandfather, Michael Purefoy, was Escheator of Warwickshire during the reign of Queen Mary Tudor, and settled at Caldecote.[345] His eldest son, William, married a daughter of Sir William Wigston, who was knighted October 19, 1553, on the same occasion as a Thomas Baskerville, who was probably another of the regicide's great-grandfathers,[346] and the regicide was the eldest son of his eldest son. I have discovered a fascinating letter dated 1608 written by the regicide's father, Francis Purefoy, giving much political gossip and news (speaking of "The sudeyne death of my L: Treasurer att the counsell table ... The Election of the Earle of Salsburye into his place ... the Earle of Northampton to bee Lord Privye Seale ..." etc.)[347] An article by David Mosler erroneously states that this Francis Purefoy "settled in Caldecote from Leicestershire in the 1540s";[348] however, Francis wasn't even alive then, and it was Francis's grandfather, the regicide's great-grandfather, who settled at Caldecote, as noted above. Colvile has found the date of purchase of Caldecote by Michael Purefoy, which was the Second Year of Edward VI.[349] The Purefoy arms accepted by the heralds in 1619 were quarterly of twelve, and consisted of arms of Purefoy, Sherford, Wellesburgh, Hardwick, Roduile, Tundin, Flounders, Limsey, Ashbrooke, Champaine, and Stevens.[350] I have copied down all the Purefoy family inscriptions, with notes of arms, in Caldecote Church, and two pages of these are to be found in the Appendix to this Chapter. The regicide had brothers the Rev. Ralph (attended Cambridge), George, Francis, Nathaniel (attended Cambridge), and another brother name unknown, and sisters Joyce (married Thomas Walley or Walley of Newton, Warwickshire, and had the regicide's favorite niece, Eleanor), Mary (married John Farmer of Ratcliffe, Leicestershire), Elizabeth, and another sister whose name is unknown. Purefoy outlived all his issue and by 1659 settled Caldecote on his nephew, William Purefoy, by indentures. We know this because of the unusual fact that the regicide's will, proved in May, 1661, survives and came into effect despite the supposed attainder and confiscation of his property.[351] This nephew, William Purefoy, was still at Caldecote in 1665 when he jointly bid £3000 per annum with Sir Arthur Coley, and they became Farmers of the Excise for the County of Warwickshire.[352]

Prominent Relations: From an inscription in the Church at Burbage, Leicestershire, it may be learned that the regicide's Aunt Magdalen was the Countess of Kent, having married the Rev. Anthony Grey, a strong puritan who in 1639 inherited the titles of Earl of Kent, Lord Hastings, Lord Waisford, and Lord Grey of Ruthvin, and died 1643 aged 86; the Countess died 1653 aged 81. The regicide's first cousin was Henry Lord Grey of Ruthin, M.P. of the Long Parliament, who became Earl of Kent in 1643. The regicide had a daughter (name unknown) who married George Abbot, M.P. and theological author, who was also a member of the Warwickshire County Committee. This Abbot, though not a soldier, held at bay with a handful of servants and his mother-in-law, an enormous force under Princes Rupert and Maurice in 1642, in one of the most extraordinary and heroic feats of the entire Civil War (described in a church inscription reproduced in the Appendix); this Abbot was not, as often claimed, a nephew of the Archbishop of Canterbury (see DNB entry which corrects this error). Abbot was extremely close to the regicide, and dedicated to him his book *The Whole Book of Job Paraphrased* in 1640; this dedication is to be found in the Appendix to the Chapter of "The Regicides and Religion". Abbot was M.P. for Tamworth from 1645 until his death February 2, 1648/9; according to the DNB, he was related to the Pickerings, and therefore to Sir Gilbert Pickering, Bart., M.P. of the Long Parliament. The regicide seems to have had another daughter (name also unknown) who became the second wife of the regicide's political crony, Colonel Godfrey Bosvile, M.P. for Warwick in the Long Parliament and member of the Warwickshire County Committee; who died 1658. Bosvile was brother-in-law of Sir Arthur Hesilrige, Bart., M.P.,[353] one of the most important political connections for Purefoy imaginable. Bosvile was also half-brother of Purefoy's old friend, Lord Brooke,[354] to whom Purefoy was himself extremely distantly related through a marriage between the Grevilles and the regicide's Leicestershire Purefoy relations. These same distant relations inter-married with the Dixwells, but Purefoy's relation to the regicide John Dixwell is too distant to warrant detailing. Purefoy was fifth cousin five times removed of Peter Temple the regicide, through Fitzherbert descent; Peter Temple's mother was a Burgoyne of Wroxhall, Warwickshire. Purefoy mentions in a letter of 1647/8 (reproduced in the Appendix to the Chapter on the Counties) his "Cosen Hales";[355] John and Christopher Hales of the Warwickshire County Committee were his cousins, one of whom he thus referred to.[356] The Calendar of State Papers Domestic errs in believing Purefoy's "Cousin Hales" to have been Sir Edward Hales, Bart., M.P.[357] Also on the Warwickshire County Committee was Gamaliel Purefoy; he was either the Gamaliel alive 1629, the regicide's second cousin once removed, or son of the same. A relation of some kind apparently was Captain Arthur Purefoy, who served in Ireland from 1646 and in 1661 was M.P. for Kells.[358] Humphrey Edwardes the regicide was probably a close step-cousin through the Baskervilles. Two brothers, Major George Purefoy and Lieutenant, later Captain, William Purefoy, of the Parliamentary side in the Civil War, were close associates and "kinsmen" of the regicide; the former was made Governor of Compton House, the captured residence of the Earl of Northampton, and addressed the regicide as "his Colonell" in 1644.[359] It is unknown what relation they were exactly; they got into terrible trouble, were examined, made prisoners, and ordered by the House of Commons to be tried by martial law, for reasons and with result that remain thoroughly obscure;[360] this seems all to have occurred before the siege of Compton House, however.

Pedigrees: "Purefoy of Wadley" in Burke's *Extinct and Dormant Baronetcies*, London, 1844, pp. 431-2. "Purifoy" in The Visitation of Warwickshire 1619, Harleian Society, Vol. XI I, 1877, pp. 254-5. "Purifoy" in *The Visitation of the County of Leicester*, Harleian Society, Vol. VIII, pp. 34-7.

OWEN ROWE. Born circa 1593 (he was aged 24 at his marriage in 1617), son of John Rowe of Bickley, Cheshire (in 1609, though probably not originally). Mother's name unknown. Apparently no relation to the Rowes of Macclesfield, Cheshire, as suggested by one genealogist,[361] since both his perfectly preserved seal[362] and his tricked arms[363] are different from theirs but show that he was related to the Rowes who were Lord Mayors of London in 1568, 1592, and 1607.[364] The same arms were borne by a family of Rowes who in 1613 were of Huntingdon but who by 1618-9 were of Cotterstock, Northamptonshire;[365] by 1663, these Rowes were of Enfield, Middlesex.[366] The regicide's father is probably the John Roe who November 28, 1637, petitioned the King against fraudulent practices in the wool trade.[367] He may very well have been a third son of Sir Henry Rowe, Lord Mayor of London who was buried at Hackney, Middlesex (eventual burial place also of the regicide), in February, 1612. This Sir Henry's daughter Susanna became Countess of Warwick, as second wife of Robert Rich, Earl of Warwick (she died January 21, 1645); Farnell has suggested that this Susanna, Countess of Warwick, "was probably [Owen] Rowe's aunt", and this is likely.[368] (Farnell in the same place is mistaken in believing Thomas Scot the regicide to have been Owen Rowe's father-in-law; Scot was father-in-law of William Rowe, not Owen Rowe.[369]) This Sir Henry's elder brother, John, married the daughter of Secretary Wilson, Queen Elizabeth's councillor, and became High Sheriff of Bucks.; their father was Sir Thomas Rowe, also Lord Mayor of London, buried at Hackney, September 2, 1570; his wife was daughter of Sir John Gresham, Lord Mayor of London, who died 1556 (see DNB).[370] These Rowes traced their descent back to William Rowe of Rowe Place in Kent in the fifteenth century.[371] The Rowe family was multifarious, complex, and bewildering in its extent. Further research would be required to arrive at a definitive survey of it. However, it is clear that the Rowes were a powerful element in the City oligarchy, a tradition in which the regicide himself very much followed. The regicide had four brothers: Scoutmaster-General Francis Rowe (not to be confused with Scoutmaster-General William Rowe, Thomas Scot the regicide's son-in-law, who was *not* one of the regicide's brothers), who married Jane .... and died in December, 1649, in Ireland;[372] Robert Rowe, John Rowe, and Arthur Rowe; he had a sister Margaret who married ......Salmon, apparently the Thomas Salmon who sued Owen and Francis for years until by 1648 they were forced to avoid him by "removing their habitations from the Cittie of London to remote places" since they were owed many thousands of pounds by the State and could not repay Salmon £600.[373] Also, close to the regicide and his brother Francis was a "kinsman" Isaac Rowe, who by 1653 was on the Board of the Bermudas Company with the regicide and their relation the Earl of Warwick.[374] On February 17, 1662/3, Administration of "goods unadministered by Owen Rowe, deceased" was granted "to nephew and next-of-kin Joseph Roe".[375]

Prominent Relations: Apart from the other Rowes already mentioned, and their manifold connections, the Earl of Warwick, as already mentioned, is presumed to be the regicide's uncle. Sir Nicholas Crisp, Bart., the immensely rich farmer of customs, trader, and royalist, was the regicide's brother-in-law through his third wife; they were apparently doubly related through the marriage of Anne Rowe, daughter of Sir Thomas Rowe (died 1686) to Ellis Crispe;[376] Ellis Crispe was the name of Sir Nicholas's father,[377] so this must be the same family.

Pedigrees: "Row, of Bickley" gives neither the regicide nor his known brothers, and is therefore probably an obscure offshoot of the family with whom the regicide's father merely happened to be staying in 1609 temporarily, *Cheshire Visitation Pedigrees, 1663*, p. 94; "Rowe of Shackelwell" and "Roe of Muswell Hill" in *Middlesex Pedigrees*, as collected by Richard Mundy, ed. by Sir George John Armytage, Bart., London, 1914, pp. 8 and 46; "Rowe" in *Visitation of London 1633-5*, Vol. II, p. 213; "Pedigree of the Rowe Family, of Hackney", fold-out pedigree in William Robinson, *The History and Antiquities of the Parish of Hackney in the County of Middlesex*, London, 1843, Vol. II, and see also pp. 8-17 with several elaborate foldouts showing effigies and monuments and arms.

Note: Reproduced in the Appendix to this Chapter is the whole text of my entry for Rowe prepared for the *Biographical Dictionary of British Radicals in the Seventeenth Century*; however, I must point out that in it I erred in assuming that Scoutmaster-General William Rowe was the regicide's brother; he appears instead to have been some sort of cousin, and thus Owen Rowe's connection with the regicide Thomas Scot is more remote than had once been thought. Also, a contemporary pamphlet which I have seen since the above was written specifically refers to the fact that Owen Rowe was related to Lord Mayor Rowe, so that was what was widely believed at the time, and was therefore probably true. (If it wer known to be untrue, it would have caused a stir, and no stir seems to have occurred.)

WILLIAM SAY. Born 1604, second son of William Say of Ickenham, Middlesex, and of Slinford, Sussex (Will proved July 3, 1613, at London), and his first wife, Anne, daughter of Sir Edward Fenner, Justice of the King's Bench (died 1612, see DNB). Noble says the regicide "was of an ancient and knightly family ".[378] This family seem to have been descended from Picot de Say, a Shropshire baron in the reign of William the Conqueror; if so, then of the same family as Geoffrey de Say, Baron de Say (1305?1359; see DNB) who was Admiral of the Fleet from the Thames Westward in 1336 and "a distinguished member of an ancient and noble family" claimed by Dugdale to have been a Judge of the King's Bench during the reign of Edward 11.[379] The Say genealogy is still confused, but the regicide was related to a variety of prominent Says of the fifteenth and sixteenth centuries, including Sir John Say, made Knight of the Bath by Edward IV in 1465,[380] and Sir William Say, made Knight of the Bath at the Coronation of Richard III in 1483.[381] The latter, who was the son of the former, died 1529, and his will has been published.[382] The regicide's uncle, Robert Say of Ickenham, was born 1576, attended Winchester College,[383] New College, Oxford, of which he became a Fellow in 1597, and obtained a D.D. degree there; his father, also Robert, had married Patience White of Christchurch, Hants., through which marriage the regicide was related to the wife (Alice) of John Lisle, as remarked under LISLE previously. The regicide's older brother was Edward Say of Blechingdon, Oxfordshire,[384] who was admitted to the Middle Temple and called to the Bar on the same dates as his brother, the regicide. The two brothers shared chambers at the Middle Temple, in Brick Court, until Edward's death in 1655.[385] Edward married Elizabeth, daughter of Jerome Keyte of Woodstock, Oxon. The regicide's younger brother was Robert Say, who had a distinguished academic career, becoming Provost of Oriel College, Oxford, in 1653, King's Commissioner in 1660, and Vice-Chancellor in 1664, dying in 1691; his portrait is preserved at Oxford. The regicide had two sisters: Jane, alive but under the age of 18 in 1613; and Patience, pointedly omitted from their father's will,[386] who married Ralph Weldon, later to become Colonel in the New Model Army.

Prominent Relations: As just mentioned, Colonel Ralph Weldon was the regicide's brother-in-law, whose father was the Kentish magnate Sir Anthony Weldon. Dr. Leonard Say, Dean of St. Paul's, was a contemporary but extremely distant cousin, as were the Earl of Bath and the Barons Mountjoy. The regicide's uncle was Sir Edward Fenner the younger, Sheriff of Oxfordshire, who was knighted August 27, 1619.[387] The regicide was apparently distantly related to the Lords Eure, giving common ancestors in the ancient Earls of Essex of the name of Mandeville. His great-grandfather Sir William Box had been Sheriff of

London. The regicide's Aunt Eleanor married William Culpepper (or Colepepper), through which marriage the regicide was connected not only with that family but the Sackvilles and the Lords Dacre.[388] The regicide was also related to the royalist Goring family, since his great-grandmother was a Goring,[389] and by marriage to the regicide Anthony Stapley, M.P., whose wife was a Goring.

Pedigrees: "Say of Ickenham" in *Middlesex Pedigrees*, Harleian Society, Vol. 65, pp. 160-1. "Say of Blechington" in *Visitation of the County of Oxford 1634*, Harleian Society, Vol. 5, 1871, p. 252. "Venour" (Fenner), in *Visitation of Kent, 1619*, Harleian Society, Vol. 42, 1898, pp. 136-7. "Say of Weston Favell and Doddington" in *Visitation of Northamptonshire, 1618-9*, ed. Walter Metcalfe, 1887, p. 134.

THOMAS SCOT. Born 1603, elder son of Thomas Scot of London and Chesterford, Essex, and also of Cambridge, and Mary Sutton. The regicide's father was son of another Thomas Scot (in turn son of a Thomas Scot) "branched from the Scots of Essex", and the regicide's family arms were quartered as early as 1612 with those of Drax and Swinburne.[390] Either the regicide's father or grandfather appears to have preceded the regicide by sixty years in being M.P. for Aylesbury (in 1585).[391] The regicide himself always signed his name Scot and he did not use quartered arms in his seal, merely those of the Scots: per pale indented, ermine and sable, a saltier counterchanged (preserved on MS. Tanner 572, ff. 338-9, in the Bodleian Library). It should be remarked that Scot's arms are incorrectly drawn in the 1750 engraving of the Death Warrant of Charles I. The fact that the regicide was so extraordinarily learned and well-educated indicates a background of learning in his family; further research into his family would be tedious and time-consuming, but would probably yield fruits. He may well have been related to the Thomas Scotts in the old DNB (which the old DNB believes may be the same man), the poet who wrote *Four Paradoxes*, and the pamphleteer who was James I's chaplain, passionately anti-Catholic, and was assassinated in 1626. It is even possible that one of these men may have been his grandfather. The regicide had a younger brother, Richard Scot, who married Mary, daughter of William Hobson of London, and who was "of London" himself in 1634; nothing further is known of him. The regicide had a sister, Mary, who married William Coltman, Haberdasher of London, prior to 1633; those Coltmans were a Leicestershire family.[392] Although the regicide's maternal relations are still a subject for speculation, one of them does seem to be identifiable: in 1656, the regicide with much opposition brought his relation the Rev. Daniel Sutton in as Vicar of Great Marlow, near his home at Little Marlow, for we know that it was Scot who expelled the previous Vicar.[393]

Prominent Relations: It has already been remarked under MAULEVERER that Scot was *not* the son-in-law of Sir Thomas Mauleverer the regicide, as several previous scholars had believed. Francis Allen, Alderman of London and M.P., appears to have been the regicide's uncle, since his aunt Elizabeth Scot married Francis Allen of London, presumed to be the same man. George Yule misconstrued an incomplete reference to this which I sent to him to mean that Francis Allen was related to the regicide through his first wife, which is simply a case of confusion.[394] The regicide was probably related to the Rev. Thomas Draxe, author of *Treasurie of Ancient Adages and Sententious Proverbes* (died 1618, see DNB) and the ecclesiastical lawyer, Henry Swinburne, B.C.L., author of very important legal works (1560?-1623; see DNB). The regicide's daughter Alice married Colonel William Rowe, Scoutmaster-General, who was closely involved with Scot in matters of import over several years; this William Rowe, as remarked under ROWE, was *not* the brother of the regicide Owen Rowe, but was apparently a cousin of some sort, and apparently not an intimate of Owen Rowe's. (The fact that Owen Rowe's brother was also Scoutmaster-General might be sheer coincidence or perhaps the post was held as a family sinecure passed from the one to the other; there is no evidence either way.) Although the regicide's first wife was daughter and sole heir of a William Allanson "Citizen and Salter of London" who was "descended out of Yorkshire", this appears not to have been Sir William Allanson, M.P. of the Long Parliament for York, but may have been a near relative of his.

Pedigrees: "Scott, of Marlow", in *Visitation of Buckinghamshire in 1634*, Harleian Society, Volume 58, p. 111. "Scott" (entry for the regicide's son William); in *The Visitation of Essex, 1558*, with later additions, p. 100. Further pedigrees may be consulted for the apparent antecedents of the regicide: his ancestors seem to have been the Scotts of Woolston Hall, Chigwell, Essex, and a branch of them later were of Rotherfield Park, Hampshire; circa 1500 they were of Chesterton, Essex. But a full survey of these early Scots would be superfluous for our purposes.

ADRIAN SCROPE. Baptized January 12, 1600/1, at Lewknor Church, Oxfordshire. Eldest son of Robert Scrope of Wormsley Manor, Oxfordshire (today in Buckinghamshire technically speaking) and Margaret, daughter of Richard Cornwall, Merchant of London. (The name was sometimes spelled Cornwell.) The regicide's father was baptized July 22, 1569, at Hambleden, Buckinghamshire, and buried February 28, 1644/5, at Lewknor. He was a Justice of the Peace and it is to be suspected that he was from time to time a vicar, and is identical with the Rev. Robert Scrope who was Vicar of Hambleden at one point; the regicide's grandfather was Adrian Scrope of Hambleden Manor (died 1578) and so the regicide's father may have presented himself with the living for a while out of religious enthusiasm, since it was hardly a financial necessity, as he had ample means. (It is ironical that Hambleden Manor was later to be a place of hiding for Charles I.) Scrope was of an ancient and distinguished family. It is noteworthy that one of his ancestors had attempted to dethrone and murder King Henry V, so that there was a precedent in the family for the act of regicide. This man was Henry, Third Baron Scrope of Masham (see DNB). Shakespeare, in *Henry V*, Act Two, Scene Two, speaks of him and his two collaborators (one of whom was by bizarre historical coincidence named Thomas Grey, just as the later regicide was to have a fellow-regicide also called Thomas Grey): "... three corrupted men, One, Richard Earl of Cambridge, and the second, Henry Lord Scroop of Masham, and the third, Sir Thomas Grey, knight, ... O guilt indeed! - Confirm'd conspiracy ... And by their hands this grace of kings must die, If hell and treason hold their promises ... the traitors are agreed ..." This ancestral aspiration to regicide can hardly have been unknown to Adrian Scrope, nor Shakespeare's line of Henry V saying "You have conspired against our royal person". The Scropes of Wormsley and Hambleden were a younger branch of the Scropes of Bolton, and the regicide was great-great grandson of Henry, Sixth Baron Scrope of Bolton. He was directly descended from Sir Richard Scrope of Bolton who was Lord Treasurer of England in 1367, and who acquired the Manor of Hambleden, which was to remain in the family for three centuries.[395] The head of the Scropes of Bolton, Emmanuel Scrope, was created Earl of Sunderland in 1627 (a title which not long after was granted to the Spencers.) The DNB contains entries for many early Scropes: Sir Geoffrey Scrope, Chief Justice and Secretary of King Edward III; Sir Henry, also Chief Justice; the first Baron Scrope of Masham, Steward of the Royal Household (died 1391); the first Baron Scrope of Bolton, Steward to King Richard II and Chancellor, 1378-80; Richard Scrope, Archbishop of York (died 1405); William Scrope, Earl of Wiltshire, Treasurer of England, 1398, executed by Henry IV in 1399; the Fifth Baron Scrope of Bolton, Governor of the Fleet, died 1498; Henry, ninth Baron Scrope of Bolton, Marshal of Army under Queen Elizabeth, took charge of Mary Stuart at Bolton, Member of Council of the North, 1574, died 1592. (The regicide's grandson, Judge John Scrope, who took part in the Monmouth Rebellion, is also listed in DNB.) Several of these men were notable for opposing royal prerogatives; for instance, the first Baron Scrope of Bolton, as Chancellor, refused to put the great seal to the many grants made by Richard II to his favorites, which enraged Richard II, but Scrope managed to face him down and is described by Walsingham as "remarkable for his wisdom and integrity".[396] The Scropes had every reason to think they were older and wiser than any mere dynasty of kings; they had stood up to kings before, so why not again? Despite the regicide having been executed, his grandson still took part in the Monmouth Rebellion. Even the royalist Sir Adrian Scrope, a distant cousin of the regicide, rebelled against authority when young, as discussed in a later chapter. It may be presumed that the Scropes did not suffer abuses of authority gladly, least of all kingly abuses.

Prominent Relations: Through his wife, Mary Waller, the regicide was connected with Edmund Waller, the poet and royalist conspirator, and more distantly, Sir William Waller and the regicide Sir Hardress Waller. John Hampden, M.P., was the first cousin of the regicide's wife; through him, Scrope was connected with the wider web of relationship which extended to Oliver Cromwell. The father-in-law of Hampden's daughter was Sir Robert Pye, M.P., whose son-in-law, Edward Phelipps, M.P., was related to the regicide Edmund Ludlow. This Pye's son, also Sir Robert Pye, was a fellow Colonel of Horse with Scrope in the New Model Army; in fact, Scrope served the younger Pye as a Captain of Horse in 1644, before risingin rank himself.[397] The regicide's sister Margaret married James Pennington, Merchant of London, who was probably an uncle of Isaac Pennington (or Penington), M.P., the radical City leader. Pearl has remarked on Isaac Pennington's acquaintance with Hampden and his circle: "Penington's choice of a country seat at Chalfont St. Peter in Buckinghamshire in proximity to Hampden, Sir Arthur Goodwin, and the other parliamentarians of this county, rather than at his paternal estates, may well indicate an acquaintance with these circles ..."[398] That is absolutely right, and probably a close relationship as well, through the Scrope family. The regicide was related to Thomas Savage, third Earl Rivers.[399] This must have been embarrassing, since Lady Rivers was a much hated Catholic.[400] Sir Gervase Scrope and Sir Adrian Scrope (his son) of Cockerington, Lincolnshire, were distant cousins of the regicide, and were both royalist commanders in the Civil War. Indeed, Sir Gervase and the regicide fought on opposite sides at the Battle of Edgehill and may even have espied each other through the smoke. Through his grandmother, the regicide was distantly related to Edmund Ludlow, the regicide.

Siblings: The regicide had two older sisters, Ursula Scrope, baptized at Lewknor, January 22, 1598/9, and Elizabeth Scrope, baptized at Lewknor, January 20, 1599/1600. He had five younger sisters: Ann, baptized at Lewknor, September 7, 1603, and married her cousin Henry Scrope of Danby, Yorkshire, she died evidently in childbirth and was buried in 1633 at Lewknor, where her daughter Anne was baptized June 3, 1633, a son Robert having been baptized there earlier, May 3, 1629 but was buried there February 28, 1644; Margaret, baptized at Lewknor, September 23, 1604, married James Pennington as mentioned above; Frances, baptized at Lewknor, April 15, 1606; Sarah, baptized at Lewknor, January 23, 1610/1; Alicia, baptized at Lewknor, January 17, 1613/4. The regicide's older sister Ursula married Nicholas Clerke of Witney, Oxfordshire, prior to 1634. His younger sister Frances married James Herbert of London (unknown if related to prominent Herberts) prior to 1634. His younger sister Alicia, or Alice, married Edward Woodward, Salter of London, prior to 1634. And finally, the regicide's eldest sister of all, evidently not baptized at Lewknor, was Mary Scrope; she married prior to 1634 Edward Curll, son of Auditor Curll and evidently a near relation of Walter Curll, Bishop of Winchester and passionate royalist (see DNB) who died 1647. The regicide's older sister, Elizabeth, married Vincent Barry of Thame, Oxfordshire, before 1634, leaving issue; her husband's first cousin, Katherine Barry, married Sir Edward Fenner the younger, Sheriff of Oxfordshire, and was thus the aunt of William Say, the regicide.[401] Adrian Scrope also had a younger brother, Robert Scrope, baptized at Lewknor, April 18, 1608, of whom nothing further is known.

Pedigrees: "Scroope, of Wormsley", in *The Visitation of the County of Oxford 1634*, Harleian Society, Vol. 5, 1871, pp. 327-8. "Scrope, of Cockerington", in Burke's *Extinct and Dormant Baronetcies*, London, 1844, pp. 474-6. *Memos of the Family of Scrope of Wormsley and Fane of Wormsley*, a manuscript compilation of 1935 by Agnes Butter (née Fane), in the possession of John Fane, Esq., of Wormsley House, who is a direct descendant of the regicide living in his house and with the regicide's portrait still hanging in the dining room. I wish to acknowledge my extreme gratitude to Mr. Fane for allowing me to make a photocopy of this document, and for helping me in several ways in my research, and extending such kind hospitality. It was a great pleasure for my wife and myself to dine with John Fane in the regicide's old dining room, and with the original oil portrait of the regicide hanging on the wall observing us. In 1985, Fane sold the house to the Getty family, and I have no idea what happened to Adrian Scrope's portrait because our correspondence with John Fane ceased after that; the oil portrait of Scrope held by the National Portrait Gallery is a different painting than the one at Wormsley because it was acquired before we ever went to Wormsley. John Fane and my wife Olivia and I used to exchange amusing notes with each other commencing 'Dear Cousin', as a kind of joke in imitation of the old family papers we had gone over together with him, so many of which began in that way.

HENRY SMITH. Born 1620, only son of Henry Smith of Withcote, Leicestershire (died 1623, the regicide then becoming a ward of the King), and …… .. Skipwith, daughter of Henry and sister to William Skipwith of Cotes, Leicestershire.[402] Despite the seemingly hopeless name of Smith, which might lead one to expect that the regicide's antecedents could never be traced, profuse and complex pedigrees do exist. A descent has been traced back to Robert de Heriz, a Norman living in England in 1074. The regicide's family insisted that their name had been changed to Smith only to inherit an estate in the fifteenth century, and that they had before that been Heriz, Herries, Harries, Hares, or however one cares to spell it (from the French name for a hedgehog). All the regicide's pedigrees, therefore, are of "Smith alias Heriz". Descendants living today still style themselves HerizSmith, and I am in touch with some whose papers and pedigrees have unfortunately not become available in time for incorporation into this survey (what with having to be sorted out, taken from storage, etc.) Arms were granted to the Smiths qua Smiths in 1499, and a crest in 1565, both grants having been published.[403] Compton Reade has also published a voluminous book full of Smith pedigrees, extensively annotated.[404] The regicide's family traced a descent from the ancient families of Zouch, Ashby, Burdet, and the Duke of Brittany, and claimed to be descended from King Henry 1.[405] The regicide's great grandmother Dorothy Cave was related to Sir Ambrose Cave (see DNB) who was an M.P., Sheriff of Warwickshire and Leicestershire., and Chancellor of the Duchy of Lancaster (died 1568). Several Smiths related closely to the regicide attained fame, especially for religious zeal. One was "Silver-Tongue Smith", well known as a preacher (see DNB under Henry). Another was Erasmus Smith (see DNB) who founded schools and lectureships. Humphrey Smith the Quaker, author of Visions, etc. (see DNB; died 1663) was probably the regicide's near cousin. And so on …

Prominent Relations: The regicide's father-in-law was Cornelius Holland, M.P., the radical who sat on the High Court of Justice but did not actually sign the Death Warrant. The brother of the regicide's great-aunt was none other than William Cecil, Lord Burleigh.

Two uncles by marriage (i.e., married to his aunts) were Sir Thomas Wilkes (1545?-1598; see DNB), M.P., Elizabethan Ambassador, Clerk of the Privy Council, etc.; and Benedict Barnham (1559-1598; see DNB), Alderman of London. His cousin was married to the daughter of Hugh, first Baron Coleraine, described by DNB aptly as "an eccentric royalist". His first cousin once removed was married to the daughter of George Bowles, Alderman of London. Other husbands of the regicide's much married Aunt Dorothy (besides Benedict Barham) were Sir John Pakington, K.B., Privy Councillor and Custos Rotulorum; Robert, Viscount Kilmorey (who died 1631; and Thomas, Earl of Kelly, K.G. (who died 1639). The regicide was thus first cousin to Sir John Pakington, Bart., M.P. in 1623 and who died 1625; and first cousin once removed to his son Sir John Pakington, Bart., M.P. in the Long Parliament who was a well known royalist.[406] Through the former of these, Smith was related by marriage to the Ferrers family, the Earl of Chesterfield, and the royalist Washington family. Through the latter, to Thomas Lord Coventry, Keeper of the Great Seal, and royalist; also, more distantly, to Lord Savile, through his wife. The regicide's Aunt Katherine Skipwith married Sir Walter Ayscough of Blyborough, Lincolnshire, through whom it is presumed the regicide was connected with Sir Edward Ayscough of Lincolnshire, M.P. of the Long Parliament, who in turn was related to many prominent people and M.P.s. The regicide's first cousin Henry Ayscough married the daughter of Sir James Harrington, Bart., the political author. One of Henry Ayscough's daughters married a Fulke Hunckes, meaning that Henry Smith was probably related to the Colonel Hercules Hunckes who stood guard at the trial of Charles I. Two other daughters of Henry Ayscough's married men called Newcomen, leading one to assume that Smith was therefore related to the Jonathan Newcomen who was a Major under Colonel Edward Aldrich in the army of the Earl of Essex.[407] Smith was related by marriage to the regicide Peter Temple, M.P. (q.v.). He was also related by marriage to Lord Grey of Groby through Lord Burleigh.

Pedigrees: See Compton Reade, *The Smith Family*, London, 1902; mention of the regicide occurs on p. 255. "Smith alias Harris" in *The Visitation of the County of Leicester*, pp. 66-7. "Smith alias Heriz" in John Nichols, *History of Leicestershire*, Vol. II, pp. 184-5.

ANTHONY STAPLEY. Baptized August 30, 1590, at Framfield, Sussex. Only son of Anthony Stapley of Framfield (died 1606), and his third wife, Anne, daughter of John Thatcher of Priesthawes in Westham, Sussex. The origins of the Stapleys are obscure, and pedigrees usually begin with the regicide's grandfather, John Stapley of Framfield who died in 1593, and like his son was also married to a Thatcher. The Thatchers were related to the royalist Gage family of Sussex, and both families were Catholic families; presumably the Catholic John Thatcher mentioned by Fletcher is the regicide's grandfather, otherwise an uncle.[408] The regicide had a full sister, Grace Stapley, who married Thomas Shirley. He had half-sisters: Margaret married John Bulman of Hartfield; ……. (name unknown) married Jo. (probably John, but could be Joseph) Staple (probably meant to be Stapley) of Twineham (possibly another mis-spelling, as this location is unknown); Anne married Thomas May of Pashley, East Sussex (who was son of Thomas May of Ticehurst).[409] The Mays were among the families "singled out by Bishop Curteys for their Protestantism and their independence", as Fletcher points out.[410] The only clue as to origins of the Stapleys is found in Burke's *Extinct and Dormant Baronetage*, London, 1844, p. 503 (wrongly paginated as 530) where Burke says: "The Stapleys of Sussex derived, according to Edward Knight, Norroy, from the Stapleys of Cheshire." Further information about the Stapley origins could probably be obtained by anyone interested who was prepared to search through the extensive archives (which include pedigrees) of the other branch of the Stapley family who were based at Hickstead Place in East Sussex; these "Hickstead Place Archives" are now on deposit at the East Sussex Record Office in Lewes.

Prominent Relations: The regicide was related to Colonel Herbert Morley, M.P. of the Long Parliament and Sussex magnate of Glynde in that his father's second wife, mother to his three half-sisters, had been Anne, daughter of Thomas Morley of Glynde. His father's first wife (apparently no issue) had been a daughter of Sir Roger Lewknor, and through this deceased step-mother, the regicide was connected with Christopher Lewknor, of Chichester, M.P. in the Long Parliament. William Hay, M.P. of the Long Parliament, was related to Herbert Morley, and thus connected to Stapley as well. James Rivers, M.P. of the Long Parliament, who died 1641, was a political and religious ally as well as relation of Stapley's.[411] Sir Thomas Pelham, Bart., M.P. of the Long Parliament, was related to Stapley, and hence Stapley was connected as well with Peregrine Pelham the regicide.[412] Further research would be needed to determine whether Stapley's brother-in-law Thomas Shirley was a prominent Shirley or an obscure one. Stapley's wife, Anne, was sister of the notorious royalist commander George Lord Goring, later created Earl of Norwich; his father, Stapley's father-in-law, was Lord Goring, who was a Privy Councillor. Lord Dungarvan and Arthur Jones, M.P.s of the Long Parliament, were the younger Goring's brothers-in-law and hence Stapley's as well.[413] Anthony May of Pashley, Sheriff of Sussex and Surrey in 1629, was the regicide's nephew; this Anthony's wife Joan Roberts was related to the Busbridge family of Sussex and also to the regicide James Temple, M.P. Thomas May, the poet and historian of the Long Parliament (author of *History of the Parliament of England*; he died 1650), for whom see DNB, was first cousin once removed of Stapley's brother-in-law, Thomay May of Pashley. The poethistorian's father, Sir Thomas May of Mayfield, who was Stapley's brother-in-law's first cousin, was the uncle of the regicide Sir Michael Livesey (his wife, Jane Sondes, being Livesey's aunt by blood). Thomas May, M.P. of the Long Parliament, and his brother Adrian May, Groom of the Bedchamber to Charles I, were both third cousins of Stapley's brother-in-law, Thomas May of Pashley.

Pedigrees: A pedigree starting with the regicide's great-grandfather in MS. Harley 6164, f. 22b, is in the British Library. "Stapley of Patcham" (the regicide's home being Patcham from about 1615), *Visitation of Sussex 1662*, p.105.

JAMES TEMPLE. Born 1606, second son of Sir Alexander Temple of St. Mary Hoo, Kent, and Longhouse Place, Chadwell, Essex, and his wife Mary Somer(s), eldest daughter and coheiress of John Somer of Rochester and Martina Ridge; it is unknown whether she was Sir Alexander's first wife or second wife. Her father John Somer was Clerk to the Privy Signet and was also of Newlands, Kent. Sir Alexander Temple was fourth son of John Temple of Burton Dassett, Warwickshire, and Stowe, Buckinghamshire, and Susan Spencer. He was knighted at the Tower of London March 14, 1603/4.[414] In the 1620s he was an M.P. who incurred the wrath of the Court and especially of the Duke of Buckingham.[415] His third wife was widow of John Busbridge of Haremare Hall, Etchingham, on the Kent/Sussex border; after marrying her, Sir Alexander often resided at Haremare and was a Sussex J.P. in the Rape of Hastings until his death, as pointed out by Fletcher.[416] Sir Alexander was Captain of the Fort of Tilbury, which was within walking distance of his earlier home (still in his possession at his death) at Chadwell, Essex. His son the regicide was to become Colonel and Commander of Tilbury Fort during the Civil War (see later chapter, indicating a distinct family sinecure). Sir Alexander's desperate exasperations with the inefficient government of Charles I may be traced in his series of petitions about Tilbury, the last one being only a few months before his death, which I have transcribed and included in the Appendix to this chapter as it shows the absurdities of Stuart policy so well. I have not transcribed the several other documents relating to this issue.[417] Sir Alexander had two other wives besides the regicide's mother. One was Margaret, Daughter of Peter Griffin of Stafford and Anne Leigh.[418] Apart from the fact that this marriage took place after Sir Alexander's knighthood was conferred, we know nothing else about it, and it is unclear whether this wife was his first or second wife. In any case, there were no issue and the marriage was brief. The mother of the regicide was a widow, and had previously been married to Thomas Peniston, one of the Clerks of the Council to Queen Elizabeth (this Thomas Peniston was father of Sir Thomas Peniston, Bart., of Leigh, Sussex, who himself married a near Temple relation, which sometimes leads to genealogical confusion); he is buried in Rochester Cathedral, as are John and Martina Somer her parents, and she herself. Sir Alexander was buried there beside her when he died in December, 1629.[419] Sir Alexander's third wife, who survived him, was Mary, daughter of John Reeve of London and the Abbey, St. Edmundsbury [i.e., Bury St. Edmunds], Suffolk. Her first husband had been John Busbridge, as mentioned above, by whom she had five children, one of whom, Mary, married her step-son James Temple the regicide! Then, after John Busbridge died, Mary first remarried a Robert Bankworth of London (who seems not to have lived long), and finally she remarried to Sir Alexander Temple. It is because of these close associations with the Busbridge family that the regicide adopted the name of Busbridge when he was trying to escape England in 1660 (see Appendix to this chapter). Dame Mary Temple's will survives, proved July 21, 1655, in which she leaves nothing to her step-son the regicide but a great deal to his children.[421] She also pointedly omits leaving anything to her eldest son Colonel John Busbridge, with whom she had actually had lawsuits over money and property.[422] As may be seen from the petition in the Appendix and the related documents, Sir Alexander Temple financed Tilbury Fort from his own pocket for many years, and was owed a great deal of money by the State. Partly for this reason, he died in debt, and his son the regicide had stood surety for him, so that quite a lot of family property had to be sold off.[423] Two of Sir Alexander's relations, Carew Saunders and Henry Whalley (brother of the regicide Edward Whalley) were executors. Both of these men were involved with the regicide for at least four years after Sir Alexander's death in a variety of property transactions together with Edward Whalley the regicide. In the Appendix to this Chapter I have placed various documents concerning these transactions, which are only a fraction of the surviving material, but are of particular interest, as they concern two regicides a good decade before the outbreak of the Civil War, when documents concerning such men tend to be scarce. The origins and history of the Temple family are dealt with under PETER TEMPLE the regicide, who was the head of the senior branch of the family. James Temple was from the junior branch of the family which were much better known and made far more mark on the world; the main family residence was Stowe, much enlarged and extended by descendants, and now well known as the public school called Stowe School. James had an older brother, John Temple, born 1603, who was killed in 1627 on the Isle of Rhé expedition, in personal combat with the French General de Blankcourt; he appears to have been one of the English officers who charged into battle regardless of the fact that his men would not fight. This is an important point: John Temple was evidently infuriated at the inefficiency of the Duke of Buckingham's absurd expedition, all the more so because his father's fort at Tilbury had been neglected in the same way and for the same reasons by the utterly incompetent favourite. It is believed that James Temple the regicide was also present at the Isle of Rhé, and he must have conceived an unconstrained and virulent hatred of the government of Charles I for several reasons: his brother's unnecessary death, his father's exasperations over many years and financial difficulties, and finally his own need to sell off his properties to pay debts incurred because the government would not pay what it owed to his father. It is notable that Sir Alexander persisted in keeping up Tilbury Fort despite official discouragement (see the one document in the Appendix and the other related ones referred to earlier), and that John Temple insisted in charging into battle nearly alone. This family of Temples were evidently determined to continue to perform what they viewed as their patriotic duties regardless of the fact that they did so without any support and suffered hardship, debts, and even death in the process. In this attitude they are typical of the families of many of the regicides who took the claims of their country seriously and who detested the foppery and dilettantism of the Stuart court. These serious, moral Puritans, were patriots of a truly disinterested kind. They could only view the incompetence and corruption and decadence of the Court with horror and contempt. This is the background to the ultimate act of regicide. The regicide had a sister who was a noted beauty and a prominent figure at the Court under James I.. She was Susanna Temple, who was Maid of Honour to Queen Anne, James I's wife. James I presented her in marriage with his own hand to Sir Gifford Thornhurst, Bart. (He was created baronet November 12, 1622.[424]) Thornhurst was of Agney Court, in Old Romney and Midley on Romney Marsh in Kent. He died December 16, 1627, and was buried with his family in the Warrior's Chapel at Canterbury Cathedral, where there are some splendid Thornhurst monuments. His only son had died an infant, as we learn from a brass inscription in Etchingham Church, which reads: "Here lies the only sonne of Sr Gyfford Thornhurst Barronett an infant by Dame Susan Thornhurst now living the only daughter of Sr Alex Temple Kt 1626". A letter of Sir Alexander Temple's survives in which he is seen to be tending to his widowed daughter's affairs in February, 1627/8.[425] Susanna remarried Sir Martin Lister (circa 1602-1670), M.P. of the Long Parliament, of Thorpe Ernald, Leicestershire, and Burwell, Lincolnshire, and became mother of the famous scientist Martin Lister. She was considered so beautiful that Granger says she was "esteemed one of the greatest beauties of the court", and her portrait by Cornelius Jansen (now one of the most glorious portraits of the period in the National Portrait Galley, London) was fiercely contended for in later generations: "John Churchill, duke of Marlborough, offered a considerable sum for this picture, and lord Wilmington was very desirous of purchasing it, but neither of them could procure it."[426]

Note: I was coauthor with Professor Robert Zaller of James Temple's entry in the *Biographical Dictionary of British Radicals in the Seventeenth Century*, and that entry is included in the Appendix to this chapter. (Since that entry states that James Temple was "of Clapham", I wish to point out that the Clapham intended is the village near Arundel in West Sussex, and not the Clapham at London; the regicide for some years lived at Michelgrove in Clapham, Sussex, as custodian of the property and and guardian of the heir of the royalist Shelley family.[427])

Prominent Relations: As already mentioned, the regicide was brother-in-law of the M.P. Sir Martin Lister, who was a moderate anti-royalist but secluded at Pride's Purge; Lister in turn was, through his first wife, a brother-in-law of the M.P.s of the Long Parliament, Thomas, Viscount Wenman, and Arthur Goodwin.[428] The regicide was first cousin of the royalist M.P. of the Long Parliament, Sir Alexander Denton, who was in turn brother-in-law of Sir Edmund Verney, M.P. The regicide went to extraordinary lengths to save his Denton relations during the Civil War, as was testified at the Restoration.[429] The regicide was a distant cousin of Peter Temple, M.P., the regicide. James was also nephew of Lord Saye and Sele, and first cousin of Col. Nathaniel Fiennes, and James Fiennes, who were both M.P.s. Another first cousin was Sir Peter Temple, Bart., M.P. of the Long Parliament who was named to the High Court to try the King but did not take up his seat. The regicide was related to Simon Mayne the regicide, who was nephew of James's first cousin once removed. The regicide was first cousin once removed of Sir Thomas Parker, M.P. of the Long Parliament, and through him was related by marriage to Sir Hardress Waller the regicide.[430] Parker's wife was daughter of Henry Lord Dacre.[431] The regicide's first cousin Susannah Temple married Lieutenant General Thomas Hammond, Lieutenant General of the Ordinance for the New Model Army, who sat on the High Court to try the King but did not sign the Death Warrant. Hammond was brother of the royalist divine, Rev. Dr. Henry Hammond, and was uncle of Colonel Robert Hammond of the New Model Army. At the Restoration, the regicide invoked the name of Rev. Henry Hammond in his favour.[432] This cousin Susannah Hammond was daughter of the regicide's uncle, John Temple of Frankton, Warwickshire; another daughter of this John Temple, Anne Temple, married Colonel John Busbridge of Haremare Hall (she was buried June 4, 1652, at Etchingham), who was the stepbrother of James Temple the regicide, as well as the regicide's brother-in-law (since the regicide married his own stepsister). In the Appendix to this chapter I give a document describing the apprehending of James Temple the regicide. This describes him assuming the name of Busbridge (his wife's surname as well as his step-parents' surname), and asking confirmation of his identity from his first cousin Thomas Temple of Frankton, whose own sister was married to Colonel Busbridge as mentioned just now. Unfortunately for the regicide, his cousin was at London and his cousin's wife Rebecca (daughter of Sir Francis Carew) pretended not to know him, either out of fear or unfriendliness (the Carews were royalists). The regicide was thus betrayed by this woman, since with her help he could have made his escape; all she would admit was that "one Busbridg did marry one of her husbands sisters". The regicide was related by marriage to the regicide Henry Smith, whose aunt Margaret Skipwith of Cotes, Leicestershire, married James Temple's first cousin Sir Matthew Saunders of Shankton, Leicestershire, brother of the Carew Saunders who had been so closely associated with the regicide in the 1620s and 1630's .The sister, Millicent Saunders, of these two cousins, married a Ralph Whalley, and it is presumably through this connection that James Temple was related by marriage to the regicide Edward Whalley, with whom he was related also through the Penistons and with whom he was closely associated, as seen by documents in the Appendix. It is an extraordinary thing indeed, but the regicide was through his second wife son-in-law of the Dutch Admiral Martin (Maarten) Tromp, and brother-in-law of the Dutch Admiral Cornelius (Cornelis) Tromp.[433] What is even more extraordinary is that the regicide's daughter Mary Temple married Admiral Cornelius Tromp: This younger Tromp was created a baronet by Charles II in 1674/5, and died 1691, and if there were any descendants, they seem to have forgotten about the baronetcy, which languishes without a claimant.[434] Another daughter of the regicide named Susanne who married as his second wife Clement Chevalier of the Island of Jersey, and their house is today the Chamber of Commerce for Jersey. They had a son named Temple Chevalier (1674-1722), who settled at Aspall in Suffolk in 1702. Susanne obviously met her husband in Jersey during her imprisoned father's lifetime, as she and her mother and other of the regicide's children were living there because James was in prison for so many years in Jersey, and in those days prisons did not provide food, which had to be brought to them daily by their families outside. The regicide was related to George, Sixth Lord Eure (died 1672), who was a Lord in Cromwell's House of Lords, since Lord Eure's grandmother Margaret Temple was the regicide's great-aunt. It is thought that the Brett marriage through which this relationship existed connected the regicide to the M.P. of the Long Parliament, Henry Brett, and therefore also - of all people! - the Duke of Buckingham whom the regicide's father so hated! The regicide was first cousin twice removed of Colonel Sir John Lydcott, of Oxfordshire and Sussex (knighted October 3, 1609[435]). The regicide's aunt was Hester Sandys, daughter of Miles Sandys, Clerk of the Crown. Through her the regicide was related by marriage to all of the Sandys family, which included many colonels and three M.P.s of the Long Parliament, Samuel, Thomas, and William, and the author and traveller George Sandys, who was nephew of Miles Sandys and hence first cousin once removed of the regicide. The Rev. Thomas Temple, D.C.L., recruiter M.P. for Mitchell, was the regicide's first cousin; he must not be confused with the Rev. Thomas Temple, D.D., brother of Sir John Temple, M.P. for Chichester (a recruiter). These two latter Temples were extremely distant relations, though Sir John was brother-in-law to the Rev. Henry Hammond, and thus also connected by marriage with the regicide. Captain Miles Temple of Dover, active for Parliament, was a first cousin of the regicide. Colonel Thomas Temple (later Sir), Colonel Edmund Temple, and Colonel Purbeck Temple (later Sir), were three brothers who were active for Parliament, though of the "Presbyterian" faction, and first cousins once removed of the regicide. The last-named, Purbeck Temple, testified against the regicide Henry Marten at the Restoration.[436] The regicide's first cousin Martha Temple married Sir Thomas Peniston, Bart., of Leigh, Sussex, who was also the regicide's step brother. Martha's sister, Bridget Temple, married Sir John Lenthall, brother of William Lenthall, Speaker of the House of Commons during the Long Parliament. It is worth noting that the Lenthalls ware indebted by the enormous sum of £3500 to the regicide's first cousin, Sir John Temple of Biddlesden, Buckinghamshire, in 1632.[437] My wife and I had the great pleasure of visiting Seton Gordon and his wife, the widow of Colonel Badger, when they lived at Biddlesden (which is beside Stowe), which they told us was built on a mountain of monks' skulls from the time when there was a priory there. I never saw as many snowdrops in a private garden as they had in the spring, thousands upon thousands of them in front of the house. Seton Gordon was the expert on the golden eagle, author of many books, and the finest piper in Scotland in his day. He gladly piped some pibroch for us at my request, and marched up and down in front of his house doing so in his kilt.

Pedigrees: There are four editions of the book by Temple Prime, *Some Account of the Temple Family*, published at New York between 1887 and 1899, which consist of extensively annotated series of pedigrees; each edition is different, and some material published in early editions is not reprinted in the later ones. Another similar work is *The Temple Memoirs* by John A. Temple and Harald M. Temple, London, 1925. Yet another such book is *The Rise of the Temples*, by Albert R. Temple and Danny D. Smith, third edition, Cincinnati, Ohio, USA, 1974. There are well over one hundred manuscript pedigrees of the Temples in existence from the seventeenth century or earlier. Some are in the Huntington library at San Marino, California. Many others belong to the present Baroness Kinloss, who inherited them directly from her ancestor Sir Peter Temple, Bart., M.P. of the Long Parliament, who had a personal obsession with family history and spent a fortune on genealogical research. In addition, a number of articles have appeared, and the subject is so immense that even a brief survey is impossible here. See under PETER TEMPLE for some further material, however.

Professor Robert Zaller, joint editor of *Biographical Dictionary of British Radicals in the Seventeenth Century* (1982-1984), began writing an entry for James Temple but then asked me to do it with him, so we were credited a co-authors of that entry. It is found in the Appendix. I not only wrote many entries for that biographical dictionary, but I advised on and co-authored (sometimes credited and sometimes not) various others, and Professor Zaller was kind enough to write a letter of thanks to me after the publication of the three volumes, saying that I had been 'like a third editor'.

PETER TEMPLE. Baptized October 14, 1600, at Sibbesdon (aka Sibson), Leicestershire. Third son of Edmund Temple of Temple Hall near Sibbesdon, Leicestershire (died 1618), sometime a barrister of the Middle Temple, and Elizabeth, daughter of Robert Burgoyne of Sutton, Bedfordshire, and Wroxall, Warwickshire; the regicide's parents married September 4, 1590, at Wroxall. The regicide's maternal grandfather was High Sheriff of Warwickshire in 1597 and died in 1613; his father, also Robert Burgoyne, was one of the Auditors of the Exchequer under Henry VIII for taking surrenders of the monasteries. The regicide's maternal grandmother was Judith Wroth. The Wroths, according to Burke, were "an ancient family" of Kent;[438] her father was Sir Thomas Wroth (1516-1573); see DNB, Gentleman of the Privy Chamber, M.P., etc. As for the Temple family, its history is such a complex matter that several books on the subject have served only to raise more questions than they answered. From the point of view of considering the two Temple regicides, it is essential to realize that the Temples at that time believed themselves to be descendants of Saxon Earls who were among the last fighters to resist the Norman Conquest, after the Battle of Hastings. Although often ridiculed as a fantasy-descent, this descent is distinctly possible, and may even be double. It is well known that the families of Arden and Bracebridge are descended in this manner; the Temples claimed the same descent, but even if it were not true in the Temple line as they maintained, the Temples after the time of Henry VI were also descended from the Bracebridges, through the marriage of Joanna Bracebridge, daughter of Sir John Bracebridge of Kingsbury, Warwickshire, with Thomas Temple of Temple Hall, ancestor of the two Temple regicides, and therefore the regicides were actually descended from the Saxon Earls at least in this manner, if not doubly as they believed.[439] Joanna Bracebridge brought with her as dower into the family of Temple the now-demolished Crowe Hall, with surrounding lands in the parish of Kingsbury, all of which were within walking distance of the Bracebridge family's extraordinary residential eyrie of Kingsbury Hall, the mouldering ruins of which still may be seen. These properties were still in the possession of the Temples 200 years later, and are mentioned in the will of the regicide's father (proved 1618).[440] The regicide's older brother Jonathan disposed of these properties in his will of 1619, and ordered them to be sold.[441] The descent from the Saxon Earls through the Temples and the Bracebridges was supposed to be from the same ancestors: from Leofwine, Earl of Hwicce under Aethelred II, through his son Leofric, Earl of Mercia (died August 31, 1057), and his wife, the famous Lady Godiva, through their son Earl Algar (whose brother was apparently the noted Hereward the Wake), and through his son, Edwin, last Saxon Earl of his line, who was killed in defending himself against the Normans in 1071. It was Algar's daughter, Edwin's sister, who was the ancestress of the Bracebridges. But the Temples claimed descent from Edwin himself. It is a curious fact that one of the earliest properties of the Temple family was the Manor of Blakenhall (now Lower Blakenhall) at Barton-under-Needwood in Staffordshire, near one of Algar's manors recorded in the Domesday Book; this may or may not be coincidence. The displayed eagle, arms of the Earls of Mercia, was prominently displayed as the arms of John Temple of Burton Dassett and Stowe, grandfather of James Temple the regicide, on his memorial placque at Burton Dassett Church in Warwickshire. The proper arms of the Temples are different, but even they have an origin in the indeterminate past, and it is claimed by one writer that: "As Robert Temple was certified to bear these arms in the reign of Henry III, it may be inferred that his family was one of the earliest that ever enjoyed the honour of hereditary arms." [442] Since the Saxon resistance to the Norman Conqueror was a popular theme in the Mid-seventeenth century, and cited frequently (along with Magna Charta) as an example of resistance to royal tyranny by those who wished to oppose Charles I's abuse of prerogative, it is of singular importance that the only family which produced more than one regicide, the Temple family, was convinced of its direct descent from the last and bravest of the Saxon nobles to oppose the Norman Conquest. Whether true or not, the belief in this was sufficient to motivate the Temples. A third Temple was nearly a regicide; Sir Peter Temple, Bart., M.P., was named to the High Court but decided not to sit. This Sir Peter was the leading antiquarian and genealogist of the family, and he can truly be described as obsessed in the fullest degree with the Temple genealogy. He paid countless people to research it, and he accumulated over a hundred genealogical pedigrees and MSS. which are still in the possession of the Baroness Kinloss today, not to mention others which are in other collections or are lost. He and Peter Temple the regicide, his distant cousin, were in touch about the family's coat of arms when the regicide was a mere boy of 20, or even younger (as we don't know when the contact began). Two letters of the regicide written to Sir Peter when the former was in his twenties are transcribed and included in the Appendix to this Chapter. The ancestral home of the Temples was Temple Hall, in the parish of Sibbesdon (aka Sibson), Leicestershire. Sir John Temple, M.P., who knew it well, described it in 1676 as being then "so ruinous as a great sum of money will not repair" and "so ancient that it has quite lost the name ... being now known by another denomination ..."[443] He warned his son, Sir William Temple, Bart. (the author and diplomat) against buying the house: "you must be bound to bestow several thousands upon the house, or else you had a great deal better let it alone, and never bring it back into the family again ..."[444] The actual family surname of Temple was thought by the family to have come from some association with the Knights Templar. This too was dismissed by many as a fantasy, until I discovered that Temple Hall took its name from that order after all, as it had been a subinfeudated manor of the Templars of Temple Balsall, Warwickshire, held as his own from the Templars by Henry de Temple, in 1279; he appears to be the Henry de Temple, lord of the manors of Temple and Little Shepey, in the time of king Henry I (misprint for III) and of King John in the pedigree of Temple published by Nichols, which also gives his son as John de Temple, temp. Hen. III, who is probably identical with the John de Temple of that period who was one of the leading Clerks to the Knights Templar as recorded by Thoroton.[445] The early Temples made various good marriages; with the magnate Stanley family, with the Kingscotes who were a branch of the magnate Berkeley family; with the knighted Turvile family; and Richard Temple of Temple Hall (died 1507), great-great grandfather of the regicide married Elizabeth Vincent, whose uncle Sir Thomas Malory is thought to be identical with the author of the *Morte d'Arthur*. This latter Temple was "much impoverished by siding with Richard III in the wars of that day."[446]

The Temples thus viewed themselves as having opposed, first, the Norman invader, and then, the Tudor impostor. They doubtless looked upon themselves, as the Scropes and other such regicide families seem also to have done, as repositories of the old defeated traditions and virtues, suffering anew under the exactions of the Stuarts. A couple of generations before the last mentioned Richard Temple, the family had been well off enough to lavish substantial manors upon daughters as dowries; Richard's uncle Nicholas Temple (died s.p. 1506) had been Edward IV's Escheator for Warwickshire and Leicestershire.[447] But after Bosworth Field, so near their home, the Temples were very seriously in decline. The regicide's father and uncle were both driven to the expedient of taking up the practice of the law at the Middle Temple, where they first studied and later took up chambers. When the regicide's uncle Richard Temple died prematurely in 1587, Roger Burgoyne moved into the chambers in his place; three years later, the regicide's father married Burgoyne's sister at Wroxall (as mentioned above). This did much to restore the prosperity and prestige of the Temple family, and was to help the regicide greatly in his earlier political career. The strongly Puritan religious views and activities of the regicide's father, shared with the Burgoynes and others of interest, are discussed in the later chapter "The Regicides and Religion". The regicide had siblings: Paul, baptised July 18, 1591, at Wroxall, married Alice Wydowes, admitted to Middle Temple 1611 where a fellow student was Clement Walker (later M.P.), became barrister 1613, had two sons who died without issue before him, and died 1641; Mary, baptized July 22, 1593, at Wroxall, married Robert Shelton of Birmingham (died 1642), brother of Sir Richard Shelton, Solicitor General of Charles I who died 1647, had son John born circa 1616 who married as second wife Elizabeth, daughter of Cornelius Holland the radical M.P., and she died 1646; Elizabeth, baptized April 5, 1594, at Wroxall, married prior to 1616 Henry Bannister of Upton, Leicestershire, had son Thomas Bannister who became barrister of Inner Temple in 1647; Jonathan, born 1598, admitted Middle Temple 1614, died unmarried, will proved January 9, 1619/20; younger siblings were: James, baptized April 24, 1603, at Wroxall, died without issue between 1616 and 1619; Joseph, born 1606, married October 16, 1641, Anne Sacheverell, widow, of Barton-in-Fabis, Notts.,[448] married secondly Millicent Flint, sister of

Henry Flint of New England and widow of Robert Hall (her will proved November 20, 1655), lived at The Would, Matlock, Derbyshire; Anne, baptized June 14, 1607 at Sibbesdon (Sibson), married Egerton; Benjamin, born 1610, possibly the Lieutenant Benjamin Temple serving under Col. Robert Russell on Jersey in 1646;[449] and Martha, baptized January 17, 16.., at Sibbesdon.

Prominent Relations: Through the marriage of his nephew John Shelton to Elizabeth Holland (mentioned above) the regicide was connected to Cornelius Holland, M.P. who was active in the High Court of Justice but did not actually sign the Death Warrant, and also to the regicide Henry Smith, M.P., who married another of the daughters of Cornelius Holland. This Henry Smith was on the Leicestershire County Committee with Peter Temple. The regicide Simon Mayne, M.P., was husband of Peter Temple's second cousin. The relationships to the other Temples, including the other regicide, have been remarked upon already under James Temple. Sir Roger Burgoyne, Bart., M.P. for Bedfordshire in the Long Parliament, was the regicide's first cousin once removed; he was secluded at Pride's Purge, but returned to sit in the 1656 Parliament.[450] His father, Sir John Burgoyne, Bart., recruiter M.P. for Warwickshire, was the regicide's first cousin; his election was opposed by the radicals of Warwickshire led by the regicide William Purefoy, but he was elected nevertheless.[451] The regicide's cousin, Elizabeth Burgoyne, sister of Sir Roger, married Alderman William Love, the anti-royalist Sheriff of London 1656-60, and M.P. for London, 1661, who obstructed the trials of the regicides (which, it should be noted, included his kinsman Peter Temple), as Ludlow tells us.[452] The Loves probably met the Burgoynes through the Temples, to whom they seem to have been related from some earlier alliance; a Thomas Love was practicing law at the Middle Temple as early as 1571 and gave his address at Temple Hall in Leicestershire when he accepted as bound to him the regicide's father of the same Temple Hall;[453] and the regicide's father left in his will £10 to bind his kinsman Samuel Love apprentice or for his maintenance.[454] Probably the radical M.P. Nicholas Love, who was so active on the High Court of Justice (although he did not sign the Death Warrant) was a relation, but research into the Love family would be necessary to establish this fact. James Temple would have qualified as a barrister at Lincolns Inn in 1629 (which was his London residence), which was the same year Nicholas Love was admitted there, so they not only would have known each other as young lawyers but Love may well have been admitted there at Temple's recommendation or at least gone there at his suggestion, and hence probably lodged with him for the next seven years. They may therefore have been intimate friends as well as relations. Love is often called a regicide, but he did not sign the Death Warrant; he fled to Switzerland at the Restoration and died at Vevey in 1682. Sir Peter Wroth and Sir Thomas Wroth, M.P.s of the Long Parliament, were second cousins of Peter Temple the regicide; Sir Thomas seems to have been a close political crony of the regicide, and it was presumably through Wroth that Peter Temple became so friendly with John Pyne and Robert Blake of Somerset, as we shall see in a later chapter. Sir Peter Wroth's wife was a sister of Sir Edward Dering, M.P.[455] The regicide was related to Sir Edward and William Ayscough, M.P.s of the Long Parliament, since his cousin Judith Burgoyne had married Sir William Ayscough. The regicide was related to the Thomas Cotton who was a member of the original Leicestershire Committee, but who "went away and forsooke the service",[456] through an intermarriage or two between the families three or four generations earlier. The regicide's aunt Mary Temple married, first, either Sir Wolstan Dixie, a Leicestershire royalist, or someone named Ducie, and secondly, William Bulstrode, connecting the regicide with the widespread Bulstrode clan which included the M.P. Bulstrode Whitelock. The regicide was doubly related to John George, M.P. for Cirencester in the Long Parliament, who had been Clerk of the Wardrobe, a Deputy Lieutenant, a monopolist, and a weak Parliament supporter with an extremely curious career;[457] they were first cousins in one connection and second cousins in a separate connection, and the two families had had extremely close connections with each other indeed over many years, too complicated to explain here. Temple was also a second cousin of Sir Hardress Waller, the regicide.

Pedigrees: Several mentioned under James Temple. See also "Temple". John Nichols, *The History and Antiquities of Leicestershire*, Vol. IV, p. 959.

ROBERT TICHBORNE. Born 1619, only surviving son of Robert Tichborne, Senior, of London, and Joan Bankes, daughter of Thomas Bankes of London and sister of Sir John Bankes, Knight, of London (not the later Sir John Bankes, Bart.; see below). The Tichborne family were of considerable eminence and antiquity, and the regicide himself was highly aware of the fact. He commissioned an incredibly elaborate official pedigree for himself, prepared by none other than the Garter King of Arms, and signed and attested by four additional heralds, dated 1658.[458] This amazing document consists of nine closely written folio pages in Latin, culminating in the regicide, his wife, and four children. It commences with Sir Roger de Tichborne, Lord of Tichborne, Hants., who lived in the time of King Henry II and married Mabella, sole daughter and heiress of Sir Ralph de Lymerston, Lord of Lymerston in the Isle of Wight. This ancestress established the famous "Tichborne Dole", a charitable bequest which was the occasion every year for a vast family reunion of all the Tichbornes, a history of which has been published.[459] The regicide's cousin, Sir Henry Tichborne, Bart., in 1689 said of this ancestress: "Dame Mabella de Lymerston, wife to Sir Roger de Tichborne, was of the blood of the ancient lord proprietors, or rather princes, of the Isle of Wight, some of whose lands, and that of her name, we yet possess, though above five hundred years distant from this time; and many there pay homage to us even to this day. Her virtues were so admirable that she is said to have wrought some miracles ..."[460] The following is a list I have extracted from the enormous MS. pedigree of the ancestors of the regicide who held the office of Sheriff of a county, to give some idea of the status and history of this family in abbreviated form: Hampshire: Johannes Tichbourne, 14 Edward III; Rogerus de Tichbourn, 41 Edward III; Johannes T., 6 Henry IV; Johannes T., 3 Henry VII; Nicholaus T., 1 Queen Mary; Beniamus T., 21 Queen Elizabeth; the same Benjamin, 1 James I; Wiltshire: Johannes de T., 14 Edward II; Johannes de T., 8 Edward III; Dorset and Somerset: Johannes T., 1 James I. The regicide's great-great-grandfather John Tichborne married the daughter and heiress of Richard Martin, whose great uncle had been the Judge of Common Pleas in 1418, John Martyn (died October 24, 1436).[461] Most published pedigrees give the regicide's grandparents (John and Dorothy) with no issue indicated, eliminating any connection with the regicide. Most of the Tichbornes were emphatic royalists; however, their wish not to be associated with the regicide was something more than that, since they were also deeply in debt to him financially: The regicide's mother was buried November 28, 1639, at St. Michael le Querne, London.[462] Since the regicide and his father were both Skinners, and it is possible sometimes to confuse the two of them, it is worthwhile to give a brief sketch of some aspects of Robert Senior's activities: He was a church-warden of St. Michael le Querne from 1619-1629, loaned the church £20 in 1638, and gave the church £20 in 1639.[463] In 1638 he lived in the parish, listed with a rent of £40 (second highest in the Parish), whereas in the same year the regicide was listed with a rent of £50 and lived three doors away from The Nag's Head Tavern on the South Side of Cheapside in the parish of St. Vedast alias St. Foster's.[464] Tichborne Senior was active on the Common Council of the City, and was a close friend and ally of Thomas Atkin, Mercer. When Atkin became the Alderman for Farringdon-Within on September 13, 1638, he chose Robert Tichborne, Senior, as his Deputy, and the regicide's father from that time was known as "Mr. Deputy Tichborne". The regicide himself later became Atkin's brother-in-law, presumably by marrying his sister.[465] The regicide also became Alderman for Atkin's old ward of Farringdon-Within in 1649, with Atkin's help. Apparently Robert Tichborne, Senior, was Warden of the Skinners' Company, and the regicide was himself later a prominent member of the Skinners as well; but the regicide was additionally a Draper. (The records of these guilds would probably yield additional interesting information, but have not been consulted.) In 1637, Robert Tichborne, Senior, submitted a petition to the King stating that he and Michael Holman, Scrivener, had loaned £4,780 to Sir Richard Tichborne and Sir Walter Tichborne several years earlier but that Sir Richard and Sir Walter in 1635 had obtained Royal Protection to evade legal action, that they would "pay neither principal nor interest, but reserve great estates to themselves". It was asked that the King would lift his Protection so that they might be sued; a similar petition was submitted to the Privy Council, both these petitions no doubt getting through the bureaucratic maze courtesy of Tichborne Senior's brother-in-law Sir John Bankes, Attorney-General.[466] These Tichbornes were fairly distant cousins of the regicide; Sir Richard and Sir Walter were brothers, sons of Sir Benjamin Tichborne, Bart., Sheriff of Hampshire.[467] These Tichbornes were so close to the Stuart Court that: "The old Sir Benjamin Tichborne was honoured with visits from King James the First at least four times, always on the 29th of August, Sir Benjamin's birthday, upon which the King arranged to honour the old knight with his company . ... So frequent were the visits of King James, that one of the apartments in old Tichborne House obtained the name of 'the King's Chamber', and ... the King in his progresses among the seats of the neighbouring nobility and gentry, when wearied with their ceremonious receptions and fulsome adulations, ... used to say to his attendants, he would go back to old Ben (Sir Benjamin Tichborne) and his honest hospitality ..."[468] The regicide's father was a second son, and had an older brother, the Rev. John Tichborne, D.D., concerning whom more research would probably uncover some interesting facts, but this has not been attempted.[469]

Prominent Relations: The Tichbornes mentioned above, royalists, and their immediate family and relations are not detailed here because they would not have been on good terms with the regicide. The regicide's grandmother and great-aunt were sisters, both Challoners, but they were of the Sussex family of that name from Lindfield, and *not* related to the regicide Thomas Chaloner, M.P. The regicide's first cousin Anne Bankes married (July 5, 1631) Edmund Waller, the poet, M.P., and royalist conspirator. The regicide was thus related by marriage to the wife of Adrian Scrope the regicide, to Sir Hardress Waller the regicide, to Sir William Waller, to John Hampden, M.P., and the set of relations that went with them all. Although in the 1650s the regicide was married to Alice Johnson of Norwich, he appears to have had a first wife who was sister of his father's old friend and crony, Thomas Atkin, as mentioned above. Pearl has published a brief biographical sketch of Atkin (whom she calls Atkins);[470] he was Warden of the Mercers Company, Lord Mayor of London 1644-5, M.P. for his old home town of Norwich in the Short Parliament and again (1645) as a recruiter M.P. of the Long Parliament, named to the High Court but did not sign the Death Warrant, was knighted by Cromwell, etc. One of his daughters was sister-in-law to Robert Brewster the Elder, a recruiter M.P. in the Long Parliament, who was also brother-in-law of Miles Corbet, M.P., the regicide. Tichborne was related to the prominent businessman, Sir John Bankes, Bart. D.C. Coleman, in his book about this man, has a footnote which says: "In a letter of April 1660 Banks had spoken of Lord Tichborne as 'my very hon. good friend and kinsman'. I have not discovered what this kinship relationship was."[471] (The regicide was involved in many business ventures with this Sir John.) Coleman seems to have spent little time on the Bankes family genealogy, and gives a parsimonious account of the family which is far from satisfying. The regicide's uncle was the other Sir John Bankes, who was knighted June 7, 1631,[472] by which time as a lawyer of Gray's Inn he had recently become Attorney General of the Duchy of Cornwall for the Prince of Wales, a post which he held until 1635. Bankes on February 24, 1640/1, was required to surrender the offices first granted to him in 1625 of Steward and Keeper of the Court Leet, Liberty, etc., of all manors in Yorkshire of the Monastery of St.

FURTHER DETAILS OF THE FAMILY BACKGROUNDS

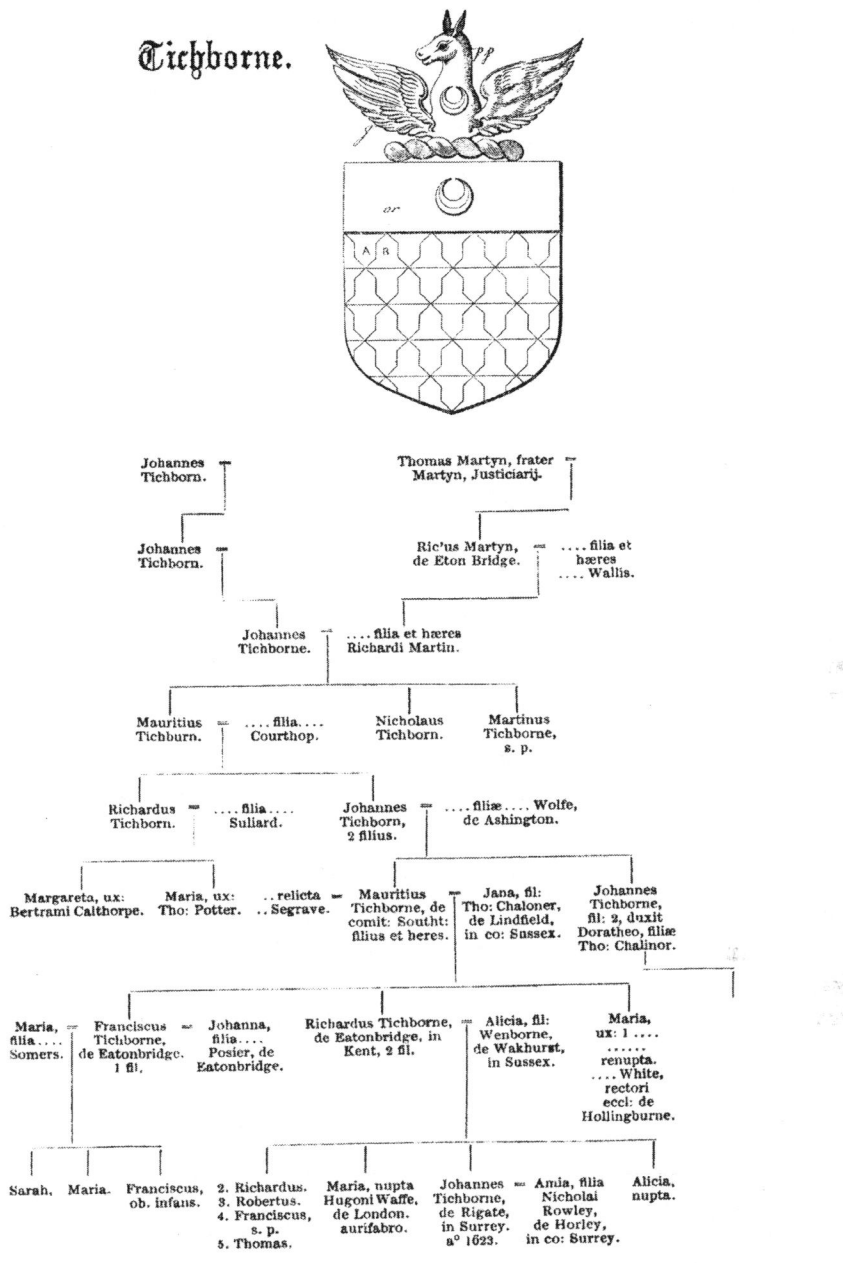

The coat of arms of Robert Tichborne the regicide, and one of the pedigrees of the family; the John Tichborn at right, three lines up, who married Dorothy Challinor, is the regicide's grandfather. This comes from the Surrey Visitation of 1623 printed in Volume II of the Surrey Archaeological Collections.

Mary's near York.[473] Had he fallen from favor? Through this Bankes, the regicide was related to Daniel Blagrave the regicide, since Bankes's daughters Joan and Alice married John and William Borlase, Blagrave's cousins. The regicide was related to James Temple the regicide, since his father's first cousin Francis Tichborne of Edenbridge, Kent, had married Mary Somer(s) as his first wife, apparently the niece of James Temple's mother Mary Somer(s).

Siblings: The regicide had three sisters: Katherine, married Edmund Mountjoy of Wethersfield, Essex, and London, second son of Allen Mountjoy of Copford, Essex and Mary Beckingham, leaving issue by 1634 Katherine and Mary;[474] Joanna, married George Smith of Gray's Inn; Elizabeth, married .... Haman (Hammond?), merchant of London.

Pedigrees: The enormous MS. pedigree mentioned above is MS. Harleian 5800, ff. 38-42, in the British Library. The regicide signed his own entry in the *Visitation of London 1633-5*, 'Vol. II, p. 289, showing his arms quarterly of eight, with an abbreviated pedigree going back only to his grandfather. His single arms are tricked in another MS. Harleian MS. 1105, f. 36a, in the British Library. The regicide's grandparents (showing no issue yet) appear in pedigrees in *Visitation of Kent, 1574*, Harleian Society, Vol. 75, pp. 37-8; and Surrey Visitation of 1623, in *Surrey Archaeological Collections*, Vol. II, under Tichborne, unpaginated.

JOHN VENN. Baptized April 8, 1586, at Lydeard St. Lawrence, Somerset. Second son of Simon Venn of Lydeard St. Lawrence, Somerset (buried April 24, 1613) and Maude Lawrence (parents unknown). The historian John Venn in 1904 described the regicide's family as sprung "from an old yeoman stock which may be traced back, in that parish or the adjacent one of Bishop's Lydeard, to about the beginning of the fourteenth century . ... Their names do not appear in any Visitation of Somerset."[475] The Venn family, therefore, seem to have been rather similar to the Horton family traced earlier, except that the Venns can be considered of slightly greater antiquity. The Venns and Hortons appear to have been sturdy, somewhat immoveable, yeomen who stayed where they were, doing nothing of particular significance, for centuries. But even doing nothing of significance, if done for long enough, can become a tradition generating some pride, if always done in the same place, and in the same sturdy style. When circumstances arise suddenly for that sturdy style to be applied towards something unexpectedly significant, the results can often be spectacular. It may be no coincidence that Horton and Venn showed themselves to be spectacularly successful in military exploits and bulldog determination, traits perhaps to be expected from people who had done nothing of significance with a fierce concentration for generations. It is interesting that the regicide's brother Simon Venn was described in 1633 as "a man of great estate and much feared by reason of his terrifying speeches and hard dealing, etc."[476] When one of the family eventually sold the Manor of Lydeard St. Lawrence to the Duke of Somerset, the price was £1950, and that was only part of the family property. So the Venns were highly prosperous. Most of the regicide's life was spent in London as a merchant, though he had an active and apparently lucrative trade furnishing "the western parts of this kingdom, with Ireland and Wales, with commodities", as he expressed it in 1637.[477] His family had had a foothold in London business since at least 1560, the earliest surviving entry in the parish register of All Hallows, Bread Street, for the baptism of a son of his father's first cousin, John Venn, Citizen of London (died 1591). Perhaps, therefore, as his immediate family used the same arms, the regicide's family was somehow related to Sir Richard Venn (Fenn), Alderman, Sheriff and Lord Mayor; after all, this Lord Mayor and the regicide were both in the City's Honourable Artillery Company together for many years and must at the least have known each other well and presumed some relationship. The regicide's siblings were: Agnes, born 1582, married George Pratt in 1602; Simon, baptized August 9, 1584, married Katherine (who was alive 1650), died March, 1640/1, had one son and three daughters; Thomas, born 1591; Edith, born 1593; Edward, born 1594, died 1620; Katherine, no details; Ann, married William Doggett and was alive, 1650, as were her husband and six children.[478]

Prominent Relations: Apparently none, unless the prominent Venns of the Lord Mayor's family were relations. However, the regicide's son became Mayor of Bridgwater and wrote the book *Military Discipline* published in 1672.

Pedigrees: Venn alias Fenn pedigree (one should always remember that both spellings were used interchangeably for this surname), *Visitation of London 1633-5*, Vol. II, p. 308. Pedigree of the "Venns of Lydeard St. Laurence", opposite p. 231 in John Venn, *Annals of a Clerical Family: Being Some Account of the Family and Descendants of William Venn ...*, London, 1904.

Acknowledgements: I am grateful to Mrs. Kate Walton of Lydeard St. Lawrence and the Day family of Pyleigh Manor, Lydeard St. Lawrence, for their generous help, and for making available information, including the description of the regicide's brother quoted above.

THOMAS WAITE. Baptized September 1, 1615, at Wymondham, Leicestershire. Only known child of Henry Waite of Wymondham, Leicestershire, and Susanna Gulson, also of Wymondham; they married in 1614.[479] Wymondham is near the border of Rutland, the small county with which the regicide was to have most of his political and military associations. The regicide's maternal grandfather and uncle were both Rectors of Wymondham: the Rev. William Gulson, M.A., Rector from 1578 to 1614, patron Queen Elizabeth; aged the Rev. Nathaniel Gulson, D.D., Rector from 1628 to 1647, patron Charles I. Further research on these clerics has not been attempted. The origins of the Waite family are somewhat obscure; they have been described by a local historian as "a very substantial yeoman family in Wymondham".[480] The signature or name of a Thomas Wayte, perhaps an ancestor, has been noted in a deed of January 16, 1547, and in several succeeding deeds, all of the Warwickshire area. A Richard Wayte of Leicestershire, obviously a relation, matriculated at Lincoln College, Oxford, aged 19, on July 24, 1580, and obtained his B.A. at Brasenose on February 28, 1583/4.[481] The regicide used arms granted to the Waite family in 1612, and for that and other reasons, we know him to have been closely related to, and possibly grandson of, the grantee of those arms, Thomas Waite, His Majesty's Receiver for Warwickshire and Leicestershire in the period 1612-37, and possibly earlier and up to Waite's death in 1642.[482] This Thomas Waite was from Keythorpe, Leicestershire, died in 1642, and had as his executor, his son Captain Francis Waite, a Parliamentarian officer, who in 1653 was actually imprisoned in the Fleet for debt and petitioned Cromwell to intervene in his eleven years' lawsuit to try and collect some money owing to him from his father's debtors.[483] There is some possibility that the Receiver mentioned above was actually two people, a father and son both named Thomas, with the grantee of arms in 1612 being the elder. If so, then he could be the regicide's grandfather Thomas, who died circa 1614.[484] In that case, it would be an uncle of the regicide's who continued to act as Receiver and had the son Captain Francis; the grandfather would, however, have had also a son John, Bachelor of Law in 1633, who jointly with his father erected a screen in Wymondham Church (now vanished) with an inscription which read "Ex dono Thomae Waite et Johannis Filil 1638", both leaving £5 to the church in their wills.[485] The regicide's uncle Thomas would have had also a son John, admitted to Gray's Inn November 24, 1637, son of Thomas of Keythorpe, and therefore a first cousin of the regicide, attending the same Inn of Court three years after the regicide was admitted there.

Prominent Relations: None that we know of, except the Receiver(s) mentioned above, and the Parliamentary militia Captain Francis Waite, who appears to have been an uncle or first cousin. An apparent aunt, Jane Waite, was the second wife of the Rev. Abraham Wright (born 1611), Vicar of Okeham, Rutland. Since the regicide beome a Governor of Okeham School, there may have been some interaction between them of local significance.[486]

Pedigrees: A pedigree of the Waite family commencing with the regicide and extending through many later generations has been compiled and printed privately, as part of a book called *Pierce: A Family Record*, by Harry Pierce, of Langdale, Westmorland, in 1943. (See pp. 63-8). This was made available to me by the kind offices of a descendant of the regicide, my friend, the late Richard Constable, who owned a copy of this rare book.

SIR HARDRESS WALLER. (Knighted by Charles I at Nonsuch, July 6, 1629.[487]) Only known child of George Waller of Groombridge, Kent, and his second wife, Mary Hardres, daughter of Richard Hardres and Mabel Wroth. (Mary Hardres had two previous husbands: Cheney Hales of the Dungeon, Canterbury, Kent, married in 1593; and Sir William Ashenden.) The regicide's father died 1622, and his mother apparently died 1612 and was buried at Speldhurst. Firth believed that the regicide "was born about 1604" (old DNB entry). The birth date of 1604 is confirmed by a MS. pedigree.[488] First wife of the regicide's father (leaving no issue) had been Elizabeth Sondes, daughter of Sir Michael Sondes of Throwley, Kent. The Wallers were an ancient and distinguished family which can be traced back at least to the reign of Richard II, in the MS. pedigree mentioned just now. However, from an unsuspected source, the enormous MS. pedigree of the regicide Robert Tichborne referred to under TICHBORNE above, we have fascinating light on an even earlier ancestor, Thomas Waller, alive in the 19th year of Edward III - aleady possessing arms - whose great-grandson really established the family's fortunes in the dramatic way now described: "Richard Waller of Gromebridge in Sussex [now in Kent] Esqr serving in ye warres in France in ye time of Kinge Henry ye 5th did take Charles Duke of Orleance fathr to Lewis ye 12th & kept him Prisoner in England 25 yeares during wch time hee built that goodly house wch yett remaineth at Grombridge & afterwards paid for his randsome foure hundred thousand crownes hee was Grandchild to Charles ye 5th & died 1464".[489] Thus did the Wallers secure themselves for the future by kidnapping the father of a king: The regicide's great-grandfather William Waller was Sheriff of Kent in the 22nd of Henry VIII, died January 18, 1555, buried at Speldhurst. His grandfather Sir Walter Waller was born 1543, and knighted 1572; his older son, Sir Thomas Waller, Lieutenant of Dover Castle, was father of the first cousin of the regicide, General Sir William Waller. On his mother's side, the regicide was descended from the ancient Hardres family who seem to be traced back to a Robert of Hardres "recorded in a Survey contemporary with Domesday", through a Philip de Hardres of the time of King John, down through another Philip who was a benefactor to Canterbury Cathedral and whose arms were hung in the cloisters there. That was as early as the reign of Henry III, and his father was the first Waller listed in the Visitation of the family taken in 1619. Two of the family were listed as gentry in the reign of Henry VI. There were several good marriages, and the martial tradition was not lacking, as the regicide's uncle Thomas was at the siege of Boulogne with Henry VIII. The regicide's grandfather Richard was Sheriff of Kent in the 30th of Elizabeth.[490]

Prominent Relations: General Sir William Waller was the regicide's first cousin. Richard Ingoldsby the regicide was brother-in-law of the regicide's daughter Anne, who married Sir Henry Ingoldsby, Bart. William Lenthall, Speaker of the House of Commons, was described by the regicide in a letter as his "kinsman".[491] The regicide's maternal great-great grandfather married a sister of the Sir John Colepeper of his day, so the regicide was distantly related to the Colepepers, including Sir John Colepeper, the royalist M.P. The regicide was related to the Oxendens of Kent, since his great-aunt Mary was daughter of Edward Oxenden of Dene, and this led to a distant association by marriage with the regicide John Dixwell. The regicide's first cousin, Sir Thomas Hardres (1610-1681, see DNB), was Serjeant at Law, and a post-Restoration M.P. The regicide was a second cousin of Peter Temple the regicide as well as Sir Peter and Sir Thomas Wroth, M.P.s, through his descent from the Wroths. His father's first wife was the aunt of the regicide Sir Michael Livesey.

Pedigrees: British Library: MS. Add. 5711, ff. 129-30.

VALENTINE WAUTON (WALTON). Born 1594. Son of Nicholas Wauton and Elizabeth .... Apparently he had a brother George Wauton and possibly other siblings. The family background of Wauton is extremely controversial and confused. A hostile post-Restoration account runs like this: "Thomas Wauton esquire was seized in fee of the said Manor (Great Stoughton, Huntingdonshire) who had issue Sir George Wauton, Bridgett, Frances and Jane. Sir George Wauton had issue two sonnes R: and Tho: - Sir George Wauton settles the estate primo Jacobi - levies a fine, makes a Deed of Uses: and made Sir Oliver Cromwell sole trustee; afterwards makes a will: and makes the said Sir Oliver Cromwell sole executor; having first settled the manor upon the Heirs males lawfully begott by Sir George Wauton who then were liveing, for want of such issue, to the heirs males lawfully begot of the body of John Wauton; and for default of such issue, to the heirs males lawfully begott of the body of Thomas Wauton esquire then deceased Grandfather to Sir George Wauton. Sir George's Grandfather had issue: Tho: and John: who died without issue male: for want of issue to John and Thomas Wauton then the said Manor was to discend and come to ye right heirs of Sir George Wauton for ever. The issue male being extinct, Bridgett Frances and Jane then surviveing Sir George, and sisters, were the Coheirs and heirs at law ... That the Said Manor of Greate Staughton was iniuriously collusively and coruptly Detayned from the Coheirs by Sir Oliver Cromwell who was sole Trustee: and Sole Executor to Sir George Waulton who found out Valentine Wauton as said one of the name not of kindred - or lineall discent to Sir George: makes private estates being posest of the Manor and the Evidences of the estates: findes Valentine Wauton now attainted of Treason, to bee a boy then, as then said to bee of the name of Wauton though not of kindred, to whom Sir Oliver became Guardian for many yeers, kept the proffitts of the estate as Trustee, Executor, and Guardian and then marries this Valentine Waulton attainted of treason to his Neece, sister to Oliver Cromwell the Diabolicall Traytor: and soe the Manor was setled upon Valentine and that broode by Sir Oliver Cromwell and not Sir George Waulton; Suites at lawe and Enquiry have bin Comenced: Composicions have bin offered by Sir Oliver in his life tyme to the husbands of the Coheirs: ... ther are Deeds and Decree in chancery that hath bin Declared and Decred that the Coheirs are heires at lawe to Sir George: Primo Jacobi (1603). ... The said Manor was uniustly and coruptly obtayned and settled by Sir Oliver Cromwell, a Trustee, setled by him upon one whom nee called Valentine Wauton: who hee maried to his neece and soe defrauded the Coheirs ..."[492] A very different light is given to this matter by reading the surviving will of Sir George Wauton, proved 1606 by Sir Oliver Cromwell, the sole executor. Wauton's will is extremely long and liberal, giving money to countless godchildren, servants, and friends and kinsmen, as well as bequests to the poor.[493] He pointedly excludes his sisters Bridget and Jane and their families (actually, Jane didn't have any), whom he must have disliked pretty intensely. He does mention his sister Frances, but not in a very affectionate fashion, saying: "Item I geve and bequeathe to Thomas Throckmorton my brother in lawe and to Frances his wife forty pounds." The only other relations who are mentioned in any way at all are cousins. The regicide is not mentioned anywhere, nor is his father Nicholas. Sir George then makes his wishes for the Manor known: "I doe ordaine constitute and make my honorable good frend Sr Olyver Willms als Cromwell knighte the sole Executor of this my laste will and Testament to whom ... I geve all the rest of my goods and Chattles moveable, and unmoveable whatsoever, to this end and purpose that hospitalitie shalbe kepte in the mannor house of greate Stoughton, and to geve that entertaynemente he maie convenyentlie to my antiente frendes for the space of Three yeares nexte after my decease." It is quite clear from this that any sons of Sir George were either already dead or in disgrace, and apart from the one bequest of £40, the sisters and their families are very decidedly excluded. Also, Sir Oliver Cromwell having "kept hospitality" at the Manor for three years for the "antient frendes" was free to keep and enjoy the Manor and everything that went with it to himself without further claims by any Wautons whatsoever. Far from conspiring to defraud any Wautons, Sir Oliver seems to have gone to incredible trouble to find a distant cousin, Valentine Wauton, take him on as an adopted son, raise him well, marry him to his niece (the marriage to Margaret Cromwell took place June 20, 1617, at Huntingdon, at St. John's), and hand over the Manor to him: This looks more like generosity than greed. There was nothing to prevent Sir Oliver selling it all off and keeping all the money: Sir George is buried in a splendid effigy tomb at Great Stoughton Church, erected at great expense by Sir Oliver Cromwell, with an effigy which is striking and handsome, and which I have photographed. Sir George had been knighted by James I at Whitehall, August 20, 1604, along with Philip Cromwell of Huntingdonshire.[494] In his will, Sir George left this Sir Philip a gold ring, and did the same to Henry, Richard, and Robert Williams alias Cromwell (the last mentioned being the Protector's father). As for the Wautons and their history, the arch-royalist Mark Noble confesses they were a "very ancient and knightly family".[495] He also writes that they were "seated at Great-Stoughton, in Huntingdonshire, which manor, with other considerable estates, they had long enjoyed from marrying the heir-general of Sir Adam de Cretings, of Cretingsbury, who distinguished himself in the wars of k. Edw. III. in France; John de Wauton, or Waweton, was a knight of the shire in the parlements held in the 43 d, 46th, and 47th years of that king's reign, and in the 1st and 5th of k. Rich. II.'s, as was Tho. Wauton, or Wawton, in the 20th of the same reign, and in the 2d of k. Hen. V."[496] It is worth noting that the above-mentioned Sir George Wauton, whom we have discussed at some length, inherited the Manor of Great Stoughton not from his own father as falsely alledged in the post Restoration document, but from a cousin, William Wauton, whose will, proved 1558/9 luckily survives.[497] William's brother Gilbert, the sole executor, was given the remainder of William's lease in the manor. The ins and outs of all this are extremely complicated. But one crucial point to be noticed in William's will is that he mentions a brother Nicholas, and leaves money to all his children. This may well be the father or grandfather of the regicide, since no trace of any other Nicholas can be found in direct connection with Great Stoughton. But here we must leave this tangled web, and wish others who may research it *bon chance*.

Prominent Relations: Oliver Cromwell the regicide and later Lord Protector was, as we have seen, Wauton's brother-in-law. It is hardly necessary to list the many relationships which followed from this one, and included many regicides, as Cromwell's relationships are so well known. The regicide Thomas Pride's daughter married Wauton's son Robert Wauton, with a handsome dowry of £3000, and they had issue, who became the regicide's heirs (if it were not for the attainder); this marriage occurred in 1656, so that Wauton and Pride became connected in this way very late in their careers.[498] Sir Oliver Luke and Sir Samuel Luke, M.P.s of the Long Parliament, were the regicide's cousins in a double connection, and Sir George Wauton left a gold ring to his "cozen Nicholas Luke esquire", apparently the father of the two M.P.s, who was additionally related to the Oliver Lord St. John of Bletshoe to whom Sir George Wauton also left a gold ring.[499] The regicide was possibly related to a royalist Lieutenant-Colonel Wauton or Walton captured and examined in January, 1646/7, by General Mytton.[500]

Pedigrees: None which are satisfactory in showing the regicide's precise relationship to the other Wautons; this is still a vexed question.

EDWARD WHALLEY. Born circa 1601. Second son of Richard Whalley of Kirkton Hall (at Screveton), Screveton Hall, and Flintham Grange, Nottinghamshire, and his second wife (married July 12, 1595) Frances Cromwell, daughter of Sir Henry Cromwell of Hinchinbroke, and aunt of Oliver Cromwell the Protector. The regicide's father was Sheriff of Nottinghamshire 1595-6, and M.P. for Boroughbridge in 1602; he died circa 1632. He was married three times but had no issue by his first and third wives. His first wife was Anne, daughter of George Horsey of Digswell, Hertfordshire. His third wife, whom he married

October 29, 1626, was Jane, daughter of William Styrrop of Cambridge. The regicide's father is described by Thoroton as "a Person of great Parts and Action: he was a Knight of the Shire and one of the most splendid Sheriffs of the County: but being much incumbered and engaged in Suits, the latter part of his Time was not prosperous."[501] His widow remarried an Edward Coleby. The history of the Whalley family is an enormous subject. The surname is derived from Whalley in Lancashire: "where the Family has resided from the time of the Conquest. Wymarus was one of King William's warriors at the battle of Hastings, for services on which occasion the Conqueror conferred upon him the Lordship of Whalley, A.D. 1067."[502] From this family descended the regicide's branch, and the regicide's arms were similar to those of Whalley Abbey (except that the abbey arms has whales with "the heads of croziers issuant from their mouths" because of the association with the Church and bishops).[503] An ancestor, John Whalley, was Sheriff of Derbyshire and Nottinghamshire under Edward III apparently for ten years, between 1351 and 1361.[504] The ancient and now demolished manor house of Kirkton Hall was the main seat of the Whalleys, though they owned many other handsome manors. Kirkton Hall once stood near Screveton Church, where there are fine tombs and monuments of the Whalleys, which I have (despite poor light) successfully photographed in many views. Kirkton Hall came into the Whalley family from the marriage of Elizabeth, daughter and heiress of Thomas Leek (or Leake) to Richard Whalley, the regicide's four-times-great grandfather, during the reign of Edward IV. Richard Whalley of Kirkton, the regicide's great-grandfather, has an entry in DNB, and was a very remarkable and noted figure. He "much distinguished himself at the tournaments held in the reign of k. Hen. VIII. which probably greatly ingratiated him into that monarch's favor,"[505] and obtained magnificent grants of land and property including Welbeck Abbey. He was an M.P. many times, held important offices, was employed by Thomas Cromwell in connection with the dissolution of the monasteries, and was even given the Manor of Wimbledon which had belonged to Queen Katharine Parr. "In the first year of the reign of k. Edward VI, he represented Scarborough in parlement; and during the splendor of the duke of Somerset, in the reign of k. Edw. VI. he had great influence, as he was nearly related to, and much trusted by, his grace: but the fall and ruin that overtook that great subject, was sensibly felt by mr. Whalley, who was his steward; but to whom he proved true; for when he was examined respecting his grace's intention of getting himself declared protector in the ensuing parlement, he as stedfastly denied it as the earl of Rutland affirmed it ... his misfortunes and imprudences involved him in debt, to the amount of the enormous sum of 48,866 l. 13 s. 4 d. but which he discharged in the first year of the reign of q. Eliz. by selling his fair seat and noble manor of Welbeck: after having experienced the frowns of two soverlgns, he obtained the smiles of Eliz . ... his riches at one time were superior to most private subjects in the kingdom; and notwithstanding the many losses he sustained, he left a prodigious fortune to his descendants."[506] He came so near to being made Earl of Nottingham that the patent was actually drawn up. His tomb is in Screveton Church, with a fine effigy. This man died 1583 and was grandfather of the regicide's father. Some letters of the regicide's father survived until the 1880s, when one was printed, but I have so far been unable to trace any of them today, or indeed letters written by the regicide's sisters which were with them. These were in the 1880s amongst the MSS. of the Barrington family; Lady Barrington in the 1620s was Richard Whalley's sister in-law, and recipient of several letters from him of a most fascinating nature, which I still hope one day to find. One particularly important one, dated March 17, 1623/4, is printed in its entirety by Lowndes, who said of it: "...it is very long, but it is necessary to give the whole of it, to shew his extraordinary style of writing."[507] The letter displays a deeply ingrained habit of Biblical quotation, and everything in his personal life is interpreted in terms of religion. Although he had not yet married his third wife, and presumably still had some spark of life in him, he begins the letter by saying: "Although my life is waxen ollde wth heavines & my yeares wth mourninge, for Innumerable Trobles are come about mee, & my Sinnes have taken such hollde oppon mee, that I am not hable to looke upp & thereby myne owne Familier frends whome I trusted, have conspired against mee ..."[508] It is essential here that we clear up a very serious misunderstanding. Lowndes says of this letter and the others which I cannot as yet trace: "In other letters he complains still more of his eldest son, accusing him of spending all his time in rioting and gambling. This son was Edward Whalley, the violent republican and regicide."[509] However, Lowndes seems to have been unaware that Richard Whalley's eldest son, still alive at this point, was not the regicide, but his older brother, Thomas Whalley. Richard Whalley says in his letter which is printed that "all my younger children" are well disposed, which must include the regicide. He specifically identifies the regicide's brother Henry as well-disposed by saying: "I have atte my Sonne Henries (a good Sonne) a very faire paire of Brasse Andirons ..." It is unfortunate that Lowndes has made this mistake, but at least we are in a position to correct it. There does remain the small possibility that in the unprinted letters which I still cannot find, Richard does mention Edward by name as the rebellious son, but Lowndes does not say so, and we must suppose not, otherwise the statement just referred to would appear not to make sense. However, the rebellious son really was something: His father speaks of "the unspeakable sorrowes & cares that he now doth to mee ... hee wholly plotteth againste mee whilest the great open Enemy is workinge to thruste us both out of all, as he will ere long for my councell is derided & his proud stomache to domyneer over his Father will sodenly bring a confucon ..." It appears, then, that far from being a rebellious son who set himself against authority, as many would have the regicides be, Edward Whalley the regicide stood by his pathetic old father in adversity. The older brother who rioted and gambled was Thomas Whalley, born circa 1600, and he died in his father's lifetime in 1628. He married and had issue by Mary, daughter of Thomas Peniston of Rochester, Kent; she remarried Richard Draper of Flintham, Notts., having further issue. (A slight correction to previous statement of Richard Whalley not having issue by his first wife is that he did have a previous son, Thomas, by Anne Horsey, but he died young.) The regicide had three sisters: Elizabeth, married William Tiffin, mercer and Citizen of London; Mary, married Robert Kellaway, Secretary to Edward Lord Littleton, Lord Keeper of the Great Seal under Charles I; and Jane, married the Rev. William Hooke, and had issue. Hooke lived in New Haven, Connecticut, in America, until 1656, when he returned to England, and when Whalley and Goffe fled to America at the Restoration, Goffe's wife and children lived with Jane Hooke in England.[510] The regicide's younger brothers were: Henry Whalley, a lawyer who became Judge Advocate of the army in Scotland in 1655, M.P. for Selkirk and Peebles in 1656 and 1659, married Rebecca Duffell, daughter of John Duffell of Rochester and sister to the regicide's own first wife, had issue, moved to Ireland at the Restoration, became Recorder of Galway in 1663, and died in Dublin in 1667;[511] Lieutenant Robert Whalley, Oliver Cromwell's lieutenant when Cromwell was a Captain in the Eastern Association, later a Major in the Low Countries, died without issue. It should also be remarked that the regicide's sister Mary was married also (either as a first or a second husband, but in any case in addition to the Robert Kellaway mentioned above) to Sir Thomas Eliot. Several letters from her to Lady Barrington were preserved in the 1880s (also not yet traced, and one of them was published by Lowndes, in which Mary asks for the pathetic sum of £5, being obviously in the most desperate poverty and under "a great and havvye Burden that lies on me".[512] I have not yet identified Sir Thomas Eliot.

Prominent Relations: The regicide was a first cousin of both Oliver Cromwell and John Hampden, M.P. William Goffe the regicide was Whalley's son-in-law, having married his daughter Frances. Whalley was of course related to the regicides Valentine Vauton, John Jones, and all the other relations of Cromwell. Whalley's second wife was sister of Sir George Middleton, who had a curious career; at first he was a servant of Charles I, whom he came to hate, he then sided with Parliament and served as a captain of horse, submitted to the Protectorate but acted as a spy for Charles II on the Protector, was detected, tried and condemned in 1656 but saved by the regicide's wife from execution, left for exile where he became an open royalist.[513] James Temple the regicide was doubly related by marriage to Whalley through the Penistons and the Saunders, and as we have seen under James Temple, the two regicides were closely connected a decade before the outbreak of Civil War, having complex property dealings together and with the regicide's brother, Henry. The regicide's aunt was Lady Joan Barrington, wife of Sir Francis Barrington, the first baronet. Sir Thomas Barrington, Bart., M.P. of the Long Parliament, was thus the regicide's first cousin. Sir John Barrington, Bart., recruiter M.P., was the regicide's first cousin once removed. The regicide's father was, through his first wife Anne Horsey, great-uncle to Captain John Horsey of the New Model Army, who served in the 7th Regiment of Foot, under Col. Thomas Rainsborough, and was killed in 1645 at the siege of Sherborne.[514] (My numbering system of New Model regiments is explained in the chapter "The Honourable Members from the Army".) The regicide had an uncle, the Rev. Thomas Whalley, D.D., and another, the Rev. Walter Whalley, D.D., who may have held high church views (it is known from the regicide's father's printed letter discussed earlier that his brothers were "conspiring" against him, which indicates serious estrangement, possibly religious conflict.)

Pedigrees: *The Visitation of Nottinghamshire 1662-4*, Thoroton Society, Vol. XIII, 1950, p. 64. *Miscellanea Genealogica et Heraldica*, Vol. II, p. 321. *The Visitation of Huntingdonshire 1613*, Camden Society, Vol. 43, p. 35. *Visitation of the County of Nottingham*, Harleian Society, pp. 117-8. John Throsby, ed., *Thoroton's Nottinghamshire*, 2nd ed., 1790, pp. 248-9, under Screveton and Kirketon, gives a lengthy pedigree. Rev. Samuel Whaley, *English Record of the Whaley Family and Its Branches in America*, Ithaca, New York, 1901, pp. 12-9 and *passim*; much of this is drawn from John Nichols, *History and Antiquities of the County of Leicester*, Vol. II, p. 736.

Acknowledgement: I am very much indebted to the late Myles Hildyard of Flintham Hall, Nottinghamshire, for conversations and sharing of notes and references. His intensive researches have resolved many obscure points. It would have been possible to write voluminously about the Whalleys and their various properties, if not restrained by considerations of space here.

THOMAS WOGAN. Birth date unknown, and the parish registers of Wiston, Pembrokeshire, where he was born, only commence in 1715. However, his father was born 1588 (though J. T. Peacey in the Oxford DNB says 1599, giving no reference), and from a portrait of the regicide which I have managed to discover (and it was difficult to distinguish the two portraits of the two contemporary Captains Wogan, but I finally did this) apparently done in the 1640s, in which he appears to be aged between 27 and 35, we may tentatively set a lower limit on his date of birth as 1607 and an (unlikely) upper limit as 1622. (It is possible that future research will uncover further leads, such as the date of his parents' marriage. Peacey in the Oxford DNB estimates his date at 'circa 1620', but if Peacey were correct about Wogan's father being born in 1599, since the regicide was the third son, it means that by the age of 21 John Wogan would have had three sons, and I certainly do not believe that possible. Peacey cannot be correct about both dates, and may not be correct about either.) The regicide was third son of John Wogan, M.P. of the Long Parliament, of Wiston, Pembrokeshire (1588-1644), who has an entry in Keeler.[515] His mother was Jane, daughter of Sir Thomas Colclough (knighted by the Lord Deputy, October 24, 1591[516]), of Tintern, County Wexford, Ireland. Keeler attempted to evaluate the political position of the regicide's father but overlooked the most important surviving evidence, his letter of January 20, 1642/3, which reveals him as one of the leading opponents of the royalists in South Wales.[517] However, even the Calendar reporting this document omits the most telling parts for evaluating John Wogan's personal position.[518] In the original document, the elder Wogan clearly speaks of his opposition to "the malignant parties of this kingdom", from whom "wee are like to suffer only for ower loyalty to ower king and common welth", and writes for help "as I am a true lover of my king and cuntrie and a member of the high court of parlament".[519] (The letter is from his seat at Wiston.) The Wogans seem to be able to trace their ancestry back to 230 A.D., and Gwraldeg, King of Garthmadryn (now Brecknock), down through Marchell, their sole heiress, who married Aulach, son of Coronawg, King of Ireland, down through Cawdraf, King of Ferreg and Brecon, and then very many generations later, through Maenarch, Prince of Brecon, who married an Ellen whose ancestors can also be traced back to about 500 A.D., their grandson Gwgan actually having dates (1080-1150) and marrying Margaret Gwys, great grand-daughter of someone called Wizo the Fleming, and daughter of Walter FitzWitz of Wiston, which presumably then remained the seat of these ancestors of the Wogans.[520] If all of this be true, then the regicide had no less than 1400 years of family history behind him, and the conviction that, as a descendant of many kings, he was not a whit inferior to the king whose Death Warrant he signed. The earliest ancestor of the regicide of whom there is certainty unencumbered by speculation is Sir John Wogan (born 1255, who has an entry in DNB). He was Chief Justice and Governor of Ireland, where he held land as early as 1284; he led a most colourful life, entrusted with countless royal missions by Edward I and other kings. There are several pages about him and the descendants and properties he left by Francis Green in his extremely long account of "The Wogans of Pembrokeshire".[521] The regicide's family were descendants of this man's third son, Sir Walter Wogan. As Green has said: "The Wogan family in early Norman times was one of the most influential among the magnates in Pembrokeshire, and its sphere was not merely confined to that county, but extended to Ireland as well as into England. The history of the family is therefore of great interest, as members of it were sheriffs of that county and of Cardiganshire, to say nothing of other offices …"[522] The regicide's four-times-great grandfather, Sir John Wogan, did "good service to Richard III",[523] and his son, also a Sir John Wogan, was a Gentleman Usher of the King's Chamber, and later sheriff of Cardiganshire in 1541 and 1555 and of Pembrokeshire in 1543 and 1550-54, his main seat being at Wiston.[524] The regicide's great-grandfather Sir John Wogan was sheriff of Cardiganshire in 1563 and for Pembrokeshire in 1567 and 1572; a letter of his to Lord Burleigh survives, written from Wiston, 1572, in which he evinces an energetic concern for communicating local concerns to the court: "hit ys my duetye being shiriffe of the shire to advertise her Majestie or some of her highnes most hon'able counsaill of every thinge or cause which doth concerne her majestie's comoditie by any maner measnes." - though in this instance, his bringing a discovery of treasure trove to light seems to   be a bit grovelling.[525] This man's widow and her new husband sued the regicide's grandfather Sir William Wogan for "wrongful, violent, and unnatural practices" when he seized land his mother had sold to someone else.[526] Various passionate acts seem to have been in the family tradition; the regicide assisted his own younger brother in abducting a girl, as described in a moment. The regicide had two older brothers: John Wogan was the eldest. He married Diana, the daughter of George Luttrell of Dunster Castle, and was engaged in messy lawsuits against his brother-in-law Thomas Luttrell for rent on the property of East Quantoxhead and the manor (still standing, known as Court Place, in Somerset); these matters were scandalous and most interesting, but must not detain us; John Wogan died 1642.[527] The next brother was Rowland Wogan, who married Elizabeth, daughter of Lewis Powell of Greenhill near Pembroke; he was by 1651 one of the Commissioners for Compounding in Pembrokeshire, and died 1663.[528] The regicide's sisters were: Mary, married first David Lloyd of Kilkiffeth, Pembs., and second James Lewis, son of Sir John Lewis of Abernant Bychan, Cardiganshire; Martha, married John Gwyther, and later apparently John Lloyd of Gellygelinen; Frances; Elizabeth; Anne. The regicide's two younger brothers were: James Wogan, married Margaret Picton, - she died 1682 and he died 1684; Compton Wogan, who in 1649 assisted by his brother the regicide abducted a girl, aged between 12 and 14, named Dorothy Barlow of Haverfordwest, in what seems to have been intended as an elopement but either went drastically wrong when the young girl lost her courage, or was a genuine abduction (according to her widowed mother, the girl cried out as she was seized "I am undone":), - the regicide maintained that the couple were married ("with the Book of Common Prayer") but the girl's family maintained it was not a lawful marriage, and the girl later married another Barlow, so this escapade seems to have been a very dismal failure.[529] It should perhaps be pointed out that the regicide's father had been an M.P. for Pembrokeshire in every Parliament from 1614 to 1640, and that his eldest son predeceased him. Why the regicide took on the family's expected place in Parliament as a recruiter rather than his remaining older brother Rowland doing so is unknown; it should be noted, however, that the regicide was not M.P. for his own county, but instead for Cardigan.

Prominent Relations: Hugh Owen (1604–16 70), M.P. of the Long Parliament, was first cousin of the regicide's father. Alexander Luttrell, M.P. of the Long Parliament, was nephew of his sister-in-law, but owing to the lawsuits mentioned above, cannot be expected to have been on too friendly terms with the regicide's father (Luttrell died in 1642). The Pophams, Alexander and Edward, M.P.s, were both uncles of this Luttrell, and Sir Francis Popham, M.P., was his grandfather; they, of course, as already mentioned, were distant relations by marriage of Thomas Pride the regicide. John Pyne, the Somerset "boss", was grand-nephew of Sir Francis Popham. But there is no reason to believe that Wogan would have experienced close friendships with these tenuous relations by marriage, due to the history of lawsuits. The regicide was extremely distantly related to Captain Edward Wogan, who defected to the royalists after having served in the New Model Army, and about whom a book has been written.[530] The regicide had an uncle, Henry Wogan, who married a Jane Laugharne, so that the regicide may have been thus connected with Major-General Rowland Laugharne, whose defection to the royalists in 1648 the regicide was to help oppose. The connection with the Laugharnes seems to have been double, as Hugh Owen, M.P., the regicide's father's first cousin, was the son of a Dorothy, née Laugharne, daughter of John Laugharne of St. Bride's, Pembrokeshire.[531] The regicide's sister Mary married as her second husband Colonel James Lewis of Abernant Bychan, Cardigan; he was a Sheriff of Pembrokeshire circa 1643. This brother-in-law of the regicide seems to have been on close terms with the regicide; Lewis was a Colonel under Laugharne who in 1648 brought his troop of horse away from Laugharne to fight under Horton and Wogan at the Battle of St. Fagan's, as Wogan narrates in a letter to Lenthall where he also nominates Lewis to be one of a new Committee for Cardiganshire, and also of a new Committee for Pembrokeshire and Carmarthen.[532] Further evidence of the close relations between Lewis and Wogan may be found in a document I discovered amongst the regicide Henry Marten's papers in Leeds, and which I have transcribed and placed in the Appendix to this Chapter, with the caution that it is a very biased royalist's view of things, and how and why it came into Henry Marten's possession is anybody's guess.

Pedigrees: A vast, annotated pedigree is the essence of Francis Green's article, "The Wogans of Pembrokeshire", in *West Wales Historical Record*, Vol. VI, pp. 169-232. I am indebted to Richard Glyn Wogan of Swansea, one of the last surviving descendants of the Wogans of Wiston, for much information and help, and a copy of a gigantic pedigree which he has drawn up, entitled "The Wogan Family", drawing on many sources including the preceding. There are other pedigrees, including 17th century MSS., but Green has incorporated much of what they have to say in his survey.

1. Mary Frear Keeler, *The Long Parliament*, American Philosophical Society, Philadelphia, 1954, p. 85. It might be mentioned here that Keeler errs in believing that Alured died in 1659; whereas he really died in 1651; CJ.VII,7b and 39a.
2. W. D. Pink, "Alured of the Charterhouse, Co. York". *Yorkshire Genealogist*, ed. by J. Horsfall Turner, Vol. I, Yorkshire, 1888, p. 4. Matthew Alured was "aged about 41" in 1654/5, and of Walkington, Yorkshire, as we know from *CSP Ireland - Adventurers*, p. 313.
3. Pierre Legouis, *Andrew Marvell*, Oxford University Press, 1965, p. 19, where Legouis says: "Who recommended Marvell to Fairfax as a tutor for his only child, then twelve years old? We cannot tell; possibly another Yorkshireman." For mention of the Marvells, see the will of the regicide's father in the Appendix to this Chapter, and notes to it.
4. Bodleian Library: MS. Tanner 602, ff. 512-3 and 504, transcribed for Appendix to the chapter on "Regicides and the Counties". See also in the Public Record Office: S.P. 28/ 142/ 11, dated September 4, 1650, bearing the same arms. Also see 1654 grant mentioned: MS. Harl. 1105, ff. 15b and 36b, in British Library.
5. Alfred Harbage, *Annals of English Drama 975-1700*, revised by S. Schoenbaum, London, 1964, p. 96.
6. D. Brunton and D. H. Pennington, *Members of the Long Parliament*, Archon Books, 1968, p. 34.
7. C. H. Josten, ed., *Elias Ashmole, 1617-1692*, Oxford University Press, 1966, 5 vols., p. 472, n. 4.
8. Robert Zaller and Richard Greaves, eds., *Biographical Dictionary of British Radicals in the Seventeenth Century*, 3 vols., Harvester Press, Brighton, Sussex, United Kingdom, 1982-1984.
9. We know this from the entry in the admissions register of the Inner Temple (see discussion of Blagrave in chapter on "Regicides and the Law"). The regicide's mother, surname unspecified, is mentioned only in the Blagrave/Southcott Pedigree, p, 238 of *The Genealogist*, Vol. V. Durston does not mention her, having been unaware of this reference.
10. Christopher Durston, *Berkshire and Its County Gentry 1625-49*, Ph. D. thesis deposited in Berkshire County Record Office, Reading, Vol. II, p. 21.
11. Pedigree mentioned in footnote 9.
12. Brunton and Pennington, *op. cit.*, p. 139.
13. Durston, *op. cit.*, pp. 22-3.
14. *Ibid.*, p. 23.
15. *Ibid.*
16. See for instance in the Public Record Office: C78 (Chancery Decree Rolls), Roll 6232, under February 12, 1654, an immensely long document which I have transcribed in its entirety but have no reason to include here. This document reveals five brothers and at least two sisters of the regicide.
17. Josten, *op. cit.*, pp. 491, 594, 605, arid 631.
18. Donald Wing, Short-Title Catalogue of Books Printed 1641-1700, New York, 1972, Vol. I, p. 18. Jonathan Blagrave and Obadiah Blagrave listed here are probably relations.
19. *Victoria County History*, Berkshire, Vol. I, p. 365.
20. Pedigree in *Yorkshire Archaeological and Topographical Journal*, Vol. IX, 1886, facing page 401.
21. William A. Shaw, *The Knights of England*, Sherratt and Hughes, London, 1906, Vol. II, p. 148.
22. Rev. C. B. Norcliffe, in "Paver's Marriage Licenses", *Yorkshire Archaeological and Topographical Journal*, Vol. XI,1891, p. 243,n. 32.
23. "Yorkshire Stuart Fines", *Yorkshire Archaeological Society Record Series*, Vol. LVII I, 1917, p . 95.
24. Shaw, *op. cit.*, p . 150.
25. *Ibid.*, p. 175.
26. "Pedigree of Bradshaw-Isherwood, of Marple Hall" (no pagination) in Joseph Foster, *Pedigrees of the County Families of England*, Lancashire, 1873, Vol. I.
27. In unpaginated Introduction to "A Letter from John Bradshawe of Gray's Inn to Sir Peter Legh of Lyme", *Chetham Miscellanies*, Chetham Society, Lancashire, 1855, Vol. I.
28. A. Craig Gibson, "Original Correspondence of the Lord President Bradshaw; with Other Documents Illustrating His Personal History", *Transactions of the Historic Society of Lancashire and Cheshire New Series*, Vol. II, Liverpool, 1862, pp. 41-74.
29. At head of pedigree mentioned in footnote 26.
30. *The Last Will and Testament of John Bradshaw*, London, 1659, p. 5.
31. John Burke and John Bernard Burke, *Extinct and Dormant Baronetcies of England, Ireland, and Scotland*, London, 1844, p. 100.
32. See pedigree in *Ibid*. See Keeler, *op. cit.*, p. 126.
33. Shaw, *op. cit.*, p. 246. Burke's *Baronetcies, op. cit.* p. 100, J. J. Alexander, "Exeter Members of Parliament", *Transactions of the Devon Association*, Vol. LXI, 1929, p. 213.
34. Burke, *op. cit.*, p. 100.
35. Keeler, *op. cit.*, p. 211.
36. Information kindly provided by James H. Hayes, of Kelowna, B. C., Canada, whose wife is believed to be a descendant of Gregory Clement.
37. *Archaeologia Cantiana*, Vol. X, pp. 194 and 196.
38. *Ibid.*, Vol. XXIV, p. 197.
39. Public Record Office at Kew: T51/6.
40. Thomas Colyer-Ferguson, ed., *Marriage Registers of St. Dunstan's, Stepney, Middlesex*, London, 1898, Vol. I, p. 102. CSPD 1627-8, pp. 170-1. CSPD 1631-3, p. 253. CSPD 1634-5, pp. 139-40. CSPD 1636-7, p. 508. CSPD 163 7, pp. 295-6. G. W. Hill and W. H. Frere, *Memorials of Stepney Parish*, London, 1890-1, p. 170. Shilton and Holworthy, *op. cit.*, p. 214. The regicide himself was married at St. Dunstan's, Stepney, in 1630.
41. Shilton and Holworthy, *op. cit.*, p. 220.
42. HMC 4th Report, p. 68a; House of Lords Record Office: Main Papers, May 27, 1641, Petition of Elinor Street, widow.
43. Public Record Office: PROB 6/ 34/ p. 91 or 96 his administration; p. 7 or 9 is administration of Nicholas Clement of Plymouth. Another highly probable relation is John Clement, a prominent merchant of Plymouth, some of whose letters of 1633 are preserved at Plymouth and concern the very same matters which preoccupied the regicide in his business (see HMC 9th Report, p. 271a and 270a).
44. Frederic W. Weaver, *Somerset Incumbents*, Bristol, 1889, p. 431. A. G. Matthews, *Walker Revised*, Oxford, p. 310.
45. Personal communication from Dr. Robert W. Dunning of the Victoria County History of Somerset, December 11, 1978.
46. According to the pedigree referred to in the text. However, this Hardwick does not appear in the Index to Shaw's *Knights, op, cit.*

47. I discovered this information in the Archives of the National Portrait Gallery. In their box containing Cook are two single sheets containing the information: one, an engraving of Cook marked "presented" has anonymous and elaborate MS. notes below the portrait stating it; the other is a curious and anonymous printed sheet entitled "Chief Justice Cook,1608 1660" containing the same information in association with a re-engraving of Cook ("Iohann Coock") from a "gross Caricature ... from a German 'History of the Anabaptists' in the British Museum". George Yule, in his original entry for Cook for the *Biographical Dictionary of British Radicals in the Seventeenth Century* (in press) repeated this information. However, the editors rewrote Yule's entry and removed this and the name of Cook's mother, presumably for reasons of space; Yule had got this information and much else about Cook from me. The relationship with Harrison certainly requires further investigation before it can be fully accepted as fact. The extraordinary difficulties of consulting material in the College of Arms have hampered this enquiry. For purposes of the tables at the end of this Chapter, the Cook-Harrison relationship is taken as genuine.
48. Mark Noble, *The Lives of the English Regicides*, London, 1798, Vol. I, p. 146.
48A. *Op. cit.*
49. G. E. Cokayne, *The Complete Baronetage*, Exeter, 1900-09, Vol. I, p. 44.
49 A. Burke, *op. cit.*, p. 127.
50. *Ibid.*, pp. 124-6.
51. Shaw, *op. cit.*, p. 74.
52. *Ibid.*, p. 96, where the regicide's own knighthood is recorded, also.
53. "Journal of the Siege of Rouen", in *The Camden Miscellany*, Vol. I, Camden Series, 1847, p. 34.
54. *Complete Baronetage, op. cit.*, Vol. I, p. 44, note a.
55. W. Paley Baildon, "Compositions for Not Taking Knighthood at the Coronation of Charles I", *Miscellanea* Vol. I, *Yorkshire Archaeological Record Series*, Vol. LXI, 1920, p. 107.
56. *Yorkshire Archaeological Society Record Series*, Vol. ,VIII, 1917, pp. 62 and 186. For other fines where he was described as baronet only, see pp. 13, 152, and 219.
57. For the two Widdringtons see Keeler, *op. cit.*, pp. 393-4.
58. *Ibid.*, p. 127.
59. *The Speeches, Discourses, and Prayers of .. Barkstead .. Okey . Corbet*, 1662, p. 24.
60. Shaw, *op. cit.*, p. 151 .
61. *Ibid.*, p. 92.
62. *Ibid.*, pp. 92 and 64.
63. Corbet Family Pedigree (large sheet), MS. 15577 43 B, in the Norfolk Record Office at Norwich.
64. Burke, *Baronetcies, op. cit.*, pp. 132-4. Also Burke's *History of the Commoners*, Vol. III, p. 189. And see Burke's *Extinct Peerage* under "Corbet".
65. Same as footnote 63.
66. MS. MC/ 46/ 4/ 1 & 2, in the Norfolk County Record Office, Norwich.
67. Shaw, *op. cit*, p. 181; otherwise the Sir John Meade knighted in Ireland, January 28, 1621/2, at p. 178.
68. *Complete Baronetage, op. cit.*,Vol. I, p. 220.
69. Keeler, *op. cit.*, p. 142.
70. *Ibid.*, and p. 246.
71. *Ibid.*, p. 263.
72. *Ibid.*, p . 264.
73. *Ibid.*, p. 126.
74. Public Record Office: S.P. 63/ 290 215 -220.
75. See for instance CSPD 1645-7, p. 601. Also, Bromfield was again imprisoned Feb. 9, 1659/60, -see CJ. VII. 837b and 847a.
76. *A Perfect Summary*, No. 10, 20 Sept. to 27 Sept.,1647, p. 80.
77. Shaw, *op. cit.*, p. 147. He is described at that time as being "of Co. Gloucester". He must not be confused with his cousin John of Culworth, Northants., who was knighted in 1624 (Shaw, p. 184).
78. Shaw, *op. cit.*, p . 76 .
79. *Ibid.*, pp. 32-3.
80. Blair Worden, *The Rump Parliament*, Cambridge University Press, 1974, p. 100.
81. *Ibid.*
82. Keeler, *op. cit.*, p . 217.
83. *Ibid.*, pp. 175-6.
84. John Aubrey, *Brief Lives*, ed. by Oliver Lawson Dick, Penguin Books, London, 1972, p. 238. (Life of Sir Charles Danvers.)
85. *Ibid.*, p. 239.
86. Keeler, *op. cit.*, p. 211.
87. *Ibid.*, p . 21-2 .
88. *Ibid.*, p. 210.
89. *Ibid.*, pp. 284-5, and DNB for Danvers.
90. Shaw, *op. cit.*, p. 117.
91. Franklin B. Dexter, "Dixwell Papers", *Papers of the New Haven Colony Historical Society*, New Haven, Connecticut, Vol. VI, 1900, p. 337.
92. *Victoria County History, Warwickshire*, Vol. VI, p. 63.
93. British Library: MS. Add. 24,120, ff. 250-1.
94. Shaw, *op. cit.*, p. 194.
95. Burke, *Baronetcies, op. cit.*, p . 161 .
96. *Ibid.*, pp. 161-2.
97. Dexter, *op. cit.*, pp. . 370-3.
98. *Ibid.*, and *passim*.
99. Brunton and Pennington, *op. cit.*, pp. 50-1.
100. Alan Everitt, *The Community of Kent and the Great Rebellion 1640-60*, Leicester University Press, 1966.
101. *Op. cit.*

102. Alexander Harris, *The Oeconomy of the Fleete*, Camden Series, New Series, Vol. 25, 1879, pp. 128 and 192. Also, *Visitation of London 1633-5*, Vol. XVII, Harleian Society, Vol. I, p. 236.
103. A.B. Beaven, *Aldermen of the City of London*, 1908, Vol. I, p. 125, and Vol. II, p. 80.
104. HMC 7th Report, pp. 158b-159a.
105. Keeler, *op. cit.*, pp. 306-7.
106. Josten, *op. cit.*, Vol. III, pp. 940-1.
107. *Debrett's Peerage, Baronetage, Knightage and Companionage*, London, 1888, p. 178.
108. House of Lords Record Office: Main Papers, September 23, 1645, which was the date the Lords concurred. The order originated September 10th in the Commons, for which see CJ. IV. 269a. See HMC 6th Report, p. 77b.
109. Noble, *op. cit.*, Vol. I, p. 201.
110. Shaw, *op. cit.*, p. 214, knighted at Shrewsbury September 21, 1642. Another Ottley (Christian name unknown) was knighted at Oxford by Charles I, November 10, 1645 (Shaw, p. 126.) The only other possibility is most unlikely: an extremely elderly (if still alive!) Sir John Oteley knighted July 23, 1603 (Shaw, p. 126).
111. Public Record Office: PROB-6-34p. 259 (f. 270).
112. Same reference as footnote 106.-
113. Essex Record Office: MS. C/SR 28516 and 29344.
114. CCAM, p. 307.
115. British Library: MS. Add. 26,758, f. 14.
116. Arms of Ewers of Middlesex, see MS. Harl. 1105, f. 2a, and for Ewers of Herts., see MS. Stowe 697, f. 109 b, both in British Library.
117. MS. Harl 1105, f. 3b.
118. *New England Historical and Genealogical Register*, Boston, 1915, Vol. LXIX, p. 358.
119. Noble, *op. cit.*, Vol. I, p. 102.
120. CSPD 1653-4, p. 386.
121. Pedigree of Watkins in *Visitation of London 1633-5*, Harleian Society, Vol. XVII.
122. Taken from Burke, *Baronetcies, op. cit.*, p. 199.
123. House of Lords Record Office: Main Papers, June 23, 1660. See HMC 7th Report, p. 106a.
124. Public Record Office: S.P. 29/ 9/ 94. II.
125. Recorded in the Pedigree of Fleetwood in Vol. II of *Den Introducerade Svenska Adelns ättartavlor*, Elgenstania, Stockholm, 1926.
126. *Notes and Queries*, 10th Series, Vol. I, p. 423.
127. *Ibid.*, pp. 422-3, foonote.
128. *Visitation of Buckinghamshire, 1634*, Harleian Society, Vol. 58, p. 55, where Chaloner is incorrectly given as "Chatteret".
129. Shaw, *op. cit.*, p. 56.
130. HMC 3rd Report, p. 153a (Salisbury MSS.)
131. Thomas Robson, *The British Herald*, Sunderland, 1830, Vol.. I (unpaginated; it is alphabetical). A contemporary Augustus Garland, alias Tapsfield, was alive and a minor in 1636 at Sevenoaks in Kent (see *Archaeologia Cantiana*, Vol. 20, 1893, p. 25), of unknown relation.The regicide's father is mentioned in an inscription over the east door of the second court of Fishmonger's Alms Houses, Newington, in 1636, with Isaac Pennington and three others as being Wardens of the Alms Houses (College of Arms: MS. I.C.B. 84, f. 61v.)
132. John Rylands Library, Manchester: Rylands Eng. MS. 300/22, for Augustine Garland (W.D. Pink's MSS.)
133. James Phillips, "William Goffe the Regicide", *English Historical Review*, Vol. VII, 1892, pp. 717-20.
134. Public Record Office: S.P. 18/ 129/ 99.1.
135. James Phillips, *op. cit.*, p. 719.
136. British Library: MS. Lansdowne 823, ff. 165-6.
137. See the various arms of these families describes in Robson, *op. cit.*, Vol. I (unpaginated; alphabetical).
138. Public Record Office: S.P. 18/ 67/ 226.
139. *Ibid.*: S.P. 16/ 510/ 26.
140. *Ibid.*: S.P. 28/ 129/10.
141. *Remonstrance of the Commission Officers and Private Soldiers of Major General Goffs Regiment*, London, April 26, 1659, p. 1.
142. HMC *Report of MSS. of F. W. Leyborne-Popham*, 1899, pp. 114-5.
143. Rev. Henry E. B. Arnold, "A Sussex Family during the Commonwealth", Sussex County Magazine (a scarce periodical available in the Sussex Record Office), Vol. 10, pp. 668-72, and 740-3. Also G. L. Goff, *The Memoirs of the Goff Family*, Vol. I, 1895 (a bound typed MS. Volume loaned to me for some time by the regicide's descendant, Col. Robert Goff), pp. 19-21.
144. Arnold, *op. cit.*, pp. 669-70.
145. Phillips, *op. cit.*, p. 7'18.
146. Arnold, *op. cit.*, p. 6 70.
147. Public Record Office: S.P. 16/ 232/ 23; S.P. 16/ 233/ 4; and S.P. 16/ 534/ 14.
148. Guildhall Library, London: Guildhall MS. 11593/ 1, f. 48.
149. *A Second Narrative of the Late Parliament*, London, 1658, p. 13.
150. One is given in footnote 140. The other two are S.P. 18/ 128 110 and John Thurloe, *State Papers of*, ed. by T. Birch, London, 1742, Vol. V, p. 215.
151. Arnold, *op. cit.*, p. 671. G. L. Goff, *op. cit.*, pp. 39-43.
152. House of Lords Record Office: Main Papers, June 29, 1660.
153. Robert K. G. Temple, "Ludlow Finds His Voyce", *Cromwelliana*, 1980-1, p. 31.
154. *A Letter to the Lord Grey of Groby*, printed for Andrew Coe, London, March, 1643/4.
155. Title page of *Ibid.*
156. T. Pape, *Newcastle-under-Lyme in Tudor and Early Stuart Times*, Manchester University Press, 1938, p. 154.
157. HMC 7th Report, p. 71.
158. Pape, *op. cit.*, p. 175.
159. John Hewetson, *Memoirs of the House of Hewetson or Hewson of Ireland*, London, 1901, p. 204.
160. *Ibid.*, p. 204 and p. 206.

FURTHER DETAILS OF THE FAMILY BACKGROUNDS

161. British Library: MS. Sloane 1519, ff. 166-7 (letter to Fairfax of 1647).
162. Public Record Office: PROB-6-25, p. 2.
163. CSPD 1650, p. 512.
164. T. C. Dale, ed., *The Inhabitants of London in 1638*, Society of Genealogists, London. 1931, pp. 6 and 173.
165. L. G. H. Horton-Smith, "The Hortons of Leicestershire: The Three Lines", *Transactions of the Leicestershire Archaeoloqical Society*, Vol. XXIII, 1947, p. 3; and same author, "The Hortons of Leicestershire" in *Transactions*, Vol. XXI I, 1944-5, pp. 98 and 115 .
166. CCC, p. 172.
167. CCC, p . 753 .
168. Public Record Office: PROB-11-215, p . 38.
169. *Ibid*.
170. Sir Charles H. Firth and Godfrey Davies, *The Regimental History of Cromwell's Army*, Oxford University Press, 1940, Vol. I, p. 82.
171. *Notes and Queries*, July 31, 1943, pp. 74-6.
172. Refer to footnote 168.
173. Public Record Office at Kew: T 51/ 1, pp. 16-7.
174. Somerset Record Office at Taunton: MS. DD/SAS, C/1193, 5/3, Vol. 3, p. 44 (Genealogical Collections of Rev. Frederick Brown).
175. Shaw, *op, cit.*, p. 161 .
176. From biographical sketch of him in Keeler, *op. cit.*, pp. 227-8.
177. Captain A. E. Lawson Lowe, "Owthorpe and the Hutchinson Monuments", *The Genealogist*, Vol. II, p. 305.
178. *Visitation of Nottinghamshire 1569/1614*, Harleian Society, Vol. IV, 1871, pp. 115-6.
179. Lucy Hutchinson, *Memoirs of the Life of Colonel Hutchinson*, London, 1806, p. 326.
180. Keeler, *op. cit.*, pp. 227-8 and 348.
181. *Ibid.*, p. 348.
182. *Ibid.*, p. 228, p. 193, and p. 164.
183. Shaw, *op. cit.*, p. 166.
184. Burke, *Baronetcies, op. cit.*, p. 277.
185. This cousin had loaned money to the son of the regicide Colonel John Moore, as is mentioned in a letter from the regicide's brother, Henry, January 30, 1645/5; L.258 of the Moore MSS. Calendared by J. Brownbill, *Calendar of … Papers of the Moore Family*, Record Society … Lancs. & Ches., Vol. LXVII, 1913, p. 131.
186. Mark Noble, *Memoirs of the Protectoral-House of Cromwell*, London, 1787, Vol. II, pp. 183-4.
187. Robert Dunlop, *Ireland under the Commonwealth*, Manchester, 1913, pp. 250-1, 308-9, 622-4, and 637-8 (and consult Dunlop's Index for further material).
188. *Ibid.*, p. 624.
189. CSPD 1659-60, p. 19 (the MS. is in the French Correspondence, not S.P. 18).
190. Firth and Davies, *op. cit.*, Vol. II, p. 646.
191. Shaw, *op. cit.*, p. 246.
192. CSPD 1659-60, p. 78.
193. Firth and Davies, *op. cit.*, Vol. I, pp. 193 and 195.
194. *Ibid.*, Vol. II, p. 568.
195. Keeler, *op. cit.*, pp. 147-8.
196. Entries in Bulstrode Whitelocke's *Annals* for May 3, May 18, June 30, and July 5, 1671. (This work while being prepared for publication by the British Academy, was made available to me by Ruth Spalding, to whom I am grateful for this and a great deal of further information from this source, which she was kind enough to allow me to consult in typescript; all occasions when information from this source is used are noted in footnotes, or text.)
197. Keller, *op. cit.*, pp. 149-50.
198. Borthwick Institute of Historical Research, University of York, have the original, indexed in Appendix to Vol. 24 (1898) of Yorkshire Archaeological Society Publications.
199. Cornelius Brown, *Lives of Nottinghamshire Worthies*, London, 1882, p. 182, n.
200. See Bernard Capp's entry for him in the *Biographical Dictionary of British Radicals in the Seventeenth Century* (in press), and his book *The Fifth Monarchy Men*, Faber & Faber, London, 1972, p. 252; and see Index.
201. *A True Narrative of the Proceedings of Parliament, Council of State, General Councell of the Army, and Committee of Safetie: from the 22 of Septemb. until this present*, 1659, p. 70.
202. Henry Cary, *Memorials of the Great Civil War in England*, London, 1842, Vol. I, pp. 237-40.
203. Phillimore, *Nottinghamshire Marriage Licenses*, Vol. I, under the date. More about the Bainbridges and their connections with the Ireton family may be found in Robert W. Ramsey, *Henry Ireton*, Longmans, London and New York, 1949, pp. 4-6.
204. Shaw, *op. cit.*, p. 216.
205. Thomas Ireton's will is PROB-11-224, pp. 2-3, in the Public Record Office.
206. *Bye-Gones Relating to Wales and the Border Countries*, First Series, July, 1872, p. 75. (The British Library callnumber for this obscure periodical is P.P. 6019. fh.)
207. A. H. Dodd's entry for John Jones, the regicide, and his family, in *The Dictionary of Welsh Bioqraphy Down to 1940*, Hon. Society of Cymmrodorion, London, 1959, pp. 472-5.
208. *Ibid.*, and see for instance *Notes and Queries*, 4th Series, Vol. X, p. 317, which is one of several instances where the 18th century account of Pennant is accepted; in my opinion, correctly.
209. *Bye-Gones, op. cit.*, December, 1872, p . 109.
210. *Ibid.*, February, 1873, p . 134.
211. *Ibid.*, pp. 134-5.
212. *Ibid.*, November, 1873, p. 236.
213. *Ibid.*
214. *Ibid.*, December, 1883, p. 336.
215. *Notes and Queries*, 8th series, Vol. XII, p. 102.
216. *Bye-Gones*, op. cit., December, 1872, pp. 109-10.

217. Edmund Ludlow, *A Voyce from the Watch Tower*, ed. by A. B. Warden, Camden Fourth Series, Vol. 21, London, 1978, p. 248.
218. "Account of the Sales of Bishops' Lands, Between the Years 1647 and 1651", *Collectanea Topographica & Genealogica*, Vol. I, 1834, p. 8. Mentioned also in *Notes and Queries*, 4th Series, Vol. X, p. 317.
219. Keeler, *op. cit.*, pp. 273 and 284.
220. *Ibid.*, pp. 110, 281, and 402-3.
221. CSPD 1660-1, p. 442. (S.P. 29/ 25/ 49; Dec. (?), 1660). Mentioned in *Notes and Queries*, 4th Series, Vol, IX, p. 426.
222. *Notes and Queries*, 8th Series, Vol. XII, p. 102.
223. *Bye-Gones, op. cit.*, February, 1873, pp. 134-5; also, *Notes and Queries*, 8th Series, Vol. XII, p. 101.
224. Joseph Mayer, "Inedited Letters of Cromwell, Colonel Jones, Bradshaw, and Other Regicides", *Transactions of the Historic Society of Lancashire and Cheshire*, New Series, Vol. I, Liverpool, 1861, p. 300.
225. *Durham Visitation Pedigrees, 1575, 1615, and 1666*, ed. by J. Foster, p. 215.
226. *Ibid.*
227. Pauline Gregg, *Free-Born John*, Harrap, London, 1961, p. 360.
228. John Rylands Library, Manchester: Eng. Ms. 136. Firth and Davies, *op. cit.*, pp. 264, 266, 273-7.
229. Gregg, *op. cit.*, p. 360.
230. Bodleian Library: MS. Tanner 592, ff. 537-8. (Letter from them and two others, dated September 17, 1646, at Durham.)
231. *Acts of the High Commission Court within the Diocese of Durham*, Surtees Society, Durham, 1858, pp. 249-50.
232. Samuel R. Gardiner, *History of the Great Civil War 1642-49*, London, 1891, Vol. III, p . 433 .
233. In his entry for Robert Lilburne in the *Biographical Dictionary of British Radicals in the Seventeenth Century* (1982).
234. Margaret M. Verney, *Bucks Biographies*, Oxford, 1912, p. 140.
235. Shaw, *op. cit.*, p. 139.
236. Sir John Oglander, ed. by Francis Bamford, *A Royalist's Notebook*, Constable, London, 1936, p. 123.
237. *Ibid.*, p. 159.
238. Mark Noble, *Protectoral House, op. cit.* Vol. I, p. 373.
239. Keeler, *op. cit.*, p. 252. The DNB also errs, calling him "second son".
240. Shaw, *op. cit.*, p. 241.
241. Oglander, *op. cit.*, p. 83.
242. House of Lords Record Office: Main Papers, October 24, 1644.
243. Those mentioned are at Shaw, *op. cit.*, Vol. I, pp. 114, 119, 128, 140, and 142. See Index under Lisle for the rest.
244. Keeler, *op. cit.*; pp. 145-6.
245. Bodleian Library: MS: Eng. Hist. C. 487, p. 160 (1033).
246. Either birth date may be construed. from the mutually contradictory information in *Archaeologia Cantiana*, Vol. XIV, 1882, p. 380.
247. Shaw, *op. cit.*, Vol. II, p. 95.
248. John Aubrey, *The Natural History and Antiquities of Surrey*, Vol. I, p. 206.
249. Shaw, *op. cit.*, Vol. II, p. 30.
250. Four of them were knighted between 1346 and 1380, - see *Ibid*, pp. 6, 8, and 10. One and perhaps two of these men are direct ancestors of the regicide.
251. Much of this information on Livesey's ancestry comes from *Archaeologia Cantiana*, Vol. XXVI, 1904, pp. 326-7.
252. Burke, *Baronetcies, op. cit.*, pp. 410-1 .
253. Keeler., *op. cit.*, pp. 304-5.
254. *Ibid.*, pp. 105-6.
255. Keeler, pp. 260-1.
256. Shaw, *op. cit.*, Vol. II, p. 99.
257. George S. Fry, *Abstracts of Wiltshire Inquisitiones Post Mortem*, The Index Library, London, 1894, Vol. 23, pp. 94-7.
258. See Keeler, *op. cit.*, pp. 105-6, and CJ. II. 563b-564a.
259. CSPD 1641-3, p. 362; CJ. II. 713 b .
260. Edmund Ludlow, *Memoirs*, ed. by Charles H. Firth, Oxford, 1894, Vol. I, p. 35.
261. *Ibid.*, p. 28.
262. *Ibid.*, Vol. II, p . 14.
263. *Ibid.*, pp. 225 and 236, and footnote by Firth.
264. Somerset Record Office, Taunton: MS. DD/ PTV 219 40.
265. Public Record Office: S.P. 16/ 519/ 124.
266. Ludlow, *Memoirs, op. cit.*, Vol. II, p. 66.
267. Keeler, *op. cit.*, pp. 376-8.
268. Ludlow, *Memoirs, op. cit.*, Vol. II, p. 281.
269. Shaw, *op. cit.*, Vol. II, p. 160.
270. The father is at p. 9, Vol. II, and the regicide at p. 659 of Vol. II, of Anthony à Wood, *Athenae Oxoniensis*, London, 1721.
271. *Ibid.*, Vol. II, p. 9.
272. C. M. Williams, "The Anatomy of a Radical Gentleman; Henry Marten" in Donald Pennington and Keith Thomas, eds., *Puritans and Revolutionaries*, Oxford University Press, p. 119.
273. Mrs. J. C. Cole, "Some Notes on Henry Marten, the Regicide, and His Family", *Berkshire Archaeological Journal*, Vol. 49, 1946, pp. 26 and 41. (The article runs from p. 23 to p. 41.)
274. Durston, *op. cit.*, Vol. II, p. 101.
275. *Notes and Queries*, Second Series, Vol. 19, pp. 376-7; Sixth Series, Vol. 5, pp. 474-5; *Gentleman's Magazine*, November, 1830, p. 430.
276. Wood, *op. cit.*, Vol. II, p. 9.
277. The College of Arms Library: MS. Vincent, Berkshire 143, f. 81.
278. The quote is from a letter of June 4, 1655, which is f . 33 in Box: 78 of the Loder-Symonds-Marten MSS. in the Brotherton Library, University of Leeds, Five of George's letters to Henry are jointly and briefly calendared on p. 398 of *HMC Thirteenth Report, Appendix, Part IV*, 1892 .
279. *HMC Report, Ibid.*, p. 398.
280. Shaw, *op. cit.*, Vol. II, p . 177.

281. *HMC Report* as in footnote 279, p. 398.
282. Shaw, *op. cit.*, Vol. II, p. 82.
283. *Ibid.*
284. Noble, *Regicides, op. cit.*, Vol. II, p . 34.
285. Pedigree of "Mauliverer of Allerton-Mauliverer" in MS. *Collection of ... Descents of .. Families* by John Hopkinson and Thomas Wilson, in York Minster Library, York.
286. Shaw, *op. cit.*, Vol. II, p. 12.
287. *Ibid.*, Vol. I, p. 146.
288. *Ibid.*, Vol. II, p. 55.
289. *Ibid.*, Vol. II, p. 68.
290. Keeler, *op. cit.*, pp. 271: and 283.
291. Burke, *Baronetcies, op. cit.*, p. 565.
292. Public Record Office: PROB-11-130-p. 190 (f. 88).
293. Bodleian Library: MS. Rawlinson B.77, ff. 127a-128b.
294. *Visitation of Buckinghamshire in 1634*, Harleian Society, Vol. 58, p. 90.
295. British Library: MS. Add. 5,497, f. 91 (not f. 80 as the library card index mistakenly says). The property transaction mentioned could be the subject of lengthy explanation, but there is no space for this.
296. John Throsby, *Thoroton's History of Nottinghamshire*, 1790, Vol. II, p . 274. And see CSPD for June 7, 1603 .
297. Public Record Office: PROB-11-!36, pp. 315-6 (f. 103) .
298. *Records of the Borough of Nottingham*, Quaritch, London, 1889, Vol. IV, pp. 205 and 245-6. (Further references to him are pp. 248, 268, 269, 270., 272, 274, 279, 281, 285 bis, 289, 301, and 322.)
299. Keeler, *op. cit.*, p. 277.
300. *Transactions of the Historical Society of Lancashire and Cheshire*, 2nd series, Vol. XIII, p. 2.
301. *Ibid.*, New Series, Vol. XXVII (Vol. 63), 1912, p. 95.
302. *Ibid.*, footnote, 2.
303. *Ibid.*, New Series, Vol, II (Vol. 38), 1889, p. 149.
304. Shaw, *op. cit.*, Vol. II, p. 84.
305. Burke, *Baronetcies, op. cit.*, p. 360.
306. *Transactions Lancs. Ches., op. cit.*, Vol. 63, 1912, p. 104.
307. *Ibid.*, pp. 112-4.
308. Keeler, *op. cit* ., p. 92.
309. *Ibid.*, pp. 248 and 372.
310. Liverpool Record Office: Moore MSS. 1051, 1062, 1276.
311. This is done in the pedigree published in *Middlesex Pedigrees*, Harleian Society, Vol. 65, pp. 1146 (the MS. being MS. Harleian 1551, f. 79, in the British Library).
312. Shaw, *op. cit* ., Vol. II, p. 155.
313. *Ibid.*, Vol. I, p. 23.
314. Public Record Office: PROB-11-223, p. 203.
315. *Westminster Abbey Registers*, Harleian Society, Vol. X, 1875, p. 290 and footnote 2, that page.
316. Personal communication during 1981.
317. An interesting document from him in 1637 may be found in the Public Record Office: S.P.16/ 3 52/ 17r and v.
318. Keeler, *op. cit.*, pp. 301-2; Henry Pelham is pp. 299-300; the regicide himself is pp. 300-1.
319. *Ibid.*, p. 302.
320. Kingston upon Hull, Yorkshire, Record Office: MS. L.481.,
321. James Savage, *Genealogical Dictionary of First Settlers in New England*, Vol. III, Boston, 1860, p. 468.
322. Noble, *Regicides,, op. cit.*, Vol. II, p. 129.
323. *Visitation of the County of Devon, 1620*, Harleian Society, Vol. VI, 1872, p. 218.
324. *Journal of John Winthrop*, Boston, 1853, Vol. II, p. 178n.
325. Savage, *op. cit.*, p. 467. The regicide had a brother-in-law in New England in 1642 (perhaps indicating that he married his sister while he was there?), named Thomas Fowle (Bernard Bailyn, *The New England Merchants in the Seventeenth Century*, Harvard University Press, 1955, p. 87 and n.; - information courtesy of B. Capp.)
326. Public Record Office: S.P. 28/ 50/ 127~and 128 (the latter has John Potter's signature).
327. Not found in surviving Bishop's Transcript in Somerset Record Office at Taunton, but given in *Index Listings from Somerset Bishops' Transcripts* (under Pride and Pryde) from *Dwelly's Parish Records* in Somerset Record Office. (In many cases, Dwelly omits important data, but in this case he adds it!!)
328. Somerset Record Office: MS. DD/SF 3948.
329. *Somerset Record Society*, Vol. LXII, p. 32.
330. *Mercurius Elencticus*, September 3, 1649.
331. Guildhall Library, London: Guildhall MS. 158604, f . 173v.
332. *Journal of the Governors* is HA1/ 5. f. 85 dorso, in the Archives of St. Bartholomews Hospital, London. I obtained this ref. from "A Seventeenth Century Hospital Matron: Marqaret Blague", by Nellie Kerling, in *Transactions of the London & Middlesex Archaeological Society*, Vol. 22, Part 3, 1970, p. 32.
333. Frederick and Ivor Popham, *A West Country Family: The Pophams from 1150*, Sevenoaks, Kent, 1976, pp. 22-3, 34-5, 40-1, and 58-9, for relevant pedigrees.
334. Cossington Bishop's Transcript in the Somerset Record Office, Taunton. Unfortunately the day and month have been torn away.
335. Public Record Office: S.P. 28/ 142/ 5, dated February 22, 1650/ 1.
336. Keeler, *op. cit.*, p. 311.
337. Everitt, *op. cit.*, pp. 60, 127, 244-5.
338. *Ibid.*, pp. 127 and 244-5.
339. House of Lords Record Office: Main Papers, January 19, 1647/ 8 (and see LJ. IX. 667).
340. *London Marriage Licenses* (ed. Joseph Foster, London, 1887) records the 1632 marriage of Searles Prowde (aged 22) with Anne, daughter of John Denne, deceased. We know this is the son of the Colonel because the monument in Canterbury Cathedral was erected by him, as it states in its inscription. Searles's mother Mary Prowde was of the parish of St. Bartholomew the Great in London at the time of his wedding, though he himself then lived in Canterbury.

341. House of Lords Record Office: Main Papers, February 22, 1647/8.
342. CCAM, p . 813 .
343. The regicide's father, Francis Purefoy, was 49 years old at his death in 1613, according to the memorial inscription in Caldecote Church reproduced in the Appendix to this Chapter.
344. Burke, *Baronetcies, op. cit.*, p.431 .
345. *Ibid.*; see also Appendix.
346. Shaw, *op. cit.*, Vol. II, p. 68.
347. Letter to Sir John Newdigate, April 26, 1608, from Gray's Inn. B.451. in the Newdigate MSS. at Warwickshire Record Office, Warwick.
348. David F. Mosler, "The Other Civil War, 1642-1659", *Midland History*, Vol. VI, 1981, p. 61.
349. Frederick Leigh Colville, *The Worthies of Warwickshire*, Warwick, 1870, p. 599.
350. *Visitation of Warwickshire, 1619*, Harleian Society, Vol. XII, 1877, p. 254.
351. Public Record Office: PROB-11-3 04, pp.177-8.
352. Public Record Office at Kew: T51/ 13, f. 27, and T51/ 12, f. 234.
353. Keeler, *op. cit.*, p. 112.
354. *Ibid.*
355. Public Record Office: S.P. 16/ 516 7.
356. Mosler, *op. cit.*, p. 60.
357. CSPD 1648/9, p. 5.
358. Robert Dunlop, *op. cit.*, p. 633, where this Purefoy is described as "apparently of a Warwickshire family".
359. E.268 (12) in British Library: *A Letter from Serjeant Major Purefoy ... to His Colonell Colonell Purefoy A Member of the Honourable House of Commons*, February 7, 1644.
360. CJ. III. 86a, 202a, 302b, 309.
361. *Herald and Genealogist*, Vol. II, pp. 61-3, 156-7.
362. On the Death Warrant of Hamilton, Goring, Capel, et al., Main Papers, March 6, 1649/50, in House of Lords Record Office.
363. Bodleian Library: MS. Rawlinson B.48, f.29b.
364. See pedigrees of Middlesex Rowes given in main text.
365. *Visitation of Northamptonshire, 1618-9*, ed. by Walter Metcalfe, 1887, p. 130. *Visitation of Huntingdon, 1613*, Camden Society, 1849, p. 92.
366. *Visitation of Middlesex, 1663*, ed. by Joseph Foster, privately printed, London, 1887, p . 30.
367. CSPD.1637, p. 571.
368. J. E. Farnell, "The Navigation Act of 1651, the First Dutch War, and the London Merchant Community", *Economic History Review* Second Series, Vol. XVI, 1963-4, p. 442n.
369. *Ibid.*, p. 442'
370. "Pedigree of Rowe Family of Hackney", fold-out in William Robinson *The History and Antiquities of the Parish of Hackney*, London, 1843, Vol. II. This pedigree is by no means complete.
371. See Rowe of Middlesex pedigrees listed in main text.
372. His death is reported by Oliver Cromwell, December 19,- see HMC 7th Report, p. 74a; Francis's will survives in the Public Record Office: PROB-11-211, pp. 209-10 (f. 28 Pembroke, old reference), proved by the regicide, February 5, 1649/50.
373. Salmon's Petition, Main Papers, April 19, 1648, in House of Lords Record Office; LJ. X. 90, 3145; Petition of Owen and Francis Rowe, with appended Certificate of Sums Due, Main Papers, March 4, 16478, in House of Lords Record Office.
374. Isaac is mentioned in Francis's will; see footnote 372; J. H. Lefroy, *Memorials of the . . Bermudas*, Vol. I, p. 675, Vol. II, pp. 58 arid 61.
375. Under PROB-6 in Public Record Office.
376. See fold-out pedigree mentioned in footnote 370.
377. Burke, *Baronetcies, op. cit.,*, p. 140.
378. Noble, *Regicides, op. cit.*, Vol. II, p. 164.
379. Entry for Geoffrey de Say, in Edward Foss, *A Biographical Dictionary of the Judges of England 1066-1870*, London; 1870, pp. 588-9.
380. Shaw, *op. cit.*, Vol. I, p . 135.
381. *Ibid.*, Vol. 1. pr 141.
382. *The Topographer and Genealogist*, London, 1846, Vol. I, pp. 41221.
383. Thomas F. Kirby, *Winchester Scholars*, London, 1888, p. 153.
384. His pedigree may be seen in *Visitation of the County of Oxford, 1634*, Harleian Society, Vol. 5, 1871, p. 252.
385. *Middle Temple Records*, London, Vol. III, p. 1085.
386. Public Record Office: PROB-11-122, p. 48 (f. 72 Capell, old reference).
387. Shaw, *op. cit.*, Vol. II, p. 174.
388. Eleanor was left C20 in gold in the will of the regicide's father (see footnote 385); *vide: Visitation of Kent, 1619*, Harleian Society, Vol. 42 1898, p. 63.
389. See entry for Sir Edward Fenner in Foss, *op. cit.*(foonote 379), pp. 247-8.
390. See the Scott pedigrees listed in main text.
391. George Lipscomb, *The History and Antiquities of the County of Buckingham*, London, 1847, Vol. II, p. 25. It hardly needs to be pointed out that Lipscomb is incorrect on p. 11, in footnote 4, regarding Scott's antecedents.
392. Pedigree of Coltman in *Visitation of London, 1633-5*, Vol. I, p. 183 (*op. cit.*), states Mary's father-in-law was from Fletney, Leicestershire. Several of the family are mentioned also on p. 66 of *Miscellanea Genealogica et Heraldica*, Second Series, Vol. I, London, 1886. Other Coltmans were from Blaby, Leicestershire, as may be seen on p. 1272 of Joseph Foster, ed., *London Marriage Licenses 1521-1869*, London, 1887 (1622 Squire-Coltman).
393. Lipscomb, *op. cit.* (foonote 391),Vol. III, p. 601.
394. In Scott's entry in *Biographical Dictionary of British Radicals in the Seventeenth Century*, in press.
395. A. H. Stanton, *On Chiltern Slopes;. The Story of Hambleden*, Oxford, 1927, pp. 19-21.
396. Burke, *Baronetcies, op. cit.*, pp. 474-5.
397. Firth and Davies, *op. cit.*, Vol. I, p. 103.

398. Valerie Pearl, *London and the Outbreak of the Puritan Revolution*, Oxford, 1961, p. 184.
399. A. H. Stanton, *op. cit.*, (footnote 395), p. 23.
400. Gardiner, *op. cit.*, Vol. I, p. 14.
401. Pedigree of "Barry of Eynsham" in *Visitation of the County of Oxford, 1634*, Harleian Society, Vol. 5, 1871, p. 326.
402. I have additionally found a marriage of 1618 between Thomas Skipwith of Prestwold and Cassandra Bluett of Cates, in *Leicestershire Marriage Licenses 1570-1729*.
403. *The Topographer and Genealogist*, London, 1858, Vol. III, pp. 255-60.
404. Compton Reade, *The Smith Family*, London, 1902. The regicide is mentioned on p. 255.
405. Ref. to footnote 403.
406. Lipscomb, *op. cit.*, Vol. II, pp. 14-5.
407. Godfrey Davies, "The Parliamentary Army under the Earl of Essex, 1642-5", *English Historical Review*, Vol. 49, 1934, p. 48. The Ayscough pedigree is in *London Visitation Pedigrees, 1664*, Harleian Society, Vol. 92, 1940, pp. 11-2.
408. Anthony Fletcher, *Sussex 1600-1660: A County Community in Peace and War*, Phillimore (re-issue and re-title), 1980, pp. 49, 54, 97-8, 100.
409. See the May pedigree in *Visitation of Sussex,1634*, Harleian Society, Vol. LIII, 1905, pp.104-6.
410. Fletcher, *op. cit*., p. 24.
411. Keeler, *op. cit.*, pp. 349 and 323 .
412. *Ibid.*, pp. 302 and 349.
413. *Ibid.*, p. 193.
414. Shaw, *op. cit.*, Vol. II, p. 130.
415. Public Record Office: S.P. 16/ 50/ 17. See CSPD 1627-8, p. 23.
416. Fletcher, *op. cit.*, p. 354. See also CSPD 1623-5, pp. 209 and 232.
417. Public Record Office: S.P. 16/ 50/ 17; S.P. 16/ 53/ 97; S.P. 16/ 5399; S.P. 16/ 54/ 55. See CSPD 1627-8, pp. 23, 54, 62.
418. *Visitations of Surrey 1530-1623*, 1899, p. 135 (under "Griffin").
419. Rev. Edward Hawkins, "Notes on Some Monuments in Rochester Cathedral", *Archaeologia Cantiana*, Vol. XI, 1877, pp. 1-9.
420. *Visitations of Surrey 1530-1623*, 1899, p. 148, under "Abdey" (Dame Mary Temple's mother was Elizabeth, daughter of Roger Abdey, of Tickhill, Yorkshire.) See also William Berry, *County Genealogies. Pedigrees of ... Sussex*, London, 1830, p. 3.
421. Public Record Office: PROB-11-248, p. 306 (f. 302).
422. Temple Prime, *Some Account of the Temple Family*, Appendix Volume, New York, 1899, pp. 79-81, reproducing a Chancery Bill of February 14, 1650/1, by Dame Mary Temple against her son, John Busbridge.
423. *Ibid.*, p. 78, extracts from Sir Alexander's will, proved December 19, 1629.
424. Burke, *Baronetcies, op. cit.*, p. 523.
425. Canterbury Cathedral Archives: Canterbury Letter Number 69.
426. Rev. J. Granger, *A Biographical History of England*, first edition, London, 1769, Vol. I, Part II (actually the second of four vols.), p. 554.
427. CCAM, p. 527. The regicide was already living at Michelgrove on May 4, 1646, when his eldest son John was admitted to Lincoln's Inn. See later discussion of James Temple's guardianship of the Shelley heir.
428. Keeler, *op. cit.*, p. 254.
429. HMC 7th Report, p. 156b.
430. William Berry, op. cit., p. 12.
431. *Ibid.* See also Keeler, pp. 295-6.
432. HMC 7th Report, p. 156a.
433. John A. Temple and Harald M. Temple, *The Temple Memoirs*, London, 1925, p. 48.
434. Burke, *Baronetcies, op. cit.*, p. 543.
435. Shaw, *op. cit.*, Vol. II, p. 148.
436. *An Exact and Impartial Accompt of the . . Trial ... of Twenty nine Regicides*. London, 1660, pp. 2479.
437. Temple Prime, *Some Account of the Temple Family*, 2nd edition, New York, 1894, p. 59.
438. Burke, *Baronetcies, op. cit.*, pp. 586-7.
439. *Visitation of the County of Leicester, 1622*, pp. 167-8 (pedigree of Temple). See also pedigree of Bracebridge, p. 43,, although it doesn't go back very far. See also J. Tom Burgess, *Historic Warwickshire*, 2nd edition by Joseph Hill, London, 1893, p. 273, but especially pp. 69-75. See also "Arden formerly of Longcroft" in Burke's *Landed Gentry*, 1952.
440. Temple Prime, *op. cit.*, Appendix Volume, pp. 13-18.
445. *Ibid.*, pp. 18-23.
442. John A. Temple and Harald M. Temple, *op, cit.*, p. 194.
443. Thomas P. Courtney, *Memoirs of ... Sir William Temple, Bart.*, London, 1836, Vol. II, p . 86.
444. *Ibid.*, p. 87.
445. John Nichols, *The History and Antiquities of Leicestershire*, Vol. IV, p. 959, and also Latin passage from Inquisition of 7 Edward I about Temple Hall. John Throsby's *Thoroton, op. cit.*, Vol. I, pp. 3289. I am indebted to Mrs. Eileen Gooder for the information about the connection with the Templars, ref. PRO: E.358/19 Rot 41 (1308).
446. John A. Temple and Harald Temple, *op. cit.*, p. 30.
447. *Calendar of the Fine Rolls*, Vol. XXI, London, 1961, pp. 101, 124 (twice) and 140.
448. Phillimore, *Nottinghamshire Marriage Licenses*, Vol. I.
449. CJ. IV. 523a and 584b..
450. Keeler, *op. cit.*, pp. 122-3 .
451. David Underdown, *Pride's Purge*, Oxford University Press, 1971, p. 35.
452. Ludlow, *Memoirs, op. cit.*, Vol. II, p. 302 and also Firth's footnote, with further refs.
453. *Middle Temple Minutes of Parliament*, London, Vol. I, p. 178.
454. Temple Prime, *op, cit.*, Appendix Volume, p. 16.
455. Keeler, *op. cit.*, p . 401 .
456. (Peter Temple), *An Examination Examined*, London, 1645, p. 15.
457. Keeler, op. cit., pp. 184-5.
458. British Library: MS. Harleian 5800, ff. 38-42.

459. "F.J.B.", in *Herald & Genealogist*. London, Vol. 4, pp. 65-71, 113-20.
460. *Ibid.*, p. 67.
461. Edward Foss, *A Biographical Dictionary of the Judges of England*, London, 1870, p. 437. See also "Tichborne", *Visitation of Kent, 1574*, Harleian Society, Vol. 75, p. 37.
462. Guildhall Library, London: MS. 10,107A, f . 151 verso.
463. Guildhall Library, London: MS. 28952 (St. Michael le Querne Churchwardens' Accounts, 1605-1718), ff. 39v, 45r, 52r, 55r, 59v, 66v, 70v, 74v, 78v, 82v (his signature occurs here), 113v, and 126v.
464. T. C. Dale, ed., *The Inhabitants of London in 1638*, The Society of Genealogists, London, 1931, Vol. I, pp. 60 and 152.
465. CSPD 1653-4, p. 3. (S.P.18/38/2).
466. Public Record Office: S .P. 16/ 538 30 and 31. See CSPD 1625-49, Addenda, p. 559.
467. *Herald & Genealogist*, Vol. 3, p. 424.
468. F.J.B.", *op. cit.*, pp. 118-9. Descendants of the Tichbornes in the female line still own the ancient Tichborne Park in Hampshire.
469. He is mentioned in MS. Harleian 5800 (foonote 458).
470. Pearl, *op. cit.*, pp. 311-3 (and see Index).
471. D.C. Coleman, *Sir John Banks: Baronet and Businessman*, Oxford, 1963, p. 22, n. 4.
472. Shaw, *op. cit.*, Vol. II, p. 199:
473. Public Record Office: E.316/ Box 15/ Bundle 27/ Piece 1453.
474. *Visitation of London 1633-5, op. cit.*, Vol. II, p. 118.
475. John Venn, *Annals of a Clerical Family*, London, 1904, pp. 311 and 223.
476. Notes on "The Venn Family" in the possession of the Day family of Pyleigh Manor, Lydeard St. Lawrence.
    This quotation comes from a Bill in Chancery by George Streat, February 19, 1633, case of Streat versus Venn.
    I am indebted to the Day family for the information.
477. CSPD 1637, pp. 51, 59, 147. (S.P.16/355/5,5.I., and 47; also S.P.16/ 3 57/60.)
478. See the regicide's will of 1650 in the Public Record Office: PROB-11—213, f. 123 (old numbering folio).
479. *Leicestershire Marriage Licenses 1570-1729*, under Wayte.
480. Ralph Penniston Taylor, *St. Peter's Church Wymondham Leicestershire: A History and Description*, Wymondham, 1976, p. 7.
481. *Notes and Queries*, 4th Series, Vol. X, p. 88 (1872).
482. Grant of arms recorded in MS. Harleian 1422, f. 37b, in the British Library. Waite's submission of accounts in 1637 recorded in S.P. 16/ 537 62, in Public Record Office; see CSPD 1625-49 Addenda, p . 568.
483. John Nichols, Leicestershire op. cit., Vol. III, pp. 460-1. Captain Francis Waite's Petition is S.P. 18/ 131 88, mentioning that his father died in 1642 (the petition is dated 1653), thus identifying him with the Thomas Waite who died in 1642 as mentioned by Nichols. Other relevant documents are S.P. 18/ 131/ 88.II (Barons of the Exchequer Report of May 9, 1648) and Petition and Order relating to this case in Main Papers, January 25, 1647/8, in the House of Lords Record Office, calendared at HMC 7th Report, p. 5a.
484. R. P. Taylor, *op. cit.* (footnote 480), p. 7.
485. *Ibid.*
486. See "Wright of Okeham" in *Visitation of Rutland 1681-2*, Harleian Society, London, 1922, p. 7.
487. Shaw, *op. cit.*, Vol. II, p. 196.
488. British Library: MS. Add. 5711, ff. 129-30.
489. British Library: MS. Harleian 5800, f. 41 r.
490. All of this information is taken from *Archaeologia Cantiana*, Vol. IV, 1861, fold-out page of Hardres pedigree (not paginated).
491. Bodleian Library: MS. Nalson VIII, 108. (Portland MSS. deposit.)
492. Huntingdon County Record Office: MS. DDM 28/81, pp. 1-2.
493. Public Record Office: PROB-11-107, pp. 25960 (f. 33 Stafforde).
494. Shaw, *op. cit.*, Vol. II, p., 135,
495. Noble, *Regicides, op. cit.*, Vol. II, p. 307.
496. Noble, *Protectoral-House, op. cit.*, Vol. II, p. 221.
497. Huntingdon County Record Office: Will of William Wautton, gentleman, of Great Stoughton, proved January 19, 1558/9.
498. Huntingdon Record Office: MS. DDM/ 28/8/4.
499. See the will given in foonote 493. See also MS. Harleian 1531, f. 39, in the British Library, and the published *Visitation of Bedfordshire*, pp. 39 and 179.
500. Bodleian Library: MS. Tanner 59/2, ff. 677-8.
501. John Throsby, *Thoroton, op. cit.*, p. 250.
502. George Streynsham Master, *Some Notices of the Family of Master*, London, privately printed, 1874, Appendix I, "Family of Whalley",, p. 98.
503. *Victoria County History of Lancashire*, Vol. VI, p. 382.
504. Noble, *ProtectoralHouse, op. cit.*, Vol. II, p. 135 and foonote.
505. *Ibid.*, pp. 136-7.
506. *Ibid.*, pp. 137-8.
507. G. Alan Lowndes, ed., "The History of the Barington Family", *Transactions of the Essex Archaeological Society*, New Series, Vol. II, 1884, p . 30.
508. *Ibid.*, p. 31.
509. *Ibid.*, pp. 30-1.
510. See William L. Sachse, "The Migration of New Englanders to England 16401660", *American Historical Review*, Vol. 53, 1947-8, p. 258, and fn. 36. See John Langdon Sibley, *Biographical Sketches of Graduates of Harvard University*. Vol. I, 1873, pp. 557-8. A letter of William Hooke's to John Winthrop, dated 1657, and containing extremely interesting comments, is printed in *Collections of the Massachusetts Historical Society*, Third Series, Vol. I, 1825, pp. 131-4. Further references, concerning the post-Restoration period, would be out of place here.
511. See *Notes and Queries*, 4th Series, Vol. III, 1869, pp. 591-2.
512. Lowndes, *op. cit.* (footnote 507), p. 29.
513. Noble, *Protectoral-House, op. cit.*, Vol. II, p. 153n.
514. See MS. pedigree of Horsey in Somerset Record Office at Taunton: MS. DD/SAS, C/1193, 5/3 (Vol. 3 of Rev. Frederick Brown's Genealogical Collections).

515. Keeler, *op. cit.*, p. 399.
516. Shaw, *op. cit.*, Vol. II, p. 89.
517. Bodleian,Library: MS. Nalson, Vol. II, ff. 144-5 (Portland MSS.)
518. *HMC Portland MSS.*, Vol. I, pp. 92-3.
519. *Op. cit.*, as in footnote 517.
520. This is all taken from a MS. pedigree of Richard Glyn Wogan, mentioned in main text under Pedigrees; suggestions of its authenticity are also made, however, by Francis Green, *West Wales Historical Records*,Vol. VI,. p . 172 .
521. *Ibid*., pp. 169-232.
522. *Ibid.*, p. 170.
523. *Ibid.*, p. 195.
524. *Ibid.*, pp. 197-8.
525. *Ibid.*, p. 203. (The MS. is MS. Lansdowne 14, f. 33, in the British Library.)
526. *Ibid.*, p. 204.
527. *Ibid.*, pp. 214-5 (where Quantoxhead is called "Quantegg").
528. *Ibid.*, pp. 216-7.
529. *Ibid.*, pp. 212-4.
530. Sir Frederick Maurice, *The Adventures of Edward Wogan*, London. 1945.
531. Keeler, *op. cit.*, p. 291.
532. Bodleian Library: MS. Tanner 571, ff. 62-8.
533. Kent Archives Office at Maidstone: MS. U270/T264.

CHAPTER TWO, APPENDIX TWO

Transcribed Manuscripts and Full Texts Prior to Editorial Abridgement of the Biographical Dictionary Entries

THE LAST WILL AND TESTAMENT OF HENRY ALURED, FATHER OF JOHN ALURED THE REGICIDE.

"Harthill D.", proved May, 1628, deposited at the Borthwick Institute of Historical Research of the University of York.

In the name of god Amen Aprill ye sevene Anno dni 1628 I Henry Alured of ye Charterhouse neere Kingston upon Hull esqr finding my body something weakened by an infirmity where with it hath pleased god for some dayes to exercise me, & hence drawne to Consider ye incertainty of my life & Continuance in this pilgrimage, & yet by ye mercy of god injoying pfect remembrance do make & ordeine this my last will & testament in maner & forme following. ffirst I bequeath my soule Into ye hands of my gracious god ye father of spirits wth full Confidence & Comfortable assurance of his everlasting favour in & by ye sole merits of Christ my Saviour in whome God hath said unto my soule that he is my salvation, who is able to keepe that wch is Committed unto him even till ye day of ye Lord Jesus. ffor my body when I shall sleepe wth my fathers my desire is it may be buryed in or neere ye sepulchre of my fathers in ye Chancell belonging ye Trinity Church or Chappell in Kingston upon Hull. for that temporall estate wch it hath pleased god to Commit unto my disposition my will is it be disposed as followeth. ffirst I bequeath unto my daughter Anne Alured fifty pounds in money, & eight beasts whereof foure are kine the other foure steeres & yong Cattell. I give unto her also twenty pounds worth of houshold stuffe as it shalbe indifferently praised, wch stuffe shalbe that wch Mrs Whincop (?) & Mrs Marvell shall thinke most Convenient for furnishing her house. unto my sonne Christopher Alured I give five pounds in money unto my daughter Averill Alured I give fifty pounds in money. unto my sonne Mathewe Alured I give five pounds in money. unto my daughter Sarah I give fifty pounds in money. And to my sonne Latimer I give five pounds in money besides one hundred pounds wch I have received for his use as a legacy that was given unto him by his godfather Mr Latimer, deceased My some Christopher & my daughter Averill together wth their porcons I Commit unto ye Care & tuition of my welbeloved brother Mr Thomas Alured: In whose hands my will is their porcons shall remaine untill they shall respectively accomplish ye age of twenty one yeares or shalbe lawfully marryed wth the Consent of their said uncle & tutor: My sonne Mathewe & his porcon, & my sonne Latimer & his porcon & said debt I give & bequeath to the Care & tuition of my dearely loved Sister Mrs Lucy Darley intreating her to take them into her disposition & imploy them to schoole so long as she shall thinke it Convenient & after to dispose of them as she shall thinke fitting: And to that purpose I will their porcons shall Continue in her hand untill they shall respectively accomplish ye Age of twenty one yeares or shalbe lawfully marryed, wth the Consent of their said Ant & tutrix My daughter Sarah wth her porcon I Commit to ye Care & tuition of her sister my daughter Anne Alured who I doubt not will be Carefull of her education, & to yt purpose my will is that her porcon shall remaine in the hands of her said sister & tutrix untill she shall accomplish ye age of twenty yeares or shalbe lawfully marryed w ye Consent of her said sister.

ffurther my will is that my yonger Children aforesaid viz: Anne, Christopher, Averill, Mathew, Sarah, & Latimer shall have & receive their severall legacyes aforesaid respectively in full Contentation of their severall filiall parts & porcons out of my psonall Estate because I have otherwise provided for them Competent pferments out of my Lands. ffurther I give and bequeath unto ye poore brethren & sisters of ye Hospitall Called Gods—house twenty shillings. And to ye poore of Kingston upon Hull I give forty shillings. All the rest of my goods & Chattells reall & psonall, moveable & unmoveable, plate, Jewells, household stuffe, Cattell & leases not bequeathed formerly my debts being payed and my funeralls discharged I give and bequeath unto my some John Alured whome I make Constitute & ordeine the sole Executor of this my last will & testament thereby absolutely revokeing all former wills & testaments whatsoever either written or nuncupative. In witnes whereof I have hereunto set my hand & seale ye day & yeare first above written. And my mind further is yt the said legacyes given to my yonger Children as is aforesaid shalbe payd when they shall severally accomplish ye age of twenty one yeares, or be lawfully marryed And if Any of them dye befor that age or marriage then the said legacyes unto them respectively given are to Cease & be reteined in the hands of my executor Hic testibus,

RICH: DARLEY iurat	HENRY ALURED
RO BARWICKE	(with seal)
THOMAS NORTON iurat	
ANDR : MARVELL	

NOTES: The Andrew Marvell who signed above as a witness to this will was the father of the poet of that name, and the Mrs. Marvell mentioned in the will is obviously his wife, and the mother of the poet. In 1624 the elder Andrew Marvell had become master of the Hull grammar school and about the same time became Master of the Charterhouse, which adjoined the Alureds' house of the same name, and lecturer at the Trinity Church mentioned in the will. Young Andrew Marvell was born in 1621 and was about seven years old at the time of this will, and therefore contemporary with some of the younger children, who were obviously his playmates. Their mother Frances Alured had died two years before, and was buried at Sculcoates (the village outside Hull where the Charterhouse was situated) June 22, 1626. This is the reason why she is not mentioned in the will and why the children are orphans. From the fact that Henry Alured refers to his previous wills, including nuncupative oral ones, it would appear that he had had considerable bouts of illness in the past, perhaps associated with whatever was responsible for his wife's death. For a noncupative will is only made orally by someone who thinks he is on his deathbed. Since the eldest son John Alured, later to be a regicide, had been baptized April 4, 1607, at Preston, this new and final will of Henry Alured's was made just a few days after the twenty–first birthday of his eldest son. Until John became 21, this will would have been an impossibility and the family narrowly missed, by only a matter of days, becoming victims of the rapacious plunderings of the notorious Court of Wards. John Alured's first wife in 1631 was to be Mary Darley, daughter of the above Richard Darley. His aunt Lucy Alured had previously married Francis Darley of Kilnhurst; she is mentioned in the will, and the two families were thus already connected. Both Richard Darley and Sir Robert Barwicke (above) were later to be on the Committee at York during the Civil War, and also on the Committee for the Northern Association.

THOMAS CHALONER
CONSOLIDATES THE
FAMILY ESTATE AT
GISBOROUGH (1650)

Public Record Office: S.P. 46/ 109/ 69
(Papers of the Trustees for the Sale of
Fee Farm Rents)

viiivo Augusti 1650.

By ye Trustees for Sale of the ffee ffarme Rentes &c.

Whereas Thomas Chaloner Esqr Contracted with Us upon the xxixth day of Aprill last; on behalfe of himselfe and Henry Sherbrooke Esqr for The ffee ffarme of ye Mannor of Gisborne als Gisbrough in ye County of Yorke p annum CXV l. Vs. IIIId. [116 pounds, 5 shillings and fourpence] and hath paid into ye Treary [treasury] ye whole purchase money paieable upon ye said Contract; as may appear by two writings under ye hands of Thomas Andrewes ffrancis Allein and John Dethick Aldren of ye City of London Trers [treasurers] appointed by ye Act to receive the same bearing date the thirteenth day of May and seaven and twentieth day of July last past.

It is this day Ordered, that ye severall and respective Owners Occupiers and Tennants of ye said Mannor doe from henceforward pay ye abovesaid ffee ffarme Rente wch shall grow due and paieable for ye said Mannor from and after ye said seaven and twentieth day of July unto ye said Thomas Chaloner and Henry Sherbrooke Esqrs or their Assignes, at such usuall daies and times, as ye same shall from time to time grow due and paieable. And a Coppie of this Order left with ye said Owners Occupiers or Tennants of ye said Mannor shall be their sufficient Warrant and Discharge for ye paying of ye said ffee ffarme Rente unto ye said Thomas Chaloner & Henry Sherbrooke Esqrs, or their Assignes accordingly: And further Ordered that Mr Ar Serle discharge the said Mannor in his Rentalls and Records from paying ye said ffee ffarme Rente unto ye State from and after the said xxviith day of July; And that he give notice hereof unto ye Receivor Bayliffe, or Collector of ye pmsses, that they demand not, nor distreyne ye said Mannor for the said ffee ffarme Rente accrueing from ye said xxviith day of July; but that they leave ye same to be received by the said Thomas Chaloner and Henry Sherbrooke Esqrs, and their Assignes according to this Order.

EWER (or Ewers, Ewre, Ewres, Hewer, Hewers, Eure), ISAAC (b.c. 1612, d. 1650), Civil War Officer and Regicide, was a close relation and possibly son of Richard Ewer of Hatfield Broad Oak, Essex, and seems to have been related to the Ewer families of Pinner, Middlesex, and Cheshunt, Herts. (the head of the latter, William Ewer, having been Serjeant at Arms to Charles I). Noble's assumption (Noble, I, 202) of a relationship to Lord Eure remains unproved and would probably be distant. Ewer's immediate family were fairly substantial householders at least; he himself was assessed for 9 shillings Ship Money when still a young man (T/A 42, Essex Record Office); in 1636 he was one of "two honest persons" in his parish to be named Surveyor of the Highways. Richard held this position in 1634 and provided his own team of labourers, horses, and carts (Q/SR 285/16 and 293/44, Essex Record Office). Ewer lived at Hatfield by at least 1633 (D/Dba Al, p. 128, Essex R.O.), and by that year had married an

Essex girl, Joan Thurloe, sister of John Thurloe, later Cromwell's Secretary of State. Their son Thomas Ewer was baptised in August 1634, at Hatfield (D/Dba, Aug., 1634, Essex R.O.) and a daughter Joanna was under 16 on August 1, 1649, when Ewer made his will (PCC Wills, Prob–11–215, p. 150), by which same date Ewer's wife (who had been still alive in 1637) was dead. Ewer's relations with his brother–in–law were close, and Thurloe was named his sole executor in his will "to whom I leave the care and tuition of my said two children in the Lord intreating him to have a tender care of them", and whose eldest son John was a residual heir in Ewer's will. Ewer had brothers John and William, the latter of whom had a son, Captain Isaac Ewer, by 1655 employed by Thurloe as under–clerk to John Milton (CSPD, 1653–4, 386), whom Thurloe warmly recommended to Henry Cromwell in 1656 (Thurloe SP, V, 46–7) pointedly adding "he is the only person of my kindred, that I have ever moved for in a case", and emphasizing that the nephew had previously been dependent on his uncle the regicide "who brought him into Ireland, and upon whom he did rely". The recommendation was, surprisingly, unsuccessful, and so this nephew subsequently accompanied instead Sir Philip Meadowes, a protegé of Thurloe's, on his diplomatic mission to Denmark in 1657, and afterwards to Sweden in 1658, becoming entirely privy to the diplomatic confidences (Thurloe SP, VI, 508–9; VII, 651–2). After this the regicide's namesake was admitted to Lincoln's Inn, became a barrister, and by 1692 Keeper of the Black Book, dying in 1694 (PCC Wills, Prob–11–422, pp. 41–2).

Ewer was Captain of a troop of horse as early as 1643 (Egerton MSS. 2647, f. 31). By March 10, 1645, he was a Major of Dragoons under Manchester and was ordered to march to the aid of Brereton (CSPD, 1644–5, 337). By 1647 he was the Lieutenant–Colonel of Col. Robert Hammond's regiment of foot in the New Model Army (Peacock, Army Lists, 103). He succeeded Hammond as Colonel of the regiment 2 October 1647 (Clarke Papers, II, 57n.). Hammond, short of men in his new post at the Isle of Wight, requested that Ewer reinforce him, which Fairfax then ordered 16 March 1648 (CSPD, XXII, 30). On April 27, the Common Council of the City sent a sheriff to address the House (CJ, V, 546a), who said that Ewer had been overheard on April 20 at Windsor plotting with Colonel Grosvenor and other officers the disarming of the City and the threatening of it with plunder in order to extract by force the sum of £1,000,000 (Gardiner, GCW, III, 361; Whitelocke, Memorials, 1735 ed., 302–3). The House appointed a committee (including six future regicides) to look into these allegations. Less than a month later, Ewer's military importance was vividly demonstrated when on May 25 he addressed a letter to Lenthall reporting his successful taking of Chepstow Castle, which had been seized by royalists under Sir Nicholas Kemmish (Tanner MSS. 57/1 preserves the original). Ewer's letter was read in the House on May 29 (CJ, V, 576b), and ordered to be printed (Ewer, A Full and Particular Relation of the ... Taking of Chepstow Castle ..., 1648). Col. Edward Whalley the Regicide wrote 11 June 1648 to Fairfax asking to be reinforced by Ewer's regiment at Witham, Essex (CSPD, XXII, 27), for, being latterly an Essex man himself, he would have known that Ewer's home was a few miles away and Ever would know the terrain well. Cromwell had ordered Ewer to Coventry some days earlier (Clarke Papers, II, 101), but now Fairfax ordered Ewer to go immediately to Whalley's aid (CSPD, XXII, 111, 113–4) against the 5000 men under Lucas and Goring. But the royalists by June 12 had made their way into Colchester and the famous siege was about to commence. At the siege Ewer took up a position to the west of the town with two other regicide colonels, Ingoldsby and Scrope. At the surrender, with the regicides Ireton and Whalley, Ewer held the discussions with Norwich and Capel (Gardiner, GCW, III, 463). Ewer seems then to have been made military governor of Portsmouth (Clarke Papers, II; 54). Ewer now became active in politics, through the Council of Officers of the Army. He was prominent at the Council meeting of Nov. 16 (Ibid., II, 54, 274) and was then named to a committee of nine to put Ireton's Remonstrance of the Army into a proper draft for submission to Parliament. This committee's leading members were all future regicides: Ireton, Whalley, Constable, Scrope, and Ewer. Four days later, Ewer took the final draft of the Remonstrance to Parliament in person, addressed the House, and requested that they take the proposals into speedy consideration (CJ, VI, 81). The Remonstrance chiefly called for the King to be speedily brought to justice, with other radical measures (A Remonstrance and Declaration of the Army Presented ... by Colonell Ewres ..., 1648). The next day, Fairfax gave special orders to Ewer (Clarke Papers, II, 54–5) to go and sound out Col. Hammond in the Isle of Wight, who had the King in custody. Ewer was the perfect choice, being Hammond's friend and former subordinate. Ewer had still not arrived in the Isle of Wight by November 26 (Tanner MSS. 57/2, 429–30) but was there by the morning of November 28 (Ibid., 435–6), and persuaded Hammond by some extraordinary means despite "his overriding trust to Parliament" (Ibid.) to leave with him for Windsor. However, on the road, Major Cromwell came along with a letter for Hammond from Parliament, which he then delivered to him. It enjoined him to remain in the Isle of Wight, and so Hammond wrote an immediate reply saying "I shall yield immediate obedience by making my urgent return thither" (ibid., 433–4): At this point, Ewer was forced to put his old commander under arrest and even to forbid him sending his letter until the next day from Bagshot (Ibid.) Ewer's subordinate officers, left behind at the Isle of Wight, dealt with the far less challenging job of removing the King to Hurst Castle (Clarke Papers, II, 54–5, 59–61; 63–4; CJ, VI, 91b; Whitelocke, Memorials, 1735 ed., 357a–b, 358b, 359a). A description of Col. Eyre, commander of Hurst Castle, by a royalist (Herbert, Two Last Years of Charles I, ed. 1702, 85–6) was for long mistakenly thought to be of Ewer (as in the DNB; Gardiner, GCW, III, 526). Ewer was named to the High Court of justice to try the King, attended with considerable regularity, and signed the Death Warrant. After the trial, his regiment was assigned to the region of Kent (CSPD, 3 March 1649). Then on April 20 occurred the drawing of lots for regimental service in Ireland, and Ewer drew one marked "Ireland", and privately was very distressed, "not knowing whether God may ever bring me back again to see my children whom I must leave behind me young and undisposed of" (Will, op. cit.) Ewer's martial exploits in Ireland were what one would expect from a soldier of his calibre (Whitelocke, op. cit., 428b, 429a, 448b) and he is last heard of 31 October 1650 marching towards Kilkenny (Gilbert, Aphorismical Disoovery, III, 224), not long after which he died, for his will was proved at London the following 25 February by John Thurloe, who became the guardian of Ewer's orphans (Will, op. cit.)

R.K.G. TEMPLE

GARLAND, AUGUSTINE (or Augustus) (b.1602, d.c. 1665), Regicide and parliamentary radical, MP 1648, 1654, 1659 (Queenborough), was the only son of Augustine Garland, a well known and very prosperous London attorney, and his first wife Ellen Whitteridge, dau. of Jasper Whitteridge of London. Garland was part French, his paternal grandmother having been a Frenchwoman of Calais surnamed Carden. The Garlands had once been of Hayes in Kent (Visitation of 1634, I, 301). Garland was baptised at St. Antholin's Budge Row, London, 13 January 1602; his father remarried Alice Johnson, widow, née Cliff (daughter of a London draper) 16 January 1604, at St. Dunstan's, Stepney, Middlesex. Garland had one full sister and two half-sisters (all married). He was on bad terms with all of them as well as his father according to his father's will (P.C.C. Wills, Prob–11–176, p. 67) proved by one of the half sisters on January 27, 1638. In the will Garland is given less than any of the sisters (if their dowries are counted), palmed off with £550 and outlying houses and lands beyond London. These, however, were to be instrumental in Garland's acquiring a political base, for he was to become MP for Queenborough in Kent, one of these locations (election writ issued 10 May 1648: CJ, V, 556a). Garland was admitted pensioner to Emmanuel College, Cambridge, at Easter, 1618. He later attended Cliffords Inn and then was admitted to Lincoln's Inn 14 June 1631 (and was hence contemporary with John Dixwell the Regicide); he was called to the bar 29 January 1635, which is an extraordinarily short time interval, considering that the normal time required to qualify as a barrister was seven years. He was appointed JP for Essex 19 December 1645 (HMC 10th Report, Appendix IV, 508–9). In August 1644 Garland was residing at Great Ilford, Essex, where he was assessed for £150 (CCAM, 457); in June 1646 he was recorded as being parishioner and residing at Barking, Essex (T/B 84, Essex Record Office). Garland was still single at the age of 32 but eventually married (name of wife unknown); his wife, however, died of smallpox in childbed 22 August 1648 (Obituary of Richard Smyth, p. 26), only three months after Garland's election as a recruiter to Parliament.

There seems to be no evidence whatsoever of Noble's contention (Noble, I, 249) that Garland "for some time quitted the law to join the parliament army". There was another contemporary Augustine Garland, probably a near cousin (Archaeologia Cantiana, XX, 25) alive and a minor in 1636 in Kent, mistakenly thought by Brunton and Pennington to be the regicide (Members of Long Parliament, 51), but he was thoroughly obscure. This Augustine had a brother John, possibly identical with the Captain John Garland whom Noble may have mistaken for the regicide; in 1644 he was denounced for preaching extremely radical views in religion (Tanner MSS. 61, 110–1) and later took a prominent part in the battle of St. Fagan's.

Garland led a student riot at Lincoln's Inn in 1635 (Black Books, 326–31), but not in company with Adrian Scrope the Regicide as believed by Underdown (Pride's Purge, 221); his companion was Sir Adrian Scrope of Lincolnshire, later royalist, a distant cousin of the regicide Adrian Scrope, who had attended the Middle Temple 18 years earlier. The episode at Lincoln's inn, which included breaking the bench table in the hall of the Inn, was precipitated by penal action against Nicholas Love, later a member of the High Court of Justice. From his entry into Parliament in June, 1648, until Pride's Purge, Garland is only mentioned once in either the CJ or the CSPD, and that is 23 September 1648 as co–Commissioner with John Nutt for the Assessment of Kent (CJ, VI, 30b). But suddenly, on December 13, 1648, exactly a week after the Purge, and in company with his old friend Nicholas Love, Garland explodes upon the scene (CJ, VI, 96a). From this time on, he is without exception the most active, energetic, one might almost say frantic, MP. An attempt to evaluate his contribution to political developments then would take great space. W. D. Pink (Pink MSS., Ryl. Eng. MS., 300/22–3) was so impressed by Garland's gargantuan achievements in the House that he took the trouble to count the committees of which Garland was a member. Between Pride's Purge and April, 1653, Garland sat on no less than 202 committees. And between 9 May 1659 and 13 February 1660 he sat on a further 48. That makes a total during his four and a half years in active politics of 250 committees, meaning that he joined roughly one and a half committees per week. This is all the more extraordinary because for many of them (such as the Committee for Compounding) he was no passive member, but time after time is given the real work to do, and "the report shall be made by Mr. Garland" becomes one of the repetitive formulae of the Commons Journals. It was Garland who read to the House the ordinance for appointing a High Court of Justice to try the King (CJ, VI, 110), and he was singled out to draft and report the amendments to it, which he did literally during a single night (Ibid.) He himself sat on the Court and signed the Death Warrant. Under Cromwell he was shown no favour despite being the person who in the 1654 Parliament proposed that Cromwell be crowned King (Clarke Papers, III, 16), a motion enthusiastically seconded by Henry Cromwell. It would seem that Garland's motives in this were to legitimize the military usurpation, as he seems to have been a thoroughgoing republican. Garland's importance was not noticed in print until Worden (Rump Parliament, 39) pointed out that "(He) seems to have attended more debates than any other member except the Speaker, becoming the Rump's most assiduous committee–man and toiling incessantly over the drafting of legislation ..." His phenomenal activities still await even a cursory assessment. At the Restoration, Garland surrendered, was tried, and imprisoned. He is last heard of in 1664 awaiting transportation to Tangier (CSPD,.31 March 1664).

R.K.G. TEMPLE

The Last Will and Testament of
RICHARD HARRISON,
grandfather of the regicide
Major–General Thomas Harrison
Proved at Lichfield May 17, 1625,
and preserved in the Lichfield Joint
Record Office.

the therd daye of June Ao dni 1623.

In the name of god Amen I Richard Harrison of Newcastle undr lyme in the County of Stafford Butcher beinge of good and pfect memorie and understandinge thanks be given to god for the same, doe make and ordaine this my last Will and Testamt in wryting in maner and forme followinge Vizt I bequeathe my soule into the hands of Almighty god my maker and redeemer & my body to be buryed in the Church or Chappell of Newcastle under lyme aforesd Itm my Will is and I give and bequeathe unto Dorothie Harrison my wyfe ffive pounds to be paide in money in Consideration of her Joynture & thirds and in respecte of the love I beare unto her, & had my estate beene better, I would have lefte her a better porcon, Itm I give and bequeathe to Alice Beatie my daughter Ten shillings in money to be paide her in full of her Childs pte of my goods, Itm I give & bequeathe unto Elizabeth ffisher my daughter ffive pounds to be paide her in money in full of her Childs pte of my goods Item I give and bequeathe unto my daughter Margrett xiis to be paide her in money in full of her Childs pte of my goods Itm I give and bequeathe unto Raphe Harrison my sonne Tenn shillings in full of his Childs pte of my goods, Itm I give and bequeathe unto Richard Harrison my eldest some all my land to him his heires and assignes for ever wth the rest of all such goods Cattels and Chattels quick & dead as shalbe remayninge after my decease, my debts beinge paide and my funerall expenses discharged, Itm I doe nominate & appoynt the saide Richard Harrison my some executr of this my last Will and Testamt In witnes whereof I have hereunto put my hande & seale

In witnes of us
Tho: Beardmore
Tho: Johnson
Willm Lindopp
Proved by Richardus Harrison Jur:
attested by Ro: Master
(May 17, 1625).

(Attached:) A list and pfect Inventory of all the goods Cattells and Chattells of Richard Harrison of Newcastle Underlyme in the County of Stafford Butcher deceased viewed and prised the xi th daye of Maij Anno dni 1625 by Randall Shaw Sammell Bagnall and Thomas Bagnall.

Imprimis bedds and beddinge	v l	Summe total, Lxxi l xvi s viii d
Itm Brasse and Pewtar	iii l	
Itm Joyned bedde and bedsteade	iiii l	debts owinge the Testator
Itm Naperie (?)	iii l vi s viii d.	John Addames ii l

Itm a presse .	1 l	Thomas Broade
Itm Chattells	x l	& John doody iii l
Itm Cables formes Cheste & Treeneware (?)	ii l	[The latter is crossed out]
Itm Implemts of husbandrie	iii l	
Itm Cheanes (?) and Iron Ware .	x l	
Itm Apparrell of the dead and money in his purse	x l	

The Last Will and Testament of WILLIAM HORTON, father of the regicide Colonel Thomas Horton. Proved 1638, 27 August (No. 155) at the Leicestershire Record Office.

Feb 14 1637/8 In the name of God amen I William Horton of Gumley in the Countey of Lecester yeoman, being weake in body but pfect in memorye blessed be God, doe here make my last Will and testamt as in forme following, first I bequeath my soule into the hands of allmightie God that gave it, and my bodey to be buryed in the Churchyard of Gumley, Item I give to the poore of Gumley 10s, It I give to my eldest sone John Horton 1s, It I give to my sone James Horton 1s, It I give to my sone Andrew Horton 1s, It I give to my sone Robert Horton Twentey five pounds, It I give to my sone William Horton tenn pounds, It I give to my daughter Elizabeth Horton Thirtey pounds, It I give to my daughter Marey Horton twentey nobles It my will and pleasure is that theis 4 legasies that is to say of 25 l, 30 l, 10 l, 6 1/6s/0d, shall be paid within one twelve monethes after my departure out of this mortall life, It my will is that my daughter Marey Horton shall have one bedd in the lodging parler with a fether bed and other furniture there to belonging, allsoe my will and pleasure is that my wife Isabell Horton shall have the use of the said bedd so long as shee liveth, my debts and Legasies being paid and my funerall discharged the rest of my Goods I give to my wife Isabell Horton, and my second sone Thomas Horton Whom I make and ordaine my full executers in wittnes of this my last Will and Testamt I have heare sett too my hand

WILLYAM HORTON

RICHARD INGOLDSBY'S
RESTORATION PETITION
FOR HIS ANCESTRAL HOME
(1663)

Public Record Office: S.P. 29/ 71/ 11
Calendared p. 98, CSPD 1663/4.
The date of this Petition is
March, 1662/3.

To the Kings Most Excellent Matie
The humble Peticon of
Sr Richard Ingoldesbye
Most humbly sheweth and
acknowledgeth/.

Yor princely Grace and goodness to him, and that yow have bin gratiously pleased to comand That hee should receive the prsent benefitt of a purchase which he made in the late unhappy time of the Mannor of Ingleby in the County of Lincolne/.

Which during a Lease for three Lives in being, at the time of his purchase and all yett Liveing, yeelding 94 l 5s {£94 and 5 shillings} p Annum, And when that Lease ends is 227 l 0s 9d {£227, 10 shillings and ninepence} p Ann upon a further Improvemt As by a Certificate of the Lord Treasurer annexed may appear, That he is a most humble Suitor to yor Matie soe farr as may stand with yor Royall pleasure, as a further bounty to yor Peticoner to afford him the full benefitt of that his purchase, (hee being admitted into the same condition with the Cold Streamers, And Gratiously to graunt him the said Mannor and the present rent, In such Mannor as to yor Matieshall seeme meete/.

And according to his duty, He and his shall ever remaine obliged to pray for yor Maties long life and prosperous Reigne/.

                                        RI: INGOLDESBY.

(ANNEXED to the above, though unpaginated, and hence
f. 11. I., is a LETTER TO THE KING FROM LORD SOUTHAMPTON THE LORD TREASURER, about the Petition:)

May it please yor Matie

Though I looke upon Sr Richard Ingoldesby as an unfortunate young man, when by some Relations to the Great Usurper, hee was drawne into their serivce, yet because I find the like sense in himself, And that hee was soe active in that buisines.of the surprizall of Portesmouth and that fortunate Rencounter where he took Lambert prisoner, I cannot but bee willing to give him any advantage hee may iustly pretend unto, And yor Matie upon yor happy returne, having perticulerly comannded that hee should receave the benefit the Coldstreamers were admitted into I finde hee was in the late tymes only a purchaser of the Mannor of Ingelby in the County of Lincolne wch I beleive hee was the rather ledd unto, for the names sake;

Now the state of the case lyes thus.

There is a Lease of that Mannor for the present in graunt for the lives of Sr Edward Heath George Heath and Robert Heath (sons of Sr Robert Heath late Lord Cheife Justice) undr the yerely rent of 94 1 5 s [£94 and 5 shillings] And by Survey of the late pretended Parliament; upon improvement valued at 227 1 9 d [£227 and ninepence] over and above the said Rent, during these lives, that Lease cannot bee invaded, But yor Maty may grannt him the Rent reserved to yor Matie wch is 94 1_5 s for one & thirty yeres (as you have done to some Coldstreamers) Reserving only twelve pence in the pound for Rent. But hee pretending further to ye Revercon of this Lease, And Sr Edward Heath the present Tenant having likewise addressed himself to mee, that hee may not have a lease graunted over his head to any other and pretends yor Mats warrant to have the same graunted him in Fee, wch is contrary to my Instruccons and I cannot concurre in (and his terme being at present so long is not very capable of being renewed) I must humbly submit it to yor Matie whether you will extend yor Grace to Sr Richard Ingoldesby whom I find strongly affected to receave this favour from yor Maty And who wilbe very long beforehee can come to enioy that part of yor Mats favor. And I conceave, the name of the place much affects him in the Suit.

Southton Howse   T. SOUTHAMPTON
Aprill the 21 1663

WILL OF SIR RICHARD INGOLDSBY THE ELDER (FATHER OF THE REGICIDE) – (1656)

Bodleian Library: MS. WILLS 62/ 2/ 36. SPECIAL NOTE: As I transcribed this will, which is in a terrible state of disintegration, further bits kept falling from it, so that some words I was able to read have since perished. The document was not carefully preserved by the library, and the poor conditions in which it was kept are responsible for its state. (I have restored missing words which are obvious within square brackets.)

[In the] name of God Amen; The ffourteenth day of July one thousand six [hundred and fifty sixe. I, Sir Richard Ing]oldsby of Lethenborow in ye parish of Buckingham [Knight, being w]eake in body but of a good perfect & disposeing [memory (thanks be to God?)] do hereby revoke all wills by me formerly made [and doe make this my last will and testam]ent in manner & forme ffollowing; ffirst I [commit my soul unto Almightie] God [&] my body to ye earth to be decently bu[ried] .... [to]geather with my Auncestors assuredly trustinge [in our glorious Saviour and Rede]emer Christ Jesus my sinns are Remitted; And I ....nted to my soule, And be made (together with ....[And as concerns] my estate which (through Gods goodness) remain[es in my possession: I]tem I give & bequeath unto my dearly beloved wife [Elizabeth all those my goods] & Chattles whatsoever reall & personall moveable [and immoveable] ....ty soever which I now have, or may or shall have att y[e tyme of my death at Lenthenboro]w aforesaid or else where in any other place or places what[soever And for this my last will and te]stament I doe make Constitute & appoint my said wife Dam[e Elizabeth Ingoldsby my, sole and fu]ll executrix/ Richard Ingoldsby, Signed Sealed and [published in the presence of]................meston Tho: Boyes George Langley John Richar[dson?] .

[Oliver Lord] Protector of ye Commonwealth of England Scotland Irela[nd] .... [t]o all whome these prsents shall come Greeting Know yee that [In the yeare of] or Lord God one thousand sixe hundred fifty sixe before ye [Court for Probate of Wills and] Adscons Lawfully authorized that ye Last will & testament of [Richard Ingoldsby of Lenthenb]orow in ye parish of Buckingham in ye County of Bucks. Knight ....which will is to this prsents annexed, Administracion of all & sing[ular] .... & how may any manner of way concerne him or his said will ....Relict & sole & full executrix named in ye said will, shee [(being duly sworne to?) Ad]minister ye same goods Chattles & debts, according to ye tennor [of] .... be made a true & perfect Inve of all & singular ye good[s] ....may come to her hands possession or acknowlidge .... Admytor when she shall be assigned or Lawfully ....[authoris]ed to performe at or before ye La..............................ye Seale of ye Courte for pbate of wills ....[aforejsaid.]

LETTER FROM COLONEL CHARLES FLEETWOOD AND HIS MAJOR, THOMAS HARRISON, TO ROBERT SCAWEN, CHAIRMAN OF THE COMMITTEE OF THE ARMY (1645)

Public Record Office: S.P. 16/ 539, Part 3/ 290
Calendared p. 679 of
CSPD Charles I Addenda 1625–49.

Sr.

The Generall pleased to order the reducemts of Maior Ingoldsbies troope towards the recruite of or Regimt according to wch this Gentleman (the Leiutenant of that troope) brought to us his men, and what horse they had of the States; Wee recvd from them foureteene horse & 13 backs & breasts, theire horse very Poore & weake, wch in reguard of theire greate dutie wee could not expect otherwise; There did appear divers more horses, but the officers of the troope (whom wee know to bee faithfull & worthy) attest the same to bee the souldiers owne, wherefore wee cannot require them from them: Wee presume to signifie to you or experience of the referrings both of the officers & soldiers of this troope, orselves having beene sharers in the extreame hardshipp wch they have passed through this winter, & witnesses to theire good behavior in severall undertakings, wherefore wee are confident you wilbee induced to owne them as objects of yt respect you are pleased to afford anie others in theire case, wch wilbe fully represented to you by this bearer. Sr Wee are

24th May. 1645.   yor humble & affectionate servants

                                                                                  CHARLES FFLEETWOOD
                                                                                  T HARRISON

[The following note has been appended to document by Robert Scawen, and is intended for Francis Allen, Treasurer–at–War:]

Mr Alleine The Comttee doth desire that Maior Ingolsby & Leut Gardner, the Cornett & Quarter Master of this Troope may Receive the 14 dayes though not Rectified as the officers dismissed.
                                                                         ROB: SCAWEN

(NOTES: The Major Ingoldsby referred to above is Oliver Ingoldsby, uncle of Oliver Cromwell, who later knighted him, and brother of Richard Ingoldsby the regicide. It should be specially NOTED that the Index of the Calendar volume errs in assuming this Major Ingoldsby to be Henry Ingoldsby, which he is not. Henry was yet another of the Ingoidsby brothers fighting for the Parliament who became a Colonel and a Baronet, but this is not he. The reason why we may be certain that the above officer is Oliver Ingoldsby is that there is an additional document UNCALENDARED occurring next to the above signed by him giving further details of the above circumstances, specifying sums, and identifying the Cornet as Robert Ashfeild and the Quartermaster as William Aris.)

PETITION OF RICHARD INGOLDSBY (1660)

House of Lords Record Office: Main Papers, June 11, 1660. Calendared in HMC 7th Report, p. 95b, as Number 14 of "Papers Relating to the Act of Indemnity".

To the right Honoble the Lords in Parliamt assembled

The humble peticon of Colll Richard Ingoldesby

Humbly sheweth.

That whereas Sr Hardress Waller became indebted unto yor petr in the yeare of our Lord 1658 in the sume of 2000 1 sterI. by Iudgemt in his Matys Court of Common pleas in the Kingdome of Ireland As by the Records of the said Court may Appeare the said Sr Hardress not being able to pay and discharge the said debt on the day appointed did for the satisfying thereof by Deed of Bargaine and Sale beareing date the 20th of Aprill last past Convey divers of his Goodes and Chattells upon yor petr By vertue whereof yor petr became Interested in the said Goods and Chattells and did seize upon and mark the same for his owne use and yor petr being furthr ready to dispose therof for the paymt of the said debt his Matys Comissioners for the prsent mannageing of the Affaires of Ireland did seize upon the said goods and Chattells for the use of his Maty whereas the property thereof was legally altered and vested in your said petr. And that for good and Vallewable Consideracons as afore said without the least fraud or Coven Intended against his sacred Maty

May it therefore please yor honors that yor petr may bee restored into the possession of the said goods and Chattells so illegally taken from him and the rather for that some of the said goods are of a perishing Nature & will be lost if not timely disposed off.

And yo r pet! (as bound)
shall ever pray &c

RI: INGOLDESBY.

ANNEXED DOCUMENT:

Provided that this act nor anything therein contained shall not extend to invalidate one Judgmt of the summe of two thousand pounds in the Court of his Majesty's Common please in Ireland 1658 by Richard Ingoldesby agt Sr Hardresse Waller nor to make voide one deed of Bargaine and Sale dated the twentith day of Aprill one thousand six hundred and sixty made by ye said Sr Hardresse Waller to the said Richard Ingoldesby of his goods and Chattells for and towards the satisfaction of the said debt and Judgment

(NOTE: By this amendment to the Act, the Lords granted Ingoldsby's petition.)

The Last Will and Testament of
JOHN IRETON, OF IRETON,
DERBYSHIRE,
Great–great–great grandfather of
Henry Ireton the Regicide (1534)

Lichfield Joint Record Office:
"Ireton 56". Proved April 13, 1534.

In dei nomine the v day of June the yere of or Lord God M CCCCC XXXiii

I John Ireton of Ireton Beyng seke in Body of holle mynd and pfecte memory make my [last will and testament in manner and forme (this part of the page being perished)] following

ffyrst I gyffe and bequeathe my sowle to almighty god to hys blessed moder saynt mary and to all the holly Company of hevyn and my body to be Buryed where it shall please god and I gyffe and Bequeathe in the name of my pryncypall to the ii parsons of mogynton x s Itm to the Church of mogynton a mke [i.e., one mark] or ells a kowe worth a mke. Itm a prest to syng for me a yere at Ireton havyng xliii s iiii d and hys food. Itm to saynt mary howse of Coventry & sent Chadds howse of lychfeld to eyther of them viii d Itm to the Chappell of querdon ii s Itm to the Chappell of Lyttell Eyton ii s Itm to the Church of Ketelston [Kedleston, home of the Curzon family, his in–laws] v s Itm to the freres of newarke xx d Itm to Marget Warren a kowe and a heyffer Itm to each of my servts xiii d Itm to John Cokeram a yong ram Itm I wyll that the Challys vestements books wt oder adornaments belongyng to the Chappell wyth a salf of sylver & a cuppe wyth a covr Remayne as eyrelomys [i.e., heirlooms] The Resydue of all my goods not Bequeathyd I gyffe and Bequeathe to John Ireton my son and to German Ireton hys son to be devyded betwes them by evyn porxons whom I make & ordeyne my feythfull executors And they shall kepe Arthur Ireton the scole to such tym he be off lawfull age to be prest and yf hys mynd be not to be prest he to have the land whych I gaffe hym for terme of hys lyfe And yf his mynd be to be prest they shall have the sayde lande beyiyng the Cofte aforesaid

Beyng present at this testamente makyng Master Nicholas Stokesley Canon of lychfeld and Sr Richerde Pars parson of Mogynton wyth others

(NOTES: Little Eyton is probably Little Eaton, 22 miles north of Derby. It might possibly be Little Ireton. Querdon is probably Quarndon, 22 miles north of Derby. "Mogynton" might be Mocking Hazel Wood, an extraparochial and now uninhabited district of St. Briavel's parish in Gloucestershire near –the Forest of Dean. If so, this might be the "Hazelwood" associated with some later Iretons rather than the Hazelwood in Derbyshire, but this all seems rather unlikely. As for Sir Richard Pars, he does not appear under that name or any conceivable variant of that name (Peirce, Pearce, Parrys, Percy, etc.) in William A. Shaw's The Knights of England, although he could conceivably have been knighted July 1, 1523, by the Lord Admiral "for hardiness and noble courage" after the taking of Morlaix, on which occasion ten knights are named followed by "and divers others". Otherwise prior to 1500 the lists of knights become somewhat vague, several men identified not by name but by their shields! But there is no doubt that in the will, Parsons is definitely described as "Sir".)

ROBERT LILBURNE TRIES TO SAVE HIS EMBARASSING BROTHER BY OFFERING HIS EMIGRATION TO AMERICA (1649)

From a Letter of Intelligence sent from Whitehall and preserved in William Clarke's Notebook; Worcester College, Oxford: Clarke Mss. Vol. XVI (Shelf 2. No. 16)

August 23, 1649. Yesterday Col: Lilburne attended ye Councelle of State about his brother Lt Col: L: who is to bee tried too morrow att Guildhall the Jury being Impabnelled & Scaffolds erected but ye business was by them referd to ye Parl to whom an offer was made in behalf of ye Lt Col: for hee & as many of his pty as were willing to goe into America if they wold wave his tryall but ye house refred him to tryall.

August 27, 1649. Sr A Comon of Oyer & Terminer being granted to Justice Keeble & Justice Thorp Jeram [Jermyn] Barron Gates & other Judges of both houses & divers Aldermen of London for tryall of Lt Col Lilburne in Guildhall Wednesday Thursday & ffriday last ye Comon was onely red & the Grand Inquest Impannelled Keble gave ye Charge & ye ground – Inquest on ye Thursday found ye bill ye Prisoner then being brought to ye Barr refused to hold upp his hand alleging there was noe ground for yt as hee ordered in any Englysh law.

Yesterday after full hearing from 9 in ye Morn: to 7 att night ye Jury brought in her Verdict & found him not guilty wch filed ye people being a great Numbr both in Hall yard & streets wth acclamacons of ioy yt hee was quitted some of them were of his owne opinion others of ye Cavaleer principles glad of any occasion to express a dislike of ye pceedings of Parlt I was prsent all ye 3 daies & could fill a Volume – but this is too tedious for my weekly Intelligence.

MAYNE (or Meyn, Meyne, Meine), SIMON (1612–1661). Regicide and parliamentary radical, MP 1645, 1659 (Aylesbury), was son and heir of Simon Mayne, High Sheriff of Bucks., and Coluberry Lovelace, sister of the first Lord Lovelace (1564–1634) and widow of Richard Beke (or Beake) of Hurley (d. 1606); she d. 10 Jan. 1629. The Regicide was baptised 17 Feb. 1612 at Dinton, Bucks. Mayne had a sister, Coluberry, who m. Thomas Bulstrode, son and heir of Henry Bulstrode of Hedgely, Bucks. The Regicide was widely connected: Henry Marten the Regicide was his mother's nephew by marriage to her niece; he was doubly related to the Lovelaces (his aunt was also one); Col. Richard Beke, MP, was his nephew; Robert Lilburne the Regicide was his niece's husband; James Temple the Regicide was his aunt's first cousin; and Oliver Cromwell was his nephew's uncle by marriage. Mayne m. 21 May 1633 Jane Burgoyne of Beds. (1614–1641) and secondly a widow apparently named Elizabeth (surname unknown) by whom he had an only son, Simon, b. c. 1644, who m. Elizabeth Browne (b. c. 1647) of Herts. in 1668/9, had issue, and became a judge. The Regicide had no less than eight step-brothers and sisters named Beke. Aged 5, his father left him in his will (P.C.C. Wills, Prob–11–130, p. 190) Dinton Hall upon his mother's death, which occurred when the Regicide was aged 16, and after 15 years a lease of the parsonage of Ladenham (Luddingham) and Cuddington, Bucks. The

Regicide also inherited further lands. Dinton Hall itself still stands and is a sizeable mansion. Mayne could be described as being of the greater gentry and highly prosperous. Ten minutes away by horseback lived Richard Ingoldsby the Regicide, and twice that distance away was one of the homes of Thomas Scot the Regicide.

Mayne was admitted to the Inner Temple in Nov. 1630 (contemporary with John Downes the Regicide) and became a county magistrate (Robert Gibbs, "The Regicides of Bucks.", Recs. of Bucks., Volume 87). In 1642 he signed a petition to Charles I to disband his army, and served on Berks. County Committee (probably through Beke connections). A document dated 27 Oct. 1643 (Add. MSS. 5497, 91) shows Mayne securing property already under lease to him from the sequestered owners, the Dean and Chapter of Rochester, with Henry Marten as intermediary (CJ, III, 291a; Sloane MSS. 856, 23b–24a).

Mayne was elected to Parliament as a recruiter with Thomas Scot for Aylesbury in 1645 (their Husks. regicide colleagues Ingoldsby and George Fleetwood did not join them in Parliament for another two years). Scot and Mayne set about getting the affairs of Bucks. into their iron grip, and a remarkable document survives showing the forcefulness and confidence displayed by Mayne in 1648 when he was running the Bucks. County Committee (Add. MSS. 5494, 28–9). The first draft (21 Sept.) was followed by a second (23 Sept.) where he got his first cousin Henry Beke and George Fleetwood the Regicide to back him up (who was by then MP) in replying to requests for accounts of all real and personal estates of delinquents sequestered between 1642 and 1648 inclusive, according to ordinances of Parliament of 9 and 15 Aug. Mayne replied to this seemingly reasonable request of the Treasurers at Guildhall in London by brazenly reminding them of a Parliamentary ordinance of 1644 empowering his committee with full disposal of Bucks. sequestrations, says he is using the profits to finance a militia troop of horse and to pay arrears of former Bucks. soldiers who, he tartly adds, "hitherto have not been necessitated to wait at the Parliament's doors with petitions for the same, as from many other counties they have done." Mayne's absolute refusal to meet the requests of Parliament was only mitigated after Pride's Purge, when he did allow his County Treasurer to send in a token specimen account covering only a single month in the spring of 1649 (ibid. 30–1). Mayne ran a tight ship and his attitude is in sharp contrast to many of the county committees who meekly submitted reams of accounts for inspection (Beds., for instance, sent in a most respectful letter and 25 lengthy, meticulously neat pages of exhaustive accounts). Two months later, Mayne was named by Parliament a Bucks. commissioner for the assessment (CJ, Vi, 87b).

Mayne was named to the High Court of Justice to try the King and attended many of its meetings, not being slow to sign the Death Warrant, for his signature precedes those of three of his Bucks. colleagues (Chaloner, Fleetwood, and Scot), which seems to belie the story he later told (Somers Tracts, VII, 456–7) that Thomas Chaloner had made him sign the Warrant and had boasted "that he was the man that made Mr. Mayne a man of courage end resolution". Mayne published this after Chaloner was safely on the Continent, but kept back Chaloner's actual name at his own trial (Noble, II, 66). During the Protectorate Mayne continued with the Bucks. Co. Committee (ibid., II, 65). He returned to Parliament in 1659, languishing there in his customary parliamentary obscurity. On Aug. 12 he was granted 8 days' leave of absence to attend a trial in Bucks. (CJ, VII, 756b) and must have been in the House on Sept. 30 because he was not fined for absence (Ibid., 789–90). But Mayne, comfortable as a large fish in a small pond, was remarkably timid in the larger councils of the nation and appears never to have served on a parliamentary committee or to have been a teller for a vote in the House. He remained very much a local boss and the High Court was his one flash onto the greater stage, subsiding very much into the pan. This one action was, however, sufficient cause for his surrender, trial, and imprisonment at the Restoration. He died In the Tower of illness on 13 April 1661, and was buried at Dinton Church on 18 April. Quite soon afterwards his son regained his confiscated lands and the family continued at Dinton as before.

R.K.G. TEMPLE

MOORE, (or More, Moor), JOHN (1599–1650), Regicide and parliamentary radical, MP 1640 (Liverpool), was eldest son of Edward Moore (JP by 1611, Sheriff of Lancs. 20 Nov., 1620, MP for Liverpool in 1st Parl. of 1625) of Bank Hall, Walton, Lancs. (now the Liverpool dock area), and Katherine, dau. of John and Margaret Hockenhull (or Hocknell) of Prenton, Cheshire. The Moores were an extremely prosperous and ancient Lancs. family; in their dower house, the Old Hall (formerly Moore Hall), an ancestor, Sir John de la More, had resided in 1235 (Trans. Hist. Soc. Lancs. & Ches. 2 Ser. XIII, 2). By the 17th century the Moores apparently had an astonishing 27 quarterings to their arms (Ibid., LXIII, 98), and Sir John Meldrum described them, not surprisingly, as "an ancient family" in recommending Moore for command (CSPD, 2 Nov. 1644). Moore's ancestors had been MPs for Liverpool on and off since 1307 (Trans., op.cit., LXIII, 104). Moore had three brothers and four sisters, his uncle was Major General Ralph Assheton (MP for Lancashire), his pre-war friend and godfather of his son was James, Lord Strange, later Earl of Derby (J. Brownbill and K. Walker, A Calendar of … Papers of the Moore Family, Rec. Soc. Lancs. & Ches., LXVII, 1913, p. 183), and the Viscounts Moore of Drogheda (later Earls of Drogheda) were "kinsmen" with whom he had cordial relations (Moore MSS. 1061, 1062, 1276 in Liverpool Rec. Off.). His wife's uncle was the Earl of Meath, and Roger Kirkby (d. 1644), MP for Lancs., was her cousin (Visit. Lancs. 1664–5, Chetham Soc. Vol. LXXXIV, p. 169). Moore was admitted Lincoln's Inn 17 Aug. 1638, at request of Hugh Rigby, Reader, being contemporary there with the regicides John Hutchinson, Augustine Garland, and Henry Smith. Moore m, late in 1633 Mary, dau. of the royalist Alexander Rigby (Admin. 1 Sept. 1650, PROS–6–25, P. 135 in PRO where it is wrongly indexed) of Burgh and Leighton, Lancs., who must not be confused with his contemp. and cousin the MP of same name (q.v.), and Catherine, dau. of Sir Edward Brabazon (Visit. Lancs., op. cit., p. 244). Around the time of the marriage, Moore bought out his mother°s share in Bank Hall and the family estates for £10,000 in cash (Moore MS. 306 at Liverpool Record Office). Moore from then on resided at the moated and "new" Bank Hall (erected 1382). His Articles of Marriage dated 2 Oct. 1633 survive (Moore MS. 920 MOO 2179 at Liverpool Record Office), in which Mary is to bring a dowry of £1200 in installments. However, Moore had still not received all of this by the time of his own death 16 years later, as he says in his will (Moore MS. 920 M00 844 at Liverpool Record Office), when in addition his wife's royalist father (who had compounded 16 Jan. 1647; CCC, pp. 1650–1), brother William, and deceased relation Hugh (mentioned above) were all Moore's debtors for hundreds of pounds. Moore's eldest son was Captain Edward Moore, cr. Baronet 1 Mar. 1662 (delayed cr. until 22 Nov. 1675; Complete Baronetage, p. 70), who m. 1st Dorothy, dau. of royalist Sir William Fenwick, and 2nd Mary Ben, and this baronetcy continued (listed under the spelling of "More") until it became extinct 21 May 1810, with the 5th Baronet. Moore's other children living 1650 and mentioned in his will were Alexander, Thomas, and Katherine (unmarried). Moore is not mentioned in the old DNB and was only a name to Noble, who thought he hadn't signed the Death Warrant (Noble, II, 85–6). There were four Moores in the Long Parliament, two of them colonels, and three more Moores who were not MPs but were also colonels, adding to the confusion. Moore became JP by 1624, Bailiff of Liverpool in 1630, and Mayor in 1633. A warrant from him and another JP of 17 Nov. 1634 regarding relief for the poor indicates an early social conscience (Brownbill, op. cit., p. 202, MS. 1394). Moore was elected MP in the Long Parliament in 1640 for Liverpool, where he immediately made an impression, by Dec. 4 was on a small committee, and on Dec. 5 "Mr. Jo. Moore, and all the merchants of the House" are added to the Committee for Monopolies, indicating his importance as one of the wealthiest traders; ship owners, and land developers in the House (CJ, ii, 44b, 45b), His connections with seafaring lead to his appointment Dec. 10 to an important committee concerning the securing of navigation in the Mediterranean, and the prisoners of the Turks and corsairs, which was soon expanded to consider treaties with Spain (CJ, II, 48). On Dec. 11 Moore joined a committee on postal services which neophytes Oliver Cromwell and the regicide Valentine Wauton only joined on Feb. 10 later on, as their first Parliamentary committee (CJ, II, 49b, 82a). Moore kept extensive parliamentary diaries (not referenced by Keeler; missed by nearly all scholars because indexed at the British Library only under "More" and not under "Moore"). Six vols. survive, commencing 6 Nov. 1640, and which he headed "A journal of the transactions of the House of Commons at the time the right of ship money was debated" (Harleian MS. 541. ff. 62–118, is Vol. I; Harleian MSS. 476–80 are Vols. II–VI, ending on 28 Feb. 1642). Moore's handwriting is appalling and these diaries are extremely difficult to read. A 449–page Victorian transcript of Vol. II (Harleian MS. 476) only, by W.A. Shaw, covering the dates 23 Feb. 1641 to 21 April 1641, is MS. 451 at the Rylands Library, but ironically it is as difficult to read as the original! Moore pledged £1500 in 1640, £500 in 1641 (Keeler, p. 277), and £300 in April, 1642 (CJ, II, 520x; T. Heywood, Moore Rental, Chetham Soc. XII, 1847, p. xii), and in June, 1642, pledged two horses for the imminent defense, the same as his uncle Assheton (N. & Q., 1st Series, XII, 359). 21 Aug. 1641 the Commons sent Moore, Rigby, Assheton, and Kirkby (who were all related to one another) to Lancs. to "disarm recusants" (CJ, II, 267b), which was a major problem as Lans was heavily Catholic in parts. 10 Feb. 1642 Lord Wharton was nom. by the Commons Lord Lieutenant of Lancashire (Ibid., 424b), approved by the Lords Feb. 12 after controversy (G.F. Trevallyn, Saw–Pit Wharton, Sydney, 1967, p. 42). He hesitated in naming his Deputy Lieutenantss (Ibid., 45) so the Commons recommended to him Moore, Rigby, and others 24 Mar. 1642 (CJ, II, 495b). 13 April 1642 More was sent with a letter to Brereton in Cheshire (Ibid., 524b). He and his fellow–DLs then were ordered on June 9 (Ibid., 615a–b, 618a, 620b) to proceed to Lancs., where they were commissioned Deputy Lieutenants on June 13 (Trans., op. cit., XXXVIII, p. 152, Item 27) and where they then were involved in the first actions of the Civil War three months later. Lord Strange, who had already seized powder at Liverpool, sent a demand for the surrender of ten barrels of powder kept in his own house at Manchester. Moore and the others rushed to Manchester to secure it for the Parliament, and mustered and trained the local citizens there (Letter of 25 June 1642 from Moore, Assheton, and Rigby, printed in Severall Letters from the Committees In Severall Counties To ... Lenthall, London, 27 June 1642; see also CJ, II, 641–2). On July 4, what appears to have been the first actual small battle of the Civil War took place (which may never have been noticed by historians) when Lord Strange attacked Manchester. Moore and the other DLs "drew out ten small companies, and set them in a fair battalion against (the enemy)" and defeated Strange after two or three hours, who withdrew leaving 27 men dead (The Beginning of Civil–Warres in England, London, 9 July 1642) Thus did these Lancs. DLs, later famed as commanders, make their fighting debut eight days before Parliament had even appointed a General. By July 25, Moore, Rigby, and Assheton were back in London (CJ, II, 689b). Moore became the Parliament's police officer on Aug. 6, as Colonel of Guards "Horse and Foot in London, Westminster, and Southwark" (Trans., op. cit., XXXVIII, p. 154, Item 45), and on Nov. 24 he searched Westminster and all Middlesex for deserters from Essex°s army (CJ, II, 861b). Early in 1643, Moore, back in

Liverpool, recommends that four small ships sail for service at Lancs., and the Committee for the Navy order this on Feb. 3 (CSPD, 1641–3, p. 556). Moore was named a Lancs. sequestrator on April 1 (Moore Rental, op. cit., p. xvi). Soon Moore is searching for malefactors again in London, and on May 30 is granted a whole regiment exclusively for searching for and seizing of arms "in such places as he ... shall think fit" (CJ, III, 121a). His duties also included commanding forts and out–guards around London (Ibid., 152b). On June 9 he is ordered to search the trunks of the French ambassador (Ibid., 121a), and house–searches by him were common (Ibid., 125a–b). On June 13 one of Moore's ships, formerly captured by royalists, is returned to him by Parliament (Ibid., 127a). He fell seriously ill (Ibid., 152b, 156a–b), and on August 18 he accepted commissions as Colonel of Foot and Captain of Horse for Lancs. and left his police duties to go to Liverpool. On Nov. 12, he warned Parliament of ships about to bring rebels from Ireland, and the House responded by asking Warwick to make Moore Vice–Admiral for Lancs. and Westmorland on Nov. 22 (Ibid., 317b), which was done, and within weeks Moore has seized several enemy vessels (HMC 10th Rep. Appendix IV, p. 69, Warwick to Moore; HMC Portland MSS. I, 156, otherwise original Nalson MSS. III. 84, in the Bodleian) During this time, Moore's clerk was Adam Martindale, who has left an interesting and vivid account of tine experience (Life of Adam Martindale Written by Himself, Chetham Soc., 1845, pp. 36–41 and, p. 81). 3 Feb. 1644 Sir Thomas Fairfax wrote to Moore desiring him "that according to former letters you would take care there be a very vigilant eye had for the guarding of the seas near you & your preventing the landing of Irish who are now daily expected", and "dispersing the enemies forces in what garrisons they have in Wirral ..." (Moore MS. 920 MOO 320, Liv. Rec. Off.) In March, the citizens petitioned Fairfax for Moore to be made Governor of Liverpool (HMC 10th Rep., App. IV, p. 66). Rigby and Assheton laid siege to Lathom House, but when Assheton was ordered away, Moore rushed from his duties at Liverpool to replace him (Ibid.,pp. 71–2). Rupert's movements forced Moore back to Liverpool by the end of May (CSPD, 28 May 1644, p. 173), and his 600 men were reinforced by 300 more from Warrington by June 13 (Ibid., p. 231), but Rupert's forces totalling 12,000 – 13,000 men (Ibid., p. 257), after several repulses and a brilliant defense (CSPD, 11 June 1644), overwhelmed Liverpool and massacred 360 unarmed men (Martindale, op. cit., p. 41). Marston Moor left the Lancs. royalists exposed, and on Aug. 26 Lt.–Gen. Meldrum commenced a siege of Liverpool with inferior force. (CSPD 29 Sept. 1644), and Liverpool capitulated under Sir Robert Byron on Nov. 1 (Surrender articles printed in HMC op. cit., 95–6). The next day, Meldrum appointed Moore Governor once again, saying he was "a great lover of the cause" (CSPD, 2 Nov. 1644 3 HMC, op. cit. p. 73), confirmed by Essex by Nov. 11 (Ibid., p. 74). Meldrum said that Moore had fought extremely fiercely and "the mariners did stick to him", and "no man has been more forward, industrious, or diligent in this service (CSPD, op. cit.). Moore then immediately re–fortified Liverpool, "which, upon my reputation, has been made one of the strongest seats of war in this kingdom by Col. Moore" said Meldrum (Ibid., 4 Nov. 1644). Liverpool's Mayor and Common Council 11 Mar 1645 sought Moore's aid as MP, indicating their congenial relations (HMC, op. cit., p. 75), and officially thanked him 14 Oct. 1645 (Ibid., p. 76). Moore's Lancs. militia commissions ceased 24 July 1645 (Trans., op. cit., XXXVIII, p. 154, Item 45) and he continued to serve as MP in London, serving on many committees including that of the Admiralty (CJ, IV, 244b, 295a, 281a, 297a). On 21 July 1645, the Committee of the Navy contracted for naval use of Moore's merchant ship the "Moorcock" (named after Moore's family crest), for which Moore received £406 on 1 June 1646 (CSPD 1645–7, p. 292; HMC, op. cit., p. 79). On Nov. 22, Moore and Assheton journeyed to Lancs for six weeks, in time for the surrender of Lathom House on Dec. 4 (HMC, op. cit., p. 76; CJ, IV, 352a). Moore returned to Parliament and more committees (Ibid., 505a, 526b, 574b, 575b), hit familiar police investigation duties (Ibid,, 582b), and other work (Ibid., 595b, 603a, 612b, 613b, 617b). On July 9, the House decided to send Moore and his regiment to Ireland (Ibid., 612a).

The Lords delayed their concurrence, and only on Aug. 18 did Moore leave London (Ibid., 625b, 647a). His last act before leaving was to submit a petition on Aug. 12 to the Committee for Compounding on behalf of the hundreds of widows and orphans of Liverpool for compensation to be paid to them out of the compounding of the Lancashire royalist Lord Molineux (CCC, p. 1344). Half of Moore's regiment were shipwrecked in Dec., and only 70 men and 14 officers reached him in Ireland (Moore Rental, op. cit., p. xxxii). Moore took up headquarters at Strangford in County Down and petitioned in Feb. 1647 and again in Aug. for relief for his men (CJ, V, 95b, 282a). He was Governor of County Louth and of Dundalk, and as a Commissioner for Ireland he was named with four others to treat with Ormonde and take over his government (Firth and Davies, Regimental History of Cromwell's Army, p. 651; CSPD 27 Feb. 1647; R. Dunlop, Ireland under the Commonwealth, I, 1256). Moore had a prolonged and acrimonious quarrel with Col. Monck about this time in Ireland (HMC, op. cit., 82, 89, 90). On July 28, Moore was ordered to the relief of Trim (Ibid., p. 83), and an interesting diary survives of this campaign (Ibid., pp. 83–5), which was extraordinary in that Moore defeated the enemy and killed over 6000 of them for a loss of only two men of his own. Another military diary from October also survives (Ibid., pp. 86–88). Moore returned to England in January 1647/8, his personal and regimental finances desperate, and made many efforts to discover and obtain money from compounders (Ibid., p. 90; CJ V. 380b, 577b, 696; CCAM pp. in chronological order: 581–2, 592, 597, 632, 179, 684, 946, 839–40, 989, 529, 1046, 886, 1012, 777). Moore's Committee of Prisoners, of which he was chairman, was specially revived "to meet constantly" to dispose of the thousands of prisoners flooding the country in 1648 (CJ, V, 589a, 629a, 632b, 635a; CSPD 1648–9, pp. 110, 114, 124, 127, 139, 190, 221, 280, 294, 307, 124). Moore resumed searching rind arresting and seizing people and goods with as many soldiers as he wanted almost entirely at his own discretion, making him one of the most powerful men in England (Ibid., pp. 131–3, 136, 148, 152, 154, 156, 157, 162, 163, 166, 167, 175, 209, 211, 254, 288 – not 287 as wrongly indexed –, 325). As co–chairman of a committee to examine soldiers' accounts, Moore "had always the most tender regard (for) the poorer sort" (CCC, p. 147). In June Moore helped seize 20 royalists to force a prisoner exchange for the Essex Committee (Ibid., p. 125), in July he helped investigate the Surrey insurrection (CJ, V, 631b), and became chairman of a committee to regulate sequestered estates (Ibid., 641b, 658b, 662b), while continuing his usual duties (Ibid., VI, 34a, 57b, 60b, 67a, 72a, 87a; V, 657a, 670a, 661b, 663b, 665a, 676b, 680b, 681b, 692a; VI, 5a–b, 10a; CSPD, 26 Sept. 1648). Moore naturally survived Pride's Purge, and two of his wife's letters to him in June, 1647, tell how his friends, the MPs Giles Green and Alexander and Squire Bence, were scheming against him, and that "Your friend Green ... is your arch enemy". She adds: "But have patience, you shall see them purged, some (who) are unjust must out" (HMC, op. cit., pp. 98–9). Green and the two Bences were indeed purged, and it is tempting to think that personal information from such a guardian of public order as Moore may have tipped the scales in some cases such as these. On Dec. 13, Moore was one of the small radical group appointed to investigate the printing of a secluded members' protestation (CJ, VI, 97b) and on his own initiative Moore began seizing enemies of the Rump as he saw fit (Ibid., 103x). He was quickly added to the Committees for the Army, for Advance of Money, and for settling Courts of Justice (Ibid., 107b, 113b, 112a–b) and helped raise money and in other business (Ibid., 114b, 116a). Moore was appointed to the High Court of Justice to try the King, attended nearly all the meetings, and signed the Death Warrant. Immediately after the King's execution, Moore was called upon to investigate those "designing any evil" against the members of the court (CSPD, op. cit., pp. 352–3). He was added to Committees for delinquents, the Excise, and seditious publications (CJ, VI, 127b, 131b, 137b), and on Feb. 10 to disband the Lancs. militia and send part of it to Ireland; he is still disposing of prisoners, and joins Committees for sequestrations in South Wales and of Complaints and with two others prepares an act for adjourning Lancs. assizes and avoiding inconveniences this may bring, and to consider sales of Crown property to raise £120,000 for the forces (Ibid., 141b, 149b, 151a, 153b, 160a–b). On March 27 Moore's tender for carrying 1000 foot and 400 horse to Ireland areas was referred to the Committee for Ireland by the Council of State, as were his plans for recruiting his regiment for Ireland on April 3 (CPD, 1649–50, pp. 56, 66). He wrapped up his business in the Comnons and investigatory duties (CJ, VI, 175b, 178b – leaving a committee he joined at p. 160 –, 180b, 181b) and left London for Liverpool (CSPD, op. cit., pp. 73, 97). He returned to London in May (Ibid., p. 121) and resumes his work (CJ, VI, 201a, 202a), on May 7 reports concerning the losses of Liverpool and arranges for his town to be paid £10,000 (Ibid., pp. 203a, 207a), on June 8 is giver power to screen everyone bound for Ireland (Ibid., p. 535), then business in the House which he had been handling is referred to others (Ibid., p. 207a). On June 22 the Council of State requests of him an account of his entire career as Vice–Admiral (CSPD, op. cit., p. 203). About the end of June, Moore embarked for Ireland from Liverpool, dispatching his regiment "at his own charge" (Ibid., p. 207), in the role of one of the Comissioners for Ireland (Trans., op. cit., XXXVIII, p. 154, Item 40). Two accounts by Moore survive of the extraordinary victory of Baggotrath on Aug. 2, to Lenthall (Tanner MSS. LVI, 84, in the Bodleian) and to Whitelocke (Whitelocke MSS. X, 26–7, at Longleat), saying in the latter "I do verily believe it was the absolutest victory that ever was got in this kingdom and the least loss of our side", giving interesting details of this crucial battle which preceded Cromwell's arrival in Ireland. Cromwell soon sent Moore to England for three months to raise more men (HMC, op. cit., p. 93), and on Sept. 6 Moore was again chairing his Committee for Prisoners and receiving correspondence about it from Fairfax (Ibid., p. 94). With Venn, Scot, Ludlow, and Purefoy, Moore also helped run the Committee of the Army (Egerton MSS. 2618, f. 40), while urging his brother Robert at Liverpool to "hasten away all the soldiers" to Ireland (HMC, op. cit., p. 94). By Oct. 31 he succeeded In squeezing £500 of his considerable arrears out of Parliament (Ibid.), was equipped for returning to Ireland Nov. 3 (Ibid.), settled his regimental accounts Dec. 8 (Ibid.), and by Dec. 13 had arrived at Dublin (Perfect Diurnall, 24 Dec. 1649), of which he was made Governor (Prownbill, op. cit, p. 207, Item 1421). 3 May 1650, Moore wrote his last letter to his son from Trim asking for his grey suit, his new coat, and some biscuits (HMC, op. cit., pp. 4–5). Then he and Col. Reynolds marched to lay siege to Tecroghan Castle, a few miles north–west of Trim. It surrendered June 16, but by that time Moore had already sickened and died either of pleurisy or a fever (Moore Rental, op. cit., p. 95). Moore's son Edward notes "His burial cost me eight hundred pounds" (HMC, op. cit., p. 95). Moore's Will (op. cit.) was read in Parliament 23 July 1651 in a successful plea for posthumous arrears (CJ, VI, 608b), but never proved, possibly because the eldest son was not sufficiently favoured. Instead, this son took out letters of admin. in Nov. 1650 (PROB–6–25, p. 164, at PRO). An account of Moore in the VCH for Lancs. (IV, 19–22) is biased, misleading, and inaccurate, and even Heywood's lengthy account is frequently inaccurate, far from complete, and distinctly unfair. Moore has been ignored or maligned but never properly described; suggestions that he was grasping, incompetent, and dishonest are untrue. He was one of the most energetic, resourceful, and important of all the radicals of his lifetime, had sympathy with the poor, and bankrupted himself in the interests of his country's liberty.

Papers: LIU; Liverpool Record Office.
T. Heywood, ed., The Moore Rental, Chetham Society, Vol. XIIs(1847) HMC Tenth Report, Appendix IV, pp. 59–152 (MSS. of Capt. Stewart)
J. Brownbill and K. Walker, eds., A Calendar of ... papers of the Moore Family, Vol. LXVII, Record Society for ... Lancashire and Cheshire (1913)

R.K.G.TEMPLE

NORTON, SIR GREGORY, Bart. (b.c. 1603, d. 1652), Regicide and parliamentary radical, MP 1645 (Midhurst), was son of Henry Norton of Charlton, Wantage, Berks., and Elizabeth, 4th dau. of William Nelson of Chaldeworth, Berks. His uncle, Sir Dudley Norton, was secretary for Ireland under Elizabeth. His great–great–grandfather Sir Anthony St. Leger (d. 1559) had also been Lord Deputy for Ireland. And his third cousin Sir William St. Leger (d. 1642) was MP, Privy Councillor, and President of Munster. These many Irish connections would explain why the Regicide, when he was created a baronet on 27 April 1624, aged about 21, was made a Baronet of Ireland. Norton had an only brother, Horden, who died young prior to 1623. (Visit. Berks. 1623; Middlesex Pedigrees; Harl. Soc. Vol. 65, 114–6; Complete Baronetage, I, 257–8; Ashmole MSS. 852, 278–9 in Bodleian; Harleian MS. 1551, f. 79.) Norton married Martha, dau. of Bradshaw Drew, Esq., of Densworth in Sussex. After his death she remarried Robert Gordon, 4th Viscount Kenmure, at St. Paul's, Covent Garden, 20 Oct. 1655. Kenmure died 1663; she died 1671. Norton had two sons and a daughter, Elizabeth, b.c. 1621. The elder son, Gregory, b.c. 1623, matric. Jesus College, Cambridge, 1638, and d. 1652 before his father. The younger son Henry thus became the 2nd Baronet. The baronetcy is only presumed to be extinct.

Norton was admitted to Gray's Inn 3 Aug. 1629, contemporary with John Alured and John Bradshaw the Regicides as well as John Cook who was to prosecute the King and his younger brother James Cook. At time of his admission he was of Hampden, Bucks., and was still there 15 Nov. 1640 (CCC, 2363), making him a near neighbour of Adrian Scrope the Regicide. He then became JP in West Sussex in 1640, when he was living at West Thorney near Chichester; he continued to be a JP there until his death. In 1639 Norton received a demand from the King that he provide money for the expedition against Scotland (CSPD, 1639, p. 83). In mid–1644 he was assessed for £500 (CCAM, 404). Norton was elected as recruiter MP in 1645 for Midhurst in Sussex, the other MP for which was William Cawley the Regicide. They seem to have coordinated their activities (Tanner MSS., 59/2, 665). On July 24, 1645, Norton was added to his first parliamentary committee (CJ, IV, 212a; LJ, VII, 504) with Humphrey Edwardes the Regicide, who was to become his most intimate friend and, because Norton disinherited his son, his heir (P.C.C. Wills, Prob–11–223, p. 203). Norton was in high favour quite soon, for on Sept. 20 he was ordered to be given £1000 and Sir Roger Palmer's sequestered house at Charing Cross for his residence (CCC, 25). The money did not all materialize (CCC, 1715–6), so a year and a half later, Norton reported a concealment in compounding by the royalist Sir Henry Hastings, from the resultant confiscation of which Norton finally got the rest of his £1000 (ibid., 1760). He apparently overdid it, however, for six years later his widow was ordered to repay £516 excess which he received (CCAM, 1122–3). A few days after Pride's Purge, Norton begins to appear on crucial committees of the Rump with other hardcore radicals, suppressing critical publications, and with four other regicides he joins the Commission of Revenue to consider the custody and conditions of the King (CJ, VI, 96b, 97b, 98a). He is then added to the Commissioners of Compounding (ibid., 99a). Norton was named to the High Court of Justice to try the King, attended nearly all the sittings, and signed the Death Warrant. He afterwards received Richmond Palace for himself as well as much of the Kings furniture (Noble, II, 102). He was appointed to a number of further committees (CJ, VI, 127b, 168b, 171a, 178b, 180a, 352a, 363b). However, he died early and was buried 26 Mar. 1652 at Richmond, Surrey. His disinherited son, Sir Henry, managed to achieve a reconciliation with his mother (C35/20/79, in PRO) by 1655, and married Mabella, daughter of Sir Richard Norton, Bart., 14 Oct. 1656 at St. Margaret's, Westminster (it is unknown if she was a relation).

THE PUREFOY FAMILY

Monumental Inscriptions from the interior
of Caldecote Church in Warwickshire:

On the wall at the rear of the church are two memorial plaques with arms and crest:

On left:
MICHAEL PUREFAY
VIXIT ANOS 73. MESES 4 DIES 8
OBIIT 22 IULII ANNO DNI. 1570.
(Surmounted with Purefoy crest
and uncoloured quartered arms.)

On right:
IOCOSA PUREFAY
VIXIT ANOS blank MESES blank DIES blank
OBIIT 6 MAR ANNO DNI. 1585.
(Surmounted with crest of a stag and
uncoloured quartered arms.)

To the left of the altar is a dual monument erected in 1617 by the regicide William Purefoy to his father and grandfather and which features two kneeling effigies – Francis and William, with their arms (not Azure, three stirrups or, but rather Sable three pairs of clasped hands argent) and crest (a hand dexter clasping a …… sable), and also their arms with those of their spouses (one being Ermine a double chevron, below gules, above azure with three 5–pointed stars argent, and the other being Azure a chevron argent inter three roundles argent). The former Purefoy arms show a crescent in field for difference. The inscriptions are as follows:

FRANCIS PUREFEY SONE OF
WILLM & CATHERINE MARRIED
ELEANOR DAUGHR OF IOHN
BASKERVILLE OF CURDWORTH IN
YE COUNTIE OF WAR, ESQr &
HAD ISSV BY HER 6 SONS
& 4 DAUGHR HE LIVED 49
YEARES & DIED Ye 27 OF
APRILL 1613.

WILLM PUREFEY SoNE OF MICHAEL
& JOYCE MARRIED CATHERIN DAUGHR
OF SR WILLM WIGSTON OF WOOLSTON
IN Ye COUNTIE OF WARWICK KNI: &
HAD ISSV BY HER 6 SONS & 5
DAUGR HE LIVED 88 YEARES &
DIED Ye I OF SEPR 1615.

GVLIELMVS PVREFEY
FILIVS PDICTI FRAN
CISCI & ELIANO HOC
FIERI FECIT. 1617.

To the right of the altar are these inscriptions, surmounted by a kneeling praying effigy (the sword at his side broken both ends when seen in 1977). Arms at the top show Purefoy quartered Azure three stirrups argent with Sable three pairs of clasped hands argent, on one side, and various quarterings on the other side (the left–and right shields differ).

MICHAEL PVRLFEY ON
LY SONN 0 F THOMAS
WHO WAS 4th SON OF MI
CHAEL PVREFEY & IOYCE
HE LIVED A BACHELOR
65 YEARES & SO DIED YE
23 OF AUGUST 1627.

GAMALIEL PVREFEY ONLY
S ONN OF GEORGE THE 5
SONN OF MICHAEL AND
IOYCE EXECUTOR AND
COSEN GERMAN TO
THIS MICHAEL PVREFEY
CAUSED THIS TO BE MADE
IN MEMORIE OF HIM. 1629.

Behind the right choir stall in Caldecote Church is a monument to GEORGE ABBOTT the son–in–law of William Purefoy the regicide which says underneath:

THIS MONUMENT WAS ERECTED TO HIS MEMORIE BY HIS DEARE MOTHER & EXECUTRIX IOHANE PUREFOY THE WIFE OF COLONELL WILLIAM PUREFOY HIS BELOVED FATHER IN LAW THE 28 DAY OF AUGUST, ANNO DOMIN1, 1649.

The text of the actual monument itself is as follows:

HERE LIETH THE BODY OF GEORGE ABBOT LATE OF CALLDECOATE IN WARWICK SHIRE ESQr. WHOSE EMINENT PARTES, VERTUS, & GRACES, DRAWNE FORTH TO USE (?) IN HIS EXEMPLARIE WALKING WTH GOD HIS TENDERNESS TO ALL THE MEMBERS OF CHRIST, WHO FREQUENTLY FLED TO HIS CHARITY IN THEIR WANTS, & COUNSEIL IN CASES OF CONSCIENCE. HIS EXACT OBSERVATION OF THE SABBATH WCH HE VINDICATED BY HIS PEN, AND ON WCH AUG 21, 1642 GOD HONOURED HIM IN THE MEMORABLE & UNPARALELED DEFENCE OF THIS ADIUYNING HOUSE WTH 8 MEN (BESIDES HIS MOTHER AND HER MAIDES) AGAINST THE FURIOUS AND FIERIE ASSAULT OF PRINCE RUPERT & MAURICE WTH 18 TROOPES OF HORSE & DRAGOONS. HIS PERSPICUOUS PARAPHRASE ON THE BOOK OF IOB AND PSALMES HIS IUDICIOUS TRACTS OF PUBLICKE AFFAIRES THEN EMERGENT HIS KNOWNE INTEGRITIE IN PUBLICKE INPLOYMENTS RENDRED HIM ONE OF A THOUSAND FOR SINGULAR PIETY WISDOM LEARNING CHARITY COURAGE & FIDELITIE TO HIS COUNTRY WCH HE SERVED IN TWO PARLIAMENTS THE FORMER AND THIS PRESENT WHEREOF HE DIED A MEMBER FEBRU: THE 21TH 1648 [1649] IN THE 44TH YEARE OF HIS AGE.

This inscription is surmounted by no effigy, but by various arms.

ROWE (or ROE), OWEN (b.c. 1593, d. 1661), Civil War officer and Regicide, was son of John Rowe who in 1609 was of Bickley, Cheshire, but no relation to the Rowes of Macclesfield, Cheshire, as has been suggested (Herald and Genealogist, II, 61–3, 156–7), for Rowe's seal perfectly preserved on the Death Warrant of Hamilton, Goring, Capel, et. al. (6 Mar. 1649, House of Lords Library), as well as his tricked arms (Rawlinson MSS. B. 48., f. 29b) leave no doubt of his relation instead to the Rowes who were Lord Mayors of London in 1568, 1592, and 1607 (Visit. Cheshire, 1663, pp. 95–6; Visit. Midds. 1663, 30; Middlesex Pedigrees, ed. Armytage, 8, 46). Rowe's father was possibly the John Roe who 28 Nov. 1637 petitioned the King against fraudulent practices in the wool trade (CSPD, 1637, 571). Rowe's father bound himself for £100 to Edward Pickering 11 Aug. 1609 to put Rowe to apprentice for the Haberdashers' Company (MS. 15,860/3, Guildhall Library), and Rowe eventually became a liveryman of the Haberdashers (Rev. T.C.C.Dale, Members of the City Companies in 1641, typescript in the Institute of Historical Research, London), a silk merchant, was on the Common Council before 1638, and was a prominent resident of Coleman Street in the City, where, with Isaac Pennington, he was a leading parishioner of St. Stephen's and member of its committee to select communicants (Archaeologia, L, 23, 25). By the mid–1630s Rowe had a share in the Massachusetts Bay Company, owned a house, town lot, and cattle in Boston, as well as property at New Haven and 200 acres of farmland in Massachusetts, and had the intention of settling there (John Winthrop, Journal, 1853 ed., I, 475). He even had sent his eldest son Nathaniel to America in 1635 ahead of him. In 1630, acting as agent with John Alcock for the Bermudas Company, Rowe sold 700 lbs. of tobacco in London (J.H. Lefroy, Memorials of the ... Bermudas, I, 515), both of them becoming by Oct. 13, 1644, members of the Company's governing board (ibid., 590), and then Rowe became Deputy Governor of the Company, an office he lost in 1647 (ibid., 623, 702) but regained again in 1655 and held until the Restoration (ibid., 675; II, 65, 87, 128, 285). Rowe's colleagues on the board included the Earl of Warwick and the radicals Cornelius Holland, Lord Say and Seale, Francis Allen, and Sir John Danvers the Regicide (who was Governor in 1651: ibid., II, 20). Isaac Rowe, a "kinsman" mentioned in Rowe's brother's will (PCC Wills, Prob–11–211, pp. 209–10), was on the board by 1653 (ibid., I, 675; II, 58, 61). Rowe was always dynamic and active in his concerns, and his Bermudas interests were no exception (CSPD, 1651, 454–5; Lefroy, op. cit. II, 23–4, 42, 84–5), and he tried to restrain the royalists in those colonies (Ibid., II, 87–8). His lands and property there were confiscated at the Restoration along with those of Holland and Danvers (ibid., II, 56–7, 164–5, 655–6, 679).

From the time he was a young man, Rowe was attracted to military affairs. He became a Lieutenant of the City's Hon. Artillery Company 26 Oct. 1619 (G. A, Raikes, Ancient Vellum Book, p. 31). He later became Captain and then by 3 May 1642 (not 1643 as in the old DNB and Valerie Pearl, London and the ... Puritan Revolution, p. 324) was Serjeant–Major of the City's 5th (Green) Regiment under Alderman Col. John Warner, with his brother Francis Rowe as 2nd Captain under him (Rawlinson MSS. op. cit, f. 25a). By Dec. 31, 1642, he was a Lieutenant–Colonel (CCAM, 7) in charge of the City's arms and ammunition magazine at the Tower. The Houses authorized Rowe to spend £5000 to buy arms for Parliament 6 Sept. 1643 (CSPD, 1641–3, 484; LJ, VI, 207). He became the central arms administrator for Parliament under the command of Essex (CSPD, 1644, 25) and had under him the officers of the ordnance (Ibid., 92). Rowe continued in this role until at least July, 1645 (CCAM, 368, 1495–6; CSPD, 1625–49 Addenda Vol., 661; 1644, 169–70, 302–3, 422, 425, 476, 508; 1644–5, 7, 28, 164, 230, 244, 259, 323, 348, 605), during which time he was the acknowledged expert in the country for judging the condition of arms (a crucial matter at a time when entire shipments of hundreds of muskets or firelocks were sometimes found worthless or faulty just prior to a battle), and supplied thousands of arms of every variety, even dealing with arrowheads, to troops all over the country, inspected and loaded arms into the ships for Ireland, and was responsible for organizing his own shipments and deliveries inland. This argues an incredible degree of efficiency and reliability in Rowe, of whom no complaints seem to have been made in his most exacting job. The City then chose Rowe to go as a Commissioner to Ireland, which the House approved 18 Aug. 1645 (CJ, IV, 245b). By 1646 he was back in England and was commissioned Colonel of the City's Green Regiment (Rawlinson MS., op. cit., f. 29b) and 7 Aug. 1646 he was granted by Parliament £2000 "for his long and faithful service" (CCC, 43; CJ, IV, 607a), but only after he had petitioned for some payment. Parliament appointed Rowe 23 July 1647 one of the Committee for the Militia of London, with his old associates Pennington, Warner, and Allen, and with Robert Titchborne the Regicide and others (Rushworth, VI, 634). Rowe and his brother Francis were now in desperate financial straits due to their not receiving their wages for many years, and 4 March 1648 they petitioned the House for £6,457 owing to Owen from the state, to keep them both from debtors' prison for Francis's debts to which Owen also stood surety (HMC 7th Report, App., p. 13; LJ X, 90), £200 of which was owing to their brother–in–law Thomas Salmon, who had been suing Francis for 2 years and 12 April 1648 petitioned the Lords about it (HMC Rep., op. cit., p. 19b; full document in the House of Lords Library). Francis was by now Scoutmaster–General of the New Model Army; but he died in Dec. 1649 at Youghall in Ireland (HMC Rep., op. cit., 73–4) and in his will (op. cit.) named Owen as his executor, and Owen proved it in London 5 Feb. 1650.

Rowe was named to the High Court of Justice to try the King, attended nearly all its meetings, and signed the Death Warrant. Rowe also signed the Death Warrant 6 March 1649 of Hamilton and others (op. cit, and HMC Report, op. cit., 71). For the conflict with the Scots, the City raised a single regiment of horse as a militia force, and Rowe was its Colonel; it was finally ordered disbanded 17 Sept. 1651 (CSPD, 1651, 436), presumably having seen service in the North under the general command of Harrison (Samuel Gardiner, HCP, I, 298, 407). Rowe was named 16 Oct. 1651 to the commission for court martial of twenty

English prisoners (CSPD, 1651, 479; Gardiner, op. cit, I, 466–7). Rowe had been appointed to a committee to attend the Council of State regarding officers' pay (ironical, since he rarely if ever received his own), and was summoned in this duty again 30 Dec. 1651 (CSPD, 1651–2, 84). In company with Major William Robinson 19 Oct. 1652, Rowe made a remarkable bid to take over the inland and foreign letter offices, and offered £10,000 cash for control of all postal services, submitting a detailed proposal to the Council of State listing charges of all routes (Egerton MSS. 1048, ff. 158–9). A committee of the Council of State which included Vane and Hazlerigg flavoured Rowe's proposal and submitted it to the full Council, but the House had other plans for the postal services, and after six months with no decision, Robinson withdrew the proposal (CSPD, 1652–3, 108–11). Rowe was appointed 8 June 1653 to a position at the Customs House (CSPD, 1652–3, 393, 478). As a commissioner of oyer and terminer he was summoned to the Old Bailey 17 Aug. 1653 (CSPD, 1653–4, 92). He was a trustee for the sale of Deans' and Chapters lands and on Mar. 2, 1654, he, Titchborne, and others, as such made difficulties for Cromwell over the Protector's order for settling some lands (CSPD, 1654, 4). Charles Fleetwood and the regicides John Jones and Miles Corbet tried 8 July 1654 to persuade Cromwell to allow Parliament's grant of lands in Ireland to Rowe (CJ, VII, 317a) to go through in satisfaction of the long–standing public debt to him of £5065 (Rawlinson MSS. A. 16. ff. 115–6). Rowe was appointed 25 Mar. 1656 a Commissioner for the Peace in London under the Mayor, Skippon, and Barkstead (CSPD, 1655–6, 238). But Barkstead's true feelings about Rowe were well expressed in a letter to Thurloe 12 Aug. 1656, where he names him, Titchborne, Bradshaw, and others as being, according to a spy of his, conspirators against the Protectorate, although he takes care to cover himself by saying, that some of them may be being used unknowingly (Thurloe, SP, V, 304). In 1659, again commanding his Green Regiment, Rowe opposed Monck (Valerie Pearl, op. cit., p. 324). Rowe married three times and had many children (Herald and Genealogist, op. cit.) and his brother married the daughter of Thomas Scot the Regicide; Sir Nicholas Crisp, Bart., the royalist, was Rowe's brother–in–law by his 3rd wife. At the Restoration, Rowe was tried and imprisoned, died in the Tower 25 Dec. 1661, and was buried on Dec. 27 at St. John's Shacklewell, Hackney, the traditional burial place for the Rowes (William Robinson, History and Antiquities of ..,. Hackney, II, 8–11, 17, 28, foldouts etc.)

R.K.G.TEMPLE

PETITION OF THE FATHER
OF JAMES TEMPLE
ABOUT THE CONDITION OF
TILBURY FORT (1629)

Public Record Office: S.P. 16/ 530 122
Calendared CSPD
Addenda 1623 –49, p. 361.

To the right honoble the Lordes and others of his Mats most honoble Privey Counsell.

The humble peticon of Sr Alexander Temple knight Captaine of his Mats fforte of Tilburie in the countie of Essex, and John Smyth Captaine of his Mats fforte of Milton nere Gravesend in the Countie of Kente.

Humbly sheweth, That whereas the said fortes of Tilbury and Milton are in great ruyne and decaie for want of reperacons, as for lacke of Barapitts [parapets], Pallasadoes, Platformes Gates and watch–houses for places of rest for the Gunners and other Officers, whereby they daylie endewer a greate deale of hardnes, the said fforts beinge altogether open and uncovered, neither are they fitt for any serviceable use; but that the decayes thereof lye open to the view of all nacons comeinge that waie, And that the petrs have for the space of theis 12. yeares bene humble Sutors for repairinge the same; but as yett there noe amendment made;

And whereas also yor petrs wth 10 Gunners and 2 Porters servinge under them in the said fforts are behinde and in arrere of their paie and entertaynement the some of 824 l [£824] or thereabouts ended at Christmas last; by want whereof the said Officers are growne very poore, theire wives, children and families being readie to perishe And forasmuch as the necessitie of their service is such in theis stirringe times, that they are forced to watch day and nighte; And for that the petrs have wasted a farre greater some of money then their entertaynment cometh unto in dayly sollicitacon as well for repreacons to be made in the said forts, as for the payment of theire Allowances, but cannot as yett obteyne the same.

Their humble suite therefore is; That yor good Lpps will take the same into yor honoble Consideracons, And to be pleased to give some present order for the speedie repairinge of the said fforts wth needfull and necessarie reparacons As also to vouchsafe to grant them some settled order for the paymt of their said entertaynements so longe arrere and behinde, out of the Loane moneys wch are to be collected wthin each of the said counties, or otherwise, as yor Lpps shall thinke fitt, whereby the petrs and the other officers may be enabled to performe his Mats due service, as also to preserve their wives Children and families for pishinge, wch otherwise they are in greate hassard to susteyne; And forasmuch as in former times of warre; the said fforts have bene strengthened wth supplies of men out of each County wch by occasion of peace hath of late bene discontynued; And now in regard of the hostilitie of these tymes it were requisite a speciall care were had The petrs humbly offer the same unto yor Lpps grave consideracons and direccons. And will ever pray etc.

LETTER DESCRIBING THE APPREHENDING OF JAMES TEMPLE (1660)

House of Lords Record Office:
Main Papers, June 18, 1660
Calendared: HMC 7th Report, p. l0la.
(Addressee unknown)

Honoble Sr

Notice being given unto me on Wednesdaie night last, that there was a suspitious person in the house of one Humfrey Hale of Stivichall in the countie of this Citie of Coventry I acquainted one Mr Snell one other of the Aldermen of Coventry therewth, and wee being Justices of the peace of the Citie and county of Coventry did take one of the Sheriffs of the Citie and Lieutenant Thomas King, and some others wth us; and repaired to the house of the said Hale and begirting the house, wee found there a gentleman (unknowne to us) and demanding of him his name, and whether he was going answeared that his name was Busbridg, and that he was for Ireland, saying he was kyn to Mr Temple of ffranckton in the countie of Warwick, and desired that he might go to Mr Temple who would satisfie us what he was, whereupon wee sent him wth Lieutenant King to ffranckton, Mr Temple of ffranckton being at London, Mrs Temple said she did not know this gentleman, but said one Busbridg did marry one of her husbands sisters, so the gentleman was brought to us at Coventry, and wee committed him to the Sheriffe, and wee not having anie matter against him, were put to it what to do with him. But yesterdaie upon our farther examining of him, at length. he confessed that his name is James Temple, and that he was a Parliament man, and was one of them that were the late Kings Judges.

All which I make bould and thought it my dutie to Certifie unto your honor, and that this James Temple is still in the custodie of the Sheriffs of Coventry to be ordered as the Kings Matie shall appoint. Thus wth my bounden dutie, remembred to yo r honor I humbly take leave and remaine

Sr Your honors humble servant

Coventry this 16th of June   HENRY SMITH
                                  1660

(NOTE:. Mrs. Temple of Frankton knew very well who James Temple was, but lacked the courage to back up his story. This must have so disheartened him that he ended up confessing his true identity. Discussion of the relation between James Temple and the Temples of Frankton is given in the main text, along with an explanation of why James Temple used the name of Busbridge.)

TWO ORDERS IN CHANCERY CONCERNING JAMES TEMPLE, CAREW SAUNDERS, AND EDWARD WHALLEY (1633)

Essex County Record Office:
D/DRU Acc. 183; T1 (234) and (235)

ORDER OF JUNE 5, 1633

Mercurij quint die Junij Anno Regni Caroli Re nono
Inter Jacobo Ravenscroft Ar Quert
Jacobo Temple Carew Saunders et Edw Whalley gen defendts/

fforasmuch as the right honoble the Lord Keeper was this prsent day informed by Mr Moreton being of the plts Counsell That the defendts Temple & Saunders having in December 1630 sould unto Thomas Ravenscroft the plts ffather a Parke and Certaine lands in Essex and having drawne him to give the greater prise for the same uppon agreement that they would take back a Lease thereof

for 10 yeares at the Rent of 340 pound wch they did accordingly and gave bonds of a great penalty for payment of the said Rent and pformance of the Covennts in the said Lease, Since wch tyme the plts ffather being dead and the prmisses descended to the pltf the said defendts Temple & Saunders break their Covennts & Bonds And the said Saunders being become a Bankrupt and the said Temple utterly declyned in his estate have made a fraudulent assignment of the said Lease to the defendt Whalley their kinsman – & agents & the said defdts by Confederacye amongst themselves have destroyed the Parke & the deere therein and the Warren uppon the prmisses and have ploughed upp the said Parke being 300 Acres whereas by their Covennt in the said Lease they are to ploughe onely 200 Acres & no more & have also ploughed upp diverse Marsh grounds wch have been allwayes used for meadowe & pasture and doe Continue to plough up the said ground and to Comitt waste and spoyles upon the prmisses, ffor releife wherein the pltfe having exhibited his Bill in to this Crt the defendte Whalley hath put in a frivolous plea and demurred thereunto. It is therefore ordered That an Iniuncon bee rewarded against the said defendts their Srvants agents workemen and Assignes to forebeare to ploughe up any of the grounds in the said Parke or any of the said Marsh grounds or to fell any Tymber trees growing uppon or cawsing any further waste upon the prmisses untill the said defendts have dyrectly answered the plts bill & this Crt taken other order to the Contrary And Sr Edward Clarke Knight, one of the Mrs of this Crt shall Consider of the said plts bill & the said ple & demural & thereuppon report to this Crt whether the said plea and demurral be such & put in uppon good ground or not yf not then a Spa [subpoena] is awarded against the said defendt to make a dyrecte & plein Answere to the plts Bill./ (SIGNED etc.)

NOTES: There was probably both political and religious basis to the obvious enmity here. As may be seen from CCAM, p. 599, James Ravenscroft was a fanatical Roman Catholic who gave people crucifixes and persuaded women to become nuns: He can hardly have been congenial to the Puritans Temple and Whalley!

ORDER OF JUNE 7, 1633

Whereby an Order of the fifthe of this moneth an Iniuncon was awarded againste the Defendts theire servants and agents workemen and assignes to forebeare to plowe upp any of the grounds in the Parke or any of the Marshe ground or to fell any tymber trees groweing & or cawsinge any further waste uppon the prmisses untill the Defendts should have answered ye other Order to the contrary uppon aproveing of the matter this presente daye before the righte honoble the Lord Keep by Mr Madison beinge of the Defendts Counsell It was alleadged that the Defendt Temple doth disclaime to have any Intereste in the demised landes and the Defendte Whalley by answeare sett forth that hee holdeth the same withoute any Truste and that hee Inioyeth the same for his owne benefitt and touchinge the Parke grounds the same are newely imparked and hath beene all plowed wthin these seaventeene yeares and other persons have some grounds dispsed intermixt in the parke & grounds and by the Covinante of the lease the Defendte Whalley hath liberty to plowe 200 acres of the parke and that as hee hath plowed as yet but 150 acres of the Parke and there beinge aboute 9 score acres of Marshe grounds hee hath plowed onely 32 acres And by the instance of the County it is conceived to bee a poynt of good husbandry and beneficiall as well for the Lanlord as tennante to plowe upp such grounds besides the Defendte by his lease oughte to have necessarie books (?) Whereuppon it is thought meete and Ordered that the defendts shall accordingly wthoute offence to the Iniuncon take necessarie books (?) accordinge to his lease but yf hee take more hee will then be in contempt neyther is this Defendt to plowe upp any more of the Marshe grounds then is allready plowed untill the Defendte canne showe better matter towards this Courte thereunto and as touchinge the other grounds in the Parke his Lordshipp beleaves the Defendte att libertie to plowe upp soe much as by the Covinante of his lease is allowed but noe further and in respecte the Defendte Temple hath disclaymed as aforesaid It is Ordered that the said Temple shall bee examined as a witnesse in this Cause unlesse cause bee showed to the Contrary by this daye fortnighte And whereas by the former Order the consideracon of the Defendts plea and demurrer stands referred to Sr Edward Clarke knighte one of the Mrs of this Courte and the Defendte hath worded his plea and demurrer and answered It is Ordered that the said referrence bee discharged but the Defendte in respecte thereof shall paye unto the plte such costs as the sixe Clarks not towards their Cause shall thinke fitt to assesse./

(SIGNED differently than the preceding order.)

SALE OF A LEASE BY JAMES
TEMPLE THE REGICIDE
TO HIS KINSMAN EDWARD
WHALLEY THE REGICIDE
(1632)

Essex County Record Office:
D/DRU TI/ 233
(Indenture of September 1, 1632)

THIS INDENTURE MADE the firste daie of September Anno dni 1632 And in the eight yeare of the raigne of or Soveraigne Lord Charles by the grace of God kinge of England Scotland ffrance and Ireland defender of the ffayth,etc:

Betweene James Temple of Lincolnes Inne in the County of Midds Esquire and Carewe Saunders of London Merchant of the one ptie And Edward Whalley of Chadwell in the County of Essex Gentleman of the other ptie. WITNESSETH That Whereas Thomas Ravenscrofte of London Esquire by an Indenture of Lease under his hand and seale bearing date the Three and Twentith day of December In the Sixth yeare of the raigne of our said Soveraigne Lord Charles the kings Majestie that nowe is of England & ffor the Consideracon therein mensoned did betake to farme lett and sell unto the said James Temple and Carewe Saunders ALL that his Capitall Messuage Tenment and ffarme Called or knowne by the name of Longehouse place with the appurtenances lying and being in Chadwell in the County of Essex And all those his severall Messuages Tenements and ffarmes with their appurtenncs Called Sleepers Cowpers and Longehousewick And all his severall Moyetyes of the Manner of Barrow als Barrowe Hall with the Appurtenncs in the said County of Essex And alsoe all that his Parke and inclosed grownd Called Chadwell Parke or by what other name the same be called lying and being in the townes parrishes or hamletts of Chadwell Orsett and little Thorocke or any of them in the said County of Essex And all other the lands Tenements and hereditaments of him the said Thomas Ravenscroft in Chadwell Orsett little Thorrocke or elsewhere in the said County of Essex Together with all buildings outhowse Barnes stables Orchards Gardens Wayes easments Comons Waters ffishings liberties ffree Warren priveledges profitts emoluments advantages and hereditaments with their appurtenncs to the said Messuages lands and prmises and every or any of them belonging or appertayning or accepted taken occupied used or enioyed as pte pcell or member thereof, Excepte as in and by the said recited Indenture of Lease mensoned to be excepted. TO HAVE AND TO HOLD all the said Messuages lands Tents hereditaments and other the premises with their appurtenncs, excepte as is before mensoned to be excepted, unto the said James Temple and Carewe Saunders their executors and assignes ffrom the ffeast day of St Michaell the Archangell last past before the date of the same Indenture of Lease unto the end and Tearme of Tenne yeares ffrom thence next ensuying and ffully to be Compleate and ended. YEILDING AND PAYING therefore yearly during the said Tearme unto the said Thomas Ravenscroft his heires and assignes the yearly rent of Three hunded and fforty poundes of good and lawfull money of England att the ffeast dayes of Thannunciason of or Blessed Lady St Mary the virgin and St Michaell the Archangell by even and equall porcons To be paid att or within the nowe dwelling howse of the said Thomas Ravenscroft situate in ffenter lane in the suburbs of the City of London And alsoe yeilding and paying unto the said Thomas Ravenscrofte his heires and assignes one ffatt Bucke and one ffatt doe of either season To be delivered at the place of payment aforesaid yearely during the said Tearme or Within the space of Eight dayes nexte after demannd As by the said recited Indenture of Lease amongst divers Covennts grannts clauses articles and agreements therein Conteyned whereunto due relacon for more certainty being had more plainly and at large it doth& may appeare.

NOWE THIS INDENTURE ffurther Witnesseth That the said James Temple and Carewe Saunders for divers good Causes and Consideracons them thereunto especiallie moving and more especiallie ffor that the said James Temple and Carewe Saunders have fformerly lett all the premisses before recited, unto the said Edward Whalley ffor the whole Tearme aforesaid upon the Condicons hereafter expressed by lease poll HAVE grannted bargained sold aliened assigned sett over and Transferred And by theis prsents doe fully Cleerly and absolutly grannt bargaine sell alieme assigne sell over and Transferre unto the said Edward Whalley as well the said recited Indenture of Lease and all and singular the premises thereby letten or meant menconed or intended to be thereby letten and every parte and pcell thereof with their and every of their appurtenncs and all Writtings Counterpts of Leases and meane Conveyances thereupon made and all rents yssues and yearly and other profitts Whatsoever referred or arising out of upon or by all every or any Leasor Leases demise or demises grannt or grannts Whatsoever heeretofore made of the prmises aforesaid or of any pte or pcell thereof As alsoe all the right Estate title interest terme of yeares to Come possession revercon use benefit propertie Clayme and demand whatsoever of them the said James Temple and Carewe Saunders or either of them of in and to the same by fforce and virtue of the said recited Indenture of Lease or by any other waies or meanes Whatsoever TO HAVE HOLD and enioy all and singular the prmises before by their prsents grannted bargained sold aliened assigned sett over and Transferred or meant menconed or intended to be hereby grannted bargained sold aliened assigned sett over and Transferred and everie pte and pcell thereof with their and everie of their appurtenncs unto the said Edward Whalley his executors administrators and assignes ffrom the daie of the date of theis pnts fforthwards ffor during and untill all the rest and residue yett to come and unexpired of the said Tearme of Tenne yeares of and by the said recitedIndenture of Lease grannted or lymitted be ffully Compleate and ended In as large ample and beneficiall manner and forme to all intents purposes and Construcsons as they the said James Temple and Carewe Saunders or either of them nowe have or hath or as they their executors or administrators or any of them may might Could should or of right ought to have hold or enioy the same by fforce & virtue of the said recited Indenture of Lease by any waies or meanes howsoever AND THE SAID Edward Whalley for himselfe his executors and administrators and ffor every of them doth Co'vennt pmise & grannt to & with the said James Temple and Carewe Saunders & either of them their and either of their executors and administrators & to & wth evrie of them by theis pnts That he the said Edward Whalley his executors administrators or assignes shall & will from tyme to tyme and att all tymes hereafter for and during the the residue yett to come and unexpired of the said Tearme of yeares in and by the said recited Indenture of Lease grannted or lymitted well and trulye pay and pforme All and evrie the rents payments duties and Covennts in and by the said recited Indenture of Lease reserved & menconed wch from henceforth shall growe due to be paid done and pformed on the Leasees or Tennts pte and behalfe for and in respect of the prmisses thereby letten And Thereof shall and will ffrom tyme to tyme And att all tymes hereafter Cleerly acquite defend discharge & well & sufficiently save and keepe harmelesse the said James Temple & Carewe Sounders & either of them their and either of theire executors & administrators and everie of them of and ffrom all & all manner of Actions suites distresses Coste Charge damages troubles molestacons encumbrances demands Whatsoever which shall or may att any tyme or tymes heereafter arise happen growe or be for touching or in any wise Concerning the same or any of them or any pte or pcell thereof. IN WITNES whereof the pties aforesaid have to theis pnts under Inferchangeably sett their hands and seales the day and yeare ffirst above written 1632

JAMES TEMPLE   CAREWE SAUNDERS

Sealed and delivered in the prnce of

THO: NELSON
HEN: WHALLEY

NOTES: Carew Saunders and James Temple were first cousins. Henry Whalley was the brother of Edward Whalley. Thomas Nelson was probably of the family of Nelsons who intermarried with the Temples somewhat later on. (The details of the Nelson–Temple relations are of no concern in this context and are not necessary to explain). It is to be noted that James Temple, who had been admitted to Lincoln's Inn in November, 1622, by 1632 had chambers there and was evidently practising as a lawyer. It is to be assumed that the preceding document was drawn up by him (after all, why hire another lawyer if he were one himself?); in this connection, it is worth noting that this document is rather more pedantic and fulsome than most indentures, and seems to indicate that he had a meticulous and scrupulous sense of fine detail. Document 225 in this series at the Essex Record Office shows that James Temple was practising and based at chambers at Lincoln's Inn as early as December 20, 1630, neatly two years earlier. In document 226 in the series, dated December 20, 1630, Henry Whalley, who above is a witness, was an actual party to a conveyance to Thomas Ravenscroft in company with James Temple, Carew Saunders, James Temple's mother, Sir Nicholas Crespe the trading magnate, and two others. Henry Whalley was trained in the law too, since in the 1650s he became Judge Advocate.

TWO LETTERS OF PETER TEMPLE AS A YOUNG MAN TO HIS DISTANT COUSIN SIR PETER TEMPLE, BART.

Huntington Library in California:
Stowe MSS. STT 2026

To the Right Honll and my Very Lovinge Cosen
Sr Peter Temple at Mr.................Brittons house
In drury lane These bee dd [delivered]

Lond[on]

Sr
Pleas my Service Remember, these are to intreat you to beare wth mee for the xx l [£20] that is now dew to you from mee if Conveniently you may halfe a yeare Longer for trewly mony is very Sparse wth mee yet But then I hope I shal be better provided; and in soe doinge I shal thinke my selfe more bound unto you for your Loane; And Conserninge our Armes I Cannot yet find out any that Cann give mee any light in them but I will still enquier about them, thus intreatinge you to let mee heare a word or two from you about the mony hoping that you are in good health I leave you to the safe protexion of the Allmyghty & dooe ever Rest

Temple Hall this
ixth of March 1621

Your Poore yet Lovinge
Kinsman to Command

PET: TEMPLE

Huntington Library:
Stowe MSS. STT 2027

Sr
I am very Sory that I have bin soe ill a debtor unto you as to keepe you soe longe about your monny, but Verrely Sr I was anie severall times at your lodggings to have payd it unto you but you weare not wthin; but upon Thursday next I doe propose to be in London and then will I Repaire to your Lodggings and will give you satesfaction; Thus my Service beinge Remembered unto you beinge glad to heare that you are in good health I leave you to god Restinge

Isselworth [isleworth] this
prsent Tewsday. 1624

Your poor yet Lovinge
Kinsman to Command
PET: TEMPLE

(NOTES: Peter Temple, later the regicide, was born in October, 1600, so at the times when he wrote the above letters he was 21 and 23/24 respectively. His father had died in 1619, and an older brother, Jonathan, in 1619. But his older brother Paul Temple was alive and at this time possessor of Temple Hall, the ancestral family home. Peter had married Phoebe Geering between the times of the two letters. Sir Peter was head of a younger branch of the Temple family and was a keen compiler of geneaological and heraldic information about the family.)

A ROYALIST ATTEMPTS TO MAKE A CASE AGAINST THOMAS WOGAN AND JAMES LEWIS

University of Leeds, Brotherton Collection: Loder–Symonds MSS. Vol. 93, page 25.
Calendared p. 392 of HMC Thirteenth Report, Appendix, Part IV.

(NO DATE) PRESERVED AMONGST THE PAPERS OF HENRY MARTEN.

Colonell James Lewis (a cheife promoter of ye sequestracon of Sr Hugh Owen and Letting his Demaynes to Capt. Thomas Woogan his Brother in Lawe) being Sheriffe of the County of Pembrocke did send his servant to ye King whoe procured a Comission of Array, & for his service therin and other his Services for ye King hee goeing to Oxford, obtayned a graunt of the wardship of his sisters only sonn from the Kinge from & against the will of the mother his sister wherby hee hath gotten ye possession of an estate of about 2000l p ann ever since June 1643/

That in 1644 hee being taken prisoner in wch Condicon hee continued about 6 months, afterwards pretended to be, for the parlt & yt hee would rayse a regimt, of wch hee never mustered above 52 men, as by the Comissary for musters oath, yett hee hath raised & receaved of the Country & State att least 10000 l [£10,000] & being a Comissionr for disbanding hath Debenters for himselfe & such Capts: as he named of yt regimt (having all of them been against ye Parlt) of a far greater sume

That ye last summer sessions, bonds of great penaltie being putt in sute against him & Mr Maurice Canon another Brother in Law of Capt Wogans and his, by Sir Hugh Owen, hee & other his Confederates did to obstruct iustice therin and ruyne as far as they could the sd Sr Hugh Owen sequester him in October last, & ymediatly thereon before Sr Hugh Owen could have any notice thereof did lease his estate to Capt Thomas Wogan (his Brother in lawe) a member of Parliamt, the chardge denyed as by oath may appear by collour of wch sequestracon the estate is kept from Sr Hugh Owen notwthstanding the order of Parlt for restitucon./

(NOTES: The Order of Parliament referred to in the last sentence was made May 30, 1649. See CJ, VI, 220a, where Oliver Cromwell personally reported to the House from the Committee of Complaints that it was the resolution of that Committee that Sir Hugh Owen was a person comprised within the Articles of Anglesea, "and accordingly ought to be discharged of Delinquency and Sequestration". On July 9, 1649, Sir William Masham reported to the House from the Council of State a Petition of Sir Hugh Owen; see CJ, VI, 256b. This had been ordered by the Council of State on June 27; see CSPD 1649–50, p. 208. Thomas Wogan's sister Mary Wogan's second husband was James Lewis of Abernant Bychan, Cardigan; he was recommended by Wagon to Lenthall on May 13, 1648, as a fit member for the Cardigan Committee for Militia and Sequestration There is no evidence as to why Henry Marten had this document in his keeping.)

TRANSCRIBED MANUSCRIPTS

CHAPTER THREE, PART ONE
Two Courtier Regicides

The early careers of the regicides have hitherto been unknown in the same way that their family backgrounds were. Clearly, the five regicides unlisted in the DNB were blanks, which I was able to fill in when I wrote their entries for the *Missing Persons* supplementary volume of the old DNB, as described in the previous chapter. However, as the entries which I wrote for the DNB were very heavily cut by the editor, and especially the material on their early careers, I have published the full texts as submitted, in the Appendix to Chapter Two, so that the extra unpublished information is now publicly available. Those five entries cover the entire careers, not just the early careers, of those five regicides.

Most of the regicides were previously so shadowy that what little was known about their early careers served more to tantalize than to satisfy. It is always important to know the background of a historical figure, but in the case of the regicides, the urgency of such knowledge is all the greater. For what the regicides did was so momentous, bold, and controversial, it is essential to find out as much as possible about the backgrounds of the men before they sat on the High Court. Had they long-standing grievances against the Crown? Had they long histories of rebellious or radical opinions and actions? Had they been imprisoned? Had they suffered from the imposition of illegal prerogative measures? These are the things we need to know if we are to reach any understanding of the act of regicide.

Another category of enquiry opens as well: had any of the regicides actually been associated with the Court? Could any of them have been courtiers? And if so, with what factions did they consort, and why were they estranged from court circles and the King?

As it happens, two of the regicides were not only courtiers, but one of them had even been Gentleman of the Privy Chamber to Charles I. Both of them had associations with the Essex rebellion under Elizabeth, both of them were aligned with the factions of Prince Henry and Queen Anne, both were estranged from James I, and both of them had every reason to hate everything the monarchy stood for in the end. I refer to Sir John Danvers and Sir William Constable, Bart. Constable actually took part in the Essex Rebellion along with Danvers's older brother, and whereas the older Danvers had been executed, Constable's life had been spared by Cecil. As for Sir John Danvers, he was Prince Henry's closest and most intimate friend, sharing his bedchamber with him for seven years (a fact never before known). I have been able to reconstruct the life stories of these two extraordinary men, from newly discovered documents which are transcribed for the Appendix to this Chapter. When attempting to understand the act of regicide, no better study could be attempted than to follow the courses of two courtiers' disillusion with the Court which went to the extremes of actually conniving at the execution of the King. The stories of Danvers and Constable are astonishing in many ways, and following them we twice recapitulate the history of the first half of the 17th century as seen from their perspectives. It is a most illuminating exercise.

Equally illuminating are some of the discoveries we make of the early backgrounds of other regicides., which are presented in a subsequent chapter to this. Several of them were associated with the setting up of 'parliaments' of one kind or another during the long years when Charles I refused to allow the country to have a real Parliament. Danvers was a key member of the Virginia Company, which set up a parliament in the New World during these years. And in the chapter on 'The Regicides and the Law', we shall discover that three other regicides were involved in setting up mock-parliaments during this time at the Inns of Court where they were students. In that later chapter will be found the accounts of the early careers of the 'legal regicides' (one judge, ten barristers, two attorneys, and others). Also, in yet another chapter, 'The Regicides and Religion', will be found the account of the regicide John

Blakiston's struggles with the ecclesiastical courts in the 1630s, together with a large amount of new documentary evidence. This present chapter, therefore, omits the early careers of the regicides other than the two courtier regicides.

We are fortunate that because they had long-standing associations with the Court, much documentation survives for both Danvers and Constable. Nothing like so much documentation has been found for the non-courtier regicides. Of course, Danvers and Constable were also older than most of the regicides and much had happened in their eventful if unhappy lives before 1649. If we appear to treat Danvers and Constable disproportionately, it is because a disproportionate amount of material has been found for them. But comparable studies are to be found of Bradshaw, Cook, and others, when we turn to the chapter 'The Regicides and the Law'.

We shall discover that many of the regicides had suffered imprisonment under Charles I. We shall see also that many of them had endured financial hardships due to prerogative acts of seizure. These acts were in several cases so outrageous – not to say monstrous – that any reasonable person at the time could only have been horrified. Many of the regicides certainly had direct, personal reasons to be outraged at Charles I. For instance, Thomas Chaloner, who had to flee the country for several years to avoid being hung on the orders of Archbishop Laud, came of a family which had had £100,000 stolen outright from them by the King. And yet Chaloner's father had been the man entrusted with the care and education of Prince Henry. (He also must have known Sir John Danvers well.)

But we shall see that anyone who had been close to Prince Henry was anathema to both James I and Charles I. Indeed, such people were hounded and persecuted beyond belief. Years of devoted service to the Crown in the person of the then-heir to the throne was rewarded by being robbed, pillaged, and harried by a relentless father and brother of the dead prince. The evidence of the regicides thus treated raises profound questions regarding the Court and the different court circles which go beyond the scope of this work. But this information was unexpected, and historians of the Stuart monarchy and its institutions could hardly have been expected to know of it, coming as it did from a study of the regicides. The general tension between King James and Prince Henry's circle has of course been known by historians for a long time. And this was a matter expressly discussed by contemporaries, as we see in the remarkable posthumously published memoir of the Court of James I by Sir Anthony Weldon (died 1645) of Swanscombe, Kent, a courtier of James I.[1] His son, Colonel Ralph Weldon, commanded a regiment of foot (which had originally been a Kentish militia regiment) in the new Model Army; at the end of the Civil War, he was succeeded as colonel of this regiment in 1646 by Colonel Robert Lilburne. (It is worth mentioning in passing that Weldon's loyal Lieutenant-Colonel Nicholas Kempson or Kempston was married to Elizabeth Ludlow, the sister of Edmund Ludlow the regicide.)[2] The publication of this vivid, detailed, and devastating exposé of the Court immediately after the execution of Charles I can hardly have been accidental, and was doubtless encouraged by some of the regicides and their close friend and colleague, the author's son. It is particularly noteworthy that Weldon's book stresses the merits of Prince Henry and the hostility between his friends and the courtiers round the King.

Several regicides had not experienced persecution under James I and Charles I personally, but had witnessed it in close members of their families. We shall see several examples of this in this chapter. But we must also keep in mind some examples which are not repeated here, as they have already been mentioned in the previous chapter, as for instance the fact that Miles Corbet's brother died as a result of wrongful imprisonment for refusing to pay a subsidy under Charles I. We shall see that Edmund Ludlow also lost a brother in prison. And I have found evidence of early opposition to the Crown from many regicides, including several who endured persecution. The regicides were, as we shall see, men whose patience had been tried … and tried … and tried.

We shall commence our survey of the early careers of the regicides by considering one of the most interesting of them all, Sir John Danvers. He was a highly cultured courtier, intimately acquainted with many of the leading royalists. At first glance it may seem incredible that such a man should sign the Death Warrant of Charles I. By attempting to get to the bottom of the apparent enigma of Danvers, we are in a sense cracking the hardest nut of all amongst the regicides. If we can understand *his* motives for the act of regicide, then surely the rest can only be easier to understand.

Sir John Danvers

Danvers is strangely absent from most of the scurrilous literature of the period. By scurrilous literature is meant the popular and widely circulated pamphlets and accounts in news sheets which contained malicious gossip and attacks on public figures. It might have been thought by us that he would be an ideal target for satire, but he does not seem to have crossed the minds much of the satirical writers. At the Restoration, Danvers is mentioned in the scurrilous pamphlet *Mystery of the Good Old Cause* simply for challenging his brother's will (a subject explained later).[3] George Bate gave prominence to the same dispute over the will, but specifically says of Danvers: 'he sided with the Sectarian party, was one of the King's Judges and lived afterwards some years in his sin without repentance.'[4] Bate goes further and says that at the end of his life, Danvers befriended the scholar and cleric Dr. Thomas Fuller, and by listening to his sermons 'was instructed to repent'; Bate likes to think that he did repent, but of that there seems to be no other evidence.

The one proper description of Danvers in a satirical pamphlet which I have been able to find is from *Oliver Cromwell The Late Great Tirant His Life-Guard*, published five years after Danvers's death but showing no awareness that Danvers was not still alive! The passage runs:

'Sir *John Danvers*, an empty tub, that makes the greatest sound; a boys gay bubble blown in the ayr, and broken; a true Courtier, that would fain seem something, when he is nothing, nay, one that is worse than nothing, being all over perfidious & ungrateful.'[5]

What we may conclude from this is that the author or a friend of the author's had seen or met Danvers and reported his personal *manner*. He was definitely, as we know from other sources, a 'true courtier' indeed. And his manners, no doubt of the most refined and delicate, according to the custom of his social circle, could seem somewhat affected, especially by the coarser standards of the 1650s. He might well have seemed 'a boy's gay bubble blown in the air', in comparison to the gruff soldiers who emerged from the battles of the Civil War and became Danvers's colleagues in Parliament and on the Council of State. But we may also agree with the scurrilous writer just quoted, from what we shall learn in our survey of Danvers's career, that he did indeed make a lot of noise, and 'would fain seem something', since he was an extraordinarily active and alert man, often coming forward with innovative suggestions and ideas. In the Appendix to the chapter on Regicides and the Law may be found

Danvers's letter to Bulstrode Whitelocke, in which he takes it upon himself to suggest the entire makeup of the Hale Commission for law reform!

Danvers was born circa 1585. The old DNB and the *Biographical Dictionary of British Radicals in the Seventeenth Century* both err in stating that he was born in 1588. In fact, he is described as being 'aged 16' when he was admitted to Brasenose College, Oxford, on July 16, 1601, so that he was thus born between July, 1584, and July, 1585. But Danvers's connection with politics had begun four months earlier than his admission to Oxford, for in March of the same year, his eldest brother, Sir Charles Danvers (see DNB), was beheaded on Tower Hill for his leading part in the Essex Rebellion, which attempted to overthrow Queen Elizabeth I. As will be described later when we discuss his early career, the regicide Sir William Constable was another participant in that Rebellion.

Whether he liked it or not, the sixteen year-old John Danvers was involved in politics, because his brother's (and hence the family's) estates were seized as a result of his brother's arrest and execution. Their father had died when John was only eight, and Charles was the head of the family at the time of his arrest. John's other brother, Henry, had already spent five years as an exile in France, but he now became the head of the family. (He was later to become the Earl of Danby, and for him see the DNB.) The Danvers boys had a very devoted mother. As their cousin John Aubrey says in his *Brief Lives*: 'To obtain Pardons for her Sonnes she maryed Sir Edmund Carey, cosen-german [*first cousin*] to Queen Elizabeth but kept him to hard meat [*i.e., gave him a very hard time*].'[6] But even this protective marriage, which had brought the two older brothers back from exile in France (to which they had fled because of a family feud with the Long family, in which various people had been killed), was insufficient to protect the Danvers family from the wrath of the Queen after the Essex Rebellion collapsed.

Fortunately for the Danvers boys, it was not long before the old Queen died, and a new era dawned. The correspondence between the Essex Rebellion leaders and the Stuarts in Scotland brought its rewards to such as the Danvers brothers when James VI of Scotland came down to claim his English throne as King James I. In the very month of the coronation, Henry Danvers was declared heir to the forfeited estates by James I.[7] A year later, John Danvers was made the Ranger of Blackmore and Pewsham Forests, which brought him a small annual income. (For details, see Danvers's 'Statement of Losses' transcribed in the Appendix to this Chapter.) He was still only 19. But the enthusiastically predatory homosexual James I must have been charmed by his good looks, which were so striking that Aubrey tells us:

'He had in a faire Body an harmonicall Mind: In his Youth his Complexion was so exceedingly beautiful and fine that Thomas Bond Esqr. (who was his companion in his travels) did say, that the People would come after him in the Street to admire him.'[8]

Further advancement in the world of the Court was rapid in coming. In 1604 or 1605, John Danvers, aged only twenty, was named Gentleman of the Privy Chamber to the young Prince Henry, heir to the throne. The Prince was at that time a young lad of only eleven. For the next seven years, until the Prince's tragic death, John Danvers was the Prince's constant companion and friend, sharing his apartments with him and in 1605 going with the Prince to live at Oxford, where Henry studied at Magdalen College. Danvers was knighted at Whitehall on March 3, 1608/9, for his continuing royal services. Only eight months before the death of Prince Henry, Danvers was combining his royal service with some further education of his own, and by request of Recorder Thomas Wentworth, he was admitted to Lincoln's Inn, March, 1611/12. That Danvers had more than a superficial interest in the law, indeed a deep and profound interest in it, may be seen in the chapter on Regicides and the Law, and its Appendix.

Considerably before this, in 1608, aged 23, Danvers had married a widow with ten children who was more than twice his age, and as Aubrey puts it: 'old enough to have been his Mother.'[9] His older brother Henry was furious. Aubrey tells us: 'He married her for love of her Witt. The Earl of Danby was greatly displeased with him for this disagreeable match.'[10] Apart from anything else, this wife was past child-bearing age, so that there could not be any children of the marriage, which indeed there were not. Henry, Lord Danby as he was to become, was unmarried and died without issue. So Sir John was running the risk of bringing the Danvers family in that branch to an end by this marriage to such an older woman.

Who was she? She was Magdalen, daughter of Sir Richard Newport, and widow of Richard Herbert. Among her children were the poet George Herbert and the famous Edward, Lord Herbert of Cherbury. The latter was a curious sort of step-son to have, since he was actually two years older than his step-father!

This is what Lord Herbert of Cherbury says of his mother in his *Autobiography*:

'And for my mother, after she lived most virtuously and lovingly with her husband for many years, she after his death erected a fair monument for him in Montgomery church; brought up her children carefully, and put them in good courses for making their fortunes, and briefly was that woman Dr. [John] Donne hath described in his funeral sermon of her printed.'[11]

Nowhere does Herbert mention her remarriage to Sir John Danvers, and Lord Herbert was definitely unhappy about her marrying a man younger than he was, and he took against Danvers. In the Appendix to this chapter will be found transcribed several letters to Lord Herbert of Cherbury from Sir John Danvers and his wife. The most revealing of all is the one Magdalen wrote to her son in 1625, in which she strongly defends Sir John against what must have been pretty strong insinuations from her son, and rapping him on the knuckles tells him in no uncertain terms:

'And to tel you further of Sr John Danvers Love which I dare sweare is to no man more … mistake him not but believe me there was never a tenderer hart or a lovinger minde in any man then is in him towards you who have the power to Commaund him and all that is his.' [*As in my transcriptions of all quotations from original documents, I have rendered the bars over the 'n's and 'm's as double-n or double-m.*]

Anyone who bothers to read through the letters of Sir John Danvers to his step-son will realize what fantastic lengths of toil and trouble Danvers was willing to run to for the sake of this complaining, jealous, and always unsatisified young adventurer. For years on end, Danvers acted as his step-son's banker, loaned him money, negotiated financial credit, saw to his bailiffs, kept his end up at court for him, made sure he shared credit and repute for patronage even when he had nothing to do with it, kept his friends and contacts sweet for him, and looked after his interests with the fanatical care and attention of a devoted father. While Danvers himself was on the verge of bankruptcy (to be discussed in a moment), he never mentioned his own financial problems to Herbert, but instead went on trying to offer himself as surety for his step-son even though it was the height of absurdity to put himself at even greater financial risk when he was himself on the verge of financial collapse anyway. Danvers was clearly desperate to earn Herbert's affection and approval. But no matter how much he craved it, his actions cannot be explained purely on that basis. We are forced to the conclusion that Danvers was the sort of man who could and would be bothered to help others; in short, a truly generous spirit.

As we shall see through further examination of Danvers's history, in this and other chapters, Blair Worden was misled through insufficient evidence to declare that Danvers was a very unsavoury character. This verdict by Worden is one which in my opinion cannot possibly be supported by the evidence. Worden wrote of him:

'There are four rumpers [of the Rump Parliament], ... whose behaviour does leave a decidedly unpleasant taste in the mouth. The most prominent politician among them was Sir John Danvers. ... Aubrey's claim that Danvers ... sat in the High Court of Justice to please Cromwell was probably accurate.'[12]

By singling out Danvers as one of the four most unpleasant members of the Long Parliament in its purged form as the Rump Parliament, and classing him with the criminal embezzler Lord Howard of Escrick, Worden has done a drastic disservice to our understanding of Danvers and the politics of the period. We shall be discovering quite a different side of Sir John Danvers as we proceed. And it is well worth taking the space to do so, for surely a close examination is justified of the one regicide accused by Worden of being a kind of monster. And as for John Aubrey's attribution of motive to Sir John Danvers's sitting on the High Court, it is extraordinary that Worden should have taken that seriously. It is patently evidence that Aubrey, as a fiercely loyal royalist, was desperately embarrassed by his cousin's 'apostasy' as he saw it, and sought to make some excuses for the republicanism of Danvers which he himself could not comprehend and did not wish to face. How can it be accepted by Worden that Danvers wished to please Cromwell, of all people? Cromwell did not become Protector until three and a half years later. There is no evidence of any kind indicating friendship between Danvers and Cromwell. But we may accept the opinion of George Bate, quoted earlier, that Danvers 'lived afterwards some years in his sin without repentance'. Indeed, his passionate view that the execution of Charles I was justified seems to have been shared by his daughter and adopted by his son-in-law, who was later to be arrested for it (this is a subject of later discussion).

This is not the place for a discussion of the character of the fascinating Lord Herbert of Cherbury, concerning whose marvellous *Autobiography* I fully agree with Hope Mirrlees is 'that incomparable account of manners and ideas in the first half of the seventeenth century'.[13] But it is to be noted that Herbert only mentions Danvers once in that work, and nowhere admits that he was his step-father. He merely says of him:

'I weighed myself in balances often with men lower than myself by the head, and in their bodies slenderer, and yet was found lighter than they, as Sir John Danvers, knight, and Richard Griffiths, now living, can witness, with both of whom I have been weighed.'[14]

Since Herbert chooses to tell us no more of Danvers than this, at least we gain some idea of Danvers's size and shape, being both slender and a head shorter than his athletic son-in-law. It is ironical that Danvers, who appears not to have been very 'sporty', lived for seven years with the highly athletic and passionate sportsman Prince Henry, and then had a son-in-law of the same type.

At the age of 25, two years before the death of Prince Henry, Danvers made his political debut, by being returned M.P. for Arundel in the Parliament of 1610. Probably the attacks on the royal prerogative in that Parliament and the spectacle of learned M.P.s discoursing upon the law of the land on the floor of the House caused him to become interested in law. His experience as a young

M.P. may therefore be the reason why he decided to enter Lincoln's Inn, so that he could learn more of the subject and arm himself for a role in future Parliamentary situations. He was to be a Member of every Parliament from 1610 until 1653, and he must have loved it. In the Parliament of 1614, his princely patron being dead and the seat at Arundel obviously bestowed on someone else in greater favour at Court, Danvers fell back on the seat for Montgomery, home of the Herberts and apparently in the gift of his step-son Lord Herbert. Pressure from his mother and the need to show gratitude for financial support by Danvers would have been sufficient to persuade Herbert to bestow the seat upon him.

Danvers was noted for his love of gardens, a fancy he shared with his brother Henry, who established the wonderful Botanic Gardens at Oxford, which are still very much in existence. We cannot take space here to discuss Danvers's gardening, which is a pity. His gardens at Chelsea and later at Lavington in Wiltshire were justly famous. The former had enjoyed the consultation and shared enthusiasm of Francis Bacon, who was a close friend of Danvers. Under the heading of 'Spontaneous Plants', in his work *Observations*, John Aubrey records the shared gardening interests of Bacon and Danvers by this remark: 'Try by compounding severall sorts of earth &c. diggd very deep, to produce several sorts of plants. Sir John Danvers assured me from his knowledge, that my Lord Bacon was wont to doe this in the garden at York-house.'[15] In *Brief Lives*, under the listing of Bacon, Aubrey also says: 'I remember Sir John Danvers told me, that his Lordship [Bacon, who became Lord Chancellor and was also created Lord Verulam and Viscount St. Albans] much delighted in his [Danvers's] curious pretty garden at Chelsey …'[16] In another chapter we shall consider Bacon's seeking of Danvers's opinion on one of his books prior to publication. Aubrey also records that Danvers was a friend of Chief Justice Sir Edward Coke, the courtier Sir Henry Lee, the playwright Ben Jonson, and in later years was often in the company of his step-son Lord Herbert.[17]

It is well known that Prince Henry took a delight in gardens, and concentrated on them especially at his favourite abode, Richmond. It is quite probable that the Prince's interests in gardening were aroused and encouraged by the Danvers brothers, for not only John but Henry Danvers as well was very close to Prince Henry. Aubrey tells us of Henry Danvers that he was 'a very great favourite of Prince Henry,'[18] though until now, it seems to have been unknown to all historians that Sir John Danvers was the Prince's companion of his Chamber. Henry Danvers had travelled in Europe and observed the gardens, and Sir John Danvers had also done so. Sir John's continental travels must have taken place between 1603 and 1604; in other words, between leaving Oxford and taking up service with Prince Henry. The travels must have been truly extensive and taken several months. Aubrey tells us: 'He had well travelled France & Italy, and made good Observations … 'Twas Sir John Danvers of Chelsey … who first taught us the way of Italian Gardens … He had a very fine Fancy, which lay (chiefly) for Gardens, and Architecture. The Garden at Chelsey in Middlesex (as likewise the house there) doe remain Monuments of his Ingenuity. He was a great acquaintance and Favorite of the Lord Chancellor Bacon, who took much delight in that elegant Garden.'[19]

It is highly probable that Danvers toured Europe again when he was older, but no evidence has so far been found to place this trip in his life history. If he acquired sufficient knowledge of Italian gardening to introduce the style to England (something unknown to gardening historians at present!), it is difficult to imagine him having done so sufficiently when he was only a teenager just out of Oxford. One reference he makes to his own European travels occurs obliquely in one of his letters to Lord Herbert (see Appendix), where he says to Herbert who is travelling in Europe: 'I doe somewhat know the trouble that ariseth by want [of money] in other countreys.'

It is worth casting our eyes through some of the documents in the Appendix, to see who some more of Danvers's friends were. He bought the Moore House in Chelsea [so called because it had been the residence of Sir Thomas More (1478-1535)] from the Earl of Lincoln, whose letter seeking deeds and papers on Danvers's behalf is in the Appendix; Lincoln was apparently on good terms with Danvers, and was an opponent of the court and of the Duke of Buckingham. Looking through the letters to Lord Herbert between 1614 and 1620, we find that Danvers was on good terms with the international financier Philip Burlimachi, and was either a friend or acquaintance of each of the following: Sir Robert Rich, who succeeded as second Earl of Warwick in 1619; Sir Thomas Roe; Sir Walter Raleigh (whom he must have come to know intimately along with Prince Henry, to whom Raleigh was a mentor), Sir Lewis Watson, the friend of Buckingham; possibly Sir Robert Sidney who was later Earl of Leicester; Sir Isaac Wake; Sir Thomas and Lady Vachell of Colley, Berkshire (parents of the recruiter M.P. to the Long Parliament, Tanfield Vachell); and evidently on fairly intimate terms with Sir Edward Cecil, the favourite of Buckingham and later Viscount Wimbledon. In addition, we know that Danvers and his wife were very intimate with Dr. John Donne, the cleric and poet, who gave a funeral or obituary sermon for Lady Danvers full of praise for her character, and which he could not deliver without bursting into tears in front of the whole congregation at St. Paul's, according to Izaak Walton, who was present.[20]

It is worthwhile taking a moment to pause over the name of Sir Walter Raleigh. It is well known to all historians of the period that Prince Henry as Prince of Wales often visited Raleigh in the Tower of London, to the great fury of King James, who hated Raleigh and had imprisoned him there. He would likely have been accompanied on these occasions by Sir John Danvers. Let us just consider some of the happier details which are likely to have featured during these visits. Raleigh would presumably have been well fed and able to keep his own cook, as a long term resident in the Tower. He would have offered the Prince and Danvers in the good weather his favourite summer drink which he called Cordial Water, the recipe for which he gives as follows: 'Take a gallon of strawberries [likely to be the small wild strawberries, or *fraises de bois*, still commonly used in France in this very same way] and put them into a pint of aqua vitae; let them stand for four days, then strain them gently off, and sweeten the liquor as it pleaseth thee.' And in the cold weather, he would have offered them his favourite winter drink, Sack Posset, the recipe for which he also gives: 'Boil a quart of cream with quantum suffcit of sugar, mace, and nutmeg; take half a pint of sack, and the same quantity of ale, and boil them well together, adding sugar; these, being boiled separately, are now to be added. Heat a pewter dish very hot, and cover your basin with it, and let it stand by the fire for two or three hours.'[21] We can imagine the two boys sitting attentively beside their mentor, in front of the fire in the winter time, waiting for the Sack Posset to be ready to drink. Amongst the sentiments expressed by Raleigh in these meetings were likely to be ones in favour of Parliaments. Raleigh wrote a dialogue on this subject which was smuggled out of the Tower and kept secret until 1628 when it was mysteriously printed 'in these distracted times', as it says on its title page, and as 1628 then extended to March 31 of what we now call 1629 (New Years Day being then March 31), it seems that this treatise on parliaments appeared just in the month when Charles closed down the Parliament and commenced what was to be his eleven years of unconstitutional 'prerogative rule' without calling any Parliament at all. The work is called *The Prerogative of Parliaments in England*, and it ran to 65 pages. The place of publication was obviously London, but this was disguised by the pretence that it was published on the continent. The British Library has a copy stating that it was printed at Hamburg. I have a copy of the work, which is not in the British Library, pretending to be printed at 'Midleburge' in the Netherlands. As most copies of this work would have been seized and burnt in 1628, my copy may possibly be a unique variant, as may also the British library's copy pretending to come from Hamburg. One does really wonder whether Danvers had anything to do with this. He served in the 1628 Parliament in a position of some prominence, being joint MP for Oxford University with the famous judge Sir Henry Marten (father of the future regicide Henry Marten). Can it be a coincidence also that in 1642 at another crucial juncture, the same work was mysteriously reprinted once again? Someone opposed to the Crown was doing this on both occasions, and what prominent Parliamentarian besides Danvers would have had access to a secret work by Raleigh which had been smuggled out of the Tower, perhaps with the connivance of Prince Henry himself? (It is odd that this important tract is not listed in the list of Raleigh's works in that unreliable source, Wikipedia.) But to conclude, there can be no doubt that Danvers had been influenced when young by Sir Walter Raleigh, and if he did not actually arrange the printing of Raleigh's tract, we can safely assume he would certainly have discreetly promoted it and handed it out, and known very well who did arrange to get it printed. It says pointedly on its 1628 title page 'Written by the worthy (much lacked and lamented) Sir Walter Raleigh, Knight, deceased ... Preserved to be now happily (in these distracted times) Published.' We should keep in mind how bitterly this must have stung King Charles, for he knew that his own older brother had fraternised with this brilliant man whose work was now being published to spite and oppose him all these years later.

It should be stressed that the new evidence which I have found in the private correspondence of Danvers show unmistakably that after the death of Prince Henry, Danvers continued to be intimately informed of the state of Sir Walter Raleigh's writings. This suggests that Danvers continued to visit Raleigh in the Tower, or at the very least that he was one of a small confidential group who were aware of the intimacies of Raleigh's writing activities, some of whom must have been in direct contact with Raleigh in the Tower. (Using Occam's Razor, it is evident that the simplest explanation of this is that Danvers visited in person, as he must have done for years with Prince Henry, doubtless being viewed by the guards at the Tower as a routine visitor and what we today call 'a regular'. The important evidence comes from Danvers's letter to his step-son Lord Herbert of Cherbury dated November 26, 1614, which is transcribed from the original and found in the Appendix to this chapter. At that time Cherbury was on the continent and Danvers was dealing with his rentals and financial affairs for him at home, as well as sending him frequent accounts of what was happening in general. In this letter, Danvers speaks of Raleigh (which he spells Rawley, which is in fact still its correct pronunciation even today) as follows (expressed in modern spelling here):

'Sir Walter Rawley's Chronicle is set forth in his own style which is excellent but he hath prosecuted the story of the world but to part of [as far as] the Romans' time and seems to have neglected the latter [subsequent times] by the death of Prince Henry for whose sake only he had endeavoured it.'

The chronicle referred to is Raleigh's book *The Historie of the World*, which does indeed end during the Roman period. This explicit testimony proves that Raleigh wrote this at the direct request of Prince Henry, and that after the death of the prince, he saw no point in continuing. Danvers was presumably present on the very occasion when Prince Henry made his original request that Raleigh write the book. This testimony also proves that the intention was to bring it up to a much later date, presumably the contemporary time, a project sadly abandoned when the whole project must have seemed pointless to Raleigh, who could not envisage how it could ever be published, considering his disgraced position and King James's hatred of him. Raleigh evidently handed over his manuscript of *Historie* to a trusted friend for smuggling out of the Tower. Danvers is one of the small number of people who might have been that intermediary. The work was then published in an edition bearing the date of 1614. However, all copies must have been confiscated and destroyed, because even the British Library does not have one. Little is therefore known of this first edition, although the printer's name is known. All surviving 'earliest' copies of the work apparently date from the second attempt to get the work into print, in 1617. Presumably, precautions were taken then to ensure that these could not also be confiscated and destroyed, as some copies of that edition do survive.

It is not unlikely that Danvers was used as a messenger to Raleigh from Prince Henry on numerous occasions over the years, and that he probably carried books and papers to him as gifts from the Prince, to make it possible for Raleigh to write such an ambitious project on world history. His cell must have been piled high with copies of Thucydides, Herodotus, Livy, Plutarch, Xenophon, Polybius, and all the others imaginable, lavished upon him by Prince Henry with no expense spared. After all, he could not possibly write a world history without such standard reference materials, so he must have had them. And since a prince cannot be expected to carry armloads of such stuff to the Tower personally, they must have been carried by Danvers.

But now we return to Danvers's career after the prince had died. For some reason which we do not know, Danvers was apparently not offered the Montgomery Parliamentary seat for the Parliament of 1621, and had to look elsewhere. It was probably through his wife's large circle of friends at Oxford that he was able to secure the seat for Oxford University. Faulkner records: 'this Lady ... was highly esteemed for her great and harmless wit, cheerful gravity, and obliging behaviour, which gained her an acquaintance and friendship with most people of eminent worth or learning in the University of Oxford, where she lived for four years, to take care of the education of her eldest son. ...'[22] Probably Danvers first met his wife at Oxford, since the end of her and her son's time at Oxford would have overlapped with Danvers's first year there. And, returning to live in Oxford himself as companion to Prince Henry, Danvers must inevitably, through his royal associations, have made many prominent friends there himself in his 20s. Indeed, as the boon companion of the heir to the throne, his connections at Oxford must inevitably have been of the very highest.

He had also become deeply interested in colonization. Perhaps it was the inspiring conversation of Sir Walter Raleigh which first turned the young Danvers's mind towards colonization activities. But however it happened, Sir John Danvers became one of the most enthusiastic and active members of the colonizing Virginia Company. He was sufficiently important in the Company by July, 1620, to be taking on the responsibility of introducing vines and encouraging the continuing development of the silk worm industry in the colony, and also encouraging the expansion of its tobacco growing, possibly as a hedge against the King's notorious attitude towards tobacco, and his outrageous tax demands on that plant. We know that silk worms were initially introduced in to Virginia during the winter of 1614/15, as Raphe Hamor records in his book published in late 1615, *A True Discourse of the Present Estate of Virginia*:

'The silke wormes sent thither from England, in seeds the last winter, came foorth many of them the beginning of March, others in April, Maye, and June, thousands of them grown to great bignesse, and a spinning, and the rest well thriving of their increase, and commodity well knowne to be reaped by them, we have all most assurance (since sure I am) no Country affordeth more store of Mulberry trees, of a kind with whose leafe they more delight, or thrive better.'[23]

The idea of introducing vines into Virginia appears to be novel, since there is no mention of vines in the 1615 report by Raphe Hamor. It is known that Danvers was a passionate gardener, and that he and his friend Francis Bacon visited one another's gardens and exchanged botanical tips. Danvers may have been responsible for suggesting the vines. Danvers would also have known a lot about mulberry trees, because they were cultivated extensively in Chelsea, where he lived, and adjoining Fulham. Few people realize that a few ancient mulberry trees survived into the 20th century from the vast mulberry orchards of those days, or perhaps they were the 'children' of the old ones. But I have myself seen some of these ancient trees in the back gardens of houses in the area, including the house of a friend who lived in Edith Grove in Fulham. Her husband having been a historian, so that she was aware of the ancient vanished gardens, she and I sometimes discussed the partial survival of the old mulberry trees and marvelled at them. It was well known to all the older residents that the trees were much older than the houses. (I do not know whether any of these trees are still alive in the 21st century, as all my older friends who had them have died.)

By that time, Danvers's step-son Lord Herbert had become Ambassador to France. (It is likely that during this period, Danvers and his wife took the occasion to visit Herbert and stay at the Embassy in Paris, but no evidence of this survives, unless it is mentioned in diplomatic papers which I have not perused.) And from Danvers's letter of July 27th to Herbert at Paris, we may see with what excitement Danvers was personally organising and directing considerable aspects of the Virginia colonization programme. (See Appendix.)

Fortunately for us, a curious document has survived which enables us to prove that Danvers was of the very faction within the Virginia Company which we would have suspected. This document, 'Information against Sir John Danvers', presented by a merchant named Anthony Wither, is transcribed and may be found in the Appendix. The Wither document is tentatively dated 1631 by the compilers of the *Calendar of State Papers*, which merely lists it (I have transcribed the original document in the Appendix). Wither says that Danvers was in the Virginia Company sixteen years earlier when he, Wither, entered it. Therefore Danvers would have been a member as early as 1615, according to this dating of the Wither document, and of course must have been a member for some time before, since he was already the member of a group. Wither says that upon his own entry, Danvers 'would needs take me into his especiall acquaintance, & I being yet of noe ptie [party], he drewe me to be of Sr Edwyn Sandes [Sandys's] ptie wth him ...'

This is precisely what we would have imagined. And from an account of the Virginia Company we read, perhaps without surprise, just what the party of Sir Edwin Sandys was and stood for:

'During this time (1617-1618) a great change had come over the Company at home. An energetic and public-spirited party had been formed, opposed alike to Sir Thomas Smith and to Lord Rich. Their leader was Sir Edwin Sandys, a member of that country party which was just beginning to take its stand against the corruptions of the court policy. Side by side with him stood one whose name has gained a wider though not a more honourable repute, the follower of Essex, the idol of Shakespeare, the brilliant, versatile Southampton. ... The next year, 1619, was remarkable in the annals of the colony. It is hardly an exaggeration to say that it witnessed the creation of Virginia as an independent community. From the beginning of that year we may date the definite ascendancy of Sandys and his party, an ascendancy which was maintained until the dissolution of the Company, and during which the affairs of Virginia were administered with a degree of energy, unselfishness, and statesmanlike wisdom, perhaps unparalleled in the history of corporations. ... About the same time ... a step of greatest importance was being taken in Virginia. ... At one step, Virginia, from being a little better than a penal settlement, ruled by martial law, became invested with important, though not full, rights of self-government. ... On the 30th of July, 1619, the first Assembly met in the little church at Jamestown. ... Every freeman appears to have had a vote, and each county and hundred returned two members. Besides these were certain private plantations which possessed the right of returning members. ... The Assembly did not confine itself to deliberation and legislation. It evidently regarded itself as having the powers of a civil and criminal law court. ... In England the Company under its new government set to work with an energy before unknown to it, to improve the condition of the colony. A committee was appointed to codify the existing ordinances of the Company, and also to frame a code for Virginia.'[24]

One of the new ordinances was that the holders of land must 'cultivate a certain quantity of other commodities'[25] (other than tobacco and sassafras) – an ordinance perhaps suggested by Danvers, who was so energetic in trying to find such commodities, and introduce them into Virginia. It thus seems very likely indeed that vines were his suggestion, so that raisins, if not wine, could be produced in Virginia.[26] Under Sandys, also, energetic missionary activities were supported with the Indians, and religion came to be seen as far more important in the equation that had previously been the case with the Company.

It is important to note that the Earl of Southampton, the most prominent member of the Sandys party in the Virginia Company, had been a most intimate friend to the Danvers brothers. In the DNB entry for Sir Charles Danvers we see that Southampton was since 1593 their special protector and gave refuge to Charles and Henry in their flight after the feud with the Long family which led to their exile in France. The DNB entry points out: 'It was generally admitted that Danvers's intimacy with Southampton led him into the conspiracy [of the Essex Rebellion]. He confessed on the scaffold to a special hatred of Lord Grey, merely on the ground that Grey was "ill-affected to Southampton".'

It therefore takes little imagination to conceive that Sir John Danvers and the Earl of Southampton, sitting beside each other time after time at meetings of the Virginia Company, must have enjoyed the most cozy and intimate of friendly relations, in continuation of a family friendship which had existed for over a quarter of a century. It need hardly be indicated that Southampton was a leader of what is often called the 'country party'. In 1621 he was imprisoned. After release from prison, he absented himself from meetings of the Virginia Company in order to placate the King and all of his enemies at court. Akrigg, in his biography of Southampton, mentions the following story:

'The Marquis of Hamilton and the Earl of Pembroke solemnly affirmed to the Earl of Southampton, that they heard Gondomar [Diego Sarmiento de Acuña, 1st Count of Gondomar, 1567-1626, who was Spanish Ambassador until 1622, and who had great influence over James I] say to the King, "That it was time for him to look to the Virginia courts which were kept at the Ferrars' house, where too many of his Nobility and Gentry resorted to accompany the popular Lord Southampton and the dangerous Sandys."'[27]

In 1622, the King even adopted Danvers's promotion of silk worms to berate the Company, insisting that they stop growing so much abominable tobacco and change over to silk worms. The fact that that was exactly what Danvers had been trying to take the precaution of doing for the past two years was conveniently ignored by the irascible monarch.[28] It is worth recording here what Hamer said about Virginia's tobacco in 1615:

'I dare thus much affirme ... of Tobacco, whose goodnesse mine own experience and trial induces me to be such, that no country under the Sunne, may, or doth afford more pleasant, sweet, and strong Tobacco, then I have tasted there, even of mine owne planting, which, howsoever being then the first yeer of our trial thereof, wee had not the knowledge to cure, and make up, yet are there some now resident there, out of the last yeers well observed experience, which both knew, and I doubt not will make, and returne such Tobacco this yeere, that even England shall acknowledge the goodnesse thereof.'[29]

A fuller account of the Virginia Company involvements of Danvers used to be impossibly difficult, with the only surviving copy of the Company's records being in Washington, D.C., and none in England. In recent years, fortunately, the Records have been published in four volumes, and a searchable digital text has also been put online. We may take note that: 'Several of the leading members among the new [Sandys's] party in the Company were already obnoxious to the court. Sandys, Digges, Selden, and Sir Nathaniel Rich, were at once members of the Virginia Company and of the country party in Parliament. Southampton was a close ally of Essex, whose temper and family history marked him out as a patriot leader. Spain, ... was doing her utmost to embroil the Company with the King, and her ambassador, Gondomar, had already taught James that "a seditious Company was but the seminary to a seditious Parliament."'[30]

Let us just note more carefully just what it was that the Virginia Company was doing to make itself so obnoxious to the King. Wright and Fowler have summed it up in a sentence, remarking upon the Assembly which was made possible by the ascendancy of Sandys's party in the Company: 'This was the first legislative assembly called together in North America and marks the beginning of American popular government.'[31] – What a fearsome reminder to the home country, which at the time had no functioning Parliament of its own, and certainly nothing remotely resembling popular government! Is it any wonder that the King looked upon the Virginia Company as a nest of sedition? Those men could not force him to grant them a Parliament, but they could erect one of their own in the colonies!

Eventually, the King took the most drastic action possible, after a series of other assaults upon the Company which we shall not detail here. And here it is Sir John Danvers who emerges as the hero of the hour. The events are dramatically described, and dramatic indeed they were:

'King James began to scheme for the dissolution of the Virginia Company, which was odious, because its prominent members believed in freedom of debate, and in the submission of a minority to the will of a majority expressed through the ballot box. One of its secretaries, Edward Collingwood, hurried from London, and told Danvers that three merchants of that city had visited him and endeavoured to obtain papers and information which might be used against the corporation, and as the King might send officers to seize the records, he suggested that exact copies be immediately obtained.

'A man of loose life, but a fair and ready writer, a clerk of Collingwood, was secured by Danvers to aid in this work, and was locked up in the chamber where he wrote, so that he might not be tempted to divulge the secret.

'After the transactions were copied on folio paper, to prevent interpolation, each page carefully compared with the originals by Collingwood and then subscribed "Com. Collingwood", Danvers took them to the president of the company, who was Shakespeare's friend, Henry

Wriothesly, Earl of Southampton. The earl was highly gratified in the possession of a duplicate copy of the company's transactions, and expressed it by throwing his arms around the neck of Sir John, and then turning to his brother, said: "Let them be kept at my house at Titchfield; they are evidences of my honour, and I value them more than the evidences of my lands."[32]

The total length of what had been copied amounted to seven hundred and forty-one pages! The scribe and Danvers must both have had severe writer's cramp after all that. These copies commissioned by Danvers are now in the Library of Congress, having passed to that library from the personal library of Thomas Jefferson, the second President of the United States. The original records, as Danvers had feared, were seized and destroyed, evidently on the orders of the King. If it had not been for this extraordinary preemptive action by Sir John Danvers, the entire early history of the colony of Virginia would be unknown.

One now begins to appreciate how Danvers's attitudes towards the royal government were shaped. Danvers associated for his entire life and career, from the time he was a child, with those persons who favoured liberty, Protestantism, expansive trade and colonization, and a containment of the tyranny of the crown.

In this connection, let us recall the words of the Earl of Essex, leader of the ill-fated Rebellion: 'I will always owe duty to her Majesty as an Earl Marshal of England, and I have served her as a clerk, but cannot as a slave. You bid me give way ... but I cannot yield truth to falsehood. What! Is it impossible for crowned heads to do wrong, and so to stand accountable to their subjects? Was any power below of an unlimited nature?'[33]

Whatever one's interpretation of the Essex Rebellion, it cannot be denied that these words could serve as a motto for the Parliament in the Civil War, and indeed for the ultimate act of regicide. And they are words which could have been well known to the regicides Sir John Danvers and Sir William Constable, whose involvement in the Essex Rebellion was in the latter case personal and direct, and in the former case a matter of deepest family loyalty of continuing intimacy with leaders of the Rebellion and other like-minded men. What would such a man think when the King forcibly dissolved the Virginia Company, for instance? For, as Doyle has said so succinctly:

'Morally and politically, indeed, the abrogation of the Virginia charter was a crime. It was one of the earliest of those efforts in which the Stuart reigns were so fruitful, efforts to wrest the process of law to the arbitrary purposes of the Crown. It was part of that policy which sent Raleigh to the scaffold, and which sought to make England the friend, almost the vassal, of the oppressor whose rod she had broken [Spain].'[34]

From the background of a sympathetic affiliation with the Essex Rebellion protagonists, Danvers moved into the circle of the Prince of Wales and all those who clustered around him in opposition to the spirit of James's rule. Danvers's attitude towards James requires little imagination, when we consider the Prince's own. All historians of the period will be familiar with Prince Henry's contemptuous aspersions on his father when he said of Sir Walter Raleigh that only a king like his own father would keep such a man in a cage (referring to the Tower of London, where Raleigh was imprisoned by order of James I). How little James mourned upon the death of his son is another notorious fact. This may seem strangely inhuman, but we need to keep in mind that it was believed in some quarters that James was not the biological father of either of his 'sons', Prince Henry or Prince Charles. It is well known that James was homosexual, and was not inclined towards women at all. However, homosexual kings throughout history have forced themselves to breedwith their queens out of duty. But there is some reason to believe that James could not bring himself to do this, and that he arranged for his queen, Anne of Denmark, to become pregnant by other men, whom he then arranged to be killed, so that they could not claim paternity. According to the 'informed gossip' of the period, the father of Prince Henry was either a Mr. Stuart, who was burned alive afterwards in his house, or more likely was the Earl Gowrie, who was also later killed by James in his own house, not long before Henry's birth, under the pretext of a 'Gowrie Conspiracy' which was wholly invented. This information is recorded in a remarkable book by John Baron Somers, entitled *The True Secret History of the Lives and Reigns of All the Kings and Queens of England*, which he published in 1725. I own two copies of this extraordinary book, and to say that it is shocking would be an understatement. Somers says that he wishes to 'rake into the Dunghil of his Life', and he proceeds to quote at length from a memoir 'by one of his Contemporaries'.[35] It is worth quoting some of the remarkable passages:

'For his [James's] Person, a Man might sufficiently and truly make a Volume, only to tell of his Laziness, and his Uncleanness, but I cannot do't, without fouling too much Paper. ... He was the greatest Blasphemer in the World, would Swear faster than Speak, and curse the People by the Clock: And it appears by the whole Course of his Life, that he was a most malicious Hater of this Nation [England]. ... King James was married to Queen Ann of Denmark, a Lady beautiful but too strong to be joined with a weak spiny Prince; but in a little time, finding his Deficiency [inability to have sex with her], what she wanted in him, she made up elsewhere; placing her delight first in one Mr. Stuart, of the House of the Earl of Murry; but his haunting her Chamber too sedulously, caus'd such a jealousie in the King, that he imparted his thoughts to the Marquis of Huntley, who between 'em got this Stuart out of the way, causing his House to be burnt, and himself in it. After whose Death, the Queen made use of the Earl of Gowry, a Lord of comely Visage, good Stature, and an Attracting Mein, to satisfy her unruly Appetite ... [the King] causing Ramsy, afterwards Earl of Holderness, with some others, to murther Gowry in his own House ...Not long after Gowries Death, Prince Henry was born in Edenbrough [Edinburgh]... As to Queen Anne, tho' she was none of the most Celebrated Vertues, yet some grains of Allowance ought to be given her: For tho' the King sometimes gave her a Visit; yet he never lodg'd a Night with her for many years, for his faculty lay another way, being more addicted to the love of Men than Women ...'[36]

The first of the books revealing secrets of the Court of James I seems to have been the memoir written by Sir Anthony Weldon, which was published in 1650, apparently at the initiative of his son, Colonel Ralph Weldon, and which I mentioned earlier. As a courtier of James I, Weldon revealed a great deal about London court life but was not informed about the earlier Scottish court life, so that the information just quoted above from Somers about the murders of Mr. Stuart and Lord Gowrie in Scotland (while James I was still merely James VI of Scotland) are not mentioned by him and comes from another source altogether. However, the revelations by Weldon of the personal habits and inclinations of James I collaborate what Somers has to say, and are even more bizarre:

'The King ... would not endure his Queen and his children in his Lodgings ...'[37]

'(The King) ... did not much desire to be in his Queenes company ...'[38]

' ... it was most true ... that the King loved Beasts better than men, and took more delight in them ...'[39]

' ... Bawdery ... did infinitely please the Kings humour ...'[40]

' ... hee never washt his hands, only rub'd his fingers ends sleightly with the wet end of a Napkin ... his walke was ever circular, his fingers ever in that walke fiddling about with his codpiece ... he would never change his cloathes till very ragges.'

'... Hee was not very uxurious [not a good husband], though hee had a very brave Queen that never crossed his designes, nor intermeddled with State affaires, but ever complied with him'

'... (but) he was ever best, when furthest from the Queen, and that was thought to be the first grounds of his often removes [living separately from her], which afterwards proved habitual. '

'...Hee ever desired to prefer mean men in great places ...'[41]

Weldon's book was followed the next year, in 1651, with a lengthy historical account of the first fourteen years of the reign of King James, which was a very unfavourable summary of events, but did not contain personal descriptions of the person and habits of James.[42] The author of this work remains unknown.

I have noticed some places in the book by Lord Somers which contain direct borrowings from Weldon's book. For instance, the story of how Sir Walter Raleigh, through his knowledge of medicine and chemistry, cured Queen Anne of a serious illness of which her doctors had despaired of her life, is told by Somers[43] in a close paraphrase of the words used by Weldon in 1650.[44] However, an intensive study and comparison of these various publications attacking the Court, character, reign, and person of King James I are really a separate matter from our purposes here, and more properly concern the history of an earlier generation, so that I shall leave this subject, having extracted what was needed. I should merely add that the paternity of Charles I is a matter which gives one pause as well.

The rumours that Prince Henry had been poisoned were another notorious fact. Weldon certainly insisted that he had been poisoned. The only question seemed to be, was Prince Henry poisoned on the instructions of his own 'father', or independently by the Earl of Somerset. Although it appears fashionable today to believe that Prince Henry died of typhoid fever, my own opinion, for what it is worth, is that he was poisoned by Somerset. Perhaps I should justify my opinion by pointing out the weakness of the typhoid hypothesis. In 1882, a distinguished medical man, Sir Norman Moore, MD, made a close study of the case and reported that the only disease he could think of which could explain the symptoms of the Prince was typhoid. However, there is a serious problem. In order to adopt this hypothesis that Prince Henry died of typhoid, it is necessary to accept that his was 'the earliest case of typhoid fever on record in England.'[45] This comes too close for my liking to creating a disease to explain a death. It stretches credulity too far to claim that the first case of typhoid in the country was contracted by the Prince of Wales. I believe that only people motivated by a desire to assert that Prince Henry was under no circumstances a victim of poison could possibly go so far as this. Occam's Razor demands that we resign ourselves to the simpler solution: that Prince Henry was indeed poisoned.

It was not merely Justice Coke who believed that Prince Henry had been poisoned. It was evidently the belief of leading radical M.P.s of the Long Parliament. Blair Worden discovered an unpublished manuscript of Algernon Sidney's at Warwick Castle, in which

Sidney claimed that James himself poisoned his son. I have examined this manuscript, which I hope will be published some day. (It was indeed subsequently published.) Its title is *Court Maxims*, and it is intensely satirical. It is a savage, devastating attack on royal prerogative, written with acid sarcasm. It is worth quoting the brief sentences summing up a few of the maxims, since they are here so apposite:

'The Fourth Court Maxime: "Monarchy is not secure unless the Nobility be suppressed effeminated & corrupted" ... The Sixth Court Maxime: "No man is to be employed that will not wholly depend upon the will of the King." ... The Thirteenth Court Maxime: "The King's designs are at home: He hath reason to suspect men of virtue, valour & reputation: and he is oblig'd to destroy them he suspects."'[46]

Henry, Prince of Wales. His premature death, probably murder, in 1612 meant that his younger brother became King Charles I.

This is not the place to discuss Algernon Sidney or his ideas. But the above sarcastic sentiments may be well presumed to have been in the minds of Prince Henry and his friends as they visited Raleigh in his 'cage' in the Tower of London, - a man 'of virtue, valour & reputation' in the process of being destroyed. The Sixth Court Maxim had, as we saw earlier, already been uttered in different words by the Earl of Essex. The strength of feeling in Prince Henry and his friends may be seen as well from his violent outburst in defense of his friend Phineas Pett, and against those unctuous courtiers against whom the Prince and his party had such a virulent hatred: 'Where bee now these perjured fellows that dare thus abuse his Majesty with these false informations? Do they not deserve hanging?'[47] Surely, if the King did not poison his son, there was no shortage of 'perjured fellows' at the Court who would gladly have done so.

It may, I think, be presumed without too much risk of being wrong, that Danvers himself (especially as he was a friend of Coke, whose opinion was firmly on the side of poison) believed that his beloved Prince had been poisoned. If the rumours of poisoning were kept alive for so many decades, which they were, all and sundry concerned with them would have turned repeatedly to Henry's closest companion, Danvers himself, with questions about the matter. And it is difficult to believe that Danvers would have discouraged such ideas, but much more likely that he believed them himself. Perhaps it does not really matter. But it is worth mentioning, especially because if Danvers really believed it, it would explain all the more his personal attitudes towards the crown and the court. Although speculation, it is speculation well worth making. And there is one other thing to remember: as Gentleman of the Bedchamber to Prince Henry, Danvers would have known the young brother Prince Charles very well indeed, and vice versa. This makes King Charles's remark at his trial that he did not recognise any of his judges disingenuous at best, since he must have recognised Danvers, who had been an intimate, in their private living quarters, of his brother, his mother, and himself for seven years, and who later became a Gentleman of the Privy Chamber to Charles himself! By pretending not to recognise him, the King may well be giving us indirect evidence of bad blood having existed between them since he was a child. Certainly the stuttering, shy, unnaturally small Prince Charles was not an impressive child, and stood in stark contrast to his effusive, extrovert and highly athletic older brother. As someone who was never expected to come to the throne, Charles was apparently never taken very seriously when he was young, and appears to have been looked upon with feelings bordering on contempt by many at the time. We have to keep in mind that Danvers, who knew Charles better at the personal level than any other regicide, may have despised him as a person from his childhood, as well as disapproved of him as a monarch.

Let us consider now Danvers's offices and finances, and the persecution and denial of money under which he struggled after the death of Prince Henry, his friend and protector. The first point to be stressed is that Danvers received not one penny payment and not one reward for seven years' service to the Prince of Wales. He says this himself in his 'Statement of Losses' (see Appendix). He mentions this briefly at the very end, knowing full well how little good it would do him at court to remind the King that he had been his elder son's companion and friend. It is clear that he only mentions it at all because of the outrageous nature of the simple fact that seven years' total dedication to royal service should receive not a penny's payment. The fact that Prince Henry's intimate coterie should be so treated in itself speaks volumes, and shows the deep aversion and hatred with which King James viewed the threat which the Prince had posed to his policies and even to him personally. It also shows his continuing antipathy towards the Prince's associates.

There is the possibility that Sir John Danvers, notoriously so good-looking, may have spurned sexual advances by the King. The King would not easily have forgiven such a thing. But of this we can presumably never have any knowledge. If such an advance had take place in the Prince's lifetime, it would probably have increased the Prince's contempt for his father. There is certainly a possibility that Sir John was at the centre of some such incident, for Sir John's brother Henry did not experience the same disfavour at Court as Sir John did, suggesting that the antipathy was to Sir John alone. In fact, the contrast could not be greater, because only a few months after Prince Henry's death, Henry Danvers (by then Lord Danvers) obtained a grant in reversion to become Keeper of St. James's Palace, which had been Prince Henry's last residence.[48] This seems a most extraordinary thing to happen while his younger brother was being financially persecuted by the King, as if out of personal spite.

As soon as James was inactive in the final year of his reign, and continuing when Charles came to the throne, Sir John was aided by his brother in trying to make a comeback at court. This suggests that it was James who personally had 'blacked' him. Sir John only submitted his 'Statement of Losses' (see Appendix) in 1624, as James's control over the government had waned and events were under the control of the Prince of Wales (Charles) and Buckingham. Danvers clearly knew how hopeless it was to try to get any money from the crown as long as James was in control of things. In the Appendix is the document signed by James ordering Danvers's payment of annuity and arrears, which was dated 1620. However, as I point out in my notes to the document, the King must have secretly countermanded the order, since it was never carried out in his lifetime. Although thoroughly in character, this behaviour of James's does indicate antipathy towards Danvers which was of the more furtive rather than open variety. Was it simply because Danvers had been Henry's companion, and the King felt guilty of making a public show of his hatred on that basis? Was it that Danvers had repelled a sexual advance, another cause for concealing antipathy in public? The situation is rather strange, and one cannot resist the conclusion that the persecution of Danvers by King James was something to which the King could not publicly admit, but which he relentlessly pursued in secret. Since Buckingham himself seems to have held no grudge against Danvers, and Danvers even sought his aid, and (as seen in Danvers's letter of July 31, 1623, to Secretary Conway, transcribed in the Appendix) received fervent expressions of support from Buckingham, we cannot help but conclude that the King held a very strong and immoveable personal grudge against Sir John Danvers, the reasons for which he concealed.

The King's order to pay Danvers (see Appendix), which was never carried out, mentions that Danvers's annuity had been unpaid since about 1616. The 'Statement of Losses' by Danvers gives a horrifying catalogue of financial sufferings under the oppression of the crown's prerogative. James had, to the detriment of both Danvers brothers, forced them to surrender their rights in the forest of Braden. Then, although Sir John was Ranger of Blackmore and Pewsham Forests, the King simply went ahead and cut all the trees down, so that the forests ceased to exist, depriving Sir John of another bit of his income. Then a far more violent and extraordinary royal abuse was committed, costing Danvers in excess of £3000, about a year after Prince Henry's death. Sir John's brother Henry transferred to Sir John a piece of valuable land in Westminster where a large building development had been completed, consisting of many new or renovated houses. Further building was still going on. Suddenly, the King ordered that all the houses be pulled down! This was in complete defiance of a specific royal grant made before Sir John acquired ownership. The intention appears to have been a malicious, intentional, and vicious persecution of Danvers. But it was not only Danvers who was left with a pile of brick rubble on his hands: 'the Tenants fled ... most of them were undone,' Danvers tells the crown in his document. So first Danvers had all his trees cut down by the King, and then he had all his houses pulled down by the King. What does this tell us? The conclusion seems obvious.

The King then intervened against Danvers yet again, and once again illegally, to prevent the Danvers family enlarging or building upon their estates in Yorkshire. To cover up the brutal grabbing of the land by the King, a token annuity was offered, and then this unpaid annuity was settled by way of a composition which was even smaller, and then Henry Danvers transferred this to Sir John, and as soon as that happened – guess what? Not a penny was paid even of that small sum. So the Yorkshire land was seized for alum exploitation and no compensation ever accrued to the Danvers family, apparently. But one thing is certain, that as soon as Sir John Danvers was designated the recipient of the compensation by his brother, payment was stopped.

Is it any wonder that Sir John Danvers may have felt himself a persecuted man? At every turn, he found doors shut in his face, money which was rightfully his denied to him, houses he had built torn down before his eyes, land he owned rendered useless or seized by brute force. – And what was his crime? He had served the royal family for seven years without pay, – evidently an unforgivable sin!

By 1626, the last year of his wife's life (when she may well have been seriously ill), Danvers was so desperate for money that he was reduced to borrowing £30 from the funds of his church at Chelsea! He meticulously paid interest on this, but by 1629 had to borrow a further £10! He was so desperately broke that, although he paid vast amounts of interest over the years, it was not until just before his death in 1655 that this money was repaid by him to the church. He had been in debt to his own church *for 29 years* for just a few pounds. By 1655 he had paid interest to the church which was far in excess of the £40 he had borrowed, so that the church had much more than doubled its money.[49]

How insufferably galling it must have been for Danvers to have to go cap in hand to his own church for a few pounds in cash when the King had been responsible for seizing illegally many thousands of pounds of his money! When one understands the true background of Danvers's poverty, and how it was really caused, one cannot but be sickened by the royalist propaganda which sought to portray him as opposing Charles I in order to ingratiate himself with the Parliamentarians to recompense himself financially for 'ruining himself through extravagance'! In any case, if that were so, Danvers would not have been so foolish as to defy the King's warrant as early as April, 1640 (see relevant document transcribed in the Appendix). What advantage was there for Danvers at that date to defy the King and refuse to carry out his Deputy-Lieutenant duties? Danvers was interrogated by the Attorney General and 'what further course will be taken against him time will try'.

Danvers had made a modest come-back which began as King James lay on his death-bed. Amongst the warrants and appointments put through in the King's name by Buckingham 'in his Maties presence' (whose attention can hardly have been of the most acute!) on March 23, 1624/5, shortly before the King's death-rattle, was a warrant for Sir John Danvers to be made a Deputy Lieutenant for Middlesex.[50] A few weeks later, Sir John was included with his brother Henry (Sir John being a substitute for Henry Osborne, who was ruled out as being under the age of 14!) as joint Keeper of St. James's Palace (and, presumably, St. James's Park as well). A legal document drawn up by Danvers in September in connection with his duties is discussed in the later chapter Regicides and the Law. Danvers took his duties very seriously and worked in connection with the Earl of Dorset keeping highways in repair.[51] Also, as the DNB points out, Sir John managed to be named Gentleman of the Privy Chamber to Charles I, doubtless through the influence of his brother, of Buckingham, and other friends and contacts at court whose help had long been rendered useless by James I's implacable antagonism to Sir John.

The attempt to come to terms with the monarchy under Charles I, however, obviously led eventually to a complete collapse in Danvers's willingness to go along any more with the royal pretensions. He refused to contribute towards the Bishops' War against Scotland[52] and, as we have seen, defied the King's warrant in 1640. Danvers was set upon a course of inevitable opposition to Charles I.

Four fascinating letters survive from Danvers in the crucial months of July and August, 1642. They are addressed to his friend Sir Robert Foster, the Judge, who was to become a royalist. This friendship, and other relevant letters of Danvers's, are discussed in the chapter on Regicides and the Law. I have not transcribed the four letters to Foster[53] because so much of their contents is to be found in the Calendar.[54] But some important passages and remarks are omitted in the Calendar, which shed some light on Danvers's attitudes. For instance, omitted is the passage in his letter of July 18, where he says to Foster:

'I have troubled you but to long whyles my cheife hope is that somewhat according to a Spanish tale when two armies were neere one the other a Combate was challenged & ready to be performed betweene a Castilian & one of Arragon. One Drawing his sword cryed Long Live the King of Castyle. The Other presently cast downe his weapons & embraced his adversarye crying Long Live wee two. And soe god send you a happy iurney & returne to meet wth Your lops assured loving friend & servant, J DANVERS.'[55]

Anyone not consulting the original would be unaware of this crucial indication of how Danvers viewed the coming Civil War. He is letting Foster know that they should continue to be friends despite the looming conflict.

Similar sentiments are repeated at the beginning of Danvers's letter to Foster of August 7th, and these too are omitted from the Calendar. Danvers says:

'I am very willing to lett you finde my love & respect pursuing you and although the turbulent tymes may controvert yet I may tell you what I heare as matter of fact.'[56]

Also omitted in the Calendar is a passage where Danvers attempts to reassure Foster about his judiciary office and position:

'Your Perticuler now under faier censure of the Most judicious & Powerfull in these Partes seems the more happy in how much as few deserve better Esteeme for your Place or profession any where Else.'[57]

That Danvers really believed this, we learn from a letter of his to Sir Edward Dering, transcribed in the Appendix to the chapter on Regicides and the Law, where fuller discussion is to be found. Just as Danvers appears to have persuaded Lord Herbert of Cherbury to 'come in' to the Parliament in the 1640s, so he is seen here trying to keep Foster from bolting to the royalists. Also omitted by the Calendar in Danvers's final letter to Foster is the end, where after speaking of the King and Parliament still having some hope of uniting, he adds:

'… which God grant. Wherein your integritye hath begotten Confidence of your right assistance.'[58]

But Danvers's efforts to keep Foster sweet for the Parliament, hold onto his friendship, and use that friendship to try and make a path for mediation between the two hostile sides, all seem to have ended in failure. The Civil War was to become far more brutal to friendships and to sweet reason and mediation than anyone could have foreseen. While there was no doubting which side Danvers was on, it is clear that he took his leave of many good friends and parted with much cultured and valued company with the deepest regret, and made considerable efforts to hang onto them to the bitter end.

The personal friendships of Danvers, even up to the Civil War, reached so high that one good friend was Charles Louis, the Elector Palatine, who sent him personal greetings in a letter of late 1640 from the Hague.[59] Charles Louis was a young lad of only 23 at the time. This friendly greeting suggests that Danvers had known his mother Princess Elizabeth Stuart (sister to Charles I) very well during his time with her older brother (who was older than her by two years), Prince Henry. (Charles was six years younger than Henry, four years younger than Elizabeth.) For Elizabeth's son to be so friendly to Danvers suggests that Danvers and Elizabeth had been affectionate friends when young and that this tradition of friendship had passed on to the younger generation with Charles Louis. Certainly, Danvers was promoting the interests of Princess Elizabeth soon after she became Queen of Bohemia by marrying Frederick V. She was crowned on 7 November 1619, and Robert Brenner records Danvers as having been a member of 'an informal English pro-Bohemian party' in 1621, along with the Earl of Essex, the Earl of Southampton, the Earl of Warwick, and others.[60]

And this brings us to the last but hardly the least item in Sir John Danvers's early career: his relationship with his royalist brother, Henry. Much has been made of this, from Danvers's contemporaries down to the present day. What ensued was to provide the entire basis for discrediting Danvers in the eyes of historians. And it is therefore crucial to establish the true facts, in order to clear the clouds from the issue. Danvers's own cousin, John Aubrey, says that Danvers 'to null his brother, Early of Danby's, will, he, contrary to his own natural inclination, did sit in the High Court of Justice at the king's trial.'[61] This is quoted by Blair Worden, who says it is 'probably accurate'.[62] Underdown accepts this and more, saying: 'Sir John Danvers ... ruined himself by his architectural and horticultural extravagance. In 1648-9 he was trying to recover his fortunes by overthrowing the will of his royalist brother, the Earl of Danby, who had left all his property to a sister, Lady Gargrave.'[63] Everywhere one turns, one finds Danvers accused of trying to overturn this will in which his brother left everything to their royalist sister Lady Gargrave, with whom Sir John was on very bad terms.

However, a closer inspection of this matter reveals a different version of events. The first thing to note is that Aubrey (who was a royalist) undermines his own case by giving the information that: '(The Earl of Danby) never married; and by his Will made 1639, settled his Estate on his hopefull Nephew Henry D'Anvers (only sonne of Sr John Danvers) snatch't away (before fully of age) to the great griefe of all good men.'[64] Obviously, the heir to this son who predeceased his father was Danby's brother, Sir John Danvers. What happened was that the Earl of Danby was upset that his brother took sides against the King, and made a will just before he died in 1644 leaving everything instead to Lady Gargrave. Sir John was quite right in saying that he should have inherited everything, for indeed he would have done if Danby had not made the new will because he didn't approve of his brother's politics, and the only relation whose politics he did approve of was the fanatically royalist Lady Gargrave. Sir John, who had spent his life being robbed time and again for political reasons, obviously felt that he had had enough. So he challenged the will. It was not as simple as it sounds. Lady Gargrave herself admitted that her brother Danby had settled things on her in his final will 'for her life only', and not absolutely. In addition, in the final will, Danby had left some lands to Sir John.[65] There was the further complication that Danby had been sequestered by Parliament for being a royalist; Danvers wished this to be taken off and himself acknowledged by Parliament as heir, leaving Lady Gargrave to prove her case to the contrary at law if she could (assisted by other royalist relations, the Osbornes and Major Legg).

Long before this dispute began to take up so much of the time of the House of Commons, Danvers had tried to have the issue resolved at a lower level in the Parliamentary Committee of Sequestrations, as may be seen from the countless entries about the case in that Committee's Order Books. That Committee took a painful and pedantic course, referring to the County Committees of Oxfordshire, Wiltshire, Northamptonshire, and Yorkshire, seeking vast numbers of witnesses, arranging cross-examinations and so on *ad nauseam*.[66] All of this was really unnecessary, and appears to have been a means of delaying a decision by a Committee which was too timid to make a ruling. Prominent people such as Nathaniel Fiennes were dragged in for questioning, and the whole matter became a *cause celèbre* so entangled that sorting it out seems to have become impossible. The future regicide John Lisle, who was a legal expert, officially reported on the case to the House of Commons after having chaired an investigatory committee which had been set up for that special purpose:

'The effect of (Danvers's) peticion is humbly to shew yow That he is brother and heire to the Earle of Danby late deceased who in his life time was sequestred by authority of Parliamt for adhering to the kings party. And further sheweth that before the differences betwixt King and Parliament the Earle of Danby bore so grate love, and brotherly affeccion to him that he severall tymes offered to leave all, or the most part of his personall estate to him, and to leave all his Land to descend to him after his decease.

'That merely for his adhering to the Parliament by the advice of Sr Edward Hide and other Enemyes to the Parliament, the Earle is wrought upon to make his Will lately at Oxford, wherein there are endeavours to disinherit Sr John Danvers of the greatest part of his brothers estate.'[67]

This evidence about the involvement by Sir Edward Hyde, alias Lord Clarendon, is very important. For Hyde has provided some of the most damning testimony against Danvers in his *History of the Rebellion*, We see here that Hyde was a thoroughly biased, conflicted, and unreliable source of independent information about Sir John Danvers, a fact which no one has appreciated before, due to John Lisle's Report not having been previously known.

Clarendon/Hyde before the Civil War shared many friends with Sir John Danvers, such as John Selden, and they must have known one another. However, they cannot have been friends, because Hyde, who was apparently involved in a sustained campaign to undo Danvers financially, was prepared to add insult to injury by blackening Danvers's reputation as well in his *History*.[68] Clarendon and Aubrey between them have led subsequent historians to claim of Danvers that he was not acting on principle at all, and 'to extricate himself from his difficulties (he) identified himself with the regicides'.[69] The passionate royalist Mark Noble was all too eager to take up the cudgel, since his appallingly unreliable book *Lives of the English Regicides* was not a work of history but one of propaganda, designed to curry favour with the Establishment of his own day by heaping odium and vituperation upon the erstwhile subjects of his biographical sketches, with all pretence at objectivity so flagrantly abandoned that no one could possibly mistake its purpose. Noble quotes Clarendon with delight in describing Danvers's 'nefarious conduct', saying of him that 'his whole aim now centered in obtaining the estate of his late brother, Lord Danby ... by fraud ... which he had lost by his wilful and ungrateful conduct.'[70] Noble seems oblivious of the fact that he had admitted by the very words just quoted that Danvers had lost the estate as a penalty for siding with the Parliament. But evidently to Noble, and to most of his then readers, 'wilful and ungrateful conduct' – i.e., opposing the King –deserved the worst of fates, and at the very least the loss of one's estate. It does not seem to occur to Noble that in admitting this he is contradicting himself, since he cannot have it both ways; on the one hand, Danvers deserved to be cut off by his brother, and on the other hand Noble wishes us to believe that Danvers only sided with the Parliament in order to get back the estate which he had already lost for the very same siding with Parliament. This lack of logic is all too common in the 'arguments' put forward in partisan rants. But such absurd circular reasoning should not be taken seriously by modern historians, as they have been wont to do until now.

Any arguments that Danvers got lenient treatment from the Commonwealth and was heaped with riches for opposing the King fall to the ground entirely when the truth becomes known, which has not previously been the case. In the later chapter on 'The Regicides and Committees', and its Appendix, further discussion of this matter will appear, and many letters will be given from the Commissioners for the Advance of Money and the Commissioners for Compounding. In these, it will be seen clearly that Danvers was hounded and harassed by the Commissioners as if he were the worst kind of enemy of the State. So much for favour being shown! But of far greater interest in the context of this discussion we should note that the basis on which the Commissioners pursued Danvers was information given in to them by a Gilbert Hyde, probably a relative of Clarendon's who may have been acting of Clarendon's instructions. (Clarendon would doubtless have known some information about Danvers's financial affairs from fellow royalists at Oxford, where there were so many people who knew them both.) The fellow-informant of this Gilbert Hyde was one Arthur Mallock, probably related to Edward Hyde's friend Judge Thomas Malloch/Mallock/Mallet.[71] Arthur Mallock was from Axmouth and was one of the people interrogated for evidence against Danvers's friend Sir Robert Foster (Danvers's correspondence with whom was mentioned earlier), and was apparently related to the Robert Mallock whom Foster had condemned for high treason, so that a deep personal grudge or hatred was probably involved between Mallock and Foster, and because of Danvers's close friendship with Foster, a profound antipathy may well have existed between Mallock and Danvers as well.[72] And to show just how hostile the Commissioners really were to Sir John Danvers, they rewarded these two unpleasant informers with £600 in cash which they extorted out of Danvers personally, thus pre-judging the case which they were supposed to be impartially investigating by paying people very large sums for providing evidence against him. The proceedings smell intensely of a campaign of persecution against Danvers by bitter personal enemies. Paying hostile informants handsomely and dragging out the investigation with needless consultations with numerous county committees all over England, concerning essentially irrelevant matters, suggests a set-up.

Blair Worden, without looking sufficiently deeply into the matter, has accused Sir John Danvers of 'ruthless pursuit of his private interests in the House, a trait which might have been less unattractive had he not also failed to repay the large sums he owed to the state.' Worden then adds confusion to confusion by attacking Danvers in company with Sir Thomas Jervoise and Robert Wallop, saying they 'worked in unison, and whose financial interests were tied up with those of Danvers'.[73] This is not only misleading and unfair to all three men, it is inaccurate. The truth is quite different. Although this is really a matter for the later chapter on 'Regicides and Committees', we shall explore the matter here as briefly as possible because the charge of Worden has to be answered.

The two men just mentioned, Hyde and Mallock, had reported to the Commissioners for Advance of Money and the Commissioners for Compounding that Danvers owed £3000 to a royalist named Angell Grey, who had been sequestered according to them, so that the £3000 was thus really owing to the State by Danvers as a result. The Commissioners wrongly accepted this testimony on trust and gave one fifth of the sum to the two men as an informants' commission. The Committee then ruthlessly pursued Danvers for the

£3000 which he was, of course, far too broke to repay entirely. He did manage to pay the Committee £1000 of it and kept asking for more time to try to raise the rest of the money.

As a much later document reveals, however, this entire set-up of Danvers was based upon a blatant lie which was clearly contrived as a dishonest campaign of persecution intended to destroy him. The real truth was admitted by the mysterious Angell Grey in a post-Restoration Petition which he filed, and which I have transcribed in its entirety and included in the Appendix. In this document, Angell Grey admits that he had really compounded as a royalist for his Estate in the 1640s and that it had never been sequestered at all. Hence, Danvers never really had owed £3000, or even three pence, to the State. But by this time, Danvers had been dead for many years and nobody cared. The testimony accepted as 'evidence' against Danvers which was so readily accepted and paid for by the Commissioners was invented. Since it should have been an easy matter for the Commissioners for Compounding to look into their records (records which were not available to anyone else) and see for themselves that Angell Grey had already compounded, so that nothing was therefore owing to the State by Danvers, the conclusion seems inescapable that Danvers was 'framed' on a false charge by the Commissioners, who concealed the evidence, which was solely in their control, which would have proved his innocence. There was undoubtedly a conspiracy against Danvers.

So Danvers knew that he didn't really owe the money at all, but he could not persuade anyone of the truth, and instead the false testimony against him was accepted without question. But the story gets even worse. In his Petition, Angell Grey freely admits that the £3000 never was his at all, but had merely been held by him on trust for somebody else, and that Danvers knew this. So Angell Grey didn't even own the money in the first place, so that *even if he had been sequestrated, which he had not,* Danvers would still not have not have owed anything to the State. The plot against Danvers was thus constructed entirely of lies.

At the time all this was going on, Danvers was not only an M.P., but also a member of the Council of State, which was ruling the country. Does this sound like favouritism? Like someone in a high position enriching himself at the expense of the State? Danvers was not even receiving a salary for being a member of the Council of State. But rather than getting paid anything for his public services, he was instead being hounded by the State mercilessly and to ruination for a huge sum which he did not even owe.

Despite paying over £1000 of the phantom debt in order to get the Commissioners off his back, they pursued him relentlessly and threatened to send bailiffs around to levy money from his property and recover funds from the sale of his seized personal possessions. The State, which owed Danvers a great deal of money, finally was persuaded to pay a portion over to him. A House of Commons order was made to pay Danvers £500 of his massive arrears, out of the Earl of Winchester's sequestered estate. Danvers turned to Jervoise and Wallop for assistance at this point, getting them to inform the Commissioners that this payment of £500 had now been authorised by the Commons. He asked if he could give them this £500 towards his debt by having the payment passed direct to the Commissioners. *But they refused to accept it.* Instead of taking the £500, they insisted they would send round the bailiffs. The only reason why Jervoise and Wallop were brought into the picture was to act as intermediaries on behalf of Danvers to try to persuade the Commissioners to accept a payment of £500. It is this alone which Blair Worden has construed as evidence for his pure fantasy of the fortunes of Danvers, Jervoise, and Wallop, being 'tied up' with each other. Worden tries to make out that the three men were in a cabal and were up to no good, that they were scheming to defraud the State, and he lumps them in the same category with the embezzler Lord Howard of Escrick. On the flimsy basis outlined above Worden describes these four men as being the most abominable men in the Rump Parliament. Lord Howard was well known for being a crook, but he had no connection with the other three men. The only 'crime' committed by Jervoise and Wallop was to act as emissaries for their friend Danvers by going to the Commissioners and asking them if they would accept £500 as part payment for a debt which their friend didn't even owe. As for Danvers, his 'crime' was that he was falsely accused of a debt to the State and 'framed' by political and personal enemies. So much for Danvers and his two friends as being three of the four most dishonest MPs in the Rump Parliament! Later, Sir John Danvers really would be financially ruined, and his story got worse and worse. But that is for a later chapter, and we have now come to the end of our account of the early career of Sir John Danvers. There is further discussion of him, with transcribed documents, in the chapter on 'The Regicides and the Law'.

The original oil painting is lost, but this drawing of it survives. Sir John Danvers was 55 years old when the Civil War began, and this boy is clearly very young, perhaps even a teenager. If it be really Sir John Danvers, then it must date from 1601 at the time of the Essex Rebellion, when he was 16. Since his older brother took a leading part in that Rebellion, for which he was later executed, the young John may also have suited up in armour with the expectation of joining in the action, or may even have taken part and later concealed the fact in order to save his own life. Certainly this boy could be 16, and he has the boyish good looks spoken of by John Aubrey.

The face represented here is clearly copied (in reverse) from the larger drawing. Note that by this later date, the copy of the painting had passed from the ownership of John Cames of Spitalfields to Robert Stearne Tighe (1760-1835), an Irish historian and writer, and Fellow of the Royal Society.

Sir William Constable, Bart.

Turning now to the oldest of the regicides, who was about 73 when he signed the Death Warrant of Charles I, we consider Sir William Constable, Bart. Occasionally in history someone prominent in one era survives to play a prominent role in a succeeding era. But when a historian encounters such a phenomenon, it can give him an uncanny feeling. Sir William Constable was, not to point too fine a point on it, a living fossil.

Whereas Sir John Danvers was a Jacobean courtier, Sir William Constable was an Elizabethan one! Having taken part in an attempt to overthrow Queen Elizabeth in the Essex Rebellion, he lived to help overthrow the monarch-after-next. One cannot ignore this remarkable continuity. The same man who commanded a platoon of halberdiers in 1601 with a revolutionary intent also set his hand to the Death Warrant in 1649 with a revolutionary intent. It is impossible that Sir William Constable can have been unaware of the fact that he was, 48 years later, realizing his youthful aim of toppling a monarch. What kind of feeling comes to a man who realizes a design after half a century of waiting? One most presume, the most sublime satisfaction. We might say of Sir William that he was the regicide who tried twice, and who succeeded the second time.

Sir William was the son and heir of Sir Robert Constable of the Manor of Flamborough, of Holme Manor, and of Spalding Manor, Yorkshire, and Anne Hussey, daughter and heiress of John Hussey of Driffield, which is in the East Riding of Yorkshire and only a short horse ride from Flamborough, riding northeast past Bridlington. (It has sometimes been wrongly claimed that Sir William's mother was Dorothy Widdrington, but she was his grandmother, not his mother.) He must have been born circa 1575. The only known baptismal record which could be him is dated 24 August 1574. But that was at St. Peter's Church, Limpsfield, Surrey, a tiny village south of Croydon with no known Constables. No parents were listed in the baptismal record. Could the regicide's parents have been staying with the gentry family there named Holmeden? As a renowned soldier, who had been knighted by the Earl of Sussex and had prominent friends in various parts of the country, as well as myriads of relations not all of whose names we know, this offers itself as a possibility. Other scholars who have knowledge of the Holmeden family history might be able to help with this matter. Was one of the Holmedens a military comrade? A relative? A friend? These are all imponderables. And the regicide's baptismal record could be lost, with this one being a false lead. We may never have certainty concerning Constable's birth date. A suggestion made in the Oxford DNB that Constable was born in 1590 was shown to be false in the Appendix to Chapter Two. Basically, the Oxford DNB author suggests that there was another Sir William Constable who was slightly older than the regicide. But that is impossible, because no William Constable was knighted after 1513 apart from the one who was knighted in 1599. And we have documentary proof that the regicide was a knight as well as (after 1611) a baronet. If the regicide had been born in 1590 he would have been nine years old in 1599. And since there was no other Sir William Constable, Knight, alive in the 17th century than the regicide, there is only one possibility, that the regicide was not knighted in the field in Ireland aged nine as some kind of infant Hercules, but was, as other circumstances require, born circa 1575, as stated above.

Sir William's family were extremely prosperous greater gentry, with an ancient lineage. They were descended from Ivo Constantine of Normandy and Ivo Lord Vescy, as well as the Barons Halton or Haillton (one of whom died in 1189 at Tyre on Crusade.) Several of their ancestors had been Sheriffs of Yorkshire or Members of Parliament. The earliest recorded ancestor to be knighted was Sir Robert Constable of Flamborough, who was knighted by Edward I. His son,

Sir Marmaduke Constable, was High Sheriff of Yorkshire under Edward III. The regicide was descended from an Earl of Britain, a Lord Darcy, and Lord Fitzhugh and was related or connected to an Earl of Lincoln, the Lords of Clavering, the Lord of Warkworth, Lord Conyers, and so on. His six times great-grandfather Sir Robert Constable had been High Sheriff of Yorkshire under both Henry VI and Edward IV, and his son and the regicide's five times great-grandfather had been an MP and Knight of the Shire for Yorkshire under Edward IV. Several generations of the Constables had been knighted in the field for valourous conduct, and they had over the centuries faithfully carried on the martial traditions of the family as brave warriors who fought for King and Country. Sir William was to be no exception to these traditions, and was to be in effect its culmination, except for one thing: he was indeed for Country and was prepared on numerous occasions to fight to the death for it, but as events were to show, he was not necessarily for King or for Queen. If it came to a choice between his Country and an oppressive monarch, he twice did not hesitate to choose his Country. A manuscript pedigree of Sir William is preserved in the Bodleian Library as MS. Rawlinson B. 74, 94b and 95a, for those who might wish to pursue the genealogical details. There are also printed pedigrees,[74] and further manuscript pedigrees are probably preserved in the College of Heralds, though they are less accessible.

Constable's wife, who survived him briefly after his death in 1655, was Dorothy Fairfax, the eldest daughter of the elder Sir Thomas Fairfax, who became the First Lord Fairfax of Cameron and died 1640. They married on February 15, 1607/8, at Newton Kyme, near Tadcaster in North Yorkshire. Lord Ferdinando Fairfax, the second Lord Fairfax, was thus Constable's brother-in-law, and Sir Thomas Fairfax, who was in command of the New Model Army, was Constable's nephew.

The relations between Constable and his wife and all of the Fairfaxes, at least three generations of them, appears to have been intimate and cordial throughout their lives. This is shown by the correspondence and by the evidence of their joint actions and close cooperation over many decades. In addition, there are various references to some of the younger Fairfaxes living with the Constables. For instance, Constable says in a postscript to his letter to Ferdinando of November 14, 1635 (from his then residence at Sheer's Court, Aldersgate Street without Aldersgate): 'My wife, your son [the later Sir Thomas in the New Model Army] and daughter, and myself, would all be shut up in [i.e. join together in] this short salute.'[75] Dorothy's father, Thomas, the First Lord Fairfax, left amongst the legacies in his will: 'Item: I give to my daughter, the Lady Constable, 40l [£40], to be bestowed in some remembrance of me.'[76] Dorothy's brother Ferdinando, the Second Lord Fairfax, left amongst the legacies in his will: 'Item, I give unto Sir William Constable, Baronet, ten pounds; and to his wife, my dear sister, one hundreds pounds.'[77] In considering Sir William Constable's life, it therefore needs always to be borne in mind that his life went on essentially in tandem with the lives of the Fairfaxes, and that the intimacy between them did not abate in any way until the end of 1648, when Sir William sided with the radicals of the Army led by Henry Ireton and Oliver Cromwell, whereas his nephew Sir Thomas Fairfax stepped back and declined to take part, largely, as it is thought, under the influence of his wife, whose political views were well known to be 'Presbyterian', i.e. moderate and in favour of compromise with the King. Thus, Sir Thomas did not turn up at the High Court of Justice to try the King, despite being named to it. His wife, however, was in the women's gallery. And when she heard her husband's name called out in a roll-call of the appointed members of the High Court, she shouted at the top of her voice: 'He has more wit than to be here!' She went on interrupting and loudly protesting until she had to be ejected from Westminster Hall because of the disturbance she was causing to the proceedings. It is doubtful if at this stage of life, she and Sir William Constable, who was sitting below her as a member of the High Court and whose name had been called out in alphabetical order before her husband's, were any longer intimate.

This is ironical, in that it was Sir William Constable who had taken great pains over the course of two years to negotiate the complexities of and permission for her marriage to his nephew. The young lady, as she then was, of 1635, was Anne Vere, daughter of the widowed Lady Vere. Young Thomas Fairfax dutifully allowed himself to be matched with her in an arranged marriage which appears not to have had his personal enthusiasm. Instead, the fierce warrior who was to command the New Model Army followed the wishes of his father and his grandfather, and permitted his uncle Sir William Constable to broker the marriage, the chief attraction of which to the Fairfax family was the girl's dowry, which on no account was to be less than £4,000. This was subject to continual haggling. Sir William threw himself into these negotiations with reluctance because he was preoccupied with his own problems, but he conscientiously carried out this duty, though that portion of the correspondence which has been published shows him to have been under constant pressure, and subject to exhaustion. In his letter to Ferdinando of November 14, 1635, he says, for instance:

'… though I could not this day inquire out a fit messenger, hearing now at night of one, though late and weary, with some disadvantage to myself, I choose rather to give you this in part than to defer till I could give you a more perfect account, which I shall seek to do with as much speed as the business and the slow agent [a Dr. Gouge] can conveniently afford. Thus, Sir, for this time, without further ceremony, good night.'[78]

It does not take a seismic detector to sense Sir William's exhaustion and that he is near to exasperation over the whole matter. He was also far too familiar with the unreliable nature of debts from the Crown, as he informed Ferdinando that Dr. Gouge on his behalf 'asked the lady (Vere) herself what portions are intended to her two daughters who are yet unmarried. Her answer is that she intends to each of them 3000l or 4000l, according as she shall like of the party; and that there is no haste on her part of having them bestowed, since the longer they stay, the better she shall be able to do for them, my lord having left her indebted. Yet she hopes, by means of some moneys due to her from the King, to better her daughters' portions, in some reasonable time.

'The second thing which I desired to do was, that my wife or myself, or both of us, might have had a sight of these two young gentlewomen; but my lady having been out of town, and daily expected, is not yet come, except it be this very night.'[79]

How Sir William must have had to hold his tongue when told about Lady Vere's hopes of getting some money back from the King! The Crown had owed him £8,000 for years, and he never got a penny of it (see below). Nearly two months later, on January 6, 1635/6, Sir William wrote a much longer letter to Ferdinando. He began:

'I know not well where to begin to sum up to you an account of the successes of your twofold treaty [with Lady Vere, managed by Sir William]. What I had not time to write before, my wife hath informed you of as well as she could, by which you may judge in what terms the business now stands on all parts. Mrs. Barrow was lately with my wife, and was pleased to ask my opinion whether the countess [Lady Vere] not writing an answer to my lord's last letter, would not be taken for a neglect. My answer was, that I was not skilled in those civilities between great persons, but I presumed there would need no more than what had been signified to him already … Mrs. Barrow seemed to think that her lady might be wound up to some few hundreds about 4000l, if the conditions for present maintenance might be made more suitable … Since this, I made a journey hither [from a temporary residence at Missenden in Buckinghamshire, presumably Great Missenden rather than Little Missenden] to London, one chief end of my journey being in hope to have met with Dr. Wright, by whom my lady Vere had formerly treated with me, and expressed more of her mind than I could then have from herself ... (but) I understand that Sir Roger Townsend [husband to Lady Vere's eldest daughter] (at whose house in Norfolk my lady Vere now is), died the last week, my letter to my lady coming to her in the midst of that distraction some few days before his death. ... my lady purposeth shortly to be here, if the increase of the plague here do not hinder her; howsoever, as soon as these present distractions of hers give leave, she will send to me, and I shall accordingly advertise you. Thus abridging all the ceremony which should end my letter, according to my paper, I must here abruptly end this confused story, and return this day to Missenden.'[80]

Later, on February 9, Sir William wrote again to Ferdinando on this matter. He expressed his annoyance with Lady Vere because his nephew Thomas upon going to see her 'had only a civil entertainment with gravity and reservedness'. He tells more details of the situation and then says: 'I shall, within a day or two, wait upon my lady, and then I doubt not to find her less reserved than her grave way of treating afforded at the first, being so slowly pressed on my part.'[81]

Sir William's 'slowly slowly' approach worked, and finally in June of 1637, approximately two years after the commencement of this arid dance of formalities and rather sordid financial haggling, the arranged marriage of young Thomas Fairfax and Anne Vere took place at last, doubtless to the great relief of all concerned. What a burden this must have removed from Sir William's shoulders, upon whom had fallen the entire responsibility of the nuptial negotiations! Anyone wondering why Sir William Constable and Sir Thomas Fairfax were so close in later life, and how Sir William could just walk in and sit down at the Council of Officers of the New Model Army and take a leading role and sign a revolutionary Order to Parliament when he was not even a member of the New Model Army (see the account of this later on), need only call to mind that he was the wise uncle with whom Sir Thomas had often lodged as a young man and who had persevered for two years in arranging his marriage for him, and Thomas must have been in the habit of being as deferential to him as he had always been to his father and his grandfather. Indeed, I would go so far as to suggest that it was this very character trait of allowing powerful martial men who were close to him to dominate him with their advice which led Fairfax to be so malleable in the hands of someone as dominant by nature as his deputy, Oliver Cromwell. And that goes a long way to explain a great deal about the history of the seventeenth century in England.

Having dealt with his relationship with the Fairfax family, we must now turn back to Sir William himself and consider the course of his early life, with all its drama, its passing glamour, his great hopes, and his extremely bitter disappointments. He seems not to have bothered to attend university. We have already seen that the Constables followed a martial tradition. It is thus not surprising that our first trace of him occurs in a military context, where as a young man in his mid-teens he is prominent in the siege of Rouen in 1591 under the Earl of Essex (whose Rebellion he would later join). Coningsby, in his journal of the siege, records: 'But yet in the meane while ... they made certaine shott of artyllerie out of the town upon us, and slewe an horse with a falcon shott under one mr. Constable and brused his thigh verie sore; and wonderfullie they came out that afternoone in great nombres, and we expected some greate consequente ...'[82] At this siege, Constable was able to become friends with a number of important comrades-in-arms: Sir Thomas Fairfax (grandfather of the New Model General), who 17 years later would become his father-in-law; Sir Henry Danvers, older brother of the regicide Sir John Danvers and who afterwards became Earl of Danby; Sir Oliver St. John, Sir Robert Cary; and not least, the Earl of Essex, their Commander.[83] It is not unlikely that Constable was a Captain, with the rest of these young adventurers of high birth, since his description in the Journal as 'Mr.' does not mean he was not 'Captain', it being Coningsby's habit to refer to the captains as 'Mr.', as the fancy took him.[84] Otherwise, he may have begun as a lieutenant to one of the captains, and then been promoted to Captain on the battlefield. In any event, he was certainly Captain William Constable by the time he wrote a letter to the Earl of Essex on November 3, 1595, which survives in the Salisbury MSS.[85] A letter also survives from Constable to Edward Reynolds, Essex's Secretary, dated September 30, 1598.[86] The next year, Essex took Constable to Ireland with him, where he knighted Constable on July 12, 1599, as mentioned earlier. A letter survives from Constable to Reynolds dated August 2, 1599,[87] and another dated August 15, 1599.[88] A year and a half later, Constable joined his patron, Essex, in the abortive Essex Rebellion, and he was imprisoned with the other participants. He was lucky not be executed. He was arraigned and tried for treason and was found guilty, but he did not suffer the death penalty. An account of his trial survives.[89]

Robert Devereux, 2nd Earl of Essex (1565-1601), who led the failed Essex rebellion of 1601 in an attempt to overthrow Queen Elizabeth I. Constable avoided execution for his minor role in it. But the older brother of Sir John Danvers was beheaded for his role, and so was the Earl of Essex himself.

Constable owed his life at this time to Sir Robert Cecil, as he makes plain in a letter he wrote to him years later, on February 9, 1604/5:

'... my fortunes, which depend upon your continuing to support the remnant of a wretched life, which yesterday three years [February 8, 1600/1, the date of the Essex Rebellion] was forfeited had not your Honour above my merit preserved me (when your enemy unworthy of any grace), which has firmly tied me unto you. It pleased my Lord of Southampton at Woodstock to witness the presentation of my fidelity to you; and since then he lives not that shall better use his sword in your service.'[90]

It is to be noted that Constable offers not his wits but his sword in Cecil's service, showing that he views himself entirely as a man-of-arms; indeed, there is something quaintly feudal about Constable's attitude and fealty, conceiving of his sword as being at the disposal of his patron. It is significant that Constable mentions Southampton in this context. There is considerable likelihood that Cecil, who schemed for the Stuart succession, tried to spare as many of the Essex rebels as he could for use in his and the Stuarts' interests upon the death of the Queen. And he may well have made a 'deal' with Southampton in the Tower, arranging to have his death sentence commuted in return for the recruitment of the support of those Essex rebels who could reasonably be saved for later purposes.

In the old DNB, C. H. Firth points out that Constable was released on bail by an order of March 20. However, Firth erroneously believed that Constable was never tried, an error perpetuated in the entry for Constable by Constance Rynder in the *Biographical Dictionary of British Radicals in the Seventeenth Century* (Harvester Press, 1982), a biographical dictionary to which I myself contributed numerous entries. No previous historian appears to have been aware that Constable was indeed tried and that he then received an official pardon for his crime on July 26, 1602.[91] (Fourteen Essex rebels were all given pardons on that same day, including Sir Christopher Heydon, who, possibly grateful to the celestial rays from the planets for his survival, the next year published his book *A Defence of Judiciall Astrology*, and whose work in astrology was to be continued and promoted by Elias Ashmole and William Lilly long after his own death in 1623.)

Two letters of Constable's to Cecil from the crucial year of 1601 survive, dated May 6 and August 5.[92] Constable seems to have suffered a drastic impairment in his estate as a result of his role in the Essex Rebellion, probably through confiscations or huge penal fines. His most urgent task, therefore, upon regaining his freedom, was to try and concentrate on 'the bettering of my fortunes'.[93] However, things looked up when Cecil negotiated the succession of James VI of Scotland to the English throne. By 1604/5, Constable was able to entreat Cecil for 'the impost of tobacco in Ireland, which might support my estate till my better deserving to attain to better'.[94] He obviously felt apprehensive about the role of a courtier, nervously remarking to Cecil about 'my plainness, for I have not the compliments of the Court', and indeed knew that he suffered as a result, for he adds: 'which makes my wants as they be'.[95] But despite his apprehensions of inadequacy, Constable was such a success with King James that, less than a month later, Sir Thomas Lake wrote to inform Cecil that Constable's petition to the King, which had been drawn at Cecil's direction, had met with such success that the King 'could like well to pleasure the gentleman'.[96] Probably at Cecil's suggestion, Constable had dropped the idea of the tobacco impost for Ireland and settled on quite a different alternative. The alternative seems to have come to his mind through his connection with relatives by marriage from the Newcastle area, the Selbys (related through his grandmother's family, the Widdringtons) and their circle of acquaintance. Constable was given inside information by someone or other from the area that there was widespread corruption in the coal trade, whereby the King was 'defrauded of custom by the shipmasters, who, by corrupting keelmen who bring the coals aboard, ship more chaldrons than they pay custom for, and that the coalsellers receive money for.'[97] King James was naturally thrilled at the prospect of getting more money from the custom duty on coal, so on March 29, 1605, within days of reading the petition, the King wrote to the Mayor of Newcastle appointing Constable the first officer there for measuring coals.[98]

Now Constable seemed on the way 'to amend his poor estate',[99] for the King said he could have a groat for every chaldron of coal reaching London from Newcastle under his inspection.[100] But the Mayor, Aldermen, and Coalowners of Newcastle wrote a brilliantly obstructive letter on April 12 to the King, in effect saying that if this new plan went through, they would have to give up the coal business altogether! They pulled out all the stops, citing a special Act of Parliament from the reign of Henry V (surely forgotten by all but themselves!) and gave breathtakingly gloomy prognostications of what this innovation would mean, concluding that 'the trade would not be able to bear it, and we should be forced to give over the same.'[101] But just in case the King might think that they merely objected to the person of Sir William Constable, the letter obsequiously added: 'The gentleman, whom it has pleased your Majesty to recommend to us to be the first officer for that purpose, is one well known and born amongst us, and so generally well thought of and beloved here that if his suit were but indifferent we would have given him reasonable satisfaction therein, much more upon your Majesty's commendation.'[102]

Faced with such a sugar-coated rebuff, Constable seems to have been frustrated of any hopes of immediate office, and appears to have decided to hang around the Court for a while, in the hopes of building on his success with the King. His martial skills came in handy here. He was very much in the social swing at Court in 1605 when he was included amongst the most select group of courtiers to take part in a special fight at foils, along with the Duke of Lennox, the Earl of Sussex, young Lord Willoughby de Eresby (who was to become his close friend), Sir Oliver Cromwell, and other luminaries.[103] Probably in compensation for the Newcastle deal falling through, Constable was drafted into the royal household, becoming one of the King's servants, the chief of whom was Lord Haddington. In this role, Constable formed his friendship with Sir Edward Bushell, who was to become a Gentleman of the Bedchamber to Queen Anne.

Constable was admitted to the Inner Temple on April 20, 1605, presumably in order to add the cachet of a little learning in the law to his background. His was a 'special admission' on the same day along with his Court companions, the Earls of Arundel, Oxford, Essex, and Northumberland, the Bishop of London, several attendants of Prince Henry, and other Court favourites. At this time, he was described as 'of Lambton, Knight'. This must refer either to Lambton in County Durham or to Lampton in County Middlesex, a village and park which survive between Hounslow and Heathrow Airport today. It was not uncommon then for people busy with affairs in London to have residences in that part of Middlesex, as for instance the lawyer-regicides John Bradshaw (at Feltham) and William Say (at Ickenham) were later to do. This group of courtiers admitted to the Inner Temple in 1605 cannot all have been serious about the law. It is doubtful if any of them were. As to whether Constable studied law at the Inner Temple, or whether this 'special entry' was just a polite social formality, further research in the Inner Temple records might reveal. It is possible that some of these men became enrolled there in order to be able to use or acquire Inner Temple chambers as places of residence for themselves, conveniently within walking distance of Whitehall, or otherwise a short boat ride away by the river. We cannot dismiss the possibility that Constable studied some law, but neither can we feel too confident of it. There is something very strange about this mass-admission of dignitaries, and there must be a political story behind it which we do not know.

It did not take Constable and his friend Sir Edward Bushell long to realize that men of his sort were more likely to be in sympathy with the Queen or the Prince than the effete and homosexually predatory James, to resist whose advances could be dangerous. Constable, whether on his own or through Bushell, seems to have struck up a very successful relationship with Queen Anne, and through her to have gained a substantial reputation in her old home town of Copenhagen. On January 8, 1606/7, Constable and his friend Bushell wrote jointly to King James proudly speaking of 'the confidence they have in the King of Denmark's favour towards them' and asking James to give them £300 'for the services they have willingly rendered in the past.'[104] However, this appeal seems to have brought no result.

If he had not fully realized it before, now was the time when Constable must have begun to see just how fickle the Stuarts were about actually handing over cash. By the end of the year, Constable could count himself lucky that in exchange for his father, Sir Robert Constable, handing in the letters patent that he had possessed to the fee farm of the Manor of Chopwell (on the border of north Durham), William was able to have a new grant of them (forests excepted, and with a proviso for coal mines if discovered, etc.)[105] Things were beginning to look black. Within a fortnight, Constable called in the heavy guns in an attempt to improve his situation. He persuaded his most prominent crony, the Earl of Southhampton, to write a letter on his behalf to the Earl of Salisbury, which was Cecil's new title.[106] This probably means that Constable had neglected to cultivate 'old crook back' with sufficient ardour and needed Southampton's help. Even the business of Chopwell was getting pretty complicated, with the Earl of Dorset, the Lord Treasurer, referring some details to Cecil (Salisbury) for clarification; it seems that the Constables, father and son, had been foiled again. Whereas Sir Thomas Lake had certified the grant to Constable on behalf of the King, the King himself seems to have ignored that and made a direct personal grant of the property to a Mr. Dudley, and this was doubly sad since the Constables appear to have dropped a lawsuit over the property in order to please the King and thereby receive the grant. But they appear to have been tricked, and it seems that the Constables were knowingly cheated, having given up a suit for something, handed in their letters patent to the property, and then been left with nothing in the end. One cannot be certain of this without a closer scrutiny of all of the documents, so the matter remains open for now.[107]

By now Constable was beginning to become extremely desperate for some money. It is difficult to untangle the complicated financial dealings of the Court, in order to understand all of this clearly. However, from a letter of Sir Thomas Lake to the Earl of Salisbury in 1608, it appears that Sir William Constable was owed the enormous sum of £8,000 by the King. This debt had already been compounded by the Crown to a promise of £4,000 in ready money, and Constable was now driven to requesting 'that his Majesty will grant him two of that four'.[108] But this was not to be. The Stuarts may have made pretty promises, but they rarely if ever did pay up. And Constable was to discover the horrendous consequences of putting his trust in the Crown. By the middle of 1609, Constable had been committed to prison by someone he calls 'my greatest enemy' for a debt of £760. He wrote desperately to the Earl of Salisbury for relief, saying that if he could only raise £200 he could clear that debt, and needed another £800 for 'the rest of my creditors'. He pleads: 'Might I by your favour obtain this good by his Majesty's grant of 2000l of his part of the debts which I have under the privy seal, that by sale or otherwise I might obtain 1000l or 800l, I should perpetually pray for your happiness. Could I effect my liberty now, I would leave my poor means in England to satisfy the rest of my creditors, and live myself, wife and family, of my company at the Brill.'[109]

This indicates that Constable was already an active –though *in absentia* – Captain of Foot in the English cautionary town of the Brill in the Low Countries. (Brielle, as it is known in Dutch, is in the province of South Holland, at the Hook of Holland, west of Rotterdam. In 1598 it was the birthplace of Admiral Maarten Tromp, later to be well known to the English, since he commanded the Dutch Fleet in the first Anglo-Dutch War of 1652-3, in which he was killed. One wonders whether during his fights with the English, he remembered the English soldiers he had seen as a boy at 'the Brill', possibly even a young captain named Constable. One of Tromp's daughters was to become the second wife of Constable's future colleague, the regicide Colonel James Temple, MP, whose own daughter Mary by his first wife would then marry the Admiral's son, Cornelis Tromp, another famous Dutch Admiral, who was made an English baronet in 1674. Such are the multiply-crossing threads of fate.)

Sometime before June, 1610, Constable appears to have obtained his release from the debtors' prison by means of a special writ of *habeus corpus*.[110] He was to return to the King's Bench Prison later, but for the moment he was free. It seems that he spent about a year in the prison. He does not seem to have had much luck in collecting money from the Crown. How the Crown came to owe him £8,000 is not clear, but there is some indication that Constable had, through his role as a servant to the King, become personally liable for that amount of palace bills. That could explain why he had a certificate with the privy seal to certify the amount owing to him. As a naïve young man unwise in the ways of the Court, he may have been 'suckered' into advancing those huge sums from his own pocket upon the assurance that he would be repaid speedily. This might have seemed to a trusting soul a fine way to ingratiate himself with the monarch, and lead to advancement. But alas, what a hard lesson to learn, to be imprisoned for subsidising the King's extravagances, and to have lost a manor property as well. Constable wrote to the King in desperation asking for 'an extended rent which is laid upon a lordship that is to descend to petitioner' to be relinquished by the Crown.[111] We do not know the result of this modest request.

During his respite from prison, Constable busily organised an expeditionary force of English soldiers of fortune to go and fight in the Danish wars under his friend Lord Willoughy de Eresby, who was about seven years younger than Constable and something of a greenhorn regarding warfare. (He was Robert Bertie, 14th Baron Willoughby de Eresby, who in 1626 was to be created Earl of Lindsey, and who would die in 1642 at the Battle of Edgehill, fighting as a royalist. At this battle, Constable would command a regiment fighting against the royalists, and one wonders whether the former close friends glimpsed one another on opposite sides at that fateful encounter.) Constable used his friendship with the Queen to expedite this. He still held his office of Captain of Foot at the Brill, and managed to get Salisbury and the Privy Council to sign a Warrant for payment of his wages (this warrant is transcribed in the appendix) on September 30, 1611, which were owing since April 1st. This was despite the fact that Constable 'hath been absent from his said Charge by reason of his attendance upon his Ma:tie being one of his Highnes Privey Chamber'. Shortly afterwards, and probably before any wages could reach him, Constable was again thrust into the King's Bench Prison for the same old debts. (His 'greatest enemy', whose name we do not know, must have sought a fresh Order for this.) This was a disaster; he had nearly organised the force for the Danish King and was now prevented from completing the job. However, he kept his head and wrote a superb letter to Queen Anne (transcribed in the appendix) pointing out that he was to be at the rendezvous of the forces for Denmark by the end of the month but could hardly be so if he could not get out of prison. Despite his drastic poverty, and the fact that he was confined in a cell with what must have been the barest of necessities, he actually used an ink for the letter which appears to have had particles of gold suspended in it! It is ironic in the extreme to read a letter written by a future regicide in which real gold ink is used to write the word 'Majesty' over and over again! It is even more amazing that he defied his circumstances by writing in gold from his prison cell, as if he were a leisurely prince sitting in a palace rather than a man incarcerated for debt. When I held this letter in my hand, I was amazed to see that the gold glistens as freshly today as it must have done in 1611. Normal ink fades, but apparently not gold ink. There is a real problem from the point of view of chemistry as to how this gold ink was made. It is extremely difficult to keep gold particles in solution or in suspension without their settling. It was only in the 20th century that a technique was developed using electricity in an unusual manner to accomplish this. Gold ink in 1611 might have had to be made at the moment of use. Gold can be dissolved into solution briefly by *aqua regia*, an unstable mixture of nitric acid and hydrochloric acid. The hydrochloric acid gives the necessary chloride ions to the gold particles. It is dangerous to do this, however, because *aqua regia* can explode. A single gold particle needs to be surrounded by at least 135,000 chloride ions in order to remain in solution. Each individual chloride ion is square, and they all fit together perfectly to form a complete layer or skin around the gold particle. One's mind thoroughly boggles to imagine Sir William Constable sitting in a dank prison cell with a candle beside him and a small table and chair, mixing the two acids together and then adding some gold powder, to produce an ink which would only remain in solution for a short while, and then writing the magnificent letter to the Queen with its brilliantly glistening gold. One does not know whether to laugh or to cry at such a scene. Perhaps I move in the wrong circles, but I have never seen another letter written in gold ink from the seventeenth century, not even one written by a king or a queen. Constable's astonishing bravado is like something from a romantic novel.

In his letter to Queen Anne, despite the fact that he showed himself the true courtier by its style and presentation, Constable's tone is remarkable for its lack of grovelling. Even when he says '(I) most humbly on the knees of my heart do beg', he does so like a proud soldier, that he 'may be as ready with as brave a troop to go to these royal wars as any other'. He suggests to the Queen that he be allowed by the King to surrender the privy seal now acknowledged to be worth £2,000 (a quarter of its original value, as already mentioned), for £600, or otherwise to be allowed two years to work off his debts by military service.

Apparently, the Earl of Rutland owed Constable £200. Constable wrote another letter, dated November 17, 1611, to Lord Willoughby (transcribed in the appendix), asking him to persuade Rutland to pay this debt. He also continued with his task of organising the Danish expeditionary force from his prison cell! He did this by giving the young Willoughby a string of advice and directions in the most tactful manner. Constable was worried that Willoughby was not wise enough in the ways of war to select the right captains and other officers for the remaining vacancies. Constable also told the Queen that the men he could have persuaded to join the force were holding back because 'they are doubtful of my liberty'.

The eventual issue of all this business is not at all certain. The State Papers Denmark would have to be searched carefully, and some documents might be in Danish. It might even be necessary to search the Danish Archives in Copenhagen for the ultimate truth of what happened, or, more likely, did not happen. I am not aware that Lord Willoughby ever really did go to fight for Denmark. I have not pursued this matter further. In the absence of documents which may remain yet to be discovered, we are left to say that nothing is heard of Sir William Constable until nearly a year and a half later. Whether he remained in his prison cell for most of that time is unknown. But by the spring of 1613, he appears to have been at liberty and in England.

On May 18, 1613, Edmund, Lord Sheffield (he was the 3rd Baron), came to Constable's aid. He knew Constable in a military capacity because he had been Governor of the Brill. Sheffield was to be created the first Earl of Mulgrave in 1626, the same year in which Constable's other friend Baron Willoughby would become the first Earl of Lindsey. (It was clearly a good year for creating earls.) Sheffield was Lord Lieutenant of Yorkshire, Constable's home county, from 1603 to 1619, and they would have had a very considerable circle of friends in common and known each other for years. Sheffield (as Mulgrave) would later join the opposition to the Court, and share Constable's political sympathies, unlike Willoughby (as Lindsey). On May 18, Sheffield, in his capacity as Lord Lieutenant, commissioned Constable to be a Captain of an East Riding trained band. Constable's Yorkshire associations were always primarily with the East Riding, where his Manor of Flamborough was located, for instance. Constable rounded up 95 men to constitute his company, and I have found his official Muster Roll, dated September 27, 1613, which I have transcribed for the appendix.

Though these duties in connection with a trained band may have been tedious to Sir William, and Sheffield probably turned to him out of necessity because of his military expertise, there may have been a bit of money in it for Constable, and in any case it was a good moment for Constable to become militarily active again. In 1611, Sir William had bought a baronetcy for £2,000, only a few months before he was imprisoned for the second time. The baronetcy 'Constable of Flamborough' was created by James I on June 29, 1611, the first year of their invention. It is often supposed that it became extinct upon Constable's death on June 15, 1655. (He was buried on June 21 in King Henry VII's Chapel at Westminster Abbey.) This is what John Burke presumed in his *Extinct and Dormant Baronetcies of England* (London, 1838, p. 126), where he states that Constable 'had no issue'. However, in the six-volume *The English Baronetage* of 1741, it is stated at p. 55 of Volume IV that Constable's baronetcy became extinct by attainder (i.e. in 1660, posthumously, because of his having been a traitor, which suggests that it survived his death and that he had a son). This raises interesting questions. Did Constable have any children? We have already seen that in a letter of 1609 to the Earl of Salisbury, Constable specifically speaks of 'myself, wife, and family'. But what family? I have come across one source (a hand annotation by a genealogist added to a printed pedigree, apparently in the 19th century) which stated that he had 'an only child who died in 1608', but that is a year earlier than the letter mentioning a 'family'. There is another tradition that he had a son called William who attended Eton and survived the Restoration. Since these are matters of tangential interest to our main historical purposes, I have not attempted to arrive at a definitive solution to them. It may be that only certain parish registers of Yorkshire might contain the answers (unless there are some clues in some of the unpublished Fairfax MSS). In any case, Constable's properties, what remained of them, were confiscated at the Restoration. If there were a surviving son, as there was no property left and no title surviving, since it had been declared extinct by attainder, he would probably have kept his head down or indeed, like other children of regicides, gone to America in search of a new life.

Purchasing a baronetage in order to become Sir William Constable, Bart., when he was already Sir William Constable, Knight, may have been a foolish act, but he was playing the game of prestige for high stakes. God knows where he got the money for the purchase, as he was so broke. But by the end of 1613, he was to need the prestige of his new title. For in the scramble for military commands, there was fierce and unrelenting competition. About that time, the Earl of Northampton wrote to Sir Thomas Lake trying to prevent Constable from regaining his captaincy at the Brill. Northampton wrote, rather pompously: 'I had forgotten good Sir Tho Lake to require you to let his Mty [Majesty] knowe that my Cosin Horace Vere is advertised that Sir William Constable meanes to procure his Matis Letter for a place in the Brille under him which he hath promised longe since to Sir H Peyton a gentleman of great valoure and sufficiency in that charge. Wherefore both he and I in his behalf are humble sutors to his Maty to Leave the gifte of those places which by patent appertayn to his owne election as it pleaseth him to deale likewise in Flushinge with that governors – It toucheth his credit very muche to be defeated in this …'[112]

It is an interesting psychological insight that we are told that if Vere does not get his way it would 'touch his credit'. i.e. damage his reputation, and he would 'be defeated'. Such were the macho posturings of the day, as the grandees strove with one another to be cock-of-the-walk. To have his will obstructed meant to such a man that he had been 'defeated', an unbearable humiliation. In playing this game, any slight boost up the social ladder, such as gaining a baronetcy, could aid a man such as Constable who was struggling in Court circles against peers of the realm and their social swagger. Society in 17th century England was snobbish to an extreme degree, and rank was fundamental to the self-esteem and social and economic prospects of everyone. Quarrels about who had the right to sit above someone else at table could even be the cause of a duel leading to one of the parties being killed. But for Northampton to suggest in his letter that Vere would be 'defeated' if he did not have his way was certainly a particularly extreme form of pressure, as it made a matter intensely personal which should not have been so. After all, it was only a foreign military captaincy that was at issue, and it was not a matter of state importance at all. Northampton and Vere were thus guilty of what we today call 'hyping' their case.

As for Sir Henry Peyton, about whom all this fuss was being made, he was a Gentleman of the Privy Chamber to Prince Henry, a member of the Virginia Company, a grandson of the Earl of Bath and son-in-law of the Duke of Somerset. Constable was clearly up against 'the Establishment'. This helps us to understand his need for a baronetcy, as he could never hope to afford the purchase of a peerage, which could have cost him approximately £10,000 (the price paid to the Crown for the Earldom of Warwick in 1618). When the Fairfaxes later obtained a Barony, the price was considerably lower than that, but to become an Earl you needed either to go to bed with the King (as did Robert Carr, who was made Earl of Somerset for his prowess in intimate circumstances) or pay at least £10,000 in cash.

It needs to be stressed that the summary of Northampton's letter from which I have just quoted which appears in the relevant Calendar is so misleading that it seems to say that Sir Horace Vere, Governor of the Brill, is Constable's cousin rather than Northampton's cousin, and it is thus important to stress that that published summary must not be relied upon.[113]

It is interesting that Sir Horace Vere (later Baron Vere of Tilbury, who died 1635, and was a tough professional soldier) did not want Constable to serve under him, and had received information underhand to try and stop it. But Northampton was unsuccessful with his imperious request, and for once Constable got what he asked for. He was at the Brill almost immediately, by the beginning of the year at the latest. Possibly he leapt into the post quickly before it could be taken away from him by further intrigues, even though it meant crossing the Channel in what must have been the worst possible weather. So drastically did he leap into the post, in fact, that he was sent straight into battle before it would seem he could even have caught his breath. Perhaps the furious Vere sent him out to fight the minute he arrived as an act of spite. In any case, practically as soon as he set foot in the Brill, Constable was so seriously wounded in battle that it was thought that he could not possibly live, and rumours spread that he was dead. As early as January 5, 1613/4, John Chamberlain was already writing from London to his friend Sir Dudley Carleton at Venice: 'Sr William Constable is dead at the Brill and his companie geven by the k [King] to a Scot, but Sr Horatio [Horace was also called Horatio] Vere had bestowd yt before on a sonne of Sr Edward Conwayes, wch stands goode.'[114] (In the *Calendar of State Papers* Chamberlain's sense is misleadingly given, another Calendar fault which needs to be kept in mind.[115])

There is something deeply disturbing about this situation. Not only were the vultures flocking around picking at the bones of Sir William before he was truly dead, but it looks very much as if Vere, incensed at Constable's arrival, sent him into some absurdly dangerous engagement the moment he got there, in the hope that he would get killed. While Constable lay with what was thought (hoped?) to be a mortal wound, Vere must have entered into communication with London stating that he was dead already, and he furiously fought to get his own (and *new*) favourite appointed Captain over one of the King's Scottish favourites. He must have thought that by declaring Constable dead there could be no possibility of London delaying to see if Constable might recover, and he must have urged the military necessity of ongoing fighting. After all that fuss about Sir Henry Peyton, Peyton was no longer even mentioned. Instead, Vere's new choice for the captaincy was a son of Sir Edward Conway, later to become Baron Conway and then Viscount Conway, and who would succeed Vere as Governor of the Brill until the Brill was handed back to the Dutch in 1616. (Conway died in 1631.) One suspects that Vere must have been involved in some form of what we would today call financial corruption, though the buying and selling of offices and even military posts was so common in Stuart England that the parties involved probably gave little thought to it being corrupt, and it would just be a way of life for them, as natural as the reckless behaviour of modern casino-bankers expecting their bonuses. If Vere had not been corrupt, and hoping to gain money from the captaincy appointment, why would he make first one pretence one minute to keep Constable away, the supposed claim on it by Peyton, and then the next minute make a completely new pretext, the supposed claim by a son of Conway? It would seem that he did not particularly care who became Captain as long as he could oblige someone powerful at Court and get some money in his pocket for doing so. Otherwise it is difficult to see why he would struggle so hard first to keep Constable away, and then to keep a Scottish favourite of the King away. He was clearly playing a high game, and was not someone to tangle with.

Constable must have been so sorely wounded that he was unable to resume his captaincy, and we hear no more of him at the Brill. Vere would appear to have got his way, and Constable was presumably lucky to survive at all, and to limp home when well enough to travel. His fortunes had now reached such a low point that the ancestral lands would have to go. The year 1614 saw the first of what was to be a sad series of sales of family property, as Constable settled down in Yorkshire and tried to keep himself out of debtors' prison. The idea of trying to get any money out of the Court appears to have been given up in disgust. Cecil (Salisbury), in any case, was dead, and could help Constable no more. Indeed, Cecil himself had died deeply in debt. Such was the financial ruin which the extravagant Court could bring upon even the most powerful of its figures.

Constable had married Dorothy Fairfax as long ago as February 15, 1607/8. Possibly it was Dorothy's dowry which was the first to go. In 1614, Sir William and his wife jointly sold the manor and entire village of North Duffield, near Skipwith, a dozen miles southeast of York. In addition to the manor house, this included thirty houses and twenty cottages, two mills, rights of markets and fairs, the fishing rights in the Derwent, and the right to the ferry over the Derwent.[116]

Constable had now settled down into county life. But all was not quiet. In fact, through his work as a Justice of the Peace, Constable came into conflict with other Yorkshire personalities, which was to land him in a suit in the Star Chamber. Constable was not an ordinary JP, but was the *custos rotulorum* for the East Riding, and he presided over the quarter sessions of January, 1614/5, at which twenty other lesser JPs were present. This particular sessions was the occasion for a great tumultuous scene. The combative Sir Thomas Hoby, a JP with a history of feuding with all of his neighbours (and from surviving accounts of him appears to have been mentally unbalanced), may have been apprehensive that Constable, so recently settled at home, might 'overtop' him, as the expression was at that time, by having greater prestige in the eyes of some at Court than he. G. C. F. Forster has written an account of the events which followed.

Forster says that 'Hoby enjoyed the patronage or support of the Court'. But, he says, 'men like Hoby ... (used) public office for private conflict'. Hoby brought a suit in the Star Chamber 'alleging various malpractices in the conduct of business, unruly behaviour and partiality towards recusants. He complained against four other justices, Sir William Constable (the *custos rotulorum*), Sir William Hildyard, John Hotham (later Sir John), and John Legard, accusing them of conspiring together to prevent the punishment of recusants.'[117] As far as Constable is concerned, we must not jump to the conclusion that he was by any means a crypto-Catholic. He was in the fact the very opposite. Forster is at pains to say: 'some of the gentry attacked by Hoby were Protestants and one, Sir William Constable, was, like Hoby himself, a strong Puritan.'[118] Forster also explains that 'allegations of the misuse of judicial powers in this way were frequently no more than a pretext used to undermine the credit of fellow-justices seen as rivals.'[119] The actual Star Chamber documents concerning this case are extraordinarily voluminous. For Constable alone there are pages and pages of closely-written material.[120] They identify Constable as living at this time at the ancient family home of Flamborough, on the coast of Yorkshire at Flamborough Head. I have not transcribed these lengthy Star Chamber documents, which await analysis by some future researcher. They are lengthy depositions signed in turn by Constable, Hildyard, and Legard. Deciphering the Star Chamber clerk's handwriting is a challenge worthy of the efforts of an Alan Turing.

During 1616, in company with his brother-in-law Ferdinando (later Lord) Fairfax, and two other friends or relations, Constable purchased from his friend the Mouncktons the Manor of Thorpe Parva, with lands in Hayton and Bielby near Pocklington, with various houses and a windmill.[121] But Constable and other newly-made baronets were getting restive about their patents for their baronetcies. On June 20, 1618, seven years after Constable was created a baronet, he and Sir Thomas Wentworth seem to have organised a petition from themselves and six other baronets (including a Peyton, a Savile, a Tufton, a Twysden, and Sir Edward Hales, later to be an MP in the Long Parliament with Constable). It was sent to Sir Julius Caesar, Master of the Rolls. Caesar, who was evidently in sympathy with them, has written on the document: 'Divers Baronets complaining that their patents are not yet inrolled notwthstanding they have long sithence payed the fees.' The baronets moaned to him that 'Haveinge longe suffered the iniurie not to have or Pattents inrolled in or rankes according to the Usuall manner & his Ma:ties Covenant ...'[122]

Presumably Caesar, as Master of the Rolls, quietly remedied the grievance, and enrolled the patents. It is an interesting thing to see that these men had to all appearances been singled out for what was rather outrageous treatment. Having paid £2,000 to be baronets, they were then denied the patents for seven years! This may well have led to a great deal of embarrassment for them, with jealous neighbours accusing them of holding spurious titles, being impostors, and so forth. Wentworth, later the notorious Earl of Strafford, was at this point clearly a close friend and associate of Constable's; we shall see in a moment that they were involved in a joint property transaction.

In 1620, Constable, Ferdinando Fairfax, and others sold to Sir John Savile, one of the Wentworths, Sir Robert Monson, and another man, the land, manor, and houses at Thorpe Parva and surrounding area, which they had bought in 1616, probably as a speculative venture.[123] We can presume that this property speculation must have made a satisfactory profit for Constable and his partners.

Early in 1622, possibly encouraged by his success with the Thorpe Parva venture, Constable made what must have been a disastrous business decision. He and his then friend Sir Thomas Wentworth (later Earl of Strafford), with two others, bought a gigantic mass of properties from some of the other Wentworths. Wentworth himself must thus have masterminded this and brought Constable in with him. They purchased no less than five manors, fifty messuages, 37 cottages, four watermills, one windmill, and lands and rents in thirteen locations.[124] Probably Constable and Ferdinando Fairfax had made a cosy profit from their previous transaction, and Constable naively thought that property speculation was a sure-fire way to riches. It must have gone terribly wrong. By the next year, 1623, Constable and his wife were forced to sell to Thomas, Earl of Kellie, a considerable portion of their lands at Holme in Spalding Moor in Yorkshire.[125] This was part of a depressing series of sales of the Constable ancestral lands. Sir William was eventually to see his entire patrimony dissolved before his eyes. He would be forced to sell up the estate at Flamborough, which had been in his family since the days of King William Rufus, and retreat to what was left of Holme at Spalding Moore, thereby bringing to an end 450 years or more of occupation of most of the 'family soil'.

Let us pause for a moment to see life from Sir William Constable's point of view, at this sad juncture. His finances were no longer just alarming, they threatened the dissolution of his entire estates and his way of life, as well as the destruction of four and a half centuries of family heritage. Having spent many years fruitlessly playing the courtier and fighting for his Country and for Protestantism in foreign wars, Constable had little to show for it but two spells in debtors' prison, a loss of at least £8,000 in ready money to the voracious Crown, serious war wounds, a shattered career at Court and on the field, an expensive baronetcy which the King had nearly reneged on entirely and delayed for at least seven years after taking the money for it, a trained band in Yorkshire which he probably had to finance himself, a frivolous suit in the Star Chamber which must have cost a fortune in legal fees (the result of the suit, by the way, is unknown, and may have involved fines), and the prospect of rusticating meaninglessly in the countryside with a lot of squabbling local squires who staged tumultuous scenes whenever he tried to preside over the quarter sessions, shouting at each other and defying his orders to the clerk of the peace or even his pleas to adjourn for lunch.[126] For a man of spirit, used to tackling problems with a sword in his hand and a company of soldiers at his back, Constable must have been subject to increasing and overwhelming frustrations. How could a man of action like Constable just sit there and allow this sort of thing to go on and get worse? Clearly, he could not. It was not just his own situation, but the whole system which was somehow all wrong. He took the plunge and decided to enter politics. It must have seemed clear to him that the next battlefield upon which he must enter was that of Parliament. When the Parliament of 1626 was convened, Sir William went down to London, no longer as a failed courtier or someone looking for a captaincy in a foreign war, but in that newfangled combat role, *the opposition MP*. Constable was to find over the next quarter of a century that this was how to enter upon the national stage at last, and that one did not have to be a court toady to do things of note. Opposition to the effete and recklessly extravagant Court was the alternative, and opposition was what he would practice!

In *The Biographical Dictionary of British Radicals in the Seventeenth Century,* in her entry for Sir William Constable, Constance Rynder makes the strange claim that Sir William became MP for Knaresborough in the 1624 Parliament. However, I can find no evidence of this, as the two MPs for Knaresborough in that Parliament were Sir Henry Slingsby and Richard Hutton. This was the Parliament summoned February 19, 1623/4, which lasted to

May 24, 1624, was prorogued and then reassembled on November 2, 1624 until February 16, 1624/5, and was officially dissolved on March 24, 1624/5, upon the death of the King. A few of Constable's friends were MPs in this Parliament, including his father-in-law Sir Thomas Fairfax (for Hedon, then known as Heydon), and Sir Thomas Wentworth (for Pontefract). Three months after the dissolution of that Parliament, a new one was to assemble, on June 21, 1625, which only lasted for three weeks, dissolving on August 12, 1625. Constable's brother-in-law Sir Ferdinando Fairfax joined this brief Parliament as one of the two MPs for Boroughbridge, Sir Thomas Fairfax continued to represent Hedon, Sir John Hotham became MP for Beverly, and the Knaresborough MPs remained the same as last time. Thus more of Constable's friends were entering Parliament and seeing it as a venue for their public purposes. A few months later, the 1626 Parliament assembled, on February 6, 1625/6, which sat until June 15, 1626, when it was dissolved. It was in this Parliament that Constable made his entry onto the national political stage. He did so in style as one of the two 'Knights of the Shire' for Yorkshire, the name by which the two MPs representing each county were known, as opposed to the ordinary MPs who represented boroughs. His colleague in this highly prestigious position was Sir John Savile. They were both returned on January 16, 1625/6. Sir Thomas Fairfax had held this position in the three-week Parliament, and appears to have stepped aside in favour of Sir William and happily gone back to representing his borough seat of Hedon. Sir Ferdinando Fairfax and Sir John Hotham represented the same seats as before. This group of friends thus had arranged for Sir William to join them. Unfortunately for them, their mutual enemy Sir Thomas Hoby persisted all of this time as an MP for Ripon, so perhaps they all held their noses as they passed by him in the House. The five months of this Parliament were frustrating for the Members, due to the continuing obstinacy of the Court regarding public grievances.

In 1627, Sir William was sent to prison once again! This time it was for refusing the demands of the Court to contribute to a 'forced loan' (which would never be repaid, hence it was pure extortion, but it was called by the King a 'loan'). Constable and his friends, led by Sir John Eliot, MP, had demanded in Parliament the impeachment of the corrupt Duke of Buckingham, the King had dissolved Parliament to prevent this impeachment, and then attempted to levy the forced 'loan' on the populace in defiance of Parliament. Many brave patriots throughout England refused to contribute and were sent to prison for their civil disobedience, which they considered a badge of honour. Constable had shown his political colours, and made himself a public enemy of the Crown. He had thus effectively reverted to his position as a young man who had participated in the Essex Rebellion. The three leading loan-resisters in Yorkshire in the Spring of 1627 were Sir Thomas Wentworth, Sir John Hotham, and Sir William Constable. All three of them were imprisoned for several months for refusing to pay their loan contributions, and they were only released on January 2, 1627/8.[127] Two months after this, Sir William went up to serve in Parliament for the second time.

In the 1628 Parliament, which sat from March 17, 1627/8 to March 10, 1628/9, Sir William was returned (on February 26) as MP for Scarborough. Sir Ferdinando Fairfax held the same seat as before, but his father Sir Thomas Fairfax did not stand for Parliament. On May 4, 1627, Sir Thomas was created the first Baron Fairfax of Cameron, but despite not standing, he was eligible to sit in the English House of Commons because the title was a Scottish one and not an English one. Thus, when Ferdinando became the second Lord Fairfax of Cameron, he was able to sit in the Commons. (The First Lord Fairfax died in 1640.) Andrew Hopper informs us that the Barony of Cameron was purchased by Sir Thomas from the Scottish heralds for £1500.[128]

Constable's two prominent jail-mates, his other friends Sir Thomas Wentworth and Sir John Hotham, were both returned to Parliament again, Hotham for Beverly, and Wentworth triumphantly elected by a defiant Yorkshire electorate as one of the two Knights of the Shire. However, Wentworth was then called to the Upper House as Lord Wentworth (his place in the Commons being taken by Sir Henry Savile), just as Sir Thomas Fairfax appears to have been called as Lord Fairfax. It seems that the Court was trying to disable them to sit in the Commons by elevating them to a less dangerous place where the Court's supporters held undisputed sway, just as another of the Court's favourite tricks was to appoint troublesome fellows to be Sheriffs of their counties, as they were then prevented from leaving their counties to serve as MPs, and that kept them safely away from London. (I must emphasize that I can give no assurance about the legal status of either the first or second Lord Fairfax as regards their sitting or not sitting in the House of Commons or the House of Lords, and that any remark I make on that opaque subject may be entirely mistaken, so that I have to leave it open. See my remarks about this below.)

At just about the time Wentworth had been imprisoned in the preceding year, and before he himself was imprisoned, Constable wrote a letter to his brother-in-law, Sir Ferdinando Fairfax, from London. This I have transcribed for the appendix. In it, Constable boasts of his having been a member of the opposition in the 1626 Parliament, by saying that the Chancellor had read out to Constable and his friends 'a longe lecture to us of our errour in not hearkening to his moderate advise in ye parliamt.' He describes how all the resisters, amongst whom he is delighted to be one, are trying to 'have a iudiciall triall in ye kings bench whether they have committed any offence or no.' Constable was thus in the thick of a major challenge to the Crown's prerogative, attempting to force a ruling in common law which would overturn the prerogative law. Constable's letter is full of exuberance at the exciting state of affairs, and he jauntily says to Fairfax: 'The prisons are ye only merry places in ye town & ye air, as ye matter is now used is one & ye same to all.'

After the 1628 Parliament, the long years of prerogative rule began, and Constable's evident enjoyment of the political fray was necessarily curtailed. That he was virulently hated now by the Court may be seen from the fact that on June 16, 1630, Constable was, incredibly, asked to compound for not taking a knighthood! He was expected to pay this ludicrous fine despite the fact that he had been knighted thirty-one years earlier and thus already held the title, and despite the fact that he had paid £2,000 to the Crown for a baronetcy 19 years earlier. Not only had the previous king held back his patent for the baronetcy after taking his money, but now the new king, Charles I, was insisting that Constable compound by a large sum for not accepting the title of Sir which he already held twice over![129] As a means of persecuting opponents of the Court, surely this one truly reached the heights of absurdity. Constable was understandably irritated, and he refused to compound and pay his fine.[130]

After the dissolution of the 1628 Parliament, there would not be another until 1640, and the King began his long twelve years of unconstitutional rule 'by royal prerogative' without a Parliament, in defiance of tradition and to the outrage of a large proportion of the population of England, including Sir William Constable and so many like him who would eventually find themselves in arms against him in a devastating civil war.

Constable's financial position continued to deteriorate. In order to survive financially, he had to sell the ancestral estate of Flamborough to the Earl of Kingston, and much of what remained at Holme.[131] The estate at Flamborough had been acquired by Constable's direct ancestors circa 1200. By selling it, he was therefore bringing to an end nearly four and a half centuries of continuous family occupation of 'the home of the Constables'. One can only imagine his feelings about this. He was a man steeped in tradition and family pride. Now he had to part with the house where he had been brought up as a boy, where his forefathers had lived further back than memory, a house no doubt filled with portraits of his forebears, with their suits of armour (as so many of them had been soldiers), probably with their spears, halberds, and swords, and coats of arms with multiple quarterings hanging proudly on the walls (we know this kind of decoration, especially in an old hall, to have been the habit of similar men of the time, such as the regicide Colonel John Moore, MP, whose entry I contributed to the DNB *Missing Persons* volume). All of this had to be moved or dispersed. And whom did he blame? Of course he would have blamed the Court. He had a privy seal certifying that the Court owed him £8,000 of his own money. But instead of paying him, the Court wished to fine him for not accepting a knighthood when he already had one! And they imprisoned him and his friends for refusing to pay unconstitutional taxes and levies. Here we see the genesis of the rage and fury of the oppressed county gentry who were to bring their four foot ten inch-high, stuttering little monarch to his fate at the hands of the public executioner, to atone for what he had done to the country and, not least, to themselves.

It should be remarked in passing, to help understand the pressures under which Sir William had always laboured, that Holme had been forfeited to the Crown by his father, Sir Robert Constable, during the reign of Henry VIII, for reasons which remain obscure.[132] It would be interesting to discover why Sir William's father had fallen so foul of the Crown in his day that he had suffered forfeiture of a considerable part of his estate. The family's finances had probably been initially shattered by that earlier blow. Recovering the lands at Holme, probably under Elizabeth, must have cost a fortune, and the Constables had to keep finding a fee farm rent to pay to the Crown every year for their own lands, which must have been extraordinarily galling.[133] There is evidence that Sir Robert Constable had recovered his lands by 1576, the year after the presumed birth of the regicide.[134] As a sidelight, it is interesting that in 1631, Sir William made an agreement with the freeholders within his manorial jurisdiction at Holme that he would enclose 60 acres of Holme Moor in return for which he offered them an enormous number of gates to let their grazing animals in and out, no less than 160 gates for 'Ewes and other great Sheepe', 64 gates 'for Ky & other great Beasts', and so on. And he also agreed with the freeholders that certain parts of the Common would be 'much oppressed' if certain grazing practices were continued, and therefore 'That none shall graze any Turnes upon Westwood, but for Fewell for ye Manour-house or other Dwelling House of him, his Lady, his heirs and Assignes of ye Sd Manour of Holme …'[135]

This document serves as a necessary reminder that no matter how active a man might be in politics, on the bench, or at the head of his band of soldiers, a country gentleman more often than not had his head full of ewes and rams, gates and posts, fences and hedges, bulls and cows, horses, stables, ploughs, firewood, fishponds, dovecotes, and tenants. Unfortunately, Constable's very fair and considerate agreement with his neighbours, which seems to have been to the advantage of them all, appears to have been but a preparation for selling the property. Having consolidated such matters, Sir William four years later sold Holme for £6,500, in 1635, and set about his plans to emigrate to the New World. He planned to go to Connecticut with his friend Sir Matthew Boynton of Barmston, to join the Puritan colony there and start a new life free from the oppressions and corruption of the Stuart Court, and where the oppressive and intolerant religious writ of Archbishop Laud did not run. Boynton had sent his servants on ahead. But the government put up so many obstacles that the emigration to Connecticut had to be abandoned. Others who had intended to emigrate to Connecticut were Oliver Cromwell, John Hampden, Sir Arthur Hazlerigg, and John Pym. Charles I arranged for an Order in Council to be made forbidding their departure. One might say that by doing so he guaranteed that some of his bitterest enemies remained in England when he might easily have got rid of them just by letting them leave. Thwarted in their desire to go to America, in 1637 Constable and his wife left England to live in the Low Countries instead. They remained there, apparently at first in Haarlem and eventually in Arnhem, until 1640, when the election of the Long Parliament and the good things of which it gave promise brought them hurrying back to England, to take some part if possible in the good work ahead. No doubt Constable was urged on by his many friends, who wanted his company and assistance.[136] There is no doubt that chief amongst these was Ferdinando, now Lord Fairfax, Constable's brother-in-law.

After twelve long years during which the people had no voice in Parliament, the King was forced to call one because he had exhausted all his illegal ways of raising money and needed Parliament to raise some for him. So in 1640 he summoned a Parliament, the so-called Short Parliament, which was convened on April 13 but which was dissolved by the King on May 5, having sat for only 28 days. If the King thought this Parliament was not to his taste, he was certainly to get a shock with the next one, which was even worse for him. In the Short Parliament, the younger John Hotham was elected for Scarborough, a borough which Constable had represented in 1628, and his father Sir John Hotham was returned for Beverly. Elected for the first time as an MP was the future regicide, John Alured of Hull (a close friend of the Fairfaxes), representing Hedon. Sir Ferdinando Fairfax was elected for Boroughbridge. Constable did not stand for this Parliament, evidently not being back to Yorkshire in time. Elected for Knaresborough was a hated enemy of the Fairfaxes, Henry Benson. Constable's brother-in-law Sir George Wentworth was elected for Pontefract.

After the dissolution of this 28-day-wonder, it would be six months before the next Parliament was called by the reluctant monarch. This Parliament was the Long Parliament, convened on November 3, 1640. It would sit until expelled at gunpoint by Oliver Cromwell on April 20, 1653. This Parliament would bring another future regicide into the Commons, Peregrine Pelham, as MP for Hull (who replaced Sir John Lister on January 18, two months after the Parliament convened, because Lister had died), and John Alured was re-elected for Hedon. (I might point out that I wrote the DNB entries for both Pelham and Alured for the DNB's *Missing Persons* volume, as they had had no entries at all before that in DNB and little was known of them by historians.) Another future Yorkshire regicide, Sir Thomas Mauleverer, Bart., was elected to Parliament for the first time, to sit for Boroughbridge. Constable's brother-in-law Sir George Wentworth of Woolley was re-elected for Pontefract, to sit alongside his third cousin who was also called Sir George Wentworth, and who was the younger brother of the Earl of Strafford. Pontefract was thus represented by two MPs of exactly the same name and title, which may have been a unique historical occurrence in the history of Parliament, though I have not researched the point. The Long Parliament contained other MPs of the same name as each other (Peter Temple and Sir Peter Temple, Bart., for instance), but they did not represent the same constituency in the way that the two Wentworths did.

Ferdinando Lord Fairfax, Constable's brother-in-law, was elected one of the two Knights of the Shire for Yorkshire. His father, Thomas, the First Lord Fairfax had died on May 2, 1640, and at that time Ferdinando had become the Second Baron Fairfax. But despite being a peer, he was elected to serve in the Commons by the people of Yorkshire in what appears to have been a monumental act of defiance against the Court. He sat in the Commons until his death in 1648. I have not researched the question of how this was possible. The future regicide Lord Grey of Groby was allowed to sit in the Commons, but his title was a courtesy title because he was the son of an earl (who of course sat in the Lords), and in any case Groby was not even eighteen years old when he was elected. The mystery of Lord Fairfax sitting in the Commons for eight years is one for the heralds, or at least for someone cleverer than myself, who find it mystifying.

Constable's brother-in-law Ferdinando Fairfax, who lived at Knaresborough himself, was a determined opponent of the MP who was re-elected for Knaresborough, Henry Benson. The seat to which Benson was elected was the same seat to which, after much difficulty, as related below, Sir William Constable would eventually be elected in his place. The story of all this was a remarkable scandal of crime, corruption, and, as we shall see, even some high comedy. The enmity between Benson and Fairfax went back a long way. The earliest overt account of it which I have discovered is found in a letter to Ferdinando Fairfax dated May 21, 1641 from his salaried client Thomas Stockdale, who kept Ferdinando informed of events and dealt with all manner of serious problems on his behalf, acting effectively as what we would today call a rather high-powered personal assistant and trouble-shooter. In this letter, Stockdale relates the following story of what happened when he went to dinner at Henry Benson's house at Knaresborough:

'Upon Monday last my wife and I were invited to dine at Harry Benson's, and we went, and there met Sir Francis Trapps, Mr. Robert Trapps and his wife, Mr. John Plumpton and his wife, and a captain of his regiment, and Mr. William Hill, that hath relation of service to your lordship. After dinner I perceived Harry Benson having got Mr. Hill apart, began to bluster out that the town of Knaresborough were about to petition the Parliament against your lordship, touching some monies raised for the trained soldiers of that town, for which a lay (ballot) was cast, and your lordship signed and subscribed some directions to the lay-bill. I coming accidentally to the discourse, wished Mr. Hill (who seemed moved with it) not to trouble himself, for I conceived it a matter of no importance; and that if Mr. Benson should attempt anything in it, I would procure more hands of the town to subscribe a petition in contradiction, (declaring that the town was not grieved with any such matter, nor did not complain of it,) than he should procure to subscribe his request, with which Mr. Benson was something moved, but passed over it in a jesting fashion. What he shall attempt I will counterwork, if I hear of it any more. But however, though he never moved further in it, I apprehend the proposing such matter to proceed from an ancient cankered ill affection in him to your lordship.'[137]

It is perhaps worth noting that there was a royalist officer named Lieutenant Trapps taken prisoner during the siege of Gloucester in 1643.[138]

It is possible therefore that these Trapps were of the same family and same sympathies. I mention this because the name is so rare and I have not encountered it elsewhere in England at this time.

Stockdale's next mention of Benson is from Knaresborough, in a letter to Ferdinando dated June 18, 1641:

'Our Parliament man of Knaresborough (Mr. Benson) hath been here about eight weeks; it seems there is no great want of his assistance in the House. The last week I met him, and asked him what he had done in the petition for the town about the military charges. He told me that the town let the matter rest; and that he was the only man that dissuaded them from proceeding in it; so I conceive he finds it will amount to nothing, and therefore waives the pursuit of it. I have got copies of some letters of his which I intend to show your lordship, as soon as I can have the happiness to see you, either there or here; that if they will conduce to any good purpose, there may be use made of them ...'[139]

Knaresborough was a borough which had been in the Bensons' control, in a manner described in a moment, but Fairfax and Thomas Stockdale decided to oust him from his seat. They were successful in this.[140] Benson was exposed as extraordinarily corrupt, and voluminous evidence was presented to the House proving that he had been running an extensive protection racket, aided by William Dearlove, who although he was described by Miles Corbet in the House of Commons as Benson's son-in-law , was really his step-son (see discussion below). The Commons took the most unusual step on November 2, 1641, of not merely expelling Benson from the House, but also of pronouncing him 'unfit and uncapable ever to sit in Parliament, or to be a Member of this House hereafter'.[141] The Committee which had investigated Benson's conduct was under the chairmanship of Robert Reynolds, MP, who also reported the results of the investigation. Upon Benson's expulsion, a writ was issued to the Sheriff of Yorkshire to call a new election for the seat at Knaresborough. This was Constable's chance to get back into Parliament again, so he stood for the seat. Benson had the utter gall to put his corrupt step-son William Dearlove up for the seat, despite Dearlove's having been clearly implicated in the family's criminal protection racket. By what were thoroughly corrupt and dishonest means, this family rotten borough proceeded to return Dearlove as the new MP.

On November 11, Thomas Stockdale wrote to Ferdinando Fairfax in London informing him:

'Of other matters I shall write to-morrow, if I get leisure, for it is like to be a troublesome day; the new burgess [MP] is to be elected at Knaresborough, for which William Derelove stands, and intends by faction to carry it; of which I shall give your lordship account hereafter.'[142]

The next day, on November 12, Stockdale as promised wrote to Ferdinando describing what happened at the new Knaresborough election:

'We have had the election this day of a new burgess in Harry Benson's place: the faction raised by Mr. Benson carried it in number of voices from Sir William Constable, for they were thirty-three, and Sir William Constable had but thirteen. But when the election was made, and all men polled, I demanded of John Derelove (who is substitute bailiff this day) that he would make return for us that had elected Sir William Constable, and I alleged that the election of William Derelove was illegal, because he is deputy-steward and judge of the court, and therefore the burghers durst not give their voices for fear of him; and ours being a legal election ought to be returned, which the said bailiff denied to do. So we staid our company together, and made an indenture and sealed it, electing Sir William Constable, which we have sent by Sir William Constable; which is as far as I can now relate. What shall be done by the sheriff I cannot write; but some friends of Sir William Constable's must take order that there may be a caveat entered to keep William Derelove out until the matter be examined, and when it shall appear that Mr. Derelove is deputy-steward and bailiff, and deputes his brother for this time, to make himself capable of election, then I hope the indenture which we have sealed for Sir William Constable will be received and he be admitted into the House.

'It will appear that he [Dearlove, or 'Derelove' as Stockdale spells it] is deputy-steward and bailiff in the Queen's Court, for his patent is sealed with the Queen's great seal kept by her Chancellor, and is of record here, and needs no other proof. And he is a man of no estate; we know not here of any thing he hath, either lands or goods, save only his office; and it is against reason that he that hath nothing of his own to give should have power to give away other men's estates or any part of them, which you know the Parliament hath, of which he would be a member. ... Your lordship and I do divide [share] the blame and malice of putting out Henry Benson and opposing William Derelove's coming in, and I am sore threatened for it.'[143]

A week later, on November 19, Thomas Stockdale wrote at much greater length and more clearly about the matter to Ferdinando:

'Upon Friday last I gave your lordship a confused relation of our more confused election at Knaresborough, and of my public protestation against the illegal choice made by the greater part of the burgesses who elected William Derelove their steward and bailiff. Since which time I have heard nothing from Sir William Constable nor any other, what success he had with the sheriff, nor how he hath returned the indenture, which we sealed and delivered to him, testifying our election of him. I then wished him to return it to the Parliament, in case the sheriff refused to return it with the writ; and I doubt not but the other election of William Derelove being examined will appear illegal and contrary to the order of the House, and so Sir William Constable shall be admitted, and the other shut out.

'The business was ill carried from the beginning, else we should have had all the voices of the town for Sir William Constable. But Sir Henry Slingsby sent word on Saturday to Henry Benson that he was put out of the House, and on Sunday writ to him a letter to the same purpose; and thereupon Henry Benson, and his sons, the Dereloves, spoke to all the boroughmen on Sunday morning for their voices, which they (being then ignorant of the cause) did promise to William Derelove; and so Sir Henry Slingsby by that unadvised intelligence deprived both himself and all men else of power to help Sir William Constable; for of the thirteen voices that elected Sir William Constable there were but two of Sir Henry's tenants, whereas he expected above thirty voices of his dependants. [*At this period, Slingsby's political motives were not yet clear, but it later became clear that Sir Henry was a royalist, and he was beheaded for it in 1658. When Slingsby was disabled to sit in the House because of his royalism in 1642, it was none other than Thomas Stockdale who was eventually elected MP in his place, thus joining Sir William Constable as the other borough MP for Knaresborough.*]

'Now that which remains to be done, if it be not already done, is to make it apparent that Derelove's election is illegal, and not to be allowed for these reasons, viz., first, William Derelove is both bailiff and steward of the borough, and hath jurisdiction of judicature over the Towns-Men, so that none of them dare give their voice freely against him, as many have declared, because he vexeth and oppresseth his opposites [those opposed to him]. The patent granted by the Queen making him bailiff and steward, you will find in the Queen's Court upon record; for it is under her great seal kept by her Chancellor. The next exception is, that if Henry Benson were unworthy, then of necessary consequence William Derelove must be so also, he being the same man, only passing under another name, and dressed in other clothes, for he is his son [son-in-law], and hath his daily maintenance and dependance on him alone, and is guided by him in all his actions. And if Henry Benson were thought to give intelligence to the recusants, then this man will do the same, and grant protections too ... And for his estate, we know he is not worth sixpence in the world, but is maintained by his father-in-law's arts, and hath neither lands nor goods in possession nor expectation of descent ... we know him extremely poor and needy, and a man of mean parts and shallow capacity, and besides, he is bred in the base ways of his father-in-law, who hath already been censured by the House. The last exception against the election of Derelove is, that he being bailiff and steward of the borough, did for that day substitute his brother, John Derelove, to be bailiff, for this only end, that he himself might seem capable of the place of burgess [MP]; and I conceive he hath not power to substitute a bailiff, and if one, yet not so many substitutes, for his brother Thomas is also a substituted bailiff under him, and so is one Thomas Wakefield; and if he hath power to substitute so many, yet John Derelove, who took upon him that day to execute and return the writ, is not capable of office, being but twenty years old in May last.

I doubt not but these exceptions, rightly managed, will stop his entry into the house, and make way for Sir William Constable.'

'The next matter to be taken into consideration, is how to ease the town of their insufferable bondage under Benson, the Dereloves, and William Conyers ... The exception they [the Benson clique] take at Sir William Constable, are, that after the election made and the indenture sealed, he caused us who gave our voices with him, to dine with him at his inn; and they say that he spoke against the Common Prayer-book; and their saucy attorney, Nixon, who hath yet paid no poll-money, gives him the phrase of "Puritan" in most despiteful manner and language. ... When I had written thus far, I was told that Harry Benson begins now to abate all of his confidence, that William Derelove's election will be allowed by the Parliament. But he saith that if it be not, yet Sir William Constable shall not have it; but that he will put it upon a courtier, (meaning the place of burgess [MP]), because I shall not have my ends, whom he terms his enemy.'[144]

One week later (it seems to have been his habit to write to Ferdinando Fairfax every Friday when there was a post), on November 26, Stockdale wrote further:

'Upon Friday last I received your lordship's letters, which have in some measure settled my confidence, that our factious election at Knaresborough will be rejected; and, if Sir William Constable be not admitted upon this election made of him, yet at least we shall have a new day for it; but truly I think, if any new writ come before these great officers (stewards and bailiffs) be removed, we shall have much opposition to any fair election. The only help must be to give us timely warning, that we may prepare our friends and wellwishers, that they may not be surprised or forestalled, as they were at the last election, by Henry Benson and his sons.'[145]

On December 3, Stockdale wrote again to Ferdinando saying:

'Here is a rumour at Knaresborough of a new election, and Henry Benson hath sent about the town; but I hope we shall first have a new bailiff. ... Your lordship's letter even now received, makes me doubt that William Derelove shall be admitted to sit in the House before the election be examined, which seems to relish either of some extraordinary favour, or else the very active labouring of friends. ... Sir William Constable tells me this day, that his [Dearlove's] patent of office contains a farm of the profits of the place at 20l rent, which must of necessity occasion great oppression, seeing he only reaps the benefit; and being judge, it will be conceived he will decree whatsoever may advantage himself. I wish I had sight of the copy of his patent, that I might enquire of such abuses, as the form of his patent hath encouraged him to commit, in hope to escape undescried.'[146]

Sir William Constable meanwhile submitted a petition to the House of Commons protesting the election, and the House voted that the petition be referred to Reynolds's former committee for consideration, 'to take into consideration the Misdemeanours and Offences of William Dearlove, ... And this House holds it fit, That the said William Dearlove do forebear to sit as a Member in this House, till the said Committee have made their Report of their Opinion to this House: And they are to ... have Power to send for Parties, Witnesses, Writings, or Records.'[147] This took place on December 7, 1641.

Thomas Stockdale wrote to Ferdinando on December 16, 1641, giving the latest news about this:

'Touching the misdemeanors of William Derelove in his office, I have this day sent to Sir William Constable certain heads or particulars, with some names of witnesses, to prove each abuse, and also the relation which Foster, the bailiff, is able to charge him with; and I have desired him to send them to your lordship, because I have not leisure at this instant to transcribe them. And though John Derelove (who is found faulty by the Parliament for abuse touching Henry Benson's protections) be not the new-elected burgess, as it was conceived, yet that John Derelove is the man who, being substituted bailiff by his brother William Derelove at the time of the election, did return his brother; and I think he is no fit man for a judicial place whose honesty is blemished before the Parliament, and whose ability or capacity is questionable, being under twenty-one years old. It seems now that other men think Derelove's election cannot stand; for yesterday Mr. Thomas Moore, the feodary, told me that one Mr. William Middleton, who hath some estate in Ripon, but lies in the south for the most part, told him that very day, that Derelove was to be turned out of the House, and that Mr. Bryan Palmes intended to stand to be burgess for Knaresborough, and that Mr. Palmes had writ to Sir Francis Trapps to make way for him; and I suppose that Harry Benson will side with that party.

'So your lordship sees plainly there is a kind of necessity either to draw in Sir William Constable upon the election we have already made, or delay the new election till Derelove, for his misdemeanors, be cast out of the bailiff's place, unless you desire to have Mr. Palmes brought in.'[148]

The Parliamentary committee appears to have asked Sir William for evidence of his assertions in his petition. Stockdale then actively assisted Sir William with documentary evidence to support his petition, as he says in his letter to Ferdinando of January 7, 1641/2:

'The last week I sent Sir William Constable such proofs as he desired, to justify his petition against Derelove's election. Amongst others, some were to prove that he did exercise the place immediately before and presently after the election. If he need more particulars than I have already sent him, he may instance, that about fourteen or twenty days before the election, my cousin, Tom Vavasour of Newton, came to William Derelove, and desired warrant to arrest Mr. Christopher Townley (then in Knaresborough), and Derelove himself carried Vavasour to his office (as he termed it), and there writ and subscribed the process, and delivered them to him and took his fees as bailiff and steward for the arrest. They make proud boasts amongst this deluded people what great friends William Derelove hath in Parliament and Court; and William Conyers saith, that if William Derelove be rejected, yet he will be elected; for one of them, he saith, will have it. But they are neither worthy of the place, nor worth so much labour as they impose upon your lordship in reading their follies. I still hope that when Sir William Constable shall appear in his own cause, his opposite's unworthiness will then appear more visibly to the House. He set forward this last week, and I hope is safely arrived at London before this day, which I should much rejoice to hear, for we had extreme ill weather when he set out, which agrees not with the weak constitution of his health.'[149]

This is the first evidence we have of the state of health of Sir William, who by this time was approximately 67 years old. On January 21, Stockdale wrote again to Ferdinando, saying:

'Upon Tuesday last we had a meeting here at Knaresborough, about the review of the poll ... We hear nothing yet of Mr. Benson's deputy-burgess [Dearlove]; I suppose the House hath so many weighty matters in hand that it cannot attend him. I know of no protections that Benson had granted until of late, and now I hear of six or seven, thereabout, and in time more will be discovered. ... I had almost forgotten to tell your lordship that on Tuesday last, about ten o'clock at night, one Stamford, a pursuivant [a junior officer of arms], came into Henry Benson's house, to arrest him by some warrant, as I conceive, from the Parliament; but his intention being discovered, his wife, his sons, and family, fell on him, and beat the pursuivant, and would not suffer him to take Mr. Benson, who in the scuffle had the opportunity to escape, and now is removed as they say to some other place.'[150]

In his next Friday letter of January 28, Stockdale reported the latest events of this saga to Ferdinando:

'I have sent answer to Sir William Constable, touching the petition against William Derelove: I intend it shall be with him the next post, if not sooner. I could not attend it altogether myself, because of my resort to York about this business of the country [county], so I left it with Richard Rodes [the Vicar of Knaresborough], who promiseth to get me more hands to it, for I only moved half a dozen principle men that signed it.'

'Here is Tom Parker, that was William Derelove's man at London; he came home on Tuesday last; he says his master is not yet admitted into the House, but he hopes every day to be received, and that thirty-two more are kept out as well as he is. I had a private advertisement that William Derelove doth not in this business altogether follow the advice of his friends upon whom he most reposeth in other occasions; because, he hopes to get into the House by help of the contrary faction, out of which phrase something may be gathered, that he either is a great politician, or else he is notably deluded.'

'The new order of the House for apprehending Benson and his sons that rescued him, it seems excuseth his wife, in favour of her sex, which is a most noble consideration; but if they knew what monstrous, rather than masculine, acts she hath heretofore performed, in the like rescues of the same person, they would have punished her the rather for this. Yet, truly I think it is punishment enough to separate them, for it is partly her pride and wicked disposition that misguides him in many particulars, and caused him to set up her son [William Dearlove, son by her previous marriage] to be burgess.'[151]

On February 4, Stockdale wrote to Ferdinando again:

'On Monday last, Stamford, the messenger [who had previously been beaten up, and this time when he returned was backed up by other men to assist and protect him] came to apprehend Henry Benson and his sons, but failed [again] in his attempt; for they had warning of his coming, both by their servant Tom Parker, who lay at York to watch when the messenger should come there, and also, as report goes, from Mr. Robert Trapps and Mrs. Plumpton. And although I think the messenger needs not much care for missing of them, because his fees will increase by it, yet to hear how Mrs. Benson (who feared she had been in the warrant) hid herself in William Barroby's hogsty, and what hard shift old Harry and his two young shifters made to hide themselves from the messenger and his assistants, would make us a pretty comedy. Sir John Goodrick assisted Stamford in the search; for I was surprised that day with an extreme fit of sickness, which, upon contraction of cold, often seizes on me, and holds me for twenty-four hours together. ... I am constrained to inclose this [a letter] to Sir William Constable, with the petition about Derelove, because I have forgot where his lodging is, and I presume your lordship will see him every day.'[152]

The gangsters of Knaresborough had thus created a high comedy, with the bullying wife hiding herself amongst a neighbour's hogs in a pig sty. And one is tempted to say, that was where she truly belonged.

On February 12, Stockdale wrote a further report to Ferdinando, as the pursuivant had now been replaced by a sergeant's deputy (perhaps a rougher and stronger character) in yet another attempt to arrest Benson: 'The serjeant's deputy could not find Henry Benson yet ...'[153]

And four days later, on February 18, Stockdale's account of the saga continued in another letter to Ferdinando:

'I send your lordship also the substance of some part of a letter from William Derelove to John Bullock, which was taken by the constable and watch at Knaresborough on Friday last; and I being then at York, it was carried to be opened by Mr. Rodes the vicar of Knaresborough; by it your lordship may understand something of that man's ways and friends. ... Henry Benson himself being either gone away, or not to be seen at home; and his son Tom Derelove is at London, and John Derelove fled we hear not whither; yet new deputies keep the court, though I am persuaded without sufficient authority, if it were examined ...'[154]

On February 25, there was more from Stockdale:

'Henry Benson is fled, as all men think; and it is said by some that he is gone to Nocton, which is Mr. Townley's house in Lincolnshire, and there lurks.'

'Mr. Cockhill, of London Bridge, wrote the last week to some friends of his to make way to get himself elected burgess of Knaresborough; for he writ that Derelove was absolutely rejected by the House, and that a writ would come presently for a new election. But this I should not believe until I hear it from your lordship.'

'I beseech your lordship let Sir William Constable know that, for certain, William Derelove, as he went from hence to the Parliament, lighted at Plumpton, and stayed there an hour, his brother John and Tom Parker in his company, and Mr. John Plumpton set him from thence to Wetherby, and there parted with him, which shows apparently an entire affection with the popish parties. This is related to me by Dick Tenant, a paviour [*a word for a workman who lays paving*] of Knaresborough, who followed Derelove to Plumpton.'[155]

The matter of Sir William's petition was meanwhile being neglected in committee, probably because of the political inclinations of the committee chairman Robert Reynolds (see below), so that on the following February 22, the House once again had to order Mr. Reynolds to revive his committee and hear the business of Knaresborough.[156] Immediately, Benson and Dearlove took active steps to try to fight back. Thomas Stockdale wrote to Ferdinando Fairfax on March 11:

'I do now understand that William Derelove's sentence is past, for upon Friday last, 4th of March, Samuel Flesher came from London by post to Knaresborough, and brought with him a letter from William Derelove to William Conyers, dated the 2nd of March; and therein he writ that his election was utterly disabled and he rejected by the Parliament [*this must refer to inside knowledge of the Reynolds committee's decision, perhaps from Reynolds himself, as this information had not yet been presented to the full House*], and therefore desired for the good of the town, that all the inhabitants would sign a petition to the Parliament, (which petition he sent ready drawn) desiring the House to pardon their former errors, and to grant them a writ for a new election. And withal, he advised they should write a letter to Sir Henry Slingsby to prefer their petition; and then he desired that all who gave their voices with him [i.e., everyone who had voted for Slingsby] should be moved to promise at the new election to give their voices for William Flesher, the linen-draper in St. Lawrence Lane. This was the substance of his letter, and I perceive it is done with a purpose to hinder Sir William Constable's admission into the House; for it was instantly gotten signed by William Baroby [the owner of the famous pig sty], brother-in-law to Flesher, with assistance of Benson's faction, and sent up by post the same day it was brought. But my hope is that Sir William Constable is already admitted, who wanted only the formality of the bailiff's hand, which he may now be ordered to put to the indenture, if the House please, for it is evident the other election was factious and unlawful. And now this part of the country do owe thanks to the Parliament, and more particularly to your lordship, for discovering and purging the House of such unworthy members as Benson and Derelove, who are well known to have only used religion for a cloak, and law, to oppress and deceive where they had power.'[157]

(This gives information on Slingsby's true political stance which had eluded Mary Frear Keeler in her book *The Long Parliament*.[158])

Miles Corbet, MP, later to be a regicide, shortly afterwards on March 19, made a very long report of the business to the House, which is printed at length in the *Commons Journal*.[159] In his report, Corbet went out of his way to describe Sir William Constable as 'one of great Esteem and Integrity'. Reynolds may have been less keen on Constable, for political reasons, as Reynolds was a 'moderate' and Constable was a 'radical'. Corbet explained to the House that Reynolds had 'gone out of Town; but hath left his Notes with me; to the end that, if the House be pleased to give me Leave to report the same, I might do it …' This is an interesting example of how at that stage, only the chairman of a committee was supposed to deliver the committee's report to the whole House. It also indicates that Corbet may have been trying to expedite the business against Reynolds's dragging his feet. Corbet delivered such a ferocious, no-holds-barred, frontal assault on Dearlove, that he must have scorched the beards of his colleagues with the fiery blast he let forth. No wonder Reynolds absented himself, - he probably ran for cover, knowing what was going to have to be revealed. A zeal for political reform may be detected in what Miles Corbet proceeded to explain to a doubtless astounded House.

Corbet detailed the corrupt means by which Dearlove had been returned as an MP. Knaresborough was, he said, a liberty within the Duchy of Lancaster, of which Benson had ten years before procured the bailiwick and given it to Dearlove. This meant that Dearlove (who lived in Benson's house and was wholly his creature, having no means of his own) held the courts of the liberty which 'hath the Returns of Writs'. Dearlove sat and held his own court in the liberty a few days before the election, using various stooges including his brother and an infant, as well as Benson's henchman who had run the protection racket. He had his brother, whom he had constituted deputy to the court, to return him as burgess (MP) for the borough's seat. He didn't bother to wait for the election, but elected himself beforehand! He used various forms of pressure to get some local people's 'votes', - people 'that durst not displease Benson'. The Friday following [March 25, 1641/2], an actual election was held at Knaresborough, where Sir William Constable 'was by many able men of the Borough propounded, and returned to be Burgess'.

As if exposing all this were not enough, Corbet went on to excoriate Benson as 'late an Evil Member of this House … also sent for as a Delinquent [meaning a royalist]: But the Serjeant's Man that went for him was beaten; and Benson, that had been an unworthy Member, yielded no obedience to this House; but caused or suffered himself to be rescued from the Serjeant.' Corbet said that upon Benson's expulsion, the House had intended 'to put a better Man in his place: But Benson declaring himself that he would oppose them that had opposed him, did resolve this House should have no better Man in his Room, but Wm. Derelove his Son-in-law …'[160]

After hearing all this, there was nothing the House could possibly do but declare Dearlove's election 'an undue and void Return … (to) be taken off the File.' But we must remember that the House was still filled with many passionate royalists, Constable was a well-known opponent of the Court, and Dearlove and Benson had been identified by Corbet as 'delinquents', i.e. royalists. Corbet reported that Reynolds's committee had resolved on two votes: that the election of

Dearlove be declared void, and 'That the Sheriff of the County of Yorke shall return up the Indenture, by which Sir William Constable was elected; and that Sir William shall be admitted to sit as a Member of this House for the Borough of Knaresborough.'

Incredibly, this latter decision of the committee was not accepted by the House! Not only did the royalists present try to block Constable's entry to the House, but the vast ranks of wavering MPs known contemptuously by contemporaries as 'the neuters' must have joined with them, presumably terrified at the prospect of having another fiery spirit like Corbet coming in to rock the boat and force awkward issues to be faced. So the House simply left it at that: Dearlove was obviously too appalling, and could not be admitted. But no action whatever was to be taken about filling up the vacant seat for Knaresborough. Constable was to be ignored, or, at least, for as long as possible. The House moved on with alacrity to consider a Hertfordshire petition and the remainder of the day's business was allowed to drown out any further consideration of the issue for the time being.

The last published report we have of the election situation by Thomas Stockdale is in his letter of April 1 to Ferdinando. There he says:

'It grieves me much that noble Sir William Constable should be kept out of the House by the interposition of Derelove's most unworthy election. I know not how prejudicial his admission may be to the privileges of the House, by making this a precedent for elections that shall hereafter want formality. But if a special order could be conceived by the House to allow Sir William for this time, in respect of the corrupt carriage of Benson, and the factious election and return of Derelove, and the petition of the boroughmen pressing his admission, though illegally elected and returned; it would but deter others from like courses, and countenance that religious noble gentleman [Constable], whose reputation suffers in failing of his desire to serve his country.'[161]

Nothing was able to be done about resolving Sir William's election until the royalist MPs had largely fled London and abandoned their seats in the House in the summer of 1642 as the Civil War loomed. I have explained and presented the documentary evidence elsewhere to show that the first battle of the Civil War took place on July 4 and 5, 1642,[162] which is earlier than most think (the conventional date for the commencement of the Civil War being August 22, when the King raised his standard at Nottingham), and I cannot repeat that information here. It was thus more than a month after that, on August 17, 1642, that something was done at last about Sir William's situation and the Knaresborough seat. On that day, Miles Corbet once again got to his feet in the House to raise the matter. While Robert Reynolds remained silent, this time Corbet sought no approval nor offered any apology for speaking for a committee of which he was not the chairman (and this was perhaps a constitutional 'first'). Corbet then went ahead and gave another committee report on the Knaresborough situation. We know for certain that Robert Reynolds was actually present while this happened, because the *Commons Journal* records that he acted as a teller on another motion only a couple of minutes before. (He had just acted as a teller against a radical measure proposed by Corbet's friends and allies Henry Marten, a future regicide, and Alexander Rigby.) Reynolds having clearly refused to speak about Knaresborough and thus allow the radical Constable into the House, Corbet took matters into his own hands and humiliated Reynolds before the entire House. By standing up and giving the report which his cowardly or biased chairman had been suppressing for months, he showed all the MPs present the contempt he had for Reynolds's cowardice, hypocrisy, and contempt for democracy. The implication was that Reynolds was part of a conspiracy to prevent the voters' will from being implemented and an elected MP from being seated.

Reynolds retaliated by creating a blatant diversion. The proceedings were suddenly Interrupted by 'other business' during which Reynolds got himself appointed to be a messenger to the Lord General (the Earl of Essex) before the matter of Constable could actually be put to the vote of the House. But Corbet was not to be defeated by such rude tactics. He got to his feet again and faced down this interruption. Corbet was so forceful and insistent, despite Reynolds's attempt to create a diversion, that the House was forced to vote. The result was that the House decided that Constable's election was 'a good Election, and that he ought to sit as a Member: And that the then Sheriff be required to amend the Indenture of Return.'[163]

I should at this stage add some clarification to the relationship between Henry Benson and William Dearlove. Mary Frear Keeler, in her book *The Long Parliament 1640-1641, A Biographical Study of Its Members*, includes an entry regarding Henry Benson, though not one for Dearlove or for Constable. In her account of Benson, whose dates she gives as 1579-1643, she states that at the age of 54, having been a bachelor until then, he had married Elizabeth Dearlove, widow of John Dearlove of Pannal. She then continues: 'Through this marriage he acquired three step-sons who later assisted him with his affairs. By 1641, perhaps earlier, William Dearlove, was bailiff and steward of the manor of Knaresborough for its owner, the queen. The family's hold on the borough was described as corrupt ... He was not an active member of the House ... Benson was charged in parliament with having abused his privileges as a member by selling protections to persons not his servants in and about London and even in more distant parts. Benson did not deny the charges, protesting merely that he thought his actions legal, but the House voted on 2 November 1641 to expel him as "unworthy and unfit" to be a member. An attempt to have his step-son, Dearlove, replace him failed.'[164] Keeler does not mention Sir William Constable or anything about what happened after the attempt to have Dearlove replace Benson failed. I do not regard Keeler's account of Benson and Dearlove's corruption as being remotely adequate, for she does not mention the Duchy of Lancaster connection and its court, or the control of writs and electoral returns, at all, which are far more important than the Manor of Knaresborough, because they are of the very essence of the electoral malpractice and corruption. If one does not realize that Benson was able to 'elect himself', one does not understand the true nature of the corrupt election, and of this Keeler shows herself to be wholly ignorant. It is therefore high time to put the record straight, especially as it explains for the first time since 1642 how Sir William Constable really got into the Long Parliament. In her entry for Constable in the *Biographical Dictionary of British Radicals of the Seventeenth Century*, Constance Rynder merely states that Constable was elected to the Long Parliament for Knaresborough in 1642 'after a disputed election', without giving any further information. David Scott's entry for Constable in the Oxford DNB is also wholly inadequate. This story, therefore, has never before been told.

The date of Constable's election to the House is given as November 12, 1641, in the standard reference work *Parliaments of England, 1213-1702* (p. 497, published by the House of Commons in 1878). There is nothing recorded there as to when he was able actually to take his seat and be admitted to the House. There is no index listing for the *Commons Journal* for Sir William Constable taking his seat. Although as of August 17, 1642, Constable was officially acknowledged as having been elected to the House, the formalities still had to be attended to before he could actually take his seat, and the amended indenture of return which was necessary before he could do so did not reach the House until November 8, 1642, nearly a year after the election. On that day, the *Commons Journal* records as the day's first item of business for the House:

'A Warrant from the Sheriff of the County of Yorke to Mr. [John] Rushworth, to amend the Indenture of Return for Knaresborough in the County of Yorke, according to an Order of the Seventeenth of August, was this day read; and allowed of: And the Clerk of the Crown called to the Bar with the Indenture: And Mr. Rushworth went down to the Bar; and, according to his Deputation from the Sheriff, he there amended the Indenture of Return.'[165]

It has been important to give the true facts about Sir William Constable's election to the Long Parliament, because the case has been misrepresented both by C. H. Firth in the old DNB and by W. D. Pink.[166] Pink says of Constable that he was 'unsuccessful at the poll but was admitted as member by resolution of the House.'[167] It is untrue to say that he was unsuccessful at the poll, since he was a victim of poll fraud. Firth and Pink were entirely unaware of this.

Constable's formal legitimacy as an MP of the Long Parliament thus dates from November 8, 1642. And he took his seat on that day, as we shall see.

There is a further intriguing insight into the true situation that summer. An interesting letter to Constable survives, dated June 4, 1642, from his old friend Sir Matthew Boynton, Bart., with whom he had intended to emigrate to Connecticut in 1635, and who was eventually to become a recruiter MP for the Long Parliament. This letter is transcribed and included in the appendix. It shows that, following Dearlove's election being thrown out by the House, Constable was performing many of the 'constituency duties' of an MP in London regardless of the fact that he had not yet been admitted to the House and was not yet able to sit. For, as may be seen from Boynton's letter, Constable was obviously regarded by the leading Yorkshiremen on Parliament's side who had attended the great Haworth Moor Rendezvous in support of Parliament's cause as the chief figure of their stamp then present at London. It was to Constable that the Haworth Moor Petition was sent, for presentation to both Houses of Parliament. This proves that far from sitting on his hands awaiting events, Constable was in the thick of the struggle months before he could officially take his seat in the House. In short, he was totally undeterred by the irregularity of his position from taking the fullest possible part in the Parliamentary cause, as a ringleader of a campaign to deluge the Houses of Parliament with anti-royalist petitions from his county. So despite being kept from taking his seat by the machinations of Robert Reynolds and others, Constable was actually fulfilling the functions of a constituency MP regardless, and he was doing so from outside the House. One can also be certain that he was frequently meeting and conferring with other Yorkshire MPs who shared his views, and there must have been many a long conference between them held in some ale house near the Parliament, as he waited, and waited, and waited, to be allowed in. At one earlier point in his life, Constable had roomed at an inn called The White Hart in the Strand, and this may be where they all gathered over their beer. The White Hart was at 296 Strand, which must be the exact location where Constable stayed. This is the western corner of Savoy Court leading into the Savoy Hotel, and is no longer a pub, and the ancient building is gone.

By July, however, Constable was forced to leave London and return to Yorkshire to prepare for the coming civil war. He raised a regiment of 1200 foot and was named a Colonel. He had this regiment formed and in active service as early as July 27. He was thus one of the earliest Parliamentary officers, and one of the most forward to take the field. He was the first regicide to be appointed a colonel. This information has been made available as the result of my discovery of an important and fundamental source, which I have named The Mounting Book of the Parliamentary Army. It will have struck readers of the old DNB that Parliamentary officers' civil war careers begin in a vague haze, with few dates of commission or first service. This vacuum need no longer afflict our study of the period. The Mounting Book is the central repository of such information, drawn up personally for the Treasurer of the Army, and it enables us to view the earliest military activities of many leading personalities with precision at last. Dates, numbers of men, and sums of money are now available which previously could only be the subject of speculation. Initial extracts from the Mounting Book relating to the regicides during 1642 may be found transcribed for the appendix. From this it may be seen that Sir William received money as a colonel for his regiment two days before Oliver Cromwell received money for his troop as a captain. On August 18, the Treasurer of the Army paid Constable on behalf of his regiment of 1200 men the sum of £1,244/ 16/ 00.

It had been my intention to edit and publish the entire Mounting Book, but the tumultuous and hysterical reaction to the findings of my research many years ago, and the violent insults and personal abuse to which I was relentlessly subjected somewhat cooled my ardour. And although I had the entire support of Lord Scarman in my cause, he was in the end powerless against 'the Swamp'.

Constable had achieved nothing short of a minor miracle in raising and arming 1200 men by July 27, 1642. This was a major feat of military expertise and organisation, especially as we know that in mid-June he had been far away in London dealing with entirely different matters. He must have accomplished this astonishing feat, therefore, in about one month.

Only ten days after being paid, Constable's regiment was assigned for service in Ireland.[168] This idea probably arose in London because Constable was so early in making an organised regiment available. However, the idea did not come off, because the services of Constable and his regiment were too urgently needed at home for what had clearly now become the Civil War to permit them to depart for Ireland. Fortunately, there would never again be any suggestion that Constable should be sent off to Ireland.

The Earl of Essex, appointed as Parliament's general, recognised Constable's seniority and experience at once. He named him as one of the seven members of his Council of War.[169] Sir William's 'blue coats' regiment of foot was brought south by the Earl of Essex during the autumn, and took part in the Battle of Edgehill, on October 23. This was the Civil War's first major pitched battle between the royalists and the parliamentarians. The list of officers in Constable's regiment was published in 1642 in a pamphlet entitled *The List of the Army raised under the command of his excellency, Robert, Earl of Essex and Ewe*. I have acquired an original copy of this 1642 pamphlet which was sold by the Fairfax family and, having been bound singly in modern times, bears the bookplate of Lord Fairfax of Cameron. It is therefore highly likely that this copy personally belonged either to Colonel Sir William Fairfax, who fought at Edgehill and was killed in 1644, or to Sir Thomas Fairfax, who was later to head the New Model Army and was Constable's nephew. In either case, it is not impossible that Constable himself handled it and looked at his own listing in it. This extremely rare and crucial pamphlet was reprinted (with slight emendations such as re-spellings) in 1863 by Edward Peacock in his booklet, *The Army Lists of the Roundheads and Cavaliers, Containing the Names of the Officers in the Royal and Parliamentary Armies of 1642*. In his book, Peacock neglects to index this important development. I have a copy of Peacock, and it is interesting to compare the two, namely the original pamphlet and Peacock's reprint of it. Sir William Constable's regiment is to be found on pages 39-40 of Peacock. The original pamphlet of 1642 is unpaginated. In his edition, Peacock has added a few notes, two of which have been added for Constable's regiment, one for Constable himself, and the other for his regimental chaplain William Sedgwick. In both editions of the pamphlet, Constable's Lieutenant-Colonel is named Robert Grain. However, in his book about the Battle of Edgehill, Brigadier Young calls him Robert Graeme, i.e. Graham in modern spelling, and says of him and of Constable's Major Henry Frodsham:

'(Constable's) lieutenant-colonel was probably a Scots soldier of fortune, while his major had been in both the Cadiz and [Isle of] Rhé expeditions. ... Certainly the regiment had no reason to be ashamed of its part at Edgehill. It was one of the ensigns, Arthur Young, later a captain, who had taken the Banner Royal.'[170]

So from the examples of his Lieutenant-Colonel and Major we can see that Constable had turned to old comrades who had a history of being professional soldiers to help him form and command his regiment. It is interesting that Henry Frodsham had been in the Duke of Buckingham's disastrous 1627 Isle of Rhé Expedition. On the hill opposite Edgehill, where the base of an old 16th century windmill of theirs still stands, at a place known as Burton Dassett, lived the family of a young officer named John Temple who had died at the Isle of Rhé after leading a brave charge and engaging the French commanding general in hand to hand combat. The Temples would have watched the Battle of Edgehill from their own hill. They would have seen the moving formations of men below in the valley, watched the silent puffs of smoke and then heard the delayed sounds of those cannon and guns. The younger brother of that John Temple whom Frodsham would certainly have known well, was James Temple, soon to become a Parliamentary Colonel, then a recruiter MP, and then a regicide alongside Constable. So do the threads of fate often intertwine.

A contemporary account of the Battle of Edgehill which was sent and read out loud to Parliament, and ordered by them to be printed, may be found in John Rushworth's *Collections*. It records an extraordinary incident regarding Constable's regiment during the battle:

'... their [the Royalists'] Foot, which appeared to us, divided into nine great Bodies, came up all in Front, and after some playing with the Cannon on both sides, that part of it which was on their Left, and towards our Right Wing, came on very gallantly to the Charge, and were as gallantly received, and Charged by Sir Philip Stapleton and Sir William Balford's [*sic,* Balfour's] Regiment of Horse, assisted with the Lord Robert's and Sir William Constable's Regiments of Foot, who did [drove] it so home thrice together, that they forced all the Musqueteers, of two of their [the royalists'] left Regiments, to run in and shrowd themselves within their Pikes [*i.e., the main foot soldiers' weapons were long sharp pikes, and the smaller squadrons of men placed in front of them with actual guns, namely muskets, panicked and ran and hid behind their own pikemen*], not daring to shoot a shot ...'[171]

Brigadier Young adds this account:

'The [King's] Lifeguard meanwhile was locked in combat with Constable's Regiment. Sir Edmund Verney, the Knight Marshal, ... was struck down by Ensign Arthur Young [of Constable's Regiment] and the [royal] standard was snatched from his lifeless hand.'[172] This capture of the King's Standard was a powerfully symbolic act which made a tremendous impression upon the public when they learned about it. It was what in the jargon of today would be described as 'an iconic moment'. The psychological impact of this, both upon the soldiers themselves and the public at large, can probably not be overestimated. Amongst royalists, Verney achieved almost a martyr's status, and became known as 'the Standard Bearer' who died holding aloft the symbol of his King. There is even a book bearing the title of *The Standard Bearer* which is a biography of Sir Edmund Verney, written by Peter Verney and published in 1963.[173]

Constable must have gone to London after the Battle of Edgehill and have taken his seat in the Commons on November 8, 1642, the day he was accepted by the House as having been duly elected as an MP. We know this because he was appointed to a crucial committee the very next day, and ordered along with his fellow committee-members to meet for the convening of the committee in the Court of Wards that very afternoon of November 9. The committee was charged with raising cavalry forces throughout the country and taking any other measures which they considered necessary for the safety of the Kingdom (thus effectively replacing a pre-existing Committee for the Safety of the Kingdom, which the House must have decided was ineffectual), and it consisted of twenty men, three of them future regicides (the two besides Constable being Henry Marten and Lord Grey of Groby). Several distinguished grandees were on this committee, such as Denzel Hollis, Bulstrode Whitelocke, Sir Arthur Hazlerigg, Sir Henry Vane, and John Hampden. The Committee was charged as follows: 'This Committee, or any Four of them, is appointed to consider how a Body of Horse may be raised, besides that Body that is appointed to attend the Army already raised: And likewise to consider of any thing else, that they shall conceive necessary for the Safety of the Kingdom, and to present it to the House ...'[174]

Although he took part in the Siege of Reading, Constable's main military exploits during the Civil War, prior to 1645 and the formation of the New Model Army in which he was prevented from becoming a Colonel of Foot by the Self-Denying Ordinance, took place in the North, where he did very good work and, after the East Riding was settled into the control of Parliament, Fairfax sent him into the North Riding, where he took and held Whitby and other places.

The newsletter *Mercurius Civicus* reported in its Issue 39 for the week of February 15-22, 1643/4:

'Also on Tuesday February 20 there came a Messenger to the Parliament from [Colonel] Sir John Meldrum, who confirmed the former Relations concerning the Lord Fairfax, in inlarging his quarters twenty miles towards Durham, and Sir William Constables successe both at Whitby and Malton neere York...'[175]

The Yorkshire historian Jack Binns gives some further information about these raids:

'In February [1643/4], operating out of Hull, Sir William Constable made a series of raiding incursions deep into Royalist territory, up the coast as far as Whitby and inland to Pickering, Malton, and even Stamford Bridge, only six miles from York.'[176]

Eventually, Constable would be appointed Lieutenant-General of Horse under Fairfax (he was described as Lieutenant-General in March of 1644/5, though we do not know the date of his appointment), which was the highest military rank possible below that of commanding general of an army.[177] Despite becoming a Lieutenant-General, everyone tended to continue referring to him as Colonel, which must mean that he was too polite to correct them. He also served as Military Governor of Gloucester between 1648 and 1651. (He thus acted at different times in his career as Governor of two towns on opposite sides of England, Hull and Gloucester.)

On July 4, 1643, the House of Commons added Sir William to the Committee for the Safety of Hull. In addition, the House ordered 'Sir William Constable to have the Command in Chief of the Forces of Horse and Foot, in the East Riding by Commission from and under

Lord Fairfax.'[178] From the summer of 1643, therefore, Constable had the role of a Lieutenant-General in Fairfax's Army of the North, so that was probably when he was officially given that rank.

Constable was often someone who was turned to when things became critical. This happened in the summer of 1643, as this entry in the *Commons Journal* for July 20, 1643, records: ...

'That Sir Wm. Constable shall have power to beat up his Drums in the Counties of Suffolk and Norfolk, for raising of Voluntiers, to the Number of a Thousand, to go to the Relief of my Lord Fairfaxe; whereof the Three hundred, now raised in Suffolk, and formerly appointed for Newcastle, are to be accounted as Part; the said Regiment of One thousand Men, to be under the Command of Sir Wm. Constable.'[179]

By August, Constable was at Colchester. On August 26 he wrote a letter from there to Sir Thomas Barrington at Chelmsford, saying:

'I made bold to direct a few hasty lines to you; since that, I had this morning opportunity to acquaint divers of ye deputy lieutenants whom I found mett here wth the request wch ye house of Commons have recommended to this county & some others for a contribution for ye supply of my Lord ffairfax. ... & if you please to dispose those dragooners this way wch they have been pleased to propound to you, I hope by Gods assistance & some frendly help from these Counties to be inabled to make my way through Lincolnshire wth a party of horse & dragoones, though I send some foote by sea.'[180]

On September 20, 1643, Sir William commanded his Regiment of Foot as part of Lord Robartes's (aka Roberts) Brigade under the Earl of Essex at the battle of Newbury. None of the Fairfaxes or Yorkshire officer friends of Constable seem to have participated in this battle with him. It is unclear how and exactly when Constable managed to make his way across England so quickly to join the forces of the Earl of Essex. Only three weeks before the battle of Newbury, as we have just seen, he was at Colchester in Essex with some horse and dragoons. But at Newbury he had no horse and dragoons, he was commanding an entire regiment of foot only. He must have left the horse and dragoons behind and made his way westwards with only a few companions, riding furiously, and it seems he must have joined Essex prior to Essex's arrival at Newbury, since the Roberts Brigade was entrusted with guarding the few small pieces of ordnance (four small cannons known as drakes) which Essex had with him, his heavy ordnance having been left behind in Gloucester. This means that Constable's regiment had to have come eastwards with Lord Essex, meaning that he had joined him previously, perhaps at Cirencester. (It cannot have been at Hungerford, because Essex stayed there for only an hour and rushed on with his Army at precipitate speed.) We do not know where Constable got the soldiers from to form his regiment. He must have whipped his regiment into shape within only a few days' time. But then, he was used to that sort of thing. One presumes he must have brought a trusted Lieutenant Colonel and Major with him on his hurried journey across England, but we seem to have no information about who was in his regiment at Newbury. Nor do we appear to have information of where Roberts and his other colonel, Francis Martin, had come from or when they had joined Essex either. The surviving information about this battle at Newbury (known as 'the First Battle of Newbury') is confusing and incomplete. I have never visited the location and tried to make sense of the topography, which would be necessary in trying to interpret the descriptions of the battle. It seems that no one has ever completely sorted it out.

A reference to Constable's military role in this major 1643 battle appeared in the pamphlet *A True Relation of the Late Expedition of His Excellency, Robert Earle of Essex for the Relief of Gloucester with The Description of the Fight at Newbury*, published by the Commons authority, of which I am fortunate to own a copy.[181] The pamphlet describes Lord Robartes's (called 'Roberts') Brigade of infantry as consisting of three regiments, that of Lord Roberts himself, that of Sir William Constable, and that of Colonel Francis Martin. The pamphlet also specifies that this Brigade's role initially was to attend and guard the train of artillery as it made its way 'to be neere to his Excell: [Essex] looking from the hill, towards Newbury' prior to the battle beginning. The Roberts Brigade was then left 'with four or five small pieces [of artillery] just where the Enemy advanced, who gave them so warme an entertainment that they ran shamefully, and my Lo: Roberts possest the ground which the Enemy came first up unto …'

Having repelled the initial royalist assault, the Brigade was supported on its left by Major General Skippon and others, 'upon the high way that came from Newbury just upon us, upon which way 4 Drakes [artillery pieces] were likewise placed, and well defended; … Colonel Mannerings [aka Mainwaring, a surname which is still today pronounced 'Mannering'] regiment [from the City of London] was placed on the right hand between the hill and my Lord Roberts his Brigade. This Regiment his Excellency after a while commanded away, to the relief of his own Regiment … The fight all along the valley (more than half a mile in length) was continued as long as in any other part of the Army, which was til ten a clock at night … this same evening his Excell: drew up the Army to Theale, and taking some refreshment there, marched the next morning being Friday with the whole Army to Reading, where we stayed till the Sabbath was past, and gave publique thankes for the great victory.'

A lengthy description of the battle which appears not to have been noticed by various historians (or perhaps any?) was written by John Vicars in his little-known but utterly fascinating book, *Jehovah-Jireh, God in the Mount, or Englands Parliamenterie-Chronicle*, published in 1644 and consisting of 434 action-packed pages. (I am fortunate to have a copy of it, so I can read the extensive text at leisure without being kicked out by a librarian.) Vicars seems to have been an eye-witness of many of the rousing scenes of action which he describes in this lengthy book. For instance, there is no doubt whatsoever that he personally took part in the destruction of the Cross at Cheapside, and his account reads like a modern London *Sunday Times* special reporter's account of how the huge monument was dismantled and of the violent behaviour of the crowds, with many minute details noted such as what happened with the melted lead of the images of the saints and popes. Although it is clear in many parts of his book that his accounts of numerous battles and skirmishes were drawn from pamphlets and letters of intelligence (he states this openly), on other occasions he seems to have been present. As for his account of the battle at Newbury, one cannot escape the impression that Vicars was actually travelling with the Army at this time and was an eye-witness of at least those portions of the battle which he could see. Here is a portion of his account:

'… thus this noble and magnanimous Generall marched on, breaking through all straits and disadvantages, with his most resolute Armie… until they came within about two miles or lesse of Newbury, where his excellencie understood the enemy was at hand, and indeed so at hand as to necessitate a fight or perishing, so that, that night also [as he had done previously] he was fain to lie in the field with his whole Army, the enemy having got Newbury before our Army could reach it in their march, besides the enemy was now in a country where they were too well acquainted, but my Lord not, whereby they possess themselves of all advantages, having their main body in a large plain ready to charge & receive us, whereas ours was to pass a lane in which but six a brest could march, by which means also ours were deprived of horse and Cannon, and in certain expectation of a strong party to charge us in our Rear, which to looke unto Major [i.e., Major General Philip] Skippon, was called off from the front of our Armie, we seeing (I say) no way but to fight or perish every mothers sonne. And this Tuesday night the King sent a challenge to the Lord Generall, to give him battall the next morning: which notwithstanding all these forementioned great disadvantages was accordingly performed. Thus on the Wednesday morning by breake of day the enemies foot was come to the hill, and by six a clock both their horse and foot were put into battalia, and all their Ordnance planted, and they gave us an over-shot to summon us to the fight: But notwithstanding all these gained from us, blessed be our God (as here now we shall see) there is nether wisdom, policie, nor strength against the Lord. ...But to goe on, we hereupon called a councell of war, and though our much weariness and want of victuals [no one in the Army had eaten that day or the day before for want of supplies] might have been sufficient motives to have caused us to have declined the battail that day; yet such was the noble and renowned courage of his Excellencie, that to try his souldiers minds, he rod from Regiment to Regiment, and out the question of a battail to the Souldiers, telling them the enemy had all the advantages, as the hill, the Town, the hedges, the lains, and the river; but they all most unanimously and bravely cryed out, *Let us fall on them, we will by Gods assistance beat them from them all*, And indeed, in six hours fight our foot with the assistance of our horse gained them all [It is to be remembered that Sir William Constable's regiment was one of foot, and is part of the force here referred to.], and then we planted our Ordnance on the top of the hill [this would have been done by the Roberts Brigade], where the Kings Ordnance began to play on us, & then we were on equall termes with the enemy for ground, onely it fell out herein unhappily that the Citie Regiments (contrary to his Excellencies direction and intention) were first and most desperately engaged and lay open to the enemies Cannon and horse too, which might have been a sad business (had not God admirably preserved them) the best of an Armie being usually kept for the turn of the day. And ... it fell out ... they losing for a long time ...none but their tatterdemalion Welsh & roguish Irish [perished in the front of the royalists], whiles we lost Citizens of a City no whit inferior to Rome it selfe in its greatest glory: But ours did most admirably valiantly beat the Kings foot from hedge to hedge, and so scattered them that hardly a foot Soldier of theirs was to be seen, save onely the dead bodies of them slain on the ground, they having also drawne off about 37 cart loads of their slain before we got the hill from them. The fight began about six in the morning, and held till neer 12 at night. Our word for distinction [i.e. password] in this fight was *Religion*; and theirs was *Queen Mary*, enough to have set the dullest Protestants on fire with zealous indignation ... Now the enemy seeing their foot was (as was aforesaid) utterly routed, and they like to lose their Ordnance, wheeled about with a great body of horse, and about three quarters of a mile below the hill fell upon the Rear of our Army where our carriages were, which occasioned us to withdraw a part of our army from off the hill to assist the bridge that was so engaged, who cut off many of the Kings horse, but in the interim the enemy drew off their Ordnance to Newbury, and carried away 30 carts loads of wounded men. In this fight Sir Philip Stapleton [commander of the chief Brigade of horse which included Lord Essex's own regiment] did most valiant service with the Lord Generalls Regiment, charging the enemie five times, Yet in all the time of the fight our souldiers could not get any water to drinke. As for his most noble Excellencie the Lord Generall, during this whole battail he behaved himself with as much noble and valiant resolution as ever did Generall in any battail, himself in person leading up the City Regiments, and when the enemies horse had broken through them, he rallied them together, and most courageously led them on again. The courageous and resolute Lord Roberts his Souldiers [which included the Constable regiment] were the first who began this terrible and bloudy battail with this provoking enemie, and performed the onset bravely, making the rest of our Army to make even a running match, and sweat again with haste to relieve them. Noble Colonel

Tucker [a Lieutenant Colonel serving under Lord Roberts who was evidently commanding the artillery, or 'Ordnance'][182] in the midst of the fight having himself fired one peice of Ordnance upon the enemy, and ayming to fire the second time (being himself a brave Cannoneer) was shot in the head with a Cannonbullet by the enemie. ....'[183] And so on at great length for some pages more.

Further descriptions of the battle, with curious details, are also to be found in a brief 1646 book about Lord Essex, of which I have a copy.[184] This supplies information not known from other sources. As for the Roberts Brigade, it tells us: 'The first that gave the charge was the most noble L. Roberts, whose action(s) do speak him higher than our Epithets. He performed it with great resolution, and by his owne example shewed excellent examples of valour to his Regiment. The Cavalry of the Enemy performed also their charge most bravely, and gave in with a mighty impression upon him. A prepared body of our Army made hast to relieve him. Upon this two Regiments of the Kings Horse with a fierce charge saluted the blew [blue] regiment of the London trained Bands, who gallantly discharged upon them, and did beat them backe, but they being no whit daunted at it, wheeled about, and on a suddaine charged them againe, our Musketeers did again discharge, and that with so much violence and successe, that they sent them now, not wheeling but reeling from them, and yet for all that, they made a third assault, and coming in full Squadrons, they did the utmost of their endeavour to breake through our rankes, but a Cloud of bullets came at once so thick from our Muskets, and made such a havocke amongst them both of men and horse, that in a feare, full of confused speed they did flye before us, and did not more adventure upon so warme a service.'[185] So having been part of the initial foot charge of the battle, Constable's regiment would have been in the thick of all of what has just been described.

Another account is also to be found in a pamphlet of October 7, 1643, which gives yet more details unavailable elsewhere. Constable is mentioned on p. 15 of this pamphlet. But it is not necessary to recount at greater length the complex course of this huge battle of about 30,000 men which lasted from early morning until midnight, except to say that it was a victory for the Parliament, and that Constable's regiment was important from the very first charge, fought fiercely, and very much helped to gain the victory.

After the Battle of Newbury, Parliament's army under Essex headed eastwards and returned to London, passing Reading and Windsor. Essex arrived in London on September 25, four days after the end of the great battle, where he received the thanks of both Houses of Parliament, and doubtless Sir William Constable sat in his seat in the Commons to join in that accolade. But the follow-through of the great victory was hopelessly incompetent, and as early as October 3, the royalists seized Reading, which Essex's army had passed only a few days previously. As Gardiner sarcastically says of this: 'Charles could hardly have been in a better position if he had been the undoubted victor at Newbury.'[186] Essex retreated to Windsor, where he based himself for the time being. It is doubtful that Constable joined him, except perhaps briefly for the reallocation of his regiment, passing over of command to another colonel, and retrieving any of his senior officers whom he might have brought with him when he had rushed to join in the struggle at Newbury. After all, he would be needing them soon in Yorkshire.

On January 21, 1643/4, Constable, the regicide Sir Thomas Mauleverer, and numerous other officers joined Sir Thomas Fairfax at Manchester to march to the relief of Nantwich in Cheshire, as David Evans relates:

'On January 21st Sir Thomas Fairfax, Sir William Fairfax, Sir William Brereton, Sir Thomas Mauleverer, Sir William Constable, Col. John Lambert, Col. John Bright, Col.

Richard Holland, Col. John Booth and Col. Ralph Ashton [aka Assheton] marched with twenty-eight – thirty Troops of Horse, five Troops of Dragoons and c. 3,000 Foot to relieve Nantwich. ... On January 25th 1644 [i.e., 1643/4] Lord Byron's forces were caught between the relief force and the garrison at Nantwich and destroyed. After the fighting and mopping-up Sir Thomas, Sir William Fairfax, and Col. Christopher Copley remained in Cheshire, helping with the securement of a number of small royalist garrisons at Crewe, Keele, and Adlington. By February 8th Sir William Constable had rejoined Lord Fairfax in Hull.'[187] Sir Thomas Fairfax continued to be stuck in Cheshire, but on February 24 he wrote to the Earl of Essex from Manchester saying he was leaving for the North because he had been 'ordered by my father to march into Yorkshire'.[188] He was badly needed there.

Evans gives a description also of Constable's activities during February and March with Lord Fairfax:

'At Hull Lord Fairfax had started to expand out of the city. Sir William Constable had taken ten Troops of Horse into the North Riding, being followed by Lord Fairfax with c. 2,000 Foot. Bridlington and Whitby were taken, Scarborough, Malton and Stamford Bridge were raided and their garrisons disagreeably shaken. ... By about March 12th Lord Fairfax's forces under Sir William Constable had stormed Tadcaster and taken it.'[189]

As C. H. Firth recounts in Constable's entry for the DNB, '(Constable's) greatest exploits ... took place in the spring of 1644. In February he took Burlington, assisted in the capture of Whitby, retook the town of Scarborough ... defeated Newcastle's forces at Driffield and Malton ... In March he also captured Tadcaster and Stamford Bridge.' Gardiner explains that as Sir Thomas Fairfax was detained at Chester, his father Lord Fairfax did not have the benefits of his assistance in Yorkshire, and indeed had been 'able to muster no more than 5,000 foot and 3,000 ill-armed horse'. But as the East Riding of Yorkshire was now safely under Parliament's control, doubtless in large part due to the efforts of Constable, who was an East Riding man, Lord Fairfax 'had been able to despatch Sir William Constable to overrun the North Riding. To capture Scarborough was beyond Constable's power, but he had secured Whitby without difficulty.'[190] And later he did after all take Scarborough, so that it turned out not to be beyond his power after all.

Constable's activities in April are described by Evans:

'By April 8th Lord Fairfax, Sir Thomas Fairfax and Sir William Constable had joined together at Leeds. One report suggests that the total force had sixty Troops of Horse present, another report gives the numbers as 4,000 Foot and c. 2,500 Horse, a third report swops these figures around.

'What could have happened is that Lord Fairfax left Hull on April 5th and marched with c. 2,000 Foot and c. 500 Horse or c. 2,000 Horse! Sir William Constable either had already joined Lord Fairfax by this stage, adding maybe c. 300 Horse as it seems that c. 200 Horse were left at Whitby and an undisclosed force left in Bridlington. Hull was left with probably 7 – 800 men to secure the garrison. Sir Thomas Fairfax was widely believed to muster c. 2,000 Horse and Dragoons whilst Col. Lambert and Col. Bright were reported to command 700 Foot and c. 500 Horse. Thus it seems possible that some 4,000 Horse and Dragoons and c. 3,000 Foot were mustered under Lord Fairfax's command.'[191]

In 2004, a useful book by David Cooke appeared entitled *The Civil War in Yorkshire*, complete with many helpful maps and photos of relevant sites, which endeavours to paint a continuous picture of the struggle there. In contrast to the briefer work by David Evans ten years earlier, which refers to him many times, in Cooke's book Sir William Constable receives almost no attention, being mentioned only in two places in the entire book. But the first of those mentions is most informative for us:

'By the end of February [1644] pressure had begun to grow on the royalists in Yorkshire. From Hull, Lord Fairfax's men were growing more daring, as opposition to them lessened. In early February Lord Fairfax had ordered Sir William Constable to carry out a mounted raid in the East Riding, which reached as far north as Pickering. Belasyse despatched a large force of cavalry to intercept Constable, but they were unable to locate him. Constable did not have the same problem, and surprised three regiments of Royalist horse in their quarters, capturing a large number of prisoners, before returning to Hull.'[192]

After that, a bit later in the spring of 1644, Constable acted as Governor of Hull. A letter of his dated May 25, 1644, to Speaker Lenthall is preserved amongst the Portland MSS. at the Bodleian.[193] In that brief letter he wittily says he is sending Lenthall a 'present'. The 'present' was two prominent prisoners, Sir John Ramsden and Colonel John Bellasys (Bellasis). The latter was a runaway and (in 1642) disabled royalist MP, who had represented Thirsk in Yorkshire in the Short Parliament and again at the beginning of the Long Parliament. Ramsden had represented Pontefract in the Short Parliament. Constable's wry humour goes further. He says:

'I have not hitherto taken the boldness to present you with a few lines from hence having nothing worthy of you, but this present which I now send you gives me a little more boldness being a proper service to the house to send you your members. I have only the sending of these, but shall be glad to bring you in more of the same quality.'

By these insouciant and amusing turns of phrase we may sense the strong sense of humour which Constable must have had, as such dry wit is rarely if ever to be found in letters to the Speaker. (I have read many dozens of letters to Lenthall, and I have never found another which dared to make a joke of any kind.) From this I draw the conclusion that Constable was not one to be in awe of any authority. Of course, we have already seen that in his 'letter in gold' to Queen Anne. Perhaps because making a joke to the Speaker was not considered solemn enough, Constable's letter does not appear to have been read aloud to the House, and remained a private matter. However, the *Commons Journal* records for May 31, 1644, the arrival of Ramsden and Bellassyse, and because they were considered as renegade MPs, the pronouncement is made that they:

'… be forthwith delivered into the Custody of the Serjeant of Arms, to be brought hither to the Bar [of the House].'

When later in the day this was done, they were rebuked with the greatest harshness and sent to the Tower:

'Resolved, &c. That Jo. Bellassys, and Sir Jo: Ramsden Knight, shall be forthwith committed Prisoners to the Tower, being committed upon High-Treason, for levying War against the King [*this was a formality of language, since obviously they had been fighting on the King's side in the royalist forces*] and Parliament; and shall there continue Prisoners, until the House take further Order.

'Mr. Bellassys, and Sir Jo: Ramsden, were both of them, one after another, called in to the Bar: And Mr. Speaker acquainted them "with the Horror and Grievousness of the Offence, for which they were brought thither; which was no less than, at one Blow, to endeavour the Ruin of Religion, Liberty, the Privileges, and very Being of Parliaments, and the introducing of Popery and Slavery; the Consideration whereof should strike Terror and Amazement into you: And for these grievous Crimes, of High-Treason, you are, by the Judgment of this House, committed as Traytors to the Tower, there to remain Prisoners during the Pleasure of this House.'[194]

The two prisoners were specifically ordered to be under the charge of Lord Fairfax, which meant that he had the power to dispose of them by exchange. And on August 14, at Lord Fairfax's instruction, the House released Sir John Ramsden, after two and a half months in the Tower, as part of a prisoner exchange with the royalist forces in return for Colonel Ashenhurst and his son, 'late prisoners at Stayley'.[195]

As for John Bellassys, by instruction of Fairfax, he was ordered by the House on December 6, 1644, to be exchanged for Major Carr, Captain Lister, and Captain Ayscough.[196]

Those two men were lucky to escape with only a few months in the Tower and not to be executed for high treason. But soldiers like Fairfax and Constable were highly practical people, and far more interested in saving their own men by these prisoner exchanges than in exacting vengeance on their enemies, as many of the armchair soldiers in the House might have preferred to do. That is why the prisoners were specified as being in charge to Fairfax from the beginning, for just this purpose. Constable's bantering letter to the Speaker gives something of the impression of an elderly schoolmaster gathering in naughty pupils and sending them to be caned for having absconded from the school. His offer to find more such naughty boys if the Speaker wished, and send him further 'presents' for punishment, is an extraordinarily offhand and cavalier attitude. It suggests a man who has 'seen it all before' and, as the slang expression of today would have it, 'has been around the block', and who, frankly, regards the Speaker himself as someone he can safely tease. (Constable was 16 years older than Speaker William Lenthall and apparently considered himself very much his 'elder'.)

An undated letter from Constable to Sir Thomas Barrington was written from Hull about the same time that Constable sent his 'present' to Lenthall. It is a 'begging letter' asking for money from Barrington towards the garrison at Hull (which Fairfax had entrusted to his command). He says: 'I do not doubt but to have had & shall have that favour & Countenance from you that may much advance ye assistance wch my Lo: ffairfax hopes to receave from this County. There is not one penny come in by any other way assigned for his supply [for the Army of the Northern Association] since his coming to Hull. This way of voluntary subscription is ye only present means wch ye house of Commons have recommended. I hope you will looke upon it not as a remote case but concurrent wth other wayes wch you are about for ye same publique end.'[197]

On June 25, 1644, the Committee for Both Kingdoms ordered that Lord Fairfax, Sir Thomas Fairfax, and Sir William Constable be made 'Commissioners to reside in the north to be sent down to the army there.' They further added that the three of them 'are added to the Committee appointed to join with the Committee of the Estates of Scotland.' Part of their orders were to ask the Scots for further assistance in the Civil War in England. The Committee sent formal notification on the same day to Scotland that the Fairfaxes and Constable were coming.[198] However, instead of going north to Scotland, the Fairfaxes and

Constable rushed south, evidently bringing some Scottish forces with them under the Earl of Leven, to join the forces of the Earl of Manchester in a great battle with the royalists. The Battle of Marston Moor took place on July 2, 1644, and in it, Sir William commanded his Regiment of Foot, as part of the Army of the Northern Association under Lord Fairfax. This was a battle which was a complete victory for Parliament, with 4,000 royalists killed in one day. A letter sent the next day to the Committee of Both Kingdoms gives some details of the Fairfax forces' participation:

'Not knowing but that the ill and false news of the defeat of our armies which has come so plentifully hither [at Wressle Castle in the East Riding of Yorkshire] may also have reached London to the prejudice of the kingdom, we thought fit to send you this brief and general account, which we saw under Lord Fairfax's hand, to this purpose, that after a defeat in part received by some of our forces God has graciously given us a happy and great victory, that Lord Fairfax and Sir Thos. [Fairfax] were both very well, only his son Charles was hurt; the place in which the battle was fought was about Marston Moor.'[199]

I discovered amongst the S.P. 28 papers in the Public Record Office an interesting document which gives unusual details relating to the Battle of Marston Moor, which is apparently otherwise unknown (since those papers are uncalendared). It records details of deceased soldiers, provisions, expenditures, etc., and its chief interest to us here is that it was drawn up by one of the captains in Constable's regiment. I did not copy it out and transcribe it, but I give the reference here for its future use by military historians.[200]

It was not until July 5 that a formal joint letter was sent to the Committee of Both Kingdoms by the commanders of the three armies (Scottish, Manchester, and Fairfax armies) reporting on the victory at Marston Moor. The details of their great victory are described as follows:

'... the issue was the total routing of the enemy's army, with the loss of all their ordnance to the number of 20 [pieces], their ammunition, baggage, about 100 colours [banners], and 10,000 arms. There were killed upon the spot about 3,000 of the enemy, whereof many were chief officers, and 1,500 prisoners taken, among whom there are above 100 officers, in which number is Sir Charles Lucas, Lieut.-Genl. To the marquis of Newcastle's horse, Major-General Porter, and Major-General Tillyer, besides divers colonels, lieut.-colonels, and majors. Our loss is not very greate, being only one lieut.-colonel, a few captains, and 200 or 300 common soldiers. The Prince [Rupert], in great distraction, with only a few horsemen and scarcely any foot, marched the next morning from York northward. We have now lain down again in our old leaguer before York, which we hope within a few days to gain.'[201]

Constable had a prominent role in the siege and surrender of York, as seen from Peter Wenham's book *The Great and Close Siege of York 1644*.[202] The siege of York was divided between three generals. Lord Fairfax's forces (which included Sir William Constable's) besieged the city from the East. The Western side of the siege was divided between the Earl of Manchester and the Earl of Leven. On July 11, the final storming was about to be launched against the city by the join Parliamentary forces, but as a last chance they appealed for a surrender. Then royalists inside the city grabbed this last chance to save themselves, and agreed, upon condition that it was by treaty. And as Wenham tells us:

'As a result, on Saturday, July 13, in the morning, Sir William Constable and Colonel [John] Lambert were "sent by the Lord Fairfax" into York after hostages had been sent out of the city for their "securitie and safe return". After spending the whole day in discussion the two envoys returned with a request to the three generals that Commissioners be appointed and authorised "to treat and conclude upon Articles of the peaceable surrender of the Citie". '

The Commissioners appointed were Lord Humbie [Sir Adam Hepburn, Lord Humbie, MP, a royalist], Sir William Constable and Colonel [Edward] Montagu. The discussions were lengthy but eventually terms were agreed. There were four signatures to the formal Agreement Concerning Terms of Surrender: Lord Fairfax, the Earl of Manchester, Lord Humbie, and Sir William Constable.

Despite the huge and devastating victory at Marston Moor and the success in capturing the city of York, the Northern Army under the Fairfaxes and Constable was worn out, unpaid, barely fed, and falling to pieces, as we see from the state of things only two months later. In the third week of September, 1644, Ferdinando Lord Fairfax was besieging Pontefract Castle in the West Riding of Yorkshire, and in a letter of September 20 he describes Constable's role and also the state of the Northern Army:

'The party which I sent under the command of Sir Wm. Constable, coming within view of the castle, the enemy drew secretly forth on the other side the same evening in haste, and marched to Doncaster and thence to Newark, leaving my troops to conflict with sorer enemies, their wants and necessities, which I am no ways able to supply. Their stock of patience being at length worn out, our troops are ready to disband, as some of them have done already. The means for their support in this country being drawn another way it will be impossible for me to keep together any considerable forces of horse and foot. In a very few days they will moulder away to nothing, ...' [203]

The Fairfaxes and Constable were thus barely able to keep enough soldiers together to constitute even a small fighting force, much less any kind of army during the autumn of 1644.

Despite the disintegrating nature of their fighting force, Fairfax and Constable kept trying to do what they could. The issue of *Mercurius Civicus* for the week of September 19-26, 1644, reported:

'[The House of Commons] was then informed out of the North, that the perfidious, and infamous apostate Sir Hugh Cholmley having by occasion of the late cessation gained an opportunity to supply and store himself with provision, doth now declare himself against the Parliament, although he before pretended to stand neutral. Whereupon the Lord Fairfax hath designed Sir William Constable to goe with a party to besiege Scarborough-castle, where the said Sir Hugh now is.'[204]

The situation regarding the collapsing Parliamentary Army of the North was so dire that the Fairfaxes and Constable decided that the only way for the Northern Army to survive was to reduce its size drastically. The Fairfaxes, Constable, Constable's old friend Sir Matthew Boynton (with whom he had planned to emigrate to Connecticut in 1635 in search of religious liberty), and two others, wrote a letter to the Committee of Both Kingdoms on November 7, from York. They described the situation and their plans as follows:

'The inhabitants of Yorkshire, being much exhausted by the heavy burdens on that county, have long called upon us who are here entrusted with the peace and safety thereof, to use our best endeavours for their relief. To this purpose it has often been proposed amongst us to lessen the Yorkshire horse by about 2,000, the charge of them being insupportable to this almost ruined country.'[205]

The Committee of Both Kingdoms were alarmed by this and on November 9 ordered:

'That the business of the north shall be considered on Monday morning. That when the Committee of the Lords and Commons are ready they will give notice to the northern gentlemen. And will conclude nothing concerning Lord Fairfax's army or the assessment of the northern counties until they confer with the northern gentlemen.'[206]

There was then considerable delay, and 'the northern gentlemen' found it necessary to go down to London to discuss the situation, as the Committee of Both Kingdoms ordered on November 18:

'The Yorkshire gentlemen to be desired to be here tomorrow to speak with the Committee about the staying of Lord Fairfax's horse in Lincolnshire.'[207]

Nothing is recorded about this matter for the following two days. And on November 21, the Committee ordered:

'That letters be written to Sir Tho. Fairfax for his regiment of horse to quarter on the north side of Newark to straighten that garrison.'[208]

Two days later, on November 23, the Committee belatedly ordered:

'That the northern business be the first heard on Monday afternoon, and that the Committee of both Houses be desired to meet here an hour before, at about 2 o'clock.'[209]

But once again, the matter did not occur, and was clearly being blocked by 'moderates' on the Committee who did not want to save Fairfax's army. Four days later, however, on November 25, the radicals in Parliament were able to engineer a speech to the House of Commons by Oliver Cromwell in which he tore to shreds the reputation of the Earl of Manchester, and blamed him for prolonging and refusing to win the Civil War.[210] (This would lead eventually to Sir Thomas Fairfax being appointed head of a New Model Army.) Cromwell's speech was savage, direct, and devastating. Meanwhile, Fairfax had refused to obey the Committee's order to station his horse at Newark, and the Committee stated in a letter sent to the Committee of Nottingham:

'… we have written to Lord Fairfax to send back the regiment of horse lately there, but which is now withdrawn into Yorkshire.'

And the Committee wrote to Fairfax the same day saying:

'We doubt not but you will be able to spare that regiment of horse which has lately retired into your county … we do especially recommend this service to your Lordship.'[211]

And meanwhile on the same day many depositions poured in to the Committee attacking the incompetence of the Earl of Manchester. These came from Cromwell, Henry Ireton, Sir Hardress Waller, Robert Lilburne, Sir Arthur Hazlerigg, and other officers. Open warfare between the moderates and the radicals had now broken out within the Committee, and there is no question that the Committee's refusal to discuss 'the northern problem' was a major cause of this outpouring of dissent and savage complaints. An avalanche of further incriminating depositions and complaints poured in against Manchester, with examinations of many prominent military leaders. The evidence against the Earl of Manchester was absolutely overwhelming. None of 'the northern gentlemen' joined in with any of this, and they kept their heads down, evidently by intention. It was clear that there was going to be no help for the North coming from the Committee.

On December 2, Lord Fairfax wrote to the Committee and said he had 'given order for some regiments of mine to march to the confines of Notts. And join there for the best advantage of the public service against Newark.' But he was giving only cosmetic obedience to the Committee, for he went on to say: 'The garrisons of Knaresborough and Pontefract employ most of my foot and horse.'[212] Signing off in a formal and obliging manner, Fairfax had managed to avoid getting sacked for disobedience, but he was clearly not going to cooperate fully, and the opposing forces of radicals and moderates were at a standstill as far as the North was concerned.

Sir William Constable became an active and prominent member of the Committee of Yorkshire based at York, as well as the Committee for the Northern Association, which was also based in Yorkshire. One letter from the former signed by Constable is preserved at Hull, dated May 22, 1645.[213] A letter from the latter (just as it was formed, announcing its formation and giving directions to Hull) signed by Constable is also preserved at Hull, dated June 3, 1645.[214] Constable did not have a great deal of time available to sit on committees, however, owing to his military activities. His signature on committee documents is not frequent, for this reason. It should be explained that historians have frequently mixed up the Committee of Yorkshire with the Committee of the Northern Association which was in the same county. The regicide Sir John Bourchier was extraordinarily active, indeed the workhorse and driving force, on the Yorkshire Committee, but he did not sit on the Committee for the Northern Association, for instance. The opposite is true of the regicides John Alured of Hull (who was particularly close to the Fairfax family) and Sir Thomas Mauleverer, Bart., however; they were both on the Committee of the Northern Association but were not on the Committee of Yorkshire. In addition to these two main committees, there were also committees for each of the three Ridings, which answered to and were subsidiary to the Committee of the Northern Association but not to the Committee of Yorkshire, and there was additionally a Committee for Hull (we have seen that Constable was at least for some time on that Committee). Good luck to anyone who ever tries to sort out all the Yorkshire committees! There appear to have been jealousies and competitions between them, and so far their affairs remain more or less opaque to historians. No one that I know of has ever attempted to collate the many surviving letters from these committees (although I have transcribed many), to compare them and evaluate them. I also suspect that a large number of crucial documents relating to them remain undiscovered in the Public Record Office. Surely, this is a rich field for further research. I should just mention that the North and West Ridings of Yorkshire were entirely desolated by the Scottish forces during the Civil War, who enforced their extortionate levies upon the local inhabitants at gunpoint, and the affairs of the whole of Yorkshire were in the most desperate condition for years, often with the above-mentioned committees as the only focus of attempts to save the county from total collapse. All of the committees show signs of their members having made Herculean efforts to save Yorkshire against what at times seemed to be impossible odds, and to prevent the starvation of the entire populace of the county, often spending what little of their own private money which they had left to feed and clothe the militia and preserve law and order as best they could. This great struggle for the survival of Yorkshire at that time awaits its chronicler.

The winter of 1644-1645 was extremely harsh. The House of Commons resolved on January 2, 1644/5, 'That the House be fitted and accommodated with Curtains for the Windows, and a new Chair, so fitted that it may keep off the Injury of this extreme cold Weather from Mr. Speaker, and the Members that sit near the Chair; and that the Windows be cleansed and mended …'[215]

During this time, with the freezing wind whistling round their ears as they huddled in their great coats with their beaver hats on, shivering, the Members of the House were getting on with the great work of agreement to form a New Model Army, in order to bring the seemingly endless Civil War to a close at last. This Army was to be placed under more forceful leadership, not under such grandees as the indecisive and hopeless Earl of Essex, or the monstrously vain and supercilious Earl of Manchester. The commander was to be the quiet and modest Sir Thomas Fairfax, who had had such success in the North, and who with his father Lord Fairfax and his uncle Sir William Constable had refrained from joining in the savage and public attacks on the Earl of Manchester, so that his appointment could not be seen as a reward for any complaint. By not joining in the chorus for Manchester's removal, Fairfax had preserved apparent neutrality, and thereby helped save some of Manchester's face.

Thus it was that it was decided to create the New Model Army, with Sir Thomas Fairfax as its commander in chief. As is well known, his deputy would become Lieutenant-General Oliver Cromwell. It is less well known that the New Model Army had another officer of the same rank as Cromwell, Lieutenant-General Thomas Hammond, who commanded the ordnance. However, neither of these men was in the beginning a particular friend of Fairfax, and both came from other parts of the country, having had no military background in the Northern Association.

On January 15, as John Rushworth records: '… the Commons went on in forming a New Model of the Army, which they agreed should consist in the whole of one and twenty thousand Men … on the 21st of January, the Commons proceeded to Nominate Commanders for their new Army, and appointed Sir Tho. Fairfax to be General, and Major [Major General Philip] Skippon to be Major-General.'[216]

The appointment of Fairfax was sturdily opposed by the 'Presbyterian', or moderate, faction. Upon a division, Fairfax was only appointed by a vote of 101 to 69. Skippon was appointed without a division. Also without a division, a list of prospective colonels was approved. These could not include Constable, because he had been automatically excluded by the Self-Denying Ordinance. It is interesting to note that Oliver Cromwell's name was not mentioned at all, and he is not listed.[217] In fact, Cromwell was acting as an MP at the time. As the bickering and bargaining over detail went on, Cromwell acted as a teller in an attempt to give Fairfax the power to nominate his own officers. His side went down to defeat on a vote of 82 to 63.[218] One of the tellers for the opposing side was that dyed-in-the-wool moderate and enemy of the radicals, Robert Reynolds, the man who for a year had kept Constable out of Parliament until out-manouevred by Miles Corbet, as described earlier.

John Rushworth then records under the date of February 19 the following information:

'An Express being sent to Sir Tho. Fairfax to invite him to come up to the Parliament; He on Febr. 18 came to London in a private manner, accompanied only with Col. Sir William Constable, Col. [Alexander] Rigby, Col. Sandys, Colonel [John] Alured, and some few other Officers. And next day the House of Commons sending Four of their Members to him, he was by them Conducted into the House, where a Chair was placed for him, but he modestly refused it, and stood bare while the Speaker told him what he had in Command from the House to deliver unto him …'[219]

The *Commons Journal* records that the four Members were Colonel Alexander Rigby, who had just come down from Yorkshire with Fairfax, Sir Thomas Widdrington (Constable's cousin who was also married to his niece, and hence also his nephew by marriage), Sir Arthur Hazlerigg, and Sir Peter Wentworth of Yorkshire.[220]

The same scene is described in that source as follows:

'Sir Thomas Fairfax was called in; and had a Chair set him; and the Serjeant stood by with his Mace: And Mr. Speaker, by Command of the House, acquainted him "That the Parliament of England hath commanded up your Service hither from the Northern Parts: They have heard of your Valour; and have had Experience thereof, for their Safety; and have now thought fit to put upon you the greatest Trust and Confidence, for the Security of the Kingdom, this House, religion, and Liberty, as was ever put in the Hands of a Subject. …'[221]

There was a great struggle over who would get to choose the officers for the New Model Army. Many years ago, I discovered the original manuscript of Fairfax's own officer list. I published this as 'The Original Officer List of the New Model Army', extensively annotated with notes identifying the officers.[222] This was finally agreed by both Houses on March 18.[223] Fairfax must have been very unhappy to lose Sir William Constable as his military right hand man, but the Self-Denying Ordinance made it impossible to keep him with him. Thus it was fated that Fairfax would eventually turn to Oliver Cromwell as his closest military advisor, though in the beginning Cromwell was just a colonel like so many others in the new army. (Cromwell was also an MP and the situation regarding himself and the self-Denying Ordnance is a matter I have not investigated, though it has puzzled me, because Cromwell is not a special subject of concern in this study.) This was the inevitable temporary end of Constable and his nephew Fairfax being intimate military comrades in the field together, and they had no choice but to go their separate ways. Hence it was that Sir William did not take part in any more of the great battles, such as Naseby. It has not been possible at the present state of research to know which of Constable's soldiers were amalgamated into the New Model. This could doubtless be discovered from the uncalendared S.P. 28 files in the Public Record Office, but it could easily involve weeks of searching. In principle, one could piece together an extensive account of the details of Constable's military activities during the Civil War (of which I have here provided only a sketch), together with details of his officers and own regiment, together with other regiments which also came under his command, but this would entirely depend upon finding the necessary papers in the hundreds of uncalendared boxes. Anyone wishing to do this must be prepared to spend a very long time in the inconvenient suburb of Kew. All of this kind of thing was so much easier when the PRO was conveniently located in Chancery Lane in the centre of London. But those days of ease of research, of informal staff and bending of rules and restrictions (in those days I used to be given 20 or more boxes of material at once, rather than being restricted to three at a time, and 'the rules' were ignored by a smiling and indulgent staff) are gone.

When C. H. Firth and Godfrey Davies published their monumental *Regimental History of Cromwell's Army* (which I daresay should have been 'Fairfax's Army', but no matter), in 1940, they had no system available to them to refer to and identify the different regiments.[224] They could only identify one by calling it by the names of its successive colonels, which was an incredibly cumbersome and inadequate method of proceeding. It was only when I discovered and published the original manuscript officer list drawn up by Fairfax himself in his own hand that a solution to this problem presented itself. Fairfax had used a numbering system. I was thus able to give each regiment a unique identification by calling it, say, the Second Regiment of Foot, or the Seventh Regiment of Horse. Thus all ambiguity disappeared at a stroke. Until then, the Tenth Regiment of Foot had only been known as 'The Regiment of Montagu, Lambert, Constable, Biscoe, Fleetwood, and Cholmley', a truly absurd designation! It was this Tenth Regiment of Foot over which Constable would be given command in December, 1647, in succession to John Lambert. And it was with this regiment that he would march into the town of Gloucester, where he was appointed Military Governor. This was of course after the Civil War had ended, and before the Second Civil War of 1648 had begun. The regiment's Lieutenant-Colonel Mark Grimes (or Gryme) would act as Constable's deputy Governor. The regiment and its officers from Grimes on down were radical in their politics and thus in sympathy with their colonel, Sir William Constable's, views, as is shown by a petition they signed on November 3, 1648.[225] The sympathy between Constable and his soldiers may thus owe something to some of them having served under him previously. This remains unknown at the present time. In any case, having had his soldiers taken away from him in 1645, whether or not many of them went off to war without him in the New Model Army, Constable was thus an officer without any men left. So he changed career from active soldier to active Parliamentarian and also a key member of 'the Committee at York', and would only become a serving officer again in December of 1647, as just mentioned.

After Sir Thomas Fairfax went off to head the new Model Army, his father Lord Ferdinando Fairfax remained in Yorkshire. He and his brother-in-law Sir William Constable worked closely together there along with their close colleague and intimate friend Henry Darley MP and at first also Colonel Francis Pierrepont (who became a recruiter MP for Nottingham during the spring of 1645, and immediately became a member of the Committee for Both Kingdoms at London, but was back at York briefly on May 27, 28, and 30 to sign letters with Fairfax and Constable, and back to London by June 1, returning again to York on June 21) in directing the affairs of the Committee of the Northern Association (described as 'the Committee at York' in the State Papers, despite the fact that the separate Committee of Yorkshire was also based at York). Lord Fairfax's military commission as General of the Northern Association automatically expired on May 12, 1645, and was not renewed. I discovered this information (apparently otherwise unknown to historians) from a document in the Bodleian Library which I have transcribed with notes for the Appendix to the chapter 'The Regicides and the Counties'.[226] Other members of that Committee from time to time included John Alured the regicide, William Lister, Sir Thomas Mauleverer, Bart., the regicide, Sir Matthew Boynton, Bart. MP, and Sir William Allanson MP.

Between May 20 and June 21, Lord Fairfax, Constable, and Darley (intermittently joined by Francis Pierrepont) sent numerous letters to the Earl of Leven on behalf of the Northern Association. These and numerous replies to them and letters to them from the Committee for Both Kingdoms survive in the State Papers and their contents are partially calendared.[227]

In the first week of June, the Committee for Both Kingdoms requested several times for Lord Fairfax to look to the military security of York and to arrest any ill-affected persons, of whom they said there were many in York, as they feared the King would soon come and lay siege to the city (see previous footnote). Constable is most likely to have executed these tasks.

In June of 1645, the counties of Yorkshire, Lancashire, Nottinghamshire, Northumberland, Cumberland, and the Bishoprick of Durham were all officially associated in order to further the war, and Sir William was involved in this process as a representative of the East Riding. Subsequently, at some point during July, Constable returned to London to resume his duties in Parliament and sit on Parliamentary committees.

During 1645, Constable became active on Parliament's powerful Committee for Compounding with Delinquents at Goldsmiths Hall in London, helping to raise money to pay for the war from sequestered royalist property and estates. A typical financial warrant of the Committee signed by him is preserved in the Bodleian as MS. Tanner. 59/2 (441a). It is dated August 1, 1645. Fairfax signed this warrant jointly with him, so whenever Fairfax came back to London they were closely cooperating with one another. The files of this Committee are designated S.P.23 and there are 296 volumes of them. The majority of them are calendared. I have not collected further Constable documents from them, but they must exist.

Sir William's attendance at the House of Commons and work on Parliamentary committees based in London appears to have been pretty steady during most of 1645, 1646, and 1647. We know that he must have been present most of the time because on May 2, 1646, he was given two weeks' leave to go into the country (obviously Yorkshire).[228] Only two days before, on April 30, he had been added to Parliament's Committee for the Army specifically to deal with 'the Settling and Establishing of the Pay of the Garrison of Kingston upon Hull'.[229] Probably his journey was to Hull in connection with this business. On October 23, 1646, Constable was named to a Parliamentary committee set up to consider a petition for a grand inquest of the County of Hereford.[230]

A letter from Sir William to Ferdinando (Lord) Fairfax dated May 24, 1647, has been printed. Constable speaks of 'presenting such passages [in Parliament] as were then fresh' in earlier correspondence. This suggests that Constable must have kept up a regular correspondence, keeping his brother-in-law informed of events in London and in Parliament. One wonders whether any of this presumably extensive, and doubtless highly informative, correspondence survives in the unpublished Fairfax MSS. In this letter, Constable then goes on to say:

'On Friday, our last day of sitting, there was much joy in the House, at the fair accord that seemed to be for some hours, upon the report which Lieutenant General Cromwell made from the army, divers things being voted, besides an ordinance, that day passing both Houses, for indemnity for things done through the necessity of the war; consideration had for the securing the remainder of arrears, ... This day the debate about giving satisfaction to the army by some vindication of them being laid aside by vote, the time of disbanding all the foot was voted severally for every regiment, - beginning with the General's regiment, at Chelmsford, this day se'nnight, and so proceeding with the rest at their several quarters, at several days, which will end about the 15th of June. I do not think that it is expected by any that obedience will be yielded by the soldiers, the provocations being so resented and grown to such an height; I fear we shall too soon see the issue, which God prevent.'[231]

This letter makes it very clear that Constable was in the habit of being his brother-in-law Ferdinando Fairfax's intimate eyes and ears within Parliament. If only we had more of his reports!

Sir William was not the only Constable who wrote to the Fairfaxes. His wife, Lady Dorothy Constable, often wrote to her brother Ferdinando.[232] One of her letters to him has been printed by Bell and is dated July 27, 1647. She writes to her brother in great alarm, describing how Sir William has narrowly escaped being physically assaulted and has fled London to take shelter with the Army. The intense and violent political disagreements raging in London, and the conflict between the Army and the 'Presbyterians' or moderates in Parliament, who wished to compromise and restore the King, now made it too dangerous for people of the Constables' political opinions to remain in London. She writes:

'This storm now looks black. My husband got late out of the Parliament House, not without danger. I know you will have it [fuller news] from better hands. He goes to the army, but by Windsor, or somewhere that way, to get me a house. I must presently remove. ... I will take your keys with me, for my niece removes too. I beseech you let me hear from you; if you please, send to Sir Thomas Widdrington, to Gray's Inn. [*He was Sir William's cousin, and as he was a lawyer, he lived in his chambers at Gray's Inn.*] ... This take into consideration: the King swears he will not consent: he is much cried up [*i.e. many are loud in his support*]. This company [the 'Presbyterians' dominant in Parliament] saith he shall do what he will.'[233].

An extended report of the Parliamentary events referred to by Sir William in his letter is printed by Rushworth, where all the regiments and their locations are listed.[234] The moderates in Parliament were determined to disband the Army, and the Army were determined not to be disbanded and leave the country in the hands of a faction of MPs who wished to appease the King. The Army thought they had fought and their friends had died and the nation had suffered in a long and bloody Civil War, the results of which might easily be thrown away by the weak-willed people they hated and called 'neuters'. Tensions rose very high indeed, and this political confrontation between the moderates and the radicals would remain unresolved until December, 1648, when Pride's Purge would finally result in the moderates being largely excluded from the Parliament. Meanwhile, it was unsafe for the Constables and others of their opinions to remain in London, and as we have seen, Sir William and his wife and niece who lived with them had to flee for their safety and possibly their lives. The situation only became more dangerous and tense after the King's person was seized by Cornet Joyce on June 5, and the King was taken by him into the custody of the Army, to ensure that he did not escape his existing custody at the Isle of Wight, fall into the wrong hands, and that the fruits of victory in the Civil War were not dissipated, with the King being allowed to return to London and resume his old ways. This event took place between the writing of Sir William's letter and the writing of his wife's letter. From Lady Dorothy's letter in particular we can sense much of the high drama of the situation as it stood at that time.

Rushworth has printed a very strongly-worded anonymous pamphlet dating from approximately June 5, entitled *A True Impartial Narration, concerning the Armies Preservation of the King*. The extreme crisis is referred to in these words:

'... [the 'Presbyterians' intended] to take him [the King] from thence, there being a secret design to steal and convey away his Majesty's Person, to side with some who pretend Justice, and deceive the Kingdom, ... intending to break the Army in pieces now under the Command of Sir Thomas Fairfax our General, and to raise another Army to carry on their Design, and ... all rational Men may see it by the Actions of some Men, (as Stapleton, Glynne, Greene, Erle, and others [*the leaders of the 'Presbyterians'*]) who said, *It's now come to that, that that must sink us, or we sink them.*'[235]

And so the die was cast, the struggle was essentially another civil war waged inside the Parliament itself, which would go on for another year and a half until Pride's Purge put an end to it. Prior to Pride's Purge and the resolution of the conflicts within Parliament, within only a few months of these events, Constable resumed his command of an army regiment, the Tenth New Model regiment of Foot as already mentioned, and became Military Governor of Gloucester, thus being absent from Parliament for many months and switching from his role of MP back to his more familiar military role. A letter to him as Governor of Gloucester survives in the papers of the Committee for the Advance of Money sitting at Queens Court in London, and dated October 6, 1648. The Committee speaks of receiving information from Colonel John Moore (shortly to be a regicide) and Colonel Hungerford about some assets of a royalist and Catholic named Francis Waite which they have sequestered and they ask Sir William to assist Colonel Hungerford in seizing some of them.[236] As for papers dealing with Constable's Governorship of Gloucester, these probably survive in full in the S.P. 28 papers, but have not yet been found. Certainly I would expect detailed financial accounts to be there, along with lists of persons and some correspondence. Although Constable held the Governorship until 1651, he must have delegated it often to his Deputy, for after Pride's Purge, he needed to remain in London to attend to the important business there. Constable fully sympathised with Pride's Purge and the radical cause, and his roles in London were to be highly prominent after it.

About a month before Pride's Purge, Sir William actively joined with his New Model Army friends and sat with them as a member of the Council of War, technically known as the General Council of Officers of the Army. They seemed to accept his presence as if he had been with them all along. On November 16, 1648, at St. Albans, he signed an Order of that Council jointly with four other future regicides, Commissary General Henry Ireton, Colonel Edward Whalley, Colonel Adrian Scrope, and Colonel Isaac Ewer. The Adjutant General and three other officers also signed.[237] This Order approved of the sending to the House of Commons of a Remonstrance putting forward their political demands.

We need to consider what this Remonstrance said, as it was a document of such decisive significance for the future of the nation, and it was a document with which Sir William Constable passionately agreed, on both political and religious grounds. It is impossible to go into much detail, because the document was immensely long, and when it was read out to the MPs in Parliament, it took four hours to read! It is probably best to quote a few of the remarks about it given by the late David Underdown in his excellent book, *Pride's Purge* (1971):

'It is the nearest thing we have to a manifesto of the revolution which the Army was about to begin, and therefore demands close analysis. Implicit in it are two fundamental beliefs, on which [Henry] Ireton [*the chief spokesman of the Army, Oliver Cromwell's son-in-law, and a close friend of Constable*] and the Levellers could agree in principle, however they might differ about their application: first the sovereignty of the people, buttressed by representative government and a contract between ruler and ruled, and secondly the use of divine providence as proof of the godliness or otherwise of any given course of action. This second, theological, assumption, is used in the *Remonstrance* to provide a moral basis for both the Army's recent behaviour and its current proposals. Thus the King's defeat in the second Civil War showed that "God would thereby declare his designing of that person to justice". But it is also used to buttress the doctrine of the sovereignty of the people. ... Parliament was to set a date for its own dissolution (on this Ireton and the Levellers could agree), with annual or biennial parliaments elected in the future on a reformed franchise to destroy the electoral influence of King and Lords. ... There would also be a written constitution, with a declaration of parliamentary sovereignty, and certain reserved powers. ... Parliament should consider law reform ... Essentially, Ireton had given the Levellers some vague promises for the future, in return for their acquiescence in the more limited revolution that he envisaged. Ireton's programme was limited to a dissolution of Parliament and justice against the King, followed by either a very limited monarchy or a republic, and a more rational parliamentary system, which by redistribution would put power firmly in the hands of the gentry and the middling sort ... Based as it was on a theory of contract and natural law, it would be a far cry from the traditional government by the three estates and the supremacy of the antiquated common law for which even progressive reformers in the middle group still stood. Even if Ireton could circumvent the Levellers, it would still be a revolution.'[238]

Sir William Constable was, as remarked above, one of the nine men including Ireton who signed the Order of the General Council of Officers of the Army ordering that this revolutionary document be submitted to the House of Commons as a demand for a total political change in the way the nation was run. If it had been accepted, it would have resulted in the creation of a republic by the Parliament (as it then existed), with the King's trial for treason being unavoidable. As things turned out, this would all occur, but just not quite yet. Constable's signature on this Order of the Council was thus probably more significant even than his signature on the later Death Warrant of the King. It was this document which really precipitated the English Revolution. And it is for this action that Constable may be described as a seminal political revolutionary more properly than just for signing the Death Warrant, which was a step in an ongoing process rather than an initiation of that process. The Army's *Remonstrance* was sent two days after the signing of the Order and delivered two days after that, on November 20, as described in the *Commons Journal* for that date:

'A Letter from the General, from St. Albans, of 18o Novembris 1648, was this Day read, touching a Remonstrance, to be presented to this House, unanimously agreed upon by the General Council of Officers, which the General, at the Desire of the Officers, and in Behalf of them and himself, doth most humbly and earnestly intreat may have a present Reading, and be timely considered of.

'The House being informed, That some Officers of the Army, from the General, were at the Door, with the said Remonstrance;

'They were called in: And Colonel [Isaac] Ewer [later to be a regicide] informed the House, "That the Lord General, and General Council of Officers of the Army, have commanded me, and these Gentlemen [*unnamed fellow officers*], to present this Remonstrance to this Honourable House; and desire you to take it into speedy and serious consideration." ... Ordered, That the debate upon the Remonstrance of the General, and his General Council of Officers, be resumed on Monday next [November 27].'[239]

Immediately after this, the House adjourned, and the Army officers having been dismissed not only with no response or thanks (an expression of thanks being the customary polite form for such an occasion), the whole matter was put off for an entire week (this having happened on a Monday, and the debate was scheduled for the next Monday).

A great deal of business was transacted by the House during the course of the intervening week, much of it of no national importance (individual petitions and the like), and then when Monday came, there was no debate, and the Remonstrance was ignored. What was even more of an insult to the Army was the passing of a resolution to oppose a specific order by General Fairfax. Fairfax had sent a letter to Colonel Robert Hammond, Governor of the Isle of Wight, who had custody of the King as a prisoner, asking him to report to him. Hammond sent this to the House, evidently protesting at it. The House of Commons then ordered that Hammond disregard the order of Fairfax and stay in the Isle of Wight.[240] This was the most extreme insult which could be offered to Fairfax, to countermand a direct order from him to a lesser officer. And it occurred on the same day that the House purposely refused to debate the Army's Remonstrance, but instead busied itself with such enormously important things as whether the town of Aldeborough in Norfolk should be given the status of a market town, various private petitions, permitting the Governor of Plymouth to leave London and return to Plymouth, and so on. The final resolution of the day was then:

'Ordered, That the Debate touching the Remonstrance of the Army be taken up on Friday next.'[241]

On November 29, the House wrote to Fairfax ordering him to rescind his order to Colonel Hammond, who had left the Isle of Wight and was making his way to Fairfax, not daring to disobey Fairfax's order. The House insisted that Colonel Hammond 'return back to his Charge in the Isle of Wight.'[242]

Sir William Constable was directly involved in this matter. He had signed an Order of the General Council on November 25 addressed to Colonel Hammond, and his cosignatories were Ireton, Lieutenant-General Thomas Hammond (a relation of Colonel Hammond), Colonel Thomas Harrison (another future regicide), Colonel Edward Whalley (another future regicide), Colonel Matthew Thomlinson, and Colonel [Christopher] Whitchcott [today spelled Whichcote].[243]

On November 28, Sir William signed at Windsor another confrontational Order jointly with Ireton, Harrison, Whalley, and Colonel John Hewson (another future regicide), that a Declaration be drawn up 'rendering the grounds of the Armie's advance ... that the Army should bee forthwith drawn uppe to London to quarter in or about the citty ...' The General Council approved this unanimously.[244]

The stage was therefore set for a direct confrontation between the Army and the House of Commons, with the Army to enter and surround London in order to secure their cause. It needs to be stressed that the only person to sign these orders who had not been a member of the New Model Army was Sir William Constable. No other person was invited to join the New Model officers. This is the ultimate proof that they regarded him as 'one of them', and that Fairfax had the highest confidence in him of anyone outside his immediate command. It appears that Fairfax personally presided over all these meetings of the General Council, but that it was his habit not to sign, leaving Henry Ireton to head the list of signatories. Cromwell was elsewhere while these meetings were taking place, so did not participate in them. Meetings of the General Council were now discontinued, as the Army mobilised and moved upon London from Windsor. However, a list of attendances at the General Council of the Army shows that Constable attended again on December 15, on December 21, and again on February 22, of the following year (1648/9).[245] He was thus one of the most frequent attenders, more so even than Lieutenant-General Hammond, and as for Cromwell, he only attended twice altogether. The only person who attended every meeting was Henry Ireton, so perhaps he was acting as the chairman rather than Fairfax. The conclusion is inescapable that Sir William Constable, the only 'outsider' present, was acting as one of the major presences and voices of authority in the Army's General Council, with the full concurrence of all the most senior figures of the New Model Army. To those men, he was not 'them', he was 'us'.

John Lilburne records that when he and other Levellers went to Windsor to meet with representatives of the Army, the Army had chosen as the persons to meet with them Henry Ireton and Sir William Constable, along with two other colonels, a lieutenant-colonel, and a captain.[246] It is clear that Constable was acting as if he were a colonel of a regiment, even though he had none.

Once again, the House did not debate the Remonstrance as it had promised. The Friday (December 1) came and went, and this time the Remonstrance was not even mentioned. Instead the House concerned itself with such weighty matters as French merchants, and then turned its attention to the Aldermen of the City of London. The House clearly had no intention of ever debating the Army's Remonstrance or considering the Army's requests.

Having clearly lost patience with the House of Commons, and concerned that there was a plot to seize King Charles from the Isle of Wight and put him in the hands of his supporters in Parliament, the Army seized the King themselves and moved him to a different location. This came to the notice of the Commons on Monday December 4, and the *Commons Journal* for that day records that the removal of the King was without the House's knowledge or consent. The following day, December 5, the House officially resolved that the King's proposals for a compromise whereby he would be restored to the throne 'are a Ground for the House to proceed on, for the Settlement of the Peace of the Kingdom.'[247]

Nothing could be more unacceptable to the Army than that the King be restored upon mere promises of good behaviour, as they feared that it would lead to a third civil war as inevitably as the sun would rise the next morning. So the Army decided to act. Over the course of the following two days, December 6 and 7, soldiers of the New Model Army commanded by Colonel Thomas Pride (soon to be a regicide) and accompanied by Lord Grey of Groby, a radical MP and future regicide who knew who all the Members were by sight so that they could be identified and their politics explained to Colonel Pride, took up a position at the door of the House. Most of the 'Presbyterians' were prevented from entering the House. This event is commonly known as 'Pride's Purge'. Many or most of them eventually made their way back into the House over the coming months. But for the moment, their majority control of the House of Commons was destroyed by the Purge, leaving the radical Members free to carry on the business of the House in the manner they wished. Sir William Constable's enthusiastic approval of all of this is shown by the fact that he attended three subsequent meetings of the General Council of Officers, by whose approval Pride's Purge had taken place.

Despite his constant attendance upon his officer friends, Sir William also rejoined the House of Commons during December. On December 29, he was named, along with 16 other future regicides and some others, to a Committee to consider 'An Ordinance touching the King'.[248] On January 1, he was added to Parliament's Committee for the Army, a committee from which he had been excluded while the 'Presbyterians' were in control. Another who had been excluded until then was Oliver Cromwell, and he too was added to the Committee at last.[249] The Committee for the Army seems to have tried to refuse the newly appointed members, so Cromwell, Constable, and the others, were all appointed by the House a second time on January 6.[250] On the same day, Constable was appointed to the important Committee of Indemnity.[251]

The House of Commons had now decided to put the King on trial for High Treason and for waging war against his subjects. Sir William Constable was named to sit on the High Court of Justice to try the King. The Trial commenced on January 6. Sir William did not attend the first four sittings of the Court, unless he was one of 'divers more' recorded on January 12. In any case, by January 13, he was present, and he attended the next three sessions (January 15, 17, and 18). He was not present on January 19, but he returned on January 20, and attended on every day after that until the trial ended on January 29.[252] On that day, he signed the Death Warrant for the King, who had been condemned to public execution. On that same day, the House of Commons named him, Oliver Cromwell, and others to a committee to disallow formally the vote of December 5 by the House to accept the proposals of the King.[253] This was doubtless a legal technicality which was judged necessary before the execution could take place.

Sir William would certainly have attended the execution of King Charles the next day, on January 30, though there is no record of who did so. The following day, January 31, Constable was back in the House of Commons again, and was named to a committee to draw up an Act for the trial of those royalists who remained in prison.[254] This laid the groundwork for the trials of Lord Goring, the Earl of Holland, Lord Capell, the Earl of Cambridge, and Sir John Owen. On February 3, Sir William was named to a committee to consider and prevent seditious publications condemning the trial of the King.[255] On February 8 he was named to a committee to consider suitable persons to be made Justices of the Peace throughout the country. Also named to the committee was Sir William's cousin, Sir Thomas Widdrington (who was also married to his niece), a lawyer of Gray's Inn who also held the legal and judicial position of Recorder of York, and the two of them together with Sir John Bourchier would have carried out this work in relation to Yorkshire. (The committee had different members representing different counties, John Dixwell for Kent, Daniel Blagrave for Berkshire, John Jones for Wales, and so on.)[256] On February 13, Sir William was named to a committee to reform the mint and stamp out abuses of the coinage.[257]

The next day, February 14, the House of Commons appointed a Council of State to act as the executive arm of the government and run the day to day affairs of the nation. Sir William was named to this Council of State.[258] The President of the Council of State was roughly the equivalent of a modern prime minister, and to avoid any individual becoming too powerful, this Presidency was rotated frequently amongst the Members of the Council. Twice Sir William acted as President of the Council of State during the year 1652. I have an original document signed by Sir William as President of the Council of State on October 21, 1652, signed also by John Thurloe as Clerk to the Council of State.

Parliament now turned its attention to a scandalous issue. On February 15, it was reported to the House that although Sir Thomas Fairfax and Colonel Nathaniel Rich (a New Model Army colonel) had been elected as recruiter MPs for the borough of Cirencester some time ago (the date not specified, but we know that it was January 28, 1646, replacing the disabled royalist MPs Sir Theobald Gorges and John George), the Indenture of election sent in by the Sheriff of Gloucestershire had been diverted to the Committee of Privileges, from whence it had been stolen and could no longer be found. This was all testified to the House by the Clerk of the Crown in Chancery, who also tendered to the House an affidavit confirming his testimony. Nothing could be more shocking than the proof that electoral fraud had been perpetrated at the very heart of Parliament prior to its purge in order to prevent someone as distinguished as Fairfax himself from taking his seat for a period of three years. This far exceeded in iniquity the attempts to keep Constable out of Parliament, which have previously been described and which only lasted one year, for here we have the head of the New Model Army himself being kept out of Parliament by corrupt partisan skulduggery. This was simply too much to take!

Immediately after this revelation on the floor of the House, the Commons appointed a committee of 19 MPs including Sir William Constable and the regicide Miles Corbet (the man who overcame the obstacles to Constable's admission to Parliament, as described previously) to examine this matter, find out how it had occurred, call for any persons, papers, records, etc., and see how Fairfax and Rich might be admitted to sit in the House despite the Indenture having been stolen.[259]

The result of this committee's deliberations was rapid in coming. Only two days later, Colonel Edmund Harvey reported to the House that they had found three copies of the Indenture in three different person's possession in Gloucestershire, and that the Clerk of the Crown's record of receiving the one in London which had then been stolen had also been found amongst his records.[260] There had clearly been a conspiracy involving several persons including the Sheriff of Gloucestershire and several burgesses of Cirencester, as well as 'moderates' in Parliament, to thwart the election. The house then rapidly ordered that the election of Fairfax and Rich was recognised and that they might take their seats in the House at last. Constable had thus helped his nephew Fairfax obtain his seat in the Commons at last, nearly three years to the day after his election.

On the same day, February 17, the new Council of State met for the first time. This was not an entirely successful meeting. Sir William Constable was unable to attend because he had to remain in the House of Commons at that time for the discussion of Sir Thomas Fairfax's admission, especially as Sir Thomas was his nephew and close friend, and Constable was a member of the committee to which that matter had been specifically entrusted. Of those who did attend, there was disagreement in that some of the members objected to signing the Engagement, a document supporting the principles of the new republic. Those who objected and refused to sign were peers, namely the Earl of Denbigh, the Earl of Pembroke, the Earl of Salisbury, the Earl of Mulgrave, and Lord Grey of Wark (who, while expressing his sympathy with the Engagement made known his reservations that it emanated only from a single House, namely the Commons). The true reason for this was probably that they knew very well that it was the ultimate intention to abolish the House of Lords. Only 13 of those attending this first meeting signed the Engagement, whereas the five just mentioned refused. The Council of State therefore 'did no other Act, but order the rest of the Members to be summoned there (on Monday)', as Oliver Cromwell reported to the House on that Monday, February 19.[261] On that day, the Council of State resumed, and in addition to Constable, 18 other Members of the Commons who had obviously been absent on the Saturday because of the debate and vote about Sir Thomas Fairfax in the House of Commons turned up. All 19 of these men agreed to sign the Engagement, thus saving the Council of State from a major and embarrassing crisis of appearing to lack sufficient support from its own members at the very moment of its formation. In addition to Constable, those who then signed were Cromwell, Lord Grey of Groby, Sir John Danvers, Henry Marten, William Heveningham, Edmund Ludlow, William Purefoy, Anthony Stapley, Cornelius Holland, Luke Robinson, Thomas Scot, Valentine Wauton, John Lisle, John Hutchinson, John Jones, Isaac Pennington, Sir Henry Mildmay, and Robert Wallopp. Most of these men were regicides, and they had all clearly stayed in the House of Commons to vote for Sir Thomas Fairfax's admission. This too was reported on this same day to the House by Cromwell,[262] so the reputation of the new Council of State and of the new Commonwealth was thereby regarded as having been saved. We do not know why the bad scheduling which caused this mini-crisis had occurred. Perhaps it was a devious manoeuvre by one of the peers or a clerk in sympathy with the peers, or perhaps it was just incompetence and lack of coordination. The infant Commonwealth as a republic was now safely launched.

After this, Sir William Constable became less active in the House of Commons. He continued to attend the General Council of Officers, as we have already noticed. But he appears to have transferred his efforts more to the Council of State. He must also have needed to return to Gloucester for extended periods, the Governorship of which he was to continue to hold for another two years, until 1651. By the time of the execution of the King, Constable was already approximately 74 years old, give or take a year, as we do not know the precise date of his birth, which was circa 1575. Having thrown himself with enthusiasm and glee into the proceedings of the House on a daily basis between the time of Pride's Purge and the formation of the Council of State, he was probably too old after that to be running back and forth between the two different bodies, not to mention his pressing duties in Gloucester. We must also not forget that a man of his age might well have been taken ill from time to time, despite his indefatiguable and determined energy which he showed throughout his life.

One curious thing about Sir William Constable is that he seems never to have acted as a teller during the Long Parliament (until the very last day he ever attended, as described later). Normally a man of his eminence and gravitas would have done so. I have a theory about this, which I shall mention, although it is merely a matter of informed speculation. When he was a young soldier, his horse was shot out from under him and he was wounded in his thigh. Later, at the Brill, he also nearly died of serious wounds which were not specified. I consider it likely that Sir William suffered for most of his adult life from the effects of serious war wounds. It is not unlikely that, as a result of the injury to his thigh, he walked with a limp. As he got older, he is likely to have suffered also from arthritis in his hips or knees. Tellers in the House have to be very nimble in the way they walk speedily to and fro in the Chamber. I suspect that Sir William did not wish to appear to be limping along in the House, slowing up the proceedings and calling attention to his infirmity, and that he therefore never wished to make a public spectacle of himself in that way. It would have offended his sense of dignity, and it would have been an encumbrance to the House's business. That is my theory as to why he was never a teller, and I do not regard it as an unlikely answer.

Sir William surfaces again in the House of Commons in the following summer. He was in the House on June 21, when he was named to a committee of assessment, of which he was apparently the chairman, to raise money from Gloucestershire.[263] This was clearly because of his position as Governor of Gloucester. Constable must then have returned to Gloucester to carry out these tasks.

About six months later, on January 4, 1649/50, the House read out a petition from Sir William as well as an annexed paper entitled 'The State of Sir William Constable's Case'. In this, Sir William sought the payment of his extensive arrears in a manner which is best explained by quoting from the *Commons Journal*, as it records the Resolution of the House approving and granting the requests of the petition:

'Resolved, upon the Question, by the Parliament, That the Inheritance of the Manor of Holme, with the Appurtenances, the Inheritance of Sir Marmaduke Langdale [*a prominent royalist who had fought against the Fairfaxes and Constable in Yorkshire*], wherein Sir Wm. Constable Baronet hath an Estate for Life, and the Lady Constable an Estate for Life, in remainder, in Part thereof, for her Jointure, be settled upon the said Sir Wm. Constable and his Heirs; reserving the Fee-farm Rent of One hundred and Thirteen Pounds Four Shillings and Five-pence to the State, in Consideration of Seven hundred and Fifty Pounds, Part of One Thousand Pounds granted to him by Ordinance of Parliament, of the Second Day of April 1645 [*but never paid*] out of the said Manor; as also of the Sum of One thousand Pounds, of his Arrears for Pay, charged, by Ordinance of Parliament, upon the lands of Wm. Middleton Esquire, in North-Duffeild, he being a Papist in Arms; and in full Discharge of the aforesaid Sum, and all Arrears: And that Mr. Stephens do bring in a Bill to that Purpose.'[264]

Sir William had evidently returned to London for the winter. He is mentioned in the House again on January 29, when he was named to a committee to consider an Act for the preaching of the Gospel in Wales and for the remedying of various Welsh grievances.[265] On February 11, Sir William was re-appointed by the House to the Council of State, without the need for any vote, whereas most other appointments were contested, including even those of Fairfax and Cromwell, and some proposed appointments were sufficiently contested to require divisions with tellers.[266] On this occasion, the Earl of Mulgrave and Lord Grey of Wark were thrown off the Council of State, having presumably irritated everyone beyond endurance. In the midst of all this contention, it is interesting to see that Sir William Constable evidently had the confidence and respect of everyone.

It was not until May 1 that an Act was passed by the House 'to settle the Inheritance, and the present Rents belonging to Sir Marmaduke Langdale, on the Manor of Holme in Spalding-Moore, in the County of York, upon Sir Wm. Constable, and his Heirs.'[267] After that, documents in hand, Sir William and Lady Dorothy would have been able to return to their old home in Yorkshire, set things in order, and begin to settle in. This probably would have taken up the rest of the spring and much of the summer.

On June 7, however, Sir William was in the House of Commons with many of his Yorkshire friends to push through an important item of Yorkshire business. Fairfax was there, Sir Thomas Widdrington, Sir Thomas Mauleverer, Thomas Stockdale, Thomas Chaloner (another Yorkshire regicide), Thomas Hoyle, and others. They were all there representing the Northern Association (which would explain why Sir John Bourchier was not involved, as he was not a member of the Committee of the Northern Association). They were determined to get justice for Constance Stringer, widow of a stalwart supporter of the Parliamentary cause named George Stringer, of York. Constance Stringer submitted a petition and they were all there to support her, citing the Northern Association's Report on her case for actions by her husband of July 1644. Despite the Northern Association's recommendation to the House submitted to the Speaker on July 17, 1646, recommending payment owed to George Stringer, the matter had been suppressed by the 'moderates'. Now they were determined that Constance Stringer should get her money. The House therefore ordered payment to her of the debt of £1,603/ 18. This was clearly a matter of honour to them all, and Constable and Fairfax appear to have made a special trip to the House to see it through.[268]

Sir William was in the House again three weeks later, on June 27, to support separate petitions by Sir Henry Vane, Lady Fairfax, and the Leveller John Lilburne, which had been introduced on Lilburne's behalf by the regicide Henry Marten. Lilburne's petition necessitated the formation of a committee, which Constable joined. This is the only direct evidence I have come across which demonstrates that Constable was a sympathiser of the Levellers. It is notable that Cromwell and Ireton did not join this committee. This suggests that Constable was more politically radical than they were, and that he was more in sympathy with the regicides Henry Marten, Edmund Ludlow, Thomas Scot, Lord Grey of Groby, John Venn, Valentine Wauton (Cromwell's brother-in-law who despised Cromwell), Thomas Harrison, Sir John Danvers, Sir John Bourchier, and Sir Michael Livesey, all of whom joined this committee along with Constable in support of John Lilburne.[269] This is a rare glimpse of just where Constable really stood politically. On the same day, Constable was named to a committee to consider of how to relieve the public of the financial burdens of various government functions, which ones could be dispensed with and shut down, and of how many others might be performed at lesser cost by hiring what today we call civil servants to carry out the administrative functions on modest salaries.

Constable is not named in the *Commons Journal* again until January 24, 1650/1. Once again, he seems to have returned to London for the winter. On that occasion he was named to a large committee to consider of the persons whose financial claims should be accepted from the proceeds of the prospective sales of royalist lands which had been forfeited to the Commonwealth, it being the accepted notion that the King and the royalists were responsible for all devastation and financial losses, and that their seized assets must therefore pay the costs incurred by those faithful to Parliament. It was under just such a principle that Constable himself had been compensated for his own arrears by the return of his own former Manor of Holme, a seized royalist asset. Now he was to be one of a large group of MPs who would go through the countless petitions and claims submitted to Parliament and decide which ones should be accepted, and be granted compensation payments.[270]

On February 7 and on February 10, the third annual Council of State was appointed. Its membership contained no peers, and all of its members were from the hardest-working and most energetic MPs. The only candidate who was rejected by vote of the House was Robert Reynolds, presumably hated by most of the other MPs, and who was the man who had kept Constable out of the House years before, as related earlier. The names of Fairfax and Constable were not put forward. They were thus not rejected, they merely did not stand for office.[271] This was one of two years in which Constable did not serve on the Council of State, and he was to be elected to the next annual Council of State, of 1652. In this year, 1651, since he was approximately 77 years old and it was the dead of winter, Constable may very well have fallen ill for some time. He is not mentioned again in the House for many months. On October 2, 1651, he is mentioned only insofar as it is ordered that six companies of foot in his regiment are to be disbanded, as part of a general reduction of serving forces throughout the country. His regiment is still called 'Sir Wm. Constable's' regiment.[272] On November 25, 1651, Sir William was named once again to be a member of the Council of State.[273] Assuming his 'year off' was due to ill health, he must have recovered by now.

On October 22, 1652, Sir William is recorded as being active in the House of Commons after so many months of apparent inactivity there. And what is extraordinary is that, apparently for the first time in all the years which he had spent in the Long Parliament, he actually acted as a teller. There were only 38 Members present and voting in the House on that day. He turned up to act with regard to a matter concerning Sir John Hippisley's personal estate. From what one can gather of the brief explanation of the matter, he seemed to want to reduce Hippisley's interest in it from life to only 21 years. He was joint teller in favour of this reduction with another elderly regicide, Colonel William Purefoy of Warwickshire. However, they lost in a vote of 24 to 14, with the tellers for the other side being Colonel Algernon Sidney and Sir Thomas Wroth.[274] It is doubtful if we will ever fully understand what this particular issue was. William Purefoy, who had also been a regicide, was a fellow member of the Council of State with Constable.

On November 24 and 25, the members of the new Council of State for the fifth year were elected. Sir William is not reported as standing for election again. On this occasion, the names of the candidates together with the number of votes each received are listed, which is an interesting indication of the relative popularity of and regard for each of the candidates. (For instance, the regicide Thomas Harrison got the least votes, possibly because he was so well known to be a religious fanatic. The person receiving the most votes was Oliver Cromwell.)[275] So Sir

William, aged about 78, must have decided it was time to retire from active politics. Sir William's appearance in the House of Commons on October 22 is his last recorded. The Long Parliament came to a close on the following April 19, 1653. It seems therefore that on his last active day in the House of Commons he did what he had never done before, and for the first and the last time, in a very thinly attended House, he actually acted as a teller. And that was to be his Parliamentary swansong.

Sir William clearly kept his regiment of foot intact after he left Gloucester. There is no specific evidence as to what Sir William thought of Cromwell's usurpation of 1653, but unlike many of his close republican friends, he did not withdraw all contact with the new Cromwellian regime. He was not a Member of either the 1653 or 1654 Cromwellian Parliaments. In any case, Knaresborough was abolished as a borough, and the Parliamentary representation system was entirely changed. So his standing as an MP came to a close in 1653 with the forcible closure of the House at gunpoint by Cromwell's troops. The fact that Constable did not wholly disassociate himself from the Cromwell regime is probably due to the fact that he was so close to all the Army officers, including Cromwell himself.

When trouble arose with the Scots, Constable continued to serve, at least in name, as a military officer on behalf of the Cromwell regime. On January 4, 1653/4, a letter from Dalkeith states that 'the regiments of horse of Major-General [John] Lambert and Commissary General [Edward] Whalley, and the foot regiment of Sir William Constable are on their march to Scotland.'[276] Constable was by this time approximately 78 years of age! Firth and Davies were unaware of this document, and they believe that this all happened three months later. They write:

'... in April 1654 seven companies of Constable's were ordered to Scotland to assist in the suppression of Glencairn's rising. In February the regiment had been raised from 700 to 1,000 men, and was commanded by Lieutenant-Colonel John Biscoe [on behalf of Constable, who seems not to have gone to Scotland in person] and Major William Style. Five companies arrived in May, "but not a penny of mony with them; soe that although they came up yesterday wee have bene forc't to lend them mony out of the Treasury," complained Monck on 4 May 1654. A week or two later two other companies put in an appearance.'[277] Later, five more companies of Sir William's regiment, numbering about 350 men, were sent north to join the rest, as an intercepted letter preserved in the Thurloe Papers informs us.[278] In December, 1654, two companies of this regiment were recalled to England.[279]

I have come across no record of Sir William being active in any public business after 1653, except for the military actions carried out in his name in 1654. He was not only getting very old, his health may well have been poor. Sir William died, aged about 80, on June 14, 1655, at his then residence in the Strand at London.[280] A week later, his body was solemnly interred in great state at Westminster Abbey. A report in the periodical *Mercurius Politicus* recorded the extraordinary event, involving an immensely long procession of dignitaries extending all the way from Westminster Abbey to the Strand, and thus somewhat resembling the annual Remembrance Day parades of today, which take hours to pass and head in precisely the same direction down Whitehall:

'The ceremony was performed with very great solemnity, there being a class of mourners between each pendant of arms, six pendants being carried by six gentlemen of his nearest kindred, the hearse carried in a chariot, his two horses covered black, and led by mourners. The hearse was attended by the officers of the army, his Highnesses gentlemen [*by 'His Highness' is meant the Lord Protector, Oliver Cromwell]*, and many other persons of honour and quality, with horse and foot, from the Strand to Westminster, where he was interred in Henry the Seventh, his Chappel, great vollies of shot being given answerable to the merit of so honorable a person.'[281]

The fact that six pendants of coats of arms were carried by six near relations (two of whom were bound to have been his nephew General Fairfax and his first cousin and husband of his niece, Sir Thomas Widdrington), confirms what I suggested much earlier in speculating about the interior of the Manor of Flamborough. These pendants were not made for the purpose of the funeral, but were old heraldic displays from a family home, showing the many quarterings of arms in which people of that time took such pride. It may be concluded with near certainty that they had once been displayed by being hung on the walls of the Great Hall at Flamborough, and had probably been rescued from trunks and proudly hung once more at the Manor of Holme which had been so recently retrieved by Sir William.

Sir William's burial is recorded in the Register of Westminster Abbey, under the date of June 21: 'Sir William Constable: in K. H. 7th's Chapel.'[282] Joseph Chester, who edited and annotated these for publication, has added a note to accompany this entry, which records the fact that Sir William's will, dated December 13, 1654, was proved July 18, 1655, by his relict Dame Dorothy, who was the eldest dau. of Thomas, first Lord Fairfax. He left no issue, and the title became extinct.'

Lady Dorothy did not long survive her husband. She died March 9, 1655/6. Chester records of her that she 'was buried in the church of St. Mary Bishophill, Senior, York.'[283]

At the Restoration, the body of Sir William was exhumed and thrown into 'a common pit' adjoining the churchyard of St. Margaret's, beside the Abbey, along with that of the regicide Admiral Richard Deane, and the Protectorate figure and member of Cromwell's Council of State, Colonel Humphrey Mackworth, who had also been buried in King Henry VII's Chapel. Sir William's estates were ordered to be confiscated and were given to King Charles II.

The pit into which the body of Sir William was cast may have been common, but the man himself was uncommon. And that is what matters.

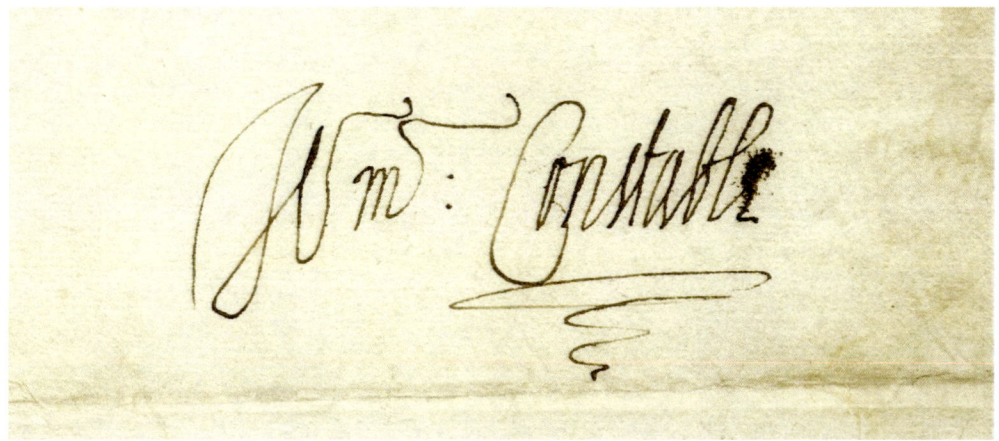

No likenesses of Sir William Constable are known to survive. This is his signature.

1	[Sir Anthony Weldon] as 'Sir A: W:', *The Court and Character of King James*, London, 1650. This is a very rare book indeed. On the fly leaf of the copy which I own has been written in a contemporary hand: 'Sir Anthy Weldon'. The handwriting is somehow familiar to me, as I believe I have seen it on important documents which I have inspected in the course of my researches, and I believe it might be possible to identify it. In any case, it is definitely a hand current in 1650. This book was reprinted in 1651 and then again in 1652 by a different London printer under the title *A Cat May Look upon a King*. I have not compared the text of the two books, but the third edition is 105 pages whereas the first edition is 197 pages. There was another reprint in 1689 under the original title.
2	Robert Temple, 'The Original Officer List of the New Model Army', *Bulletin of the Institute of Historical Research*, Vol. LIX, No. 139, May 1986, p. 59 and n. 66.
3	Anonymous, *Mystery of the Good Old Cause*, London, 1660 (Wing M3191). This pamphlet was reprinted by Hotten in 1863 and by the Aungervyle Society in 1883. Very few copies of the original exist, though I have one in my personal collection.
4	George Bate, *The Lives, Actions, and Execution of the Prime Actors ...*, London, 1661, p. 134.
5	Anonymous, *Oliver Cromwell The Late Great Tirant His Life-Guard*, London, 1660, p. 4.
6	John Aubrey, *Brief Lives*, ed. by Oliver Lawson Dick, Penguin, 1972, p. 238.
7	See DNB entry for Henry Danvers.
8	John Aubrey, *op. cit.*, p. 240.
9	*Ibid.*, p. 239.
10	*Ibid.*
11	Edward, Lord Herbert of Cherbury, *Autobiography and History of England under Henry VIII*, Ward, Lock & Co., London, undated, p. 18.
12	Blair Worden, *The Rump Parliament*, Cambridge University Press, 1974, p. 100.
13	Hope Mirrlees, *A Fly in Amber*, London, 1962, p. 147.
14	Herbert, *op. cit.*, p. 80.
15	John Aubrey, *Three Prose Works*, ed. by John Buchanan-Brown, Centaur Press, Sussex, 1972, p. 341.
16	Aubrey, *Lives, op. cit.*, p. 175.
17	*Ibid.*, pp. 226, 350, 338, and 292 respectively.
18	*Ibid.*, p. 237.
19	*Ibid.*, p. 240.
20	Recounted in Walton's *Life of George Herbert*; mentioned by Thomas Faulkner, *An Historical and Topographical Description of Chelsea*, 1829, Vol. I, p. 173.
21	Anonymous but known to be George Edward Roberts and Henry Porter, *Cups and Their Customs*, second enlarged edition, London, 1869, pp. 23-4.
22	*Ibid.*
23	Raphe Hamor the Younger ('late Secretarie in that Colony'), *A True Discourse of the Present Estate of Virginia, and the Successe of the Affaires There till the 18 of June, 1614,*. London, 1615, p. 35.
24	J. A. Doyle, *The English in America*, London, 1882, pp. 208-16.
25	*Ibid.*, p. 216.
26	I may here introduce an ironical personal note. My grandfather, also called Robert Temple, had a farm in Virginia where he had 500 vines. Because my grandmother was a teetotaler, she would not permit him to make wine. He therefore sold the whole crop every year for raisins, which is how I know about raisins growing in Virginia.
27	G. P. V. Akrigg, *Shakespeare & the Earl of Southampton*, London, 1968, p. 163.
28	*Ibid.* It should be noted by those who wish to explore this subject further that the Index to Akrigg's book is peppered with references to Sir Charles Danvers and Henry Danvers.
29	Hamor, *op. cit.*, pp. 34-5.
30	Doyle, *op. cit.*, pp. 219-20.
31	Louis B. Wright and Elaine W. Fowler, *English Colonisation of North America*, London, 1968, pp. 40-1.
32	*Notes and Queries*, 4th Series, Vol. III, p. 225.
33	Alexander Charles Ewald, *Stories from the State Papers*, London, 1882, Vol. I, p. 264.
34	Doyle, *op. cit.*, p. 242.
35	[John Baron Somers][, *The True Secret History of the Lives and Reigns of All the Kings and Queens of England*, 2 vols., sometimes bound as one, London, 1725, Vol. I, p. 290. (I have two copies of this work, one bound as one, and one as separate volumes.)
36	*Ibid.*
37	Weldon, *op. cit.*, p. 135.
38	*Ibid.*, p. 41.
39	*Ibid.*, p. 53.
40	*Ibid.*, p. 56.
41	*Ibid.*, pp. 177-97, the section entitled 'The Character of King James'.
42	Anonymous, *Truth Brought to Light by Time: or, the History of the First 14 Years of King James I*, London, 1692. I have this reprinted edition, but not the original of London, 1651.
43	Somers, *op. cit.*, Vol. I, p. 313.
44	Weldon, *Mysteries of History*, pp. 38-9.
45	C. J. S. Thompson, *Mysteries of History*, 1928, p. 96.
46	Algernon Sidney, *Court Maxims*, a post-Restoration manuscript now owned by and deposited at the Warwick Record Office. I have transcribed part of it.
47	Hope Mirrlees, *op. cit.*, p. 268.
48	CSPD 1611-18, p. 187.
49	Thomas Faulkner, *op. cit.*, pp. 140-3.
50	Public Record Office: SP 14/ 185/ 100. (Item 5 on first page.) See CSPD 1623-5, p. 508.
51	CSPD 1625-6, pp. 9, 23, 422, 443.
52	John Rushworth, *Historical Collections Containing the Principal Matters Which Happened ...1639 until ...1640*, London, 1721, Volume II, Part II (Volume III as bound), p. 915. Other future regicides in the same list of refusers were Henry Marten, Sir Gregory Norton, Bart., and Anthony Stapley, as well as Sir Henry Ludlow, the father of the future regicide Edmund Ludlow.

53	Public Record Office: SP 16/ 491/ 75/, 85, 104, and 105.
54	CSPD 1641-3, pp. 355-6, 359-60, 366-7, and 367-8.
55	Public Record Office: SP 16/ 491/ 75.
56	*Ibid.*: SP 16/ 491/ 104.
57	*Ibid.*
58	*Ibid.*: SP 16/ 491/ 105.
59	CSPD 1640-1, p. 121.
60	Robert Brenner, *Merchants and Revolution: Commercial Change, Political Conflict, and London's Overseas Traders, 1550-1653*, Cambridge University Press, 1993, p. 249.
61	Aubrey, *Lives, op. cit.*, p. 239.
62	Worden, *op. cit.*, p. 100.
63	David Underdown, *Pride's Purge*, Oxford, 1971, p. 246n.
64	Aubrey, *Lives, op. cit.*, p. 237.
65	House of Lords Record Office: Main Papers, March 15, 1647/8 (Petition of Lady Gargrave).
66	See for example: S.P. 20/ 2/ 9, 48, 64, 204, 221, 231, 243, 427, 437, 441, 467, and so on and on.
67	House of Lords Record Office: Main Papers, March 15, 1647/8 (Report by John Lisle).
68	Earl of Clarendon, *History of the Rebellion*, 1849 ed., Vol. IV, p536.
69	*Notes and Queries*, Second Series, Vol. 2, p. 449.
70	Mark Noble, *Lives of the English Regicides*, London, 1798, Vol. I, pp. 166-7.
71	Hyde and Mallock were arrested and put into the Tower at about the same time in 1642. See HMC 5th Report, p. 161b.
72	HMC 6th Report, p. 19a. For an affidavit of Gilbert Hyde on another matter, see p. 81b.
73	Worden, *op. cit.*, p. 100.
74	See for instance 'Constable of Flamborow' in Surtees Society, Volume XLI, p. 68. And consult the indices of the Society of Antiquaries.
75	George W. Johnson, ed., *The Fairfax Correspondence. Memoirs of the Reign of Charles the First*, London, 1848, 2 vols., Vol. I, p. 297.
76	*Ibid.*, Vol. II, p. 426.
77	*Ibid.*, Vol. I, p. xciii.
78	*Ibid.*, Vol. I, p. 297.
79	*Ibid.*, Vol. I, pp. 296-7.
80	*Ibid.*, Vol. I, pp. 297-300.
81	*Ibid.*, Vol. I, pp. 302-3.
82	Sir Thomas Coningsby, *Journal of the Siege of Rouen, 1591*, ed. by John Gough Nichols, in *The Camden Miscellany*, Vol. I, 1847, p. 34.
83	*Ibid.*, p. 6.
84	See *Ibid.*, p. 33 for 'Mr. St. John', and p. 28 for 'Mr. Cary', etc.
85	HMC 5th Report, p. 278a.
86	HMC 6th Report, p. 254b.
87	*Ibid.*, p. 260a.
88	*Ibid.*, p. 260b.
89	HMC 3rd Report, p. 293b.
90	HMC Salisbury MSS., Vol. 17, p. 49.
91	Sir Thomas Duffus Hardy, *Syllabus ... (to) "Rymer's Foedera"*, London, 1873, Vol. II, p. 829.
92	HMC 6th Report, pp. 271b and 273b.
93	HMC Salisbury MSS., Vol. 17, p. 49.
94	*Ibid.*, p. 50
95	*Ibid.*, p. 49.
96	*Ibid.*, p. 86.
97	*Ibid.*, p. 126.
98	CSPD 1603-10, p. 207.
99	HMC Salisbury MSS., Vol. 17, p. 126.
100	*Ibid.*, p. 133.
101	*Ibid.*, p. 134.
102	*Ibid.*
103	*Ibid.*, p. 594.
104	*Ibid.*, p. 113.
105	HMC Salisbury MSS., Vol. 19, p. 296, and CSPD 1603-10, p. 384.
106	*Ibid.*, p. 373.
107	*Ibid.*, p. 377.
108	HMC Salisbury MSS., Vol. 20, pp. 300-1.
109	HMC Salisbury MSS., Vol. 21, p. 85.
110	CSPD 1603-10, p. 621.
111	HMC Salisbury MSS., Vol. 22, p. 13.
112	Public Record Office: SP 14/ 75/ 29.
113	CSPD 1611-18, p. 212.
114	Public Record Office: SP 14/ 76/ 2.
115	CSPD 1611-18, p. 220
116	*Yorkshire Fines for the Stuart Period (Vol. II)*, Yorkshire Archaeological Society Record Series, Vol. 58, 1917, p. 13.
117	G. C. F. Forster, 'Faction and County Government in Early Stuart Yorkshire', in *Northern History*, Vol. XI, 1976 for 1975, pp. 70-86.
118	*Ibid.*, p. 85.
119	*Ibid.*
120	Public Record Office: STAC. 8/ 175/ 4.
121	*Yorkshire Fines, op. cit.*, p. 62.

122	British Library: MS. Lansdowne 163, ff. 88-9.
123	*Yorkshire Fines, op. cit.*, p. 152.
124	*Ibid.*, p. 186.
125	*Ibid.*, p. 219.
126	Forster, *op. cit.*
127	J. T. Cliffe, *The Yorkshire Gentry from the Reformation to the Civil War*, London, 1969, p. 293. A report of Constable's behaviour may also be seen in SP 16/ 60/ 52. See also *Acts of the Privy Council 1627-8*, pp. 17, 75, and 217. The warrant to arrest Constable and Hotham was not issued until September 9, and their appearance before the Privy Council was on October 6. Even when they were released from prison on January 2, 1628, they were ordered to remain confined to their county of Yorkshire.
128	Andrew Hopper, *'Black Tom': Sir Thomas Fairfax and the English Revolution*, Manchester University Press, 2007, p. 13. This book is marvelously informative about the Fairfax family, but it does not contain much about Sir William Constable, alas.
129	W. Paley Baildon, 'Composition for Not Taking Knighthood at the Coronation of Charles I', *Yorkshire Archaeological Journal*, Vol. 43, 1971, p. 154.
130	W. L. F. Nuttall, 'The Yorkshire Commissioners Appointed for the Trial of King Charles the First', *Yorkshire Archaeological Journal*, Vol. 43, 1971, p. 154.
131	*Ibid.*
132	Public Record Office: T51/ 7, f. 231.
133	*Ibid.*
134	British Library: MS. Add. 40,132, f. 71.
135	*Ibid.*, f. 35.
136	Nuttall, *op. cit.*, p. 154.
137	George W. Johnson, *op. cit.*, Vol. II, pp. 107-9.
138	John Vicars, *Jehovah-Jireh, God in the Mount or Englands Parliamentary Chronicle*, London, 1644, p. 403.
139	*Ibid.*, Vol. II, pp. 112-3.
140	Mary Frear Keeler, *The Long Parliament 1640-1641, A Biographical Study of Its Members*, American Philosophical Society, Philadelphia, 1954, reprinted 1965, pp. 107-8.
141	CJ, II, 301.
142	George W. Johnson, *op. cit.*, Vol. II, pp. 286-7.
143	*Ibid.*, Vol. II, pp. 260-2.
144	*Ibid.*, Vol. II, pp. 262-7.
145	*Ibid.*, Vol. II, p. 268.
146	*Ibid.*, Vol. II, pp. 290-1.
147	CJ, II, 334b.
148	George W. Johnson, *op. cit.*, Vol. II, pp. 216-7.
149	*Ibid.*, Vol. II, pp. 295-6.
150	*Ibid.*, Vol. II, pp. 321-3.
151	*Ibid.*, Vol. II, pp. 345-6.
152	*Ibid.*, Vol. II, pp. 347-9.
153	*Ibid.*, Vol. II, . 363.
154	*Ibid.*, Vol. II, p. 366.
155	*Ibid.*, Vol. II, pp. 376-7.
156	CJ, II, 449a.
157	George W. Johnson, *op. cit.*, Vol. I, pp. 382-3.
158	Keeler, *op. cit.*, entry for Sir Henry Slingsby, p. 340.
159	CJ, II, 488.
160	*Ibid.*
161	George W. Johnson, *op. cit.*, Vol. II, pp. 394-5.
162	Robert Temple, 'When Did the English Civil War Really Begin?', awaiting publication.
163	CJ, II, 724b and 725a.
164	Mary Frear Keeler, *op. cit.*, pp. 107-8.
165	CJ, II, p. 843b.
166	John Rylands Library, Manchester: Ryl. Eng. MS. 299/557.
167	*Ibid.*
168	CSPD 1641-3, p. 366.
169	Edward Peacock, *The Army Lists of the Roundheads and Cavaliers*, London, 1874, p. 47. (Peacock neglected to index this.)
170	Peter Young, *Edgehill 1642, The Campaign & the Battle*, The Roundwood Press, Kineton, Warwickshire, England, 1967, pp. 255-6. (Kineton is the nearest village to the site of the Battle of Edgehill, and the Roundwood Press was a small private press run by Gordon Norwood, who lived there, whom I knew fairly well, who was keen on Civil War battles as well as local history. I also knew Brigadier Young slightly. He was an enthusiastic military historian.)
171	John Rushworth, *Historical Collections*, London, 1692, The Third Part: Volume the Second, p. 36.
172	Young, *op. cit.*, pp. 120-1.
173	Peter Verney, *The Standard Bearer: The Story of Sir Edmund Verney Knight Marshal to King Charles the First*, Hutchinson, London, 1963.
174	CJ, II, 845a.
175	*Mercurius Civicus, London's Intelligencer*, Number 39 for the week of February 15-22, 1643/4, modern annotated publication ed. by S. F. Jones, Tyger's Head Books, no place, 2013, Volume 2, p. 52.
176	Jack Binns, *Yorkshire in the 17th Century*, Blackthorn Press, Pickering, 2007, p. 79. Binns refers to a Ph.D. thesis by Jennifer Jones at this point, entitled *The War in the North: the Northern Parliamentary Army in the English Civil War, 1642-1645*, York University, Canada, 1991. I have not seen this thesis, which must be interesting.
177	CJ, IV, 88b.
178	CJ, III, 154b.
179	CJ, III, 175b.

180	British Library, Egerton MS 2647, ff. 177-8b. [Barrington Papers, Vol. IV]
181	Anonymous but apparently by or on behalf of the Earl of Essex himself, *A True Relation of the Late Expedition of His Excellency, Robert Earle of Essex for the Relief of Gloucester with The Description of the Fight at Newbury*, printed at London by order of the Commons 7 October 1643, p. 15.
182	We know these details about this officer, of whom little else is known, from the pamphlet *A True Relation of the Late expedition of His Excellency, Robert Earle of Essex, for the Relief of Gloucester, with The Description of the Fight at Newbury*, London, 1643, p. 16.
183	John Vicars, *op. cit.*, pp. 416-8.
184	Robert Codrington, *The Life and Death of the Illustrious Robert Earle of Essex*, London, 1646. (50 pages long)
185	*Ibid.*, p. 33.
186	Samuel Gardiner, *History of the Great Civil War*, London, 1886, Volume One, 1642-1644, pp. 278-9.
187	David Evans, *The Battle of Marston Moor 1644*, Stuart Press, Bristol, 1994, p. 2.
188	George Fox, *The Three Sieges of Pontefract Castle*, The Old Hall Press, Leeds, 1987, p. 9 (a transcription of the entire letter).
189	*Ibid.*, p. 3.
190	Gardiner, *op. cit.*, pp. 371-2.
191	Evans, *op. cit.*, pp. 3-4.
192	David Cooke, *The Civil War in Yorkshire: Fairfax versus Newcastle*, Pen & Sword Books Limited, Barnsley, South Yorkshire, 2004, reprinted 2011, p. 98.
193	HMC Thirteenth Report, Appendix, Part I, MSS. of the Duke of Portland, p. 178. (MS. N. III, 118.)
194	CJ, III, 511b and 512b.
195	CJ, III, 589a.
196	CJ, III, 716a.
197	British Library, Egerton MS. 2650, ff. 218-9b.
198	CSPD 1644, p. 275 and 277.
199	CSPD 1644, p. 303.
200	Public Record Office: S.P. 28/ 267 Part 1/ f. 1. In the same bundle at f. 10 may be found a certificate signed by Constable relating to Captain Symon Askwith, who was under his command in Yorkshire; it is dated 19 December 1646. Detailed information about another of Constable's captains, Captain Stephen White, may be found in S.P. 18/ 72/ 5.I-II. This folder contains a letter of White to John Lambert (by then Lord Lambert) dated 1654, and a Report concerning his company of foot as part of Constable's Regiment of Foot, dated May 29, 1654. These documents have the signatures not only of White but also of the regicides Edward Whalley and William Goffe, and of a Major Haynes, but not of Constable. They give some history of the regiment, and of White recruiting extra men previously. I have copies but have not transcribed these documents, regarding them as of marginal importance here.
201	CSPD 1644, p. 311.
202	Peter Wenham, *The Great and Close Siege of York 1644*, The Roundwood Press, Kineton, Warwickshire, 1970, pp. 90-95.
203	CSPD 1644, p. 521.
204	*Mercurius Civicus, op. cit.*, Vol. 2, p. 246. (Issue 70)
205	CSPD 1644-1645, pp. 104-5.
206	CSPD 1644-1645, p. 108.
207	CSPD 1645-1646, p. 130.
208	CSPD 1645-1646, p. 137.
209	CSPD 1645-1646, p. 140.
210	CSP 1644-1645, p. 143.
211	CSPD 1645-1646, pp. 145-6.
212	CSPD 1645-1646, p. 172.
213	T. T. Wildridge, ed., *The Hull Letters*, Hull, 1886, pp. 76-7.
214	*Ibid.*, p. 80.
215	CJ, IV, 8a.
216	John Rushworth, *Historical Collections*, London, 1722, The Fourth Part, Volume One [i.e., Vol. 6], p. 7.
217	CJ, IV, 26.
218	CJ, IV, 43b.
219	Rushworth, 1722, *op. cit.*, p. 13.
220	CJ. IV, 53a.
221	CJ, IV, 54b.
222	Robert Temple, 'The Original Officer List of the New Model Army', *Bulletin of the Institute of Historical Research*, Vol. LIX, No. 139, May, 1986, pp. 50-77.
223	Rushworth, 1722, *op. cit.*, p. 13.
224	Sir Charles (C.H.) Firth and Godfrey Davies, *The Regimental History of Cromwell's Army*, Oxford, 1940, 2 vols.
225	*Ibid.*, Vol. II, p. 400.
226	The document in the Bodleian Library is MS. TANNER 60/2, ff. 459-60. It is dated February 18, 1645/6, and is addressed to Speaker Lenthall from Francis Pierrepont, William Lister, and John Alured of the Committee for the Northern Association. William Lister was one of the few people who was a member both of this Committee and its rival, the Committee of Yorkshire; both were based at York!
227	CSPD 1645-1646, pp. 505, 506, 509, 517, 520, 523, 528, 532, 542, 546, 551, and 603-4; replies and also letters from London: 508-9, 512, 516, 530, 531, 536, 537, 543, 548, 551, 553, 554 (from the Committee for Both Kingdoms saying: 'We desire your Lordship to look carefully to the security of York, and to put it in so good a posture as you may be able to hold out against the attempts of the enemy in case they should appear before it; June 1)', 559 ('secure such persons in York as are suspected'; June 3) 599, and 606.
228	CJ, IV, 530a.
229	CJ, IV, 527b.
230	CJ, IV, 703a.
231	Robert Bell, ed., *Memorials of the Civil War Comprising the Correspondence of the Fairfax Family*, London, 1848, 2 vols.; Vol. I, pp. 347-8.

232 I have found two other published references to her letters to her brother Ferdinando in George W. Johnson, *op. cit.* These are Vol. I, p. 297, where Sir William himself in a letter dated January 6, 1635/6, mentions to Ferdinando the letter which had been sent to Ferdinando by Dorothy Constable a short time before; and Vol. I, p. 362, where Ferdinando in a letter to his father dated May 17, 1639, says: 'I received a letter from my sister Constable, by this post ...' The correspondence between brother and sister seems to have been frequent and continuous, from what one can gather, and I suspect that many more of Dorothy Constable's letters must survive in the Fairfax MSS, as indeed must many more of Sir William's.
233 Bell, *op. cit.*, Vol. I, pp. 378-9.
234 Rushworth, 1722, *op. cit.*, pp. 493-4.
235 *Ibid.*, pp. 513-7.
236 Public Record Office: S.P. 19/24/24.
237 C. H. Firth, ed., *The Clarke Papers*, Camden Society, London, 1894, 4 vols.; Vol. II, p. 54.
238 David Underdown, *Pride's Purge: Politics in the Puritan Revolution*, Oxford, 1971, pp. 125-6.
239 CJ, VI, 81a-b.
240 CJ, VI, 88b-89a.
241 CJ, VI, 90b.
242 CJ, VI, 91b.
243 *Clarke Papers, op. cit.*, Vol. II, p. 56.
244 *Ibid.*, p. 61.
245 *Ibid.*, pp. 272-2.
246 *Ibid.*, p. 262.
247 CJ, VI, 93a-b.
248 CJ, VI, 106a.
249 CJ, VI, 107b.
250 CJ, VI, 113b.
251 *Ibid.*
252 J. G. Muddiman, *Trial of Charles the First*, Edinburgh and London, no date, pp. 193-227, being extracts from 'Bradshawe's Journal' included as an appendix. These attendance lists were originally published in John Nalson, *A True Copy of the Journal of the High Court of Justice, for the Tryal of K. Charles I*, London, 1684.
253 CJ, VI, 124b.
254 CJ, VI, 126b.
255 CJ, VI, 131b.
256 CJ, VI, 134a.
257 CJ, VI, 139b.
258 CJ, VI, 141a.
259 CJ, VI, 142a.
260 CJ, VI, 144b-145a.
261 CJ, VI, 146b-147a.
262 Ibid.
263 CJ, VI, 239b.
264 CJ, VI, 343b. The Mr. Stephens was either Edward Stephens or Nathaniel Stephens, who were first cousins. Both were from Gloucestershire, and hence closely associated with Sir William's activities there as Governor, and both were Middle Temple lawyers skilled at drafting documents. Mr. Stephens, whichever ot the two it was, must therefore have assisted in drafting the petition, submitted it to the House on Sir William's behalf, and acted as Sir William's intermediary and representative in getting him his arrears in this way. Thus, Sir William was able to regain his old Manor of Holme in lieu of the cash owing to him, and at the same time secure the financial future of his wife in the form of her jointure in the event of his death. His arrears must have amounted to much more than is stated, but long experience had taught him to be happy to settle for what he could get of state debts owing to him. (It should be noted that Mr. Stephens might also have been a recruiter MP named William Stephens, though this is probably less likely.)
265 CJ, VI, 352a.
266 CJ, VI, 363a.
267 CJ, VI, 406a.
268 CJ, VI, 421b.
269 CJ, VI, 432-3.
270 CJ, VI, 528a.
271 CJ, VI, 531b-533a.
272 CJ, VII, 24b.
273 CJ, VII, 42b.
274 CJ, VII, 193a.
275 CJ, VII, 219b-221a.
276 C. H. Firth, Scotland and the Commonwealth, Edinburgh, 1895, p. 305 n.1. I might add that my copy of this book is signed by Firth, the only example I have ever seen of a book signed by him personally.
277 C. H. Firth and Godfrey Davies, The Regimental History of Cromwell's Army, Oxford, 1940, 2 vols., Vol. II, p. 401.
278 Thomas Birch, A Collection of the State Papers of John Thurloe, London, 1742, 7 vols.; Vol. II, p. 413. Although most of the Thurloe Papers are deposited in the Bodleian Library in Oxford, I have about 200 of them in my private collection, which were never part of the main body of papers acquired for the Bodleian.
279 Firth and Davies, op. cit., II, 401.
280 Mercurius Politicus, Number 262 for 14-21 June 1655, p. 5419b.
281 *Ibid.*, pp. 401-2, where it is quoted, the reference given being to Mercurius Politicus, 14-18 June 1655, pp.5419, 5435.
282 Joseph Lemuel Chester, ed., The Marriage, Baptismal, and Burial Registers of the Collegiate Church or Abbey of St. Peter, Westminster [the official name of Westminster Abbey], London, 1876, p. 148.
283 *Ibid.*, n. 9.

CHAPTER THREE, PART ONE APPENDIX

Transcribed Manuscripts

STATEMENT OF LOSSES BY SIR JOHN DANVERS (1624)

Public Record Office: S.P. 14/ 161/ 69
Calendared CSPD 1623-5, p. 204,
where it is dated March,1624.

28. ffebr. 36. Eliz.

The late Queene by her Letres Patents leased all Starnelinges dotards and the Lopps and shreadinges of Trees wthin the fforest of Braden in the County of Wiltshire to Charles Henry & John Danvers for their lives successively the one after the death forfeiture or surrender of the other, rendring a small Rent. Charles being dead it pleased the Kings Matie for the benefitt of the surcharge of Deare there, to induce a surrender thereof from Henry now Lo: Danvers, whereby, thoughe the whole right of the premisses doe legally accrue and would bee valuable to Sr John Danvers for his life, yet hee nether hath nor doth receave any benefitt thereby.

30. Sept. 2. Jac.

The Kings Matie, by letres Patents, was pleased to grant a yearly ffee of 15 l 13 s 4 d [£15, thirteen shillings, and fourpence] to Sr John Danvers for his life as Ranger of the fforests of Blackmore and Pewsham, wch thoughe his Matie hath since beene pleased to disaforrest yet the ffee remaynyng still due according to his Matie Covenant, hath beene behind for the space of 4. or 5. yeares nor had Sr John Danvers any part or recompence by the said disaforesting.

17. Octo. 10. Jac.

His Matie was pleased by letres Patents to give Licence to Sr Henry Nevill to build upon a parcell of ground in Westminster, notwthstanding any Proclamations to the contrarye: by wch priveledge, money being induced took divers long leases of divers pcells, and in respect of that dispensation, undertooke to build thereupon wth brick, and to give improved Rents. Theis lands by these meanes thus built upon & improved, the Lo: Danvers [Sir John's brother, created Earl of Danby in 1626] purchased according to this improvement and afterwards (upon conditions) conveyed them to Sr John Danvers, who expecting the continuance of ye improved Rent, and an encrease to bee made by new building according to his Maties Grannt, divers of ye howses so built and in building, weere, contrary to that Grannt, pulled downe and hindered by a violent course (through misinformation or wrong suggestions) that therein was prosecuted under the authoirty of ye Comission for Buildings in my Lo: Chancelors Elsmr tyme [Sir Thomas Egerton, Lord Ellesmere and Lord Brackley, was Lord Chancellor from 1603 until shortly before his death in 1617]; by wch meanes many of the Tenants that had leases fled, or denyed to pay their Rent, others that had before agreed, refused to build or inlarge their howses, most of them weere undone, others by their examples discouraged, would neyther farme the howses nor Lands, And Sr John Danvers in respect of the present losse of Rent, and impediment of the future improuvment, wch otherwise might have been made by the benefitt of his Maties Graunt, is priudiced to the value of 3000 l at least.

The Lo: Danvers on the behalfe of his Mother, for his Maties benefitt and the bettering of ye Allom workes in Yorkeshire was dealt wthall to desist from erecting upon his owne or his Mother's land there, and in respect thereof (though ye profitts of his owne would have yeilded him much more) yet hee was to have but 200 p Ann and those out of the profitts of those his Maties workes, to this the Earle of Suffolke then Treasurer assented but afterwards by way of Composition drew this 200 l p Ann downe to a some of 600 l to have beene payd then in hand, wch the Lo: Danvers did not refuse, but consigned both it and the benefitt of that Buissines to Sr John Davners,.who as yett hath not receaved any satisfaction for ye same.

His Matie hath beene pleased heretofore to consider the state of Sr John Danvers pension of 500 l p Ann granted for valuable consideration, his cheefe maintenance and Patrimony and was induced to expresse his pleasure by his gratious letres, both to the late Commissionrs for ye Treasury about the end of their Commission, and likewise to my Lo: Treasurer Montague in the beginning of his Treasurershipp, that in some assured way, and wth expedition hee might bee satisfied ye Arrearages, and allso bee duely payd from tyme to tyme heareafter: Neverthelesse there remaynes above seven yeares arrearages, nor can hee tell what to expect of that yearly payment for his Maintenaunce.

Sr John Danvers was servant to Prince Henry of his privy chamber in ordinary above 7 yeares togeather, attended services of Trouble and Charge, and neither before nor since obtayned any reward or favor for the same.`

NOTES: This document is written in the same hand as S.P. 14/ 117/10, the order to which King James appended his reluctant signature (see preceding document in this Appendix).

Charles, Henry, and John Danvers mentioned in the first paragraph of this document are the three Danvers brothers in descending order of age. All have their own DNB entries. Sir Charles was executed for his part in the Essex Rebellion. Henry became Lord Danvers and then later Earl of Danby (two years after the date of this document).

Historians seem never to have noted that Sir John Danvers the regicide was Prince Henry's constant companion for seven years, which is a point of considerable importance (discussed in main text). The harsh treatment of Sir John Danvers may be presumed to have something to do with his close association with the deceased Prince and all that that Prince stood for. It is one more striking illustration of the unnatural dislike the King had for the memory of his own older son.

It is significant that Danvers mentions his connection with Prince Henry only briefly, at the end. He was obviously aware of how little it would count in his favour.

THE LETTERS OF SIR JOHN AND LADY DANVERS TO EDWARD, LORD HERBERT OF CHERBURY (1614-1620)

First letter: Public Record Office:
PRO 30/53/7/13-14.

Sr now I can immagine you are in Italy I will give you ye best account I am able of your businesses. and bycause I think you are most desirous to know the conclusion of warr or peace as wheron your resolution doth much depend I will tell you that after divers uncertaine newses the peace is as they say firmly concluded yet though I have forbonne visiting those lords for your purpose during the time of such uncertaine allarmes I thinke it fitt to lett them know your desire to be continued in their good opinions wch when you find a fitt occasion you may doe well to second by your letters. Your letters frm Heidleberg were deliverd safely both to me and from me. and I hope you have fownd my letters sent to Venice off three severall dates. I receaved your letter by Mr Harwood the 22th of November the pistolls are not yet come. Your Bayliffe James Williams came unto me the 13th of this present moneth and payd me 60 ll 13 s [£60, 113 shillings] the rest due uppon Williams Williams account I know not when I shall receave he being in suit for some part of it as James Williams makes his answere. and as it appeeres by casting up James Willms notes you will have more att his hands then was expected wch will discharge anny reckonings wch you refferd me to pay my self out of your December rents. yet if Will: Willms doe not make up the some very shortly I shall stand ingaged for all the rest of that 220 ll [£200] you gave me order to dispose. for yesterday did I speake wth Mr Townsend who is very hopefull of his liberty wthin few dayes wch hath ingaged me to performe your pleasure by taking up the rest of the money. I have payd Phillip and that before I receaved your money bycause he was in distress being arrested for suretyshipp. Your rents in northwalles are soe slow coming in as that your mother hath not yet receaved all of your brothers anuities and doth more doubt the next payment to helpe her needs. James Williams promised to send up those rents for December out of wch I will see the 20 ll [£20] taken up at Augsbourg discharged and the rest sent according to your direction. S Burlimacha his letter unto you that the 20 ll is payde will be a sufficient testimonye to make good your letter of Credit wch I will procure for you. Concerning the rest Mr Pruthero doth and will write unto you and by all our letters you may perceave the wont your busines hath of you. and if the desire of your frends may invite you more I can assure you they much desire your returne. When I shall heare from you from Venice you will give us some tast of the lyking you have to that contrey and perhaps hasten home to return againe howsoever I will not divine your minde but shall be the more glad the sooner I see you well. Your Tenants and officers I feare will presume to much of your pacience and by that means frustrate (it may be) your dependance of supply by those rents. I doe somwhat know the trouble that ariseth by want in other contreys. wch though I have not reason to suspect on your behalf yet I desire you would use soe much dilligence in your directions as notwthstanding the failling of these rents you might still preserve a good part of your letter of Creditt. Now Sr for news. in the first place I will tell you that all your frends are well or as you left them. There is hope your Cosen Newports wife shall be brought a bed in march. Yong Mr Detton hath left his two wards in wch busines your servant R: Griffith hath and doth labor in the much want of his noble masters help and countenance. Sr Robert Rich [who succeeded as second Earl of Warwick in 1619] hopefull to be imployd and honorable conditions yeelded him by the Duke of Savoy doubts the conclusion of this peace in Germany may make him take the secure way to doe the like. Sr Thomas Roe shall have 3000 ll [£3000] a yeere given him by the merchants and be sent Embassadore into Persia very shortly. The state of our Virginia is like to succeed the better for a good fishing is found on that Cost by wch meanes the Plantation will be much increased wth much less charge then yet was hoped. the lotery for that Purpose proceeding to be drawne att the end of trinitie terme. the Company for that Collony had obtayned the councells letters into all sheirs to invite their adventures towards soe worthy a worke. but have deferrd the execution or sending of them in respect of some endevors of theirs to advantage yeir benevolence to his Masty wch hat not bin according to expectation and refusd in divers Countyes Westward. but ever protesting a ernest desire to supply his maiesty by a usuall course as by parliment. My self amongst many others feele the kings wants neither doe I heere of much amendment therin but by Parliment wch is not spoken of though Divers Proiects have bin handled and reiected for their inconvenience, the King had a fall wth his horse att Newmarkett and was bruisd Mr Mayer is gone unto him but writes word of good amendment of him Sr Walter Rawleys Cronicle is set forth in his owne stile wch is exellent but he hath prosecuted the story of the world but to Part of the Romaines time and seems to have neglected the latter by the Death of Prince Henry for whose sake only he had endevord it. his sonn Mr Walter Rawley having quarrell wth Mr Robert Knowles that was att Juliers are by the Kings attorney brought to answere in the starr Chamber after the example of the Boucher and Barber who were there finde of wch there is a booke in Print wch I thinke you saw before you went. Sr Lewis Watson [see DNB; a friend of Buckingham's, eventually created Baron Rockingham in 1645] being but for want of a word or two troth plight as they say unto Mr Watsons daughter is now in sute wth her bycause she hath forsaken him and will have Sr Robert Sidney [see DNB, later second Earl of Leicester, did not marry this girl but in 1616 married instead Dorothy Percy] Sr Lewis Watson being aptly perswaded by his frends to desist from such unusuall courses houlds himselfe (as they say) soe much ingaged by vowes as untill by due order of court it be declared he thinkes himself conscionable bound from marrying an other woman though she take an other man. besides wch makes it seem more straing for all sides it is knowne that not long after this performed contract she was in bed wth Sr Lewis Watson these things are soe strainge that one cannot tell what will become of the Case. I am willing to entertaine you in councell you see for these are things one is unwilling to write. I only hope it may be to cross some melancholick thoughts and give you satisfaction of my desire to say or performe any acceptable thing unto you. You shall receave heer inclosed twoe letters I have receavd from your lady. I have sent you other before. I pray lett me have a particuler of your receipt of this Packett. You shall receave an other letter from Sr Francis Newport. an other from Mr Richard Newport. an other from your Mother. and lett me not forgett to tell you that my lady Rich hath lately an other Daughter. and now I have as it were out of order strived to fill my paper I will tell you that there are secrett reports of declaration of Sr Horace Veres Patent to be Coronell Generall over the English wch you know hath long bredd dispute and some discontent. and now is it time that I make an end wherefore wth as much affection as can make me serviceable unto you I will remaine

London
the 26th of November   Yours
1614 stilo Anglo: JO: DANVERS

Second letter:
Public Record Office:
PRO 30/ 53/ 10/ 1-2.

Al magrs William Herbert In frensay
[William was Edward's younger brother through whom this was evidently forwarded]

    Sr
I receaved a letter from you of your purpose to stay the returne of your moneys att Turin and direction for speedy securing of your bills for that place. I had written unto yu the last weeke that I did ingage my credit to Signior Burlimacha and wrought that he sent then away order wherby yr credit might be increased and you furnished when you soe pleased I have thought good to persever in that shortest course (especially since it tends to your returne speedyly.) and have againe causd him to renew his order for feare of the miscariing of those letters in the meane time having noe certaine dependency on your bayliffs payment I have sent to Sr Francis Newport [Lady Danvers's brother, and Edward Herbert's uncle] according to your direction wch eithr now or when time shall best serve shall be reservd or payd for your purpose. and for the matter of warr I shall wish yr owne presence. for I have not thought it convenient in these times of grand faction to move any other then I writ unto you I have donn: on such reasons as I will reserve till an other time. On saterday last Sr Arthur Ingram [see DNB and Keeler; wealthy merchant and Secretary of the Council of the North] was by the lord Admrll Treasorer, Chamberlayne, Knolles and Wotton sworne Cofferer having payd 2500 ll [£2500] for Sr Robert Vernons release. This wrought soe much in the stomacks of a number that of custom were wont to live in asured hope of the Place, as that they all cam unto the king and told him that if he did permitt a strainger thus to purchas the honor and profitt for wch soe many of his Mastyes servants had spent their time and estates in hope on and that the advancing of men in their turns did extend to advantage the estates of one an other, his service would be left by many and the honor of his house much impayred. and in respect of the honor wch they conceaved to loose by this Proceeding they would freely pay him back his money that things might be continued wthout president to the disadvantage of all ye king housould servants. The king was att the time much displeased especially telling him that though it might have bin once putt upon them in the queens time yett had a general court of the house: to wch was the kings promise adioyned. That ther should thence fourth noe such thing be admitted his Maysty sayd he would dilligently take it into his consideration. and they doe not want to solicite the crossing of this new officer. and soe depends it uncertainly Now I will tell you that I have sent away your inclosed letters we are all some what after the old manner and doe hartely wish you well and Heer wth him that will be ever redy to serve you.

the 2d of March 1614   JO DANVERS
london

Third letter:
Public Record Office:
PRO 30/ 53/ 10/ 3-4.

Sr

I hope you have ere this receaved two letters by the way of Venice wch were to one and the same purpose you did desire them. and att both times did require Sgr Burlimacchi to send his directions for renewing your credit to what you should want. not much exceeding the proportion you did propose unto your self to spend abroade. I have againe bin wth him. and according to your desire have procurde his directions for your creditt att lyons and att Paris. I doe expect his letter wch I will enclose wth this and renew it att Mr Wakes returne. Yesterday I did receave the 150 ll [£150] by your appointment wth a direction from Sr Francis Newport [Herbert's maternal uncle] to tell you that now he hath imployd for you all the money you had in his hands. 200 ll [£200] therof I have deliverd to Sgr Burlimaccha. the other fifty I have taken to pay my self about soe much wch I had disbursed for you towards the hundred pounds imployd for Mr Townsend. and your other occasions wch I had nor have not receaved from your Bayliffes. to whom I have causd Mr Pruthero to wright divers times and wee can have noe answer. I have written to Mr Charles Herbert [presumably the younger brother of Edward who was a Fellow of New College, Oxford, but died young, and hence another step-son of Sir John Danvers] alsoe to call on them. I will still hope that the next terme may bring some good news of them. in the meane time I have done what I can. and I thinke you shall not be disapointed of your receipts where you are. for I am soe sencible of my frends wants beyond seas as I was willing to offer my self and if it had not servd, to have procured other of my frends. to have given Sgr Burlimacha satisfaction. but I find him an honest free Gentleman. wch hath made me especially since he is like to be before hand wth you in payments, referr the advantages of exchaing to be agreed on by your selves att your return or att the repaying of him: the letter was offered from him for 500 ll [£500] wch I did not thinke fitt to enlarge and to inteate for it since you are as I immagine on your returne. or to remaine soe neere att hand as your directions and farther assistance may soone be procured. wch is all I can say of your businesses. Now of the world that is to say of the news in these parts. it is att that pass as one may expect rather then perceive any chainge of things. and of forraine busines the case is very suspitious. I will write unto you againe by Mr Wake who attends ye coming of your Savoy Embassador. You shall receave heerwth 6 letters from soe many of your frends. wth an other of Creditt to Lyons. and Paris. now wth my harty well wishes for your happines I will rest Yours

London.
the 8th of Aprill 1615

JO. DANVERS

Fourth letter (from Lady Danvers):
Public Record Office:
PRO 30/ 53/ 10/ 5.

12th May 1625. Lady Danvers to her Son Sir Edw. Herbert

To my best beloved sonn Sr Edward Herbert Knight

My deare sonn.

it is strange to me to here you to complayne of want of care of you in your absence when my thoughts are seldom removed from you which must assuredly set me aworkinge of any thinge may doe you good. and for writinge, the one of us yf not both never let messinger pass without letters. your aboad is so short in any one place and we so unhappy in givinge you contentment as our letters com not to your hands. which we are sory for. And to tel you further of Sr John Danvers Love which I dare sweare is to no man more. he is and hath beene so carefull to keep you from lake of money now you are abroad as your Bayliffs faylinge payment as they continually doe and pay no man. he goeth to your Merchaunt offers him self and all the power he can make to supply you as your occasions may require. mistake him not but beleeve me there was never a tenderer hart or a lovinger minde in any man then is in him towards you who have power to Comaund him and all that is his. Now for your Baylifs I must tell you they have not yet payd your Brothers all there Anuities due at Midsomer past. and but half due at Christmas last and no news of the rest. this yf advauntadge were taken might be preiuditiall to you and it is ill for your Brothers. and very ill you have such officers I hope it will bringe you home and that is all the good can com of this. your sister Johnes hath brought a boy she is so weake as she is much feared by those abouts her. [This is Herbert's eldest sister, Elizabeth, of whom he says in his Autobiography: "Elizabeth, my eldest sister, was married to Sir Henry Jones, of Albemarles, who had by her one son, and two daughters; the latter end of her time was the most sickly and miserable that hath been known in our times, while for the space of about fourteen years she languished and pined away to skin and bones, and at last died in London, and lies buried in a church near Cheapside."] my Lady Vachell lyes now adyeinge the bell hathtwice gon for her. your wife and sweet Children are well. and herein I send you little Florence letter to see what comfort you may have of your deare Children. [This daughter of his did not survive to adulthood, the only daughter who did so being named Beatrice] let them my Deare sonn draw you home and affoorde them your care and me your comfrot that desire more to see you then I desire any thinge ells in the world. and now I end with my dayly prayers for your health and safe retorne to Your ever Lovinge mother

    MAGD: DANVERS -   12th May 1615.

I have received the Pattent for your Br: William. and Sr John hath beene with the ambassador. who stayes for Sr James Sandaline his cominge. [Evidently Sir John Danvers had obtained for Herbert's younger brother, William, a commission in the forces in the Netherlands; Herbert says of this brother in his Autobiography: "... (he) then went to the wars in the Low Countries, but lived not long after".]

Fifth letter:
National Library of Wales,
Aberystwyth: MS. Powis Castle 314A.

Sr

    heering by a letter your mother receved from the Hage that you desired your letters should be directed to Sr Henry Wootons House. I have now performd it though all that I can say is but an advertisement that I sent a Packett and letters of Creditt for you to Amsterdam instantly upon receipt of yours by Mr Calvert. wherin I did give you account of your busines. and tolld you might find others Packetts att the abbay of St Martin in Paris where your brother is wth other Letters of Creditt and likewise divers letters of your frends unto you. these unless they be very certaine where to find you will be kept till you come there or send for them I know not whether it be news unto yu of your Cosen Newports knighting [Richard Newport, knighted at Theobalds, June 2, 1615; in 1642 he was created the first Baron Newport, was a royalist, fled to France where he died; see DNB and Keeler's entry for his son Francis Newport, a royalist M.P. of the Long Parliament] in wch busines you have your part of ye obligation. Your mother and I yett hold our iorney into Shropshiere Mr Dekam (?) hath the revertion of Sr Thos. Parryes place. [the Ambassador to France, who died the next year; see DNB] my lo: Treasurer is a little on ye mending hand and was led betweene two yesterday to take the ayre. the Bishop of Winchester they say shall be councelor and lord Privie seale. I receaved a letter from Sr Edw: Cecill wch tould me you were hasting homwards it makes all of us glad and shall make me the breifer because these are in hasard of speedy coming to yr hands. I hope you have receaved some of those letters I sent you and that I shall ever be worthy of your true love. wch is the ernest ambition of

                                    JO: DANVERS

    Charing cross the 24th of June 1615 st: Angl:

Sixth letter:
Public Record Office:
PRO 30/ 53/ 3/ 31-2.

Sr Jh: Danvers my Lo: Amb: 1627. Jul: 1620.   London.

Rd: 12. Aug: 1620./ Paris.

To the right hoble Sr Edward Herbert Knight of the Bath. Ambassador from his Msty wth the French king att Paris.

My lo:

The last Letter I wrote in the maner you aprove acquainted you wth those things as remaine in a sort after the same state nor is ther ought else I can now think on to be added. Wherfore I will divert to my Cheife Errand & on the behalf of the Virginia Company intreate your favor that some industrious dilligent servant of yours may be imployed to procure hither skillfull vignerons about 5 or 6. & as many skilled in nourishing of silk wormes. Wch Plants of the best vines especially of Frontigniack [*Frontignac, a heavy sweet table wine of France, made of muscat grapes, which was a great favourite in England at this time; the vines he speaks of would be muscat grape vines*] and 3 or 4 or more ownces of the most kindly silk worm seeds all to be transported into Virginia there to improve. It is much desired that i or two of each were heere to goe either att the mids of August or beginning of September. Ships being setting out about those times & a frend of Mine an Extraordinary worthy honest man goes in the first shipp thither & there means to reside as theire Comander in that State in the second goes some other worthy men as Captaine Chester a greate sea Captaine & a brother of Sr John Brown [Sir John Browne was twice Sheriff of Dorset and Vice Admiral, and died on the Isle of Rhé Expedition, being father of the radical M.P. of the Long Parliament, John Browne, whose entry in Keeler see, there being nothing in the old DNB; Sir John had been knighted July 23, 1603, amongst the enormous crowd of knights made at the coronation of James I] wth divers of my acquaintance. wee shall send allsoe in October.   soe that noe time betweene this & that will be amiss. you may assure they shall be used very well & whatsoever you please to promise or disburse for their wages entertainment or for their Voyage hither shall be duly performed & discharged according as your letters shall direct though it be to double their usuall wages had in their owne Contreys. alsoe if you find convenient to stipend some of the better experienced more largely who may be allsoe a means to draw over others your recomendation shall be obeyed. I have sent you heerin inclosed a letter (from one serves me as butler) unto his father who is a greate Nourisher of Silk wormes & skilld about Choice of Vine Plants. who I presume will be induced to offer to doe you service heerin. and I have sent you books & such declarations as wee give abroade wherby you may discover our hopes & somewhat perceave you may doe an acceptable pleasure to many & alsoe assist to soe glorious a worke. if you direct them unto me I shall not be much farther then chelsey whither I am removing tomorrow & will give order att Mr Telliers they shall be provided for att theire coming. I hope the same hast I have written in will cause this beare noe long date in comming & soe wishing you all maner of good I rest

Charing cross
27th of July 1620

Yours assured to serve you
J DANVERS

if you be assured of the seed that its of the best kind a pownd will not be too much. if you please to send a footman wth this letter perhaps it will hasten the effect wee desire. ther is one Mr Perronyn dismentaine dwelling in the Isl of the Pallace to whom this letter inclosed is directed. who will be apt to serve you in this busines.

INFORMATION AGAINST SIR JOHN DANVERS (1631?)

Public Record Office:
S.P. 16/ 206 57. Calendared
(one sentence only)
in CSPD 1631-3, p. 238, where it
is identified as a statement by
Anthony Wither, similar to his
statement against Nathaniel Stephens,
J.P., of Gloucestershire (Piece 56), and
dated tentatively 1631.

Concerning Sr John Danvers

About 16 yeeres since when I first came into ye Virginia Companie Sr. John Danvers would needs take me into his especiall acquaintance, & I being yet of noe ptie, he drewe me to be of Sr Edwyn Sandes ptie wth him, wch acquaintannce he hath sought to presearve until now by many Mutuall passages betwixt us.

At ye first being Commissioner for Clothing he wrott letters on my behalf & in Comendacons of yt busines unto all his freinds in Wiltsheeire & spoake ye like to them afterwarde in my hearing

Sr Edward Bainton & ye three other Justices being upon his Maties hearing in Councell Comannded to be prosecuted in ye Star=chamber, upon Sr John Danvers entreatie, I forbeare for a while to prosecute: Sr Edward Bainton being his Nephew & Mr Bailey another of ye Justices being his kinsman, upon a second & third Comand from his Matie & ye Board yt he must prosecute, then he entreeted me to prosecute Sr Edward Bainton onely, & to forbeare Mr Bailey & ye rest./

He employed me at this tyme in a treatie betwixt my Lord Craven & himselfe in a busines of noe smale importannce./

[Five lines of the MS. are here crossed out, but by diligent study could probably be deciphered; however, this has not been attempted.]

he finding by our often consultacons formerly had, in how bigge a strayne Sr ffrancis Seymer [Sir Francis Seymour, for whom see DNB; created Baron Seymour of Trowbridge in 1641, and a prominent royalist] had ingaged himselfe against my Commission, & yt himselfe had many busines standing out against ye Seymers conceived hope to make to himselfe advantage by a treatie & union wth yt howse against my Comission

ffirst he treated wth ye Seymers at London & thereupon obteyned yt all suits betwixt them should be referred to Mr Glanfeild to be compromised, & to make it probable yt my busines & my selfe were made by Sr John Danvers ye price of this reconsiliacon, it appeareth by Sr ffrancis Seymers Carracter, & Sr John Danvers contrarie & unwoonted manner of carriage, as followeth./

ffirst ye Lords having ordred yt Markett spinning should be confyned unto ye Markett spinners in one howses it being yo greatest reason of ye falsities & abatemets made in White-cloth, his brother ye Earle of Danby [underlined in another hand each time this name occurs in the document] solicited dyvers pticuler Lords (as I am informed) to make stopp of yt point in the proclamacon then in hand wch he accordingly effected./

Heere upon ye Marchats peticon ye Lords againe about ye Markett spinning, & obteyne to have it referred to ye consideracon of ye Iustices of peace in theire seaverall Clothing devisions:

Sr John Danvers by comming himselfe sundry times home to my Lodging importuneth me yt I would pretend a fitnesse of ye place & yt it would wth most convenyencie expedite ye service to have ye handing of ye Markett spinning by ye Iustices to be at a generall quarter Scessions in Wiltsheire & not in ye pticuler Clothing devisions, & by reason many Clothiers dwelt in ye quarter about ye Towne of Chippenham to have ye quarter Scessions held these, pro hoc vice tantum would be for ye ease of ye Countrie wch Towne he said my Lord his brother & himself much favored, & desyred to benefitt, by reason theire Lands lye neere adioyninge, wch I utterly refused, but Sr John coming home to me soe often I pceived he meant to put his whole strength upon this busines, both to prevaile wth me by vertue of our inward acquaintannce, & to defend it (as I thought & he promised against Sr ffraniis Seymers opposition & leading power at ye Scessions, where upon I yeilded to second my Lorde of Danby & his endeavours for removing ye quarter Scessions to Chippenham according to theire desire./

Sr John Danvers according to his usuall custome writeth Letters downe to his frends in Wiltsheire of his comming to ye Scessions about Markett spinning, & as I am lately informed by an Neighbour of his in ye Countrie (a very intelligent pson) yt the letters did signifie his dislike there should be any alteracon made in ye busines of Markett spinning, whereupon his frends in ye Countrie raise a cry before hand against any endeavours & proceedinge in yt busines./

Sr John Danvers commeth to Chippenham before hand to confirr wth me as he promised, but rideth into ye Towne as ye Bench were satt, & goeth from his horse to ye Bench, where he kept himselfe setting contynually both fore-noones & after-noones, yt soe I might have noe opportunitie soe much as to speake wth him a worde in private: But one daye as they were setting downe to dynner, he sent to me to bring in ye Lords letters to ye Iustices wch I did & delivered them to his hands relying on him still to ye uttermost; ye letters being delyvered, & after dynner reade by ye Iustices, ye busines of Markett spinning was appointed by them to be heard after supper in ye private chamber where they supped./

After supper ye busines being called for my selfe setting downe at ye lower end of ye table and Sr francis Seymer who mannaged ye whole busines setting upper most ye difference was greate betwixt us, Sr John Danvers Clarke being placed at my backe gave ayme & intelligence to Sr ffrancis Seymer of all private speeches betwixt my selfe & ye Clothiers at ye lower end, & often as I was speaking he was observed by dyvers to use many gestures towards Sr ffrancis in derision of me, wch was ye first manifest token I had of Sr John Danvers being of ye contrarie side: I went to him ye next Morning earely at his Lodging, Where after large & unusuall tyme of attendance I was admitted to speake wth him & complayned of his Clarks carridge towards me, he answered me wth a deepe silence & called others to speake wth him yt soe I might wthdrawe./

Sr John Danvers not onely failed to muster upp those helpes of Iustices wch at first he promised me, but satt himselfe moste all ye tyme ye busines was in debate, but at theire conclusive meetinge wch against my consent & liking was resolved should be at Salsberry [Salisbury] there my selfe being knowne not to be in Towne Sr John Danvers spoke against my busines all he could, my servannt was there put unknowne & heard him, he at last undertooke to carry the Iustices answere to theire Lorpps Letters, & to back the same by his brother & himselfe to his uttermoste power./

And as he rodd on his way to London therewth he sent for me to come speake wth him to ye end I should forbeare to acquaint ye Lords against ye Iustices manner of carridge in this busines, but (to use his owne words) to geive them here after now a tapp & then a tapp as I should fynd occasion./

KING JAMES ORDERS
SIR JOHN DANVERS
TO BE PAID HIS ANNUITY
AND ARREARS (1620)

Public Record Office:
S.P. 14/ 117/ 10

JAMES [signature of the King]

Right trustie and right wellbeloved Councellors wee greet yow well. Whereas we have heretofore granted unto Sr John Danvers kt. an Annuity of five hundred pounds by the yeare for a valuable consideration; In regard whereof, and for that it is the onely meanes hee hath for his Maintenance, hee hath made humble suite unto us to give order hee may receave aswell the Arrearages of his said Annuity, wch hath beene unpayd for these three yeares and a halfe, as that some course may bee setled for the better payment thereof hereafter. And hath propounded for the payment of his arrearages that a Talley may bee stricken upon the ffarmers for his use and discharge of that debt out of the remainder of the Rent answeared unto us out of the ffrench and Rhenish wynes, And for his better payment hereafter, that the 500 l [£500] payd into our Exchequer upon the Rent of unwrought clothes may bee assigned unto him, and a Talley stricken accordingly from tyme to tyme for the same. Wee have therefore thought fitt to recommend his case unto yow to take some course eyther by that way wch hee propoundeth or any other assured meanes wch yow shall find out that hee may bee payd both the arrearages and whatsoever shallbee due hereafter from tyme to tyme wth all the expedition that may bee. dated 9th of October 1620.

directed To the Comisioners of the Treasurie.
ffor Sr John Danvers.

NOTES: As may be seen from subsequent documents, the above order was not carried out five years later: It is possible that the King himself connived at the frustration of this order, which he did not wish to deny or refuse openly. That would have been quite in character. It is difficult to see how the order could resist all attempts at fulfillment, and pleas to various and sundry, including Buckingham, unless the King secretly cancelled the order behind Danvers's back. The King's signature at the top of the document is so faint, only half visible due to the quill running dry as he wrote, that one can barely resist the temptation to conclude that he did not sign with any enthusiasm, could not be bothered to dip the quill again, and that the lack of ink indicates an equal lack of willingness to give any money to Danvers. The document is in the same hand as S.P. 14/ 161/ 69 (see later).

THREE EARLY LETTERS OF
SIR JOHN DANVERS (1620/1-1623)

First letter:　　　　　　　　　　Public Record Office: S.P. 14/ 119/ 34.
　　　　　　　　　　　　　　　　Calendared CSPD 1619-23, p. 215.
　　　　　　　　　　　　　　　　(Addressee not named)

　　　　　　　　　　　　　　　　S. Jh. Danvers. 18. Jan. 1621　　London

Sr

　　　　　　　　　　　　　　　It was my good fortune to deliver your letter & relation to my lo: Chamberlayne Since I can assure you he tooke your respect in very good part. and wth the assurance that twice he came to me desiring I would not fayle to thanke you on his behalf. I hope my letter shall be wellcome. nor must I shew doubt of your worthy acceptance of any lynes from a more impertinent frend then my self am unto you & therfore on my owne behalf doe likewise salute you & thank you for those former curtesies towards me you have bin ready to performe. & as it is sometimes an assurance that a man will pay a debt when he enters into a greater obligation soe my desire you will take notice of a kinsman of myne one Mr Withypole now gone over wth the Mareshall de Cadenett and both in his respect to my lor Ambassador & his other addresses for his course of lyfe to afford him your favor & good advice shall bind me for your love to rest in hast.

　　　　　　　　　　　　　　　　　your assured ready frend

　　　　　　　　　　　　　　　　　J DANVERS

18 1h Jan: 1620

My Cousen Withypole was once designed for my lo: Amb: attendance but an Extraordinary occasion diverted that wth noe less thanks to My lo: Amb:

NOTE: Amongst the Dropmore MSS. is a letter of Sir John Danvers to the then Marquis of Buckingham, dated February 2, 1619/20, begging for help in obtaining payment from the King, the same matter with which the following two letters are concerned:

Second letter:　　　　　　　　　Public Record Office: SP. 14/ 149/ 105
　　　　　　　　　　　　　　　　Calendared CSPD 16235, p. 39.

　　　　　　　　　　　　　　　　To Secretary Conway.

Right hoble

What I might say of your worthines inducing my confidence in your favor, I may fitly referr to your owne able judgement of your self & me your servant, &　soe fall to the point of my present desire att yr Noble hands. Having bin, Sr an ill or not importunate Solicitor of my owne busines as well as by my harder fortune, I stand oppressed in the nature expressed in this paper of my greivances inclosed. & notwthstanding that for more easye passage, I only sought & petitioned for payment of my Pension, &, that I divers tymes obtayned his Mattes just recomendation in substance as is recited in this enclosed copy of his gracious letter, & that my lord Treasurer hath usually promised to cause me payd att least what hath fallen due unto me since his tyme of Tresoreship: Yet nothing performed. My humble suit is that you will be pleased to lett his Msty understand the state of my cause & how neere driven by necessity as leaves me neither means nor credit in my much indebted estate, & theruppon Move his Msty to some such manner of consideration & benignitie as may produce some speedy payment for my releife. I know noe way but by such kynde of comand to my lord Treasorer as he will not refuse. or as your Noblenes may conceave pertinent for effecting my desire. be it in any proportion great or smale in present or certaine assignacion wch I may turne over to satisfie my Creditors. Noble Sr you may measure the pleasure yw shall heerin doe me by your apprehension of the state of my case & I shall answere your favor wth the best measure of my ever thankfullnes & acknowledged obligation I can be able to express. Soe craving pardon for my troubling you, wch I chose to doe in writing rather then Speech, that both your (Progress) leisure & this noate of remembrance might concurr to the helping of yours

    Sr   Your everhonored & humble Servant

Chelsey 30th of July   J. DANVERS
                                                          1623 .

Third letter: Public Record Office:
                                              S.P. 14/ 149/ 106
                                              Calendared beside previous,
                                              CSPD.1623-5, p. 39.
                                              Also to Secretary Conway.

                                              Sr John Danvers

R Hoble

Since the writing of my other letter [the preceding] It came in my minde to express unto you some passage of favor from my lord Duke of Buckingam wherby you may conceave your frendly pleasuring of me to be a service or respect to his Grace, wch remembred to his MSty may prove perswasive on my behalf &that I may the less seeme to force words of curtecie for my owne advantage I shall deliver the very termes as I remember My lo: Duke the weeke or fewer dayes before his departure towards Spaine spoke on some occasion of me to my lo: of Kensington & Sr William Croft & sayde Comend me to your frend Sr John Danvers desire him to have yet awhyle patience till his Mstyes greater busines now in hand be somewhat setled. Let him be assured I will care for him effectually, as Onewho not only for his owne desert but alsoe as to whom I think my self much indebted for his curtesies & respectiveness towards me divers wayes. This much gave me confidence enough to trust that his Graces soe speedy returne as hee presumed would have provided for my good before now. but Tyme doth soe invade uppon my indebted estate as presseth me to importune seasonable releif by your favor & mediation & by that apprehension of applyable reasons wch your Noble judgement may out of what I have written or otherwise conceave pertinent to be sayde on my behalf who shall be bound unto yw as willingly I shall ever rest

                                                          Sr

                                              Your affectionate & faithfull
31th July 1623   frend & servant

                                              J DANVERS

NOTES: Possibly the "paper of my greivances inclosed" with the letter of July 30th is the document, S.P. 14/ 161 69, included in this Appendix. Conway may have held it back until the following March for good reasons. In October, 1623, Buckingham and the Prince returned to England, and after that, Buckingham went through his phase of befriending leaders of the "popular" party, of which Danvers may be assumed to have been a member. In February, the 1624 Parliament opened and the Earl of Pembroke, a relation of Danvers's step-son Sir Edward Herbert, expressed satisfaction with Buckingham's account of the Spanish marriage negotiations, on the floor of the House. This may have seemed like a propitious moment to put forward Danvers's Statement of Losses. Possibly the King's Order to Pay Danvers (not carried out at the time), document S.P. 14/117/10, also included in this Appendix, is the "enclosed copy of his gracious letter" referred to in Danvers's letter of July 30th, and the compilers of the Calendars of the State Papers, not realizing this, put it with the material for 1620, in accordance with the date written on it.

DOCUMENT CONCERNING
SIR JOHN DANVERS'S PURCHASE
OF HIS HOUSE AT CHELSEA
(1618)
Public Record Office:
S.P. 14/ 97/ 132. Calendared,
CSPD 1611-18, p. 548.

June 1618
E: of Lincolnes Ire ffor deliveringe certaine
Writings to Sr John Danvers
To Sr Clemannt Edmond
To the right worll Sr Clement Edmunds knight
Clearke of his Mstyes most honorable Pryvie
Councell these.

Sr

There are amongst my Evidences some writings only belonging unto a certaine Portion of land in Chelsey Called the Moorehouse Purchased by my lord my father from one Mr Roper, wch I have sould to Sr John Danvers and stand bound to deliver him all the Evidences and wrytings therunto belonging. Now for that I am importuned by him to performe my covenant & he having some present occasion to make use of his writings I desire you will doe him and me the pleasure to take a fitting course such as you think the readiest way that they may be delivered unto Sr John Danvers. I presume (since att the sight of them they will appeere not to concern any others) it shall not cost you much labor to performe my request. wch I shall notwithstanding take as a curtesye from you & soe rest

your very loving frend

TH LYNCOLNE

NOTES: The signatory is Theophilus Clinton, Earl of Lincoln. He had a history of opposing Buckingham and the Court. His association with Sir John Danvers can have done Danvers no good in the Court's eyes. The "present occasion" which Danvers had to consult and peruse every possible bit of paper relating to his property in Chelsea was doubtless in order to arrange mortgages and loans from creditors, which would require the relevant documents for their security. Danvers's pension had not been paid since 1616 and by now he must have been at extremities of financial desperation. The Earl of Lincoln must have realized now desperate Danvers's plight was, in order to bother the Clerk of the Privy Council for the relevant papers like this. (Why the Privy Council had Lincoln's papers is a matter to which I have not sought the answer.) Danvers's house in Chelsea, More House, was also later called Danvers House. (See Danvers's entry in DNB. Faulkner, citing Lysons, maintains that Danvers was in possession of this property "as early as the reign of Elizabeth" (see Thomas Faulkner, An Historical and Topographical Description of Chelsea and Its Environs, Vol. I, p. 172, citing Lysons, Vol. 2, p. 123. This seems an extraordinary thing indeed, since Danvers was only in his teens then, but we have seen in his Statement of Losses that he was already sharing with his brothers under Elizabeth residual rights in the forest of Braden in Wiltshire. It is more likely that Danvers acquired the property in Chelsea upon marriage with his first wife in 1608, and that her money, combined with his pension, encouraged him to feel financially secure enough to do so. (She was, after all, a distinguished older woman who could be considered to require a house of such distinction to match her own status.) But whether the acquiring of the property took place then or earlier, Danvers's sudden need for deeds and evidences in 1618 must indicate the need for a mortgage. The house at Chelsea was the location of Danvers's famous Italianate Garden at Chelsea, succeeded and excelled later by Danvers's garden at West Lavington in Wiltshire, a property which came to him with his second wife.

SIR JOHN DANVERS DEFIES THE KING'S WARRANT (1640)

Public Record Office:
3.P. 16/ 451/ 45
Calendared p. 68, CSPD 1640,
where it is dated April 24, 1640.
The document is a copy,
and bears no signatures.

Memorandum. That wee whose names are hereunder subscribed, beinge required by Some of the Deputy Lieuetenants of the County of Middlesex to attend Sir John Danvers Knight (beinge allsoe one of the Deputy Lieuetenants of the said County) To desire his hand to certaine Warrants made for the Levyinge of Twelve Hundred men, And for money to Coate, exercise and Conduct them; As likewise to provide Thirty able horses and Tenn Porters, by vertue of his Mats most honnoble privy Councell. Wee attended the said Sir John Danvers at his house in Chelsey this present ffryday morninge the xxiiiith of Aprill 1640. And offered him the said Warrants to signe. Whereupon he read all or most parte of the Warrants wch were for the levyinge of the men. And then foldinge them upp said, That no doubt the Gentlemen who had signed the Warrants well knewe ye proportion. Whereupon offer was made to shewe him his Maties said Warrant, The Lords Letter, and ye Estimate whereon ye said warrants were grounded. But he shewed no desire to see them, Sayinge, It was needlesse, ffor he gave Creditt to the Authoritye whereupon the deputy Lieuetenants had Signed. And desired to be excused therein, for that he had not bin formerly acquainted with any parte of that Businesse. But beinge againe told that the Deputy Lieuetenants requested his hand to the said Warrants, He answered, That he was sicke for a moneth togeather, after the lres yssued from ye Lords. And sithence the beginninge of the Parliament he had bin extraordinary bussie; Wherefore haveinge not bin at any meetinge concerninge that Service, he left it to those who had hitherunto agitated the same. Addinge further yt he did not speake it to the end it should be conceived he refused to signe them, But because he had not medled with yt service at all. And said further, that for his parte he had formerly signed some Warrants for Sumons, but to his remembrance had not Signed any warrants of that nature.

(NOTES: Within days, on May 6, the Council had ordered: "Sir John Danvers to be sent for by a messenger and examined by the Attorney General." - see p. 120, Calendar. Shortly afterwards, a newsletter of May 12 reported: "Sir John Danvers was questioned for not subscribing these warrants to raise this money in Middlesex, being a deputy-lieutenant, the same having been presented to him while the Parliament was sitting, and therefore he has been since examined by the Attorney General upon several interrogatories, but what further course shall be taken against him time will try." - see p. 155, Calendar. The Sir John Danvers of Northampton mentioned in June, p. 376, the same Calendar, is probably the cousin of the regicide of that name, of Culworth, Northants., who died 1642.)

ANGELL GREY'S PETITION RELATING TO SIR JOHN DANVERS'S FINANCES (1660)

House of Lords Record Office: Main Papers, June 11, 1660, consisting of Number 11 of "Papers relating to the Act of Indemnity". (Calendared HMC 7th Report, p. 95b.)

Mr Angell Greys Peticon
To the right honoble the Lords of England assembled in Parliament:

The humble peticon of Angell Grey.

Sheweth

That yor petr being of ye Kings party in ye late Unhappy Differences, the said Sr John Danvers (or some on his behalfe) in the yeare 1644 made discovery of ye said Debt unto ye Comittee for Advance of Money as a Debt due from ye said Sr John Danvers unto yor petr And notwthstanding that yor petr Compounded upon ye Articles of Oxford and inserted the said Bond & Indenture in his Particular as a Trust, and notwthstanding that ye same upon ye Suite of ye said Audelay, Henry, and Katherine Grey, was fully proved by ye Oathes of ye said Lady Elizabeth Griffin &, severall other Witnesses who were prsent at ye Sealing of ye said Bond, & payment of ye said 3000 l Yet Mr Moyer, Mr Moore, Mr Uptone, Mr Rice Williams & Mr Cary [Samuel Moyer, Richard Moore, John Upton, Rice Williams, and Edward Carey, who in 1650 were appointed as civil servants to act as Commissioners for Advance of Money and of Compounding, in replacement of the M.P.s who had formed those two Parliamentary Committees up until that time, a subject discussed in the chapter "Regicides and Committees" in the main text] sitting then as Comrs at Haberdashers hall, Combineing wth the said S; John Danvers, did by illegall & unjust Orders first compell yor petr ye sd Lady Elizabeth Griffin (to avoyde the Imprisonmt of their psons) to produce the said bond & leave ye same in their Treasury And afterwards delivered the same up to the said Sr John Danvers to bee Cancelled as being fforfeited unto ye Comonwealth for yor petrs Delinquency Whereby the good Intencons of ye sd Lady Elizabeth Griffin towards his Children are not only frustrated, but yor petr alsoe (Who was but a trustee) hath been & still is forced to pay Interest for ye same to ye said Lady Elizabeth Griffin duering her life & must alsoe answere ye principall unto his Children out of his owne estate after her decease, Soe yt ye goodnes of a Kinde Grandmother towards her Children is by ye sd unjust pceedings made ye Occasion of Destroying of yor petr & his whole ffamily.

Yor petr therefore humbly prayes, That his said Case being taken into Consideracon Yor honors wilbee pleased to afford him such Releife herein as to yow in yor grave Wisedome shall seeme Meet Or otherwise to Provide that hee may bee left at Liberty to prosecute his Suite at Law or Equity agt ye sd Sr John Danvers & his Suerties & ye said Comrs at Haberdashrs hall for his iust reparacons herein, The Act of Oblivion intended to bee passed this prsent Parliamt Notwthstanding./.

And yor petr shall ever pray &c./

ANGELL GREY

NOTES: The above petition contains such outrageous lies, distortions, and devious dishonesty, that it fairly takes the breath away. Despite all this, it does, however, strangely provide additional evidence in defence of Sir John Danvers, though quite against the intentions of Angell Grey. (Danvers had of course been dead for five years by the time of this petition, as Grey must well have known). The case and its implications are discussed in the main text in the chapters on Early Careers of the Regicides, and on Regicides and Committees, in the Appendix to which latter chapter may also be found letters to Danvers from the Commissioners mentioned in this petition proving quite opposite facts to those maintained here by Angell Grey in his own interests.

WARRANT FOR PAYMENT OF SIR WILLIAM CONSTABLE'S WAGES AS CAPTAIN (1611)

British Library: Add. MS. 5753, ff. 233-4.

To or very Loving freinde Mr Richard Wright paymaster of his Mats fforces in the Lowe Contreys./././

Sr Wm Constable his Checques remitted by the 11: Warrant

Offer or harty Comendacons. Whereas Sr William Constable knight, haveing the Charge of 100 foote in his Mas Cawtionary Towne of Brill, hath ben absent from his said Charge by reason of his attendance upon his Maie being one of his Highnes Privey Chamber. fforasmuch as it is his Mas pleasure that he should receive his Entertaynement wthout Checque as yf he had ben present. These are therefore to require yow to cause payment to be made unto the said Sr William Constable of all such Checques, as are and shalbe certified unto yow under the hand of Sr William Waade knight MusterMaster, that hath ben imposed upon him and two men that attend him, from the first day of Aprill last untill the last day of this present Moneth of September. ffor wch this shalbe yor warrant. And so wee bid hartely farewell this Laste of September 1611

Yor Loveing freinds

G: Cant [George Abbott, Archbishop of Canterbury]

R. Salisbury [the Earl of Salisbury]

H. Northampton [the Earl of Northampton]

Gilb: Shrewsbury [the Earl of Shrewsbury]

Jul. Caesar [Sir Julius Caesar]

Tho: Parry [Sir Thomas Parry the younger]

Mr. Wright Paymaster

SIR WILLIAM CONSTABLE'S LETTER IN GOLD INK TO QUEEN ANNE (1611)

British Library:
Add. MS. 19, 401, f. 177.

This letter bears no date, but can be dated by context to the end of 1611, when Constable was languishing in the King's Bench prison for debt. The words underlined below are written in gold ink, which seems to have used suspended particles of real gold, which still glisters!

<u>To Her Moste Sacrede Maiesty</u>

<u>May it please your moste Sacred Matie</u>, not to be offended wth my presumption in that I am thus above pcedure importunate for your <u>Maiesties</u> most gratious favoure that in regarde of the spedie expedition for the srvice of his Royall <u>Matie of Denmarke, your most Excellent Matie</u>, wilbe pleased once againe to move the <u>kinges Matie</u>, my most Royall <u>Master</u> on my behalfe, that my most humble peticion may have some happie success Eyther uppon my surrender of the previe seale for 2000^L, to have 600^L, or so much mony Lent and my Pention detayned for the repayment of it, or yf my desertes have not merited so greate a good, that his <u>Maiestie</u> wilbe so gratiously pleased to graunt his Powerfull comaunde for the srvice of my boddye for 2 yeares, in wch tyme yf I discharge not my debtes I will yeeld my boddie to prsonn againe the Lik grace uppon Like occation hathe bene donn to some yett Living wthout retourninge to prsonn, as yf any doubte be maiede of it I shall prsente youre <u>Maties</u> vew wth sundrie prsidents in this kind. This shorte tyme for my prparation the Randevoz beinge at Calmer the Last of this munthe, and doubtinge my Leiutenant wth my Letters can not draw so many worthy valiant men into this action as my prsence in regard they are doubtfull of my Libertie; I most humbly on the knees of my harte doe begg <u>your Most Gratious and powerful mediation unto his Matie</u> for my liberty on any Condition, that I may be as reddie wth as brave a troope to goe to these royall wars as any other. For wch and all other your <u>Maties</u> goodness unto me, my prayers and faithfull dewtie shall ever be reddie, to pray for your everlastinge happiness

Your Maiesties
most humble subiect and srvante
WILLM CONSTABLE

[NOTES: On f. 10, r and v, of this volume, Add. Mss. 19,401, are comments on this document and on Constable, explaining that he had been granted a Privy Seal of £2,000 by King James, who could not pay it, and Constable is therefore trying to cash it in for £600, under the pressure of creditors. This letter is bound between documents of 1598 and 1603, but is definitely from 1611.]

LETTER OF SIR WILLIAM CONSTABLE TO ROBERT BERTIE, LORD WILLOUGHBY DE ERESBY (later first Earl of Lindsey) - (1611)

British Library: Add. MS. 37, 951, f. 1.

To the Right Honoble my Very Honoble frend the Lorde Willowbie, This.

Sr William Constable. 1611. Then Prisoner in the Kings Bench.

[A perfect seal is preserved on this document, with nine quarterings, at least one of which is itself quartered, at top left; the central arms are an eagle displayed, and at bottom right are arms, a lion rampant.]

Right Honoble,

the conveniency of this messinger doethe occation these Lines, wherein to testifie my respectfull Love I wryte yt wch is heare brewted, yt is, yt my Lorde of Southampton is privately spoken of to intende ye pcouringe of ye Prynces Care for these warrs of Denmarke: to prcure wch yf I may advise your Lp I would wishe your prsence aboute the Courte. Likewise you are Like to be prest for many Captns, howsoever good my Lo be carefull in ye Choise of all your officers yt are to Commande for it will furder ye reputations of your Command, & ye well managine of your Companyes will ad honor to our Nation, Capen Turner can gett no shippes to goe this winter for Denmarke, neither hathe he as yett herd from Sr Jos Selbie so as he will stop heare aboutes till ye Spring Unless Sr Jo. finde some Cource for to gett shippinge from Amsterdam. He & Capen Lichfeeld remembers ther humble service boethe beinge reddie to doe your Lp yt service yt is in ther power. I am so tied unto your Lp yt I trust to free myselfe to attend yow beinge asured yt by the termes end to bring my selfe wthin 300L execution wch neareness I trust will induce my Lo: of Rut. *[Roger Manners, fifth Earl of Rutland, who had been involved with Constable in the Essex Rebellion; see DNB]* to disburse 200L wch his Lp hath pmised divers tymes to doe for me, wch uppon this good occation, & your Lps honoble mediation, his Lp may be psuaded prsently to doe it. for ye manner for my freedom may not induce delaies. Good my Lo: add so much more favoures unto me as to Importune my Lo: of Rut: for this good unto me, by wch meanes I may have Liberty to attend your L^p in this service in what place your Lp may deame me worthy of wishinge all happiness to attend your L^p I am ever redie to obey your L^{ps} Commanndes & so Comannde

Your L^{ps}
Kinges bench 17th Novr: 1611.

trew frende & servante

WILLM CONSTABLE

Let me be thus much more trobles unto your Lp, as to advise yow to sende prsently for your Comission gettinge it to be for ye Generall Commannde of all Britishe forces yt shall come to those wars, wch place is not to be obtayned heare it beinge onely in ye K: of Denmarks gifte & yf yow think fitt to send aboute this business Captn Lichfeeld wilbe redie to goe uppon your directions. Capt Turner hath a kinsman to whom he hath spoken for ye pcuringe of shippinge

& victulinge of them for your troopes at such reasonable rates as your Lp will Like of, so I humbly kiss your Lps hande and am ever

Your L^ps

WILLM CONSTABLE

NOTES: It will be noted by the astute reader that this letter is written rather in the tone of an elder brother, with all its advice and directions, and so little excuse or apology for them. Lord Willoughby was actually about seven years younger than Constable, and the letter's tone indicates that between them there were many unspoken and assumed intimacies and confidences. Constable of course addresses Willoughby with all the forms due to his rank and position, but having "kissed his hand" and hoped that his lordship would "deem him worthy", Constable unmistakably lectures the young lord on how to be careful in selection of captains, and more or less instructs him to go see the Earl of Rutland straightaway to get him some money. All in the most courtly manner, certainly; but the tone is that of an older friend accustomed to steering and directing the young lord.

This letter indicates something of the involvement Constable and his friends had with the Earl of Southampton. Constable's friends were largely "comrades-in-arms" with an anti-James colouring to their attitudes. Clearly, the patronage of the Queen was useful in getting themselves fixed up with her brother King Christian IV of Denmark, as soldiers of fortune in that country's wars. But now the Earl of Southampton is trying to solicit the support of the young Prince Henry as well for their mission, for he would have more "clout" at home than his mother Queen Anne, whom James more or less ignored.

Sir John Selby was a relation by marriage of Constable, through the Widdringtons (Constable's grandmother was a Widdrington). He had been knighted in July, 1582, when he was described as "knight porter of Berwick"; the Selbys were prominent at Newcastle, and they evidently had shipping connections, and involvement in transportation of coal.

One cannot but admire the spirited nature of this letter, written as it is from the foul King's Bench prison in London, where Constable must have been in appalling conditions of stench and discomfort. He insouciantly dates his letter from "Kinges bench" as if it were a stately residence.

SIR WILLIAM CONSTABLE'S
MUSTER ROLL (1613)

British Library: Add. Roll. 66,608.

[In what appears to be an eighteenth century hand:] MUSTER ROLL of the Trained Bands.

Rolls of the Nobility, Gentry, & Parliament Men in Yorkshire.
Note of the Subsidy Men in Holden shire.

A Commission from the Ld Sheffield To Sr Wm. Constable to be a Captain of the East Riding Trained Bands. Dated 1613. with some other Things of no use.

[In a contemporary hand of 1613:]

A Muster Roule of Sr Will: Constables Company (13) 1613.

THIS MUSTER ROULE Indented made the xxvii day of September in the Eleaventh Yeare of the reigne of our soveraigne Lord James by the grace of God King of England ffrance and Ireland defender of the faith &c. and of Scotland the Seaven and ffortieth 1613 WITNESSYTHE that Srr Willm Constable Barronet, haith Receyved the day and Yeare above Wrytten of Sr Christofer Hildiard Sr Phillip Constable and Sr Henry Griffithe knights deputie Leiuetenants for the East ridding of the countie of Yorke nyntie and fyve able ffootemen, well Armed wth Common Armes and Certaine private parsons who are charged to fyend one hundred and ffyve able ffootemen well Armed, wth Private Armes, amounting in all to Two Hundred wch ar to serve under his Conductt and leading. By vertue of a Comission unto the said Sr Willm Constable directed from the Right Honorable Edmond Lord Sheffelde of the Noble order of the Garter knight and Lord Leiuetenant of thes parts and Lord President of his Maties Counsell established in the North bearing dayte the eighttenth day of May last past There severall names, and Sr names together wth the severall Townes wherein they were levied, and the sevrll Armor and Weapons wherewth they must serve hereafter followeth./

Sweapontack de dickering / Private / Hunmanby Comon / Private Bridlington du Rey Com

[Under the four headings above are given four separate columns of names, with weapons indicated, and names of towns from which the men come; these are here omitted but with the observation that the total number of muskets is 57 and the total number of callevers is 42, that 14 men were from Flamborough (none were Constables), and there is one Constable listed, at the bottom of the fourth column, a Private Robert Constable, having a corslett, and being of T.....ing du Orton.]

CHR: HILDIARD PHILLIPP CONSTABLE HENRIE GRIFFITHE In Witnesse Whereof the
    pties above named to these muster Rowls interchangeably have set their hands and seales the day and yeare above written.

LETTER OF SIR WILLIAM CONSTABLE TO HIS BROTHER-IN-LAW SIR FERDINANDO FAIRFAX (1627)

British Library: Add. MS. 18,979, ff. 7-8b.

Sr Willm Constable July the sixth
[*an excellent impression of a seal is preserved*]

To his assured goodbrother Sr Ferdinando fairfax knight at Yorke these/

Sr

I have a very fitt opportunity by this bearer, but can yet give you litle accompt how things goe wth us. save only yt wee arrived here London (very well I thank God) on tuesday morning/ & entered our appearance wth ye Clerk of ye councell yt day. ye next day wee attended, & only Sr Beuchamp St John was called & so comitted, who had been attending there before, & wee now remain in ye same state wth those who have attended some of them this six months. but it is thought yt ye Councell will not continue to sitt here longer then ye end of ye next weeke So yt it is like somthing will be said to us before yt tyme. perhaps to morrow, being a councell day/ since some of ye councell take notice of our attending. Mr Chan: of ye Duchy coming from ye councell, ye last day was pleased to entertaun some discourse wth us, & to read a longe lecture to us of our errour in not hearkening to his moderate advise in ye parliamt.

There is speech every day of a general confining of all those yt are comitted, but as yett only some few who you have heard of, yt by reason of sicknesse have made suit for it, are confined, there are many of ye other (especially all those yt are in ye fleet) yt have have [sic] a resolution not to accept of a confinemt, in yt maner as it is tendered. yt is to say, not except there warrant doe leave them as prisoners wth ye sheriffs, least by yt means they should barr themselves of ye benefitt of a heabeas [sic] corpus, wch it is said cannot be denied them ye nextt tearm, or might have been ye last tearm of it had been demanded. by yt means they looke to have a iudiciall triall in ye kings bench whether they have comitted any offence or no.

I shall shortly lett yow know more. This bearer Sr W: Hildyard can lett you know all ye newes yt is. there is nothing yett known of our great fleet he can tell you of my Ld of Canterburies confinemt, & of my Ld Peeters sonn & his busines wch might have proved a worse cause but may perhaps find a more favourable interpretation then ours. The prisons are ye only merry places in ye town & ye [*"difference of" is crossed out here*] air, as ye matter is now used is one & ye same to all. So God send us a a [sic] good meeting.

Whiteheart in ye strand   your WM: CONSTABLE
July 19th

LETTER TO SIR
WILLIAM CONSTABLE, BART
FROM SIR
MATTHEW BOYNTON, BART.
(1642)

Public Record Office: S.P. 16/ 491/ 4
Calendared, CSPD 1641-3, p. 334.

4° Junij . 1642. Sr Math: Boynton to Sr
Wm. Constable concerneinge the
Yorksheir Peticion

To my much honored friende, Sr William Constable Baronett
prsent this./

Sr
on ffryday last we attended his matie upon his summons att Huworth Moore neare York; where theire was the greatest appeerance of People that ever I saw in this County, and therfor tho you finde not manie handes subscrib'd to these Petitions which, by direction of the gentlemen I have herewithall sent you, yett itt is not that we could not have had manie thousands more, but by reason of the Peoples suddaine departure (upon a mistake) whilst we expected that they had followed us into the Towne, so that we were forced to take, onelie those few that were left:

The gentlemen desire you would prsent these Petitions with the names subscribed, to both the houses of Parlament: thus prsenting my srvice to you and my lady I rest

Yorke June 4th Your ev^r assured friend
1642.   to serve you.

                MATT BOYNTON

this bundle tho itt be nott fixed to the Petitions yett itt ptaines to the subscriptions which are anexed to them. if itt be conceyved needefull we shall sense upp handes enough./

NOTES: Unfortunately, Sir Matthew Boynton, Bart., has no entry in the DNB. It was he who had planned to emigrate to Connecticut with Constable in 1635 (discussed in main text). He was later to be elected a recruiter MP for Scarborough, but died before Pride's Purge, in March, 1647. He had sat in Parliament in the 1620s. His baronetcy, Boynton of Barmston, Yorkshire, was created in 1618, and became extinct only in 1966, though collateral branches survive.

It is noteable that Sir William Constable was looked upon by all as the best person to present the petition from the great gathering at Haworth Moor to the Houses of Parliament. He was evidently conceived of as the chief opposition M.P. from Yorkshire to remain in London during this period. There is further discussion of the Haworth Moor rendezvous in the main text under Sir John Bourchier's early career.

THE MOUNTING BOOK OF THE PARLIAMENTARY ARMY (1642)

Public Record Office: S.P. 28/143/ long, thin book bound in vellum (no number for the item); faintly discernible on the cover in faded ink are the words "Receipts and Payments", but the rest has faded too much to be read.

Extracts relating to regicides:

(NOTE: This booklet is the original, central "mounting book" of the Parliamentary Army when first formed. As such, it provides unique data regarding the dates of first commissions of countless prominent Parliamentary supporters, the number of men they had, and what their first service was. The book was kept by Captain Francis Vernon, acting as the assistant to Sir Gilbert Gerard, Bart., who in July, 1642, was appointed by the House of Commons to be Treasurer of the Army. The first payments tend to be for what was called "mounting money", which equipped troops of horse with their saddles, arms, and other necessaries. For our purposes here, the Mounting Book has been surveyed only so far as folio 37 verso, though it is very much longer. There is no doubt that this invaluable source of information should be published in its entirety, as a basic reference work for historians. I have made a beginning at transcribing and annotating it, and hope in the future to complete the task and find a publisher for it.)

f. 5 verso: August 6, 1642. Pd my Lord Grey of Grooby for advance of on half monthes pay of a troop of horse of 60 harquebusiers, £172/ 18/ 0.

f. 6 verso: August 10, 1642. Pd Capt. John Alured for mounting himself & his officers being Capt of a troope of horse, £354/ 0/ 0.

f. 7 verso: August 11, 1642. Pd Mr Henry Martine for the charge of raisinge 2000 menn whereof on thousand for Hull, £2000/ 0/ 0.
(Lord Grey of Groby paid another £42 and £104/ 7.)

f. 8 recto: August 11, 1642. Pd Capt Adrian Scroop Capt of a troop of horse for providing him selfe & his officers wth horses armes and other necessaries, £280/ 0/ 0.

f. 9 verso: August 13, 1642. (Lord Grey of Groby paid another £174/ 13 and £30.)

f. 10 verso: August 16, 1642. Pd Captaine Henry Ireton for mounting 3 corporalls - 42 - more for 2 trumpeters 1 farier & 1 sadler -32, £74/ 0/ 0. (Also paid £30 for scarfs for his troop.)

f. 11 recto: August 18, 1642. Pd Sr Wm Constable Collonell of a regiment of 1200 men for on months entertainment for himself and his officers & levy monie for his men, £1244/ 16/ 00.

f. 11 verso: August 19, 1642. Pd Captaine Oliver Cromwell capt of a troope of horse for mounting himself and his officers, £280/ 0/ 0.

[It is interesting to note that Henry Ireton and Oliver Cromwell are entered as captains of horse within three days of each other, and that Ireton was actually earlier than Cromwell in entering upon active commission and service.]

f. 13 verso: August 24, 1642. Pd Captaine Owen Rowe & Capt Bradlye for repairinge of Armes,
£500/ 0/ 0.

Pd Captaine John Lilburne for a monthes pay of his companie of 97 menn in the regiment of my lord Brooke ... he is present, £90/ 10/ 8.

[This is included here because he was the younger brother of the regicide Robert Lilburne, and entered military service first, as Captain of Foot.]

f. 15 verso: August 27, 1642. (Captain Adrian Scrope paid twice more on this date.)

August 29, 1642. Pd Capt Valentine Walton for mounting himself & Officers, £280/ 0/ 0.

f. 16 recto: August 30, 1642. Pd to Mr Henry Martine by way of imprest for the service of Hull,
£70/ 0/ 0.

f. 17 recto: September 1, 1642. Pd Captaine Adrian Scroope for 63 great saddles and bitts for his troope at 50s each sadle & bitt, £157/ 10/ 0.

[Firth was unaware of the prices in this book, of course. In estimating the cost of saddles, he only had access to later information, when saddles had become much cheaper. In *Cromwell's Army*, p. 242, he mentions that in 1645 saddles for the New Model Army were either 16s or 16s, 6d. each, and "dragoon saddles" were far cheaper. As the war progressed and more saddles were made, the price of saddles thus dropped over the course of only three years by three and a half times.]

f. 20 recto: September 5, 1642. Pd Collonell Sr Wm Constable for on mo pay and entertainmt of the officers of his regt from the 27 Augt, £542/ 16/ 0.

[Note this dates the active service of Sir William Constable to July 27th at least, since Constable had already been paid a previous month's pay on August 18th, which must have covered a month's service from July 27 to August 27.]

f. 20 verso: September 5, 1642. Capt George Austin [a captain of horse, paid on this date, but slain near Worcester by October 7th, just a month later, - see f. 28 recto; it is thought that this is the George Austin who was the first husband of the second wife of the regicide, Valentine Wauton.]

f. 21 recto: September 6, 1642. Pd Capt. Gray for 1 m°. pay of his comp of 70 sol. in Sr Wm Constables regt from the 29 Augt, £65/ 6/ 0.

[This demonstrates that Constable's was a Foot Regiment, since the term "company" was used only of foot; since we know from the entry on August 18 that Constable's Regiment had 1200 men, this indicates that from the very commencement of the Civil War foot regiments were being formed in the traditional proportions of 1200 men rather than 1000. It is peculiar that Gray's Company numbered only seventy men; this would indicate that there were a larger number of companies and captains in Constable's regiment than one would have been inclined to expect. Possibly the need to recruit rapidly meant that Constable made up his complement of 1200 from a multiplicity of partially-formed companies. If so, as the companies filled up he may have hived some off to help form additional regiments. This process might help explain some of the puzzling aspects of formation of regiments.]

f. 22 recto: September 7, 1642. Pd Collonel Henry Martin for levinge 1200 men to serve in his regt., £600/ 0/ 0. [By this time Mr. Henry Marten has become Colonel Henry Marten.]

f. 24 recto: September 10, 1642. Pd Captaine Adrian Scroope for an arreer of pay due to himself & officers from the 30 of Julie inclusive to the 25 Augt exclusive being 26 dayes, £129/ 7/ 0.

[Note that this dates Scrope's active service as Captain of Horse from July 30, whereas his first entry in the Mounting Book was August 11. This evidence indicates that the Mounting Book records date of first payment rather than date of first service, although they were not far apart.]

f. 25 recto: September 27, 1642. Pd my Lord Grey for pay of his officers & troops to the last 7bre [*a most curious way of writing September by the sound, 'sept' being represented by the number seven*], £191/ 12s. & also for on ½ mo pay for his troop to begin the 1 8bre [*again we see here October written with 'oct' represented by the number eight*] 174.13 in all £365/ 14/ 0.

f. _ 25 verso: September 29, 1642. Pd Capt. Henry Ireton for intertainmt for himself and other Officers of his troop for 2 whole monthes and 7 days endinge the 1 8bre next, £313/ 8/ 6.

[Note that this dates his active service to at least August 1st, whereas he first appears in the Mounting Book on August 16th.]

f. 25 verso: September 29, 1642. Pd Wm. Purfroy Leifft Collonel of a regimt of ffoot to be raised in this service after the rate of 20s p diem from the 30 Julie to the 1 8bre being 2 mo 7 dayes, £63/ 0/ 0. [Note that this dates William Purefoy's active service from July 30th, two months prior to his first recorded payment in the Mounting Book.]

f. 26 recto: October 1, 1642. Pd Capt Henry Ireton for on mo paye for his troope of 60 harquebs by way of imprest, £349/ 6/ 0.

[Note that Ireton's troops were armed not with pistols but with harquebuses at this early stage, though they may of course have carried a pair of pistols each as well. Later in the Civil War, the short rifles were dispensed with.]

f. 27 verso: October 4, 1642. Pd Capt Valentine Walton [Wauton] for his troop as above (money due from October 1), £174/ 13/ 0.

f. 28 verso: October 8, 1642. Pd Captaine Richard Ingoldsbye for 29 dayes paye of 100 soldrs in Coll Hambdns regt. to end ye 14 8bre, £96/ 13/ 4.

[Note that this dates Ingoldsby's active service to at least September 14th, and that he was a Captain under Colonel John Hampden possibly even earlier.]

[I ceased to extract the regicide listings after f. 31 due to the magnitude of the task. However, regicides listed between ff. 31 and 37 are: Lord Grey of Groby, ff. 31 r, 33v, 36r; Adrian Scrope, ff. 32v, 35v; Sir William Constable, ff. 32v, 35v, 37r; Valentine Wauton, f. 33 r; Henry Ireton, ff. 33 v, 35r; Oliver Cromwell, f . 34v; William Purefoy, f . 37v. After f. 37 I ceased noting them. As mentioned earlier, the Mounting Book needs to be transcribed and published in its entirety, as it is the foundation document for the formation of the Parliamentary Army. No previous historian has been aware of its existence, as it was one of my own unexpected and happy discoveries in the Public Record Office.]

CHAPTER THREE, PART TWO

The Early Careers Of The Regicides

In Part One of this chapter, we saw an account of the early career of Sir John Danvers. Much more remains to be said about Sir John Danvers later, and more documents concerning him are transcribed also in appendices of other chapters. There is for instance an account of his deep interest in the law, and his efforts for legal reform, to be found in the chapter 'The Regicides and the Law'. Also in Part One we found an account of the life of Sir William Constable, Bart. Those two men were the two 'courtier regicides', whose involvements with the Court had been intimate, so that the stories of how they turned against the monarchy are case studies in the extremes of political disillusion with the Court, a tendency which Constable had shown clearly in his youth when he took part in the Essex Rebellion against Queen Elizabeth I in 1601.

The early careers of the professional lawyers amongst the regicides are not considered here, but are described at length in the chapter 'The Regicides and the Law', where we discover that a surprising number of the regicides were barristers. (And becoming a barrister then required seven years' study in the Common Law at one of the Inns of Court.) In that chapter also, the mystery of Oliver Cromwell's 'background in the law' is explained for the first time.

Here we survey the early careers of several other regicides who are of particular interest or importance. In Part One I described how I had found the Mounting Book of the Parliamentary Army, a long thin manuscript accounts book bound in vellum, dating from 1642 and created by Captain Francis Vernon, acting as assistant to Sir Gilbert Gerard, Bart., who in July, 1642, was appointed by the House of Commons to be Treasurer of the Army. Numerous early extracts from this book, extending as far as folio 37, were transcribed by me and included in the Appendix to Part One. Those extracts record all mentions of regicides up to that point, giving their original commissioned military ranks, the dates of those commissions, and how much they and their soldiers were paid. No previous historian had ever known of the book, which is the fundamental record of the commencements of the military careers of numerous regicides. There is no doubt that this entire book, being such a fundamental source of reference, should be published, and although I had once thought of undertaking that project, the massed opposition from what one could perhaps call 'the seventeenth century historians' Establishment' accomplished its aim of preventing me from upsetting any more apple carts and exposing any more inadequacies and errors in the field. It is only now that I reveal the existence of the crucial Mounting Book.

Apart from Constable, the regicides mentioned in the first 37 folios of the Mounting Book of the Parliamentary Army are: John Alured, Oliver Cromwell, Lord Grey of Groby, Henry Ireton, Richard Ingoldsby, Henry Marten, William Purefoy, Owen Rowe, Adrian Scrope, John Venn (see below), and Valentine Wauton. All of these regicides held the rank of Captain or higher by the autumn of 1642 at the latest. Details are found in the transcribed sections just mentioned.

One considerable surprise in the Mounting Book is what it reveals about the early martial exploits of Henry Marten, who is not normally thought of as having been at any time a soldier. (It has been conventional to think that any mention in documents or contemporary publications of a Colonel Martin or Marten must refer to the later Colonel Francis Martin/Martyn, who appears to have been of no relation to Henry Marten.) However, the Mounting Book reveals that Henry Marten had personally raised 2000 men for the defence of Hull by August 1, 1642, and then by September 7th, had raised another 1200 men to serve as his own regiment with himself as Colonel. Raising 3200 men in two months is an incredible achievement, and may be the largest such effort of its kind at that stage of affairs. It shows, as if any historian were ever in any doubt, just how keen Marten was to oppose the monarchy. But here he was not just speaking against the King, he wanted personally to do battle against him, and had raised thousands of soldiers and armed them to do just that. In fact, since the Mounting Book begins in July, to have raised 2000 men by August 1, Marten must have accomplished this fantastic task in only two or three weeks.

But Marten's martial efforts go back in time even earlier. I have found an uncalendared and hitherto apparently unknown document (of which no trace remains in the State Papers) amongst the personal papers of Henry Marten which shows that on July 18, 1642, Marten was specially entrusted by the Committee of Safety with paying money to a ship's captain who brought letters from Hull. It bears the signatures of John Pym, John Hampden, Nathaniel Fiennes, Anthony Nicholl, Denzil Holles and Lord Say and Sele (father of Nathaniel Fiennes). It is transcribed in the Appendix to this Part Two. This document shows clearly that Marten had been authorised to have a special role in dealing with the crisis at Hull, under the authority of the Committee of Safety, and he was acting (in this as in the raising of troops) as a kind of active agent for the Committee of Safety in actually carrying out the Committee's most important military business at the very beginning of the Civil War.

While on the subject of Hull, which was such a flashpoint for conflict at the beginning of the Civil War due to its being the location of one of the three main magazines of arms and ammunition in England (the others being in the Tower of London and at Portsmouth),[1] it would seem to be appropriate to call attention to a fascinating document I have discovered in the Nalson MSS. at Oxford. It is a pathetic and moving letter written by the regicide Peregrine Pelham to Bulstrode Whitelocke a few days before his death pleading for financial help from Parliament. The document is transcribed in full in the Appendix. In it, Pelham mentions as his special friends a number of prominent MPs including the regicides Henry Marten and John Lisle. But for our purposes here, there is particular interest in the retrospective account which Pelham gives of his activities at Hull in the summer of 1642.

Pelham claims: 'That I kept the King out of Hull when he came in pson (although I had not such Instructions from the house) – where was a very great magazin in which I suppose I saved the State above 100,000ˡ [£100,000] ... That I had command of the Towns-Men both within the towne and without, that I raised them to salle [sally] out where they beat the Earle of Newcastle's forces, I went wth them to the Ile of Exholme [Axholme], and Gainsborough, both wch were then taken in I never tooke any peny pay, but on the contrary gave to divers both meat and mony, and my wine Sellers [cellars] were opene upon all occasions.' Pelham, who was rich before the War, had advanced thousands of pounds to the Parliamentary cause and never received any repayment, or received any payment for his years of public service other than a modest salary as MP from the town of Hull, which he represented in Parliament. But interesting as that is, what is more important is the new account we now have of who really rallied Hull and saved it for the Parliament in July, 1642. I know of no other record of this information.

A close reading of *The Troubles of England* by the royalist Dr. John Bates suggests awareness of what really happened in Hull at that moment, and which fits with what Pelham said:

'(Those opposed to the King thought that) the King in his progress to the North, intended to seize the Town and well-provided Magazine of Hull, which might be of great consequence in carrying on the War.

— 333 —

'That they might prevent this, the Faction of their own head, without any authority from both Houses, give the government of the place to Sir John Hotham, which he instantly secured with a Garrison and the assistance of some Towns-Men.'[2]

And apparently the most important of those 'Towns-Men' was Peregrine Pelham. He received his proper attention from Basil N. Reckitt in his book about Hull in the Civil War, who informs us that Pelham lived 'on the north side of Rottenhering Staith in the High Street'.[3] Reckitt also confirms that it was at a crucial meeting held between Hotham and Pelham, attended by some Aldermen, that the decision was taken not to admit the King to Hull.[4] And he specifically says of him:

'Peregrine Pelham … had played a considerable part in stiffening the attitude of the Corporation [of Hull] against the King and who had advised Hotham against his admission in April 1642, was ever active both at Hull and Westminster. He was Mayor in 1650 and was one of those who signed Charles's death warrant, but death overtook him before his year of office was completed. … At the Restoration his estate was confiscated and his widow was at one time the recipient of the bounty of the Hull Corporation.'[5]

This reveals that as he lay dying and wrote the desperate letter to Bulstrode Whitlocke, he was the Mayor of Hull, but could not bring himself to request any financial assistance from his home town, which as the Mayor he could readily have done. Certainly what Reckitt tells us fully confirms Pelham's account of his role in saving Hull. And it also gives us the sad news that his widow was left penniless and had to turn to the Corporation of Hull for some financial assistance in order to survive the loss of her home and means of subsistence after 1660.

I have found another document offering testimony for another regicide who saved a city in 1642. In this case it was William Purefoy, and the city he saved by his prompt and efficient action was Coventry. The document is transcribed for the Appendix. It shows that in the summer of 1642, Purefoy rushed to Coventry, raised forces, borrowed money on his own credit to pay and arm them, and saved the city. The certifying parties are the House of Commons!

There are also other new documents giving traces of activity at the beginning of the Civil War by some other regicides. In the Appendix I have transcribed a note written by Lord Grey of Groby in late 1642 which shows that the future regicide Peter Temple (a neighbour of Lord Grey of Groby in Leicestershire), years before becoming a recruiter MP, was acting as an agent of Grey of Groby in financial matters concerned with Leicestershire militia duties. Temple was a Colonel in the Leicestershire Militia, and though we do not know the date of his commission, he was probably already a colonel by the time of this note. Temple took delivery of money from the Treasurer of the Army at London on Grey of Groby's behalf at this time. As we saw from the extracts from the Mounting Book transcribed in Part One's Appendix, Lord Grey of Groby was the first regicide listed in it, having received his initial funds for a troop of horse on August 6, 1642, and further funds on August 13 and September 27. On January 16, 1642/3, Lord Grey of Groby was appointed by Parliament to be Major General of the army to be raised for the Association of Leicestershire, Derbyshire, Nottinghamshire, Rutland, Northamptonshire, Buckinghamshire, Bedfordshire, and Huntingdonshire, under the Earl of Essex, the Lord General.[6]

The regicide Sir Michael Livesey seems to have been a Kent militia colonel as early as August, 1642, as he was by then in command of some captains of horse. A remarkable letter of September 1, 1642, from the royalist Arminian divine, Dr. Thomas Paske, is transcribed for the Appendix. In his letter, Paske writes a commendatory description and praise of Livesey, remarking upon his 'curteous usadge'! Livesey was praised by Paske for having made strenuous efforts to control the troopers under him from offering any affront either to Paske or to Canterbury Cathedral ('Christ's Church at Canterbury', as he calls it, by its old name). Livesey actually offered protection to Paske in the carrying out of his high church religious observances, which must have been highly offensive to Livesey's personal religious principles as well as those of his junior officers. This is an extraordinary example of magnanimity and humanity on the part of a regicide who has generally been maligned and traduced by historians, and who received criticism even during his own lifetime (from royalists) for being just the opposite, namely a ruthless and violent person. Also in the Appendix I have transcribed a letter from Livesey to Speaker Lenthall of February 25, 1642/3, showing how he had taken upon himself the responsibility of seizing Sir William Sheffield whom he viewed with considerable suspicion as being about to depart for Holland. Livesey was specially commended for his vigilance by the House of Commons (see notes to the document).

The incident at Canterbury Cathedral gives us a good example of how truth could be distorted at that time for partisan political purposes. We may take the primary source material of Dr. Paske's letter of September 1 as the accurate account, especially as coming from a passionate royalist! But the incident was drastically misrepresented for propaganda purposes in the royalist publication *Mercurius Rusticus*. It printed a different letter from Dr. Paske, also sent to the Earl of Holland two days earlier, on August 30.[7] In that letter, the outrages (which were considerable) committed by the troops in the church are made to seem the result of orders from Livesey, although Dr. Paske does mention that they occurred after Livesey left the premises. The impression given by that letter is that Livesey was the villain of the event. And it was from this misreported incident that Livesey was dogged for the rest of his career with the reputation for being an unscrupulous, ruthless, and dastardly person who smashes up holy precincts. Dr. Paske's second letter of September 1, transcribed in full in the Appendix, completely exculpates Livesey from any blame. Livesey had only demanded the keys to the church in order to have his men remove arms and gunpowder which were stored there. As Paske makes abundantly clear, Livesey was absolutely horrified at the violent rioting of his men inside the church, and Paske accepted his abject apologies. The earlier version, which was publicly circulated, thus was what today is called 'fake news'. I think we can see who was responsible for this. Both letters were sent to the Earl of Holland. The one excusing Livesey from blame was held back, was never published, and survives in the House of Lords archives, where I found it. The earlier letter is not there, having evidently been given to the *Mercurius Rusticus* people by the Earl of Holland, who preferred to circulate the letter blaming Livesey and to hold back the one excusing him. They say that 'all is fair in love and war', and the Earl of Holland was apparently happy to have any excuse to attack an adversary in the war which had begun. To slander an enemy was not slander, to a partisan such as the Earl of Holland. The Earl had a reputation as an extremely slippery character. He changed sides twice during the Civil War. No one trusted him. It is hardly to be wondered at that the House of Commons voted for him to be beheaded for treason, and for helping to start the second Civil War of 1648, and that he lost his head only five weeks after the King.

During the crucial events of July, 1642, the regicide Edmund Ludlow's brother, Robert Ludlow, was very active. In a document of July 27, 1642, we read:

'Dr. Bastwick, Sir Henry Ludlow's son, and two other famous firebrands of this State … were … discovered, lad fast, and … (put in) York Castle …'[8]

Parliament ordered Bastwick, Robert Ludlow, and 'Mr. Rawlyns' released.[9]

As remarked in Chapter Two, Robert Ludlow was never released from prison by the royalists but died the next year aged only 22. Robert Ludlow was a Captain and was described as 'a stout man with whom the King is displeased.'[10] In May, 1642, the regicide's father, Sir Henry Ludlow, MP, had made extremely bold remarks against the King and was called to account by the Speaker of the House for his audacity.[11]

Considerations of space make it impossible for us to consider the early careers of any other regicides in the lengthy manner assigned to Constable and Danvers, which are given in Part One. Those two regicides were special cases; their long histories of attempted accommodation to the Court, and their drastic disillusionment with it, as well as their connection with the Essex Rebellion, made it worthwhile to treat of their early careers in a leisurely fashion. With those that remain, we can only take glimpses of some of the more interesting. I have far more information in my files than I can possibly fit into this work. It seems to make sense to concentrate on those with a history of opposition to or grievances against the Court, or alternately, the Church. (However, the story of the regicide John Blakiston's struggles with savage religious persecution by the Court of High Commission is reserved for the later chapter 'The Regicides and Religion'.)

One of the most passionate and intense opponents of the orthodox high church known as Arminianism was the future regicide, Anthony Stapley, of Sussex. He staged a truly remarkable public 'scene' in late 1639, putting himself at grave risk. Sitting as a JP at quarter sessions for Michaelmas, 1639, Stapley publicly declared to all those present that 'the altering of the Communion Tables altarwise, was an Innovation detracting from Gods Glory'. This is in the report sent to Archbishop Laud's Chaplain by Edward Burton, transcribed in full in the Appendix to this chapter. Stapley's use of his position as a Justice of the Peace to make a public declamation against Laud's religious policies (which had nothing whatever to do with the Quarter Sessions!) was an ingenious and dangerous form of open protest, in those long dark days of the eleven years when there was no Parliament. It is possible that Stapley devised this means of protest because, taking place as it did within the proceedings of Quarter Sessions, there would seem to have been no possible way Stapley's action could be considered answerable to any ecclesiastical court. But it was a drastic way of throwing down the gauntlet to the civil authorities. Being untouchable by the strict and vengeful ecclesiastical courts, would Stapley be prosecuted in Star Chamber, or what? Legal advice had probably been taken in advance, which may have assured Stapley that a technical defence could be prolonged indefinitely in a civil court. Stapley would force an illegal act of prerogative suppression from the King himself. Or otherwise escape punishment, – and, in fact, he escaped!

Fletcher has rightly said of the incident: 'Stapley was on delicate ground. He had no authority to interfere in a matter of ecclesiastical jurisdiction. His colleague William White, indeed, at once questioned "what he meant to meddle with those businesses ther, which the Bench had nothing to doe withall." ... In February, 1641, the radical Puritans, led by the knights of the shire Sir Thomas Pelham and Anthony Stapley, presented a root and branch petition to parliament in the name of the county.'[12]

In the document in the Appendix, Burton apprehensively observes in 1639 that 'Mr Staply and Mr Rivers have a strong party in the Towne, and it is much feared they will be chosen Burgesses for the Town of Lewes: God forbid the greater part of a Parliament should be of their stampe: if soe, Lord have mercy upon our Church'. – Accurate prophecy! Stapley and Jacob Rivers did indeed get into the Short Parliament (Rivers for Lewes and Stapley as Knight of the Shire), and Stapley was returned again as Knight of the Shire for the Long Parliament. And Stapley's career was to be all that royalists could have feared.

This seems a suitable place to give a list of those future regicides who were elected to the Short Parliament of 1640:[13]

John Alured
Miles Corbet
Oliver Cromwell
Sir John Danvers
John Lisle[14]
Henry Marten
William Purefoy
Anthony Stapley

That is a total of only eight future regicides. Also elected were three fathers of future regicides, shown in the same list published by Rushworth:

Sir Henry Marten (father of Henry Marten)
Sir Thomas Hutchinson (father of John Hutchinson)
John Wogan the Elder (father of Thomas Wogan)

The mention of Sir Henry Marten, father of Henry the regicide, offers the occasion to mention a curious letter from him dating from 1613, which I have transcribed for the Appendix. In it, we see that Sir Henry was on no terms of unease concerning the Archbishop of Canterbury of that day, who was, of course, pre-Laudian. The document is a curiosity and no great significance need be attached to it; I have transcribed it largely due to its very unusual provenance.

Many of the regicides can be viewed as carrying on family traditions of opposing the Court. Several of the fathers, uncles, or brothers of the regicides opposed the Court before the Civil War. These relatives could therefore be said, in a sense, to constitute the regicides' 'early careers' in a vicarious manner. Something of this has already been remarked upon in Chapter Two. Under James Temple, for instance, we observed the difficulties his father, Sir Alexander Temple, had had with the Court. The continuity was all the stronger in that Sir Alexander's vicissitudes over Tilbury Fort were inherited by his son, who was himself to become commander of Tilbury Fort during the Civil War. It is important to note that sometime prior to 1614, Sir Alexander Temple appeared on a ten page list of 'Gentlemen of Kent', where it was noted that his estate at Newlands, St. Mary Hoo, in Kent, alone was valued at £800 a year, and that took no account of his other sizeable estate across the river in Essex.[15] The sum of £800 per annum prior to 1614 was a very large sum indeed. Sir Alexander was thus an extremely wealthy man before all his troubles with the Stuart Court deprived him of his wealth.

On April 15, 1622, James Temple, aged only 16 years, was authorised to go on a Grand Tour of Europe. He was granted a pass by the Privy Council 'to travaile for three yeares and to take with him one servant and provisions, not prohibited, with proviso not to goe to Rome'.[16] Certainly this shows an intrepid spirit, for a boy of 16 wanting to go wandering around Europe for three years essentially on his own, accompanied only by a single servant. When Sir John Danvers went on his tour of Europe as a young man, as we saw in Part One of this chapter, he went with a personal friend as his companion. James's trip also could only have been possible because his family were significantly wealthy at that time. And James was only the second son, not even the family's prospective heir.

We need to take seriously the implications of this desire to enter 'the big wide world' on his own at sixteen. I say that because I underwent the same process. I also entered 'the big wide world' on my own at sixteen. That was how old I was when I entered a large Ivy League university and became the youngest person on campus, knowing no one at all, without a single friend, contact, or any family support either. As someone who also 'entered the world alone at 16' I strongly urge the psychological importance of the same thing about James Temple in terms of explaining his later career and the strength of personal independence which he displayed, having been trained up in self-reliance. On a lighter note, I can say it would have been handy for myself to 'have a servant', not to mention ample funding. (Alas, I have to add: haha.)

Since several of the regicides were significantly cosmopolitan, I think we should make a special point of considering that. Sir John Danvers and James Temple spent years touring Europe, Thomas Chaloner spent years in the Middle East, Richard Deane had seen many lands (or at least ports) as a naval officer, Augustine Garland evidently had a French grandmother, Sir William Constable and his wife spent a few years in the Netherlands as religious exiles during the Laud period, and most remarkable of all, Gregory Clement had spent most of his youth in Spain and Portugal, and subsequently spent seven years in India. That is already seven regicides, more than ten percent of their number, who were very far indeed from being 'local yokels' and whose mental horizons stretched far beyond Little England. And in saying this, I am not mentioning the intensive experience of Ireland which so many more of the regicides had gone through, some of them such as Henry Ireton even perishing there later. And we must not forget that some of the regicides were Welsh.

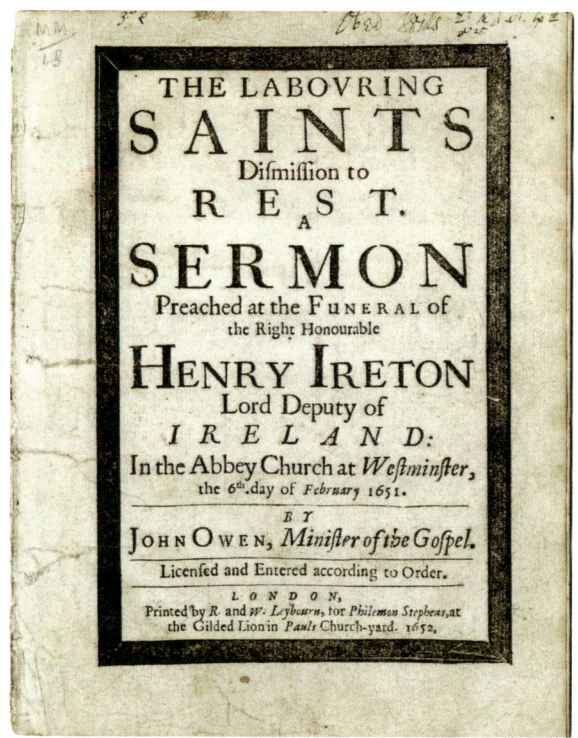

The single sheet funeral notice of Henry Ireton, who died in Ireland and was subsequently interred in Westminster Abbey. This is a scan of the original sheet, from the collection of the author. The printers were Robert and William Leybourn. William Leybourn was a key polymath Early Modern scientist, who was an astronomer, sundial maker, mathematician, geometer, and expert on trigonometry and surveying. His many books are classics of the history of science and of mathematics. It is possible that this is the only copy of Ireton's funeral notice to survive.

THE EARLY CAREERS OF THE REGICIDES

But to return to the early life of James Temple, while we are on the subject. Here is an extract from a 17th century map showing the location near Chadwell/ Shadwell in Essex (the area which is today called Thurrock) of Longhouse, one of Sir Alexander Temple's homes, which James Temple made his own home for some time. In London he used his chambers at Lincolns Inn as his home. From there, he only had to walk a few minutes to the other side of Lincolns Inn Fields where his first cousin Sir Peter Temple, Bart., lived (on the west side of that square), to have chats with his near relatives.

An interesting letter from Sir Alexander Temple to the Duke of Buckingham, dated January 18, 1626/7, survives, in which Temple makes the telling remarks, in pleading for pay for the gunners at Tilbury whom he is financing out of his own pocket:

'I will not admit the least thought yt any seeming errors of mine in Parliamt shall so farr occasion your Lo:shipps displeasure against mee, that either his Mayes service in this dangerous tyme, or those poore wretches [the soldiers of Tilbury Fort] having nothing but from hand to mouth, shall suffer for them, but that your Grace will treade under your foote all thoughts of revenge.'[17]

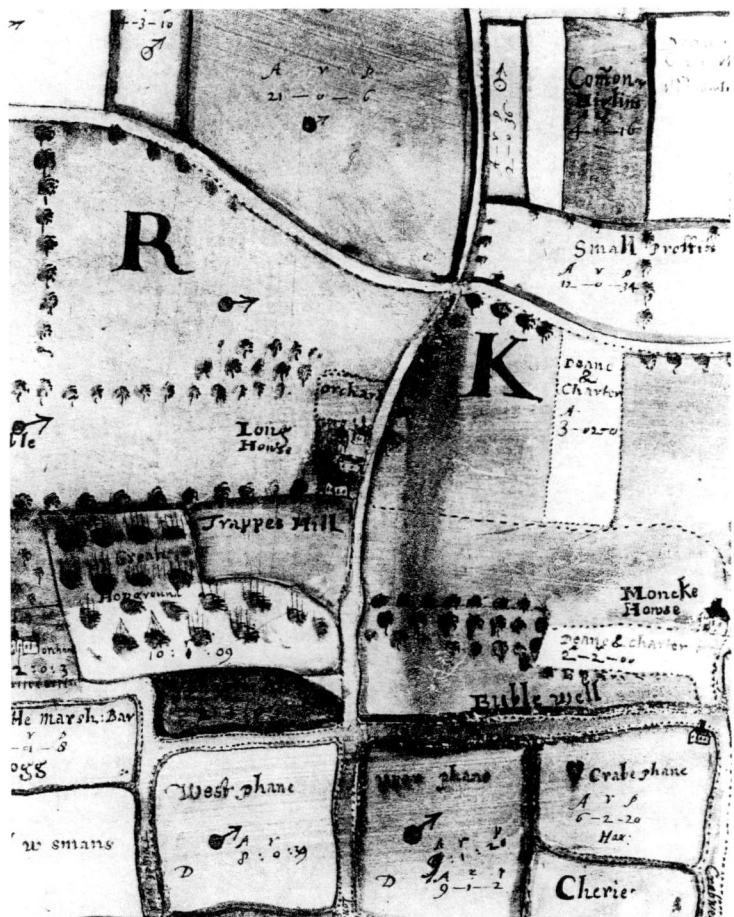

Longhouse is shown near the centre of the map, with an orchard behind it. It seems to consist of a cluster of houses in addition to the main building, which was a traditional old 'long house', a type of house which is what the name says, very long. Longhouse was the family residence used when supervising Tilbury Fort on the Thames, a fort which was within perhaps ten minutes' riding distance of the house.

It is to be noted that Temple's letter, so lacking in any form of grovelling as to be untactful, admits only to *seeming* errors in Parliament. He had obviously spoken out boldly against Buckingham in the House, and then wrote him this letter which was more a challenge than a plea; what he was seen to be saying to Buckingham in the letter was in effect: Are you such a despicable fellow as I think you are, willing to sacrifice the nation's safety to your own spite and picque?

Portrait of Sir Alexander Temple, father of the regicide, by Cornelius Johnson. Painted in 1620.

Sir Alexander had stood in the Parliament of 1625 for Winchelsea and been cheated of election. Instead, Sir Ralph Freeman and Sir Roger Twisden were elected to that borough seat. Freeman was a courtier who from 1618 was Master of the Court of Requests, and from 1629 was Master of the Mint. Sir Roger Twisden (1597-1672) was a Parliamentarian later, and probable friend to Temple, so Temple must have had his seat 'pinched' by Palmer. Temple petitioned against the fraud (see CSPD 1623-5, p. 209, and S.P.14/162/26 verso, a letter from Sir Richard Younge to Lord Zouch, saying: 'but what your Lordship did feare of Winchelsea is come to pass for there is a petition presented by Sr Alex. Temple against ye Parl. Election but I still believe it will turne to nothing because noe persons which stood for him were disfranchised before the summons of this parliament.'). In other words, the voters were disenfranchised *after* the Summons, not before, so that was considered all right. This must have enraged the voters of Sussex, since later the same year Temple was carried to Parliament in a county-wide wave of support as Knight of the Shire. Sir Alexander was also a lawyer as well as JP, and was a judge of some kind by 1627, as we see from *Canterbury Letter 69*, dated 25 February 1627/8, at Canterbury Cathedral Archive, where Sir Alexander speaks of going to the assizes soon at East Grinstead, and from the *Salisbury Manuscripts*, Vol. 24, where Edmund Bagan writes to the Earl of Salisbury on 2 November 1611 (or a previous year) in a letter dealing with matters concerning wardships, we learn that Sir Alexander was appointed by Salisbury to preside over a Commission of Inquiry into the Court of Wards, and meanwhile, in his capacity as lawyer: 'Now Sir Alexander Temple has undertaken to deal impartially in the matter, and to establish the King's title to the wardship, if it can be proved.'

Susanna Temple, the sister of James Temple the regicide, painted in 1620 by Cornelius Johnson.

A portrait of Susanna Temple, the sister of James Temple the regicide, pained in 1620 by Cornelius Johnson today hangs in the National Portrait Gallery. The painting was engraved more than once, and many famous men over the centuries bid large sums to possess it. Her first marriage was to Sir Gyfford (sometimes called Geoffrey, but that appears to be an error) Thornhurst, Bart., of Agnes or Agney Court in Romney Marsh in Kent, a neighbour of her uncle Roger Abdey. Their only child died an infant, and was buried in Etchingham Church, where the brass in the floor states: 'Here lies the only sonne of Sr Gyfford Thornhurst Barronett an infant by Dame Susan Thornhust now living the only daughter of Sr Alex Temple Kt 1626'. This inscription intimates that Susanna's husband had already died prior to the child's birth, since only the mother is described as 'now living'. In any case, Susanna was left a widow very young, and her second husband was Sir Martin Lister (1603-1670), only son of Michael Lister (died circa 1610) of Frearhead in Craven, Yorkshire, and Mary Kebell. Sir Martin's uncle was Sir Matthew Lister, President of the College of Physicians and Physician in Ordinary to Kings James I, Charles I, and Queen Henrietta Maria; he was thus uncle by marriage to the regicide's sister. Susanna, who died in November 1669, had nine children with this husband, the best known being Dr. Martin Lister, the famous scientist, who was born circa 1638 and died 1712. Their daughter Frances married Richard Jennings and was mother to Sara Jennings, afterwards the celebrated Duchess of Marlborough, who died 10 September 1736.

James seems to have continued his father's practice in wardship law at Lincolns Inn, and in the 1640s he became involved in a dispute regarding his own protective wardship for the heir to the Shelley family of Michelgrove in Sussex, who were friends of the Temples. In subsequent years, many complications arose about this. James spent some of his time residing at Michelgrove due to the wardship duties. The motive appears to have been to protect the Shelleys from the predations of the hated Court of Wards (which was abolished under the Commonwealth, doubtless with James's strong encouragement, and perhaps also with his advice).

The regicide married twice, firstly, circa 1628, to his own step-sister, Mary Busbridge, with whom he had six children, the last five baptised at Etchingham, Kent, on the Sussex border, which was the parish church of the Busbridges of Haremare Hall. The children were: Alexander, baptised April 13, 1629 (who married Mary Eyre, widow of William Eyre); James, baptised May 2, 1630; Thomas, baptised April 17, 1631; Mary, baptised September 9, 1632, and Peter, baptised December 15, 1633 (Etchingham Parish Register Extracts, deposited in the British Library as Add. MS. 6356, f. 45). Their first child John, born 1628, was admitted to Lincolns Inn, his father's old Inn, 4 May 1646, described as being of Michelgrove in Sussex, the Shelley's home, where they were all living at that time. The regicide married secondly Joanna Tromp, daughter of the Dutch Admiral Martin Tromp, and they had a daughter Susanne, who married as his second wife Clement Chevalier of Jersey (1609-1687), and they had a son named Temple Chevalier (1674-1722) who settled at Aspall in Suffolk. Susanne was living in Jersey because her father was still alive and imprisoned there and that is evidently how she met Clement Chevalier. No known record survives in England of how James Temple came to be so friendly with the Tromp family, though these records may survive in the Netherlands. His familiarity with the Dutch admirals may explain his later prominent role on Parliament's Committee of the Navy and as a Commissioner of the Navy, or otherwise that might be how he met them. One theory, and it is only a theory, is that James would have gone to the Netherlands during his European travels in 1622, which was the same year in which Maarten (Martin) Tromp returned to the Netherlands from slavery at Tunis. At that time, Tromp was 'a nobody'. Although Tromp was eight years older than James, the two may have met and become friends as young men who were then of no importance or position. In July of 1622, Tromp joined the Dutch Navy and became based at Rotterdam. If James knew Tromp from such a youthful acquaintance, that might explain why he went straight onto the Naval Committee as soon as he entered Parliament as a recruiter MP, because he would have been the only MP who had a personal acquaintance with the important Dutch admiral. Certainly there had to be a special connection between James and the Tromps, because James's daughter Mary married Tromp's son Cornelius (Cornelis) Tromp, who also became an admiral. What is the story behind all of this? We do not know. But there has to be one. Two marriages between the Temples and the Tromps goes well beyond mere chance. There had to be a close connection and friendship, but how did it arise, and when? This is one of those tantalising mysteries.

Richard Ingoldsby the future regicide was, at the beginning of the Civil War, associated with his father, Sir Richard Ingoldsby. Nehemiah Wharton has left a description of how he and three other soldiers of his company took up quarter temporarily at the Ingoldsbys' house in Buckinghamshire:

'(We) visited that thrice noble gentleman Sir Richard Inglisby, where his own table was our quarter and Serjeant-Major Barrif and his son Captain Inglisby, and several other noble gentlemen, were our comrades.'[18]

This was in August, 1642. The regicide's father was still active more than a year later, when he and two others were appointed to examine and state assessment accounts of Buckinghamshire with special reference to repairing the works and maintaining the garrison at Aylesbury.[19]

The home of Richard Ingoldsby and his father Sir Richard Ingoldsby, where Nehemiah Wharton and the other soldiers dined (as just described), still stands. (*Photo by Robert Temple*)

We have already noted in Chapter Two the infuriating experience of Robert Tichborne, Senior, the father of the regicide, in having thousands of pounds owing to him by his royalist Tichborne cousins being denied to him by the special and personal protection of the King. For, the King himself described it as 'taking Sir Walter Tichborne into his protection.'[20]

Young Robert Tichborne was a Captain in the London trained bands as early as June, 1642, when he was recorded as collecting plate and money for Parliament in Farringdon Within Ward in the City.[21] The same document records the future regicides Owen Rowe (a Captain collecting for Limehouse and Hackney) and John Barkstead (called 'Backster', collecting for St. Clement Danes, and also a Captain) as active in the same sense in June, 1642.[22] This document is mentioned in one sentence in the Calendar,[23] but its contents are not given at all, so that it is necessary to see the original. In a Letter and Declaration to the Sheriffs and

City of London dated January 17, 1642/3, the King complained of Robert Tichborne (spelled Titchburne) as follows:

'And whereas we are informed that one [Richard] Brown a Woodmonger [later Major-General], [Robert] Titchburne a Linen-Draper, and [Colonel Edmund] Harvey a Silkman, have exercised great Insolencies and Outrages in that our City, and when many of our good Subjects there have assembled together in a peaceable and modest manner, to consult about the peace and welfare of that City, the said mutinous and seditious persons have presumed to lead Multitudes of armed men against them, and by such Force have beaten, wounded, and killed our good Subjects, our will and pleasure is, That if the said Brown, Titchburn and Harvey, or either of them, shall so far neglect our gracious offer of Pardon as still to engage themselves in those unwarrantable and seditious courses, that our Sheriffs of London raise Power to suppress the said Force ...'[24]

During 1643, Tichborne was clearly one of the leading City radicals, and when the radical Salters Hall Committee for City military volunteers was formed on 12 April 1643, he became not only a member but also its leader. The Salters Hall Committee was struggling against the more conservative City Militia Committee which had its headquarters at Grocers Hall, and in an effort to dilute the trouble-making power of the radicals, the Militia Committee decided to appoint seven members of the Salters Hall Committee to their own committee, apparently as an act of appeasement. Tichborne was one of those seven men. And when Parliament decided that martial law should be declared in the City, Tichborne and two radical colleagues were put in charge of doing so. This City of London power struggle between radicals and moderates, and Tichborne's importance in it, is described by Robert Brenner at some length in his book *Merchants and Revolution*.[25] Later on, in the 1650s, Tichborne organised a syndicate for trading with the East Indies, involving as partners John Dethick, Colonel Maurice Thomson (an ancestor of the British television actor Kevin Whateley!), and the New England trader, Richard Hutchinson. Brenner gives references for further information about these trading activities, for those who might wish to learn more.[26] On January 17, 1648/9, Parliament appointed a militia commission for the City which was largely controlled by political radicals, and three regicides were members: Tichborne, Owen Rowe, and Gregory Clement (who by that time was a Member of Parliament, and is discussed later.)[27]

Sometimes it was not the father of a regicide who had had bad experiences with the Court and had thereby commenced a family hatred of the Court, but another close relative. In the case of John Alured, it was his uncle, Thomas Alured. The story is not told by Cliffe.[28] It is Anthony à Wood who tells the story:

'The works of this our Author [George] Hakewill are these ... Treatise against the match with the Infanta – This little thing, which is in MS. I have not seen. But another of the like nature I have lying by me, written by one, Thomas Allured sometimes Secretary to Ralph Lord Ever [Ralph, fourth Baron Eure] President of Wales, the beginning of which is this. ... 'Twas written to the Marquis of Buckingham, who communicating it to the King, he was so much displeased, that the Author Allured was commited to custody 10 June 1620, being a full year before Hakewill had written his Tract.'[29] Thomas Alured's letter to Buckingham was published in 1642 and reprinted in 1643, probably by his nephew. But I have found the original manuscript, addressed to Buckingham, in the Public Record Office.[30] Alured's motivation was largely religious, warning against the influence of the Papists and 'the Romish locust'.[31] I have transcribed for the Appendix to this chapter Thomas Alured's grovelling submission to the King of July 22, 1620. He commences:

'Upon the bended knees of my broaken, and sorrowfull heart, I acknowledge before God, and your Lops that I have highly offended his sacred Maiestie in a presumption of the highest nature ...'

He had already been imprisoned for forty days. He was apparently not released for months, He followed up his submission by surrendering his office of remembrancer in the Court of the Council in Wales on March 20, 1620/1.[32] He had been granted it many years previously.[33] The office was immediately granted to another man who was a royal favourite.[34] Thomas Alured may even have languished in prison for years. I have found nothing more about him until October 23, 1625, when he had arranged to obtain the favour of Secretary of State Sir John Coke, who wrote to Lord Keeper Sir Thomas Coventry recommending Alured to him as a secretary.[35] By May, 1627, Alured had recovered his position sufficiently to be able to obtain confirmation of a lease, with a partner, of several villages in Carnarvonshire in Wales.[36] Secretary Coke had apparently not persuaded Sir Thomas Coventry to take on Alured as a secretary, for in November, 1626, Alured was acting as Coke's own agent.[37] By 1628, Alured was able to become MP for Hedon (five miles from Hull, the family's home town).[38] But he would be dead before there was another Parliament called in 1640.

Thomas Alured was an extremely keen philanthropist. He offered considerable assistance to the town of Hull during the plague in October, 1637. A letter from James Watkinson to the Mayor of Hull on October 4th says of him:

'Mr. Alured I believe hath done more for us than anye of the greatt ones who are our neighbours, though they had their begininges from the Towne as well as his predecessors had. God I make no doubt will requite him his charitie, and we are tied to him if ever itt lye in our power to befd [befriend] him.'[39]

In the Hull record Office is preserved a letter from Thomas Alured to the Mayor of Hull dated October 24, 1637, in which he says he is enclosing £100 for the Mayor to distribute to the poor of Hull at his own discretion. He also describes his conversations with prominent officials wherein he tried to persuade them to come to the relief of Hull [i.e. because of the plague].[40] Thomas Alured had no children. He died a few months after this letter, and was buried in the spring of 1638 at St. Anne's, Blackfriars, London.

The outrageous imprisonment of his uncle probably incensed John Alured. For he certainly was an outspoken opponent of the Court by the late 1630s. John was a highly-motivated Puritan, who in 1633 put a Puritan preacher named John Spofforth into possession of all the tithes in the parish of Sculcoates near Hull for so long as he remained there 'as preacher of the word of God'.[41]
(Sculcoates is today a northern suburb of Hull.) Alured settled the tithes by Indenture, probably to get round the ecclesiastical courts. Young Alured had apparently been 'a most profane young gentleman' until 1630, but through the influence of the Puritan preacher Thomas Shepard 'fell to fasting and prayer and great reformation'.[42]

It was on July 4, 1638, that John Alured got into trouble with the Court. He had evidently inherited his Uncle Thomas's house at Blackfriars in London, and was staying there. On the day mentioned, he happened to say to a Gervase Clifton about the Scots that 'they were brave boyes and would make us all quake. And yt being tolde they ever could not much avayle to doe us hurt, he sd they would come to or [our] faces and yt they did well. They would reform this land by a parliamt as well as they have done theirs allreadie for the king would be forced to laye downe his taxes on their comminge in to England. And beinge told they durst nott invade us, He sd the kinge would gett nobody to fite against them for they were or owne nation and or owne bloode.'[43] Secretary of State Sir Francis Windebank noted on the back of this Information that Alured was worth £400-£500 a year.[44]

John Alured was forced to sign a submission, just as his uncle had been before him. He did so in the presence of Windebank and Sir Gervase Clifton, Bart., his accuser. The submission was a grudging and qualified one, briefly worded as follows: 'I heere say that I Jo: Alured

John Henry Alured Esq.
of Scowscottes near y.e Town and County
of Kingston upon Hull.
From an original picture at Shasted House Kent.

Previously unpublished portrait of John Alured the regicide, apparently painted in the late 1630s about the time he got into trouble with the Court. As for 'Shasted House, Kent', it is Sharsted Court near Doddington, Kent. In the eighteenth century the house was left to a man named Alured Pinke, and from him passed to a Major General Sir Alured Dodsworth Faunce. Clearly these people were descended from the Alureds, which is how they came to own the oil portrait of which this drawing is a copy. In 1966 the house was acquired by the Wade/Shepley family, and whether or not they possess this portrait is unknown.

discorsing with Mr Clifton concerning the scoch businesse I sayd I heard that the scochmen stoud upon having a parlement in Scotland & could not be soe content, but desired to have one heare tow likewise saing they were madd boys, at Grinewige [Greenwich] the 9 of July 1638 JO: ALURED In the presence of fran Windebank/ Gervas Clifton'[45]

Since Clifton is described as 'Mr.', he was not Sir Gervase Clifton, first Bart.. but his son Gervase Clifton, who when his father died in 1666 became the second Bart. This younger Gervase Clifton was an impulsive and unruly character who was in conflict with his dignified royalist father (who had been an MP repeatedly since 1614 and was one of the social magnates of Nottinghamshire), was imprisoned in 1640 for assaulting two men serving a writ upon him for unpaid debts, and disinherited of the Clifton estates in 1648.[46]

On July 25, 1638, Alured had to enter into a bond with two sponsors guaranteeing that he would appear before the Privy Council within twenty days of 'Warning to be left at his house situate in Blackfriars London, then and there to answere such matters as shalbe objected against him, and shall also then and there give his attendance upon theire Lpps and not depart thence wthout leave of that Hoble [Honourable] Board.'[47] This had the effect of making it utterly impossible for him to return to Yorkshire, so that he was stranded in London and had to neglect his estates. If he was not furious with the Court because of his uncle, he was now on his own account. His remarks about the Scots indicated that he saw quite clearly the most important advantage to be gained, - the forcing of the King to call a Parliament, which the King had refused to do since 1628, thus depriving the people of their representatives who might ameliorate the harsh, illegal royal rule by 'prerogative', there being no judicial appeal possible either, as the judges were all supporters of the Court. (This was ensured because of the total control of judicial appointments managed through the Serjeants at Law system, for discussion of which see the chapter 'The Regicides and the Law'.)

I have not managed to discover what eventually happened in the matter just discussed. In all likelihood Alured was summoned and fined. He may even have been jailed, as his uncle had been. But by early 1640 he was back in Yorkshire, where he was elected to the Short Parliament as MP for Hedon, thus taking his uncle's old seat. The Parliament convened on April 13, 1640, but was disbanded on May 5, having sat for only 28 days, which was as much as the King could tolerate.

On July 28, Alured signed the Petition of the Gentry of Yorkshire to the King, protesting against the billeting of soldiers and demanding observance of the Petition of Right. His name does not appear in the list printed by Rushworth, who added at the end of his list 'With divers others'.[48] But Alured's name appears on the original document itself, which I consulted.[49]

Alured was elected to the Long Parliament, which convened on November 3, 1640, and once again he represented Hedon. As threats of a looming war came increasingly to everyone's minds, on May 18, 1642, Alured, together with the future regicide Peregrine Pelham and others, were appointed by the House of Commons to travel to Hull and constitute themselves a Committee for Hull.[50] In July, 1642, the Committee for Hull is seen to have consisted of Alured, Pelham, and the two Sir John Hothams (father and son), as shown by a joint letter from them which is preserved in the Nalson MSS.[51] However, whereas Pelham identified totally with Hull, whose MP he was, Alured never seemed to warm quite so much to his native town. As I have pointed out in an article where I discussed Pelham's correspondence, Pelham was not on intimate terms with MPs from his own part of the country, and had difficulty getting their support for matters to do with Hull. Pelham told the Mayor and Aldermen of Hull in one of his letters plaintively: 'Those that serve for remote pts [parts] are my best friends.'[52] This indicates pretty clearly that Alured and Pelham did not get on very well. Alured directed his energies in a wider context, being an active member of the Committee of the East Riding and also the Committee of the Northern Association, the former being a division of the latter, and Alured's activities being mostly on the latter. It is important to note that this Committee of the Northern Association was entirely distinct from the Committee of Yorkshire, as explained later on in the chapter 'The Regicides and the Counties'.

As such, Alured could and did come into some conflict with Pelham and his friends of Hull, as we can see in a letter of 1645 where Alured clearly puts regional interests over those of the town.[53] In 1641, Alured had helped Fairfax disarm recusants in Yorkshire; in June, 1642, Alured was Collector of Taxes at Hull.[54] And as we can see from the Mounting Book extracts in the Appendix to Part One, by August 10, 1642, Alured was a Captain of Horse. In September, 1643, his house, the Charterhouse, outside of Hull, had to be totally destroyed by Fairfax as part of his defensive measures for the town, for which the House of Commons awarded him £5000 compensation.[55] The Civil War brought complete disaster to Alured, and doubtless hastened him to his premature death in 1651.

I mention once again at this point that until I wrote one for him, the *Dictionary of National Biography* had no entry for John Alured, who had dropped out of sight for historians except for a few people concerned with Yorkshire in the Civil War.

One regicide whose life has been well chronicled is Colonel John Hutchinson MP. His own wife Lucy Hutchinson wrote a most remarkable book, many times reprinted, *Memoirs of the Life of Colonel Hutchinson*. This work was preserved in manuscript within the Hutchinson family for a century and a half, and was published for the first time in a fine folio with Hutchinson's portrait as the frontispiece in 1806.[56] The book also contains a portrait of Lucy Hutchinson, an engraved specimen of her handwriting, and a large fold-out Hutchinson family pedigree. The regicide lived at Owthorpe near Nottingham. During the Civil War he held Nottingham Castle for the Parliament against all the odds, a full and harrowing description of which events is given in graphic detail by his wife. One of his great enemies was Doctor Huntington Plumtree. That name stuck in my mind for many, many years after reading the book, and in 2020 a document came up for sale on Ebay relating to him, which I bought; neither the seller nor any potential buyer knew who Plumtree was, so I was able to acquire this at a reasonable price. It is dated October 31, 1650, and deals with Fiskerton cum Morton in Nottinghamshire and a Chancery action. It is not sufficiently relevant to Hutchinson to include here, but I mention this as an example of the kind of thing that happens sometimes if one reads the old books attentively enough. It can honestly be said that anyone who wants to understand the period of the English Civil War needs to read Lucy Hutchinson's memoir. It is a uniquely personal document. And these days, when at last women are being celebrated as authors, Lucy Hutchinson stands out as a heroine first class. Although she and her husband were very religious and tended towards Puritanism, they were far from being austere. John Hutchinson, as Lucy informs us, always wore a beautiful lace collar rather than a plain collar, which must have grated on the nerves of his more Puritanical colleagues in Parliament. But what I find truly remarkable about the Hutchinsons is that when the paintings of the Royal Art Collection of Charles I were sold off at public auction, following his execution and the abolition of the Monarchy, they bought a painting by Titian *of the Madonna and Child*. John Hutchinson was certainly no stained glass window-smasher. Nor was he afraid to gaze upon the Virgin Mary.

The Hutchinsons were aesthetes, and they loved listening to music played on the viola da gamba. Give the Hutchinsons a try sometime! There is no point in my summarising John Hutchinson's life, as it has already been done by the person best in a position to know, his wife.

We cannot consider the early careers of the regicides without noticing that of the arch-republican, Thomas Chaloner. Chaloner's threat to the Crown and the Church was always that of his powerful intellect, his forceful speaking, and his great learning. In the later chapter 'The Regicides and Religion' much is said about Chaloner's theological learning, which he turned against organised religion in the manner of John Selden. When a royalist wanted to attack Chaloner in 1648, he fumed at him for 'the Logique Chaloner disgorg'd against the King'.[57]

The portrait of Colonel John Hutchinson which is frontispiece to the first edition of his wife's memoirs, published from the manuscript in 1806.

As mentioned in Chapter Two, Chaloner's eldest brother William died in Turkey, and his remaining older brother Edward also died young, leaving him as the eldest living son. And as discussed in the chapter 'The Regicides and Religion', Thomas himself seems to have had an intimate knowledge of the Middle East, having joined his brother as a trader at Constantinople and toured Lebanon and Israel, as they are known today, during the time of his enforced exile from England (a subject discussed at length later). Anthony à Wood also records that Thomas had 'travelled into France, Italy, and Germany'.[58] By the time Chaloner had returned from his foreign travels sometime around 1620, à Wood says he was 'a well-bred Gentleman, but ting'd, as it seems, with antimonarchical Principles, if not worse.'[59] In fact, Chaloner and his pal and drinking buddy Henry Marten seem to have been the two earliest outright republicans in England, and it may even be that Marten imbibed such ideas from Chaloner. à Wood says Chaloner in Parliament was 'a great stickler for their new Utopian Commonwealth. All which he did partly out of his natural inclination, and partly out of revenge for the loss which his Father endured (and so consequently he himself) for being deprived of the propriety of the Allom [alum] Mines in Yorkshire, which he had discovered about the latter end of Qu. Elizabeth.'[60]

William Rowe, son-in-law of Thomas Scot the regicide, in 1650 wrote to Cromwell speaking of 'Tom Chaloner, Harry Nevill, and those witts ... Tom Chaloner, Tom May (when living) and that gangue ...'[61] à Wood says of Chaloner that 'he was a boon Companion, was of Harry Marten's gang'.[62] So they were a merry gang of chums whom you could hear laughing a long way off, and who were not averse to numerous replenishings of ale.

Chaloner excited a violent controversy and caused a torrential flood of pamphlet literature in response in 1646 when he published his incisive and tightly-argued *An Answer to the Scotch Papers.*[63] It would take too long to include here a survey of this controversy and make a complete list of all of the pamphlets concerned in it. Perhaps someone will do that one day. Chaloner's pamphlet was separately entered even in the revised wing Catalogue as *A Speech Made in the House of Commons*, due to the title page of that copy having been lost and the next page having also the appearance of a title page. Thus, in the revised wing Catalogue, C1802 and C1804 are actually the same pamphlet, except that C1804 has lost its title page.[64] I brought this to the attention of Timothy Crist when he was revising the Wing Catalogue further, and he wrote to me acknowledging that I was correct, and he rectified the situation. However, a comical situation occurred when the reprint publisher EEBO Editions printed the pamphlet twice, under its two separate titles, one with a title page and one without. This proves that the reprint publishers sometimes do not bother to read what they are reprinting, since it takes only a few seconds to see that the text is identical in each of the two supposedly 'separate reprints'.

Chaloner's attitude towards the Crown is summed up in his remarks about the King in this pamphlet:

'I beseech you ... consider whether (as the case now stands) his Reception with Honour can stand with the Honour of the Kingdome, whether his safety be not incompatible with the safety of the Commonwealth, and whether that in receiving him with safety you doe not endanger and hazard the Common-Wealth; be advised least in bringing him home with freedome, you doe not thereby lead the people of England into thraldom.'[65]

And of course, he was correct, as was demonstrated when the Second Civil War came about as a result of trusting the King, who had a second go at retaining his unrestrained royal power by starting the civil war all over again.

The pamphlet war which was triggered by Thomas Chaloner was fierce and furious. I have not endeavoured to consult all the pamphlets, but I can list a portion of them. Of the ones I have consulted which attack Chaloner, all were published anonymously, but the royalist journalist Sir John Birkenhead has been identified as the author of one of them, which arouses no surprise whatever. A few can be dated. The sequence appears to be as follows:

Chaloner's original pamphlet, which was 15 pages long, was a printing of a lengthy speech which he delivered in the House of Commons on October 26, 1646, 'upon the reading of the Scotish Papers the same day'.

It seems that the first reply, which was anonymous, was written by Sir John Birkenhead, according to the British Library catalogue. A contemporary annotation states that it was published on November 16. It was: *An Answer to a Speech without Doores: or, Animadversions upon an Unsafe and Dangerous Answer to the Scotch-Papers, printed under the name of Mr. Challener His Speech, which while it offereth to reach a blow at the Scotch-Papers, doth indeed strike at the honour of the Parliament, and interest of the Kingdome of England.* (7 pp.) (E.369 (9))

On November 23, a reply, supposedly anonymous, was published justifying Chaloner's speech. The British Library Catalogue states that this was written by Chaloner. Its title is: *The Justification of A Safe and Well-Grounded Answer to the Scottish Papers, Printed under the name of Master Chaloner His Speech: which, (Whatsoever the Animadvertor affirmes) doth maintaine the Honour of the Parliament, and Interest of the Kingdome of England.* (12 pp.) (E.363 (11))

On the same day, November 23, another pamphlet supporting Chaloner was published, entitled *A Reply to A Nameless Pamphlet, Intituled, An Answer to a Speech without Doors, &c., or, A Defence of Master Chaloner's Speech*. This pamphlet was published under the initials G. G. No one seems to have identified G. G. He was most likely to have been Giles Green MP, who was a close colleague of Chaloner. (Green was later secluded at Pride's Purge.) The only other candidates for authorship within Parliament are Lord Grey of Groby, a future regicide; Gilbert Gerrard (c. 1618 - 1683, later knighted at the Restoration; there were several contemporary Gilbert Gerrards, which is why I give the dates of this one, for some were royalists); and George Gallop. They were the only G.G.'s in Parliament, and a supporter of Chaloner's in this pamphlet war was most likely to be an MP who had been present at Chaloner's speech on October 26. (It cannot have been George Goring, who was a royalist who had been secluded and was not present.) I cannot see Lord Grey of Groby referring to himself as G.G.; it just doesn't 'fit'. George Gallop was in political sympathy, but was a rather obscure fellow. The most likely candidate within parliament to be author of this tract and to hurl himself into the debate is, in my humble opinion, Giles Green. This is substantiated by the fact that Giles Green (who spelled his name Grene) sat on the Parliamentary Committee for the Admiralty with Chaloner and was later a Commissioner for the Navy with Chaloner.[66] (6 pp.) (E.362 (26))

Another anonymous pamphlet in support of Chaloner appeared next, entitled *An Answer to Severall Obiections Made against Some Things in Mr. Thomas Chaloners Speech.* (7 pages) (E.362 (27)) We know that this pamphlet was the next to appear, and that it did so between November 23 and December 4, because the next attacking pamphlet published on December 5 specifically states that it is in response to *three* pamphlets of support, of which this must therefore be the third.

On December 5 Sir John Birkenhead responded with a second attack, entitled *The Speech without Doores Defended without Reason, or, A vindication of the Parliaments Honour: in A Rejoynder to Three Pamphlets Published in Defence of M. Chaloners Speech*. (11 pages) (E.365 (5)) Although published anonymously, the author begins by admitting that he is the author of the November 16 pamphlet, which he calls his *Animadversions*. He insists upon his faithfulness to the Parliament.

Another anonymous and critical pamphlet appeared, dated 1646, entitled *The Moderator: In Reply to Mr Thomas Chaloners Speech, and the Scots Papers, Concerning the Disposall of the Kings Person.* (16 pp.) This intensely scholarly pamphlet was clearly written by one of the supporters of the 'Presbyterian' faction in Parliament, was printed by the same Francis Leach who published Chaloner's original speech and the most recent pamphlet in defence of it (*An Answer to Severall Obiections*). Furthermore, the pamphlet bears on the title page the injunction: 'Commanded to be published in all Churches and Chappels through the Kingdome'. This publication thus had the official backing of some 'moderate' MP in charge of a relevant committee who could give such an order. The pamphlet also includes two supporting documents, the first being 'A Copy of the Kings Speech Spoken before Divers of the Lords, Peeres, and Barons of the Kingdome of Scotland', and the second being 'A Copie of the Irish Rebels Protestation, of Their Fidelity to the King … made at Waterford'. This highly tendentious, strongly religious, and learned pamphlet, citing historical instances and talking about Henry VIII, etc., reads like one of the learned but ranting diatribes of William Prynne or Clement Walker MP.

Other pamphlets continued to be published. One from 1647 is entitled *Lex Talionis. Or, A Declamation against Mr. Challener, The Crimes of the Times, and the Manners of You Know Whom.* (10 pp.) It ends with A Letter to the Army commencing with: 'How can you expect an Act of Indemnity?' 'Lex talionis' means 'the Law of Retribution', i.e. as in the Biblical injunction of 'an eye for an eye, a tooth for a tooth'. This pamphlet was written by a passionate royalist, who says: 'King Charles is the essentiall head of our Politique Body' and accuses Thomas Chaloner of 'malice' and threatens that he will be executed. It refers to the Parliamentary supporters from the City of London as 'spurious scum'. In its vulgar tirade and amidst its abuse, it is interesting to note that Thomas Chaloner is singled out as apparently the leading opponent of monarchy in the author's opinion.

This is as far as I went in gathering material about this pamphlet war sparked by Chaloner. I refrain from discussing and analyzing the contents of all of these pamphlets, as that would take a treatise in itself. Although I have copies of all of them, it seemed most useful to make a list available of the ones I have seen.

Chaloner's attitudes were certainly derived in part from those of his father, Sir Thomas Chaloner, who was from 1603 the Governor of Prince Henry, and later became his Chamberlain. Queen Anne had also given Sir Thomas the management of her estates. Prince Henry so trusted Chaloner that he asked him to make experiments in defence of Phineas Pett, in the famous incident when the Prince denounced his father, the King, and those 'perjured fellows' at the Court whom he intended to hang when he got the chance. (See Sir Thomas's entry in DNB.) Sir Thomas Chaloner was thus involved deeply with the same circles as Danvers and Constable, namely the courtiers of the factions opposed to the King and his immediate sycophants such as the Duke of Buckingham and Robert Carr. (In Chaloner's time, of course, it was primarily Carr who was the problem, as he was then the King's favourite, i.e., was the young man who was sleeping with him at the time).

Portrait of Thomas Chaloner painted by Anthony Van Dyck, sometime in the 1630s.
Preserved in the Hermitage Museum in St. Petersburg.

There is another fascinating byway to pursue briefly with regard to Sir Thomas Chaloner, especially as it concerns his association with Prince Henry, and by implication it tells us also about the ambiance surrounding the young Sir John Danvers during his time with the Prince. It is probably only historians of science, or those deeply interested in that subject, who have ever heard of the Rev. William Barlow (born circa 1544, died 1625). He is sometimes mistakenly described as being Welsh, but he was English and was only born in Wales because his father was then Bishop of St. David. He is one of the most important people in the history of science in Early Modern Britain, since he introduced the words 'magnet' and 'magnetism' into the English language. He was a close friend of William Gilbert (1544-1603), born the same year as Barlow, author of the famous *De Magnete* (published 1600 in Latin), which is often viewed as the founding text of magnetism and one of the foundations of modern science. Barlow and Gilbert constantly exchanged ideas and writings, as shown by a letter of Gilbert's to Barlow which Barlow published at the back of his own book *Magneticall Advertisements* (1616).[67] According to Anthony à Wood, Barlow 'had knowledge in the Magnet 20 Years before Dr. Will. Gilbert published his book of that subject, and therefore by those that knew him, he was accounted superior, or at least equal, to that Doctor for an industrious and happy searcher and finder out of many rare and magnetical secrets.'[68] Copies of Barlow's book are very rare, and at the time of writing the only copy for sale on the internet is priced at about

£35,000, somewhat beyond the means of us ordinary mortals. I am extremely fortunate to have a bound copy of a very carefully prepared photographic printout of the book, which for research purposes is just as good as the original book. The story of poor Barlow having his work stolen from him is piteous. But here is the interesting thing for us here: Barlow made his discoveries because Sir Thomas Chaloner and Prince Henry urged him to. In fact, Barlow had become Chaplain to Prince Henry, apparently at the suggestion of Chaloner. As he says:

'… the perswasions of that learned honourable Gentleman, Sir Thomas Challenor, late Chamberlaine unto the Mirrour of honour Prince Henry prevailed most with me. Unto whom I was all the time that I attended that Prince his highnesse, for his love and curtesie, much beholding. Whereupon about seaven yeeres since [in 1609] I delivered unto him this treatise, finished almost as now it is [he is writing in 1616], saving some few additions upon necessary occasions. But that Copie was either mislaied or embeseled, that he lost it; About three yeeres since he sent earnestly unto mee for an other Copie: which also he received, promising me by his letters, that within three months hee would put it to the presse, and that it should be carefully and correctly performed: But what is become even of that also I know not; …'[69]

Barlow's work has suffered ever since from being eclipsed by the earlier publication by his friend William Gilbert. But such considerations in the history of science need not detain us. The purpose of mentioning all of this is to show even more clearly a picture of the intense intellectual atmosphere of the immediate circle around Prince Henry, which has earlier been described in the account of Sir John Danvers, especially in connection with Sir Walter Raleigh. Not only was Danvers necessarily present, as the Prince's closest companion, during all of this ferment of scholarship, but it must have been made known most clearly to Thomas Chaloner the regicide as well, for his father would have told his children in great detail of the lost world and the lost promise of the valiant young Prince. The regicide may even have met the Prince fleetingly, since he was 17 at the time of the Prince's death. Prince Henry's death in 1612, followed by Sir Thomas's death in 1615, and finally Sir Walter Raleigh's death in 1618, closed what could have been a brilliant chapter in English history rivalling even the Elizabethan Era which had gone before. The loss of 'the Golden Age that might have been' must have been felt most deeply by those most likely to know the details, two of whom became regicides, namely Thomas Chaloner and Sir John Danvers.

As just mentioned, Sir Thomas Chaloner died in 1615, the year before Barlow wrote this. So Barlow put the entire book together for a third time and sent it to Sir Dudley Digges, asking him to try to get it published. But that obviously bore no fruit, because on the title page of the book we read: 'Printed by Edward Griffin for Timothy Barlow'. So getting the work into print was clearly arranged by a close relative instead, and probably self-funded.

Much has been made by all authorities of the seizure without compensation of the Chaloner family's alum mines by King James I, and the obvious family grievance this caused. (We have already seen in Part One of this chapter that the Danvers family's lands containing alum mines were also seized by the King.) However, all the authorities both then and later have erred in ascribing the discovery of the alum mines (the first in England) to Sir Thomas Chaloner, father of the regicide. The old DNB says Sir Thomas 'about 1600, made the discovery of alum-stone at Belman Bank, Guisborough, and opened there the first alum mines in England.' And an interesting manuscript in York Minster also tells us:

'This Sir Tho. was a compleat Gentleman … He was the first that discovered the Alum Mine at Gisborough, which proving extraordinary Advantagious it was adjudged a Royal

Mine so that little Benefit came to Sir Tho. or his Posterity ... Sir Tho. Chaloner Observed the Leaves of the Oak Trees where the Mines are, to be of a deeper green than elsewhere and the Bough more spreading the boles Dwarfish but strong having little sap, and not deep rooted; also the ground clayish, variously coloured, and the path ways in the night glittered like Glass, on which he conceited there was included some valuable minerals especially Alum. Soon after it was adjudged a Royal Mine when Sir Geo. Radcliffe procured Workmen from France who advanced it. And afterwards Sir Paul Pindar paid the following annual rents for it Viz. to the King £12,5000, to the Earl of Mulgrave £1640, and to Sir Will. Pennyman £600, besides wages to 800 workmen.'[70]

I have, however, discovered a document which I have transcribed for the Appendix to this chapter showing that it was not Sir Thomas (who owned the land) who alone discovered the alum. He did it in close association with his first cousin, another Thomas Chaloner (born circa 1547), who was fourteen years older, and who was the real mineral expert of the two. This cousin expending a great part of his estate and younger years 'in many Chargeable trialls of sundry minerals, he at last discovered and found the Allom Mynes of Yorkshire', as he states in his 1615 Petition in the Appendix. The King had compensated him with an absurdly small pension but soon discontinued it. The importance of the discovery of English alum mines must not be underestimated. Alum is a mordaunt, or 'fixer', of dyes, and without it, cloth could not be dyed and retain the colours. The Pope had a European monopoly of alum, which had to be imported to England from Italy. As a necessary chemical fixative for dyes of cloth, the discovery of alum in England freed the English Protestants from dependence on the hated 'Beast of Rome' for a basic necessity of clothing and commerce. English alum thus had a political importance of the first magnitude, as well as the religious advantage. It was not just a commodity worth a lot of money. But it was that too!

In a Petition of 1657 transcribed for the Appendix, James Chaloner (younger brother of Thomas the regicide and who had also been a Member of the Long Parliament and an ardent republican) estimated his personal share of financial loss over the seizure of the mine at £10,000, and cited £6000 unpaid share of pension (supposed compensation). He also says 'the late King got 100,000l [£100,000] by his Allom works.' The illegal seizure of the Chaloner family's mines by the King was thus probably the largest and most profitable single abuse of the royal prerogative ever practiced by the Stuarts. In financial terms, it was the most outrageous act of outright robbery from a single family perpetrated in a century which unfortunately abounded in such abuses. To put it in its simplest terms, King James I stole £100,000 from his son's own Chamberlain and his wife's own financial manager. If we required any further evidence of James I's hatred of Prince Henry and his circle, and disdain for the Queen and her circle, this would be it. And it should not escape our notice that if anyone knew or suspected the truth about Prince Henry's fate, it was the Chaloner family. The incredibly vicious retribution visited upon Prince Henry's and Queen Anne's circles by the courtiers personally bound to James I, and by the King himself, has, as we have seen, several instances in the backgrounds of the regicides. We should be justified in viewing what happened partially as being the persecution of an 'honest' and genuinely patriotic and disinterested set of courtiers by a dishonest, unpatriotic, grasping and selfish set of courtiers clustered around the person of a dishonest, unpatriotic, grasping and selfish monarch. It may well be that if Prince Henry, 'the darling of Britain',[71] had become King upon the death of James I, regicides like Chaloner, Danvers, Constable and their friends would have been quite happy to be faithful royalists in his service, putting in the backs of their minds any republican notions they might have formed. It is certainly my personal view that there would have been no Civil War at all. But such matters of speculation can never be proved and are entirely a matter of personal opinion.

Before continuing with our look at Thomas Chaloner, this would be an appropriate point at which to take a hard look at the nature of the peers of England at this time, and by extension the aristocracy at large. Francis Bacon had made acerbic remarks relevant to what was happening in his essay 'On Nobility':

'For new nobility is but the act of power; but ancient nobility is the act of time. ... it is a reverend thing to see ... an ancient noble family, which hath stood against the waves and weathers of time.'[72]

And here is a sarcastic observation about kings and their 'new nobility' which is to be found in Robert Burton's *Anatomy of Melancholy*:

'... a frowne, an hard speech, ill respect, or bad looke, especially to Courtiers, or such as attend upon great Persons, is present death. ... they ebbe and flow with their masters favours. Some persons are at their wits end, if by chance they over-shoot themselves in their ordinary speeches, or actions, which may after turne to their disadvantage or disgrace, or have any secret disclosed.'[73]

Though himself newly ennobled, and thus the apotheosis of 'an act of power', Bacon was able to state what was obvious then but often lost sight of now: the difference between *artificial aristocracy* and *natural aristocracy*, as I would put it. I have often been deeply disturbed in reading discussions of 'social status' in modern historical works dealing with the seventeenth century to find the designations of 'greater gentry', etc., used without reference to whether artificial aristocracy or natural aristocracy is intended. Nor, when historians speak of 'declining gentry' (as if money were the only thing that mattered, and was the universal measure of importance) do they often enough take note of *why* a family might be economically declining. The usual implication is usually that if a family is declining, it must be desperate and will do anything to reverse the decline. This is assumed to be a motivation, and no doubt there is some truth in the idea. But let us consider the Chaloners: they declined by £100,000-worth. However, to put it like that misses the main point. The Chaloners were the object of an outrageous abuse of power by a King, as a result of which they lost £100,000. The former part of the previous sentence conveys the premise, the latters conveys the consequence. It is to the premises that we should direct more attention than to the consequences. The sociological influence in historical writing has not had an altogether healthy effect for several decades. In our eagerness to classify people in sociological categories (which is supposed to be 'scientific' but is in fact a pathetic example of 'scientism'), we can be led to overlook the more important and underlying matter of *the structure of power*. 'New peers' were 'acts of power'. There was a struggle for power going on. As pointed out in Chapter Two, very many of the regicides represented what Bacon called 'antient noble families, which hath stood against the waves and weathers of time'. Their status as expressed in sociological terms might not be at all equivalent to their other kind of status, namely their antiquity and genuineness. Such men were the natural aristocracy as opposed to the neophyte artificial aristocracy of the Court sycophants. And to show just how drastic the situation was, we now look at the peers summoned to Parliament in 1640. (Of these, 26 were bishops who were naturally supporters of the Court; these are omitted from consideration because their positions were ecclesiastically determined.) Here is the breakdown of the non–ecclesiastical peers of the different titles, showing when their titles were created:

Earls:
Pre-Stuart: 19
Made by James I: 21.
Made by Charles I: 22.
So that less than a third of the Earls were 'real', or *natural aristocracy*.

Viscounts:
Pre-Stuart: 1
Made by James I: 2
Made by Charles I: 2
Only one of these five was 'real', or *natural aristocracy*; Viscount Saye and Sele had previously been a Baron, but both his titles were created by James I. His earliest ancestor who was a peer was Lord Saye of 1313, so we acknowledge that he was anomalous and despite being of Stuart creation twice, his family were 'antient' in Bacon's sense, and he was of course a great enemy to the Court.

Barons:
Pre-Stuart: 19[74]
Made by James I: 13
Made by Charles I: 19
About a third were thus 'real', or *natural aristocracy*.[75]

We see that by the time of Charles I, less than one third of the membership of the House of Lords (omitting the bishops) represented titles created before the Stuarts. The body was thus a legislative chamber packed by the Stuarts with their sycophants, an Act of Power writ large. The Stuarts not only made peers, they created an entire House of Parliament by appointment. Two third of the peers plus 26 bishops gave the Stuarts total control over the Chamber; all those men had been created by them, and few were prepared to defy them. Naturally, with the titles, money and property tended to follow in due succession. In my opinion, when discussing such sociological matters as gentry status and categorisation, we should take account of this more fully. Until now, this crucial matter has been ignored entirely by historians.

There is an interesting connection between this kind of thinking and the Chaloner family. Thomas Chaloner the regicide's grandfather, Sir Thomas Chaloner the Elder, was the translator of *In Praise of Folly* by Erasmus. And here is what Erasmus had to say about courtiers in that book, which we may be sure was closely read by the regicide in his own grandfather's translation:

'Princes in their greatest Splendor seem upon this Account unhappy, in that they miss the Advantage of being told the Truth, and are shamm'd off by a parcel of insinuating Courtiers, that acquit themselves as Flatterers more than as Friends. But some will perchance object, that Princes do not love to hear the Truth, and therefore Wise Men must be very cautious how they behave themselves before them, in speaking what is true, rather than what is acceptable. This must be confess'd, Truth is seldom palatable to the Ears of Kings …'[76]

The regicides as a group, as pointed out in Chapter Two, represent in many cases the very ancient families, or what Francis Bacon would call 'the ancient nobility'. And the royalists, who may have been graced with grand titles and enormous estates, were 'the new nobility' who clustered around the Stuarts who had made them what they were. This is no hard and fast rule, but it is an observation with sufficient enough basis to be worth making. What is new here is the information I have gathered about the leading men of the English Revolution. It has not previously been known or realized that the regicides were so representative of the ancient families who viewed themselves as the 'ancient nobility' as opposed to the Court creatures of the Stuarts, who were upstart toadies and also monstrously corrupt.

But to return now to Thomas Chaloner. It is ironical that his older brother, the Rev. Edward Chaloner, D. D., a Fellow of All Souls College Oxford and a keen Episcopalian, who died of plague aged only 35 in 1625, had briefly been the Chaplain of Charles I, as mentioned in Chapter Two. Two years prior to his death, in 1623, Edward published six of his sermons, and six more were published four years after his death in 1629.[77] He was far from being a Puritan.

Thomas Chaloner was mentioned by Bulstrode Whitelocke in his *Annals* for the autumn or early winter of 1628, where we see that he was a drinking and jesting buddy with Edward Hyde (later the royalist the Earl of Clarendon), the later Parliament supporter Harbottle Grimston (later the second Sir Harbottle Grimston, Bart., MP), Roger Palmer (later a royalist

One of the two volumes of Edward Chaloner's sermons published after his death.

MP), and Bartholomew Hall (later Attorney of the Duchy of Lancaster and Recorder of Abingdon). The following passage by Whitelocke was given to me by my friend Ruth Spalding, though it does not appear in Whitelocke's *Diary* which she so brilliantly edited:[78]

'private Commons in the house of one Mrs Percy in Fleetstreet, with Mr Palmer, Mr Hyde, Mr Grymston, Mr Hall, Mr Chaloner & others, where they exercised their witts & learning in the imitation of Starrechamber proceedings, & sentencing with ingenious speeches, those of their company who transgressed their orders by swearing ill speaking, or the like, which they used in stead of drinking, & sometimes they putt cases together, butt detested all scurrility & debauchery.'

It is notable that Whitelocke never records in his *Diary* any contact with Thomas Chaloner or Henry Marten, whose later republican politics he despised and opposed, and as for Thomas Scot, he hated him personally.[79] Since Whitelocke was at one time accused by Scot in Parliament of secretly corresponding with the royalist Earl of Clarendon during the Civil War, which Whitelocke hotly denied, it is interesting to see this evidence that as early as 1628, Whitelocke and Clarendon (then 'Mr. Hyde') were intimate friends, and that Chaloner was then an intimate friend of both of them. These youthful friendships tended to be covered up later when the men either became political enemies or remained in some form of secret contact which was inappropriate. (Whitelocke was a very closed and furtive personality, well schooled in devious and secret activities.)

In the early spring of 1637, Thomas Chaloner made some remarks (I have not been able to discover their exact nature) which so deeply scandalized and upset Archbishop Laud, that Chaloner was arrested by Order of Secretary Coke, at the personal request of Laud. However, Chaloner escaped from custody, as we learn from James Chaloner's Petition and Deposition of April 6, 1637, transcribed in the Appendix. James was then taken into custody as an accomplice in his brother's escape, which he most strenuously denied. The information which led to Thomas Chaloner's seizure was given in by an informer from Scotland named Captain Innis, who was a sea captain. We learn this and much else from several letters of Laud's to Lord Strafford, in which Laud repeatedly expressed his rage against Chaloner and wished for him to be hanged. Wanting to hang someone for speaking in private is, I think all would agree, somewhat extreme. But here we see the 'informer culture' of the Stuart period at work just as we saw earlier in the case of John Alured, whose words about the Scots were also spoken in private. One can understand the hatred of the Court better if one realizes that under the Stuarts, one could not even speak privately without the danger of being killed for it. Such a life can readily be seen to be intolerable to people who are used to speaking freely in private. And who can defend such a state of affairs?

Excerpts from Laud's letters make for very interesting reading:

Laud to Strafford, August 28, 1637:

'As for Challenour, it was the weakest Part that ever Mr. Secretary Coke did to leave him in the hands of a Messenger, and not commit him to a very safe Prison. But what can you think of *Thorow* [Laud and Strafford used to preen themselves on being thorough, and often spoke of 'Thorough' ('Thorow') as their great joint achievement] where there shall be such Slips in Business of Consequence?'

Laud to Strafford, October 18, 1637:

'Challenour was well taken, extreamly ill let go: for, if I be not mistaken (which I may, not knowing him so much as by Face) his Hanging might have been a Paracelsian Cure [Paracelsus was a famous medical doctor] for that Liberty of Speech Men take to themselves now a-days. Certainly it is a most pestilent-natured Companion, and very well it would be to recover him, if you may; the Gallows groans for him, and I am persuaded (if all be true is said of him) first or last they will have Right at his Hands.'

Laud to Strafford, November 11, 1637:

'For Challenour, he is certainly worth nothing but the Gallows: But having made an Escape, I believe he will be wise enough to keepe out of the Way.'

Laud to Strafforde, May 23, 1638:

'Your Lordship's Letter of the 9th of January in favour of Captain Innis was by him brought me within these ten Days; and it seems that he rather suffers than otherwise for the Discovery he made against Challenour; and yet perchance had the Secretaries given him a Reward of the Espial Money [the spying fund], it would have been as well bestowed as some of the rest elsewhere. However forth of the Concordatum Money here, I will give him one hundred Pounds, and, if I can, help him to the Command of the *Whelp* [a ship] when it next falls. The Truth is, this faint Looking upon Men who do Service, is one of the true Reasons your Intelligence on that side is not so good, as I believe you find it.'

Letter to Strafford from Lord Cottington, November 24, 1638:

'My good Lord, Beside that in favour of Captain Innis (to whom I will give all Assistance when he requires it) I am to give Answer to three of your Lordship's Letters ...'[80]

Whatever Chaloner may have said, it must have been pretty strong for the mere report of it by a paid spy, and hence technically hearsay, to drive Laud into such a fit of fury as to last for more than a year and make him rage for Chaloner to be hanged for it. But Laud's reaction leads one to suspect that he may have been a psychopath of some kind, for he admits he did not know and had never seen Thomas Chaloner. To give the spy £100 in cash from ecclesiastical funds and to promise to make him captain of a ship for reporting some words spoken in private by Chaloner, which the spy in order to curry favour may well have exaggerated, is another indication of a potentially deranged mentality on the part of Laud. But whatever way one looks at this, it was not the kind of society that any reasonable person would want to live in, and the web of informers and spies set loose to roam amongst the populace and listen for private words and report them is what we all condemn in Hitler's Germany, Stalin's Russia, Ceausescu's Romania, and East Germany. Does one wonder therefore why there was a Civil War in England?

Thomas Chaloner later got his revenge on Laud. For he testified against Laud at his trial, stating that when he was in Rome [where he must have stopped off on his way to or from the Middle East], he had heard that Laud was a secret Papist whose aim was to bring papacy back into England by degrees.[81] And so it was that instead of Laud hanging Chaloner, it was Chaloner who helped to get Laud's head chopped off. Score one for Chaloner.

We may presume that Chaloner fled England for several years, and that his visit to Rome was only a small part of a lengthy stay abroad, to save himself from Laud's desire to hang him. He must have been absent from the spring of 1637 at least until 1640. Since his older brother William was at Constantinople, obviously with Turkey trade connections, we may make a fairly safe assumption that Chaloner fled to join him there. This would offer a good occasion for Chaloner's Middle East travels. Indeed, so thorough do Chaloner's travels in that region seem to have been that only a man killing time in exile would seem to have had the leisure to pursue them so fully. Chaloner's knowledge of the geography and religious traditions of the Middle East was truly extraordinary, so much so that he was able to use that knowledge to create the most erudite practical joke of his time, his booklet *A True and Exact Relation of the Strange Finding out of Moses His Tombe*, which is described at length in the later chapter 'The Regicides and Religion', and which for six months following publication fooled all of the devout divines in the entire country, as John Aubrey relates.

Chaloner's knowledge and experience of foreign trading, much of it derived from his time in the Middle East, made him one of the most knowledgeable MPs on that subject. In the opinion of Robert Brenner, Chaloner was 'perhaps the key figure in shaping Commonwealth commercial policy'.[82] That occurred at a later stage, and was not part of his early career which is our main concern here, though we shall more to say about it shortly, when we discuss the trading and political activities of the regicide Gregory Clement.

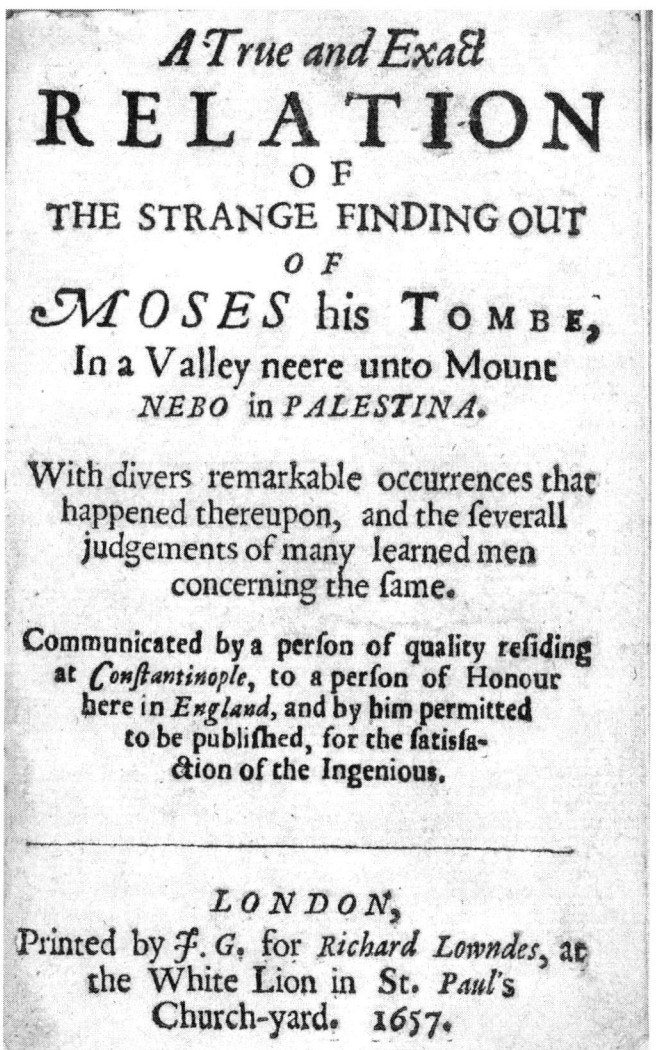

Thomas Chaloner's practical joke, which was taken seriously by everyone for about six months.
(From the original in the author's possession.)

Early in 1641, Chaloner's Yorkshire neighbours and cousins the Foulis, or Fowlis, family were prominent in prosecuting and testifying against Laud's great friend and the King's right-hand man, Lord Strafford.[83] Sir David Foulis, Bart., was even sworn as a witness in Sir John Bourchier the regicide's prosecution against Strafford.[84] For the various Foulises, see their entries in DNB, though there is not one for Colonel Robert Foulis, a letter of whose to

Thomas Chaloner has been printed by Cary.[85] Sir David Foulis, mentioned a moment ago, was Thomas Chaloner's uncle, as he was married to his mother's sister; his daughter, Honora, also married William Chaloner, the regicide's great-nephew.[86]

It is worthwhile to take a moment here to record a striking comment made by Sir David Foulis, aka Fowlis, Thomas Chaloner's uncle, about another future Yorkshire regicide, Sir Thomas Mauleverer, Bart. In testimony given in 1634, Fowlis 'extoll'd and highly commended one Maleverer, for denying to compound with the [royal] Commissioners [for a fine for knighthood], saying, He was the wisest, and worthiest man in the Country [i.e., the County of Yorkshire], and that he was a brave Spirit, and true York-shire-man, and that none durst shew himself stoutly for the good of his Country, but the said Maleverer, who was to be honoured therefore.'[87] Unfortunately, the equally brave Sir David Foulis was fined £5000 and committed to the Fleet Prison and his son Henry was fined £500 and committed to the Fleet Prison also. Thomas Chaloner's hatred of the Court cannot have diminished, considering that these men were his uncle and his first cousin. To be fined for not taking a knighthood (as a tax) when he was already a baronet, quite rightly struck Davis Foulis as absurd. The same problem faced Sir William Constable, as we saw in Part One.

A regicide who was sworn as a witness against both Strafford and Strafford's confederate, Sir George Ratcliffe, was Sir Hardress Waller.[88] Another regicide who was sworn as a witness about this time in a Parliamentary cause of consequence was John Lisle. On November 26, 1640, the House of Lords appointed a Committee to Examine Abuses of Courts of Justice and in Matters of Imprisonment.[89] On December 22, the House of Commons passed on to this Committee charges against several judicial officers, including Justice Sir Francis Crawley, 'of a very high Nature'.[90] A Mr. Westrop pressed the charges against Crawley on a matter of wrongful imprisonment, and on January 15, 1640/1, John Lisle was sworn as a witness in the case.[91] (Lisle, being a prominent barrister, may have defended Westrop at the time.)

Sir John Bourchier had had his problems with the Crown. There is a lengthy discussion of him in the chapter on 'The Regicides and the Law', with an extended account of his background and early career. But we might add here that in 1633, Bourchier was summoned before the Star Chamber for encroachment on royal lands, by command of the King, fined £1800 and kept in prison for six months.[92] Strafford knew Bourchier personally, from association in Yorkshire. He wrote on June 3, 1633, to Secretary Coke, and said:

'As concerning Sir John Bourchier his insolent Carriage, it is his daily Bread, the Man is little better than mad, one Grain more would weigh him down to a direct fury, and if any thing save him, it must be by letting him feel his fault soundly, for so, you know, they use Men in Bedlam, and then I trust, that which brings other Men into their wits may chance keep him in his.

'For the Title he can pretend to any thing in the Park, alas, good Man, he hath long since concluded himself by an Order made here in the Exchequer with his own Consent, and then judge what he can expect, and yet he hath been scolding at me these two Years, because I would not give him the King's Land; and now finally plays this May-game, to shew the King within the Government, as well as some others have done without it, that either coming or going, all Madmen and Fools in a Country will call in upon me.'[93]

The land in dispute was Galtres Park.[94] Strafford's treatment of Bourchier constituted part of the official charges against Strafford at his Trial: 'the said Earl ... did Disinherit divers of His Majesties Subjects in those parts of their Inheritance, Sequestred their Possessions, and did Fine, Ransom, Punish, and Imprison them ... namely, Sir Coniers Darcy, Sir John Bourchier, and divers others ...'[95] Strafford shamelessly lied at his Trial about Bourchier. We have already seen his remarks in a letter admitting full and complete knowledge of the whole matter. But at his Trial he said:

'That as to the Sentence of Sir John Bourcher, which is charged upon me, but not insisted upon by the Gentleman, I was no way acquainted with the beginning, proceeding or ending of the Cause, being all the while in Ireland; so your Lordships may observe with what uncertainty men can speak, that do inform in such Cases.'[96]

Well, there's a prize example of a man who can lie as easily as he can breathe!

Witnesses examined on Bourchier's behalf included Sir John Hotham, Sir George Wentworth (Strafford's brother), Sir Arthur Ingram, Henry Darley, and Michael Wharton, all of whom were MPs.[97] Also examined was Strafford's henchman Sir George Ratcliffe; and it was Bourchier personally who pressed the case against Strafford.[98] Henry Darley, MP, it might be mentioned, was close prisoner at York by Strafford's personal order until the Lords ordered his release on November 30, 1640.[99] Darley was a cousin and also brother-in-law of John Alured the regicide. Upon release from prison, he probably went straight to London to take his seat in Parliament and testify for Bourchier. Bourchier was very friendly with the Darleys, and later was side by side with Sir Richard Darley at the great Howarth Moor Rendezvous on June 3, 1642, as he mentioned in a letter which was twice printed.[100] Sir Matthew Boynton wrote to the regicide Sir William Constable describing this great concourse of the populace at Howarth Moor in defiance of the King as: 'the greatest appearance of people that ever I saw in this county.'[101] Bourchier seems to have organised this huge event largely by himself. A contemporary account gives a dramatic picture of what happened on that day:

'Sir John Bourchier being among the Freeholders, and reading a Petition, openly in the field for their approbation, to be presented in the Name of the Countie to his Majestie, thereby declaring their dislike, that those Cavaliers should be so neare the Court, as if they were kept for some design: And desiring the King to comply with the Parliament, & to dismiss them. The Lo" Savill [the royalist Thomas Savile, 2nd Baron Savile of Pomfret, later in 1644 created the 1st Earl of Sussex by the King] having notice thereof, came in a furious manner to Sir Jo. Bourchier, saying, Sirrah, what Pamphlet are you reading there; who answered, no Pamphlet, but that thing wch he could justifie, What is it some seditious Petition? I command you to deliver it; which he refusing, the Lord Savill was ready to take him by the Throate, & laying his hand upon his Sword, threatned what he would do to him if hee did not deliver it; whereupon the free-holders who approved of the same, were earnest to lay violent hands on his Lordship; but Sir John Bourchier desirous to avoid shedding of Blood (which unavoidably would have followed) delivered the same ...'[102] The British Library has three copies of this pamphlet, and attributes the authorship to Sir John Bourchier himself. At the same time, Bourchier wrote a second letter, published as a pamphlet, of which the British Library has a single copy, entitled *Die Lunae 6 Junii. The Copy of a Letter from Sir Jo: Bourchier, to Sir Thomas Barrington Knight and Baronet, from York*. It would seem that Barrington arranged the publication of this one. (Barrington was MP for Colchester in the Long Parliament, and died in 1644.) The House of Commons responded to these events by declaring Lord Savile and the Earl of Lindsey incendiaries and enemies of the State.[103] As for Sir John Bourchier, this was not his only sally into print. Although it is not listed under his name by the British Library, he was the lead author of a jointly signed pamphlet published on June 26, 1646, entitled *Truths Discovery of a Black Cloud in the North*.

Before taking our leave of Sir John Bourchier, it is worth pointing out that although he was accused by Lord Strafford of being like a madman, we can safely conclude that that description might be more applicable to the furious and violent Lord Savile.

Another organiser of crowds, - some would say mobs! – was the future regicide, John Venn. Indeed, he is probably the most famous mob leader of the Parliamentarian cause. Venn's origins were in West Somerset, but he went to London as a young man to seek his fortune. By May, 1637, he was a prosperous merchant running a large trade in 'the Westerne parte of this kingdome, together wth the kingdome of Ireland and Principalities of Wales wth sundrie Commodities', as we learn from a Petition which he submitted with nine other merchants to the Privy Council about trading conditions.[104] At that time, the ferries across to South Wales from the ports of Blue Anchor and Minehead in West Somerset were the means of transporting people and goods to that part of Wales, and Venn would have used his local knowledge and friends and contacts in his home region to arrange a successful trade with South Wales, which most London merchants would not have known how to do. It seems he used the Somerset ports also as alternative routes for trade with Ireland, eliminating the need to send goods from the more traditional port of Liverpool. This would have opened up the possibility of a considerable expansion of trading opportunities for the South West of England, particularly of livestock, cheese, cider, and grain.

We learn more of what John Venn was trading from the excellent entry for him in the Oxford DNB, written by the historian Keith Lindley:

'From at least 1621 Venn had a silk shop in Bread Street [the street where John Milton was born in 1608] and was busy establishing himself as a substantial trader in wool and silk with the west of England and Ireland. Like several future leading parliamentarians he also developed an interest in America without, in his case, ever becoming actively involved in colonial trade. He was one of the original members of the Massachusetts Bay Company, joining its governing body in 1629 and attending its meetings in England, and he was still holding company stock in 1644. He corresponded with John Winthrop in Massachusetts and had apparently considered emigrating there himself.'

Lindley has also discovered information about Venn's earliest period in the City of London:

'He was bound apprentice to the Merchant Taylors' Company in 1602 [aged 16], gained his freedom in 1610, and entered the livery in 1621. He became assistant of the company in 1638, and warden in 1641-3, ... Venn made an early impact in the civic arena. Having become a member of the Honourable Artillery Company [the City's militia] in 1614, he gained prominence in City politics for the first time in 1631 ... In 1631 Venn was chosen as church-warden of All Hallows, Bread Street, a London parish renowned for its puritanism From at least 1638 Venn was also a leading member of common council ...'

Valerie Pearl tells us more:

'John Venn first rose to prominence as a result of a disputed election in the Honourable Artillery Company. ... Venn had been nominated as an opposition candidate to Captain Marmaduke Rawden (the choice of the Court of Aldermen and later, after 1642, an ardent Royalist) for the position of Captain leader. Neither candidate was elected, for the crowd nominated a third candidate who was forcibly instituted. But in 1636 Venn was elected

Captain Sergeant-Major by the Company and at some time between 1639 and 1641 he was made Deputy President under Alderman [Sir Thomas] Soames. Venn was also a prominent member of Common Council from at least 1638. In that year he was elected to the Committee for Selling Contract lands, and to nearly all important subsequent committees set up by Common Council. In July 1640, he was elected to the most important Common Council Committee, the Committee for letting the City Lands. He was chosen one of the four Wardens of the Merchant Taylors' Company for the year 1642-3. ... He was a friend and correspondent of John Winthrop, and like Alderman [Isaac] Penington he was a well-known Puritan who lived in a parish that also enjoyed a reputation for its Puritanism.'[105]

The greatest single contribution to our understanding of John Venn is the result of many years' research by my friend Elias Kupfermann, whom I have known since childhood. In 2019 he completed his M. Phil. thesis, *The Role of Windsor Castle during the English Civil Wars, 1642-1650*, submitted to the University of Leicester, with his supervisor having been Andrew Hopper. Elias was clever enough to find 126 pages of garrison accounts for Windsor Castle submitted by Colonel John Venn which have survived in the uncalendared S.P. 28 files in the National Archives, aka Public Record Office. His masterly survey of Venn's conduct tells us much about the man, and stresses the fact that Venn used his own wealth to pay his men and sustain his garrison. He also gives a full survey of the pro and con descriptions of Venn in the pamphlets and newsletters of the time, and discusses his mercantile activities, his wife, and so forth. The thesis is so full of information which was never previously available that no one in future can carry out a satisfactory study of John Venn without consulting it.

I have transcribed for the Appendix a fascinating royalist informant's account of how John Venn organised London mobs to besiege Parliament in 1641, in opposition to the King. One particularly intriguing aspect of the document is that it reveals the future regicide and President of the High Court that tried the King, John Bradshaw, caught up in the business as a witness who disapproved strongly of the mob, and who wished to testify against Venn before the House of Commons as a rabble-rouser!

Venn was another of the regicides who had aroused the King's personal wrath early on. In 1642, the King singled out Venn and three others [Isaac Pennington, John Fowke aka Foulke, and Randall Mainwaring], saying of them that they threatened the ruin of London and were 'all persons notoriously guilty of Schism and High Treason', and that they made it impossible for him to be safe there.[106] Venn was again singled out by the King and his royalist mini-Parliament at Oxford in a declaration of March 9, 1643/4, saying Venn had 'bragg'd of having brought down the People upon the Two Houses', and that he had orchestrated the riots personally, consisting of 'multitudes of the meanest sort of People, with Weapons not agreeing with their Condition or Custom ... proclaiming the Names of several peers, as *evil and rotten-hearted Lords*', etc.[107]

Do we perhaps detect here a degree of contempt for the public, with terminology such as 'the meanest sort' and suggestions that the public in the streets were not of the correct social condition to carry arms? ('Gentlemen' wore swords at their side to show status, which must have been a bit clunky when they attended Parliament and squeezed past each other, banging other MPs' knees in finding a seat, and then sitting down behind the other MPs who wore their hats while seated, so that one could not see round or over them very well.)

On March 9, 1643/4, a very long declaration was issued by the royalist parliament-in-exile at Oxford, which was published in full by John Rushworth. It contains interesting further complaints about the anti-monarchical activities of John Venn:

'Shortly after his Majesty returned from Scotland, there being a very long Debate in the House of Commons, concerning an unparliamentary Remonstrance to be published to the People of the State of the Kingdom, which many of us then thought might prove prejudicial to the Peace thereof, Captain Venne, then a Member of the House of Commons who had before bragg'd of having brought down the People upon the Two Houses, and so drawn Resolutions from them, sent Notes in Writing under his Hand into the City, that the People should come down to Westminster, for that the better part of the House was like to be over-powered by the worser part; whereupon both at that time, and some days after, multitudes of the meanest sort of People, with Weapons not agreeing with their Condition or Custom, in a manner very contrary and destructive to the Privilege of Parliament, filled up the way between both Houses, offering Injuries both by Words and Actions to, and laying violent Hands upon Several Members, proclaiming the names of several peers, as evil and rotten-hearted Lords, crying out many hours together against the established Laws, in a most tumultuous and menacing way; this Action of Captain Venne's was complained of to the house of Commons, and witnesses offered to prove it; a Fellow who had assaulted and reproached a Member of the House of Commons in those Tumults was complained of, and shew'd to the house, in the number of those that brought a Petition to the Bar, and yet in neither of these Cases Justice, or so much as an Examination, could be obtained.'[108]

It is interesting to see how Robert Brenner, in his study *Merchants and Revolution*, describes John Venn's importance:

'The citizens' [of the city of London] petition contained between ten thousand and thirty thousand signatures, depending on the estimate. The identities of the two citizens who are named by the *Journal of the House of Commons* as presenting the petition gives a further idea as to who was leading the City movement at this critical juncture, beside the three militant London MPs, Isaac Pennington, Matthew Craddock, and Samuel Vassall. One of the presenters was John Venn, who, along with Maurice Thomson and Richard Shute, had gained prominence the previous autumn as a leading organizer of the citizens' petition of grievances. Venn, a militant Puritan and Massachusetts Bay backer, would replace Matthew Craddock as City MP when Craddock died in May 1641, and would play a leading part in the City radical movement throughout the revolutionary period.'[109]

It is interesting to consider which future regicides who were MPs in 1642 advanced money, plate, or horses for the defence of Parliament in June that year, just as the Civil War was about to begin. They were: John Venn (£100 plus a horse always ready), Oliver Cromwell (£500), John Moore (two horses), John Downes (£50), Gilbert Millington (£50), Miles Corbet (£50), John Blakiston (£50), Anthony Stapley (two horses), Henry Marten (six horses), Valentine Wauton (wrongly spelled in the list 'Warten'; £100 and two horses), and the fathers of Thomas Wogan (one horse) and Edmund Ludlow (three horses and three more later).[110]

There are two other interesting glimpses of future regicides prior to the Civil War. Humphrey Edwardes as a man of arms helped to lead a mutiny of soldiers in July, 1640, killing an officer and hanging up his dead body in the street. He and two others (one named Ludlow, and possibly related to Edmund) were ordered to be apprehended and imprisoned.[111]

In April, 1639, Sir Gregory Norton (Edwardes's great friend) refused to contribute to the Bishop's War against Scotland, and Henry Marten made his excuses to the same effect, though trying to avoid overt opposition.[112] Others who refused to contribute were Sir John Danvers, Anthony Stapley, and Sir Henry Ludlow, father of Edmund.[113]

We cannot leave our consideration of the early careers of the regicides without noticing that of Gregory Clement, who was the most widely travelled and cosmopolitan of them all. He was baptised November 21, 1594, at St. Andrew's, Plymouth. (Records also show that he was 42 in 1637 and 44 in 1639.) His parents, who married in 1590, were John Clement (born circa 1570, died aged 68 on March 12, 1643), who became Mayor of Plymouth in 1600 and again in 1614, and Judith Sparke of Upper Plymouth (born circa 1570, daughter of John Sparke, who died August 29, 1603 at Plymouth, and Julianne Cock; Judith died January 2, 1612, aged 42, at Plymouth). The regicide's Clement grandparents Robert Clement (born 1550) and Alice Parris both came from Chardstock in Dorset; Robert's father was William Clement, born circa 1525; his father was Charles Clement. The regicide was born as the second son into a family which eventually consisted of thirteen children, the last two of whom had an unknown mother following the death of Judith Clement. Much more information about Clement's relations is recounted in the Appendix to Chapter Two. At the age of 19 he lived for two years at San Sebastian in Spain, obviously as an apprentice doing his overseas service for a trading company. (San Sebastian is a coastal city on the coast of the Bay of Biscay, about twenty miles south of the French border.) Then, about 1616, he moved to Bilbao, where he lived between the ages of 21 and 25, carrying on business as a factor.[114] (Bilbao is a larger port city on the Bay of Biscay, approximately a hundred miles further along the Spanish coast from France.) He kept these trading connections all through his active life, for he signed a petition as one of the merchants 'trading to the Streights Spaine Portugal and ffrance' on January 6, 1642/3, along with Rowland Wilson, William Methold, and many others.[115] After leaving Spain at the age of 25, Clement seems to have returned to England for a couple of years. Then, on December 10, 1623, he was engaged to the East India Company for seven years. He sailed to Surat in India (in southern Gujarat) in a ship named the *Star* and remained in India until 1630.[116] A considerable amount of documentation survives concerning Clement's activities in India. He had many adventures and dealt in exotic goods such as emeralds. By October 18, 1626, Clement in company with a James Colbach was being accused of engaging in private trade, against the custom of the Company.[117] Clement spent a long time at the Moghul court in Agra, where he was by 1627 in charge of the Company's trading.[118] In January, 1627/8, Clement and his colleagues at Agra were granted an audience with the great Moghul Emperor Shah Jehan.[119]

After his seven years' engagement with the East India Company, the regicide returned to England, and on June 25, 1630, he married Christian Barter (born 1610), who was sixteen years younger than he was, at St. Dunstan's, Stepney, in London. They had three sons, James (born in Wiltshire in 1630, suggesting that his mother was already a few months pregnant at her marriage), Jacob, and Gregory. James married firstly Frances Sedley, daughter of Sir John Sedley, Bart. (2nd baronet of the Ailesford line, circa 1597-1638; he was High Sheriff of Kent in 1621), of Ightham in Kent (where the senior Clement family had been seated for generations), and secondly Sarah ….. (There is an alternative version that says that Frances Sedley married James's younger brother Gregory, and hence James would only have had one wife, Sarah.) James became a trader in what was then called 'New Netherlands', later known as New York City, had eight sons and two daughters, and died aged 60 in 1690 at Flushing, Queens, in New York. On May 5, 1724, another James Clement died at Flushing, presumably one of his sons. It was from one of the three sons of the regicide, probably James who went to

America, that the American author Samuel Clemens, better known as 'Mark Twain', claimed direct descent. (The spellings Clement, Clements, and Clemens were interchangeable even in the regicide's time.)

The regicide became an increasingly prominent trader in London and became immensely rich, what would today be called a multi-millionaire. Although he lived for some time in the parish of St. George's in Botolph Lane in the City, he later bought land in Greenwich and built himself a huge marble mansion there alongside the Thames. In 1652 he bought five more houses in East Greenwich, including a pub called The George (possibly for demolition as a building site?)[120] Clement also bought a vast country estate in Wiltshire for a huge price on July 12, 1648. I came across this particular information in the most extraordinary way. Because I like collecting and reading rare old books written by eccentric antiquaries dealing with specific English places in intensive, sometimes manic, detail, due to the amusement I get at their collecting of arcane information and titbits of otherwise unknown history, I bought an unusual such book published in the town of Salisbury in 1787. Although published anonymously, it is known that the author was E. Ledwich. It title is *Antiquitates Sarisburienses: or, the History and Antiquities of Old and New Sarum: Collected from Original Records, and Early Writers*. I had always been interested in the mysterious aspect of that strange tourist site of Old Sarum, a deserted Saxon and early mediaeval town which had been the original Salisbury, before everyone moved to New Sarum (Salisbury), where they built their cathedral. I thought this would be a good way to learn the story, and I was not wrong. But imagine my astonishment when I reached an appendix of the book and found the name of Gregory Clement staring up at me from page 306. What could the regicide possibly have to do with Old Sarum? And beside Clement's name were those of William and Thomas Barter, clearly relatives of his wife Christian Barter. What the book recorded, from an original list seen by the author, was that on July 12, 1648, Clement had purchased for the enormous sum of £8,226 seven shillings, twopence and a half penny, 'the lordship of Pottern', a village two miles from Salisbury. And for £43 seventeen shillings and fourpence, on June 3, 1648, the court leet and royalties of Pottern had been purchased by William and Thomas Barter.[121] I checked the Victoria County History website for Wiltshire and none of this information is known to them about Potterne (as it is now spelled). They say instead that the Manor of Potterne was sold in 1648 to William and Thomas Baxter of Chelsea. The sale list giving Clement's name records that the Palace [i.e. what had been the Bishop's Palace] of Salisbury was bought by William and Josh. Barter for £880 and two shillings, on September 28, 1648. So Clement and his in-laws were taking over huge property assets in Salisbury and its neighbouring areas. The list giving their names nowhere contains the names of William and Thomas Baxter. Potterne was a large and complicated parish, which for instance contained six mills. The Park seems to have been owned earlier in the 17th century by Sir John Dauntsey, a relative of the regicide Sir John Danvers. But the Potterne manor of Blount's Court was leased by the Longe family, the deadly hereditary enemies of the Danvers family; in 1643 it belonged to William Frampton, who sold it to (unknown). In trying to work all of this out, I have solved one problem: the William and Thomas Baxter known to the Victoria County History as purchasers of the Manor of Potterne were not Baxter at all, they were BARTER. They were the very same William and Thomas Barter who on the other list were recorded as buying the court leet of the same manor in the same year. What has happened is very simple: the name Barter has until now been misread by the Wiltshire historians as Baxter. At least that mystery is solved. And we now know that Clement's in-laws lived in Chelsea at that time, and we have the first names of three of them, which we did not have before. A bit of genealogical research on the internet turned up the fact that there was a Barter family living at 'Fovent, Fydleton, Wiltshire' in the sixteenth century (one of whom was named Christian, born circa 1557). Fovent is today spelled Fovant. It is a village nine miles from Salisbury. Until 1919 it was owned by the Herbert family. 'Fydleton' is now called Fittleton, another Wiltshire village half way between Salisbury and Potterne. I see from the National Archives that there was a law suit (STAC 8/183/46, undigitised) in the Court of Star Chamber against Thomas Barter and others by the Earl and Countess of Pembroke (Herbert family) for deer stealing in the forest of Gillingham, November, 1624. The Royal Forest of Gillingham near Melksham, reserved for royal deer hunting, is another Wiltshire location not far from Potterne. It is near certain that these Wiltshire Barters were the same family as that of Gregory Clement's wife. There is clearly an elaborate story to be reconstructed here about the Barters, their marital and business connection with Gregory Clement, and what they were really up to at Potterne. One descendant of these Wiltshire Barters was Governor Thomas Mayhew, Senior, born 31 March 1593 at Tisbury, Wiltshire. He became the first Governor of Martha's Vineyard in Massachusetts, where he died in 1682. His mother was Alice Barter, daughter of Edward Barter of Fovant. The Mayhew Family appear to be fairly well known in America, and books and archives exist concerning them; they are all descended from the Wiltshire Barters. One of Gregory Clement's old friends from the East India Company days (and who became its Deputy Governor in 1643, until his death), who was also a close business partner of Clement for trade with Spain, the Straights, France and Portugal was William Methold (aka Methwold; 1590-1653), who was mentioned above as a co-signatory with Clement of the January 6, 1642/3 merchants' petition regarding those countries. The same list which records Clement's property purchases in Wiltshire records William Methold as purchasing on February 28, 1648/9, the Manor of 'Figheldon', today spelled Figheldean, in Wiltshire, north of Salisbury and Amesbury. At this point, I drew a close to this fascinating side-avenue of research, despite there being much more to learn one day by some other energetic person.

Gregory Clement's wife Christian, née Barter, seems to have died in 1655, aged only 45. (I have seen this statement but without a reference given, so it cannot be said with authority.) In the National Archives there are various documents relating to Gregory Clement's legal actions. One is a bill and demurrer of 1658 relating to a Chancery lawsuit brought by Gregory Clement against Richard Glyde and (unknown) Bewley and others concerning the Estate of William Bewley of London. It is C 7/441/32 and has not been digitised. Another is a Chancery action answer from Gregory for a suit brought against him by Duncombe Colchester in 1655 concerning property in Apley, Lincolnshire. It is C 8/97/15 and has not been digitised. Another is a bill and demurrer for a Chancery action brought against Clement in 1656 by the MP William Heveningham, who had sat on the High Court of Justice with Clement and shared his political views. The case involved 'money matters'. It is C 5/31.60 and has not been digitised. There are several more of these, going back to 1638, but they may all be found listed on the National Archives website. (In searching one must be aware that there was a man named Clement Gregory whose name occurs frequently, and has no connection with the regicide.) There is a decree in Latin from the Court of the Admiralty in a case involving Gregory Clements (with an 's' added) and a partner, Maximilian Thompson, but no date is listed. It is HCA 30/840/90 and it is undigitised as well as imperfectly catalogued. I have not consulted any of these documents.

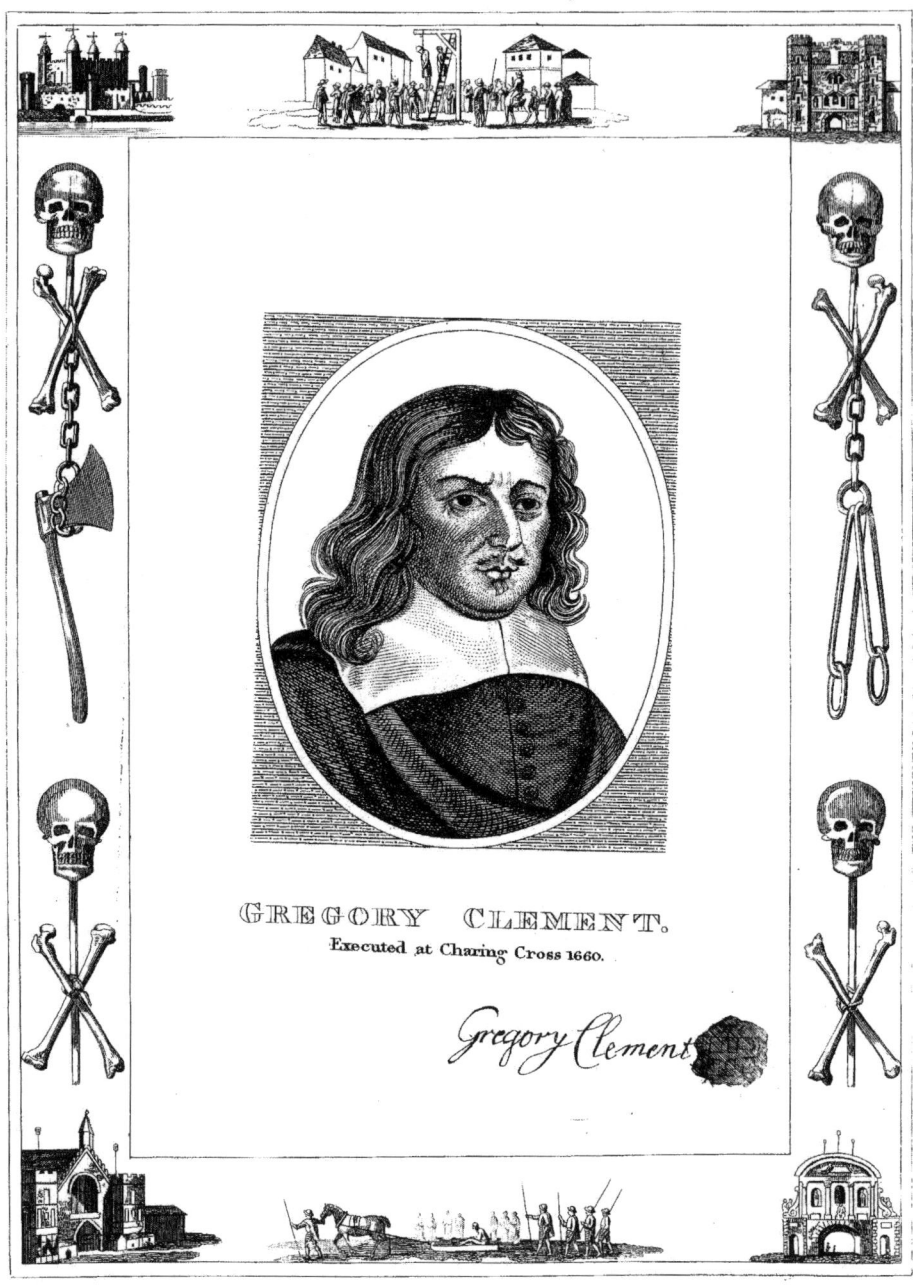

This crude depiction of Gregory Clement may or may not bear any resemblance to his real appearance, but the signature is correct, having been copied from the Death Warrant. Images of the executed regicides such as this were circulated widely at the Restoration to show the public the villains upon whom justice had been done by the newly restored monarchy.

Robert Brenner, who studied traders and merchants of the City of London so extensively, summarised some of Gregory Clement's business, commercial, and trade activities after his return to England like this:

'The composition of the Commons' committee for completing the establishment of the council of trade provides further evidence as to who was behind Commonwealth commercial policy.... In the first place, alongside Thomas Chaloner and Richard Salway on this committee sat their brothers James Chaloner and Humphrey Salway, both of whom could be counted on to support their siblings' initiatives. In addition, there were two immediate members of the new merchant leadership, Gregory Clement and Thomas Boone, as well as Francis Allein, the London goldsmith who had long worked closely with them. Gregory Clement had been in trouble as early as 1631 for illegal trading in the East Indies. Over the next two decades, Clement was one of Maurice Thomson's most important political and commercial collaborators in the trades with the Americas, in privateering, and in the Additional Sea Adventure to Ireland, and he worked with the new-merchant leaders on a long string of City and national political committees, most recently the London militia committee of September 1647 and January 1649 and the High Court of Justice that tried the king (December 1648). Thomas Boone was, like Clement, with whom he was often allied, a West Country merchant with London connections, who only recently had joined the new-merchant leadership in its Assada-East Indies interloping project. He appears to have been another of those pivotal figures who provided indispensable personal connections between the City and the parliamentary wings of the radical movement, for he was one of the closest political friends of Thomas Chaloner. Francis Allein was ...also a very close political collaborator of Richard Salway, with whom he worked constantly in the Rump, and probably of another member of the committee for establishing the council of trade, the radical Sir John Danvers. Both Allein and Danvers were active members of the Bermuda Company and served on various governmental bodies established to deal with Bermuda affairs. Finally, on this committee were John Venn, Miles Corbet [the regicide], and Dennis Bond, all well-known fiery spirits and radical supporters of the Commonwealth ...'[122]

It is important to pause here for a moment to reflect upon what it might mean for Gregory Clement to have met the Moghul Emperor in India. Shah Jehan was one of the most splendid emperors in the history of the world. He built the Taj Mahal as a memorial to his dead wife. He founded the city of Delhi. He sat on the famous Peacock Throne, the most valuable object in history. Gregory Clement met him and saw all this fantastic luxury with his own eyes. He saw grandeur and magnificence on a scale no one in England could ever dream of for a moment, in his or her wildest fantasies. Clement probably observed the Taj Mahal under construction and saw for himself that it incorporated jewels and the rarest materials in its fabric. Beside all this, how paltry and pathetic King Charles I and his pretensions to splendour must have seemed. Charles I was proud of his Rubens ceiling in his Banqueting House (albeit the public could not see it). But Clement had witnessed the golden age of Indian architecture, and seen palaces and mosques of breathtaking magnificence being built before him, seen walls of buildings encrusted with precious stones as it they were as common as the English flints used to make the walls of Norman keeps. Can Clement be expected to have taken the Stuart Court at all seriously after seeing all of this?

However there is another side to the coin. While Clement had undoubtedly been 'spoiled for life' as regards the splendour of a court, he probably had his stomach turned against monarchy while he was in India. For he was a witness to the most appalling barbarities imaginable. In a letter referring to Shah Jehan's coronation or enthronement at Agra on February 4, 1627/8,

Clement observes that to secure his throne the Shah had 'cruellie murthered all other princes of the blood, vizt. His brother Sheryare, who, notwithstanding his eyes were putt out and soe made uncapable to raigne, yet to make sure worke was afterwards strangled; and so weare Bollockie and his young brother, the miserable children of Prince Cossero. Their mother, distracted hereatt, slew hirselfe, dying with them. Tennuer and Hossang, Danu Shaughs [Shah's] sonnes, weare made away in like manner in Lahore; and lastly the yong sonne of Parveis in this place, as is crediblie affirmed by men of ranck and divulged in court. ... What success may ensue their unaturall proceedings wee leave to the divine disposures.' He adds that Shah Jehan has granted a safe passage for a caravan of the Company's gold and lace.'[123]

By March 2, Clement wrote again from Agra to the Company at Surat that 'these people prefer bribes and presents rather than petitions and he was evidently so sickened by the Court that he would no longer pursue the 'court solicitacions'. He said someone else would have to do it, but the person must be furnished 'with rarities and toys for the purpose'. He is tired of the bribes needed to guarantee safe passage of Company caravans.[124]

Only a fortnight later, Clement had the distinction of being imprisoned by the Emperor with his colleague John Bangham 'a whole daie and night prisoners in the castle'. It was apparently a dispute over the bribes for the safe passage of the caravans. 'At last, after enquirie, the King [Emperor] gave licence; and wee, giving a bribe and present to his minion, Reza Bauder, weare released.'[125] Whereas many regicides had occasion to feel bitter about having been imprisoned by Charles I, Gregory Clement could lay claim to a more exotic cause for grievance at the hands of the man who was probably the most powerful monarch in the world at that time.

Clement then got into conflict with some of the Company officials at Surat, who were extremely corrupt. Clement made several pages of formal charges against Richard Wylde, who had been President of the Company at Surat, accusing him of smuggling and embezzling the Company's money, of asking Clement to falsify records and pretend that an entire Company caravan of indigo from Agra which was delivered to Wylde had been intended instead for a Moghul official, of overrating Deccan goods sent to England and of undervaluing English gold coming out to India, and of other acts of theft and corruption. Quite a catalogue of horrors![126] Wylde retaliated, as might be expected, by ordering a cargo of peppers belonging to Clement to be seized,[127] and imposing a gigantic fine on him, doubtless realized in seized assets of all kinds, amounting to 10,000 *mahmūdīs*, which, whatever it was worth in pounds, was quite a sum.[128] According to historical currency information, one *mahmūdī* was a silver coin of 88 grains. So the amount of the fine was 880,000 grains of silver. Since a kilogram contains 15,432.36 grains, the fine was thus 57 kilograms of silver. Today, silver has a very low value, but even so, today 57 kg of silver is still worth £35,385.60. But silver has gone down to about two fifths of its value since as little as ten years ago. And in the 17th century silver had a very high value. I give these figures despite their being essentially meaningless in terms of monetary values hundreds of years later, and the only 'solid' number is the 57 kg of silver. If you imagine a one kilogram bag of flour, fill it with the same weight of silver instead, and pile those up on a very strong table, then you can 'see' the fine. (If anyone ever does this, please send me a photo.) And you can add to this a 'cargo' of peppers, presumably enough to fill the hold of a large ship.

Gregory Clement seems to have been honest, horrified at Wylde's corruption and sickened by the excesses of the Moghul Court. He came back to England in 1630 with experiences too bizarre and exotic to relate. Perhaps that is why he became a man of so few words. What could he say? Who would believe him if he tried to tell what Agra was like? Who would want to hear of the strange practices of the heathen Mohammendans? Was that the sort of thing a good English Puritan would talk about? Who would believe he had really handled handfuls of diamonds and emeralds, seen caravans loaded with gold, mounds of peppers and spices, mountains of lace, and shining white buildings of incredible beauty that floated in a heat haze of 47 degrees? After seven years in India he must have been as bronze and strange-looking as a Moor. He must have fallen into the habit of putting an alarming amount of hot peppers and spices into his food, which no ordinary Englishman could put into his mouth without choking and gasping. He could talk heathenish Urdu, Persian, Gujarati, and Hindustani, not to mention Spanish, French and Portuguese. Of what was such a man not capable? He must have scared people in London. He was immensely wealthy (some said the wealthiest man in England) and lived in a huge marble mansion on the banks of the Thames at Greenwich, where he could mix with his mariner and trader friends and keep an eye on the ships that were coming in. He doubtless had brought back from India his own private cooks and servants, wearing strange garments and speaking little or no English, but who bowed and called him Sahib. He probably ate rice instead of potatoes and coloured the rice a shockingly bright yellow with some strange fragrant spices called turmeric and saffron. He must have felt estranged from the tame surroundings of England, careful at all times of what he said, not wishing to alarm people by making wry remarks or comparisons. But when there came a chance to free England from its midget Shah Jehan, Clement must have felt a great excitement. England may have been cold and tame, but it had the spark of freedom stirring. And he gave lavishly, thousands of pounds, or tens of thousands, to encourage the Good Old Cause, - a cause for which he would in 1660 stand mute, saying not one word, making no final speech, uttering no prayer, on the scaffold. What was there he could say? Could he tell the crowd that as the executioner came towards him he was, perhaps, thinking of far-away Agra and of the barbarisms of another land? No, he would keep his own counsel.

1. For those who might wish to obtain specific details of how much gunpowder, for instance, was in those magazines, a December 1, 1641, document from the Office of Ordinance may be found in the Public Record Office, and is briefly calendared at CSPD 1641-43, p. 187. Converting the measurement called 'lasts', the total amount of gunpowder in the three magazines at that date was 10,954 hundredweight (cwt), and since a cwt contains 112 pounds, the total in pounds is 1,226,848. One and a quarter millions pounds of gunpowder was clearly worth fighting for. If Parliament had not secured the gunpowder stored in the Tower of London and in Hull, it is doubtful that the Parliamentary side could have won the Civil War. Such things are often overlooked by historians, or if not overlooked, go largely unmentioned.
2. John Bates, *The Troubles of England*, London, 1685, Part One, p. 38.
3. Basil N. Reckitt, *Charles the First and Hull 1639-1645*, Howden, Yorkshire, 1988, p. 16. It is unfortunate that Reckitt died the year following the publication of this valuable book.
4. *Ibid.*, p. 27.
5. *Ibid.*, pp. 113 and 136.
6. John Rushworth, *Historical Collections*, London, 1721, Vol. II, Part III, p. 120.
7. The account by Bruno Ryves and the letter of August 30 are to be found in Bruno Ryves, *Mercurius Rusticus: or, the Countries Complaint of the Sacrileges, Prophanations, and Plunderings, Committed by the Schismatiques, on the Cathedral Churches of This Kingdom*, London, 1685, in which the account is case Number 1 which is discussed. The pagination is pp. 116-132. However, after a short Preface, the pagination of this publication actually commences with the very same p. 116. This section occurs as an inserted book of its own, with the peculiar pagination just described, as a kind of appendix to Bruno Ryves's fifth enlarged edition of a compendium reprint volume (i.e. not with the pagination of the original newsletters which were separately issued until 1646), *Mercurius Rusticus: or the Country's Complaint of the Barbarous Outrages Begun in the Year 1642 by the Sectaries of This Late Flourishing Kingdom*, London, 1732, the main section of which terminates at p. 205, so that the bound volume contains two pp. 116-132, the first of which is the wrong one. Finally the bound volume ends with another appendix of 1685 which consists of a chronology of events, and is unpaginated.
8. CSPD 1641-3, p. 362.
9. CJ. II. 713b, 714b, and 770a.
10. Edmund Ludlow, *Memoirs*, ed. by Charles H. Firth, Oxford, 1894, Vol. I, p. 29, footnote by Firth.
11. CJ. II. 563b-564a.
12. Anthony Fletcher, *Sussex 1600-1660: A County Community in Peace and War*, Phillimore (re-issue and re-title), Chichester, Sussex, 1980, p. 93.
13. John Rushworth, *op. cit.*, Vol. III, pp. 1105-13.
14. Called 'Lisley' in Rushworth's list.
15. HMC, *Calendar of the Manuscripts of ... the Marquess of Salisbury*, Volume XXII, pp. 14 and 567. (The valuation appears only in the footnote on p. 567.)
16. *Acts of the Privy Council, July 1621 – May 1623*, p. 194; the manuscript is P.C.2/31/p.327 (old folio 160), but the original contains no more text or information than what the Calendar says.
17. Public Record Office: S.P. 16/ 50/ 17. Further petitions from Sir Alexander (apart from the one transcribed for the Appendix to Chapter Two) are: S.P. 16/ 53/ 99 (97 is an identical copy of this); S. P. 16/ 54/ 55; and S. P. 16/ 530/ 122.
18. CSPD 1641-3, p. 379.
19. CJ. III. 252a.
20. Public Record Office: S.P. 16/ 537/ 30, 36, and 42.
21. Public Record Office: S. P. 16/ 491/ 47.
22. *Ibid.*
23. CSPD 1641-3, p. 348.
24. John Rushworth, *op cit.*, p. 122.
25. Robert Brenner, *Merchants and Revolution: Commercial Change, Political Conflict, and London's Overseas Traders, 1550-1653*, Cambridge University Press, 1993, pp. 443-459.
26. *Ibid.*, pp. 505, 543-4.
27. *Ibid.*, p. 551.
28. J. T. Cliffe, *The Yorkshire Gentry from the Reformation to the Civil War*, London, 1969.
29. Anthony à Wood, *Athenae Oxoniensis*, 1721, Vol. II, pp. 124-5.
30. Public Record Office: S. P. 14/ 115/ 67 (nine pages long, plus title).
31. Calendared, CSPD 1619-23, p. 150.
32. CSPD 1619-23, p. 236.
33. CSPD 1611-18, pp. 252 and 555.
34. CSPD 1619-23, p. 236.
35. CSPD 1625-6, p. 131.
36. CSPD 1627-8, p. 180.
37. Clliffe, *op. cit.*, p. 235.
38. Brown Willis, *Notitia Paliamentaria*, London, 1750, p. 227.
39. T. Tindall Wildridge, *The Hull Letters*, Hull, 1886, p. 17.
40. Record Office of Kingston-upon-Hull, East Yorkshire: MS. L. 265.
41. Cliffe, *op. cit.*, p. 269. Cliffe seems to have been unaware of the copy of this Indenture at Hull Record Office: MS. D.832.
42. Cliffe, *op. cit.*, p. 272.
43. Public Record Office: S. P. 16/ 395/ 29r.
44. *Ibid.*, verso. And see CSPD 1637-8, p. 558.
45. Public Record Office: S. P. 16/ 395/ 30.
46. Wikipedia entry for Sir Gervase Clifton, 2nd Baronet.
47. Rushworth, *op. cit.*, Vol. III, p. 1215.
48. *Ibid.*
49. Public Record Office: S. P. 16/ 461/ 38. And see CSPD 1640, pp. 523-4.
50. CJ. II. 577b.
51. Bodleian Library: MS. Nalson, Vol. II, 43 (Deposit of Portland MSS.; see also *HMC Portland MSS.*, Vol. I, p. 41.)
52. Robert Temple, 'Discovery of a Manuscript Eye-Witness Account of the Battle of Maidstone', *Archaeologia Cantiana*,

	Vol. XCVII, 1981, p. 216. See also Wildridge, *op. cit.*, p. 134.
53	Wildridge, *op. cit.*, p. 93.
54	W. L. F. Nuttall, 'The Yorkshire Commissioners Appointed for the Trial of King Charles the First', *Yorkshire Archaeological Journal*, Vol. 43, 1971, p. 151.
55	*Ibid.*, p. 152.
56	Lucy Hutchinson, *Memoirs of the Life of Colonel Hutchinson*, London, 1806. I am fortunate to have a first edition of this work, which has in the front the bookplate of the Sixth Duke of Portland, owner of the Nalson MSS. preserved on loan at the Bodleian Library, which contain so many crucial manuscripts of this period and amongst which I have laboured a great deal.
57	*Mercurius Elencticus*, No. 27, 24–31 May 1648, p. 213. (E.445(23) in the BL.)
58	à Wood, *op. cit.*, Vol. II, p. 263.
59	*Ibid.*
60	*Ibid.*
61	John Nickolls, ed., *Milton State Papers*, London, 1734, p. 43.
62	à Wood, *op. cit.*
63	Thomas Chaloner, *An Answer to the Scotch Papers... Concerning the Disposall of the King's Person*, London, 1646.
64	Donald Wing, *Short-Title Catalogue of Books Printed ... 1641-1700*, New York, 1972, Vol. I.
65	Chaloner, *op. cit.*
66	See for instance p. 35 of (Thomas Birch,) *Letters between Col. Robert Hammond ... and the Committee of Lords and Commons at Derby-House*, London, 1764.
67	William Barlow, *Magneticall Advertisements: or Divers Pertinent Observations and Approved Experiments concerning the Nature and Properties of the Load-stone*, London, 1616. (The letter from Gilbert follows page 86.)
68	Anthony à Wood, *Athenae Oxoniensis*, London, 1721, 2 vols.; Volume One, p. 495.
69	Barlow, *op. cit.*, p. A3 of The Epistle Dedicatory (addressed to Digges; pagination only commences with the main text).
70	York Minster Library, York: MS. By John Hopkinson and Thomas Wilson, *Collections of ... Descents of ... Families*, under "Challoner of Gisbrough".
71	*Ibid.*
72	Francis Bacon, 'On Nobility', in *Essays*, Dent (Everyman Series), London, pp. 40-41. For an earlier edition: *The Essays or Councils, Civil and Moral, of Sir Francis Bacon*, London, 1701, pp. 33-34.
73	Robert Burton, *Anatomy of Melancholy*, Part I, Section 2, 4, 7. (This is page 161 in the third edition of 1628, which is the edition I have).
74	Lord Strange was included amongst these by Rushworth, but I have put him amongst those created by Charles I. Although he was son and heir of the Earl of Derby (an old title), he was created Lord Strange in his own right. His position is thus anomalous, and anyone disagreeing with my re-allocation is free to reverse it.
75	This information is taken from Rushworth, *op. cit.*, Vol. III, pp. 1156-1160. The list was also published in Anonymous (though according to the British Library, Thomas Frankland), *The Annals of King James and King Charles the First*, London, 1681, pp. 867-9. My copy of this book came from the library of Kimbolton Castle and belonged to the son (3rd Earl) of the 2nd Earl of Manchester (died 1671), who was the noted military commander for Parliament in the Civil War.
76	Erasmus, *Moriae Encomium: or The Praise of Folly*, London, 1735, pp. 62-3.
77	Edward Chaloner, D.D., *Sixe Sermons Preached by Edward Chaloner*, 1623, and *Six Sermons Now First Published*, Oxford, 1629.
78	Ruth Spalding, ed., *The Diary of Bulstrode Whitelocke 1605-1675*, The British Academy at Oxford University Press, 1990.
79	Ruth Spalding, *Contemporaries of Bulstrode Whitelocke 1605-1675, An Appendix to the Diary of Bulstrode Whitelocke*, The British Academy at Oxford University Press, 1990. There are unfortunately a number of errors in this book by Ruth, including mis-spellings. An example of an error of identification is that she believed (p. 332) that the regicide Henry Smith was named John Smith. She omitted the regicide Daniel Blagrave from this book, and indexed him in the main volume as Blagrove. She lists Lord Herbert of Cherbury as Lord Herbert of Chirbury. She failed to identify the regicide William Purefoy properly and thought he was called George. She did not realize that the regicides John Lisle and William Say were joint Vice Presidents of the High Court to try the King, which explained why they were sitting either side of John Bradshaw (p. 174). She lists the regicide Valentine Wauton as Walton or Wanton. She did not realize why Lord Grey of Groby was called 'Lord' and that it was a courtesy title of his because his father was an earl. She unaccountably calls Edward Massey 'a distinguished soldier' despite the fact that I had given her my article exposing his war crimes. Ruth and I were friends for many years and met often. We exchanged a lot of information and I deluged her with facts about the regicides. Alas, I had no opportunity to correct the above errors and several more which I have not mentioned. However, these errors should in no way diminish her scholarly reputation, for she was the most conscientious historian I ever knew.
80	William Knowler, ed., *The Earl of Strafforde's Letters and Dispatches*, London, 1739, Vol. II, pp. 99, 119, 131, 172, and 245.
81	Nuttall, *op. cit.*, p. 153.
82	Brenner, *op. cit.*, p. 579.
83	LJ. IV. 107a, 129b, 147b, 148a, 151b, 152a, 153a, 155a, 170a, 172a, 179a, 181a, 195b, 197a-b, 199b, 206a, 223a, 252a, 257a, 272a.
84	LJ. IV. 175a.
85	Henry Cary, *Memorials of the Great Civil War*, London, 1842, Vol. I, pp. 82-3.
86	John Walker Ord, *The History and Antiquities of Cleveland*, London, 1846, pp. 221 and 432.
87	Rushworth, *op. cit.*, Volume V, Appendix, p. 65.
88	LJ. IV. 117b and 121b.
89	LJ. IV. 98a.
90	LJ. IV. 114-5.
91	LJ. IV. 132b.
92	Nuttall, *op. cit.*, p. 152.
93	Knowler, ed., *op. cit.*, p. 88.

94   *Ibid.*, p. 86.
95   Rushworth, *op. cit.*, Vol. VIII, London, 1721 (*The Tryal of Thomas Earl of Strafford*), pp. 137-8.
96   *Ibid.*, p. 146.
97   CJ. II. 95b.
98   LJ. IV. 175a and 176a.
99   *Ibid.*, 100b.
100 Sir John Bourchier, *The Copy of a Letter Sent from*, London, June 7, 1642, broadside. Also printed in *Five Speciall Passages: viz., Two Petitions of the Countie of Yorke*, London, 1642, final page.
101 Public Record Office: S.P. 16/ 491/ 4.
102 *A Letter Sent to a Yorkshire Gentleman, to a Friend in London*, London, early June, 1642, p. 2.
103 CJ. II. 607b-608a (June 6, 1642)
104 Public Record Office: S.P. 16/ 355/ 5 and 47.
105 Valerie Pearl, *London and the Outbreak of the Puritan Revolution: City Government and National Politics, 1625-1643*, Oxford University Press, second and revised edition of 1964 reprinted 1972, pp. 188-9.
106 Rushworth, *op. cit.*, Volume V, p. 111.
107 *Ibid.*, p. 585.
108 Rushworth, *op. cit.*, Vol. II, Part III, p. 585.
109 Brenner, *op. cit.*, pp. 337-8.
110 Francis Kyffin Lenthall, in *Notes and Queries*, Vol. XII, 1855, pp. 337-8 and 358-60.
111 Rushworth, op.; cit., Volume III,, p. 1193.
112 *Ibid.*, pp. 912-913.
113 *Ibid.*, 914-915.
114 Public Record Office: HCA 13/ 55, f. 184verso. (reference courtesy of Bernard Capp.)
115 Public Record Office: S. P. 16/ 497/ 4.
116 William Foster, *The English Factories in India 1624-29*, Vol. III, Oxford, 1909, pp. xxiii-iv. (reference courtesy of Bernard Capp)
117 *Ibid.*, p. 145.
118 *Ibid.*, pp. 183 and 189-90.
119 *Ibid.*, p. 229.
120 Huntingdonshire Archives in Huntingdon: CON 3/6/2/6. The well known Samuel Moyer was connected with this deal. I have not consulted this intriguing document of bargain and sale, dated 24 July 1652.
121 The National Archives also contain some documents about Clement purchasing the Manor of Potterne: E 134/ 13 and 14 Chas2/Hil24. Documents are also to be found in the National Archives about Clement's properties in Ireland.
122 Brenner, *op. cit.*, pp. 605-6.
123 Foster, *op. cit.*, pp. 240-1.
124 *Ibid.*, pp. 246-7.
125 *Ibid.*, pp. 270-1
126 *Ibid.*, Vol. IV (1910), pp. 150-4.
127 *Ibid.*, p. 147.
128 *Ibid.*, p. 33.

CHAPTER THREE, PART TWO APPENDIX
Transcribed Manuscripts

WARRANT OF THE COMMITTEE OF SAFETY FOR HENRY MARTEN TO GIVE MONEY TO CAPTAIN AND SAILORS, WHO BROUGHT MESSAGES FROM HULL
(July 18, 1642)

University of Leeds,
Brotherton Collection:
Loder-Symonds MSS., Box 78, f. 5.

Die Lune. July. 18. 1642.

Mr Martin is desired to pay eighteene pounds five shillings to Mr Hill that came with letters from Hull to these purposes following. vz. for victualling his crewe (?) for one fortnight 4 l [£4] for the saide Mr Hills wages 7 l [£7] for his Mate 4 l [£4] for one of his servants 2 l 05 s [£2 and 5 shillings] in gratuity to the other five marriners in the Kings pay 2 l [£2] for the Masters Charges while he stayes in London 1 l [£1]

DENZELL HOLLES
W: SAY & SEALE
NATH. FFIENNES./
Jo: HAMPDEN:
Jo. PYM
ANTH: NICOLL

TRANSCRIBED MANUSCRIPTS

NOTES: There is no trace of this in the CSPD 1641-3 volume. The above is the original Warrant which remained in Henry Marten's hands and was preserved in the Loder-Symonds MSS. The pagination is not wholly reliable, as Box 78 contains another folio 5 besides this one. This document is not calendared in HMC Thirteenth Report, Appendix, Part IV., which Calendar seems entirely ignorant of the contents of Box 78.

LETTER FROM PEREGRINE
PELHAM TO BULSTRODE
WHITELOCKE (1650)

Bodleian Library: Nalson
MS. VIII, f. 31.
Calendared (three lines only) in
HMC Portland MSS., Vol: I, p. 546.
(This document has a
perfectly preserved seal.)

ffor my Honrble friend my Lord Whitlocke these

My Lord

When yw have convenient opptunity I desire yw to make a motion for me, yw may please to use these motives to the house to take it into there consideration/
 That I kept the King out of Hull when he came in pson (although I had not such Instructions from the house) where was a very great magazin in which I suppose I saved the State above 100 000 l [£100,000] besides the contegnments of that strong towne wch would have lost much treasure and the effusion of much bludd to have regained/
 That I had command of the Towns-Men both within the towne and without, that I raised them to salle [sally] out where they beat the Earle of Newcastles forces, I went wth them to the Ile of Exholme, and Gainsborough, both wch were then taken in I never tooke peny pay, but on the contrary gave to divers both meat and mony, and my wine Sellers were opene upon all occasions/
 That when the Scotts came first to Sunderland upon a Letter from the Comissioners there was sent by my meanes above 10 000 l [£10,000] worth of pvisions both for horse and foot, wherof about 2000 l [£2000] worth for myne owne accompt by wch I sustained great Losse, but never received any Satisfacion for that nor any other sarvice/.
 That I have lost for many yeares my trade of a marchant wch was soe considerable that I have payd Custom 2000 l [£2000] p ann: I have alsoe neer 15000 l [£15,000] debts owing me, wch will be all or a great pte lost, my debtors being Impoverished by those Warres/.

TRANSCRIBED MANUSCRIPTS

LETTER FROM PEREGRINE
PELHAM TO BULSTRODE
WHITELOCKE (1650)

Bodleian Library: Nalson MS. VIII, f. 31.
Calendared (three lines only) in
HMC Portland MSS., Vol: I, p. 546.
(This document has a perfectly preserved seal.)

ffor my Honrble friend my Lord Whitlocke these
My Lord

When yw have convenient opptunity I desire yw to make a motion for me, yw may please to use these motives to the house to take it into there consideration/

That I kept the King out of Hull when he came in pson (although I had not such Instructions from the house) where was a very great magazin in which I suppose I saved the State above 100 000 l [£100,000] besides the contegnments of that strong towne wch would have lost much treasure and the effusion of much bludd to have regained/

That I had command of the Towns-Men both within the towne and without, that I raised them to salle [sally] out where they beat the Earle of Newcastles forces, I went wth them to the Ile of Exholme, and Gainsborough, both wch were then taken in I never tooke peny pay, but on the contrary gave to divers both meat and mony, and my wine Sellers were opene upon all occasions/

That when the Scotts came first to Sunderland upon a Letter from the Comissioners there was sent by my meanes above 10 000 l [£10,000] worth of pvisions both for horse and foot, - wherof about 2000 l [£2000] worth for myne owne accompt by wch I sustained great Losse, but never received any Satisfacion for that nor any other sarvice/.

That I have lost for many yeares my trade of a marchant wch was soe considerable that I have payd Custom 2000 l [£2000] p ann: - I have alsoe neer 15000 l [£15,000] debts owing me, wch will be all or a great pte lost, my debtors being Impoverished by those Warres/.

I desire to informe your Lordship of the treu State of my condition at prsent, wch is deplorable being so0e much indebted that I can give noe satisfaction to my Creditors, wch is noe small vexsation to me, my wife and Children are altogether unpvided for, and now I am in course Phisicke, and how it may please god to deale wth me I know not; therefore now the parlaments bounty will be very seasonable, I want moneys to.keep howse, and to pay the docters; although my wife hath pawned her Pearles and Jewils, and now I intend to make sayle of my Coach and horses, wch I,confesse is very hard yt she yt hath been wife to a Vice Roy & having such a vast debt owing by the last King should goe on foote/

I doubt not but yw and others of my friends will be sensible of this my Condicion, and that yw will be Instrumental for my speedy redresse; my lord Comissioner Lile, Sir Tho: Withrington, Mr Martin, Mr Robt: Goodwin, Sir Peter Wentworth etc. I hope will give yw there best assistance if yw can have the optunity to move for me tomorow I doubt not but I shall have many of my friends in the house to second yw, I will not further troble your lordship but remayne

Westminster the 23th
december 1650/   your most Humble Sarvant,

PER: PELHAM

I desire that the Parlament will be pleased to grant me some Considerable some of mony for my prsent supply, & what more they thinke fitt out of some delinquents estates

NOTES: Four days later, on December 27, Pelham was dead and a Petition was read in the House of Commons on behalf of his family, with Pelham's friend Robert Goodwin, MP, assigned as the receiver of moneys on their behalf, and further consideration of the matter referred to a specially constituted Committee including Whitelocke, John Lisle, and Goodwin. The complete entry in the Commons Journal, VI, 516a, reads as follows:

"The humble Petition of John Bowes, Brother-in-law to Peregrine Pelham Esquire, late a Member of Parliament, on behalf of himself, and other Creditors, and the Children of him the said Peregrine Pelham, was this Day read.

"Resolved, That the Commissioners for Compounding with Delinquents be authorized and required to issue their Warrants to the Treasurers of the Receipt of Haberdashers Hall, to pay unto Robert Goodwin Esquire, the Sum of Five hundred Pounds, upon Account of the Monies due to Peregrine Pelham Esquire, deceased, for defraying the necessary Charge of his Funeral; and the Residue for the Use of the Children of the said Mr. Pelham: And that the Acquittance of the said Mr. Goodwin shall be a sufficient Discharge for the Payment thereof, accordingly.

"Resolved, That this Petition be referred to a Committee; to consider and examine what is further due to the said Mr. Pelham; and to report the same to the House, that Course may be taken for the Satisfaction of what shall appear due: Viz. unto Lord Commissioner Lisle, Lord Commissioner Whitelock, Mr. Carew, Mr. Robinson, Major Lister, Mr. Salwey, Mr. Morley, Mr. Garland, Mr. John Goodwyn, Sir Henry Vane junior, Mr. Robert Goodwin, Sir Henry Mildmay, or any Three of them: And this Committee are to meet in the Exchequer Chamber, at Two of the Clock this Afternoon; and so de die in diem: And Mr. John Goodwyn is to take care of it.")

TESTIMONIAL BY THE HOUSE
OF COMMONS (IN AN ORDER
FOR PAYMENT) THAT
WILLIAM PUREFOY SAVED
COVENTRY IN 1642.

House of Lords Record Office:
Main Papers,
(See LJ, V, p. 616.)
February 21, 1642/3.
Calendared, p. 74a, HMC 5th Report.

Die Martis 21 Febr 1642 [1642/3]

Whereas Wm Purefoye Esqr a member of this house about Sixe moneths since was appointed by this House to goe downe into the Countie of Warr and ye County of ye Citty of Coventry, for the raiseinge of some defensive fforces for the safetie of those Counties, against the Horses [sic, may be a mistake for 'Forces'] there Levyed against ye Kinge and Parlyamt And that in pursuance of the Truste in him reposed hee procured ffive hundred Souldiers to come into Coventry to defend that Citty, and to ayde ye said County of Warr against the Enemies Approachinge, and charginge ye said City in an hostile way, And for ye better effectinge of ye said Defence, by paimt of ye said Souldiers wages was faine to borrowe for ye publique use of Waldine Willington Esqr one of ye Collectors of ye Bill of 400000 l [£400,000] for ye said County of Warr the Somme of twoe hundred sixtie pounds pcell of his Colleccons. And forasmuch as this house thinkes it unreasonable that the said Mr Purefoye should bee anywise charged to pay ye said Somme of Twoe hundred sixty pounds wch was truely disbursed to verie good purpose for ye publique good in ye paimt of the said souldiers wages, wthout whose healpe the said Cittie must needs have yeelded up into the enemies Hands. It is therefore ordered and ordained by the .... and Commons That ye said Collector upon his Accompte shalbee allowed the said Somme of Twoe hundred sixtie pounds, and thereof shalbee Acquitted and Discharged for ever by ye Authority of Parlyamt And ye House of Commons doeth undertake to an Advance and pay unto the Trers appointed by yt acte of Parlyamt the like Somme of twoe hundred pounds to bee Imployed for ye uses menconed in the said Acte.

LETTER OF AUTHORIZATION
FROM LORD GREY OF GROBY
WITH REGARD TO
PETER TEMPLE
Public Record Office:
S.P. 16/ 539/ 118 (I, ff. 255-6)

ffor Mr Jessupp att Sr Gilbert Garrats Office in Whitehall these I praye

Mr Jesup

by reason of my going out of towne, which requiers hast I cannot com to reseve my money my selfe but Iv geven order to this Gentelman Mr Temple to receve it for mee there fore I pray fale not to delever it to him In soe doing this shall bee your warrant for the som of one hundred seventy fower pounds Thirteene shillings which here unto I sett my hand for your discharge

THO: GREY

december the 27th 1642

A LETTER ABOUT SIR
MICHAEL LIVESEY FROM A
ROYALIST DIVINE (1642)

House of Lords Record Office:
Main Papers, September 1, 1642.
Calendared: HMC 5th Report, p. 46a.

(Addressed to Henry, Earl of Holland.)

Right honable

In the greife of my heart I was bould to present unto yor Lop the barbarous outrages, and high impieties committed by some of the troopers in the House of God, everie particular wherof will bee made manifest. Yet that I may doe right to all, I hould it but an acte of iustice to informe yor Lop of that Apologie which Sir Michael Livesey hath since made for himselfe, who coming with his troopes to towne on Tuesday night, sent for mee, and (in the presence of the Maior, two Members of the House of Commons, and divers other gentlemen) declared that hee was commaunded by the Committee to require the keyes of the Church (which were by his direction delivered to Captain Baynes) for this end and purpose only that they might remove the armes, and powder thence, affirming that hee advised the Captain to behave himselfe civillie in the Church, and professing so much greife and sorrowe for what had happened, that upon the veiw therof hee was readie to feint, and sinke downe in the place: Wherin I am apt to beleive him, and the rather for his curteous usadge that night, and care to prevent further mischeife, requiring them not come within the precincts of the Church, and removing them from the towne early the next morning, wherby wee might the more freely attend the Service of God in the celebration of that daies ffaste. I wish that the rest could have pleaded as much in excuse of themselves: but Captain Bayns, and some of his companie seem to iustifie the fact, and in an uncivill way offered before Sir Michael and the rest for to dispute it. All which I humblie submit unto yor Lops wysdome, nothing doubting but that the two honable Houses, as well for yor Lops mediation, as out of their owne most honable disposition, will both seriously consider what wee have suffered, and speedily provyde for our

future securitie, that wee may peaceablie serve our God, in his owne House, according to the established lawes of this Kingdome.

Yor Lops most humble servant ever to bee commanded

Xts Ch: Cant.   THO: PASKE
Sept. 1. 1642

NOTES: Dr. Thomas Paske, the royalist divine, has an entry in DNB. The letter is sent from Christ's Church, Canterbury. See Lords Journals, V, 346 etc.

LETTER FROM SIR MICHAEL
LIVESEY TO SPEAKER
LENTHALL (1642,/3)

Bodleian: Nalson MS. II, 124.
Calendared (one sentence only):
HMC Portland MSS, I, p. 97.

To his most honored ffrend William Lenthall Esqr
Speaker of the hoble house of Comons present these

Mr Speaker.

After I receved a Command from a worthy member of yor house, (a brother Traytor) & in obedience went immediately to Kent where itt was my fortune to lye att the same town as a member of yor house lay, but he beinge a stranger unto mee, I had reason to examine him, for his paper, heering he was to goe beyond the seas, wch was only an order from the lords house; pardon mee I did then beginne to mistrust whether his fidelity to yor house (he being a member as he sayth) wanting of there conferm to the order or command itt might bee a false certificate; And did then sett some watchfull eye over him and his horses wch had spyed wthin an hour after wee were a bed where he was a carrying his money; one way and his horses an other; Though I am a young souldyer; yett I have beene very much instructed by an other brother Traytor att Chichester./ to have a Care of such Commodityes; Sr A seeing he was stealing away in the night I then sett a watch att his doore; to keep him until morning; and in the meane tyme take Counsell of my pillow for I was troubld much; he beinge a member of yor house where I owe soe much; noe more than all, life & fortunes; yett my thoughts to be more he was a malignant and then If I sent him upp I should have done good service to yor house; if he bee an honest man; I am confident he shalbe welcom to you; considring the affayres in hand soe I made bold wth him; and have sent him by my Coronett to wayte upon him to yor house he calls himselfe Sr William Sheffeilde if I have erred I shall willingly indure yor punishment if otherwise; Truly, for honering of yor house in respect he wanted that badge; I have then happened to doe you service.

Sr since Sr William Sheffield sais that hee could nott deceive mee any longer he then confesseth that he is noe member of yor house where upon I have disarmed him tooke 2 horses and wt moneyes he had and them intend to keepe (untell you order mee otherwise) for the publick service And further search his pocketts whereof I have found things of consequence together wth many bills of exchange wch I have sealed up; and sent by this bearer who can informe you of some other things wch I have nott tyme to relate the Ink almost long spent; and in that respect must present my selfe to you; wth these harsh and blotted, lines; Sr I cannott expect from you; but yor best surprise for my presumption Otherwise I should make bold to intrust some directions in such like orders here after or what else wherein I might serve you, (and wth the help of my god) noe man shall owe you more, wth there lives and fortunes for to serve yor hoble house Thus in all humility I take leave and rest

Gravesend this saturday   yors to serve you

February 25, 1642/3   M LIVESEY

(Postscript:) (continuation of Livesey's letter to Lenthall, Feb. 25, 1642/3:)
Sr here is one Mr (ff?) Hurly (?) I have sent upp wth Sr William Sheffield but have nott tyme to take his examination in respect of this hee my Coronett cann Informe you./

NOTES: In the Commons Journals, II, p. 979, for the afternoon session of Saturday, February 25th, we read: "A letter from Sir Mich. Livesay, from Gravesend, of this present Saturday; who sent up Sir Wm. Sheffield, whom he apprehended at Gravesend.

"Ordered, That this House doth approve of this Action of Sir Mich. Livesay, and return him Thanks for it; And do Order, That Sir Wm. Sheffield, , and .... Fairefaxe his Servant, be forthwith discharged; And that Sir Wm. Sheffield, shall have the Pass of this House to go into Holland: And that he shall have all his Horses, Money, and 'Bills of Exchange, restored unto him."

As for Livesey's curious phrase "brother traitor", this seems to have been a popular phrase amongst the Parliamentarians after the King's attempt to seize the Five Members, by turning the word "traitor" to use as a badge of honour and a token of brotherhood in resisting the tyranny of the King. Striking confirmation of this from the mouth of Sir Arthur Haslerigg is recorded in Burton's Diary, Vol. II, p. 407 top line, where in reminiscing of the Five Members, of which he had been one, he calls the others "my fellow-traitors".

ANTHONY STAPLEY'S PUBLIC
"SCENE" DENOUNCING
ARMINIANISM (1639)

Public Record Office:
S.P. 16/ 442 137
Calendared pp. 386-7, CSPD 1639-40.

Infor of Mr Stapely, for His Charge at ye Sessions - D: Burton -cond 1639

To the right worll his very worthy Friend Dr. Bray Chaplayne in Ordinary to his Grace at Lambeth House these wth Speed/ at my Lord of Canterbury his House at Lambeth

Sr
I have received yrs dated the 23th of this present month: wherby I understand that his Grace expected some pticulars of the busines I imparted to him before I went out of Towne:

I did conceive when I waited last upon his Grace that I had given him full satisfaction according to his appoyntment, otherwise I would not have left the City before I had observed the uttmost of his Commaunds:

When I first attended his Grace, I acquainted him that the Puritan Faction was growen strong amongst the Justices upon our Bench for the Eastern pt of this Countie: sterred rather by humor and faction then Justice; growen soe strong that such as are moderatly disposed whare not able to wthstand it: that Mr Staply, Mr Rivers, Mr Baker, Mr Hayes weare the Ringleaders: That it was growen to that hight, that Mr Staply at Michaelmas Sessions last (our Churches being well and peacibly composed before) possest the people in his Charge that the altering of the Communion Tables alterwise, was an Innovation detracting from Gods Glory and that some Prelates in this Kingdome did not approve of it: in these very words or to this effect:

I confesse I was not ther present, for it was ordered and plotted betweene 3 or 4 of them to be acted in this manner before the rest of the Justices being more remote could come thyther:
Ther are wittnesses enough to justify it, and I am confident Mr Staply himselfe will not deny it, For Mr White one of our Justices elder Brother to my L: of Dorsets Secretary asking Mr Staply after the charge was donne, wt he meant to meddle wth those Businesses there, wch the Bench had nothing to doe wthall, his answeare to Mr White was, that he was soe pressed by other men to doe it, that he could not deny them:

As for theire swaying of temporal Affayres in open Sessions their owne way wth difference and distinction betweene other men and those of their owne Character it weare endlesse to mention pticulars, wee are most sensible of it that see it and feele the burden: If my Lords Grace would be pleased to lett Sargeant Foster (who I understand is now a Judge) to write upon him, he is able to make a larger relation then I can write, who being a Justice heretofore amongst us for the space of many years and but newly gone from us groaned under the burden of that Faction soe long that he could noe longer endure the country:

The Towne of Lewes as well as the Sessions House is tainted with them, For at this present, not wthstanding my Lord of Dorsets and my Lord Gorings Letters and Intimations for their Creatures to be Parliament men; yet Mr Staply and Mr Rivers have a strong party in the Towne, and it is much feared they will be chosen Burgesses for the Towne of Lewes: God forbidd the greater part of a parliament should be of their stampe: if soe, Lord have mercy upon our Church:

God who knoes my heart, knowes that they are not the men I accept agaynst but their Condition: And it was the Peace of the Church and Commonwealth that moved mee to move his Grace:

To be brought forth as an Informer agaynst them will cause an implacable cloude of hatred to hang over mee not to be undergone: Yet wt I have eyther spoken or written I will make good: And I hope my Lords Grace will be pleased to have soe a gratious an opinion of mee that I would not possesse him wth an untruth; weare I in the least Degree guilty of that, I should never desire the happines to looke him in the Face agayne, and I should much concerne my selfe for making soe ill a returne for his many gratious favours conferred upon mee: May I prosper here and hereafter ackording to the Integrity of my Hart both to his Grace and the Church of England:

The same day I received yr Letter, I received another from my Lord Chamberlayne commaunding mee (wthout any request of mine) to attend in May next for Dr Cosens the Vice-Chancellor of Cambridge, if it may be wth my Lords Grace his approbation I shall the more cheerfully undertake it: I have waited many yeares for other men; but never soe happy as to waite yet for my selfe:

The last L: Keep, as soone as he was chosen tooke instantly a Survey of all the Justices in every County, and expunged divers wthout sending any cause: amongst whome Mr Hayes was one whom I have mentioned before amongst the rest: although since he hath scrambled in agayne: And soe may this Lord Keep. if he please: a thing done out of Course by his predicessors: I confesse ther being a defect of Justices at this time in that Division wher Dr Dow lives, and none soe fitt ther for that place as himselfe, I could hartely wish he weare in, that he and I might be Assistants one to the other: Wth my best respects to you; desireing you will please to doe mee wt good Offices you may to his Grace, I am

Westham Jan: 27th 1639   Yr very Loving Friend to serve you
                                EDWARD BURTON:

LETTER OF RECOMMENDATION BY. SIR HENRY MARTEN (1613)

The original of this letter is folded and bound in the back of one of the Bodleian Library's copies of HENRY MARTEN the younger's *Familiar Letters to His Lady of Delight.*

To my verie lovinge friend Mr. Roger Jones at his house - neare the North Gate in Oxford thes

Mr. Jones this bearer my good friend Mr. Henri Saunders a gentleman in speciall favor wth my Lors Grace of Cant [the Archbishop of Canterbury] hath occasion to use yor friend shippe, about an Administracion of the goods of Mr. John Cuddington to bee granted to Thomas Cuddington. I praie you doe him and the saide Thomas herein what kindness you can, whereof I nothinge doubt in respect of the love which I knowe you beare mee. And this with my hartie Comendacions unto you and yor wife I bid you farewell and Rest -

ffrom my chambers in the Comons London
[Note: this does not refer to the House of Commons, but to Doctors' Commons, where Doctors of Civil Law had their offices; the large ancient building, standing between Knightrider Street, and the north side of what is now called Queen Victoria Street, was demolished in 1867. Most of the site is now occupied by the Faraday Building.]

this vii th of Aprill   Yor verie lovinge friend
1613/

HENRY MARTEN

[In another hand is written:]

Thomas Cuddington yeoman at Ewell in Surrey.

JOHN, ALURED'S UNCLE IS FORCED TO GROVEL BEFORE THE KING (1620)

Public Record Office:
S.P. 14/ 116/ 42.

Alured submission July 22. 1620.

To the right honorable the Lordes and others of his Maties most honorable privey Councell

The humble Submission of Thomas Alured, prisoner in the fleet.

Upon the bended knees of my broaken, and sorrowfull heart, I acknowledge before God, and your Lops that I have highly offended his sacred Maiestie in a presumption of the highest nature, Which his Matie might have iustly made the occasion both of publique Example and my private undoing: Yet he hath most graciously overcome the Evill both of my punishment, and my offence with his unspeakeable goodnes, and hath so magnified his mercies towards me, that besides my many other bounden duties, my fervent, and my frequent prayers shall be Continually sacrificed, and offred up for the eternall happines of his Matie, and all his; Which though it be no more (I confesse) nor so much, as what I owe, yet it is no lesse (I vow) then I will ever performe

Most humbly beseeching your good Lops to the unexpected grace already receaved, to add this further undeserved favour to mediate with his Matie, that this close Imprisonment for 40 dayes together (though litle in regard of the quality of my offence) which hath so much Empayred your Suplt both in minde, in body, and in his poore Estate; may Expiate for his offences, And he shall ever pray both for his Maties eternall happines, and your Honors,

THOMAS ALURED

THOMAS CHALONER THE REGICIDE'S COUSIN:

THOMAS CHALONER PETITIONS FOR HIS ALUM PENSION (1615)

Public Record Office: S.P. 14/ 80/ 41
Calendared CSPD 1611-18, p. 276.

To the right ho: the Lords and others
of his Maties most ho:
Privey Councell./

The humble peticon of
Thomas Chaloner gent./

Most humbly shewinge unto yor good lls. that wheras by the expence of a great parte of his estate, and younger yeares in many Chargeable trialls of sundry mineralls, he at last discovered and found the Allom Mynes of Yorkshire, wch beinge well ordred cannot but prove both an ho: and profitable worke to his Matie, and the whole kingdome./

In respect wherof there was grannted unto him for his life by the first undertakers of the said worke, and since Confirmed by the late Lord Trer Salisbury on his Mats behalf, a small pencon of 40 marks p annum [about £40], wch hath ben duly paid accordingly untill Midsommer last. Since wch time there beinge two quarters receaved and a third at hand, the nowe ffarmors refuse to pay the same, and so have driven yor poore petr being an aged gent. of above 72. yeares old to travell on foote above 200. miles to come hither to seeke releife at yor Lpps hands.

Most humbly beseechinge yor Lpps for gods cause and iustice sake, that in a busines of so many thousands yearly value, some Course may be taken, that his small allowance may be paid him quarterly in the Countrey as hath ben alwayes used, & wthout inforcinge him to come hither for it. And (as in dutie bound) he will duly pray for yor LppS

NOTES: The discovery of this petition demonstrates that the discovery of the Yorkshire alum mines was not made by the regicide's father, Sir Thomas Chaloner the younger (1561-1615, see DNB) as universally thought. The actual mineralogical discovery was made by this other Thomas Chaloner, Gent., who was undoubtedly the man of the same name who was first cousin to Sir Thomas (son of Sir Thomas's younger brother, John Chaloner), and who was left some money by Sir Thomas Chaloner the elder (1521-1565, see DNB), in his will. Probably as the son of a younger son, this discoverer of the alum did not have the means to carry through anything or buy the land; the regicide's father probably joined forces with his cousin and providied the money to exploit the discovery. This cousin states that he is 72 years old, and the CSPD dates the petition to February, 1614/5. That would mean he was born circa 1547, and was thus about fourteen years older than Sir Thomas the younger, and 48 years older than the regicide, who was only a young man of 20 at the time of this petition.

THOMAS CHALONER ESCAPES FROM CUSTODY (1637)

Public Record Office: S.P. 16/ 352/ 42 and 42 1.
Calendared CSPD 1636-7; p. 560.

To the Right honoble the Lords and others of his Mats most
honorable Privy Councell:

The humble peticon of James Chaloner Esqr Shewinge

Whereas the petrs brother Thomas Chaloner haveing lately escaped from Edward Stockdale one of the Messengers of his Mats Chamber, to whose custody he was committed by the Right honoble Mr Secretarye Cooke; the said peticoner is therupon restrayned of his liberty upon the affirmacon of the said Messenger that he the said peticoner undertooke to finde out his said Brother and to bringe him unto him; ffor asmuch as the peticoner was now ways privy or consentinge to his said Brothers escape, nor doth knowe where he is, nor made other promise to the said Messenger then to doe his endeavor to finde him and bringe him to him, wch he accordingly did, seeking but not finding him, conceavinge in his inmost thoughts that whatsoever his brothers cause was, he by flyinge made it worse, Of the truth of which passage and for the cleeringe of his innocency therin he hath made a Voluntary Oath hereunto annexed. And for asmuch as the peticoner hath many occasions of his owne and his neere friends to followe wch suffer much by reason of his restraint, and may tend to the overthrowe of his fortunes,

> His most humble suite is that in
> tender consideracon of the prmisses
> Yor honors wilbe nobly pleased to
> give order for his enlardgemt

And he shall pray &c:

[Annexed document, 42. 1.:]

James Chaloner of London Esqr, maketh oath, That whereas Thomas Chaloner his brother who was lately restrayed in the hands of Edward Stockdale a Messenger of the Chaimber is gone from him; That hee this deponent neither knewe of his said Brothers intencon to gett out of the Custody of the said Messenger, or to absente himselfe, neither doth this depont knowe nor can imagine where his said Brother now is: And further deposeth, That soe farr was this depont from being privy or consenting to his said Brothers absentinge of himselfe, as that had he knowne or mistrusted the same, he would have Used all the meanes that in him lay to have prvented and hindred it: And lastly this depont maketh oath, That he this depont did noe way engage himselfe, nor make any promise att all to the said Messenger or any other, for his this deponts said Brothers appearance or forthcoming, But the truth is that the said Messenger comeinge on Wednesday morning last to this depont att his lodging in fleetstreet and tellinge him that his said Brother was gone from him ovr night, this depont then said to the said Messenger that hee verelie beleeved that his said Brother would not doe himselfe that disparagement as to absente himselfe, And this depont hoping to find him, then alsoe tould the said Messenger that hee would seeke him out if he could, and would returne to him within an hower and a halfe, wch he accordingly did

> Int vi die Apri: 1637.
> JO MYCHELL

NOTES: The name of Thomas Chaloner is not mentioned in the Calendar, and he is referred to only as James Chaloner's unnamed brother. The exact nature of what was going on is unclear, but further light is shed on the business by the following document:

PETITION OF JAMES CHALONER TO OLIVER THE PROTECTOR (1657)

Public Record Office: S.P. 25/ 93/ 9
Calendared CSPD 1657-8, p. 60.

(Dated August 12, 1657)

James Chaloner esqr

That before the late warre his pson was injureously secured in the Tower & His paps [papers] seized by ordr of the privy Councell he was extremly oppressed by the late King in his Allom rights so as he hath owing to him about 6000 l [£6000] as in pt appeares by privy seale yet he lost 10000 l [£10,000] at least and the late Kings gott 100,000 l [£100,000] by his Allom works. during the late Warres his estate was under sequestracon & by reason of it the kings Guarrisons & the exaccions of the Scots & other pressures attending the Warre he is brought very low Prayes for his support the paimt of 3291. 13. 4d [£3291 13 shillings and fourpence] out of the Exchecqr granted to him by privy seale in 1637 or otherwise as may stand wth the Petrs releife Uppon Reference hereof to Mr Nathaniell Bacon Capt Blackwell & Capt Deane they certify they find a transcript of a privy seale from the late King Charles of the sume of 3291 l 13. 4 payeable to him out of the Exchecqr. uppon wch nothing hath been paid as p Certifict.

[Judgement:] "the Case fitt for Parliamt "]

NOTES: This case was never raised in Parliament during the Protectorate, nor did the Council act on it. Although Chaloner's cousin Charles Fleetwood was a member of the Council at this time, so was the Earl of Mulgrave, son of an old enemy of the Chaloner family who actually was implicated in stealing the very alum mines and rights from the Chaloners of which Chaloner here complains! The Calendar describes this and the petitions from others accompanying it as "Notes of petitions referred to the Committee for Petitions on which no orders in Council appear". This petition was effectively killed.

TRANSCRIBED MANUSCRIPTS

JOHN VENN'S ORGANIZATION OF LONDON MOBS DESCRIBED (1641)

Bodleian Library: MS. Clarendon 20, f. 129.
(A deposition by an unnamed royalist MP - Hyde?)

Concerninge Capt Venn attempting to raise a Tumult in behalf of the Parlt.

It willbe proved that that day on which Mr Palmer was sent unto the Tower [Geoffrey Palmer, M.P., committed to the Tower on November 26, 1641; see Commons Journals, II, 324-5] there came into one Lavenders shopp a servant from Mrs Venn and told him that in the house of Commons they were together by the eares that the worser partie were Like to get the better of the good partie, therefore he was desired from Captaine Venn to come to Westmynster with his Armes to helpe the good partie/ accordingly he presently tooke his sword and went away: this was testified under the hand of one Mr Bradshaw a gentleman of Grayes Inn [apparently the future regicide!], and others the which I delivered into the house, and he with others where manye dayes attending att the dore to iustifie what he had sett his hand unto but they never would call him in although I moved it often. it willbe proved that this message was sent unto manye and that one going into the shopp to Mrs Venn she sitting there crying and wringing her handes for her husband whom she feared would be Kylled, asked her howe she did knowe this to be true, she answered that a very good Christian brought her word from her husband, while this man was in the shopp cometh in a Grocer whose name I cannot nowe remember with a sword by his side and a pistoll on the other, and bade her be of good compfort he and manye more would goe to Westmynster and laying his hand upon his sword saied yf this will not doe it this shall, meaneing his pistoll, many profes there are to this effect which I cannot nowe remember: it willbe proved that there came downe about 300 of them, and more still comeing untill the house did rise, Captaine Venn answeres he was att the house all that day, what his wife did he knoweth not, it willbe proved that his wife shewed his Letter brought unto her by one of the members of the house the which directed her to doe this

NOTES: It appears that the Mr. Bradshaw, Gentleman of Gray's Inn, referred to above, must be John Bradshaw, who was indeed a barrister of Gray's Inn. It is highly ironical that he should be standing at the doors to the House of Commons waiting to testify against John Venn, when later he and Venn would have the same political views. Possibly, fresh from sleepy Cheshire, Bradshaw was horrified at the organization of unruly London mobs for political purposes; his motive need be no more than an opposition to these means, and we need not infer that he was by any means necessarily opposed to the Parliament faction.

It is possible that the date of the "tumult" this first time was November 25, on which day the House was discussing "congratulating" the King and refused to expel Palmer (though he was sentenced to the Tower); on the 26th the debate was about recusants. (CJ, II, 324-5).